SHARĪ^cA IN THE RUSSIAN EMPIRE

The Royal Asiatic Society was founded in 1823 'for the investigation of subjects connected with, and for the encouragement of science, literature and the arts in relation to Asia'. Informed by these goals, the policy of the Society's Editorial Board is to make available in appropriate formats the results of original research in the humanities and social sciences having to do with Asia, defined in the broadest geographical and cultural sense and up to the present day.

The Monograph Board
Professor Francis Robinson, CBE, Royal Holloway, University of London (Chair)
Professor Tim Barrett, SOAS University of London
Dr Evrim Binbas, The Institute of Oriental and Asian Studies, University of Bonn
Dr Barbara M. C. Brend
Professor Anna Contadini, SOAS University of London
Professor Michael Feener, University of Oxford
Dr Gordon Johnson, University of Cambridge
Dr Rosie Llewellyn Jones, MBE
Professor David Morgan, University of Wisconsin–Madison
Professor Rosalind O'Hanlon, University of Oxford
Dr Alison Ohta, Director, Royal Asiatic Society

For a full list of publications by the Royal Asiatic Society see www.royalasiaticsociety.org

SHARĪᶜA IN THE RUSSIAN EMPIRE

THE REACH AND LIMITS OF ISLAMIC LAW IN CENTRAL EURASIA, 1550–1917

Edited by Paolo Sartori and Danielle Ross

SOC·REG·AS·BRITT·

EDINBURGH
University Press

Edinburgh University Press is one of the leading university presses in the UK. We publish academic books and journals in our selected subject areas across the humanities and social sciences, combining cutting-edge scholarship with high editorial and production values to produce academic works of lasting importance. For more information visit our website: edinburghuniversitypress.com

Edinburgh University Press Ltd
The Tun – Holyrood Road
12 (2f) Jackson's Entry
Edinburgh EH8 8PJ

First published in hardback by Edinburgh University Press 2020

Typeset in 11/13 JaghbUni Regular by
Servis Filmsetting Ltd, Stockport, Cheshire

A CIP record for this book is available from the British Library

ISBN 978 1 4744 4429 3 (hardback)
ISBN 978 1 4744 4430 9 (paperback)
ISBN 978 1 4744 4431 6 (webready PDF)
ISBN 978 1 4744 4432 3 (epub)

Published with the support of the University of Edinburgh Scholarly Publishing Initiatives Fund.

The copy of the cover image was obtained with the assistance of Luiza Midakhatovna Giniatullina and Igor' Vil'sovich Kuchumov.

Contents

List of Contributors vii

Introduction: The Reach and Limits of *Sharīᶜa* in the Russian Empire, *c*.1552–1917 1
Danielle Ross and Paolo Sartori

1 Islamic Education for All: Technological Change, Popular Literacy and the Transformation of the Volga-Ural Madrasa, 1650s–1910s 38
Danielle Ross

2 *Taqlīd* and Discontinuity: The Transformation of Islamic Legal Authority in the Volga-Ural Region 81
Nathan Spannaus

3 Debunking the 'Unfortunate Girl' Paradigm: Volga-Ural Muslim Women's Knowledge Culture and its Transformation across the Long Nineteenth Century 120
Danielle Ross

4 Between Imperial Law and Islamic Law: Muslim Subjects and the Legality of Remarriage in Nineteenth-century Russia 156
Rozaliya Garipova

5 Islamic Scholars among the Kereys of Northern Kazakhstan, 1680–1850 183
Allen J. Frank

6 Tinkering with Codification in the Kazakh Steppe: *ᶜĀdat* and *Sharīᶜa* in the Work of Efim Osmolovskii 209
Pavel Shabley and Paolo Sartori

7 *Taqlīd* and *Ijtihād* over the Centuries: The Debates on Islamic Legal Theory in Daghestan, 1700s–1920s 239
Shamil Shikhaliev

8 Kunta Ḥājjī and the Stolen Horse 281
Michael Kemper and Shamil Shikhaliev

9 What We Talk about When We Talk about *Taqlīd* in Russian Central Asia 299
Paolo Sartori

10 Take Me to Khiva: *Sharīʿa* as Governance in the Oasis of Khorezm (Nineteenth Century–Early Twentieth) 328
Ulfat Abdurasulov and Paolo Sartori

Index 363

Contributors

Ulfat Abdurasulov is Post-Doc Research Fellow of the Institute of Iranian Studies at the Austrian Academy of Sciences within the framework of the START Project *Seeing Like an Archive: Documents and Forms of Governance in Islamic Central Asia (18th–19th Centuries)*, funded by the Austrian Science Fund (FWF). Previously, in 2000–14, Dr Abdurasulov worked as a Research Fellow at the Institute of History of the Uzbek Academy of Sciences.

Allen J. Frank is an independent scholar based in Takoma Park, Maryland. His publications include: *The Cambidge History of Inner Asia: The Chingisid Age* (2009, co-editor), *Saduaqas Ghïlmani, Biographies of the Islamic Scholars of Our Times* (2018, co-editor) and *Gulag Miracles: Sufis and Stalinist Repression in Kazakhstan* (forthcoming).

Rozaliya Garipova is an assistant professor of Islamic Studies and History at Nazarbayev University, Kazakhstan. Her research and teaching focus on the Islamic history of Russia and Central Asia. Her current book project deals with the function and transformation of Islamic law in the Volga-Urals and Western Siberia in the nineteenth century. It traces the impact of imperial governance on the religious authority of the *ʿulamāʾ* and on Islamic family law among Volga-Ural Muslims. She has published in *Islamic Law and Society* and *Yearbook of Islamic and Middle Eastern Law*.

Michael Kemper is professor and chair of the Eastern European studies group at the University of Amsterdam. Kemper's foremost interest has been the study of Tatar and Arabic Islamic manuscripts from Russia, the Caucasus and Central Asia. Among the topics that he published about are Tatar discourses about Islam and politics, Islam and customary law in Daghestan, Sufi links between the Russian and the Ottoman empires and, most recently, the emergence of the Russian language as a major language of Islam, and the Kremlin's use of Islam as a pillar of Russian 'traditionalism'.

Danielle Ross is an assistant professor of Asian and Islamic history at Utah State University. Her research focuses on the social and cultural history of the Muslim communities of Russia's Volga-Ural region. She is author of *Tatar Empire: Kazan's Muslims and the Making of Imperial Russia* (2020).

Paolo Sartori is Senior Fellow of the Institute of Iranian Studies at the Austrian Academy of Sciences. A recipient of numerous grants and awards, Dr Sartori was VolkswagenStiftung Fellow at the Martin Luther University of Halle-Wittenberg from 2007 to 2011. In 2013 he was awarded the START prize by the Austrian Science Fund (FWF) for his six-year research project 'Seeing Like an Archive: Documents and Forms of Governance in Islamic Central Asia (18th–19th Centuries)'. He currently serves as the Editor-in-Chief of the *Journal of the Economic and Social History of the Orient.* He is author of *Visions of Justice:* Sharī^{c}a *and Cultural Change in Russian Central Asia* (2016).

Pavel Shabley is associate professor at the Kostanay branch of Chelyabinsk State University, Kazakhstan. His major research interest is the history of Islam in the Kazakh Steppe and the study of the Orenburg Mohammedan Spiritual Assembly. Among his recent publications: 'Akhund Siraj ad-Din ibn Saifulla al-Kyzyljari among the Kazakhs of the Siberian Department: An Islamic Biography in the Imperial Context', *Ab Imperio* (2012), pp. 175–208; with Paolo Sartori, 'The Fate of Imperial Codification Projects: ^{c}Adat and Shari^{c}a in the Kazakh Steppe', *Ab imperio* (2015), pp. 63–105. Currently he is working (with Paolo Sartori) on a book on ^{c}Adat and Shari^{c}a in the Kazakh Steppe.

Shamil Shikhaliev is the head of the department of Oriental manuscripts in the Institute of History, Archaeology and Ethnology of the Daghestan Scientific Center of the Russian Academy of Sciences. His spheres of academic interest include Islam in Russia (medieval and modern period), Sufism, Islamic Law and history, Islamic reform, networks of education, and the historical-philological study of Arabic manuscripts. He is the author of more than eighty works on Islam and Arabic manuscripts. He participates in the annual expeditions to Daghestani villages for the localisation, cataloguing and edition of Islamic manuscripts from private and mosque collections.

Nathan Spannaus is a postdoctoral researcher in Islamic philosophy at the University of Jyväskylä, Finland, specialising in Islamic intellectual history and religious thought. His work has appeared in *Islamic Law and Society*, *Muslim World*, *Arabica*, and *Journal of the Economic and Social History of the Orient*, and he has contributed to the *Oxford Handbook of Islamic Theology*, the *Encyclopedia of Islam* and the two-volume *Modern Islamic Authority and Social Change* (Edinburgh University Press, 2018). His monograph *Preserving Islamic Tradition: Abu Nasr Qursawi and the Beginnings of Modern Reformism* was published in 2019.

Introduction: The Reach and Limits of *Sharīᶜa* in the Russian Empire, *c*.1552–1917

Danielle Ross and Paolo Sartori

Why a History of Islamic Law in Russia?

When it comes to writing the history of Islamic law from the 1600s to the early 1900s, Russia is, perhaps, not the first state to come to mind. As of 1897, the Russian Empire's Muslim population, numbered at about 13.9 million or 11.7 per cent of Russian subjects, appears small when compared to the British Empire's approximately 62.8 million Muslims.[1] However, Russia's Muslim population was, in fact, not much smaller than that of the neighbouring Ottoman Empire, which was about 15.5 million in 1906.[2] Some early twentieth-century observers noted, furthermore, that Tsarist Russia's sphere of unmediated influence over the Islamic ecumene transcended the boundaries of the empire and expanded well into the neighbouring regions of Iran and western China. Thus, the number of Muslims who experienced some form of Russian administration may have been as high as 25 million.[3] This larger figure suggests that, in numerical terms, Russia's influence over the Muslim world in the late 1800s and early 1900s was roughly on par with that of the Dutch Empire, which boasted a Muslim population of about 30 million in Southeast Asia by 1905.[4] To compare Muslim communities numerically may be regarded as a rather dry statistical exercise. However, it is precisely when one considers comparatively the size of the Muslim community inhabiting the Russian Empire that one begins to realise that Russia was one of the major imperial and colonial forces that profoundly shaped the Muslim world in early modern and modern history, a process of transformation that continues to affect Muslim societies today.

Nor could imperial Russia's Muslim population be characterised as marginal to the greater Islamic world. Embracing diverse communities ranging from the Volga river basin, the Ural Mountains, and Siberia to the Kazakh Steppe, Central Asia, Crimea and the Caucasus, imperial Russia's

Muslims stood at the confluence of multiple cultures and political spheres. They occupied the central and northern sections of what once was the Mongol Empire, from which they inherited specific forms of governance and cultural practices. The cultures of the khanates of Kazan, Astrakhan, Siberia and Qasim, as well as the Kazakh khanate, all emerged from the fragmentation of the Golden Horde, and their history (considered either separately or collectively) offer numerous examples of traditions that can be traced back to the Mongol period.[5]

Simultaneously, the Muslim-majority regions of the Russian Empire belonged to the 'Persianate' sphere, a space otherwise known as 'the Balkans-to-Bengal complex', a cultural area in which Persian was one of the languages of learned communication enabling elites to transcend regional differences and particularisms. Indeed, Persian facilitated the circulation of Islamic knowledge across regions as far removed as Transoxiana, the Volga-Ural regions and Transcaucasia: from primers of Arabic grammar[6] and compendia of Islamic jurisprudence (*furū*ᶜ *al-fiqh*)[7] to treatises on ethics (*akhlāq*) and literary works (*adabiyyāt*) in general, writing and learning in Persian served Russia's Muslims as a gateway to advanced education and high culture, at least until a broader process of Turkic vernacularisation came to full maturation in the nineteenth century.[8]

Finally, the Russian Empire came to include important nodes facilitating scholarly traffic within the wider trans-imperial network of global Islamic education. From the mid-1600s to the 1910s, the Bukharan and Khivan madrasas and the institutes of Islamic higher education in the Caucasus beckoned to generations of Muslims coming from the Middle Volga and Siberia.[9] In addition, the Muslim-majority lands ruled by Russia by the late 1800s included the homeland of some of the most prominent scholars in the history of Islam. Suffice it to refer, for example, to the great hadith compiler Muḥammad al-Bukhārī (810–70), or the jurist Burḥān al-Dīn al-Marghīnāni (1135–97), the author of *al-Hidāya*, one of the most widely used legal manuals in the Islamic world, or Najm al-Dīn Kubrā (1145–1221), a Sufi master who operated under the rule of the Khwarazmshahs and whose piety became embedded in narratives of the Islamisation of the Mongols.[10]

Such references to the Muslim scholars of medieval Central Asia have been deployed in the past to populate the Soviet national pantheons of 'great educators'[11] or to eulogise the representatives of an ostensible lost Islamic enlightenment.[12] Both of these approaches are premised upon a selective and misleading reading of the past, which presents Central Asian Muslim intellectual activity as an exclusively medieval phenomenon that had little or no bearing on the region in the modern era. However, many of the scholars highlighted in the Soviet and post-Soviet studies of medieval Central Asia are, in fact, deeply connected to the very written traditions to which numerous Muslim scholarly communities (both inside and outside of Russia proper) continue to trace their intellectual genealogy and spiritual connections, a multifarious and long-term process that has been key to the formation of collective identities.[13] For example, in the field of Islamic jurisprudence, the preference for specific juridical works depended, among other things, on local constituencies of dynasts, who, by patronising scholarly families and facilitating their educational activities, ensured the transmission of specific legal doctrines and preserved their integrity over time.[14] For example, the spread, reproduction and transmission of the Ḥanafī school of law is usually associated with Turkic dynasties, who supported scholarly genealogies tracing back to Abū Ḥanīfa (credited as the founder of the school), a trend still notable among the Uzbek principalities of nineteenth-century Central Asia.[15] Among the most authoritative texts of said school of law, one finds the *Mukhtasar al-wiqāya fī masāʾil al-Hidāya*. Itself an abridged version of the *Wiqāya al-riwāya fī masāʾil al-Hidāya*, it was composed by Maḥmūd ʿUbayd Allāh al-Maḥbūbī, known as Ṣadr al-Sharīʿa (d. 747–1346).[16] Both works of Islamic jurisprudence were written in Bukhara by representatives of a scholarly lineage known as Maḥbūbī, a lineage that followed another Bukharan family of Muslim scholars (*ʿulamāʾ*) called the Al-i Burhān.[17] While it is plain that over the centuries the jurisprudential authority of these and other texts rested on many factors, they equally came to constitute a local intellectual tradition, and were thus regarded as part of cultural capital symbolising past prestige.

Despite the clear historical significance of Inner Asia's Muslims to the intellectual legacy of medieval Islam and the numerical significance of said communities in the colonial era, the Muslims of the Russian Empire remain minimally represented or altogether absent from broader studies of Islamic law after 1500. Histories of Islamic law in the colonial era continue to focus on Muslim constituencies under British and French rule.[18] It is of course true that global narratives of Islamic thought in the nineteenth and twentieth centuries have become more inclusive of historical actors from beyond the Arab world, but still allot little, if any, space to Muslim thinkers from Russian-ruled lands.[19] On the rare occasions that Russia's Muslims appear in synthetic works on Islamic history, their experiences are almost always refracted through the lens of modernist ('Jadid') cultural reform, an approach that obliterates anything less modern-looking, decouples the study of supposed secular sensibilities from the study of Islamic intellectual traditions and turns a blind eye to patterns of Islamic knowledge-production and circulation in manuscript form, which predated the age of steam and print.[20]

This volume takes a first step towards integrating the Muslims of the Russian Empire into the global history of Islamic law under colonial rule. Muslim juridical training, legal institutions, codification of legal knowledge and debates over legal theory, phenomena well-studied in British, French, Dutch and Ottoman-ruled lands, were as every bit as present and relevant in Russia-ruled Muslim lands. At the same time, the specificities of Russia's government, geography and the many communities over which it ruled meant that colonial rule in Russia was not merely a mirror-image of British or French empire-building. Bringing Russia into the broader study of Islamic law in the nineteenth and twentieth centuries allows historians to expand and complicate their understandings of how Islamic law, legal institutions and legal consciousness developed in the presence of and in response to different kinds of European colonial rule.

In this volume, we offer a preliminary examination of the formulation, codification, transmission and application of Islamic law in various regions under Russian rule from the 1600s to the 1910s. The contributors present a series of case studies from different regional and ethnic communities within the empire. In doing so, we seek to bring together the progress of the past three decades to illustrate where the study of Islamic law in the Russian Empire now stands and to suggest trajectories for future research.

These studies do not provide a comprehensive picture of Islamic law under Russian rule. To do so would be impossible, given the current state of the field. Although the number of historians working with Islamic law, theology and ritual in post-Soviet territory using Arabic, Persian and Turkic-language sources has grown considerably since the 1990s, this number is still relatively small when compared to the number of scholars in other historical fields. Furthermore, the neglect of 'religious' subjects during the Soviet period means that questions that have been long resolved in other fields only began to be addressed for Russia's Muslim communities in the 1990s and early 2000s. Finally, the poor state of preservation and cataloguing of non-Russian-language primary sources, although improved since the 1990s, has hampered research efforts. In specific national and regional contexts, post-Soviet restrictions on archival access still represent a colossal impediment to researchers.

The Historiography of Islamic Law in the Russian Empire

Before considering specific examples of Islamic legal practices, institutions and discourses under Russian rule, it may be useful to situate the present study within the longer history of Russian Muslim studies. The end of the Soviet Union was a turning point in the study of Russian and Soviet history in general. However, it was of especial importance for the study of the Muslim peoples of the Russian Empire and its Soviet successor. Countless archival, library and museum collections that had previously been inaccessible to foreign scholars and were open to Soviet historians only on a restricted basis were made partially or fully available. (Sadly, some collections have since been closed or restricted once again.) From the 1960s to the 1980s, religion as a subject for historical enquiry had been mostly off-limits to Soviet scholars for political reasons or unresearchable due to the limited access to relevant primary sources. Instead, the study of Russia's Muslims was structured around Soviet-era national categories and 'Marxist-Leninist' narratives of class, national and anti-colonial struggle.[21] Starting from the 1990s, it became possible to pose complex questions about popular religiosity, gender and religious practice, communal religious institutions and personnel, and mystical practices. Historians also began to examine Islam as a source of community cohesion, collective identity and social order. In turn, this historical project helped to refine our understanding of how certain cultural practices among Muslims of Russia differed from or resembled what has been observed in other parts of the Islamicate world.[22]

The 1990s also altered the study of Islam and Muslims in Russia in a second way. It drew the study of Islam in Russia into a new burgeoning historiography of Russia as an empire. The histories of Kazan, Orenburg, Samarkand or Tashkent were no longer interesting only as windows into the world of the Soviet nationalities. They now became evidence for determining whether Russia was a colonial and/or imperial project comparable to the British and French empires. Like post-1991 studies of Muslim culture in Russia, this new interest in Russian imperial rule over Muslims was facilitated by the opening of Russia's archives and libraries. However, its proponents posed a very different set of questions from those posed by scholars of Islam in Russia. Historians of Russia *qua* empire placed the Russian state – the imperial government and its policies, institutions, officials and non-state allies – at the centre of their enquiry. They concerned themselves with how Russia engaged with and regulated Islamic law and religious practice, how Russian officials perceived their Muslim subjects, how Muslims under Russian rule interacted with state legal institutions and how Muslim subjects' beliefs, behaviours and community relations were shaped by these interactions. Some of these historians proposed the existence of a holistic imperial policy towards Muslims across the empire's history or, at least, a coherent, linear evolution of the imperial government's strategies for ruling Muslim populations.[23] Others focused more narrowly on Russian rule over single provinces or ethnic groups as case studies on the effects of Russian imperial rule on the legal culture of individual Muslim societies.[24]

The studies of how Russia ruled its Muslims have turned primarily to Russian official sources – imperial law codes, records of court proceedings, ethnographic communications among imperial bureaucrats, among many other compositional genres – to gather data. In a few cases, small samplings of non-Russian-language materials or discussions of indigenous legal concepts have been used to augment information from and interpretations of Russian-language sources.[25] The interpretive outcome of this approach has been a broad acceptance among historians of the Russian Empire that the imperial government was the single most powerful actor in shaping institutions, legal culture and views on Russian subjecthood in Muslim communities under Russian rule.[26]

The authors of this volume seek to complicate this interpretation of the relationship between the Russian state and its Muslims by shifting the focus from imperial institutions to the Muslim subjects who inhabited and interacted with them. It is not the authors' intention to deny or belittle the role that the imperial government played in shaping legal institutions, practices and consciousness in Muslim societies under its rule. The unequal balance of power between the Russian government and Muslim societies as well as the centralising tendencies of the Russian imperial state gave its officials significant leverage over Muslims and the definition of their rights. However, turning our attention to Muslim imperial subjects enables historians to look beyond the somewhat narrow taxonomies through which the Russian state often rendered (and distorted) what Muslims said about and made of law. Concentrating our attention on Muslim communities and their internal dynamism allows us to re-envision the degree to which Muslims' own interpretations of Islamic law shaped imperial policies vis-à-vis Islam in Russia and abroad. The larger goal of this project is to achieve a more complex picture of Muslims' normativity under Russian rule, one in which indigenous communities were not just the passive recipients of policies superimposed on them. This, in turn, should equip us with a better understanding of the various ways in which Muslims related to Russian intervention into matters of law and the cultural and ideological issues at stake in the disputes that came to imperial officials' attention. The proposed shift of focus is not intended merely to add complexity to an already eclectic picture, but, rather, to offer a change of perspective. Indeed, it is about time that historians of Russia recognise that the various manifestations of *sharīʿa* that one can observe within the Muslim communities of the Russian Empire did not just amount to a *reaction* to the state and should not be interpreted as such. The Muslim subjects of the Russian Empire did not live their lives solely by responding to the stimuli coming from the state. Indeed, as variously demonstrated in this volume, more often than not it was the state that had to react to changing circumstances within the Muslim-majority regions of the empire. The appreciation of this complex picture can be achieved chiefly by sifting through records that shed light on the biographies of Muslim jurists, the structure of Islamic legal and educational institutions, indigenous discourses on law and morality and, more broadly, the ways in which Muslims engaged with the law to pursue justice. And this has been the chief concern of the contributors to this volume.

A recurring criticism of the work of historians who have taken a top–down approach to studying Russia's intervention into Islamic law is that they lack the background knowledge of native institutions, social networks and legal culture that is required to disentangle the language of Islamic law and Islamic intellectual traditions from the linguistic conventions of the imperial bureaucratese to provide accurate interpretations of individual legal disputes. If one relies excessively on government records, one is destined to reproduce, albeit inadvertently, the sensibilities, concerns and misconceptions of the imperial state.[27] Giving greater attention to Islamicate sources when examining Muslim legal culture in Russia can help one to avoid this pitfall.

Sustained attention to indigenous sources can also clarify the extent to which the Russian officials and institutions relied on local Muslim legal authorities and local hierarchies to govern the empire's Muslim population. The small salaried staff of the empire's Muslim spiritual assemblies, which were intended to regulate Islamic institutions and Muslim legal cases, relied upon village imams to keep the metric books containing the birth, marriage and death records critical for resolving divorces and inheritance disputes.[28] The judges who staffed the assemblies and presided over 'native courts' often received their education in madrasas, institutions that were only superficially regulated by the state.[29] Colonial administrators borrowed elements and terms from pre-conquest legal culture, sometimes without possessing a clear understanding of their meaning within Muslim societies.[30] Despite amassing copious ethnographic material on indigenous societies, imperial codification projects never extended beyond the regional level and the imperial officials who authored them often promoted their contents as local 'customary law' rather than as a system of 'Islamic law' that could be applied to all the empire's Muslim subjects.[31] Russian officials remained reliant upon Muslim legal scholars for insights on local law in the empire's Muslim provinces and such an approach became a stimulus for scholarly networks and legal debates to thrive under Russian rule.

This volume – as a whole and in its various chapters – calls for the informed and extensive use of non-Russian-language Islamic sources to reconstruct Muslim legal life under Russian rule. However, in doing so, it does not neglect relevant Russian-language sources on the subject. Nor, by privileging Islamic sources do its authors intend to suggest the existence of two parallel Muslim legal cultures – official/imperial and unofficial/native – in the Russian Empire. The authors of the present volume are not attempting to revive the paradigm of 'official Islam' (licensed spiritual personnel subordinate to state-sponsored hierarchies) versus 'parallel Islam' (Sufi and mystical leaders, folk Islam and religious practices not sanctioned or controlled by the state) proposed in Cold War-era studies of Soviet Islam.[32] Nor do we find it useful to rely on an interpretive model that explains anything related to *sharīʿa* as an epiphenomenon of two self-contained Islamic discourses, one produced by Muslim scholars and operative within ostensibly insulated Muslim communities, the other emanating from imperial agencies writing in Russian. Such a division between Muslim and Russian Islamic discourses is not only inaccurate, but also profoundly misleading, for it obscures how different and, at times, opposing historical forces of change intersected to shape the legal practices that we observe in the Islamic juridical field of the Russian Empire.[33] To speak of Russian or Muslim discourses on *sharīʿa* may be helpful to highlight the conventions informing the composition of the historical records upon which historians must rely. However, it is equally important to bear in mind that a substantial number of Muslims (including legal scholars) served the Russian state in various capacities and often spoke on behalf of both Muslim constituencies and Russian state agencies. In addition, to postulate either the self-containment of an Islamic discourse designed for Muslim communities or that such a discourse ultimately informed transactions between the empire and its Muslim subjects has little analytical traction if one does not undertake to explain the production and circulation of knowledge on Islam within society and the state apparatus.

Instead, the essays in this volume propose that Russian institutions and policies relating to the promulgation and enforcement of Islamic law (labelled as such or disguised as customary law) rested upon a deep and complex structure of native Muslim networks, institutions, practices and discourses over which the Russian government never exercised exclusive control.[34] Muslim legal consciousness was shaped not only by interactions with Russian officials, but by local practices and ongoing communications with Muslims from other regions and other empires. Muslim debates over Islamic ritual, morality, legal theory and application of the law ranged well beyond the relatively narrow set of concerns of Russian officials.

Mapping out Islam under Russian Rule

In *For Prophet and Tsar*, Robert Crews argues that from the time of Catherine the Great '[t]he [Russian] empire created a religious-centered framework for its subjects to engage with the autocracy. Rather than try to impose religious uniformity on its varied subjects, the empress and her successors devised a policy of toleration to make faiths such as Islam the basic building blocks of the empire.'[35] In making this argument, he emphasizes continuities in imperial Russia's efforts at governing Muslim populations across different eras and regions. He argues that while the details of how Islam was handled in each region of the empire varied, Russia's rulers pursued a consistent goal (the implementation of imperial rule) and acted according to a consistent set of principles (religious toleration and the belief that religion could be made useful to the imperial state).[36]

In contrast to Crews's empire-wide examination of Russia's administration of Muslim peoples, a number of other historians of Islam in Russia have chosen to focus on Russian rule in specific regions. While these historians do not deny similarities or continuities among Russian policies in different Muslim regions, they tend to emphasise the unique aspects of Russian rule in their chosen region. These regionally focused studies of Russian engagement with Islamic law can be grouped into the following subfields:[37]

The Middle Volga, Volga-Ural Region or Inner Russia

The Muslims of the khanates of Kazan (conquered in 1552), Astrakhan (conquered 1556), Siberia (conquered 1582–9) and Kasim (liquidated in 1681) as well as the Bashkirs of the Urals and service Muslims settled in Muscovy before 1552 represent Russia's oldest Muslim population and were distinguished from other Muslims of the empire by their full integration into the Russian estate (*sosloviia*) system and the disappearance of their aristocratic elite and native political institutions from 1552 to the early 1700s. Studies on Russia's policy towards Islam in the Middle Volga give especial attention to Catherine II's Enlightenment-inspired Edict on the Toleration of Faiths (1767) and the founding of the Orenburg Muslim Spiritual Assembly (1788), the latter being an institution designed to function as a 'Church' for Islam and whose personnel claimed juristic and moral authority over other scholars of Islam in the empire. Thus, historians see the regency of Catherine II as marking a transition from a policy of state persecution of Islam to one of religious tolerance and co-option of the region's *ʿulamāʾ* into the imperial project.[38] In particular, Robert Crews and Daniel Brower view Catherine's policies towards Volga Muslims as a key moment in the development of Russian official attitudes towards Islam, which decisively shaped imperial policy towards future conquered Muslim populations.[39] Other historians view Catherine's policies as facilitating an economic and cultural florescence in the Volga-Ural Muslim community, which facilitated an 'Islamic revival' in the 1800s.[40] Still others argue that it had limited direct intervention and innovation by the Russian state within Volga-Ural Muslim society until the latter part of the nineteenth century.[41]

The Orenburg Muslim Spiritual Assembly (henceforth, OMSA) occupies a central role in studies of Volga-Ural Muslim legal issues and relations with the state in the nineteenth century and early twentieth. However, there is not a firm consensus among historians on how it impacted legal consciousness and the implementation of Islamic law. Some scholars have emphasised how the intervention of a non-Muslim government into Islamic law delegitimised Islamic jurists and fuelled disputes over where true Islamic legal authority rested.[42] Crews has argued that the assembly became a tool by which the Russian state could use Muslim jurists and legal scholars to promote a vision of 'Islamic orthodoxy'.[43] In speaking of 'orthodoxy', Crews, in fact, emphasises the aspiration of certain imperial institutions to streamline the practice of Islamic law by cementing it into a simplified rendering of Hanafism.[44] It is, of course, true that the network of scholars loyal to the OMSA, to a certain extent, accrued power to impose their own opinions upon the larger Muslim society. And we do observe that local communities perceived as exceptional the authority of the *muftī* and exploited his unique status to achieve their own purposes: to uphold a certain moral position or to challenge the power of other jurists and settle scores with individuals whom they did not like.[45] However, these assertions about the OMSA and its effect on Islamic scholarly authority have been based on a relatively small number of documents. To date, no extensive study of the tens of thousands of case files held in the OMSA archive has been conducted to detect patterns and shifts in the assembly's procedures or its stance on specific legal questions, not to mention the broader effects of Muslims' petitions to the OMSA on communities at a local level.

The other pole around which studies of Islam in the Volga-Ural region have clustered is the so-called Jadid cultural reform movement of the 1880s to 1910s. Since the 1960s, historians of Jadidism have identified reform-minded Volga-Ural Muslim legal scholars such as Mūsā Bīgī (1875–1949), ᶜĀlimjān Bārūdī (1857–1921), Riḍāʾaddīn bin Fakhraddīn (1859–1936) and ᶜAbdullāh Būbī (1871–1922) as part of the Jadid movement; some of these same historians have cast earlier figures such as Abū n-Nāṣr al-Qūrṣāwī (1776–1812) and Shihābaddīn al-Marjānī (1818–89) as forebears of Jadidism.[46] The result has been a narrative in which all innovation in Volga-Ural Islamic legal thought culminated in Jadidism, the adherents of which, over several generations, shifted their attention from 'religious' matters to the creation of a 'secular' and/or 'national' society.[47] Since the 1990s, there have been significant efforts to revise this narrative by emphasising ties between Islamic legal reformism in the early twentieth-century Volga-Ural region and in other parts of the Islamic world, to raise scholarly awareness of Islamic knowledge production beyond the bounds of Jadidism and to give greater attention to the participation of so-called Jadids in Islamic legal debates.[48] However, these trends have yet to coalesce into a coherent narrative or interpretive framework for discussing the evolution of debates over Islamic law within the Volga-Ural Muslim community.

The North Caucasus

The North Caucasus was initially annexed into the Russian Empire in the late 1700s. But it was the Caucasus Wars (1817–64) and the confrontational character of the colonial encounter in the nineteenth century that mostly informed Russian imperial policies towards Islam in the Caucasus and particularly towards *sharīᶜa*.[49] By evoking the image of unruly mountaineers, earlier generations of historians once emphasised the role of Sufism in resistance to Russian rule in the North Caucasus.[50] However, recent research has demonstrated that Sufism was neither the cause of nor an organisational tool in the Caucasus Wars and the prominence attributed to it was largely a result of Russian official (mis)interpretations of local Muslim cultures.[51] The Caucasus Wars are often positioned as a turning point in Russian officials' engagement with Islam. Officials' belief that resistance to Russian rule in the Caucasus was based on so-called 'fanatic' adherence to Islam cast into doubt the Catherinian policy of using Islam to create loyal subjects. Imperial officials came to see the compilation of knowledge on Islam and local culture (rather than the cooption of Islamic scholars) as the key to harnessing native elites to the imperial project without arousing religious objections.[52] Russians therefore attempted to weaken *sharīʿa* by emphasising the importance of customary laws, which they presented as a manifestation of a pre-Islamic culture embedded in north Caucasian mountaineers. Some officials, missionaries and ethnographers pushed further, using newly gained knowledge of non-Russian languages, cultures and laws for the gradual transformation of non-Russians into citizens of the empire.[53]

Whereas historians of the Volga-Ural region have mostly concerned themselves with questions of how the OMSA and Russian courts and police forces affected the authority of Muslim jurists, historians of the North Caucasus have focused more on imperial codification projects, the development of colonial legal ethnography and changes in Islamic jurisprudence in pre and post-conquest Daghestan.[54] In particular, a few scholars have put into greater relief how the reconfiguration of Islamic legal hermeneutics were rooted in the early modern trans-regional networks of Daghestani *ʿulamāʾ* studying in the Middle East.[55] This interpretive move is significant, for it allows us to understand legal changes not just as derivative of Russian imperialism, but as the long-term consequences of the entanglement between pre-colonial and post-colonial cultures. More specifically, in the past the artificial separation between customary laws and *sharīʿa*, together with the rise of an Islamic jurisprudential critique against custom (*ʿādāt/ʿurf*), was explained as the outcome of the colonial encounter. Recent studies have suggested, instead, that such critique may have predated the Russian intervention in the Islamic juridical field of the North Caucasus and that, in fact, local jurists' rejection of *ʿādāt* could be rooted in pre-colonial indigenous attempts to re-envision Islamic legal hermeneutics.[56]

The Kazakh Steppe

Annexed piecemeal into the empire from the 1730s to the 1860s, the Kazakh Steppe encapsulates the various phases of Russia's rule over Muslims. The Junior Horde and the Bukey or Inner Horde, brought under Russian rule from the 1730s to the early 1800s, were placed within the jurisdiction of the OMSA until 1868.[57] The Middle Horde became the subject of Russian experiments in 'rational' legislation beginning in 1822 with Mikhail Speranskii's (1772–1839) 'Statute on the Siberian Kirgiz' (*Ustav o Sibirskikh Kirgizakh*), which replaced Catherine's use of Tatar intermediaries with direct administrative relationship between Kazakh elites and Russian officials.

Russia's diverse policies in the Kazakh Steppe were bound together by officials' assumption that Kazakhs were only recently and incompletely Islamicised. Imperial administrators deployed such an assumption (which historians have variously demonstrated was tendentious and flawed)[58] to hold Islam at bay, for they regarded the display of Islamic piety as a marker of a civilisation that was alien and, thus, a threat to the integrity of the Russian imperial project in Central Asia. Russian legislative projects in the Kazakh Steppe, together with their attendant emphasis on customary law (and codification thereof), were not just informed by ethnographic sensibilities, but rested, instead, on a transformative project, which was typical of colonial situations. By codifying what they termed 'customary law', Russians sought, in fact, not only to record what they encountered as they penetrated the Kazakh Steppe, but to distance Kazakh subjects of the Russian Empire from other Central Asian Muslims, who were subjects of the Uzbek khans. They did so by excluding *sharīᶜa* from the Kazakh juridical field, a cultural condition upon which Russians relied to administer Kazakhs and, also, one that they projected into the past.[59] Ironically, the codification of Kazakh customary law and its artificial separation from Islamic law were pursued during a period in which the Kazakhs (as much as other communities inhabiting the fringes of the steppe) were experiencing an increase in Islamic educational infrastructure, an intense exposure to Islamic print culture and a boom of Islamic charitable activities. These developments were aspects of a deeper transformative process, which brought the Kazakhs closer to other Muslim constituencies inhabiting the southern regions of Central Asia and the Volga-Ural region to the north.

Thus, on the one hand, one can observe how the Russian Empire promoted 'customary law courts' presided over by native judges called *biy*s and treated compilations of customary law as forming the core of the nineteenth- and early twentieth-century legal system for the Middle Horde.[60] On the other hand, the situation on the ground was much more complex: many native judges continued to receive their education in the madrasas,[61] while at the same time cadet corps at Orenburg and Omsk provided sites for training a new cadre of bureaucrats who were ethnic Kazakhs but fluent in Russian language and culture.[62]

The Governor-Generalship of Turkestan and the Protectorates of Khiva and Bukhara

The Russian conquest of Central Asia (1847–85) brought into the empire the most populous and institutionally complex of its Muslim territories.[63] The officials charged with integrating these conquered states arrived armed with, on the one hand, faith in the power of knowledge as a tool of empire and, on the other, a distrust for native religious authorities and Islamic law, a distrust conditioned by Russia's experiences in the North Caucasus. At once pessimistic about the usefulness of Islam for creating loyal imperial subjects and fearful of the violent reaction that a frontal assault on Islamic institutions and practices might provoke, the colonial administration adopted what Konstantin Petrovich von Kaufmann (d. 1882), the first Governor General of Turkestan, termed a policy of 'benevolent neglect' (*ignorirovanie*). Under this policy, Russian officials refused to recognise the role of Islam in political and public life, while at the same time they avoided actions, such as Orthodox Christian proselytising, which they judged likely to offend Muslim religious sensibilities and lead to violent uprisings. Officials' suspicion towards Islam in Central Asia was influenced, in part, by their growing awareness of the Islamic revival underway in the Volga-Ural region since the late eighteenth century. This revival had spurred an enthusiasm for Sufism and Islamic law, literature and education among Islamic scholars and the broader Muslim population that alarmed Russian officials. These officials increasingly viewed the Tatars' 'fanatical' attachment to Islam as an obstacle to promoting Russian culture and loyalty to the empire and Tatars themselves as rivals in a battle for the hearts and minds of the empire's Muslims. To prevent the 'Tatarification' of newly conquered Muslims, the government's earlier practice relying on Tatar *ᶜulamāʾ* intermediaries and cultural experts was greatly curtailed. The jurisdiction of the Orenburg Muslim Spiritual Assembly was not extended into newly conquered Central Asia and the Kazakh Steppe was removed from its authority. Laws were established to bar Volga-Ural scholars from obtaining imams' posts in the steppe and opening schools for non-Tatar students in Central Asia.[64]

In Central Asia, the juridical field of *sharīᶜa* was constrained and transformed into the system of the so-called 'native courts' (Rus. *narodnye sudy*). Russians explained this new institutional arrangement both as a continuity with past practices and a modern innovation. Indeed, although still staffed by Muslim jurists, these courts were posited as a more 'rational' alternative to pre-conquest legal institutions and practices.[65] In fact, this system allowed the dispensation of justice according to *sharīᶜa* within the precincts of courts presided only by Muslim scholars, who were appointed to the post of *qāḍī* by ballot. Therefore, the institution of the 'native courts' was something far removed from the juridical field in which Muslims operated prior to the Russian conquest. In the Uzbek khanates, the resolution of conflicts was the prerogative of the royal courts, while *qāḍī*s were authorised to hear disputes only when authorised by representatives of the dynasty in power.[66]

The long-term goal of the 'benevolent neglect' policy was the gradual transformation of 'alien' Central Asian Muslims into civic-minded Russian subjects. This goal would be achieved, according to imperial lawmakers, by offering Muslims the option of resolving their conflicts through their own 'primitive' laws and practices while simultaneously presenting the purportedly more 'civilised' alternative of Russian legal institutions.[67] For historians who study empire and colonialism in Russia, this shift from pacifying, containing and indirectly administering a conquered community to intervening directly into its institutions and legal codes to reshape its people's cultures and mentalities constitutes a break that must be explained. Some historians have focused on the concept of 'tolerance' to connect von Kaufmann's policy of non-interference in Central Asia with Catherine's earlier policies in the Volga-Ural region.[68] However, the two policies diverge in significant ways. Whereas Catherine emphasised the Islamic character of Volga-Ural Muslim society and developed an exclusive, if limited, legal framework for Volga-Ural Muslims on the basis that Islam made them confessionally and legally distinct from their Christian neighbours, non-interference sought to de-emphasise the role of Islam in Central Asian legal life and ease Central Asians towards a legal consciousness that did not include Islam. The first policy pre-supposed a Russia state inhabited by culturally and confessionally diverse subjects (including Muslims) who could be loyal to the emperor while continuing indefinitely to live according to the legal norms of their own faith and local culture. The second policy cast Islam as inherently threatening to the imperial order and aimed to create a society of undifferentiated citizen-subjects. Customary law codes and native courts became waystations on the road to eventual cultural assimilation.

Second, Catherine's and von Kaufmann's policies differed in scale. Catherine's OMSA handled cases only on a narrow range of subjects (family law, clerical licensing and the maintenance of Muslim institutions). By contrast, the 'native courts' of Russian-ruled Central Asia heard the full range of civil cases. Also, while the Muslim population in the Volga-Ural region were surrounded by and, often, intermixed with a larger Russian population, the ethnic Russian population of Central Asia remained small and, often, concentrated in designated quarters of a few large cities, where they were subject to a different set of legal institutions from the native population. These factors made Russian rule in Central Asia more readily comparable with European colonial possessions in India, North Africa and Southeast Asia than with Russian rule in the Volga-Ural region. As such, the debates among historians of Russian colonial rule in Central Asia tend to focus on how Russian governance was carried out and how native political and legal institutions were affected.[69]

When these various regional histories and historiographies are brought together, some general tendencies emerge. One of these is Russian officials' growing suspicion of Islam. Such suspicion is evident as early as the 1730s in the communications among Ivan Kirilov, Alexei Tevkelev and other officials charged with containing the Bashkir uprisings of 1734–40, and it re-emerged periodically in discussions of the government's involvement with Islamic law, culture and institutions from the 1780s through the 1850s. However, by the 1860s such suspicion had become so strong and widespread among the empire's officials that it led them to commit to legal institutions and codes that constrained the role of Islamic law or refused altogether to recognise it.

Another trend is officials' increasing interest in rapprochement (*sblizhenie*) and, ultimately, the assimilation of Muslim subjects to a Russian vision of citizenship, a goal that was to be achieved through the initial stage of enshrining cultural differences in the form of native legal institutions.[70] As one moves from the Volga-Ural region to the North Caucasus and, finally, to the Kazakh Steppe and Central Asia, it is possible to see how policy success or failure in one region informed administrative decisions elsewhere.

Despite these continuities, historians must contend with a mosaic of administrative systems across the Muslim regions of the empire. The Muslims of the Volga-Ural region were thoroughly integrated into Russia's estate system (*sosloviia*) and, after the 1860s, enjoyed the same institutions of local governance as their Russian neighbours. Parts of the North Caucasus, most notably, Daghestan, existed under civil-military administration and, periodically, under martial law. So, too, did the polities of Central Asia: the Kokand Khanate, and parts of the Emirate of Bukhara and the Khanate of Khiva were absorbed and transformed into provinces under civil-military administration, while the remaining territories of the Emirate of Bukhara and the Khanate of Khiva were preserved in truncated form as Russian protectorates.[71] The Kazakh Steppe presents perhaps the most complicated picture, divided as it was among the Governorship-General of Turkestan, the *Stepnoi Krai*, and several provinces of inner

Russia.[72] These differences in administrative structure were matched by differences in Russian officials' perceptions of the nature of Islam in various regions of the empire. Officials perceived the Volga-Ural region, the North Caucasus and Central Asia as regions in which 'fanatical' adherence to Islam posed a threat to imperial rule. Meanwhile, they imagined the Kazakh Steppe as a space in which Islam rested lightly on the population and could be easily replaced with a legal and civic consciousness of the colonisers' choosing.

This volume seeks to highlight the diversity of Russian officials' approaches to Islamic law. While it may be possible to discern broad tendencies in imperial administration, these tendencies were never sufficiently coordinated or coherent to comprise a Russian 'Muslim policy'. There is strong evidence for the existence of a 'Muslim question' in the Russian Empire, especially after the Russo-Japanese War, when the 1905 Revolution destabilised the Russian state and Russian officials came to view ethno-national and religious differences as threats to the empire.[73] However, Muslims' interactions with imperial representatives and institutions concerning Islamic legal questions differed significantly from region to region. Despite information-gathering activities at the local level, there was no effort by the imperial government to aggregate this information to create a single authoritative legal digest or to adopt a standard set of institutions and procedures across regions.

This lack of uniformity is evident if one considers, for instance, the arbitration of family law in the Volga-Ural region and the Kazakh Steppe. Despite being neighbouring regions inhabited by Sunni Muslims of the Ḥanafī legal school who often traded at the same markets, studied at the same madrasas, enjoyed some of the same Islamic literature and followed the same Sufi shaykhs, Tatars and Kazakhs remained subject to different laws and institutions concerning family law. In matters of marriage and divorce, Volga-Ural Muslims were to turn to their local imams, then, their *ākhūnd*s and, finally, the OMSA. Their cases would be resolved in accordance with Islamic (usually Ḥanafī) legal norms, as long as such norms did not contradict imperial law.[74] By contrast, Russian officials in the Kazakh Steppe dedicated much energy to creating customary law codes and native legal institutions distinct from both Islamic law and the Russian civil courts. In addition, some Kazakhs appealed their cases to the OMSA, but officials reserved the right not to recognise OMSA decisions as superseding those decisions already handed down by the native courts.[75] Comparing how the empire regulated Islamic and customary law among Tatars and Kazakhs respectively shows the degree to which Russian approaches to Islam in general and Muslim normativity in particular differed according to regional and historical contexts. Here is a case in which Russian officials used Islamic law and legal scholars to define and regulate family law for one people while trying to create a code of family law ostentatiously decoupled from *sharīᶜa* for a second people despite the geographic and cultural proximity of the two peoples to another.

If we shift our attention from family law to the law of *waqf* (Ar. 'charitable endowment', pl. *awqāf*), we again observe that institutionalised regional traditions and pragmatism mattered more to Russian administrators than formulating uniform policies. The policies that officials adopted in Central Asia did not necessarily build upon previous experiences of administering other Muslim-majority regions. From the mid-sixteenth to the second half of the eighteenth century in the Middle Volga, Siberia and northern Kazakh Steppe, for example, Russians did not legislate on charitable endowments for they did not recognise *waqf* as a category of landownership. Lands donated to *awqāf* were therefore subject to the same taxation as private ownership, a fact that de-incentivised the establishment of the kind of large-scale *waqf* complexes seen elsewhere in the Islamic world or in other Muslim-majority regions of the Russian Empire.[76]

The situation was very different in the Governorship-General of Turkestan, where the existence of *awqāf* was sanctioned by the colonial legislation. Under Russian rule, the administration of assets belonging to charitable endowments underwent a complex process of repeated surveys for purposes of taxation. In this respect, by building on local legalese, Russians disambiguated 'private' from 'public' endowments. That is, they distinguished *awqāf* established to preserve the integrity of assets from the application of the Islamic law of inheritance and subsequent devolution of property rights from endowments established for the benefit of all Muslims such as *awqāf* created exclusively to support financially Islamic institutions such as madrasas, shrines and wells. Thus, 'private' endowments were rendered subject to taxation, while 'public' *awqāf* were tax-exempt. In addition, colonial agencies pursued a policy of simplification or elimination of *waqf* administration. In some cases, multiple relatively small charitable endowments were aggregated into one and brought under the supervision of a single administrator (*mutawallī*). In other cases, imperial statutory laws legislated on Muslims' tenurial rights in such a way as to encourage *awqāf*'s expropriation by peasants or their transformation into private properties. Despite this aggressive policy, Muslim charitable endowments not only were preserved, but also some were also established anew, and this arrangement allowed for the integrity of Islamic educational infrastructure.[77]

If the Russian government demonstrated any overarching approach to governing Muslims, one might say that it was that individual regions had to be governed on their own cultural and historical terms or, rather, on such terms as Russian officials understood them. It is tempting to see in this culturally and geographically based legal-administrative segmentation a precursor to the national compartmentalisation that replaced it under Soviet rule. However, the USSR's laws, legal institutions and definitions of citizenship were far more coherent and uniform than the empire's various codes and systems for ruling its diverse Muslim populations.

The Myth of a Pristine Pre-colonial Past

Measuring the effects of colonialism on the theory and practice of Islamic law is a complex and challenging enterprise. It is one that is often affected by the ways in which we look at the Muslim world today and by our presentist concerns. In his magisterial work devoted to the history of *sharīᶜa*, Wael Hallaq posits colonisation as a key moment of transition from an egalitarian culture of Islamic law to one heavily informed by European concepts of law, modernity, bureaucracy, class and, finally, nation. According to this interpretation, conquest and/or pressure by the European powers at once halted the natural evolution of Islamic law and replaced it with something both hybrid and decidedly far-removed from pre-conquest law and culture. Colonisation engendered a rupture. The movement towards codification, the creation of state-sponsored legal institutions and hierarchies for the judiciary and the cynical use of the law by elites and colonisers became defining characteristics of the Islamic juridical field.[78] Hallaq's story is, in effect, that of a fall from a grace. Before colonialism, Muslims moved about within a legal culture that belonged wholly to them. Afterward, they not only felt compelled to measure their legal culture against those of Europe but adopted ways of thinking about the law that were derived from the cultures of their conquerors.[79] These effects of the colonial encounter on Muslims' understanding of *sharīᶜa* continue to inform much of the theory and practice of Islam in the post-colonial world.[80]

Not all historians of law in Russia's Muslim regions reference Hallaq's work, but many of them have adopted a similar interpretation while addressing the impact of Russian colonisation on Muslim legal culture, namely, that encounters between Islamic law and imperial officials tended to result in law codes and institutions that were deviations from pre-conquest legal culture, inferior to it and inherently dysfunctional. Recurring themes in the study of the legal lives of Russia's Muslim communities include the manipulation of colonial law by the colonised, the destruction or denigration of legal concepts meaningful in the pre-conquest society and corruption and/or diminished authority of native elites.[81] Such an interpretation presents three basic problems. First, in focusing on the changes that Islamic law underwent in the colonial era, it becomes all too easy to idealise and, thus, essentialise pre-colonial Muslim legal cultures. At present, scholarship on pre-conquest legal institutions, practices and discourses in many of the Russia Empire's Muslim communities is so fragmentary that broader conclusions on pre-colonial legal culture have been largely speculative.[82] Research conducted on the Khanate of Khiva, for example, suggests that practices of forum-shopping were as significant, and thus representative, of pre-colonial Muslim legal life as of Muslim legal life under Russian rule. Likewise, pre-colonial Muslim jurists depended as much upon political authorities to uphold their verdicts as colonial-era jurists did.[83] Therefore, it is inaccurate to view such activities purely as outcomes of Russian intervention. Moreover, exclusive reliance on a narrative of 'change' obscures the many manifestations of continuity that we find across the colonial divide. To acknowledge such continuities is tantamount to recognising, once again, that the age of Russian imperialism was one in which, in many Muslim-majority areas, colonial agents absorbed institutions, notions and sensibilities that had, in fact, originated from local societies and their attendant cultural practices.

Second, while colonial rule clearly influenced Muslims' perceptions of *sharīʿa* in Russia and elsewhere, it is difficult to pinpoint a specific moment at which this critical transformation from pre-colonial to colonial consciousness occurred. This problem is especially evident in the cases of the Volga-Ural region, conquered in the 1550s, but not the object of imperial experiments in applying Islamic law until the 1780s, and the Kazakh Steppe, which was absorbed piecemeal into the empire from the 1730s to the 1860s. However, it is also evident in the histories of Russian involvement in the Caucasus, Crimea and Central Asia. Russian institutions and concepts arrived through a string of conquests, declarations and projects that stretched across decades and, in some cases, centuries. Native responses were incremental, and the re-configuration of legal practice and legal consciousness was gradual. It is difficult to make a clear division between the pre-colonial and the colonial. Moreover, this before-and-after model is problematic in how it (mis)represents the consciousness of the historical actors. That a modern historian perceives a particular concept or practice as alien to 'Muslim' culture does not mean that Muslims living in that time and place perceived it as such. Assuming an objective progression from a pure indigenous culture to one transformed and corrupted by Western concepts leaves little space for understanding how Muslims could fully internalise particular practices and concepts at one moment but come to perceive them as foreign or incompatible at another.

The dominant interpretation raises a third flaw in contrasting pre- and post-conquest legal culture: it leads to an excessive emphasis on 'colonial' or 'Western' influence to the detriment of indigenous dynamism. Tendencies towards direct state involvement in the definition of the law, in the appointment of jurists and the building of a juristic hierarchy and in the control of the juridical field were not unique to Western societies. They were also present in early modern Muslim societies from the Ottoman empire to the Khanate of Khiva.[84] New substantial changes in the Islamic legal spheres occurred when a growing number of Muslim communities in the Russian Empire turned from Arabic and Persian to vernacular Turkic languages as a preferred medium to reproduce, teach and practice *sharīʿa*. The vernacularisation of Islamic law facilitated a new wave of canonisation of jurisprudential texts, produced a concomitant process of debasement of Islamic legal theory and led to a move towards the popularisation of *sharīʿa* through new compositional genres such as Sufi ethical works.[85] More broadly, it would be helpful to acknowledge that, as scholarship on South Asian history has shown, major cultural shifts occurred in Asia regardless of changes in the West. The centuries from the Black Death to the First World War were characterised by rapid political, social, economic, cultural and technological changes across the globe. Those changes included European colonialism, but many other developments as well: bureaucratisation, rising literacy, expansion, migration and integration into a global economy characterised by the mass production and mass consumption of goods and texts. Some of these developments were driven in direct ways by affairs in Europe. Others were influenced in more indirect ways by the rise of the Atlantic trade system and the rapid industrialisation of Western and Central Europe. Still others must be linked to the emergence of expansionist, commercially minded states across the Eurasian landmass from the 1400s through the late 1700s.[86] Internal developments in Islamic lands did not cease once these lands were drawn into the orbit of the expanding colonial powers.

Rather than contributing to polemics over the relative merits and authenticity of pre-colonial and colonial legal culture, this volume seeks to understand Russian Muslims' daily interactions with Islamic legal knowledge, institutions and authorities. The authors seek to examine the interaction and dynamism of both indigenous and Russian-imposed aspects of legal life while maintaining a clear-eyed view of the possibilities and limitations present in both pre-colonial and colonial society.

The Purpose and Layout of this Volume

The study of the history of Islam and Muslims under Russian rule has made great strides since the early 1990s. Scholars know much more about Russian imperial rule over Muslim communities and the internal history of those communities than was known thirty years ago. That said, the number of historians employed in the study of Islam in Russia has been and continues to be small compared to other fields and the primary sources, many of which have only become accessible in the past three decades, have received less scholarly attention than those used in the longer-established fields of British and French colonial history. Also, historians have and continue to favour particular issues, time periods and regions (especially, late nineteenth-century education reform and the Russian Empire's strategies and policies for administering Muslim populations) at the expense of others. The result of this is a situation in which some aspects of the history have been relatively well-explored while others remain largely unexamined.

Given this state of the field, composing an encyclopaedic treatment of the history of Islamic law under Russian rule would prove extremely difficult. Rather than attempting to provide a comprehensive account of the history of *sharīᶜa* in imperial Russia, this volume highlights recent developments in the study of Islamic legal institutions, personnel and practices, and points to directions for future scholarly enquiry. This volume focuses on three aspects of Russia's Muslim legal culture: (1) the training and organisation of Muslim legal experts, (2) discourses on Islamic legal theory and, especially, independent legal reasoning (*ijtihād*) and (3) the implementation and enforcement of *sharī'a* and customary law (*ᶜādat*) in various parts of the empire.

In examining the training and organisation of Muslim legal experts under Russian rule, the authors highlight the centrality of classically trained Islamic scholars to legal life in various parts of the empire and the continuities in legal training across the imperial period. In Chapter One, Danielle Ross uses manuscript and printed law manuals, madrasa programmes and writings on education to argue that training Islamic jurists remained the central mission of Volga-Ural madrasas across the imperial period despite various movements for education reform. In Chapter Three, Ross turns to Muslim women's education in the Volga-Ural region. She argues that late nineteenth-century reformers, despite their claims to champion women's education, did much to de-value women's legal knowledge and the settings in which women gained that knowledge. In order to continue to participate in discourses on Islamic law, educated women had to adopt the knowledge-transmission strategies and discursive models used by their male colleagues and relatives. In Chapter Five, Allen Frank uses Kazakh-language genealogies and hagiographies from the Kerey clan (*ru'*) to establish that Islamic law and legists played a central role in Kazakh nomadic society before the Russian conquest and continued to do so until the Russian Revolution. The sources he examines not only challenge Russian observers' rendering of Kazakh Islam as superficial, but also demonstrate strong links between the Kazakhs of the northern steppe and the neighbouring Muslim peoples, with whom they interacted through madrasas and Sufi networks. Training in mathematics, natural sciences and native language were intended to augment juridical education rather than replace it. All three of these chapters counter the narrative of Islamic cultural reform as a secularising process by emphasising the ongoing presence of Islamic legal scholars, their networks and their madrasas across the last decades of imperial rule.

In those chapters examining legal discourses, the authors focus, in particular, upon the debates surrounding *ijtihād* (independent legal reasoning) versus *taqlīd* (following established legal precedent) and how those debates developed over time. In Chapter Two, Nathan Spannaus examines how Volga-Ural Muslims' understandings of Islamic law evolved from the 1552 Russian conquest to 1917. He focuses, in particular, upon how the co-option of Muslim legal scholars by the Russian imperial state and the transformation statuses such as imam, *qādī* and *muftī* into bureaucratic offices reshaped discourses on *ijtihād* and *taqlīd* and led to the emergence of numerous divergent views on how to properly conduct Islamic jurisprudence. Such complexity of legal theory was not unique to the Volga-Ural region. In Chapter Seven, Shamil Shikhaliev presents the discourse on *ijtihād* and *taqlīd* in Daghestan from the early 1700s to the 1920s. As the Muslims of Daghestan struggled with a variety of challenges, ranging from internal community conflict to Russian conquest and economic integration, the region's legal scholars shifted their stance on the value and validity of *ijtihād,* embracing it in the 1700s, turning away from it in the 1800s and returning to it in the last years of the empire. Shikhaliev's study of Islamic legal theory in Daghestan also reveals that the choice between *ijtihād* and *taqlīd* was rarely a binary one. Daghestani jurists recognised multiple levels of independent legal reasoning and could permit some while rejecting others. This understanding of *ijtihād* complicates the reform versus tradition and innovation versus blind imitation dichotomies often found in studies of Muslim cultural reform in late imperial Russia.

In Chapter Nine, Paolo Sartori turns to legal miscellanies from colonial Russian Central Asia to re-consider the role of *taqlīd* in the region's juridical culture. He argues that, far from being a cause of cultural and intellectual stagnation, the compilation of legal precedents and the requirement that low-ranking Muslim jurists follow them created stability within Islamic legal culture. It was precisely the profound level of formalism achieved by *sharīᶜa* in the age of *taqlīd* that made colonial attempts to codify Islamic law redundant and thus incapable of producing the desired effects. Sartori shows that, despite Russian officials' and Orientalists' claim that *sharīᶜa*'s theorisation was chaotic and its practice unpredictable, Islamic jurisprudence had, in fact, developed in such a way as to produce an established chain of juristic authorities and uncontested approaches to legal hermeneutics. Thus, Sartori's study challenges the narrative that colonial conquest led to a decisive change in how Islamic jurisprudence (*furūᶜ al-fiqh*) was understood and implemented.

Finally, this volume considers how Islamic law was implemented in various regions of the empire. In Chapter Four, Rozaliya Garipova uses the case of Volga-Ural Muslim marriage and government-imposed exile to consider how contradictions between imperial law and Islamic law shaped Muslim scholarly hierarchies and domestic relationships. Furthermore, Garipova ventures into the uncharted terrain of subjectivity and probes the deep reaches of the history of emotions grafted onto legal materials. In Chapter Six, Paolo Sartori and Pavel Shabley seek to untangle Russian officials' efforts to craft a customary law code for the Kazakh Steppe. Their examination of the fate of I. Ia. Osmolovskii's compendium of Kazakh customary law demonstrates how imperial officials' perceptions of Islam and non-Russian cultures shaped the way they collected knowledge and used (or discarded) that knowledge as they attempted to design legal codes. Taking a somewhat narrower approach in Chapter Eight, Michael Kemper and Shamil Shikhaliev use a single case of a stolen (and eaten?) horse to understand how Islamic legal authority operated in Russian-ruled Chechnya. This case demonstrates how a now-legendary Sufi leader operated as a conflict mediator and arbitrator of Islamic law in the 1860s, and, in doing so, complicates our view of the conflict between customary and Islamic law in the North Caucasus. In Chapter Ten, Paolo Sartori and Ulfat Abdurasulov explore the role of the khan in conflict resolution in nineteenth-century Khiva. They contend that Muslim scholarly and juridical figures alone could not resolve legal questions. Forcing conflicting parties to bring a case to arbitration and accept a legal ruling often required the presence of a politically powerful individual such as the Khivan khan. The Khivan court and legal system were structured to facilitate the practice of subjects travelling great distances to receive the khan's justice. Sartori and Abdurasulov's work is one of the first to consider the role of Muslim political leaders in coordinating and enforcing Islamic law in Central Asia. All the cases examined in these chapters emphasise the complexities and ambiguities of formulating and implementing Islamic law under Russian rule and underline our contention that there was no single policy or method by which Muslims across the empire were ruled.

Throughout the volume, the authors stress the potential of Arabic, Turkic and Persian-language primary sources to improve our understanding of Muslim legal culture and views on Russian rule. Not only have Arabic-script sources received much less attention than Russian-language archival documents, but they represent the true frontier of the field. Our understanding of Muslim legal culture (and Muslim culture in general) continues to evolve as existing manuscript collections are catalogued and new ones come to light. In addition to drawing upon sources crafted in the Arabic-script, the essays contained herein prioritise local perspectives on Islamic legal culture over imperial ones. How Muslim peasants, jurists and officials understood and interacted with Islamic law is privileged over how imperial officials thought and wrote about it. At the same time, emic sources (Muslim law digests, madrasa curricula, personal letters from Muslim subjects, treatises on Islamic legal theory and, where possible, pre-conquest sources) are used to situate etic sources (imperial decrees, ethnographic accounts) in relation to legal concepts and practices embedded within the Muslim communities. In our view this exercise is key to enriching our readers' understanding of historical material produced at the intersections of Muslim society and Russian rule (native court records, petitions, customary law codes). By adopting these approaches, the authors highlight the continuities and diversity of Islamic legal culture in Russia and the limits of Russian officials' ability to shape it. We remind historians of Russia that, when attempting to understand the nature of imperial rule, there is much to be gained by taking non-Russian perspectives into consideration.

For scholars who operate outside Russian history, this volume seeks to return the Russian-ruled parts of the Muslim world to the study of Islamic law, and the history of Muslim culture broadly conceived. Studies on independent legal reasoning and the 'modernisation' of Islamic legal culture, for example, continue to focus disproportionately on South Asia and the Middle East. The authors recognise the interactions between Russia's Muslims and those in other parts of the Muslim world, but contend that experiences and views of Russia's Muslims on Islamic law provide for fruitful comparison with those of Muslims under British, French and Dutch rule and challenge the tendency to use the trajectory of Islamic law in British India as a model for making sense of Muslim colonial experiences elsewhere.

Notes

1. *Obshchii svod po imperii rezul'tatov razrabotki dannykh pervoi vseobshchei perepisi naseleniia, proizvedennoi 28 Ianvaria 1879 goda* (St Peterburg: Tipo-litografiia N. L. Nyritsina, 1905), vol. 2, pp. 996–7; *Census of the British Empire. 1901. Report with Summary and Detailed Tables for the Several Colonies, &c., Area, Houses, and Population* (London: Darling & Son, Ltd, 1906), p. L.
2. S. J. Shaw, 'The Ottoman Census System and Population, 1831–1914', *International Journal of Middle East Studies* 9:3 (1978), p. 334.
3. Anonymous, 'Narodnonaselenie Rossii', *Tarjuman/Perevodchik* 47 (1901), p. 1.
4. *Nederlandsch-Indië. Uitkomsten der in de Maand November 1920 Gehouden Volkstelling* (2 vols) (Batavia: Ryugrok, 1922), vol. 2, p. 133.
5. *The Cambridge History of Inner Asia: The Chinggisid Age*, eds N. Di Cosmo, A. J. Frank and P. B. Golden (Cambridge: Cambridge University Press, 2009); D. DeWeese, *Islamization and Native Religion in the Golden Horde: Baba Tükles and Conversion to Islam in Historical and Epic Tradition* (University Park: Pennsylvania State University Press, 1994); S. Kotkin, 'Mongol Commonwealth? Exchange and Governance across the Post-Mongol Space', *Kritika: Explorations in Russian and Eurasian History* 8:3 (2007), pp. 487–531.
6. A. A. Arslanova, *Opisanie rukopisei na persidskom iazyke nauchnoi biblioteki im. N.I. Lobachevskogo Kazanskogo gosudarstvennogo universiteta* (Moscow and Kazan: Kazanskii gosudarstvennyi universitet/Institut istorii im. Sh. Mardzhani Akademii nauk Respubliki Tatarstan/Institut vostokovedeniia Rossiiskoi Akademii nauk, 2005), vyp. I, pp. 86–93, nos 33, 36–9; II, pp. 32–40, nos 401–8; A. A. Arslanova, *Opisanie rukopisei na persidskom iazyke nauchnoi biblioteki im. N.I. Lobachevskogo Kazanskogo (Privolzhskogo) federal'nogo universiteta*, vyp. II (Kazan: Kazanskii federal'nyi universitet/GBU 'Institut istorii im. Sh. Mardzhani' Akademii nauk Respubliki Tatarstan/Institut vostokovedeniia Rossiiskoi Akademii nauk, 2015), pp. 43–4, No. 411, and pp. 51–2, No. 419.
7. At least three important examples come to mind. The first one is the Persian translation of the *Mukhtaṣar al-wiqāya fī masāʾil al-Hidāya* (otherwise known as *al-Nuqāya*), which was produced by one Muḥammad Ṣalāḥ b. Badr al-Dīn b. Muḥammad al-Jarzuwanī in 1530/1 under ᶜUbaydullah Khan, the Shibanid ruler of Bukhara. There exist several copies of this translation. O. F. Akimushkin et al., *Persidskie i tadzhikskie rukopisi instituta narodov azii akademii nauk SSSR (Kratkii alfavitnyi katalog), chast' 1* (Moscow: Nauka, 1964), nos 3980–3; G. I. Kostygova, *Persidskie i tadzhikskie rukopisi*

'novoi serii' FPB. Alfavitnyi katalog (Leningrad, 1973), no. 154; A. Idrisov, A. Muminov and M. Szuppe, *Manuscrits en écriture arabe du Musée regional de Nukus (République autonome du Karakalpakstan, Ouzbékistan). Fonds arabe, persan, turkī et karakalpak* (Rome: Istituto per l'Oriente C.A. Nallino, 2007), p. 82; *Tarjumay-i Mukhtasar al-Wiqāya*, MS St Petersburg, Russian National Library, T.N.S. 105, uncatalogued. The second example is a Persian-language commentary on a tract on the Islamic law of inheritance titled *al-Farā'iḍ al-Sirājiyya* and authored by Sirāj al-Dīn Muḥammad b. Muḥammad al-Sijāwandī (d. twelfth century). The Persian commentary was crafted in the Middle Volga and there exist several copies also in Central Asia. See M. Kemper, *Sufis und Gelehrte in Tatarien und Baschkirien 1789–1889: Der islamische Diskurs unter russischer Herrschaft* (Berlin: Klaus Schwarz Verlag, 1998), p. 217; A. Idrisov, A. Muminov and M. Szuppe, *Manuscrits en écriture arabe du Musée regional de Nukus*, p. 123. A third important example is represented by the fourteenth-century jurisprudential work titled *Maṭālib al-muṣallī*, otherwise known as *Fiqh al-Kaydānī*, crafted by Luṭfallāh al-Nasafī al-Fāḍil al-Kaydānī. Originally written in Arabic, this work was made repeatedly subject to translation into Persian. There exists also a Persian-language commentary by Muḥammad Amīn b. Muḥammad Imām. See ibid., p 134; Akimushkin et al., *Persidskie i tadzhikskie rukopisi instituta narodov azii akademii nauk SSSR (Kratkii alfavitnyi katalog), chast' 1*, nos 2557–70. Both the Persian translation of and commentary on *Fiqh al-Kaydānī* can be found in a jurisprudential miscellany in manuscript form now in Nukus, at the Fundamental Library of the Karakalpak Branch of the Uzbek Academy of Sciences, inv. no. VR-343. The translation was made in 1270/1853–4 while the commentary was completed in 1274/1857–8.

8. J. R. Pickett, 'The Persianate Sphere during the Age of Empires: Islamic Scholars and Networks of Exchange in Central Asia, 1747–1917' (PhD Dissertation, Princeton University, 2015); D. DeWeese, 'Persian and Turkic from Kazan to Tobolsk: Literary Frontiers in Muslim Inner Asia', in N. Green (ed.), *The Persianate World: The Frontiers of a Eurasian Lingua Franca* (Berkeley: University of California Press, 2019), pp. 131–58.
9. On the extent of the trans-regional networks of the Bukharan madrasas, see A. J. Frank, *Bukhara and the Muslims of Russia: Sufism, Education, and the Paradox of Islamic Prestige* (Leiden and Boston: Brill, 2012), passim; Kemper, *Sufis und Gelehrte in Tatarien und Baschkirien 1789–1889: Der islamische Diskurs unter russischer Herrschaft, passim*; Pickett, 'The Persianate Sphere during the Age of Empires: Islamic Scholars and Networks of Exchange in Central Asia, 1747–1917'. On the far reach of Khivan madrasas, see P. Sartori, 'On Madrasas, Legitimation, and Islamic Revival in 19th-century Khorezm: Some Preliminary Observations', *Eurasian Studies* 14 (2016), pp. 98–134; I. A. Beliaev, *Mekteby Zakaspiiskoi oblasti* appendix to *Obzor Zakaspiiskoi Oblasti za 1912–1914* (Askhabad: Tipografiia I.I. Aleksandrova, 1916).

10. D. DeWeese, 'Mapping Khwārazmian Connections in the History of Sufi Traditions: Local Embeddedness, Regional Networks, and Global Ties of the Sufi Communities of Khwārazm', *Eurasian Studies* 14 (2016), pp. 37–97.
11. E. Allworth, *The Modern Uzbeks: From the Fourteenth Century to the Present: A Cultural History* (Stanford: Hoover Institution Press, 1990).
12. F. Starr, *Lost Enlightenment: Central Asia's Golden Past from the Arab Conquest to Tamerlane* (Princeton: Princeton University Press, 2013).
13. By reproducing, and transmitting hagiographic material, specific Sufī communities and initatic constituencies were able to preserve their spiritual connection to the shrine in which the eponymous founder of a brotherhood or a saint was said to be buried, and thus keeping alive a liaison with the community tending such a shrine. The most eloquent example is given by the diasporic Naqshbandī communities in South Asia. On this topic, see J.-A. Gross, 'The Naqshbandīya Connection: From Central Asia to India and Back (16th–19th Centuries)', in S. C. Levi (ed.), *India and Central Asia, 16th to 19th Centuries* (Oxford: Oxford University Press, 2007), pp. 232–59. One, however, can observe similar phenomena among the Muslim communities in the Russian Empire, most notably among the constituents of the Naqshbandī community in Western Siberia; see A. Bustanov, 'Notes on the Yasavīya and Naqshbandīya in Western Siberia in the 17th – Early 20th Centuries', in N. Pianciola and P. Sartori (eds), *Islam, Society and States across the Qazaq Steppe (18th – Early 20th Centuries)* (Vienna: Austrian Academy of Sciences Press, 2013), pp. 69–93.
14. Ph. Bruckmayr, 'The Spread and Persistence of Māturīdi Kalām and Underlying Dynamics', *Iran and the Caucaus* 13 (2009), pp. 59–92.
15. Completed in the year 1844, the chronicle *Riyāḍ al-Dawla,* which eulogises the reign of the Qunghrat dynast Allāh Qulī Khān (r. 1825-1842), maintains that the Khan of Khiva summoned special assemblies of scholars who were required to read and comment upon four texts in the fashion of public disputations, before four authoritative jurists who acted as arbiters (*mumayyiz*). The selection of texts included Marghīnānī's *Hidāya.* See Āgahī Muḥammad Riḍā Mīrāb b. Īr Niyāz-Bīk, *Riyāḍ al-Dawla,* MS St Petersburg, Institute of Oriental Manuscripts, inv. no. D-123, fols 90a–92a.
16. A. Idrisov, A. Muminov and M. Szuppe, *Manuscrits en écriture arabe du Musée regional de Nukus,* p. 95.
17. O. Pritsak, 'Āl-i Burhān', *Der Islam* XXX (1952), pp. 81–96.
18. W. B. Hallaq, *Sharīʿa: Theory, Practice, Transformations* (Cambridge: Cambridge University Press, 2009); L. Benton, *Law and Colonial Cultures: Legal Regimes in World History, 1400–1900* (Cambridge: Cambridge University Press, 2009); M. S. Umar, *Islam and Colonialism: Intellectual Responses of Muslims of Northern Nigeria to British Colonial Rule* (Leiden and Boston: Brill, 2006); I. R. Hussin, *The Politics of Islamic Law: Local Elites, Colonial Authority, and the Making of the Muslim State* (Chicago and London: University of Chicago Press, 2016); J. Stephens, *Governing Islam:*

Law, Empire and Secularism in Modern South Asia (Cambridge: Cambridge University Press, 2018).

19. C. Kurzman's *Modernist Islam, 1840–1940: A Sourcebook* (Oxford: Oxford University Press, 2002) is one of the few surveys of Islamic thought in the nineteenth and twentieth centuries to include Russia Muslims in its narrative. However, Russia's Muslims are entirely absent from his *Liberal Islam: A Sourcebook* (Oxford: Oxford University Press, 1998). M. Q. Zaman's *Islamic Thought in a Radical Age: Religious Authority and Internal Criticism* (Cambridge: Cambridge University Press, 2012) concerns itself almost exclusively with Arab and South Asian thinkers. Likewise, recent histories of Salafism follow the development and spread of that branch of Islamic thought in the Middle East, South Asia and Southeast Asia, but not in Russian and Soviet-ruled lands. See Henri Lauzière, *The Making of Salafism: Islamic Reform in the Twentieth Century* (New York: Columbia University Press, 2015); *Global Salafism: Islam's New Religious Movement*, ed. Roel Meijer (Oxford: Oxford University Press, 2014).
20. I. M. Lapidus, *A History of Islamic Societies* (Cambridge: Cambridge University Press, 2014), pp. 684–717; M. G. S. Hodgson, *Venture of Islam, Volume 3: The Gunpowder Empires and Modern Times* (Chicago: University of Chicago Press, 2009), pp. 316–23; 'Introduction: Global Muslims in the Age of Steam and Print', in J. L. Gelvin and N. Green (eds), *Global Muslims in the Age of Steam and Print* (Berkeley: University of California Press, 2014), p. 9.
21. The imposition of these national categories in the Soviet academy left a deep imprint on the works of Western scholars, who, in the absence of unfettered access to the archives, relied heavily on Soviet historical scholarship and edited primary sources. See, for example, A.-A. Rorlich, *The Volga Tatars: A Profile in National Resistance* (Stanford: Hoover Institution Press, 1986); E. Allworth, *The Modern Uzbeks: From the Fourteenth Century to the Present: A Cultural History*; S. A. Zenkovsky, *Pan-Turkism and Islam in Russia* (Cambridge, MA: Harvard University Press, 1960); H. Carrère d'Encausse, *Islam and the Russian Empire: Reform and Revolution in Central Asia* (Berkeley: University of California Press, 1988); A. L. Altstadt, *The Azerbaijani Turks: Power and Identity under Russian Rule* (Stanford: Hoover Institution Press, 1992); M. Brill Olcott, *The Kazakhs* (Stanford: Hoover Institution Press, 1987); G. Wheeler, *The Modern History of Soviet Central Asia* (New York and Washington, DC: Praeger, 1964); A. Bennigsen and C. Lemercier-Quelquejay, *La Presse et le Mouvement National chez les Musulmans de Russie avant 1920* (Paris: Mouton, 1964); A. Bennigsen and C. Lemercier-Quelquejay, *Islam in the Soviet Union* (London: Central Asian Research Centre, 1967); A. W. Fisher, *The Crimean Tatars* (Stanford: Hoover Institution Press, 1978).
22. A. J. Frank, *Islamic Historiography and 'Bulghar' Identity among the Tatars and Bashkirs of Russia* (Leiden: Brill, 1998); A. J. Frank, *Muslim*

Religious Institutions in Russia: The Islamic World of Novouzensk District and the Kazakh Inner Horde, 1780–1910 (Leiden and Boston: Brill, 2001); A. J. Frank, *Bukhara and the Muslims of Russia: Sufism, Education, and the Paradox of Islamic Prestige* (Leiden: Brill, 2012); M. Kemper, *Sufis und Gelehrte in Tatarien und Baschkirien;* M. Kemper, *Herrschaft, Recht und Islam in Daghestan. Von den Khanaten und Gemeindebünden zum ǧihād-Staat* (Caucasian Studies vol. 7) (Wiesbaden: Reichert, 2005); A. N. Kefeli, *Becoming Muslim in Imperial Russia: Conversion, Apostasy, and Literacy* (Ithaca: Cornell University Press, 2014); *Muslim Culture in Russia and Central Asia from the 18th to the Early 20th Centuries* (4 vols), eds M. Kemper et al. (Berlin: Klaus Schwarz Verlag, 1996–8); P. Sartori, *Visions of Justice:* Sharīʿa *and Cultural Change in Russian Central Asia* (Handbook of Oriental Studies VIII/24) (Leiden and Boston: Brill, 2016).

22. R. D. Crews, *For Prophet and Tsar: Islam and Empire in Russia and Central Asia* (Cambridge, MA: Harvard University Press, 2006); J. Burbank, 'An Imperial Rights Regime: Law and Citizenship in the Russian Empire', *Kritika* 7:13 (2006), pp. 397–431; E. I. Campbell, *The Muslim Question and Russian Imperial Governance* (Bloomington: Indiana University Press, 2015).
23. R. D. Crews, *For Prophet and Tsar*; J. Burbank, 'An Imperial Rights Regime'; E. I. Campbell, *The Muslim Question and Russian Imperial Governance.*
24. A. S. Morrison, *Russian Rule in Samarkand, 1868–1910: A Comparison with British India* (Oxford: Oxford University Press, 2008); D. Brower, *Turkestan and the Fate of the Russian Empire* (London: Routledge, 2003); J. Sahadeo, *Russian Colonial Society in Tashkent, 1865–1923* (Bloomington: Indiana University Press, 2007); A. Jersild, *Orientalism and Empire: North Caucasus Mountain Peoples and the Georgian Frontier, 1845–1917* (Kingston: McGill-Queen's University Press, 2003); V. Martin, *Law and Custom in the Steppe: The Kazakhs of the Middle Horde and Russian Colonialism in the Nineteenth Century* (Richmond: RoutledgeCurzon, 2001); R. Geraci, *Window on the East: National and Imperial Identities in Late Tsarist Russia* (Ithaca: Cornell University Press, 2001); E. Pravilova, 'The Property of Empire: Islamic Law and Russian Agrarian Policy in Transcaucasia and Turkestan', *Kritika* 12:2 (2011), pp. 353–86.
25. R. D. Crews, *For Prophet and Tsar*; E. Kane, *Russian Hajj: Empire and the Pilgrimage to Mecca* (Ithaca: Cornell University Press, 2015).
26. R. D. Crews, *For Prophet and Tsar*; C. Steinwedel, *Threads of Empire: Loyalty and Tsarist Authority in Bashkiria, 1552–1917* (Bloomington and Indianapolis: Indiana University Press, 2016); W. Sunderland, *Taming the Wild Field: Colonization and Empire on the Russian Steppe* (Ithaca: Cornell University Press, 2004); M. Khodarkovsky, *Russia's Steppe Frontier: The Making of a Colonial Empire, 1500–1800* (Bloomington: Indiana University Press, 2004).

27. A. Khalid, 'Tolerating Islam', *London Review of Books* 29.10 (24 May 2007), pp. 15–16; A. Morrison, 'Crews, Robert D. *For Prophet and Tsar: Islam and Empire in Russia and Central Asia.* Harvard University Press, Cambridge, MA, 2006. viii + 463 pp. Maps. Illustrations. Notes. Index. $29.95: £ 19.95', *The Slavonic and East European* Review 86:3 (July 2008), pp. 553–7; P. Sartori, *Visions of Justice*, pp. 27–8.
28. *Sbornik tsirkuliarov i inykh rukovodiashchikh rasporiazhenii po okrugu orenburgskogo magometanskogo dukhovnogo sobraniia 1836–1903 g* (Kazan: Iman, 2004), pp. 22–3; *Materialy po Istorii Bashkirskoi ASSR* (Moscow: Izd-vo Akademii Nauk SSSR, 1960), vol. 5, pp. 564–6; M. Tuna, *Imperial Russia's Muslims: Islam, Empire, and European Modernity, 1788–1914* (Cambridge: Cambridge University Press, 2015), pp. 48–50.
29. On the history of the madrasas and *ᶜulamāᵓ* training under Russian rule, see A. Khalid, *The Politics of Muslim Cultural Reform: Jadidism in Central Asia* (Berkeley, Los Angeles and Oxford: University of California Press, 1999); A. J. Frank, *Bukhara and the Muslims of Russia*; J. R. Pickett, 'The Persianate Sphere during the Ages of Empires: Islamic Scholars and Networks of Exchange in Central Asia, 1747–1917'; M. Tuna, *Imperial Russia's Muslims*; J. H. Meyer, *Turks across Empires: Marketing Muslim Identity in the Russian-Ottoman Borderlands, 1856–1914* (Oxford: Oxford University Press, 2014).
30. An excellent example of this kind of misunderstanding is the appropriation of the term *muftī* as the title for the head official of the Muslim Spiritual Assemblies. Clearly, there was no precedent within Volga-Ural Muslim society for using the term in this manner. As elsewhere in the Islamicate world, the term *muftī* denotes only a scholar's ability to issue legal opinions (*fatwās*), and not the possession of ultimate authority over all other Muslim jurists. On the creation of the OMSA, see D. D. Azamatov, 'Russian Administration and Islam in Bashkiria (18th–19th centuries)', in M. Kemper, A. von Kügelgen and D. Yermakov (eds), *Muslim Culture in Russia and Central Asia from the 18th to the Early 20th Centuries* (Berlin: Klaus Schwarz Verlag, 1996), pp. 91–111; M. Kemper, *Sufis und Gelehrte in Tatarien und Baschkirien;* R. D. Crews, *For Prophet and Tsar,* pp. 46–8. Virginia Martin's study of imperial officials' misinterpretation and criminalisation of the Kazakh practice of *barïmta* (Rus., *baranta*) presents another example of the limits of Russian officials' understandings of Islamic and non-Russian legal language, titles and practices. See V. Martin, 'Barïmta: Nomadic Custom, Imperial Crime' in D. R. Brower and E. J. Lazzerini (eds), *Russia's Orient: Imperial Borderlands and Peoples, 1700–1917* (Bloomington: Indiana University Press, 1997), pp. 249–70.
31. Sartori, *Visions of Justice*, pp. 104, 109, 115, 184 and *passim.*
32. For a prominent example of such a strand of scholarship, see A. Bennigsen and S. Enders Wimbush, *Mystics and Commissars: Sufism in the Soviet Union* (Berkeley and Los Angeles: University of California Press, 1985). A recent,

forceful critique of the Bennigsenian approach to 'Sufism' and other forms of Islamic religiosity, which were not sanctioned by the Soviet state and thus regarded by Sovietologists as manifestations of 'Islamic resistance', can be found in D. DeWeese, 'Re-Envisioning the History of Sufi Communities in Central Asia: Continuity and Adaptation in Sources and Social Frameworks, 16th – 20th Centuries', in D. DeWeese and J.-A. Gross (eds), *Sufism in Central Asia: New Perspectives on Sufi Traditions, 15th – 21st Centuries* (Leiden and Boston: Brill, 2018), pp. 21–74.

33. For further reflections on the problems that inhere in the use of the notion of 'Islamic discourse', see P. Sartori, 'Exploring the Islamic Juridical Field in the Russian Empire', *Islamic Law and Society* 24:1–2 (2017), pp. 8–10; C. Steinwedel, 'On Sufis, Scholarship, and Many Different Discourses that Existed in the Russian Empire', *Ab Imperio* 2 (2011), pp. 345–52.
34. A prime example of what can be achieved by looking at trans-regional networks of Islamic learning, which developed beyond the control of the Russian imperial surveillance apparatus, is M. Kemper and S. Shikhaliev, 'Sayfallāh-Qāḍī Bashlarov: Sufi Networks between the North Caucasus and the Volga-Urals', in R. Elger and M. Kemper (eds), *The Piety of Learning: Islamic Studies in Honor of Stefan Reichmuth* (Leiden and Boston: Brill, 2017), pp. 166–95.
35. R. D. Crews, *For Prophet and Tsar*, p. 2.
36. Ibid., pp. 2–3.
37. We exclude from the present discussion the South Caucasus (Azerbaijan) and Crimea because, at present, the scholarly literature on legal culture and institutions in these regions is too sparse to comprise distinct historiographical discussions.
38. R. D. Crews, *For Prophet and Tsar*, pp. 37–9; D. Azamatov, 'The Muftis of the Orenburg Spiritual Assembly in the 18th and 19th Centuries: The Struggle for Power in Russia's Muslim Institution', in M. Kemper et al. (eds), *Muslim Culture in Russia and Central Asia from the 18th to the Early 20th Centuries. Vol. 2: Inter-Regional and Inter-Ethnic Relations* (Berlin: Klaus Schwarz Verlag, 1998), pp. 355–84; N. Spannaus, 'The Decline of the *Ākhūnd* and the Transformation of Islamic Law under the Russian Empire', *Islamic Law and Society* 20:3 (2013), pp. 202–41; Steinwedel, *Threads of Empire*, pp. 79–86.
39. D. Brower, 'Islam and Ethnicity: Russian Colonial Policy in Turkestan', in D. Brower and E. J. Lazzerini (eds), *Russia's Orient: Imperial Borderlands and Peoples, 1700–1917* (Bloomington: Indiana University Press, 1997), p. 116; R. D. Crews, *For Prophet and Tsar*, p. 22.
40. A. J. Frank, *Islamic Historiography*, 33–6. In his more recent works, Frank has added a further interpretive dimension to the phenomenon termed 'Islamic revival' by pointing out that, besides the stimuli coming from Catherine's policy of toleration, Central Asian, and especially Bukharan madrasas were known among Muslim communities in Russia for their elevated scholarly

status and thus represented one of the major driving forces behind such revival. See his *Bukhara and the Muslims of Russia,* pp. 4–6.

41. Tuna argues for the existence of an 'insulated safe space of the Volga-Ural Muslim domain' to characterise a relationship between the Russian state and a regional constellation of Muslim communities, in which government officials interacted with Muslim intermediaries rather than directly with Muslim subjects. This, according to Tuna, allowed Volga-Ural Muslims to inhabit an Islamic 'domain', which was minimally influenced by Russian administration and culture. This supposedly began with the founding of the OMSA and ended in the 1860s, with the Great Reforms, or in the 1870s, with the Ministry of Education's efforts to promote Russian-Tatar schools, or in the 1890s with the 'sea change' in the Russian economy. In making this argument, Tuna is effectively suggesting that the influence of the Russian state on Volga-Ural Muslim society was mitigated, diminished or lessened in the 1788–1860s period by the use of Muslim intermediaries. See his *Imperial Russia's Muslims*, pp. 55–6.
42. D. Azamatov, 'The Muftis of the Orenburg Spiritual Assembly in the 18th and 19th Centuries: The Struggle for Power in Russia's Muslim Institution', pp. 355–84; N. Spannaus, 'The Decline of the *Ākhūnd* and the Transformation of Islamic Law under the Russian Empire'.
43. R. D. Crews, *For Prophet and Tsar, passim.*
44. Ibid. pp. 182–3.
45. P. Shabley, 'Fetvy Akhuna Gumara Karasha: Muftiyat i pravovye stolknoveniia vo vnutrennoi Kazakhskoi orde v nachale XX v', *Islamology* 7:2 (2017), pp. 11–28.
46. S. A. Zenkovsky, *Pan-Turkism and Islam in Russia*, p. 24; A.-A. Rorlich, *The Volga Tatars*, pp. 48–64.
47. Ibid., pp. 65–83, 104–22; M. Tuna, *Imperial Russia's Muslims*, pp. 146–70. For a critique directed against such teleological thinking, see N. Spannaus, 'The Ur-Text of Jadidism: Abū Naṣr Qūrsāwī's *Irshād* and the Historiography of Muslim Modernism in Russia', *Journal of the Economic and Social History of the Orient* 59:1–2 (2016), pp. 93–125.
48. S. A. Dudoignon, 'Echoes to al-Manar among the Muslims of the Russian Empire: A Preliminary Research Note on Riżā al-Dīn b. Faḫr al-Dīn and the Šūrā (1908–1918)', in S. A. Dudoignon, H. Komatsu and Ya. Kosugi (eds), *Intellectuals in the Modern Islamic World: Transmission, Transformation, Communication* (London and New York: Routledge, 2001), 85–116; S. A. Dudoignon, 'Qadîmiya as a Historiographical Category: The Question of the Communal Unity as Seen by "Reformists" and "Traditionalists" among the Muslims of Russia and Central Asia in the Early Twentieth Century', in T. Kocaoğlu (ed.), *Türkistan'da yenilik hareketleri ve ihtilaller: 1900–1924: Osman Hoca anısına incelemeler/Reform Movements and Revolutions in Turkistan: 1900–1924: Studies in Honour of Osman Khoja* (Harlem: Sota, 2001), pp. 159–77; S. A. Dudoignon, 'Status and Strategies of a Muslim

'Clergy' under a Christian Law: Polemics about the Collection of the *Zakât* in Late Imperial Russia', in S. A. Dudoignon and Hisao Komatsu (eds), *Islam and Politics in Russia and Central Asia (Early Eighteenth–Late Twentieth Centuries)* (London: Kegan Paul, 2001), pp. 43–73; A. J. Frank, 'Muslim Cultural Decline in Imperial Russia: A Manufactured Crisis', *Journal of the Economic and Social History of the Orient* 59 (2016), pp. 166–92; A. J. Frank, *Bukhara and the Muslims of Russia*; N. Spannaus, 'The Ur-Text of Jadidism: Abū Naṣr Qūrsāwī's *Irshād* and the Historiography of Muslim Modernism in Russia'; R. Garipova, 'The Protectors of Religion and Community: Traditionalist Muslim Scholars of the Volga-Ural Region at the Beginning of the Twentieth Century', *Journal of the Economic and Social History of the Orient* 59:1–2 (2016), pp. 126–65; J. H. Meyer, 'The Economics of Muslim Cultural Reform: Money, Power and Muslim Communities in Late Imperial Russia', in T. Uyama (ed.), *Asiatic Russia: Imperial Power in Regional and International Contexts* (London and New York: Routledge, 2012), pp. 252–70.

49. B. Grant, *The Captive and the Gift: Cultural Histories of Sovereignty in Russia and the Caucasus* (Ithaca and London: Cornell University Press, 2009): R. Gould, *Writers and Rebels: The Literature of Insurgency in the Caucasus* (New Haven and London: Yale University Press, 2016).
50. A. Zelkina, *In Quest of God and Freedom: Sufi Responses to the Russian Advance in the North Caucasus* (London: C. Hurst & Co., 2000); U. Halbach, '"Holy War" against Czarism: The Links between Sufism and Jihad in the Nineteenth-Century Anticolonial Resistance against Russia', in A. Kappeler, G. Simon, G. Brunner and E. Allworth (eds), *Muslim Communities Reemerge: Historical Perspectives on Nationality, Politics, and Opposition in the Former Soviet Union and Yugoslavia* (Durham, NC and London: Duke University Press, 1994), pp. 251–76; A. Bennigsen and S. Enders Wimbush, *Mystics and Commissars: Sufism in the Soviet Union* (Berkeley and Los Angeles: University of California Press, 1985), p. 14.
51. M. Kemper, 'The North Caucasian Khalidiyya and "Muridism": Historiographical Problems', *Journal for the History of Sufism* 5 (2006), pp. 111–26.
52. D. R. Brower, 'Islam and Ethnicity: Russian Colonial Policy in Turkestan', pp. 117–19; I. W. Campbell, *Knowledge and Empire: Kazak Intermediaries and Russian Rule on the Steppe, 1731–1917* (Ithaca: Cornell University Press, 2016).
53. A. L. Jersild, 'From Savagery to Citizenship', p. 117; Geraci, *Window on the East*.
54. M. Kemper, ''Adat against Shari'a Russian Approaches toward Daghestani "Customary Law"', in B. Balcı and R. Motika (eds), *Religion et politique dans le Caucase post soviétique: Les traditions réinventées à l'épreuve des influences extérieures* (Paris: Maisonneuve Larose, 2007), pp. 97–119; V. Bobrovnikov, *Musul'mane Severnogo Kavkaza: Obychai, pravo, nasilie*

(Moscow: Vostochnaia Literatura, 2002); R. Gould and Sh. Shikhaliev, 'Beyond the *Taqlīd/Ijtihād* Dichotomy: Daghestani Legal Thought under Russian Rule', *Islamic Law and Society* 24:1–2 (2017), pp. 142–69. See also the chapter of S. Shikhaliev in this volume.

55. R. Gould, '*Ijtihād* against Madhhab: Legal Hybridity and the Meaning of Modernity in Early Modern Daghestan', *Comparative Studies in Society and History* 57:1 (2015), pp. 35–66.
56. Ibid. pp. 57, 65.
57. V. Martin, *Law and Custom in the Steppe*, p. 58; R. D. Crews, *For Prophet and Tsar*, pp. 221, 226.
58. A. J. Frank, *Muslim Religious Institutions in Imperial Russia*, pp. 275–304; *Islam, Society and States across the Qazaq Steppe (15th–Early 20th Centuries)*.
59. See Sartori and Shabley's chapter in this volume.
60. V. Martin, *Law and Custom in the Steppe*, 35–6.
61. P. Sartori, 'Murder in Manghishlaq: Notes on an Instance of Application of Qazaq Customary Law in Khiva (1895)', *Der Islam* 88:2 (2012), pp. 217–57; P. Sartori, 'The Birth of a Custom: Nomads, *Sharīʿa* Courts and Established Practices in the Tashkent Province, ca. 1868–1919', *Islamic Law and Society* 18 (2011), pp. 293–326.
62. V. Martin, 'Engagement with Empire as Norm and in Practice in Kazakh Nomadic Political Culture (1820s–1830s)', *Central Asian Survey* 36:2 (2017), pp. 175–94; Gulmira S. Sultangalieva, 'Kazakhskoe chinovnichestva Orenburgskogo vedomstva: formirovanie i napravlenie deiatel'nosti (XIX)', *Acta Slavica Iaponica* 27 (2009), pp. 77–101; 'Kazakhskie chinovniki Rossiiskoi imperii XIX v. Osobennosti vospriiatiia vlasti', *Cahiers du Monde russe* 56:4 (2015), pp. 651–79.
63. P. Sartori, *Visions of Justice*, pp. 47–88.
64. Ibid. pp. 117–18; A. S. Morrison, *Russian Rule in Samarkand*, pp. 55–8; D. Brower, 'Islam and Ethnicity', p. 119.
65. P. Sartori, *Visions of Justice*, pp. 89–90.
66. Ibid. Chap. 1. See also Sartori and Abdurasulov's chapter in this volume.
67. P. Sartori, *Visions of Justice*, pp. 104–5.
68. D. Brower, 'Islam and Ethnicity', p. 116; Crews, *For Prophet and Tsar*, p. 292.
69. A. S. Morrison, *Russian Rule in Samarkand*; P. Sartori, *Visions of Justice*; J. Sahadeo, *Russian Colonial Rule in Tashkent*; D. Brower, *Turkestan and the Fate of the Russian Empire*.
70. P. Sartori, *Visions of Empire*, p. 104; A. Jersild, 'From Savagery to Citizenship'.
71. A. Morrison, 'Metropole, Colony, and Imperial Citizenship in the Russian Empire', *Kritika* 13:2 (2012), pp. 327–64.
72. The administrative complexities of the Kazakh Steppe in the early 1900s are well-summarised in Mukhamat Tynyshpaev's 1905 report to the Union

of Autonomists: Mukhamat Tynyshpaev, 'Kirgizy i osvoboditel'noe dvizhenie', in *Istoriia kazakhskogo naroda* (Almaty: 'Sanat', 2009), pp. 23–34.

73. E. Campbell, *The Muslim Question and Russian Imperial Governance*, pp. 154–214.
74. On the resolution of family law cases in the Volga-Ural region, see R. Garipova, 'Married or not Married? On the Obligatory Registration of Muslim Marriages in Nineteenth-Century Russia', *Islamic Law and Society* 24:1–2 (2017), pp. 112–41; N. Spannaus, 'Formalism, Puritanicalism, Traditionalism: Approaches to Islamic Legal Reasoning in the 19th-Century Russian Empire', *The Muslim World* 104 (2014), pp. 354–78; I. Zagidullin, *Tatarskoe natsional'noe dvizhenie v. 1860-1905 gg.* (Kazan: Tatarskoe knizhnoe izdatel'stvo, 2014), pp. 38–60.
75. V. Martin, *Law and Custom in the Steppe.* The sample cases from the 1870s to the1890s included in the appendix to Martin's volume (pp. 212–20) illustrate the multiple jurisdictions that overlapped in the Kazakh Steppe and officials' preference for customary law over resolutions from the OMSA in cases involving Kazakh family law.
76. *Awqāf* in the Volga-Ural region and Siberia were not systematically documented and administered by the OMSA. For a detailed discussion on *waqf* and Muslim charity practices among Muslim communities under the authority of the OMSA, see D. Ross, 'Muslim Charity under Russian Rule: *Waqf, Sadaqa,* and *Zakat* in Imperial Russia', *Islamic Law and Society* 24:1–2 (2017), pp. 77-111.
77. For more on Russian policies on *waqf* in Central Asia, see P. Sartori, *Visions of Justice*, chap. 4.
78. W. B. Hallaq, *Sharīʿa*, pp. 355–70.
79. Ibid., pp. 1–6.
80. Ibid., pp. 549–50.
81. V. Martin, *Law and Custom in the Steppe*, pp. 1–14, 140–55; S. Sabol, *Russian Colonization and the Genesis of Kazak National Consciousness* (New York: Palgrave Macmillan, 2003); N. Spannaus, 'The Decline of the *Ākhūnd* and the Transformation of Islamic Law under the Russian Empire', pp. 202–41; Rozaliya Garipova, 'The Transformation of the Ulama and the Shari'a in the Volga-Ural Muslim Community under Russian Imperial Rule' (PhD dissertation, Princeton University, 2013).
82. This is due in large part to the source base for the pre-colonial period, which is either non-existent, or composed of non-Russian-language manuscripts in varying states of preservation and cataloguing.
83. P. Sartori, *Visions of Justice*, pp. 76–7; 93–6.
84. G. Burak, *The Second Formation of Islamic Law: The Hanafi School in the Early Modern Ottoman Empire* (Cambridge: Cambridge University Press, 2015); P. Sartori, *Visions of Justice*, pp. 95–6, 103; Metin Coşgel and Boğaç Ergene, *The Economics of Ottoman Justice: Settlement and Trial in the Sharia Courts* (Cambridge: Cambridge University Press, 2016); A. Rubin,

'Modernity as a Code: The Ottoman Empire and the Global Movement of Codification', *Journal of the Economic and Social History of the Orient* 59:5 (2016), pp. 828–56. We place the developments examined in our volume within the broader trend of challenging narratives of decline and stagnation in Muslim societies in the eighteenth and nineteenth centuries.

85. Paolo Sartori has elaborated on these topics in 'Taking Stock of Vernacularization from Kazan' to Yarkand: Entexting before Codification', paper read at the conference 'Uses of the Past in Islamic Law', University of Exeter, 28 September 2018. A seminal work in the study of vernacularisation of Islamic law is S. N. Yıldız, 'A Hanafi Law Manual in the Vernacular: Devletoğlu Yūsuf *Balıḳesrī's* Turkish Verse Adaptation of the *Hidāya-Wiqāya* Textual Tradition for the Ottoman Sultan Murad II (824/1424)', *Bulletin of the School of Oriental and African Studies* 80:2 (2017), pp. 283–304.

86. N. Levtzion, *Islam in West Africa: Religion, Society and Politics to 1800* (London: Routledge, 2017); S. Subrahmanyam, *Penumbral Visions: Making Polities in Early Modern South India* (Ann Arbor: University of Michigan Press, 2001); K. Pomeranz, *The Great Divergence: China, Europe, and the Making of the Modern World Economy* (Princeton: Princeton University Press, 2009); P. Perdue, *China Marches West: The Qing Conquest of Central Eurasia* (Cambridge, MA: Harvard University Press, 2009); R. M. Eaton, *The Rise of Islam and the Bengal Frontier, 1204–1760* (Berkeley and Los Angeles: University of California Press, 1993); J. R. McLane, *Land and Local Kinship in Eighteenth-Century Bengal* (Cambridge: Cambridge University Press, 2002); K. Kim, *Borderland Capitalism: Turkestan Produce, Qing Silver, and the Birth of an Eastern Market* (Stanford: Stanford University Press, 2016); S. C. Levi, *The Indian Diaspora in Central Asia and its Trade, 1550–1900* (Leiden: Brill, 2002); S. C. Levi, *The Rise and Fall of Khoqand, 1709–1876: Central Asia in the Global Age* (Pittsburgh: University of Pittsburgh Press, 2017); A. S. Dallal, *Islam without Europe: Traditions of Reform in Eighteenth-Century Islamic Thought* (Chapel Hill: University of North Carolina Press, 2018).

1

Islamic Education for All: Technological Change, Popular Literacy and the Transformation of the Volga-Ural Madrasa, 1650s–1910s

Danielle Ross

In the lessons on *Sharḥ-i Mullā*, a student reads [the word] '*maḥrām*',
If you leave me, my darling, my beloved will be forbidden to me.
The lessons from *Isaghūjī* are full of zeal.
I saw you, my darling, and it touched my soul . . .
When *Isaghūjī* is finished, a student begins to read *Shamsiyya*,
In heaven, my angel, your black hair will be a shawl for you.
During *ᶜaqīda* lessons, I look lovingly at the *Ḥāshiyya*,
In fact, my darling, I am in love with your ebony eyebrows . . .[1]

Introduction

In the above song, transcribed in 1915 by Ṣunᶜatullāh bin Mullā Badraddīn, an imam posted in Keche Mui village, about 100 miles east of Kazan, a madrasa student confesses his feelings for his beloved. In this confession, he references numerous traditional Arabic and Persian-language books on *ṣarf* (grammar), *fiqh* (jurisprudence), *manṭiq* (logic) and *ᶜaqīda* (doctrine). A few pages later, in the same diary, he records a list of the Tatar 'national' novels he had read in 1912.[2]

Ṣunᶜatullāh was one beneficiary of a process of rising literacy and education reform that had begun a century before he penned the song cited above: a village imam who was trained to educate people in the fundamentals of Islam, resolve Islamic legal questions, communicate with imperial authorities in the Russian language, teach children to think of themselves as part of a Tatar ethno-national/linguistic community and model new technologies, farming techniques and ideas. Ṣunᶜatullāh represented a new vision of what an Islam scholar (*ᶜalīm*) could be. Simultaneously a preacher, a schoolteacher, a legal expert, a gardener and a beekeeper, he was jack-of-all-trades who would use his broad range of knowledge to help his increasingly literate congregation navigate the pitfalls of twentieth-century life without losing touch with their faith.

Studies of Muslim education in the Volga-Ural region have focused overwhelmingly on the so-called Jadid movement of the late 1800s and early 1900s. This narrow focus and the accompanying debates over Jadidism's mass appeal and relevance obscure the broader history of Muslim knowledge transmission under Russian rule.[3] This chapter will argue that the debates and transformations that occurred in Volga-Ural Muslim men's education from the 1880s to 1917 were not unique or isolated, but, rather, represented the culmination of longer-term developments in *ᶜulamāᵓ* culture and popular religiosity. From the 1770s to the 1860s, mass-printing and cheaper paper made written texts more widely available and led to new views on literacy as being fundamental to the proper observance of Islam. By the first half of the nineteenth century, the prevalence of books and manuscripts enabled Sufi shaykhs and madrasa teachers to use a growing range of old and new written texts side by side with oral transmission to relay and reinforce Islamic values and laws among Muslim believers. This process enabled less educated Muslims to engage with their faith in new ways and to begin to venture into bodies of knowledge that had once been the preserve of the highly educated.[4] Mass production of scripture and law books and the changing relationship of the common Muslim believer to written texts necessitated changes in the role of the *ᶜulamāᵓ* from keepers of arcane knowledge to curators and facilitators who guided their students and congregants through the labyrinth of complex Islamic legal and theological writings. At the same time, the Russian government's efforts to cultivate cadres of provincial professionals (country doctors, medics, veterinarians) offered a new model of trained professionals as agents for improving popular knowledge and quality of life in rural Russian society. Finally, by the second half of the nineteenth century, European colonial dominance raised growing concerns among educated Muslims over the future of Islamic law, belief and culture.

Together, these factors fuelled a series of debates over what role an *ᶜalīm* should play in his society, what skills he required in order to play this role and how he could most efficiently acquire those skills. These debates included defenders of established educational methods and curricula as well as those who placed their faith in the promotion of rationality and 'scientific' approaches to learning, supporters of logic and philosophy-heavy study programmes as well as those who believed that scripture should be read and interpreted directly, promoters of vernacular-language translations as well as those who insisted that Islamic sacred and legal texts could only be read in Arabic, and defenders of a scholarly monopoly over Islamic law and textual interpretation as well as those who called for all believers to engage with Islamic law and theology. However, holders of all these views strove for the same goal: to create a madrasa education that would adequately equip the *ᶜulamāᵓ* and Muslims in general to sustain Islam in a rapidly changing world. Rather than a two-sided conflict that pitted champions of secularism and progress against defenders of Islam and tradition, participants in the multi-faceted debates over Muslim education in the Volga-Ural region grappled with questions of how Islamic knowledge could best be transmitted to future generations, who should exercise authority over the transmission of that knowledge and what the relationship between 'Islamic' knowledge and knowledge from non-Islamic sources should be.

Volga-Ural Muslim writers began to use terms such as 'progress' (*taraqqī*) and 'modern'/'contemporary' (*zamāncha*) in the late nineteenth century, but they had, in fact, been caught up in what might be viewed as 'modernising' processes (migration/colonisation, globalising trade, systematisation of legal culture, rising literacy) since the seventeenth century. These processes increased in both pace and scale from the beginning of the nineteenth century to 1917. Thus, it is inaccurate to speak either of a 'traditional' Muslim educational culture before the 1880s or a sudden 'awakening' at the end of the nineteenth century. The evolution of Muslim education in the Volga-Ural region was dynamic, cumulative and rooted in the broader conditions of the early modern and modern eras.

This chapter is divided into five sections. The first section examines the emergence of a coherent Volga-Ural madrasa curriculum and culture from the mid-seventeenth century to the late eighteenth century; the second section focuses on the effects of mass printing and falling paper prices on Islamic legal and popular religious culture from the 1770s to the 1860s; the third section offers a new interpretation of the debates over madrasa education and education reform from the 1850s to the 1870s; the fourth section re-assesses the impact of curriculum change in the so-called 'new method' madrasas from the 1890s to the 1910s; finally, the fifth section turns to Muslim publishing catalogues and published law books to reconstruct views on Islamic legal education at the beginning of the twentieth century.

Education from the 1650s to the 1770s: Reproducing a Stable Legal Culture

From the 1650s to the 1770s, the gradations of literacy in the Muslim communities of the Volga-Ural region resembled those of early modern Europe. Some people could read or recite from a limited number of familiar vernacular texts. Fewer were able to write in their vernacular language, and still fewer were able to read and write in Arabic and Persian, the languages of scholarship.[5] Knowledge was often transmitted orally and acquired through interpersonal relationships between masters and their students.[6] Books were hand-copied, a process that required not only knowledge and skill on the part of the copyist, but access to paper, a commodity that was not produced locally.[7] Mass-printed copies of Islamic sacred texts, textbooks, law manuals and devotional texts did not exist in the Volga-Ural region before the end of the eighteenth century. Arabic, Persian and Turkic-language manuscript books used in the region tended to be of high quality (good-quality paper and executed in a clear, if not professional, hand), but they were few in number, expensive and held primarily by the cultural elite.

With written sources in short supply, memorisation and oral transmission played a central role in the preservation and circulation of knowledge. Hints of this orality are visible in surviving written records. A book from the 1690s renders the Islamic inheritance laws into Arabic-language verse.[8] (Even after the advent of print, the rendering of legal and doctrinal information into verse remained a strategy for helping students master such material.) Another book, copied in 1757 and preserved only in fragments, explains the benefits of reciting verses of the Qurʾān. It promised specific benefits to those who had memorised specific verses.[9]

In the midst of this broader world of oral knowledge, the madrasas trained a small group of (mostly) men in reading and interpreting the sacred texts. It is impossible to say much about the structure or day-to-day operations of these madrasas, because there are no sources describing those aspects of education. What can be said is that education in the late seventeenth century and early eighteenth appears to have centred on prominent teachers rather than institutions. A madrasa gained its reputation from its *mudarris* (instructor), who was often also a Sufi shaykh. Attachment to a powerful teacher not only enabled a student to acquire professional and arcane knowledge but established his reputation as a legitimate scholar and enabled him to find employment as an imam and/or teacher.

The 1552 Russian conquest did not sever existing connections between the Volga-Ural *ʿulamāʾ* and Islamic intellectual centres, especially in Central Asia, and intellectual exchanges persisted through the 1600s and 1700s.[10] The content and organisation of the Volga-Ural curriculum from the 1650s to the 1850s reflected trends extant throughout the Sunni Ḥanafī world during these two centuries. The subjects taught in the madrasa were divided into the transmitted sciences (*manqūlat*), namely the study of the Qurʾān, hadith and jurisprudence, and the instrumental or rational sciences (*ma^c^qūlat*), comprising the skills required to analyse the sacred texts (Arabic grammar, speculative theology, logic, philosophy).[11] The manuscripts and references to textbooks that survive from the Volga-Ural madrasas of the 1650s–1770s suggest a heavy emphasis on the instrumental/rational sciences. Arabic grammar instruction (*ṣarf* and *naḥw*) was critical for mastering the rest of the madrasa curriculum and many of the surviving textbooks from the 1600s and the 1700s belong to that discipline. *Al-ᶜAwāmil al-Miᶜa*, an Arabic grammar textbook by the eleventh-century scholar ᶜAbdalqāhir al-Jurjānī, was especially popular for introducing Volga-Ural students to Arabic grammar, and, from the 1650s onward, several local scholars wrote commentaries on it.[12]

There was no unified curriculum for teaching Arabic grammar in the madrasas. Riḍaʾaddīn bin Fakhraddīn, in his biography of Manṣūr bin ᶜAbdarraḥman al-Burindiqī, claims that Kazan's teachers had previously used *Taṣrīf al-ᶜIzzī,* an Arabic grammar guide composed by the thirteenth-century Baghdadi scholar ᶜIzzaddīn az-Zanjānī,[13] to teach Arabic morphology and *Kitāb al-Miṣbāḥ fīl-Naḥw*, an abstract of ᶜAbdalqāhir al-Jurjānī's well-known Arabic grammar *Al-ᶜAwāmil al-Miᶜa* composed by Khwarazmian scholar Abūʾl Fatḥ Nāṣir bin ᶜAbdassayyid Muṭarrizī (1144–1213),[14] and one of its commentaries, *al-Iftitāḥ fī Sharḥ al-Miṣbāḥ*,[15] to teach Arabic syntax. However, Manṣūr, after his return from Bukhara in the late 1600s or early 1700s, replaced these works with *Sharḥ ᶜAbdallāh,*[16] a Persian-language book on Arabic morphology, and *al-ᶜAwāmil al-Miᶜa* and *Qawāᶜid* for syntax. Manṣūr also composed a Persian-language glossary to assist students in using *al-ᶜAwāmil al-Miᶜa.*[17] By contrast, mid-eighteenth-century scholar ᶜAbdassalām bin Ḥasan of Qarile village in Kazan province eschewed the use of *Bidān*, *Sharḥ ᶜAbdallāh*, *al-ᶜAwāmil al-Miᶜa* and *Mufaṣṣal Anmūdhaj* in favour of the commentaries *al-Iftitāḥ fī Sharḥ al-Miṣbāḥ* and *Mullā Jamiᶜ*.[18] *Taṣrīf al-ᶜIzzī* and *Kitāb al-Miṣbāḥ fīl-Naḥw* continued to be used by some teachers throughout the 1700s despite Manṣūr al-Burindiqī's effort to replace them.

The second largest group of surviving seventeenth- and eighteenth-century manuscript books belong to the fields of jurisprudence (*furūᶜ al-fiqh*) and legal theory (*usūl al-fiqh*), disciplines designated as transmitted sciences. Volga-Ural teachers relied on a wide variety of Ḥanafī commentaries and *fatwā* collections: *al-Farāʾiḍ as-Sirājiyya/as-Sirāj fīl-Mīrāth*,[19] *Mukhtaṣar al-Qudūrī*,[20] *Multaqa al-Abḥur*,[21] *Jāmiᶜ ar-Rumūz*,[22] *Būstān Faqīh*,[23] *Tuḥfat al-Mulūk*,[24] *Al-Hidāya fī Sharḥ Bidāyat al-Mubtadī*,[25] *Fatāwa Qāḍīkhan*[26] and *Fatāwa-i Hindiyya/Fatāwaī ᶜĀlamgīrī*.[27,28]

Other works taught in the Volga-Ural region before the 1770s included *Taᶜlīm al-Mutaᶜallim Ṭarīq at-Taᶜallum*,[29] a guide for students on how to learn, *Mirʾāt al-Akhlāq* on ethics (*akhlāq*),[30], *Naṣīb al-Akhbār* on the hadiths and history of the Prophet, *Tafsīr Yaʿqūb Charkhī*[31] and *Tafsīr al-Jalālayn*[32] for understanding the Qurʾān, at-Taftāzānī's *Sharḥ al-ʿAqāʾid an-Nasafiyya*[33] on doctrine (*ʿaqīda*) and *Isāghūjī* (*Isagoge*)[34] to introduce students to logic (*manṭiq*).

Based upon the list of books used in the seventeenth and early eighteenth centuries, several conclusions can be drawn about education at the Volga-Ural madrasas. First, despite the Russian conquest and the anti-Muslim policies that historians have attributed to the Russian state in these centuries, Islamic legal and theological training continued and madrasa reading lists in the conquered Kazan khanate resembled those in other parts of the seventeenth- and eighteenth-century Sunni Muslim world where the Ḥanafī legal school (*madhhab*) predominated. Instruction in Arabic grammar occupied a prominent place in the madrasa curriculum in the late 1600s and early 1700s. Books relating to specialist topics such as mathematics, astronomy and geography have survived from the period, but these topics are not as well represented in surviving manuscripts and biographical records as jurisprudence, Arabic grammar, logic and doctrine. It is likely that the region lacked the economic resources and the critical mass of scholars to support intensive study in more specialised fields. Those wishing to study them or, indeed, to study any discipline in greater depth, went to Central Asia to do so.

In the field of jurisprudence, one finds a predominance of Ḥanafī books of *furūʿ al-fiqh* in use in the Volga-Ural madrasas (*Mukhtaṣar al-Wiqāya*, *Mukhtaṣar al-Qudūrī*, *Jāmiʿ ar-Rumūz*). The prevalence of these books suggests that, as in other parts of the early modern Muslim world, Volga-Ural jurists leaned increasingly towards canonisation of earlier opinions and the promotion of a standardised set of legal stances across regional juridical networks rather than the promulgation of a new opinion for each individual case. This practice of re-stating a mutually accepted set of previous opinions to answer new questions is visible in the legal rulings of the seventeenth and eighteenth centuries.

Print Culture and Popular Literacy: 1770s–1850s

The spread of written culture in the Volga-Ural region was closely connected with the expansion of papermaking and printing in eighteenth-century Europe and the development of these industries in Russia. As a result of the rising rates of paper production in Western Europe and the imperial government's efforts to wean Russia from its dependence on imported paper, the amount of paper for sale throughout the empire's towns increased rapidly from the late 1700s to the mid-1800s.[35] From the 1770s to the 1810s, Volga-Ural Muslim culture became firmly rooted in written texts. The first people affected were the *ᶜulamāʾ* and their students, more of whom could afford to buy paper and make their own copies of legal digests and textbooks or pay others to make copies for them as paper prices decreased. The late eighteenth century was also marked by the beginnings of Arabic-script printing for purposes other than the dissemination of state official documents. In 1787, Catherine II sponsored the first Arabic-language printing of the Qurʾān in Russia.[36] In 1801, the press was moved from St Petersburg to Kazan, where it was used to print popular Muslim didactic and literary works. A total of 150,000 copies of the edition of the Qurʾān initially sponsored by Catherine were printed in Kazan from 1802 to 1859.[37]

This new abundance of written material transformed education in the Volga-Ural Muslim community. In the 1600s and 1700s, instructing the average Muslim in the tenets of Islam had been accomplished mostly through oral transmission; reading and writing had primarily been occupations of the madrasa-educated and their families. By contrast, by the early 1800s, reading began to play a larger role in popular piety. By the early 1800s, *maktab*s and madrasas multiplied across the region. There was a proliferation of Turki-language manuscript religious guides and learning aids: books of ethics, doctrine, worship (*ᶜibādat*) and catechism (*ᶜilm al-ḥāl*) and tales of the prophets. These texts laid out in writing Islamic history, doctrine, obligations and values for Muslim peasants, craftsmen and merchants. The growing importance of reading and written texts in popular religious life was exemplified by the wide circulation (in manuscript and published form) of the *Haft-i yak*, a condensed Qur'ān intended for non-scholarly readers.[38]

The rapid growth in both manuscript production and Arabic-script publications from 1800 to the 1880s suggests that the number of Volga-Ural Muslims literate in their native Turki and familiar with a small amount of Arabic rose significantly by the middle of the century. So, too, did the *ᶜulamāʾ*'s expectations of what written knowledge the average believer should master. The first decades of the nineteenth century saw the production of commentaries and adaptations meant to make popular devotional and legal texts more understandable to the non-madrasa-educated. One work that drew significant attention was *Thabāt al-ᶜĀjizīn*, a work of Chagatai-language devotional poetry attributed to Ṣūfī Allāhyār, a seventeenth-century Central Asian poet and mystic whom nineteenth-century Volga-Ural Muslim scholars identified as descended from refugees who had fled to Central Asia after the Russian conquest of Kazan. *Thabāt al-ᶜĀjizīn* already circulated widely in the Volga-Ural region in written and oral form, where it played an important role in Sufism and Islamic law. It was printed in Russia for the first time in 1802.[39] It also became the subject of commentaries by the early nineteenth-century poet ᶜAbdarraḥīm al-Ūtiz-Īmānī and other Volga-Ural Muslim scholars.[40] The most popular of these commentaries was the *Risāla-i ᶜAzīza* of Tājaddīn bin Yālchīghul (1768–1838), a re-telling and explanation composed in a language closer to the vernacular of the Volga-Ural region.[41] Tājaddīn bin Yālchīghul claimed his motivation for writing *Risāla-i 'Azīza* was a request from his daughter for a 'translation' of *Thabāt al-ᶜĀjizīn* into a language that was more understandable.[42] *Thabāt al-ᶜĀjizīn* remained popular throughout the nineteenth century, and *Risāla-i ᶜAzīza* joined it, circulating widely in manuscript form, going to press for the first time in 1847 and being re-published more than thirty times by 1917.[43]

These vernacular commentaries on the *Thabāt al-ᶜĀjizīn* were part of a larger phenomenon of adapting Sufi poetry and Islamic didactic literature for a larger readership. Al-Ūtiz-Īmānī composed 'The Nightingale and the Rose' (*Bılbıl wa gül*), a Turki-language translation of part of the prologue of Jalāladdīn Rūmī's *Masnavī-i Maᶜnavī*.[44] He was also responsible for compiling what became the authoritative edition of Qūl ᶜAlī's 'Book of Joseph' (*Yusuf Kitabı/Qiṣṣa-i Yusuf*), a popular Turki-language mystical-poetic work, which came to press for the first time in 1839.[45] ᶜAbdalmanīḥ al-Qargalī retold in Turki-language verse Farīdaddīn ᶜAṭṭār's 'Shaykh al-Basrī and Rābiᶜa' and his biography of Ibrahīm ibn Adham from 'Lives of the Saints' (*Tadhkhirat al-awliyāᵓ*) as well as 'The Dispute between the Romans and the Chinese' from Rūmī's *Masnavī*.[46] Vernacular adaptations of Persian-language literary works made texts that were already popular among the madrasa-educated accessible to Muslims who possessed some literacy in their vernacular language, but little or no training in Persian or Arabic. The newly established Asiatic Press in Kazan also contributed to the accessibility of written copies of already popular Turkic-language works. In 1802, *Fawz an-Najāt*, a Tatar translation of a Persian translation of a work on Islamic law, ethics and morality by Abū ᶜAlī Miskawayah (d. 421/1030), that had previously circulated in manuscript form, came to press for the first time.[47] *Qiṣṣa-i Sayfalmulūk* followed in 1807.[48]

In the Volga-Ural madrasas of the early nineteenth century, Persian-language Sufi poetry was a medium used to teach on morality, ethics and the individual believer's relationship with God. Shaykhs and madrasa teachers read to their students from Rūmī's *Masnavi* and *Miftāḥ at-Tawḥīd*.[49] Saᶜdī's *Gulistān* and ᶜAṭṭār's poetry were also widely read among the *ᶜulamāᵓ*. Beginning in the late 1700s, Volga-Ural scholars composed reading aids to make these Persian texts more comprehensible to their students. In the 1770s, Muḥammad Karīm al-Bulghārī assembled an Arabic–Persian–Bulgar [Turki] dictionary for the purpose of assisting Volga-Ural students in improving their knowledge of Persian and functioning more smoothly in Persian-speaking cities such as Kabul and Bukhara, where they might go to continue their education.[50] In the 1830s, al-Ūtiz-Īmānī composed the 'Brief Explanation of the Particularities of the Masnavī' (*Mukhtaṣar latāʾif al-lughat lil-mathnawī*), an Arabic-language text that clarified for students some of the more difficult words and passages of Rumi's text.[51] He also composed an Arabic-language commentary on Ṣūfī Allāhyār's Persian-language *Murād al-'Arīfīn*.[52] When viewed together, the Arabic-language commentaries on Persian-language texts and the Turkic-language translations of Persian poetry discussed previously reveal two expanding audiences for Persian literature: the Arabic-trained madrasa students and a Turkic-speaking readership outside of the madrasa.

In the first half of the nineteenth century, madrasa teachers and jurists also sought to raise the average Muslim's level of knowledge of Islamic law and doctrine. In the 1830s, al-Ūtiz-Īmānī wrote in praise of Shams-i Aḥmād Qāḍīzāda's *Tanāyiḥ al-Afkār fī Kashf ar-Rumūz wa Asrār*, encouraging all Muslims to use the work to improve their knowledge of Islamic law and to teach Islamic law to their wives and children.[53] He communicated a similar message in *Jawāhir al-Bayān*, where he argued that all Muslims should pursue basic knowledge of Islamic law, ritual and doctrine.[54]

In al-Ūtiz-Īmānī's lifetime, Muslim educational institutions in the Volga-Ural region expanded rapidly. During Russia's eastward expansion in the 1700s, new madrasas were founded in the South Urals and western Siberia. By the last decades of the 1700s, the number of madrasas and *maktab*s in Kazan province was also on the rise. These schools attracted young men who hoped to become imams and jurists, but they also drew the attention of Muslims who wanted their children to gain higher levels of education. As a contributor to the *Kazanskii Vestnik* reported in 1816, 'a Tatar who does not know how to read and write is looked down upon by his countrymen, and, as a citizen, receives no respect from others. Because of that, every father tries to enroll his children as early as possible in a school where they will learn, at very least, to read, write, and know the fundamentals of their faith.'[55]

This growing popular interest in education is evident in the history of the region's major madrasas. From 1814 to 1843, the director of Istarlībāsh Madrasa hired a specialist to plant trees on the madrasa grounds and installed an irrigation system. These improvements followed a rise in both the student population and the madrasa's revenue.[56] For the *ᶜulamāᵓ*, Muslims' growing interest in literacy and religion translated into more potential students and, ultimately, more schools and more employment for licensed imams and teachers. From 1833 to 1917, the number of mosques in the Volga-Ural region and Siberia continued to increase.[57] For the same period, the number of Muslim religious personnel licensed by the OMSA grew twice as fast as the number of mosques.[58] Mass printing, cheaper paper and vernacular adaptations made literature read by the madrasa-educated available to a widening circle of readers. The *ᶜulamāᵓ* encouraged their fellow Muslims to improve their knowledge of jurisprudence, doctrine and ethics, and those Muslims themselves viewed the ability to read texts (as opposed to only being able to recite them) as a new measure of piety.

The Linguistic and Organisational Transformation of the Madrasa (1865–81)

By the mid-1800s, the expansion of manuscript production, the rise of Arabic-script publishing in Russia, the spread of popular literacy and ongoing popular interest in Islamic knowledge and texts together laid the foundations for re-thinking the role of the *ᶜulamāᵓ* in Volga-Ural society. As a wider range of written sources on Islamic law and theology became available and more people were able to read them, the *ᶜulamāᵓ* could no longer claim to be the sole bearers of written legal and theological knowledge. For some *ᶜulamāᵓ*, this situation necessitated a change in how they should interact with the Muslim community and how they should train their students. This concern was evident in Riḍāᵓaddīn bin Fakhraddīn's description of the madrasa of ᶜAlī Ishān at-Tūntārī (1772–1874), the most prominent Sufi shaykh of the mid-nineteenth-century Volga Basin:

> There was no order at his madrasa; he did not offer the necessary lessons, particularly on religious matters and ethics, for students who were destined to become common village imams. In place of teaching them the foundations of moral admonitions and advice, he taught them classical logic and speculative theology and how to dispute based on the commentaries and super-commentaries, and they mourned at how their lives had been wasted.[59]

In the above passage, Riḍāᵓaddīn contrasts two visions of the *ᶜalīm* or scholar. The first is the *ᶜalīm* as a bearer of arcane knowledge. This kind of *ᶜalīm* acquired prestige through the public display of his knowledge and, especially, by besting rival scholars in disputes. For this, logic and exegesis were vital skills. The second vision is that of what Riḍāʾaddīn termed the 'common village imam', the men assigned to manage rural mosques, lead Friday prayers, teach the tenets of Islam to children and preside over the rituals connoting major life events. For this kind of work, mastery of logic and philosophy were less necessary than basic pedagogical knowledge.

By the mid-1800s, factors outside of the Volga-Ural Muslim communities were also changing some *ʿulamāʾ*'s views on the role of education. The expansion of Russia education during the nineteenth century included a focus on vocational and practical training for specialists (doctors, medics, military officers) who were to be posted across the empire. This tendency was evident in the first half of the nineteenth century, when both Orenburg *muftī* Gabdessalam Gabdrakhimov and Inner Horde Kazakh khan, Jahāngīr, corresponded with Russian officials concerning the training of madrasa students as doctors and veterinarians to serve the Muslim communities of Inner Russia.[60] Russian official efforts to cultivate cadres of professionals in the provinces increased with the implementation of the Great Reforms in the 1860s, which brought about the establishment of new institutes and vocational schools as well as *zemstvo*-led campaigns to improve public health, education and social services.[61]

At the same time, the governments of the Ottoman Empire and Iran responded to the growing power of the European colonial powers by promoting professional training in law, engineering, medicine, public administration and military affairs. In British India, colonial expansion led the *ʿulamāʾ* to rework madrasa education with the goal of preserving Islamic law and culture under colonial rule.[62] In both the Russian and Islamic contexts, government officials, Muslim jurists and pedagogues emphasised education as a form of investment in society and its future rather than as a path to personal gain. It was against this background that the value of the Volga-Ural madrasas as sites for training men to engage in public displays of esoteric knowledge came under fire.

The *ʿulamāʾ* and their main institution of training and socialisation, the madrasa, became the focus of mid-nineteenth-century discussions of education and its role in Volga-Ural Muslim society. For Russian officials, the Kazan *ʿulamāʾ* had long served as intermediaries between the state and Muslim populations on Russia's southern and eastern frontiers.[63] As officials in the ministries of education and internal affairs began to view education as a tool for the cultural and linguistic integration of non-Russians into the empire, they envisioned madrasa-trained jurists and imams as potential agents for spreading new ideas about Russian subjecthood in Muslim communities.[64] The *ʿulamāʾ*, for their part, viewed themselves as imparters and mediators of Islamic knowledge. The increase in popular literacy and the wider availability of written texts on Islamic law and theology posed both an opportunity for Muslims to become more knowledgeable about their faith and a danger of the spread of misinformation. Madrasa directors sought means to improve the training of future scholars and teachers and to make authoritative information on the faith more accessible.

Many of the *ᶜulamāʾ* involved in the discussions about education in the madrasas worked in Russian educational institutions and/or had contact with Russian educators. They began to think about Muslim juridical education not only in terms of internal community discussions of *ᶜulamāʾ* professional standards and community literacy, but also in relation to educational practices at government-sponsored Russian and *inorodtsy* schools. That is not to say, of course, that Muslim educational reform was merely a consequence of reforms undertaken in Russia. Rather, as educated Muslims witnessed and participated in debates over Russian education in the mid-1800s, they gained access to new ideas, tools and methods that they used as they sought to address the problems they had identified in Muslim education. It is not possible to speak of a single movement or programme of Muslim education reform from the 1850s to the early 1880s. Rather, multiple educators began to work independently and, over the decades, were gradually drawn into dialogue with one another. The independent writings and projects of the 1850s–80s gradually merged into a wider debate over education. These writings and projects addressed the same issues: (1) the benefits of instruction in the Turki vernacular, (2) the organisation of the classroom and the school day and (3) the importance of mathematics, the natural sciences and native language as distinct subjects in the curriculum.

Ḥusayn Fayḍkhanov, an early proponent of such Muslim education reforms, studied at Shihābaddīn al-Marjānī's madrasa in Kazan and attended lectures at Kazan University.[65] In 1858, he was appointed a teacher in St Petersburg University's Oriental Languages Department.[66] This employment brought him into contact with Russian scholars and educational organisations, as well as the university and library cultures of Western Europe. In letters to his former teacher, al-Marjānī, Fayḍkhanov expressed wonder at the range of scholarly writings available in Europe and the ease with which scholarly texts could be obtained.[67] He contrasted the availability of books and information in Europe with the situation in the Islamic world, where many works existed only in manuscript form and were often held only in private collections.

During his short career – he died of tuberculosis at age thirty-eight –

Fayḍkhanov challenged the foundations of the practices used to educate jurists at the madrasas. He believed that mid-nineteenth-century madrasa education had failed Muslim society. Instead of producing devout, knowledgeable scholars, the madrasas turned out social climbers, braggarts and charlatans who were incapable of comprehending the core textbooks.[68] The cause of this failure was not the books themselves, but, rather, the way in which they were taught. The teaching methods, in turn, were shaped by the way that erudition and piety were defined in Volga-Ural Muslim society. The ability to quote key books of law, grammar and theology and to triumph in public debates at *ᶜulamāᵓ* social gatherings and *munāẓara*s had become the means by which a scholar demonstrated his knowledge and piety and by which he built his reputation. For Fayḍkhanov, who imagined the ideal imam as a public servant, form had been divorced from function. Students acquired knowledge without understanding and the outward trappings of piety without personal integrity, morality or sincere belief.

Fayḍkhanov also blamed what he perceived as the failure of madrasas upon poor pedagogy and lack of organisation. He noted that instructors were primarily imams and teaching was a task that they assumed in addition to their domestic and community duties. They often lacked the training, time and expertise required to provide an effective education.[69] Teaching methods focused on self-study or on the rapid delivery of knowledge by the instructor with no mechanism for evaluation or review.[70] Students tended to follow a single teacher and some teachers forbade their students from studying with other teachers.[71] Some educational facilities were poorly maintained multi-purpose spaces conducive neither to learning nor to basic health and hygiene.[72] With no fixed programme and uncertain economic circumstances, students entered and left the madrasas at will and engaged in a variety of non-academic activities to support themselves.[73]

Fayḍkhanov's solution for the problems he perceived in Muslim education was to re-build both the madrasa curriculum and broader Muslim knowledge culture from the ground up. His purpose in calling for reform was not to purge Volga-Ural Muslim education of religion, but to restore piety and functionality to Muslim scholarly life by crafting an education system that focused on instilling understanding of the core madrasa texts. In the early 1860s, he proposed the foundation of a new kind of madrasa to be organised in the same fashion as a Russian gymnasium, with a programme of study that was divided into years and study hours. Pupils would begin their education in early childhood and advance through a regimented multi-year course of study.

The curriculum of the new madrasa would be organised by subject rather than by textbook, and a distinction would be made between 'religious' (*dīnī*) and 'worldly' (*dunyāwī*) disciplines.[74] The programme of study consisted of 149 instructional hours spread over ten years. The first year of the programme focused on imparting basic skills such as reading and writing in Turkish, *farāʾiḍ* and penmanship. In the second year, training in the Arabic and Persian languages and arithmetic was introduced. In the middle grades, students studied mathematics, natural sciences, geography, Russian language, logic, theology and *sharīʿa* (an introduction to Islamic law). Only in the last three years, after sixteen study hours of native language literacy and thirteen of Arabic-language training, were students finally permitted to study jurisprudence, hadith and Qurʾānic exegesis, all of which required advanced knowledge of Arabic language, logic and Islamic doctrine.[75]

Fayḍkhanov's innovations for the madrasa went beyond the curriculum. He proposed guaranteed salaries for all the madrasa's teachers, orders of printed textbooks and free meals for the students. These innovations set the annual budget for a fifty-student madrasa to 4,600 rubles, which was more than most *maḥalla*s could afford. The proposed addition of Latin and French teachers and other personnel who would have to come from outside the Muslim community pushed operational costs still higher.[76] Fayḍkhanov turned to the Russian government to seek funding for his madrasa. To win over officials in the Ministry of Education, he highlighted how the new madrasa would aid in the creation of a generation of *ʿulamāʾ* well-versed in both Russian and Islamic cultures, who would be able to act as intermediaries between the two. He pointed out how the teaching of 'worldly' subjects in the madrasa would reduce ignorance among Russia's Muslims and help them integrate more fully into the empire.[77] In the spirit of the Great Reforms, he argued that the imperial government owed its Muslim subjects such a school in return for their long service to the empire as enterprising merchants and loyal subjects.[78]

However, even as Fayḍkhanov tried to win over Russian officials, he also continued to emphasise the role that his madrasa would play in revitalising Islam. He believed that Muslim education in Kazan had fallen behind education in Egypt, Anatolia, the Hijaz and Bukhara, and that it could only be reformed through the adoption of the best practices used in madrasas in these societies.[79] He repeatedly emphasised the point that religious education should promote deep understanding of the spirit and meaning of legal and sacred texts and that it should yield tangible benefit for society, rather than simply producing exploitative elites.

While Fayḍkhanov pushed for a re-structuring of the madrasa, other *ᶜulamāʾ* strove to systematise Muslim education by other means. The early works of Kazan language-teacher and ethnographer ᶜAbdalqayyūm an-Nāṣirī showed concern for providing comprehensive and accessible information on Islamic history and doctrine to students and casual readers. Like Fayḍkhanov, an-Nāṣirī interacted with Russian orientalists and pedagogues in Kazan, attending lectures at Kazan University, teaching Tatar-language courses at Kazan's Ecclesiastical Seminary and, ultimately, being inducted into the Kazan University Society for Archeology, History and Ethnography in 1885.[80] However, his *Majmūᶜ al-Akhbār*, completed in 1859, was crafted for consumption by Muslim readers rather than Russian scholars. *Majmūᶜ al-Akhbār* drew information from widely read Turki, Ottoman and Chagatai-language works such as Celebi's *Muḥammadiyya*, *Altı Barmaq* and *Durr-i majālis* and combined it into a single volume with material from Abū Jaᶜfar Muḥammad b. Abū Jarīr at-Ṭabarī's Arabic-language 'History of Prophets and Kings' (*Tārīkh ar-Rusūl wal-Mulūk*). An-Nāṣirī divided this material into three sections, one on the life of Prophet Muḥammad, a second on the Prophet's companions and a third on 'Followers and Shaykhs', which included the biographies of such figures as al-Hajjāj bin Yūsuf, Abū Hanīfa, ash-Shāfiᶜī, Bayazid Basṭāmī, Ibrahīm bin Adham, Khwāja Bahāʾaddīn, al-Fārābī and Ṣūfī Allāhyār.[81] Many of these figures would have been known to Volga-Ural Muslims from Sufi poems, primers and histories of the prophets. In *Majmūᶜ al-Akhbār*, an-Nāṣirī fact-checked this knowledge, translated it into vernacular Turki and organised it so that his volume could be used either as a reference book for Muslims reading other Islamic texts or as an instructional text on its own. Although he turned to writing ethnographies, teaching Russian-language courses, compiling folktales and authoring textbooks on astronomy and geography, making Islamic knowledge accessible to a general audience remained an important part of his work. In 1890, he published 'Writings on Ethics, and Writings on the Obligations of Doctrine' (*Akhlāq risālase wa ham furūz muᶜtaqadāt risālase*).[82] His work in this field served the goals articulated by Fayḍkhanov: to replace memorisation, imitation and debate with comprehension and practical application of the principles and ethics of Islam.

In the late 1870s and early 1880s, ᶜAtāʾullāh Bayazitov, military *ākhūnd* of St Petersburg, joined the discussion on madrasa education. In 'The Book of Islam' (*Islām Kitābı*), published in 1880, he challenged both the length of Islamic education in Russia and the dominant role of the Arabic and Persian languages in Muslim religious and intellectual life. He noted that 'in our day, a lifetime is not time enough for people to acquire learning. In the past, the madrasas were full of twenty-five or thirty-year-old bearded students.' Bayazitov believed that a student should have completed their education by the age of fifteen or sixteen and be prepared to pursue a career and live as a devout Muslim. He argued that, even after ten or fifteen years in the madrasa, former madrasa students 'look at the Arabic-language books and do not understand them, and they do not go back to their teachers to ask and learn'.[83]

Whereas Fayḍkhanov blamed pedagogical methods and societal misconceptions of what constituted knowledge for the failings of the madrasa system, Bayazitov linked the long duration of religious training to the inefficiency of forcing students to pursue their education in foreign languages. He pointed out that when Turkic-speakers wished to learn anything, they had no choice but to turn to books in Arabic. To read these books, they needed to learn Arabic, but the textbooks used to teach Arabic were written in Arabic and Persian. The lack of reliable Turkic-language textbooks on Islam, Arabic grammar or any other subject hampered education or halted it altogether.[84] Like an-Nāṣirī, Bayazitov did not limit his goals to improving training for jurists. He envisioned each individual Muslim as being responsible for acquiring and disseminating accurate information about Islam. He positioned his book as serving that purpose by providing Turki-speaking students with a guide to ethics and faith written in their own language.[85]

By the 1880s, al-Marjānī adopted some of Fayḍkhanov's views on formalising administration in the madrasa. In 1881, he introduced a ten-point student code outlining authority structures and proper behaviour in his madrasa in Kazan. The code established an administrative council for the madrasa consisting of a *qāḍī* and members appointed from among the instructors and teaching assistants. Students were expected to pray five times daily and to dress and behave appropriately while attending mosque. They were supposed to behave respectfully towards one another, their teachers and visitors, to adhere to the reading schedule established by their instructors and not to progress to the next assigned book without having read the previous ones. Students risked expulsion from the madrasa if they failed to attend their scheduled lessons.[86]

Two study schedules survive from al-Marjānī's madrasa. The first consisted of four lessons of Arabic grammar (taught from *Kāfīya* and *Sharḥ Mullāh Jāmi*ᶜ), six lessons in logic (taught from *Shamsiyya*, *Sharḥ Tadhhīb al-Manṭiq* and *Sullam al-*ᶜ*Ulūm*), one lesson in philosophy (from *Ḥikmat al-*ᶜ*Ayn*), one lesson in eloquence (from *Talkhīḍ*), five lessons in theology (from *Tadhhīb al-Kalām*, *Sharḥ* ᶜ*Aqā*ᵓ*id Nasafiyya* and *Mullāh Jalāl*), two lessons in methodology of jurisprudence (from *Tawḍīḥ* and one of its commentaries), four lessons in jurisprudence (from *Mukhtaṣar al-Wiqāya*, *Sharḥ al-Wiqāya*, *al-Hidāya* and *Farā*ᵓ*iḍ*), two lessons in ethics (from *ᶜAyn al-ᶜIlm* and *Ṭarīqāt-i Muḥammadiyya*) and one lesson in hadith (from *Mishkāt al-Muṣābīḥ*).[87]

Al-Marjānī's second programme introduced small changes to this curriculum. Arabic grammar was reduced to three lessons. Logic was increased to ten lessons and Mīrzā Zāhid's commentary on *Tadhhīb al-Manṭiq* and Qāḍī Mubārak's commentary on *Sullam al-ᶜUlūm* were added to the curriculum. The number of lessons in theology likewise rose to eight, with Khayālī's commentary on *ᶜAqāᵓid-i Nasafiyya* and several other commentaries on *ᶜAqāᵓid-i Nasafiyya* being added to the reading schedule. Principles of jurisprudence was increased to three lessons.[88]

Both of al-Marjānī's syllabi emphasised the rational sciences (grammar, logic, philosophy). The comparatively smaller space occupied by the transmitted sciences (Qur'ān, hadith, jurisprudence) concerned al-Marjānī's biographer, Shahr Sharaf, who, writing in 1915, expressed distress over the 'Bukharan' character of al-Marjānī's curriculum. In his efforts to portray al-Marjānī as an intellectual father of early twentieth-century Islamic legal reform and Tatar national history-writing, he argued that al-Marjānī had increased the amount of instructional time devoted to the rational science only in response to demands from students, who believed that rational sciences such as logic were more relevant to their future careers than Turkish history or texts on social reform. Sharaf also claimed that the programmes of study reflected only al-Marjānī's 'official' lessons. He alleged that al-Marjānī habitually held extra lessons and gatherings for interested students, where he taught Qur'ānic exegesis, using *Tafsīr Qāḍī Baydāwī*, *Tafsīr Madārik*, *Tafsīr Kashshāf* and *Tafsīr Thaᵓlibī*, and hadith, using *Saḥīḥ al-Bukharī* and *Mishkāt al-Muṣābīḥ*, and praised Ahmet Midhat's *Mudāfaᶜa*.[89] This emphasis on direct work with the Qur'ān and hadiths and support for Ottoman reform was in keeping with what Sharaf, an early twentieth-century reformer, thought that educational and legal reform should look like.

Al-Marjānī's curriculum did, in fact, resemble the education that he and other Volga-Ural *ᶜulamāᵓ* received in Bukhara in the 1830s and 1840s.[90] However, Sharaf misinterpreted the significance of al-Marjānī's reforms because he viewed education reform as a change in curricular content. Fayḍkhanov and al-Marjānī's goal was not to purge the madrasa curriculum of the rational sciences in favour of the transmitted sciences or of Arabic-language textbooks in favour of Turkic-language ones, but, rather, to make madrasas more effective at teaching the existing curriculum by instituting stronger organisation, new pedagogical methods and better financial support. Al-Marjānī's student code and his study schedule were designed to achieve these ends.

Re-organising the Madrasa Curriculum (1890s–1917)

ᶜUlamāᵓ writings about education reform before the mid-1880s focused primarily on the transmission of information about Islamic law, doctrine and history. For Muslims in general, they focused on how to teach basic Turki-language literacy, doctrine, worship, catechism and ethics, as these were the fields of knowledge that they identified as critical for comprehending and applying the tenets of Islam in daily life. Some scholars pushed for all Muslims to gain at least a limited mastery of jurisprudence, but they also recognised that this was beyond the reach of most Volga-Ural Muslims, who did not know Arabic.

In the 1880s and 1890s, madrasa teachers began to change madrasa curricula in ways that blurred the distinction between basic and advanced education and divided knowledge into new categories. This was particularly evident in the treatment of mathematics and the natural sciences. Throughout the nineteenth century, mathematics was part of madrasa education, but was taught primarily as part of taxation and inheritance law.[91] However, in the 1870s, an-Nāṣirī published 'Accounting' (*Khisablıq*). An-Nāṣirī's approach to mathematics in 'Accounting' differed from mathematical instruction in the madrasas in that his textbook was composed in the Turki vernacular and focused primarily on commercial interactions and household finances.[92] 'Accounting' presented mathematics as a subject with applications beyond the jurisprudential fields of inheritance division and calculation of obligatory charitable payments (*zakat*). At the same time, the book made arithmetic accessible and relevant to the daily life of the average believer. It would be at least a decade before these trends began to take hold in the madrasas, but 'Accounting' heralded a new emphasis on numeracy in the Volga-Ural Muslim popular (non-*ᶜulamāᵓ*) education.[93]

The promotion of arithmetic and accounting in the Volga-Ural region did not equate with a general secularisation of Muslim education or worldviews. For nineteenth-century Muslim educators who promoted instruction in mathematics and the natural sciences, these disciplines represented a desirable addition to the legal-doctrinal curriculum rather than replacements for it. In the first half of the nineteenth century, the primary means for Muslims to acquire knowledge of European-style medicine, mathematics, engineering and drafting had been enrolment in a Russian cadet corps or professional school. Fayḍkhanov's madrasa proposal was one of the first efforts to challenge this division of knowledge. He envisioned a new madrasa that would teach students the grammatical rules of Arabic, Persian and Turki 'to perfection' and, simultaneously, offer instruction in the 'religious sciences' (theology, exegesis, hadith, methodology of jurisprudence, jurisprudence and Islamic philosophy) as well as enough medical training for graduates to qualify as medics (*feld'sher*).[94]

Fayḍkhanov's introduction of medicine and mathematics into the curriculum of his proposed madrasa as distinct disciplines was intended to make these subject accessible to Muslims who did not wish to venture into the Russian education system, but it also served another purpose. It was meant to demonstrate that mathematics, the natural sciences and other so-called 'European sciences' were compatible with Islamic education. In making this argument he presented several examples, including medieval Islamic scholars' embrace of the works of Socrates, Plato and Aristotle as well as modern cases such as the Ottoman Tanzimat and Rifāᶜa at-Ṭahṭāwī's Schools of Translation in Egypt.[95] A similar argument about the relationship between Islam and the study of philosophy, mathematics and natural science was presented by Bayazitov in 1883. Bayazitov presented this argument in a response to a lecture given earlier that year by the French scholar Ernest Renan, in which Renan argued that Islam was incompatible with modern science. Bayazitov argued not only that Islam in no way hampered the study of the sciences, but that many of the scientific and mathematical advancements that Europeans claimed as their own were, in fact, inherited from the Islamic world.[96] Bayazitov's essay was published in Russian, but it also found an audience in the Muslim communities of the Volga-Ural region, where it was translated into Turki and circulated among the *ᶜulamā᾿* in manuscript form.[97]

Fayḍkhanov and Bayazitov both emphasised that disciplines such as mathematics and the natural sciences were not only compatible with Islam but had been an integral part of Islamic intellectual life throughout the history of the faith. However, efforts by them and other *ᶜulamā᾿* to promote the study of mathematics and science in Volga-Ural Muslim society resulted in the evolution of these subjects as fields distinct from the legal-doctrinal disciplines of the nineteenth-century madrasa. In the 1890s, an-Nāṣirī published Turki-language textbooks on geography and astronomy.[98] In 1900, Shamsaddīn al-Kultasī published 'A Description of the New Astronomy' (*Mufaṣṣal hay᾿at jadīda kitābı*).[99] Like an-Nāṣirī's *Accounting*, these textbooks presented subjects such as astronomy, geography and mathematics as having relevance beyond their application to resolving questions of jurisprudence. At the same time, they contributed to the popularisation of knowledge that had once been reserved for the madrasa-educated. Although these two processes occurred simultaneously, they were distinct. The first involved a re-configuration of the categories of knowledge in which disciplines such as mathematics and astronomy were recognised as separate from jurisprudence. The second involved the popularisation of previously arcane knowledge.

By the late 1880s, the various trends in nineteenth-century education reform – vernacular-language instruction, distinction between religious and worldly subjects, finite education programmes with clear progression from grade to grade – came together in a new kind of madrasa. Historians have referred to some of these madrasas as 'Jadidist', but the meaning behind this term requires clarification. The directors and sponsors of some of the reformed (and reforming) madrasas were subscribers to Ismāᶜīl Gasprinskii's newspaper *Tarjuman* and took inspiration from that source to experiment with new curricula. However, the programmes they implemented were often of their own design and not prescribed by Gasprinskii. Likewise, while Volga-Ural teachers admired the range of academic subjects taught in Ottoman schools, most of them were not interested in transforming the madrasas into pure teachers' schools or technical institutes. Juridical and theological training remained the main missions of the Volga-Ural madrasas, and the curricular and organisational reforms in the Volga-Ural more closely resembled madrasa reform movements in British India than the education reform programmes in the Ottoman Empire, the latter of which were often designed to marginalise the madrasas in favour of government-run schools.[100]

Muḥammadiyya Madrasa and ᶜUthmāniyya Madrasa in Kazan, Ḥusayniyya Madrasa in Orenburg, Būbī Madrasa in Izh-Būbī village, Viatka province and Shamsiyya Madrasa in Tūntār village all implemented programmes that deviated from the education practices that had been in use in the first half of the nineteenth century. From 1895 to 1917, all these madrasas adopted the following innovations:

1) Creation of programmes of study consisting of a fixed number of years divided into grade levels. Upon successful completion of these grade levels, a student was considered to know enough to be graduated and sent into the workforce.
2) Organisation of curriculum around academic disciplines rather than core textbooks.
3) A shift from task-based learning to time-based learning. (The curriculum was divided so that the student would work on a book or a skill for a pre-determined number of study hours rather than for as long as they needed to gain mastery of it.)
4) Re-definition of learning as a teacher-directed activity and an increase in the number of hours students spent in the classroom.

5) Designation of education as a youth activity beginning in early childhood and ending by the time the student reached their late teens.
6) Grouping of the students into age cohorts both in the classroom and the dormitories.
7) Formalisation of the academic year. (New admissions were limited to certain times of the year. The academic years had designated start and endpoints. Students could no longer arrive or depart at will.)
8) The use of the vernacular language as the primary medium of instruction.
9) Separation of mathematics, the natural sciences and history from the 'religious sciences'.
10) The introduction of Russian as a foreign language.
11) The implementation of an extensive curriculum for teaching reading, grammar and composition in the students' native Turki language.

Some historians have characterised the above-mentioned innovations as 'Jadidism', but, in fact, many of them were not unique to Gasprinskii's writings on education. Rather, they came from multiple sources: the discussions of education reform during the 1850s–80s, exposure to Russian models of education and *ᶜulamāʾ*'s travels to Ottoman Anatolia, Egypt and India. Once madrasa directors began to introduce changes into their schools, they borrowed freely from one another and regularly revised their programmes.

In his article on Volga-Ural madrasas, Mustafa Tuna characterises these reforms as a secularisation of knowledge and culture: as happened in state-sponsored schools in the Ottoman Empire, 'religious' disciplines were replaced by non-religious disciplines and the madrasas were gradually transformed into normal schools or Muslim gymnasia. He argues that this led to the creation of a generation of madrasa graduates who were distanced from Islam and saw little value in it.[101] However, a close examination of madrasa programmes of study suggests a different pattern.

With seven different programmes of study surviving for the years from 1895 to 1912, Būbī Madrasa offers the fullest picture of curricular change in a single Volga-Ural madrasa. From 1895 to 1900, a strict separation was maintained at Būbī between *maktab* and madrasa education. The former was designed to provide elementary education, while the latter offered a curriculum primarily for future jurists and theologians. The graph below (see Figure 1.1) summarises the fluctuations in the madrasa curriculum from 1900 to the madrasa's closure in 1910.[102]

In past studies of Muslim education reform, the case of Būbī Madrasa has been used to support the argument that such reform was a secularising

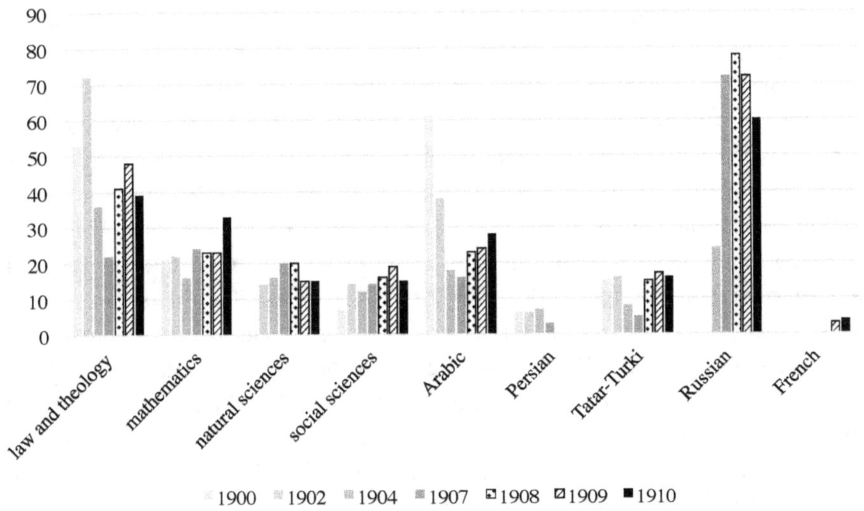

Figure 1.1 Distribution of instructional hours at Būbī Madrasa, Izh-Būbī village, 1900–10

process. However, when the data from the school's various programmes of study is viewed in aggregate, a more complicated process emerges. First, it should be noted that in Būbī's first two programmes (1900 and 1902), while some instruction in mathematics, natural sciences and social sciences was introduced, the majority of the student's week was dedicated to studying the core legal and theological subjects and Arabic language. This situation changed in 1904 not because of the introduction of additional mathematics, natural sciences and social sciences, but because of the introduction of Russian language classes, which occupied from sixty to eighty instructional hours in every subsequent program or roughly one-third of the time spent in the classroom. In 1904, numbers of instructional hours dedicated to every other discipline except the natural sciences was reduced to accommodate these Russian courses. As will be seen subsequently, this heavy emphasis on Russia language was unique to Būbī Madrasa and should not be interpreted as the norm for Volga-Ural madrasa education.

Second, while the specific classes offered in the fields of mathematics, naturals science and social science varied somewhat from 1900 to 1910, the overall number of instructional hours dedicated to these fields remained relatively stable: fifteen to twenty hours for the natural sciences and the social sciences and fifteen to thirty for mathematics (except in 1910). This suggests not a long-term trajectory of replacing the 'religious sciences' with 'secular' or 'worldly' subjects, but, rather, that the school's director deemed fifteen to twenty hours an appropriate amount of time to devote to these three fields of knowledge.

Islamic law and theology and Arabic language experienced far more fluctuation in their number of instructional hours. It is here that one of the core questions of the reform debates can be clearly seen: how many hours were required to transform a student into a jurist-theologian? In 1902, ᶜAbdullāh Būbī's answer to this question was to increase the number of instructional hours dedicated to Arabic-language instruction and core legal and theological subjects. Although, in 1904 and 1907, he severely cut back the number of hours reserved for both fields, he ultimately reversed that decision in 1908–10 by restoring to Arabic and the legal-theological subjects many of the hours that he had previously taken away. The rise and fall of Arabic-language instruction and Islamic law and theology does not suggest that either of these fields was slated for eventual removal from the curriculum. Rather, the fluctuation likely reflects Būbī's efforts to expedite the transmission of knowledge in these fields using students' native-language as a medium of instruction, new 'rationally organised', 'scientific' (European-style) textbooks and a classroom-intensive, teacher-centreed pedagogical model. When the radically reduced hours in the 1904 and 1907 programmes proved inadequate to instil mastery of Islamic law and theology even through 'modern' teaching methods, Būbī again increased the number of instructional hours dedicated to them. The attention that Būbī devoted to finding the proper number of instructional hours and the appropriate teaching methods for Arabic language and Islamic law and theology suggests that these subjects, rather than mathematics, natural science, social science or French, remained the heart of his madrasa's programme. Būbī's main goal was to train Islamic jurists who could also balance their accounting books, communicate with Russian officials and teach their *maḥalla*'s children. He was not interested in graduating doctors, engineers, lawyers or veterinarians, and his madrasa did not provide adequate depth in any of these fields to permit its graduates to pursue a career in them.

Ḥusayniyya Madrasa (see Figure 1.2), Muḥammadiyya Madrasa (see Figure 1.3), Shamsiyya Madrasa (see Figure 1.4) and ᶜUthmāniyya Madrasa (see Figure 1.5) also implemented some form of curriculum reform during the early 1900s. The directors of these schools made the Tatar-Turki vernacular the main language of instruction in their schools, divided out mathematics and the natural sciences from jurisprudence and designated them as distinct disciplines, introduced the study of history and geography of societies beyond the Muslim world and, in many cases, established courses in Russian language and literature. The distribution

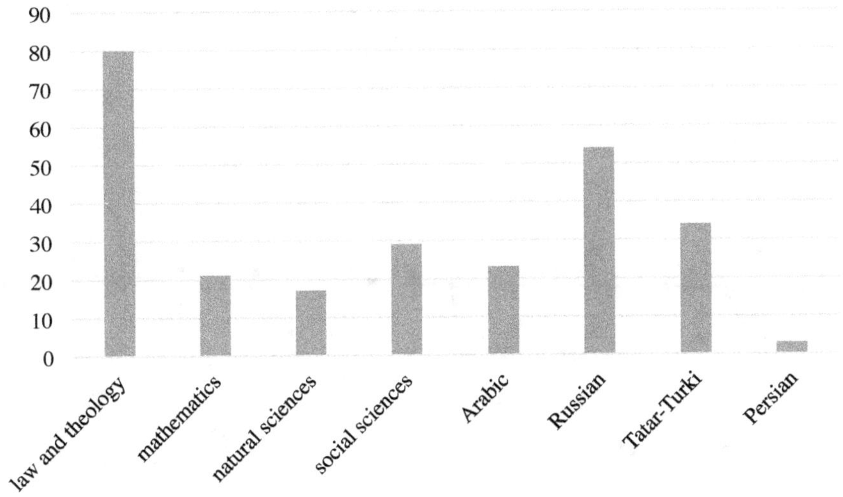

Figure 1.2 Distribution of instructional hours for Ḥusayniyya Madrasa, Orenburg, 1906–7

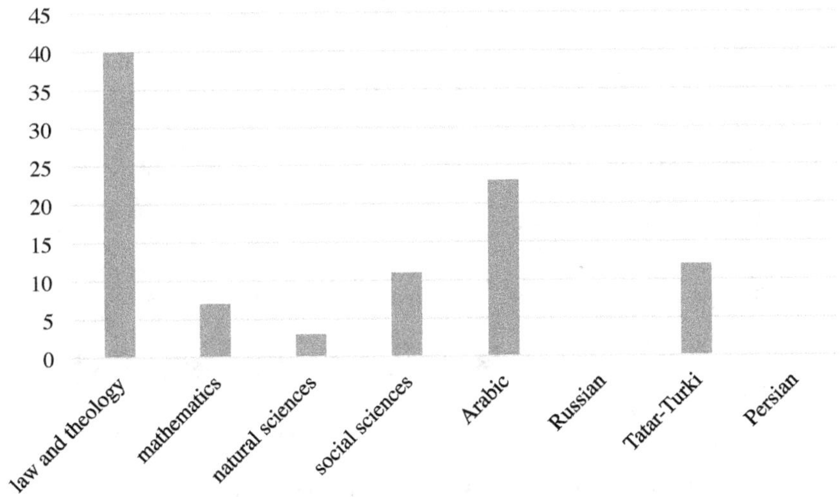

Figure 1.3 Distribution of instructional hours at Shamsiyya Madrasa, Tūntār village, 1911–12

of instructional hours by discipline in these four madrasas can be seen below.

There were marked differences in the lengths of these programmes. Shamsiyya offered only a four-year course of study for intermediate and advanced students, taking for granted that their students had attended

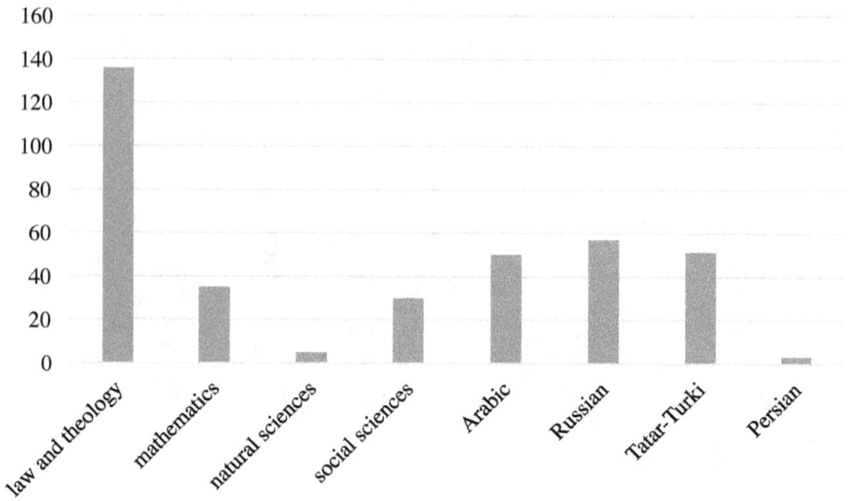

Figure 1.4 Distribution of instructional hours at Muḥammadiyya Madrasa, Kazan, 1913

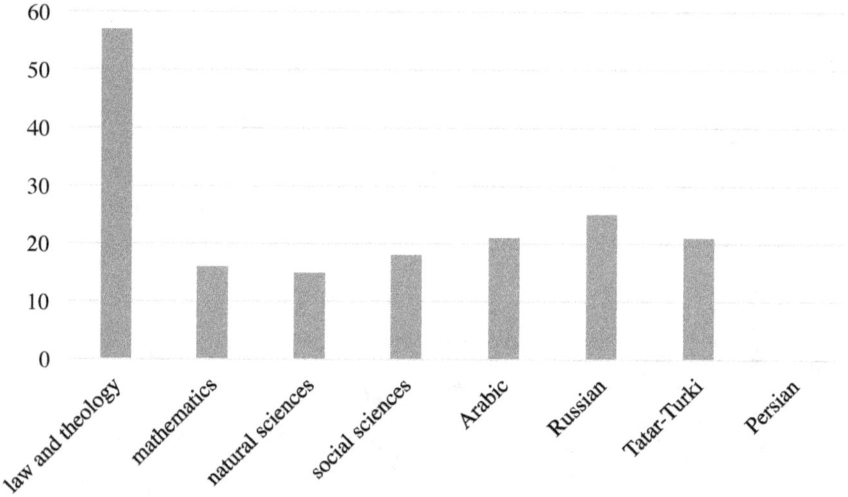

Figure 1.5 Distribution of instructional hours at ᶜUthmāniyya Madrasa, Ufa, 1917

a *maktab* for several years prior to enrolling. By contrast, Ḥusayniyya and Muḥammadiyya offered full elementary–intermediate–advanced programmes of eleven years and fifteen years, respectively. Students could enrol in early childhood and remain at the same institution until they graduated in their late teens or early twenties. Despite these differences, the distribution of instructional hours by disciple was relatively consistent among the schools. Subjects related to Islamic law and theology (Qur'ānic exegesis, jurisprudence, legal theory, hadith studies, Qur'ānic recitation, ethics, doctrine, biography of the prophet) remained prominent in the curriculum. Mathematics, natural sciences and social sciences appeared as distinct subjects, but none of these alone outstripped Islamic law and theology. At most of the schools, the total number of instructional hours dedicated to mathematics, natural sciences and social sciences was less than or equal to the number of hours reserved for teaching Islamic law and theology. Nor did instruction in mathematics, the natural sciences or the social sciences match the instruction in Islamic law and theology in terms of depth. While training in Islamic law and theology was intended to prepare students for careers as imams and jurists, training in the natural sciences, social sciences and mathematics tended to be of a general educational nature. A madrasa student received enough training in chemistry to understand the basic principles of the discipline, but not enough to pursue a career as a chemist, engineer or doctor without further training in a Russian technical institute or university.

Like Būbī Madrasa, many of the reformed madrasas invested considerable time in teaching their students the Russian language and many, although not all, devoted more hours to teaching Russian than to teaching Arabic. However, Arabic remained in the curriculum, occupying from twenty to forty instructional hours. In most of the above-mentioned madrasas, the cultivation of reading and writing skills in the students' native Turki was also made a priority. The language that suffered most as a result of introducing Russian and native-language training into the curriculum was not Arabic, which became the subject of new textbooks and pedagogical experiments, but Persian, which was radically reduced in the curriculum or eliminated entirely and replaced by French or German. The fate of Persian is explained less by secularisation than by the cultural and political re-orientation that took place in the Volga-Ural region in the late 1800s and early 1900s, as certain factions of the *ᶜulamāᵓ* began to look to Western Europe, Istanbul and Cairo rather than to the Persianate world for models of high culture and intellectual activity.[103]

Nor, by any means, was instruction in Islamic law and theology ossified by the early 1900s. As the directors of reformed madrasas sought to re-order old disciplines and accommodate new ones, they also sought to change how they taught Islamic law and doctrine. All the schools discussed above emphasised the study of three bodies of knowledge: the Qur'ān and Qur'ānic interpretation, the hadiths and jurisprudence. Logic, philosophy and speculative theology, which had been central to the mid-nineteenth-century curriculum, were severely reduced or eliminated. This transformation reflected the scripturalist tendencies of reformist teachers and directors. By emphasising the primary sources of the law and their interpretation, they encouraged their students to engage directly with those sources rather than to rely on past interpretations. By replacing Aristotelean logic and speculative theology with more courses on the history of the prophet, the Muslim community and the Islamic faith, they also encouraged historicised and rationalist readings of the core legal texts. In these schools, history replaced philology and Aristotelian logic as the main tool for interpreting Islamic law.

In summary, the programmes of study of reformed madrasas in the early 1900s do not suggest that Muslim cultural and educational reform was on a secularising trajectory. The appearance of mathematics, the natural sciences and the social sciences as discrete subjects in the curriculum occurred in combination with an increase in the number of hours students spent in the classroom. Rather than phasing out instruction in Islamic law and theology, directors sought to balance old and new subjects and to assign what they deemed to be an appropriate number of instructional hours to each subject. Islamic law and theology continued to account for the largest single disciplinary category. Islamic law and theology were the only fields in which the madrasas delivered specialist knowledge. Coverage of mathematics, natural science and social sciences was, at best, introductory and generalist. Finally, teaching of Arabic language and Islamic law and theology continued to evolve during the early 1900s, with the adoption of new pedagogical techniques and adaptation to new views on how legal interpretation was to be carried out. Such adoption and adaptation would have been pointless if reformist directors had intended to transform their madrasas into gymnasia or technical institutes.[104]

Arabic-script Publishing and Islamic Literature in the Early 1900s

Publishing and bookselling patterns in the early twentieth century also suggest that the 'worldly sciences' were seen as a complement to Islamic legal and theological knowledge rather than as a replacement for it. By the early 1900s, mass-printed books became fixtures in Muslim classrooms. As Muslim commercial publishing increased in Russia and abroad, publishers began to issue catalogues of their inventory. Bookstores and booksellers issued catalogues of their own. The contents of these catalogues give a view of the types that were for sale in Russia's Muslim communities as well as the categories into which bookdealers and their customers divided knowledge.

A 1901 catalogue advertised books sold by Muḥammad ᶜAlī Qadīrov at Kazan's Haymarket. Qadīrov's inventory for that year included 370 titles printed in Kazan, Istanbul and Cairo. These titles were divided into twelve categories: 'Qur'ān and speculative theology', 'Qur'ānic commentaries', 'Hadith', 'Sufism and ethics', 'Legal theory', 'Jurisprudence and Fatwās', 'Arabic grammar', 'Logic', 'Doctrine', 'Languages', 'History' and 'Medicine'. 'Medicine' constituted the largest single category, with 110 titles, but these included a broad range of materials, from prayer books to volumes on disease, medications and medical procedures.[105] 'Sufism and ethics' was the second largest category, with seventy-seven titles.[106] 'Jurisprudence and fatwās' was the third largest, with sixty-one titles.[107] The 'Logic' and 'Hadith' categories were smaller, but still significant with twenty-two and fifteen titles, respectively. By contrast, 'History' and 'Languages' contained only thirteen and six titles, respectively.[108]

The 1906 catalogue for the Ṣabāḥ Publishing House in Kazan offered 361 titles in Tatar, Turkish, Arabic and Persian, including forty-one titles in the category of 'Jurisprudence and fatwās', twenty-six in 'Arabic grammar', forty-six in 'Obligations and ethics', twenty-four in 'Logic', seventeen in 'Qur'ānic exegesis' and eleven in 'Hadith'.[109] By contrast, it had only six offerings in 'Geography' and four in 'Mathematics'.[110] In a separate category, it offered thirty-three different titles by ᶜAbdalqayyūm an-Nāṣirī, which covered topics ranging from theology to natural science.[111]

The 1906 catalogue for Khezmät Publishers in Troitsk offered a total of 762 titles, among them thirteen titles in 'Qur'ān and speculative theology', thirty-two in 'Qur'ānic exegesis', thirty-nine in 'Hadith', fifty-six in 'Jurisprudence' and twenty-five in 'Legal theory', forty-seven in 'Arabic syntax' and twenty-nine in 'Arabic morphology'.[112] Alongside these, they marketed fifteen titles in 'Mathematics', fourteen in 'Geography', thirty-two in 'Medicine' and ninety-five under the combined heading of 'History, Biography and Travel'.[113]

Millāt Press's 1911 catalogue of textbooks for Muslim schools was divided into two sections: Part One was for general education and younger grade levels, and Part Two was for advanced students. Of 122 titles targeted for *maktab* students, Millat Press offered nine titles on 'Hadith', seventeen under the heading of 'Catechism and doctrine', four for 'Qur'ānic recitation' and nine for 'Arabic grammar'. 'History' books (on religious history as well as national and imperial history) made up the largest single category with twenty-three titles. Other categories included 'Primers' (ten titles), 'Turkic-language readers' (eleven titles), 'Mathematics' (six titles), 'Geography' (five titles) and 'Ethics' (eleven titles).[114] The 279 offerings for advanced students were organised alphabetically by title rather than by category, but they included a wide range of subjects and titles, from texts used in the nineteenth-century madrasa such as *Sharḥ ᶜAbdallāh*, *Mukhtaṣar al-Wiqāya* and *Isāghūjī* to textbooks on geography and Russian history.[115]

From 1901 to 1911, the fields of history, mathematics and geography emerged as subjects independent from the study of Islamic jurisprudence and doctrine. However, their emergence was gradual and it did not sweep away the older categories of knowledge. Exegesis, morphology, syntax, jurisprudence, legal theory, theology, ethics and logic continued to exist as disciplines, at least as far as publishers and booksellers were concerned. The selection of literature in these disciplines outstripped that available for mathematics, geography, natural sciences and history. The catalogues indicate a great deal of continuity between the books used in the madrasas in the eighteenth and nineteenth centuries and those used in the early twentieth century. At the same time, however, the intended audience for this legal and theological training was changing.

Throughout most of the nineteenth century, the advanced Islamic legal and theological training offered at the madrasas had been available mainly to those who wished to become legists and theologians. The need for students to master Arabic and Persian served as a barrier to most Muslims' pursuit of advanced legal and theological knowledge. So, too, did the way that legal and theological knowledge was disseminated. With many manuals, textbooks and commentaries available solely in manuscript form, the only way to acquire them was to make a copy for oneself or hire someone to do so. A significant part of legal knowledge remained in oral form, with teachers adding their own insights to what was written on the page. For most of the nineteenth century, it would have been difficult for the average Muslim to teach himself anything more than the basics of Islamic law and doctrine without joining the ranks of the specialists.

By the late 1800s, mass print made the law digests and textbooks used in the madrasa ever cheaper and more easily obtainable. In 1844, Russia's Asiatic Press published the Ḥanafī law commentary *Mukhtaṣar al-Wiqāya*.[116] By the 1860s and 1870s, other law books began to come into print. By the early 1900s, *ᶜAyn al-ᶜIlm*, *Mukhtaṣar al-Qudūrī*, *Sharḥ al-Wiqīya*, *al-Hidāya*, *Isaghūjī*, *Sharḥ Mullā Jāmiᶜ* and *Sharḥ ᶜAbdallāh* were available for purchase in mass-printed form and could be acquired from any bookstore or itinerate book-peddler. Only the fact that these works were written in Arabic or Persian limited the number of people who could read them, but that barrier began to disappear as well by the beginning of the twentieth century when new Turkic-language translations and commentaries of these works appeared in print. A Turki translation of *Mukhtaṣar al-Wiqāya* appeared in 1901.[117] In the same year, Shākirjān al-Ḥamīdī published a two-volume Turki-language commentary on *ᶜAyn al-ᶜIlm.*[118] His brother, ᶜUthmāniyya Madrasa teacher Shaykhalislām al-Ḥamīdī, translated *Mukhtaṣar al-Qudūrī* into Turki in 1904.[119]

Among the purchasers of these new commentaries were madrasa instructors and their students. Vernacular-language commentaries streamlined the education process. Without such commentaries, students had to gain proficiency in Arabic before they could begin to work with the Islamic sacred texts and the major Ḥanafī law books. With Turki-language commentaries, they could begin to read legal and theological sources earlier in their education. The process by which some madrasas began to shift from Arabic manuals and textbooks to Turki translations and commentaries can be seen in ᶜAbdullāh Būbī's description of how he went about transforming the study of Islamic law at Būbī Madrasa.

> In 1896, we removed *Qawāʾid, al-ᶜAwāmil* [*al-Miᶜa*], *Kāfīya* and *Sharḥ-i Mullā Jāmiᶜ*, and we began to teach [Arabic grammar] with only [*Mufaṣṣal*] *Anmūdhaj* and *Taṭbīqat*. My kinsman, Fayzī Afande, began to teach arithmetic and Turkish grammar to the Arabic-language students. In 1897, we removed [*Tafsīr al-*] *Nuᶜman, Mīrsayyīd,* and *Khayālī* [commentary on *ᶜAqāʾid-i Nasafiyya*], and we added Turkish recitation and geography lessons . . . In 1898, we removed *Talwīḥ* and *Isāghūjī*, and added Tatar-language logic and Persian grammar. In 1899, we got rid of [*Mufaṣṣal*] *Anmūdhaj* and began to teach Arabic grammar from a Turkish-language *Taṭbīqat*, and we also added engineering and ethics. In 1900, we got rid of *ᶜAyn al-ᶜIlm* and *Tariqanī* and added *farāʾiḍ* (basic obligations of Islam) and rhetoric.[120]

The publication of vernacular translations, commentaries and guidebooks played a direct role in the reduction of the number of instructional hours dedicated to Arabic language, jurisprudence, logic, exegesis and doctrine at some madrasas. This reduction seems to have reflected less a disdain for theological and legal training than a belief that, by using different pedagogical methods and vernacular-language texts, teachers could deliver a better quality of training in fewer instructional hours. This would free up classroom time for other academic subjects that madrasa teachers and directors believed that students should learn.

The Turki-language commentaries were not intended only for future jurists. By the early 1900s, jurists occupied themselves with the production of Islamic legal and theological books in the vernacular. From 1906 to 1912, four different Volga-Ural Muslim scholars published vernacular translations of Muhammad ᶜArif Bek's '1001 Hadith Commentary' (*Meng dä ber hadīth-sharīf sharḥe*): Shākirjān al-Hāmidī (1906), ᶜAbdarrashīd Ibrahimov (1907), ᶜA. Kabīr (1910) and ᶜĀlimjān Bārūdī (1912). Three of these translations were published before the Arabic-language original was finally published in Russia in 1910.[121] As Riḍāʾaddīn bin Fakhraddīn wrote in *Jawāmiᶜ al-Kalim Sharḥe,* another Turki-language book of hadiths:

> The Prophet wanted learning to spread among all the people of Islam and explained to every capable person his/her needs and what he/she should know. For this reason, it is possible to claim that 'general education' is the first rule of Islam. Unfortunately, to this day, this first rule has not been enacted among Muslims in any period or any state.[122]

Riḍāʾaddīn presented his new Turki-language hadith commentary as part of the solution to this problem, noting that it was written to help readers understand the hadith collection *Jawāmiᶜ al-Kalim*, which had formerly been accessible only to those who had studied Arabic.[123]

Many new works on Islamic history also appeared in the early 1900s. From 1908 to 1910, Muḥammad Shākir bin Muḥammad Dhākir Sulaymānī published a multi-volume Turki-language textbook 'The History of Islam' (*Tarīkh-i Islām*), which began with the life of the Prophet and continued through the ᶜAbbasid period.[124] A significant component of this new wave of Islamic history-writing was the production of biographies of Muḥammad Ṣābirjān bin 'Abdalbadīᶜ, imam of Qazile village in Kazan province, wrote in the foreword to his 1910 'Life of the Prophet' (*Sīrat an-Nabī ᶜalayhi as-salām*), that 'knowing the holy life of Prophet, peace be upon him, is the most necessary of the obligations placed upon the *umma.* How the Prophet, peace be upon him, was born, how he grew up, what his people were like, what his social interactions were like – these, of course, are things that every Muslim should know.'[125]

Authors of these new biographies of Muhammad strove to make their subject both 'scientific' and approachable for a general audience. An example of this new trend was Sunᶜatullāh Bīkbulātov's 'The Prophet Muhammad (Peace be Upon Him)' (*Ḥaḍrat Muḥammad (ṣallā Allahu ᶜalayhi wā-sallam)*) a 355-page biography of Muḥammad complete with maps and illustrations. Rather than writing a hagiography, Bīkbulātov tried to present a historicised account of the early days of Islam, complete with explanations of sixth-century Arabian culture and politics. At the same time, however, he intended the work primarily as a self-education aid for students and general readers, noting, 'I have tried, as far as possible, to avoid using large, elevated words and philosophies. In this way, the student can draw his own conclusions.'[126]

In the quest for popular knowledge, the *ᶜulamāʾ* put themselves forward as guides and facilitators, filtering out errors and packaging difficult texts and concepts in formats more readily accessible to non-specialists. As Riḍāʾaddīn bin Fakhraddīn stated at the beginning of his 'Religious and

Social Issues' (*Dīnī wa ijtimāᶜī masᵓalalar*): 'our work is not meant to be a textbook for students in the *maktab* or a canon for jurists and those who hand down *fatwā*s . . . what is good, students will accept, and they will cast aside what they reject. Let them differentiate decisively between good and evil, it is said, and order will be achieved.'[127]

In the first chapter of 'Religious and Social Issues', Riḍāᵓaddīn discusses the sources of Islamic law (Qur'ān, hadith, *ijmāᶜ*, *qiyās*), the different kinds of proofs (*dalīl*) used to support Islamic legal decisions and the role and nature of the Qurᵓān.[128] Under Islamic knowledge that everyone should know, he includes doctrine, catechism, ethics and social relations (*muᶜāmala*).[129] He also discussed the need for mathematical, scientific and historical knowledge, arguing that it was integral to the practice of Islamic jurisprudence:

> Though it may be brief, one should make one's acquaintance with history and geography, astronomy, medicine, and the natural sciences in general. Because, without knowing history and geography, one cannot fully understand many of the stories from the Qur'ān, and, if one is not acquainted with knowledge of astronomy and nature, one cannot fully explain the meaning of the *āyāt*s of the Qur'ān that speak of the sky and the earth, of the sun and moon, of the seas and the stars, of trees and river, of the rain and grass, and of other things. There is no intelligence in making arguments using things one does not understand and cannot explain.[130]

The above statement reveals how the relationship between different kinds of knowledge in the madrasa had and had not changed since the nineteenth century. By the 1910s, astronomy, arithmetic, geometry, world history, geography, chemistry and biology were seen by madrasa teachers and directors as distinct disciplines that complemented juridical training. They believed that knowledge of mathematics and science made for more competent jurists and more pious believers.

The combination of vernacular-language legal and theological texts, knowledge of Russian and Arabic and basic mastery of mathematics, natural sciences, geography and pedagogy was meant to empower the 'common village imam', the madrasa graduates assigned to poorer urban *maḥalla*s and villages. On the one hand, such training expanded the range of services that these imams could provide to their congregations. On the other hand, it re-configured the village *mullā* as an agent of education, technological advancement and social change within his community, able to model or provide guidance on new agricultural techniques, livestock care, apiculture, European medicine and pedagogy while, at the same time, solving his congregation's legal and doctrinal questions and providing the most up-to-date readings of Islam. He was expected to do all of this within a society in which the average Muslim was becoming increasingly informed regarding Islamic law and doctrine. Madrasa students of the early 1900s were not asked to choose between 'secular' and 'religious' bodies of knowledge. Rather, like Imam Sunᶜatullāh, discussed at the beginning of this chapter, they were expected to master Islamic legal and doctrinal knowledge as well as a set of generalist skills.

Conclusion

Islamic education in the Volga-Ural region remained dynamic from the mid-1600s to the early 1900s. In the seventeenth and eighteenth centuries, the Islamic legal curriculum in the Volga-Ural region underwent a process of canonisation similar to that in the Ottoman Empire and Central Asia. This trend continued until the 1770s when technological advances (first, cheaper paper for manuscript production and, then, the printing press) made Islamic legal and devotional texts easier to obtain. Muslim participation in Russia's eastward settlement and the Asiatic trade brought new money into Muslim communities and opportunities to found new mosques and schools. These factors would lay the foundation for a century-long process of popularisation and democratisation of Islamic knowledge.

By the early nineteenth century, the push for increased popular education was driven from above and below. Muslims of all social levels came to view literacy as a mark of piety and respectability. Shaykhs, jurists and teachers urged less educated Muslims to pursue as much knowledge as they could access and comprehend. Sufism and popular religious expression flourished in oral and written form. However, the prevalence of the Arabic and Persian languages in Islamic intellectual culture and the long duration of madrasa education limited most Muslims' ability to obtain advanced knowledge of Islamic law and theology.

From the 1850s to 1917, some madrasa directors and jurists took steps to make Islamic knowledge more accessible and more relevant to future *ᶜulamāʾ* and the Muslim community in general. Their approaches included adopting Russian-style grade-levels and study schedules, replacing Arabic with vernacular Turki-Tatar as the language of instruction, writing new textbooks and introducing a broader range of disciplines into the madrasa curriculum. These changes did not comprise a secularisation of Russian Muslim education along Western European lines, but, rather, a re-consideration of what a good Muslim should know and how they could most effectively be taught. The end goal of these reforms was to create a society of well-read Muslims who were equipped to practice their religion in the rapidly changing conditions of the early 1900s and a new *ᶜulamāʾ* who were prepared to guide them in this endeavour.

Notes

1. 'Shakirdlar jırlī tūrghān jır', from the diary of Ṣunᶜatullāh bin Mullā Badraddīn (manuscript held in the private collection of the author).
2. '1912 yıl uqıghān rumanlar, millī ḥikāyat', ibid.
3. A.-A. Rorlich, *The Volga Tatars, A Profile in National Resilience* (Stanford: Hoover Institution Press, 1986); M. Tuna, *Imperial Russia's Muslims: Islam, Empire and European Modernity, 1788–1914* (Cambridge: Cambridge University Press, 2015); J. H. Meyer, *Turks across Empires: Marketing Muslim Identity in the Russian-Ottoman Borderlands, 1856–1914* (Oxford: Oxford University Press, 2014). In reaction to this tendency, scholars such as Allen Frank, Michael Kemper and Agnès Kefeli have emphasised the central role of Sufism, popular mystical texts and traditional institutions and practices in disseminating Islamic knowledge. A. J. Frank, *Islamic Historiography and 'Bulghar' Identity among the Tatars and Bashkirs of Russia* (Leiden: Brill, 1998); A. J. Frank, *Muslim Religious Institutions in Imperial Russia: The Islamic World of Novouzensk District and the Kazakh Inner Horde, 1780–1910* (Leiden: Brill, 2001); A. J. Frank, *Bukhara and the Muslims of Russia: Sufism, Education, and the Paradox of Islamic Prestige* (Leiden: Brill, 2012); M. Kemper, *Sufis und Gelehrte in Tatarien und Baschkirien, 1789–1889: Der islamische Diskurs unter russischer Herrschaft* (Berlin: Schwarz, 1998); A. N. Kefeli, *Becoming Muslim in Imperial Russia: Conversion, Apostasy, and Literacy* (Ithaca: Cornell University Press, 2014).
4. A. N. Kefeli, *Becoming Muslim in Imperial Russia,* pp. 60–1.
5. R. A. Houston, *Literacy in Early Modern Europe: Culture and Education from 1500–1800* (London: Pearson Education, 2002), pp. 3–4, 141–66; M. J. Maynes, *Schooling in Western Europe: A Social History* (Albany: State University of New York Press, 1985), pp. 11–18.
6. E. L. Eisenstein, *The Printing Press as an Agent of Change: Communications and Cultural Transformations in Early Modern Europe* (2 vols) (Cambridge: Cambridge University Press, 1979), vol. 1, pp. 64–6.
7. On the role of paper prices and availability in limiting the production of printed books, see D. McKitterick, *Print, Manuscript and the Search for Order, 1450–1830* (Cambridge: Cambridge University Press, 2003), p. 183. The technology for printing texts in the Arabic script existed in Russia in the early 1700s, but it was used only by the imperial government for the dissemination of select official decrees, and it played almost no role in indigenous cultural production; see A. G. Karimullin, *U istokov tatarskoi knigi: ot nachala vozniknoveniia do 60-kh godov XIX veka (Izdanie 2-e, ispr. i per.)* (Kazan: Tatarskoe knizhnoe izdatel'stvo, 1992), pp. 62–79.

8. 'Mīrāth', Kazan Federal (Povolzh'e) Universitet – Otdel Rukopis'ei i Redikikh Knig (KF(P)U – ORRK), 2969 AR.
9. 'Qur'ān sūrälären öyränü', Institut iazyka, literatury, i isskustvo (IIaLI), fond 39, opis' 1, delo 4498, list 2. This work was copied in a period when people holding the title of *abız* (a corruption of *ḥāfiẓ*, the Arabic term for one who has memorised the Qur'ān) held great authority within Volga-Ural Muslim communities and even took leadership roles in rebellions against the Russian government. See D. D. Azamatov, 'Russian Administration and Islam in Bashkiria (18th–19th Centuries)', in A. von Kügelgen, et al. (eds), *Muslim Culture in Russia and Central Asia from the 18th to the Early 20th Centuries* (Berlin: Klaus Schwarz Verlag, 1996), vol. 1, pp. 91–112; A. J. Frank, *Islamic Historiography*, pp. 21–47; A. Iu. Khabutdinov, *Millet Orenburgskogo dukhovnogo sobraniia v kontse XVIII–XIX vekakh* (Kazan: Iman, 2000).
10. Both Kemper (in *Sufis und Gelehrte*) and Frank (in *Bukhara and the Muslims of Russia*) have discussed at length the ties between Bukhara and the Volga-Ural Ural region, particularly for the late eighteenth century and nineteenth. Ties between the Naqshbandi shaykhs of late eighteenth- and nineteenth-century Bukhara and the *ᶜulamā'* of the Volga-Ural region have been well-established in scholarly literature. Less has been written about transregional contacts and patterns of transmission from the 1550s to the 1780s.
11. F. Robinson, *The ᶜUlama of Farangi Mahall and Islamic Culture in South Asia* (London: C. Hurst & Co., 2001), p. 42; E. Moosa, *What is a Madrasa?* (Chapel Hill: University of North Carolina Press, 2015), p. 110.
12. R. Fäkhreddin, *Asar, berenche tom* (Kazan: Rukhayat, 2006), p. 35.
13. Also called *Kitāb taṣrīf al-Zanjānī*, this work was composed in Baghdad in 1257 by ᶜIzzaddīn Abū'l-Faḍā'il bin ᶜAbd al-Wahhāb b. Ibrāhīm b. ᶜAbd al-Wahhāb al-Zanjānī. See C. Brockelmann, *History of the Arabic Written Tradition*, trans. J. Lameer, ed. J. J. Witkam (Leiden and Boston: Brill, 2016), vol. 1, pp. 292–3.
14. This work was an abstract of ᶜAbd al-Qāhir al-Jurjānī's grammar, *Al-ᶜAwāmil al-Miᶜa.* It was composed by Abū'l Fatḥ Nāṣir b. ᶜAbd al-Sayyid Muṭarrizī (1144–1213), a Khwarazmian scholar of grammar, Ḥanafī *fiqh* and Muᶜtazili dogmatics; see Brockelmann, *History of the Arabic Written Tradition*, vol. 1, pp. 305–7.
15. Authored by Ḥasan ibn ᶜAlā' al-Dīn ibn al-Aswad (d.1025/1616).
16. R. Fäkhreddin, *Asar*, pp. 42–3; A. Bustanov, 'Speaking "Bukharan": The Circulation of Persian Texts in Imperial Russia', in N. Green (ed.), *The Persianate World: The Frontiers of a Eurasian Lingua Franca* (Berkeley: University of California Press, 2019), p. 197.
17. R. Fäkhreddin, *Asar*, p. 35.
18. Ibid., p. 46.
19. This work, written by twelfth-century scholar Sirāj al-Dīn Abū Ṭāhir Muḥammad b. Muḥammad b. ᶜAbd al-Rashīd al-Sajāwandī, became the

subject of a commentary by seventeeth-century Volga-Ural scholar Yūnus bin Iwanay. That commentary, *Sharḥ-i Yūnus*, circulated in the Volga-Ural region in the eighteenth and nineteenth centuries; see Brockelmann, *History of the Arabic Written Tradition*, vol. 1, pp. 409–10; A. Bustanov, 'Speaking "Bukharan": The Circulation of Persian Texts in Imperial Russia', p. 196.

20. This manual of Ḥanafī *furū*ᶜ *al-fiqh*, composed by Abūʾl Aḥmād b. Muḥammad al-Qudūrī al-Baghdādī (d. 428/1037), was commonly taught in many parts of the Ḥanafī world, including in the madrasas of the Volga-Ural region and the Ottoman Empire. It continues to be widely used in Ḥanafī legal instruction today; see Brockelmann, *History of the Arabic Written Tradition*, vol. 1, pp. 159–60.
21. This book of Ḥanafī *furū*ᶜ *al-fiqh* was composed by Burhān al-Dīn Ibrahīm b. Muḥammad ibn Ibrahīm al-Ḥalabī (d. 956/1549), who studied in Aleppo and Cairo, and was later appointed as a teacher in Istanbul; see Brockelmann, *History of the Arabic Written Tradition*, vol. 2, p. 505.
22. This book, titled in full *Jāmi*ᶜ *al-Rumūz: Sharḥ mukhtaṣar al-wiqāya fī masāʾil al-hidāya*, is a commentary on the Ḥanafī *furū*ᶜ *al-fiqh* handbook *Mukhtaṣar al-Wiqāya*. It was composed by Bukharan *faqīh* and *muftī* Shams al-Dīn Muḥammad al-Quhistānī (d. 1546).
23. Also called *Bustān al-*ᶜ*Ārifīn*, this book of legal principles and juridical ethics was composed by Abū'l Layth Naṣīr ibn Muḥammad ibn Ibrahīm al-Samarqandī (d. 373/983), an early Ḥanafī scholar and jurist. *Bustān al-*ᶜ*Ārifīn/Bustān al-Faqīh* often appears in the same volume with another of Abū'l Layth's works on ethics, *Tanbīh al-Ghālifīn*; see M. Haron, 'Abū'l-Layth al-Samarqandī's Life and Works with Special Reference to his *Al-Muqaddimah*', *Islamic Studies* 33:2/3 (1994), pp. 319–40.
24. This collection of Ḥanafī *fiqh* is attributed to Zayn (Tāj) al-Dīn Muḥammad b. Abī Bakr b. ᶜAbd al-Muḥsin ᶜAbd al-Qādir al-Rāzī (d. late 600s/late 1200s) or to Muḥammad b. Tāj al-Dīn Ibrahīm al-Tūqātī; see Brockelmann, *History of the Arabic Written Tradition*, vol. 1, p. 416.
25. This is a compendium of *furū*ᶜ *al-fiqh* by Central Asian legal scholar ᶜAlī b. Abī Bakr b. ᶜAbd al-Jalīl al-Farghānī al-Marghīnānī al-Rishtānī Burhān al-Dīn (d. 593/1197), based on early Ḥanafī scholar Muḥammad al-Shaybānī's *al-Jāmi*ᶜ *al-Saghīr*. Called *Al-Hidāya* for short, it is one of the most influential books of Ḥanafī jurisprudence and has been used and taught throughout the Ḥanafī Muslim world, including in the Ottoman Empire, India and Russia; see Brockelmann, *History of the Arabic Written Tradition*, vol. 1, pp. 405–9; J. Esposito (ed.), *The Oxford Dictionary of Islam* (Oxford: Oxford University Press, 2003), p. 192.
26. A collection of *fatwā*s assembled by Fakhr al-Dīn Ḥasan b. Manṣūr al-Ūzjandī al-Farghānī (d. 592/1196); see Brockelmann, *History of the Arabic Written Tradition*, vol. 1, p. 405.
27. This collection of *fatwā*s was commissioned by Mughal emperor Aurangzeb

(1620–1707); see Brockelmann, *History of the Arabic Written Tradition*, vol. 2, p. 485.

28. This list is based upon biographies of seventeenth- and eighteenth-century scholars recorded in Shihābaddīn al-Marjānī al-Qazānī, *Mustafād al-akhbār fī aḥwāl Qazān wa Bulghār, qism al-thānī* (Kazan: Tipo-litografiia imperatorskago universiteta, 1900), pp. 127, 138; R. Fäkhreddin, *Asar*, pp. 40, 41, 44, as well as upon manuscript holdings in IIaLI and KFU.
29. This guide on education, the title of which can be translated as *Instructing the Learner in the Method of Learning*, was authored by Central Asian Ḥanafī scholar Imam Burhān al-Zarnujī, who died in Bukhara in the mid-1200s. It was widely used in medieval and modern Ḥanafī juridical education. See S. Günther, '"Your Educational Achievements Shall Not Stop Your Efforts to Seek Beyond": Principles of Teaching and Learning in Classical Arabic Writings', in N. A. Memon and M. Zaman (eds), *Philosophies of Education: Historical Perspectives and Emerging Discourses* (New York and London: Routledge, 2016), pp. 85–6.
30. This book on ethics was composed by Ottoman shaykh Shams al-Dīn Sivasī, (d. 1006/1597), founder of the Shamsiyya branch of the Khalvatiyya Sufi order. See H. Aksoy, *Şemseddin Sivâsî, hayatı, şahsiyeti, tarikatı, eserleri* (Sivas: [no publisher], 2005), pp. 28–9.
31. This Persian-language commentary on the opening *sura* (Sūrat al-Fātiḥa) of the Qurʾān was composed by Naqshbandi shaykh Mawlānā Yaʿqūb b. ʿUthmān b. Maḥmūd Charkhī (d. 851/1447). Charkhī was born near Ghazna and studied in Herat and Cairo, before travelling to Bukhara, where he became a disciple of Khwaja Bahāʾ al-Dīn al-Naqshband. After Bahāʾ al-Dīn's death, he travelled through what are now Uzbekistan and Tajikistan; see H. Algar, 'Čarḵī, Mawlānā Yaʿqūb', *Encyclopedia Iranica*, http://www.iranicaonline.org/articles/carki-mawlana-yaqub-b (accessed 27/1/2019).
32. This widely read Arabic-language commentary on the Qurʾān was begun by Cairo scholar Muḥammad b. Aḥmad b. Muḥammad b. Ibrahīm Abū ʿAbdallāh al-Anṣarī al-Maḥllī al-Shāfiʿī Jalāl al-Dīn (d. 864/1459) and completed by his student Abu al-Faḍl ʿAbd al-Raḥman ibn Abū Bakr ibn Muḥammad Jalāl al-Dīn al-Khuḍayrī al-Suyūṭī (d. 911/1505). Its title translates as *The Commentary of the Two Jalāls*. See Brockelmann, *History of the Arabic Written Tradition*, vol. 1, pp. 117, 154–5.
33. This commentary on Ibn Ḥafs ʿUmar al-Nasafī's work on dogmatics, *al-ʿAqāʾid al-Nasafiyya,* was written by Persian scholar Imām Saʿad al-Dīn Masʾūd b. ʿUmar b. ʿAbdallāh al-Taftāzānī (d. 792/1390). Born in what is now north-eastern Iran, Taftāzānī composed works on Qurʾānic exegesis, Arabic grammar and dogma, which enjoyed wide circulation in the early modern and modern eras, *The Oxford Dictionary of Islam*, p. 310.
34. This is an Arabic translation of *Isagoge,* Porphyry of Tyre's introduction to Aristotle's *Categories*, attributed to early Islamic writer and translator ʿAbdallāh ibn al-Muqaffaʿ (d. 138/756); see Henrik Lagerlund (ed.), *The*

Oxford Dictionary of Islam, p. 125; *Encyclopedia of Medieval Philosophy: Philosophy between 500 and 1500* (New York and London: Springer Science and Business Media, 2003), vol. 1, p. 1,058.

35. O. Mashkina, 'The Pulp and Paper Industry Evolution in Russia: A Road of Many Transitions', in J.-A. Lamberg et al. (ed.), *The Evolution of Global Paper Industry, 1800–2050: A Comparative Analysis* (New York and London: Springer, 2012), pp. 285–306.
36. A. G. Karimullim, 'Vozniknovenie rossiiskogo *knigopechatiia*', *Narody Afriki i Azii* 3 (1969), pp. 101–2; A. G. Karimullin, *U istokov tatarskoi knigi*, p. 90; E. A. Rezvan, 'Koran v Rossii', in R. A. Nabiev (ed.), *Islam na evropeiskom vostoke: entsiklopedicheskii slovar'* (Kazan: Magarif, 2004), p. 169.
37. Rezvan, 'Koran v Rossii', p. 169.
38. The first print edition of the *Haft-i yak* produced in Russia appeared in Kazan in 1801. See 'Protokol tsenzurnago komiteta pri Kazanskom Universitete uchrezhdennago 1822 goda', K(P)FU-ORRK, 4174, l. 1-2; 'Po otnoshenniiu bibliotekaria universiteta s prepovozhdenii raznykh knig' dlia khraneniia', K(P)FU-ORRK 4175 no. 1, l. 1; Karimullin, *U istokov tatarskoi knigi*, pp. 103–12.
39. 'Protokol tsenzurnago komiteta pri Kazanskom Universitete uchrezhdennago 1822 goda', K(P)FU-ORRK, 4174, l. 1–2; 'Po otnoshenniiu bibliotekiria bibliotekaria universiteta s prepovozhdenii raznyikh raznykh knig' dlia khraneniia', K(P)FU-ORRK 4175 no. 1, l. 1; Karimullin, *U istokov tatarskoi knigi*, pp. 103–12.
40. 'Gabderäkhim Utız-Imäni al-Bolgari, 'Näzmı Gabderäkhim Bolgari fī ḥaqqı Qāḍīzadä', in Ä. Sharipov (ed.), *Gabderäkhim Utız-Imäni al-Bolgari: Shigır'lär, poemalar* (Kazan: Tatarstan kitap näshriyatı, 1986), p. 37.
41. R. Fäkhreddin, *Asar*, 151; Shihābaddīn al-Marjānī al-Qazānī, *Mustafād al-akhbār fī aḥwāl Qazān wa Bulghār, qism al-thānī,* pp. 250–1.
42. Tājaddīn bin Yālchīgul, *Risāla-i 'Azīza: Sharḥ Thabāt al-ᶜĀjizīn* (Kazan: Elektro-tipografiia 'Umid', 1912), p. 3; A. N. Kefeli, *Becoming Muslim in Imperial Russia,* p. 101; A. J. Frank, *Islamic Historiography,* 95–6; M. Kemper, *Sufis und Gelehrte*, pp. 98–9.
43. Minnegulov, 'Ialchygul, Tadzheddin', p. 375.
44. Ibid., p. 324.
45. Qūl ᶜAlī, *Qiṣṣai Yosıf: Yosıf turında qıṣṣa*, ed. F. S. Fasiev (Kazan: Tatarskoe knizhnoe izdatel'stvo, 1983), p. 30; A. Kefeli, 'The Tale of Joseph and Zulaykha on the Volga Frontier: The Struggle for Gender, Religious, and National Identity in Imperial and Post-Revolutionary Russia', *Slavic Review* 70:2 (2011), pp. 373–98; N. Sh. Khisamov, 'Itogi i zadachi izucheniia 'Kyssa-i Iusuf' Kul 'Ali', *Tatarica: Studia in honorem Ymär Daher, anno MCMLXX sexagenario* (Helsinki: Abdulla Tukain kulttuuriseura, 1987), pp. 354–63; N. Sh. Khisamov, 'Qūl ᶜAlī. 'Qiṣṣai Yosıf ' dastanı', in R. F. Rakhmani (ed.), *Tatar ädäbiyatı tarīkhı* (8 vols)

(Kazan: Tatar kitap näshriyatı, 2014), vol. 1, pp. 226–39; R. Ganiev, 'Shärık yangharıshı häm Qūl ᶜAlī ijatı', *Tatar ädäbiyatı tarīkhı*, vol. 1, pp. 212–26; Sh. Sh. Abilov and N. Sh. Khisamov, 'Qiṣṣai Yosıf', in M. S. Shabaev and F. M. Zölkarnäev (eds), *Tatar ädäbiyatı tarīkhı* (6 vols) (Kazan: Tatarstan kitap näshriyatı,1984), vol. 1, pp. 115–57; Kh. Mökhämmätov, 'Yosıf wä Zöläykha' poeması', in Kh. Mökhämmätov et al. (eds), *Borınghı Tatar ädäbiyatı* (Kazan: Tatarstan kitap näshriyatı, 1963), pp. 67–96.

46. A. A. Khasavnekh, *Filosofsko-eticheskie motivy v sufiiskoi poezii Abdulmanikha Kargalyi* (Kazan: Izdatel'stvo AN RT, 2015) pp. 21, 72, 84.
47. 'Protokol tsenzurnago komiteta pri Kazanskom Universitete uchrezhdennago 1822 goda', K(P)FU-ORRK 4174, l. 1–2; 'Po otnosheniiu bibliotekaria universiteta s prepovozhdenii raznyikh knig' dlia khraneniia', K(P)FU-ORRK 4175 no. 1, l. 1; Karimullin, *U istokov tatarskoi knigi*, pp. 103–12.
48. Ibid.
49. R. Fäkhreddin, *Asar*, 140; R. Fäkhreddin, *Asar, Tom II*, eds I. Gyimadiev, R. Mingnullin and S. Bahavieva (Kazan: Rukhiyat nashriyatı, 2009), pp. 116, 121–2.
50. 'Bulghārī, Muḥammad Karīm, Bulghār-ᶜArab-Farsı suzlek', K(P) FU-ORRK, No. 12T (E426).
51. *Gabderäkhim Utız Imäni äl-Bolgari*, p. 324.
52. Ibid., p. 322.
53. Gabderäkhim Utız Imäni äl-Bolgari, 'Näzmı Gabderäkhim Bolgari fi khaqqı Qazizadä', in *Gabderäkhim Utız Imäni äl-Bolgari*, pp. 37–8.
54. Gabdrakhim Utyz-Imani al-Bulgari, 'Jawāhir al-Bayān', in Damir Shagaveev (ed.), *Antologiia tatarskoi bogoslovskoi mysli: Gabdrakhim Utyz-Imani al-Bulgari* (Kazan: Tatarskoe knizhnoe izdatel'stvo, 2007), [n.p.]. (English translation from the Arabic facsimile.)
55. 'Tatarskie uchilishcha', in *Istoriia Kazani v dokumentakh i materialakh XIX veka: Obrazovanie: vysshee, srednee, nachal'noe, kniga 4* (Kazan, Tatarskoe knizhnoe izdatel'stvo, 2012), p. 519.
56. M. Tuqaev, *Tārīkh-i Istarlībāsh* (Kazan: [no publisher], 1899), pp. 7–8.
57. I. K. Zagidullin, *Islamskie instituty v Rossiiskoi Imperii: Mecheti v evropeiskoi chasti Rossii i Sibiri* (Kazan: Tatarskoe knizhnoe izdatel'stvo, 2007), p. 142.
58. Ibid., 142–3.
59. R. Fakhreddin, *Asar*, *Tom III-IV*, ed. M. Gosmanov (Kazan: Rukhiyat nashriyatı, 2010), p. 19.
60. D. Ross, 'Muslim Charity under Russian Rule: *Waqf*, *Sadaqa* and *Zakat* in Imperial Russia', *Islamic Law and Society* 24:1–2 (2017), p. 91.
61. W. B. Lincoln, *The Great Reforms: Autocracy, Bureaucracy and the Politics of Change in Imperial Russia* (DeKalb: Northern Illinois University Press, 1990); B. B. Veselovskii, *Istoriia Zemstva za sorok let'* (St Petersburg: Izd-vo O. N. Popovoi, 1908–11); P. A. Golubev, *Viatskoe zemstvo sredi*

drugikh zemstv Rossii: Kratkii istoriko-statisticheskii ocherk kul'turnoi deiatel'nosti? viatskago zemstva v sviazi s deiatel'nostiu vsekh russkikh zemstv (Viatka: [No publisher], 1901).

62. B. D. Metcalf, *Islamic Revival in British India: Deoband, 1860–1900* (Princeton: Princeton University Press, 1982); F. Robinson, *The ᶜUlama of Farangi Mahall and Islamic Culture in South Asia.*
63. R. D. Crews, *For Prophet and Tsar: Islam and Empire in Russia and Central Asia* (Cambridge, MA: Harvard University Press, 2006), pp. 49–60; C. Steinwedel, *Threads of Empire: Loyalty and Tsarist Authority in Bashkiria, 1552–1917* (Bloomington and Indianapolis: Indiana University Press, 2016), pp. 83–5; M. Tuna, *Imperial Russia's Muslims*, pp. 39–52.
64. For example, Russian Minister of Education Dmitri Tolstoy emphasised the role of the Kazan Tatar Teachers' School in creating a new generation of Muslim teachers 'prepared to spread Russian education among their fellow Muslims living in our state', in L.V. Gorokhova (ed.), *Kazanskaia Tatarskaia Uchitel'skaia shkola, 1876–1917: Sbornik dokumentov i materialov* (Kazan: Izdatel'stvo 'Gasyr', 2005), p. 23.
65. *Bibliograficheskii slovar' otechestvennykh tiurkologov: dooktiabr'skii period*, ed. A. N. Konanov (Moscow: Nauka, 1974), pp. 276–7; Ismägyil Rämi and Räis Dautov, *Ädäbi süzlek*, p. 271.
66. R. Fäkhreddin, 'Khösäen bine Fäezkhan bin Fäyzulla bine Bikkenä bine Ismägyil' bine Tängrevirde es-Sabachaii', in R. Mardanov (ed.), *Shäkheslärebez: Khösäen Fäezkhanov: Tarikhī-dokumental' jıentıq* (Kazan: 'Jiyen' nashriyatı, 2006), pp. 514–15.
67. 'Khösäen äfände Fäezkhanov, khat 2', ibid., pp. 319–21; 'Khösäen äfände Fäezkhanov, khat 13', ibid. p. 348.
68. Khösäen äfände Fäezkhanov, 'Risāla', ibid., p. 77.
69. Ibid., pp. 77–8.
70. Ibid.
71. Ibid., p. 81.
72. Ibid., p. 76.
73. Ibid., pp. 76–7.
74. Khösäen äfände Fäezkhanov, 'Iṣlāḥ-i madāris', ibid., p. 46.
75. Ibid., p. 57.
76. Ibid., p. 56.
77. Ibid., p. 45.
78. Ibid., pp. 38–44.
79. Khösäen äfände Fäezkhanov, 'Risāla', ibid., pp. 80–1.
80. *Bibliograficheskii slovar' otechestvennykh tiurkologov: Dooktiabrskii period*, p. 224.
81. Kayum Nasiri, 'Majmūᶜ al-Akhbar', in *Kayum Nasiri: Saylanma Äsärlär dürt tomda*, 4 vols (Kazan: Tatarstan Kitap Näshriyatı, 2006).
82. ᶜAbdalqayyūm an-Naṣīr-ūghlī, *Akhlāq risālase wa ham furūz muᶜtaqadāt risālase* (Kazan: Kazan universitetınıng ṭabᶜkhānası, 1890).

83. ʿAtaʾullāh Bayazitov, *Islām Kitābı* (Kazan: n.p., 1880), p. 2.
84. Ibid., p. 7.
85. Ibid., p. 2.
86. 'Marjānī madrasase niẓāmnāmase', KF(P)U-ORRK, No. 749 AR, 46ob–48ob. A copy of this document was published in *Marjānī*, ed. Shahr Sharaf (Kazan: Maʿārif matbuʿası, 1333/1915), pp. 102–5.
87. Sh. Sharaf, *Marjānī*, p. 106.
88. Ibid.
89. Ibid., pp. 107–10.
90. R. Fäkhreddin, *Asar, Tom III–IV*, p. 146.
91. 'Farāʾiḍ Kitabı (Matematika), ʿAbdarraḥmān walade Mullā Muḥammad al-Penagarī, 1861', IIaLI f. 39, op. 1, del. 3968; 'Rukopis' na arabskom iazike (Matematika), Medrese Gabdelkarim bine Mulla Yakhuda, d. Bikbau (Menzelinskii raion), 1828', IIaLI f. 39, op. 1, del. 844; 'Rukopisnyi uchebnik po matematike, Madrasa Mulla . . . syna Khasana, d. Agryz (1800–1850)', IIaLI f. 39, op. 1, del. 866.
92. ʿAbdalqayyūm ʿAbdannaṣīr-ūghlī, *Ḥisābliq yaʿnī ʿilm ḥisāb qāʿidalar, yākī ārīfmetīkā wa ham ḥisābliq masʾalalare* (Kazan: Universitet tipografiiasy, 1873), p. 2.
93. On the spread of numeracy and accounting in Western Europe, see A. Shepard, *Accounting for Oneself: Worth, Status, and the Social Order in Early Modern England* (Oxford: Oxford University Press, 2015), p. 83; B. Lemire, *The Business of Everyday Life: Gender, Practice and Social Politics in England, c. 1600–1900* (Manchester and New York: Manchester University Press, 2005).
94. Khösäen Fäezkhanov, 'Iṣlāḥ-i madāris', p. 46.
95. Khösäen Fäezkhanov, 'Risāla', ibid., pp. 64–6, 70–1.
96. A. Bayazitov, *Vozrazhenie na rech' Ernesta Renana Islam i nauka* (St Petersburg: [no publisher], 1883), pp. 5–9.
97. *Pis'ma Nikolaya Ivanovicha Il'minskago* (Kazan: Tipo-litografiia imperatorskago universiteta, 1895), pp. 102–3.
98. ʿAbdalqayyūm ʿAbdannaṣīr-ūghlī, *Iṣṭilaḥāt Jughrāfiyya* (Kazan: Kazan universitetınıng ṭabʿkhānası, 1890).
99. Shamsaddīn al-Kūltasī, *Mufaṣṣal hayʾat jadīda kitābı* (Kazan: Tipo-litografiia Imperatorskago Universiteta, 1900).
100. B. Metcalf, *Islamic Revival in British India*, pp. 87–137; E. Ö. Evered, *Empire and Education under the Ottomans: Politics, Reform, and Resistance from the Tanzimat to the Young Turks* (London: I. B. Tauris, 2012), pp. 7–8.
101. M. Tuna, 'Madrasa Reform as a Secularizing Process: A View from the Russian Empire', *Comparative Studies in Society and History* 53:3 (2011), pp. 540–70.
102. In the graph above, the categories are organised as follows: (1) Islamic law and theology: *fiqh*, *usul al-fiqh*, *akhlaq*, *ʿaqāʾid*, debate, *tajwīd*, hadith, Qur'ānic reading, *tafsīr*, Islamic history; (2) Mathematics: arithmetic,

algebra, engineering, trigonometry and accounting; (3) Natural sciences: philosophy of nature, history of nature, natural sciences, physics, chemistry, botany, zoology, geology; (4) Social sciences: general/world history, geography, social geography.

103. S. Hodgkin, C. P. Kaiser, K. Rice, J. R. Pickett and S. Salushev, 'Persianate Cultural Legacies in the Russian Empire and USSR' (Roundtable), Association for Slavic, East European and Eurasian Studies, Philadelphia, 20 November 2015.
104. Gabdulla Bubi, 'Bubi mädräsäseneng qısqa tarikhı', in R. Märdanov, R. Mingnullin and S. Räkhimov (eds), *Bertugan Bubilar häm Izh-Bubi mädräsäse* (Kazan: Rukhiyat, 1999), pp. 33, 35, 36, 39, 46–7, 50–1, 55–7; *Madrasa-i Muḥammadiyya Programması, 1913 m./1331 h.* (Kazan: Elektro-tipografiia Milliat, 1913), pp. 8, 24–5; *Ufada berenche masjid jāmi*[c] *ḥuḍūrındagı Madrasa-i* [c]*Uthmāniyyanıng mufaṣṣal programı* (Ufa: Elektip. 'Tūrmush', 1917), p. 4; 'Madrasa-i Shamsiyya niẓāmnamase', K(P) FU-ORRK, No. 1240 T, 3ob-4; M. Rakhimkulova, *Khusainiia Medrese* (Orenburg: [no publisher], [no publication date]), pp. 18–20, 22.
105. *Asmā*ʾ*-i Kutub* (Kazan: Tipo-litografiia Naslednikov M. Chirkovoi, 1901), pp. 18–24.
106. Ibid., pp. 4–8.
107. Ibid., pp. 9–12.
108. Ibid., pp. 16–18.
109. *Baldat-i Qazānda Ṣabāḥ kitāpkhānasīnīng asmā*ʾ*-i kutubıdır* (Kazan: Knigoizdatel'stvo Sabakh, 1906), pp. 6–19.
110. Ibid., pp. 22–3.
111. Ibid., pp. 26–7.
112. *'Asmā*ʾ*-i Kutub', Khidmä näshriyat wa ṣaḥīfiyat sharikatiyaneng Troitskii (Orenburgiyya)* (Troitsk: Tipografiia Kh. Sosnovskago i F. Selyankina, 1906), pp. 8–24, 35–40.
113. Ibid., pp. 47–57.
114. *Millātneng maktab kitāplarīna makhṣūṣ asmā*ʾ*-i kutubī 1911 wa 1912-nche sana tadrīsīyya uchūn* (Kazan: Elektro-tipografiia Milliat, 1911), pp. 5–12.
115. Ibid., p. 16, 24, 28.
116. *Kitāb Mukhtaṣar al-Wiqāya fī Masā*[c]*il al-Hidāya* (Kazan: [no publisher], 1844).
117. *Mukhtaṣar al-Wiqāya tarjamase tūrkīcha*, trans. Shihābaddīn bin Mullā [c]Abdal[c]aziz Imānlībāshī (Kazan: Tipografiia T. D. Brat. Karimovykh v Kazani, 1901).
118. *Sharḥ* [c]*Ayn al-*[c]*Ilm* [c]*Alī al-Qārī (jild al-Awwal min Sharḥ* [c]*Ayn al-*[c]*Ilm)*, trans. and ed. Shākirjān b. Asadullāh al-Ḥamīdī at-Takawī (Kazan: Tipografiia Litografiia i Slovitnia T. D. Brat. Karimovykh, 1901).
119. *Mukhtaṣar Qudūrī tarjimase*, trans. Abū [c]Abdalahād Shaykhalislām bin Asadullah Ḥamīdallī (Kazan: Tipografiia Torgovago Doma Brat'ev Karimovykh, 1904).

120. Gabdulla Bubi, 'Bubi mädräsäseneng qısqa tarikhı', pp. 34–5.
121. S. Gyilajetdinov, 'Keresh süz', *Meng dä ber hädis shärekhe* (Kazan: Rannur, 2005), p. 5.
122. R. Fakhreddinov, *'Jawamigul-Kālim' Sharkhe*, ed. I. Gyimadiev (Kazan: Rukhiyat nashriyatı, 2005), p. 4.
123. Ibid., p. 5.
124. Muḥammad Shākir bin Muḥammad Zākir Sulaymānī, *Tarīkh-i Islām*, 4 vols (Kazan: Elektro-lito-tipografiia T. D. 'Br. Karimovy', 1908–1910).
125. Mullā Sābirjān Mullā ᶜAbd al-Badīᶜ-ūghlī, *Sīrat an-Nabī ᶜalayhi as-salām* (Kazan: Elektro-tipografiia Milliat, 1910), p. 3.
126. S. Bīkbūlātov, *Ḥaḍrat Muḥammad (ṣallā Allahu ᶜalayhi wāl sallam)* (Kazan: Elektro-tipografiia 'Magarif', 1914), p. iii.
127. R. Fäkhreddin, 'Dīnī wa ijtimāᶜī masʾalalär', in I. Gyilmadiev (ed.), *Dīnī wa ijtimāᶜī masʾalalär: Saylanma khezmätlär* (Kazan: Rukhiyat nashriyatı, 2011), p. 7.
128. Ibid., pp. 7–8, 14–23.
129. Ibid., pp. 10–11.
130. Ibid., p. 16.

2

Taqlīd and Discontinuity: The Transformation of Islamic Legal Authority in the Volga-Ural Region

Nathan Spannaus

In 1910, a certain Aḥmad Fā'iz Manṣūrov, imam in the village of Yaᶜqūb near Ufa, published an article in the journal *Dīn wa maᶜīshat* defending *taqlīd* as a religious necessity. He argued that following the canonical *madhhab*s – especially the Ḥanafī school, to which the overwhelming majority of Russia's Muslim subjects adhered – is essential for correct Islamic belief and practice.[1]

In many respects, the appearance of such a full-throated defence of *taqlīd* in this period is not surprising. The history of Volga-Ural Muslims in the nineteenth century and early twentieth has long been characterised by the struggle between reformers and conservatives, with the latter strongly associated with *taqlīd* and an embrace of *ijtihād* the sine qua non of the former. Although dating from the very early Soviet period, this historiographical framing remains prevalent in the academic literature, which tends to view this struggle through a social/cultural lens.[2] In this light, Manṣūrūf's article, as an example of religiously based resistance to the modernist ethos pushed by reformers since the early nineteenth century, written by a member of the *ᶜulamā'* and appearing in a major conservative newspaper, fully confirms this narrative.

From a different perspective, however, the article evinces an important – and frequently overlooked – shift in the debate over *taqlīd* and *ijtihād*. While we may accept it as representative of conservatism at the time, profound transformations to Islamic law had occurred in the region since the late eighteenth century. These eventually gave rise in the revolutionary period (1905–22) to a new context with unique dynamics at work. Particularly at issue was the makeup of Islamic religious and legal authority, the construction and exercise of which were subject to significant alteration, most notably by the introduction by the Russian government of an official hierarchy for *ᶜulamā'*. *Taqlīd* and *ijtihād* are inextricably linked with authority, and the terms and contours of debates surrounding them similarly shifted over time. Thus, rather than merely repeating a well-known view, Manṣūrov's article, in fact, offers a glimpse into how legal discourse had changed. His position, therefore, cannot be projected back onto earlier debates. This raises questions about the ostensible struggle between conservatives and reformers, as well as its historiographical salience (especially for the study of Islamic law).[3]

This chapter addresses changes in legal discourse throughout the nineteenth century and early twentieth by focusing on the interaction between discourse and institutional structures, and how the former is shaped by/within the latter. This approach is similar to the one utilised by Robert Crews, which looks at the impact of state control on *ᶜulamāᵓ*.[4] *Pace* Crews, who sees a standardisation of Islamic orthodoxy as the major consequence of government oversight of religious scholars, I argue that the prevailing change in the history of *sharīᶜa* in the imperial period is divergence, with growing diversity in Islamic discourse. Although Crews highlights ways that particular areas of law became uniform through state enforcement of norms, these were relatively infrequent and small in scope. By contrast, Muslims' notions of legal, or even basic religious orthodoxy became matters of immense contestation and controversy. This process occurred in spaces largely free of direct tsarist control. Crews, however, is right to emphasise the important role of imperial power, as government oversight of Islamic institutions altered how the *sharīᶜa* was understood and articulated and who could claim to speak for it.[5]

Both of these phenomena – the standardisation of legal practices and divergence in religious discourse – are related to the transformation of Islamic authority, which touches upon foundational elements in the historical edifice of the *sharīᶜa*. These changes gave rise to initial debates over *taqlīd* and *ijtihād* at the turn of the nineteenth century. They also led to a shift in the terms of the debate, such that, by Manṣūrov's time, conceptions of *taqlīd* and *ijtihād* had departed drastically from the earlier understanding. Therefore, an examination of how the discourse surrounding these issues changed over time provides a useful lens for addressing precisely how the construction of legal and religious authority had likewise changed.

Taqlīd ***and*** **Sharīᶜa**

Taqlīd, although frequently mischaracterised as hindering or preventing religious interpretation, was, in fact, a central element of the Islamic legal tradition. Underpinning the institution of the *madhhab* (school of law), it was an important element in the development and function of *fiqh*. It provided coherence to the law by limiting who could articulate legal discourse and how. The scholars most learned in their school's methodology were given the most interpretive autonomy.[6] It was also through *taqlīd* that legal discourse was constructed over time, with new positions based on existing ones. Wael Hallaq has labelled this 'secondary' legal reasoning, in that *fuqahāʾ* utilised their school's *corpus juris* as the textual basis for their interpretations (rather than utilising scripture, as in 'primary' reasoning), but the precise interpretive mechanisms at work were otherwise little changed.[7] *Taqlīd,* in this regard, was neither passive nor unthinking, but rather served as a kind of 'scaffolding', enabling scholars to turn their focus away from structural issues and instead devote their energies to addressing more minute, but also more advanced, questions, leading to more sophisticated scholarship.[8] *Taqlīd* as scaffolding allowed for the refinement of legal discourse as well as changes within it and its evolution over time.[9]

In this way, the prevailing 'regime of *taqlīd*' of pre-modern Islamic law represented a framework for discourses and modes of reasoning, not imposed upon scholars but created and adopted by them, a necessary development, Sherman Jackson argues, of the legal tradition in an advanced stage of its history. It required great acumen and learning from scholars, whose standing as religious authorities was based on expertise in their school's doctrine.[10] The most important *fuqahāʾ* held the status of *mujtahid fī 'l-madhhab*, one who performs *ijtihād* using the methodology of his school, in contrast to an 'absolute *mujtahid*' (*mujtahid muṭlaq*), who follows no one else in juristic method.

Intimately connected with religious and legal authority, *taqlīd* mediated *ʿulamāʾ*'s relations with broader society, primarily through the *madhhab*. Scholars' attachment to the methodology and doctrine of their school's eponymous founder served to legitimate their interpretations with laypeople (defined as those lacking an extensive *ʿulamāʾ* education), but school affiliation and one's place within their school were also a major consideration in patronage and advancement by elites.[11] The *madhhab* operated, to a large degree, as a guild, with its internal structure impacting scholars' roles as judges, authors, teachers and *muftī*s.[12] Within the school, *taqlīd* governed a *faqīh*'s interpretive autonomy, shaping what kind of legal questions he could answer and how exactly he utilised school doctrine in doing so.

Taqlīd, in this way, promoted coherence in legal discourse, which served the valuable function, as Mohammed Fadel writes, of ensuring predictability in the law.[13] In fact, this connection with society was of paramount importance. Not merely an academic endeavour performed in a vacuum, *fiqh* and legal discourse were intimately linked with the function of society and articulated in constant reference to social reality, both in prescriptive and descriptive ways.

Their manifestation in society constitutes an essential aspect of the *sharīʿa*, which Hallaq describes as 'a complex set of social, economic, cultural, and moral relations that permeated the epistemic structures of the social and political orders', and that represents 'a cultural rendering of law in practice, where cultural categories meshed into *fiqh*, legal procedure, moral codes'.[14] It shaped and regulated political and moral landscapes, commercial and agricultural economies, educational and literary practices, relations of power, spiritual lives and social relationships.

Embedded and enacted within society, the *sharīʿa* was thus upheld by a range of social actors who formed the moral community, comprising virtually all segments of society, which is implicit in the *sharīʿa*'s divine mandate. It was both broader than, and inextricably connected with, *fiqh* and the work of *ʿulamāʾ*. The latter was the domain of *qāḍī*s and *muftī*s, of course, but also other elite scholars: the authors who composed the books of law and formulated opinions that developed and moved the boundaries of legal science, the theologians who approached the law and its foundations with explicit regard for its relationship with the divine, and the master teachers who attracted followings of students and disciples who shaped the field in particular regions and settings. These roles were frequently combined in the same figures – authorship and teaching, for instance, were largely linked practices. In the Volga-Ural region, such leading *ʿulamāʾ* held the honorific title *ākhūnd* or *ākhūn*, signifying both learnedness in the *sharīʿa* and authority on behalf of the community.[15] Alongside these scholars stood more mundane teachers, Sufi shaykhs, preachers, Qurʾān reciters, elders and patrons, all of whom played an important religious and moral role within Islamic society.

But knowledge of the *sharīʿa* was not limited to a single group or scholarly class. Rather, it pervaded society. It is, therefore, difficult to place firm divisions between *ʿulamāʾ* and lay Muslims; the former enjoyed particular standing as religious authorities on the basis of their knowledge, comportment and piety – virtues that all Muslims should possess. Most *ʿulamāʾ* held no office, but they were nevertheless among those who spoke for the *sharīʿa* on the community's behalf, who settled disputes and offered guidance, and who, in turn, received deference and reverence as well as patronage and support.

The *sharīʿa*, then, was articulated and maintained by those learned in it (broadly speaking), and it ordered and permeated – even to an extent defined – Islamic society. And the two were closely linked: the *sharīʿa* shaped the function of society, which, in turn, shaped the articulation of the *sharīʿa* by *ʿulamāʾ*. The history of *sharīʿa* in the Russian Empire is one of how its meaning and function were transformed as a result of changes to society, specifically in Muslims' relationship to the Russian state, which in turn altered its articulation and the structures of authority upon which the role of the *ʿulamāʾ* was premised.

State Control

The Volga-Ural region was brought into the Russian Empire with the conquest of the successor khanates of the Golden Horde in the mid to late sixteenth century. Yet, as Matthew Romaniello has shown, Russian control of the region was not effectively established until at least the 1670s (and decades later in the Urals). Until this time, tsarist governance was thin and fragmented, relying on the pre-existing Muslim nobility, and it left considerable space for Muslims' day-to-day existence to continue as it had previously.[16] It appears that the *ʿulamāʾ* continued to serve as communal authorities and upholders of the *sharīʿa*. Indeed, the *ākhūnd* Yūnus bin Īwānāy (1636–88?), perhaps the most important local scholar of the seventeenth century, composed a *fatwā* asserting that payment of the *ʿushr* tax (a traditional Islamic tax on agriculture) was an obligation (*wājib*) in the region.[17] This *fatwā*, which itself suggests that the authority of the *ʿulamāʾ* remained operative and important, also carries the implication that the region could legally be considered part of the *dār al-Islām*, despite the presence of Russian rule.[18]

Christianisation became an explicit priority for the government in the later seventeenth century, a result of changes in the Russian state that saw membership in the Russian Orthodox Church become an essential part of tsarist subjecthood. Accordingly, dedicated efforts to convert, first, the Muslim nobility and, then, the whole of the empire's Muslim population, were implemented. These measures took on increasing hostility and severity, culminating in outright persecution in the 1740s, including the systematic destruction of hundreds of mosques.[19]

But confrontation was not the sole approach employed. In 1736, tsarist administrators in the Urals (with approval from St Petersburg) began offering official recognition to a set number of *ākhūnd*s, who, in exchange for promoting loyalty to the tsar, were allowed to operate as religious and social authorities in the region with imperial imprimatur. Thus began a system of sanction for *ʿulamāʾ* in the region – which local administrators kept free of the anti-Islam measures enacted elsewhere – with *ākhūnd*s approved by the government granted oversight over local imams and allowed to operate courts for Islamic family law.[20]

This arrangement would become the basis for empire-wide patronage of the *ʿulamāʾ*. The state abandoned the open assault on Islamic institutions after only a few years, gradually adopting more tolerant policies, particularly under Catherine the Great (r. 1762–96), who allowed the construction of mosques and barred interference by the Orthodox Church in the affairs of non-Christians. Most significantly, in 1788, she ordered the establishment of the Orenburg Muslim Spiritual Assembly, an institutional hierarchy for all mosques and *ʿulamāʾ* in the Volga-Ural region, Siberia, Kazakh Steppe and European Russia.[21]

The OMSA, headquartered in Ufa, represented a bureaucratic framework for *ʿulamāʾ*. It created a leadership for all Islamic religious 'personnel' – imams and *ākhūnd*s, but also *muʾadhdhin*s, *mudarris*es and even mosque custodians – headed by a state-appointed *muftī*, who served as both the highest Islamic authority and the Muslim community's representative within the government. All such personnel were subject to the OMSA's oversight, which was comprehensive: its purview encompassed all these regions' *maḥalla*s (mosque communities), to which these personnel were officially attached; only 'licensed' (Russ. *ukaznyi*; Tat. *ūqāzlı* or *manshūrlı*) *ʿulamāʾ*, who had been approved by both the local government for their *maḥalla* and the OMSA's leadership, could perform religious duties.

Beyond its basic functions of approving and overseeing *ʿulamāʾ*, the OMSA also served as a formal judicial body, given jurisdiction over Muslims' personal status law. Imams were tasked not only with performing marriages and divorces for the members of their *maḥalla*s, but with dividing inheritances and adjudicating disputes in these areas as well. Moreover, an appellate function was built into the structure of the OMSA, with claimants who disagreed with their imam's judgments allowed to appeal them to an *ākhūnd*, and *ākhūnd*s' judgments to the *muftī*.[22]

The judicial focus of the OMSA belies its bureaucratic character. As Crews points out, it was intended to manage the empire's Muslim subjects on the state's behalf, to serve as 'a mode of organisation to discipline the faith and its officiants and draw them into state service'.[23] At the time of its creation, it was one of the few points of contact between the government and the mostly rural and dispersed Muslim population. It was used to promote loyalty to the tsar in explicitly Islamic terms and to promulgate directives and notices from St Petersburg. Significantly, the state introduced the 'parish register' (Russ. *metricheskaia kniga*; Tat. *mītrīqa daftare*) in 1828, obliging OMSA personnel to record demographic information about their *maḥalla* to be furnished to the state.[24] Paul Werth argues that this marks Muslims' complete integration into the tsarist bureaucracy.[25] Indeed, the

OMSA was, unquestionably, a venture initiated and led by the Russian government – of which it was technically a part, existing for much of its history within the imperial Ministry of Internal Affairs – and it formed an important element of tsarist governance. Yet, it also created a space for Islamic law and the Muslim community within the state and it served as the point of interaction between the *sharīᶜa* and state power.

The empire's use of *sharīᶜa* was designed to facilitate tsarist rule. As Mahmood Mamdani has shown in his study of colonial Africa, imperialist states function not through the wholesale dismantling of extant social structures, but through selective patronage, with support for certain types of native elites (with attendant reinforcement of their elite status) and the removal of others.[26] The result is the reification of existing social categories and their institutionalisation. We can see this effect with the Russian government's patronage of the *ᶜulamāᵓ*.[27] Although scholars served as a point of connection with Muslims' pre-conquest past that continued through the imperial period, the establishment of the OMSA altered the role and composition of the *ᶜulamāᵓ*, as well as the nature of Islamic religious authority.

The OMSA represented an official, legal hierarchy, delineating who was (and who was not) a member of the *ᶜulamāᵓ*.[28] Status as a religious authority was thus defined by the state, which narrowed the category of '*ᶜulamāᵓ*' and placed scholars into formal appointments and ranks, which determined their position and power within the hierarchy. The office of *muftī* (a title that was not previously used in the Volga-Ural region) was created at the head, with the first *muftī*, Mukhammedzhan Khusainov (Muḥammadjān bin Ḥusayn al-Burindiqī)[29] (r. 1789–1824), claiming sweeping powers over the institution that his successors continued to enjoy.[30] Below the *muftī* were placed the *ākhūnd*s, traditionally the elite scholars of the region, who were now subject to the *muftī*'s oversight and directives and granted a supervisory role over the local imams and lower religious personnel. Imams, most commonly known as *mullā*s (a catch-all term denoting authority), formed the most important rank. They served as Muslims' proximate religious authorities, fulfilling virtually all functions under the OMSA's purview; thus, their duties included conventional responsibilities such as leading prayer and performing basic rituals, but also carrying out marriages and divorces, adjudicating family law disputes, and keeping records of their *maḥalla*s for the government.

The imam, although certainly long predating Russian control, was therefore reconstituted as an office (*manṣab*) under the OMSA, made to fit the new hierarchy carved out by tsarist administrators within the government and the institutional structure created. Similar transformations occurred with the *ᶜulamāʾ* broadly. The OMSA's construction through the *maḥalla* excluded religious figures lacking an appointment in a mosque, such as some Sufi shaykhs and mendicant preachers, but also informal prayer leaders. The importance of the *maḥalla* is evinced in Shihābaddīn al-Marjānī's (1818–89) regional history *Mustafād al-akhbār*, which organises scholars' biographies around mosque appointments rather than their death dates, as was conventional.[31]

At the same time, experts in *fiqh* found themselves marginalised within the religious hierarchy, whether as *ākhūnd*s or imams (whose level of education and knowledge could vary immensely), with their decisions and judgments subject to appeal to the *muftī*, who was more tsarist functionary than *faqīh*. *ᶜUlamāʾ* under the Spiritual Assembly exercised their authority by virtue of their office – that is, derived from the hierarchy itself – and not by virtue of their scholarly aptitude or moral comportment. An *ākhūnd* could overrule a subordinate imam for any reason, without needing to appeal to an argument based in *fiqh*. Likewise, the *muftī* could overrule an *ākhūnd* or imam because he was the *muftī*, and his legally binding rulings superseded any *ākhūnd*'s by virtue of coming from the highest-ranking figure in the hierarchy, whose judgment on all Islamic matters was officially supreme.[32] Squeezed between the imams and the *muftī*, the *ākhūnd* as an office underwent a marked diminution in status and function over the course of the nineteenth century.

Such reliance on the office, rather than scholarly competence, is characteristic of a bureaucracy, and, indeed, the establishment of the OMSA brought with it a considerable bureaucratisation of the *ᶜulamāʾ*. Scholars were given a specific purview and jurisdiction (namely, family law in their *maḥalla*s) and placed into formal positions, with their standing and authority determined by their rank.

This bureaucratic character was built into the OMSA from its very beginning. It was created as part of the tsarist administration – initially a provincial legal organ before being brought under direct imperial control – and it was thus backed by state power. The Russian Empire utilised religious institutions to govern its subjects, forming what Crews has called confessional governance, with hierarchies created for each of the primary religions of the empire (certain Christian denominations, Islam, Judaism and Buddhism).[33] The OMSA's structure and function were thus inseparable from the structure and function of the state, and *ᶜulamāʾ*, once appointed, were formally part of the tsarist administration, and could only be removed by the government.[34]

But, importantly, the OMSA also operated alongside other parts of the administration, creating parallel legal structures. Muslims were free (at times encouraged) to take their cases to Russian legal bodies, often with each of the disputing parties addressing their claims to different venues in search of the most favourable outcome.[35] In practice, judgments by *ᶜulamāʾ* were often contested. Muslims pursued unfavourable decisions in tsarist courts or sought help from Russian administrators with cases within the religious hierarchy. Indeed, in 1815, Muftī Khusainov petitioned St Petersburg requesting that municipal-level administrators and lower courts be barred from interfering in OMSA business. The request was denied.[36] Eventually, a series of reforms were implemented in the 1820s in order to strengthen the *ᶜulamāʾ*'s legal standing, requiring Muslims to address all disputes within the OMSA's jurisdiction to an imam, which could then be appealed to an *ākhūnd*, whose ruling on the matter was final, but if the *ākhūnd* encountered any difficulty with the case, he could refer it to the *muftī*, who would issue a *fatwā* deciding the matter.[37] It seems, however, that many cases did not follow a neat path up the religious hierarchy, as Muslim disputants continued to seek out the most advantageous venue in which to press their claims.

The question of the OMSA's standing vis-à-vis the rest of the government remained an issue throughout the imperial period. The religious hierarchy's subordination to the state was reinforced by the fact that it was dependent on the government to enforce its rulings. Tsarist officials could overrule or simply ignore a judgment by a member of the *ᶜulamāʾ*, and the enforcement of Assembly decrees and decisions was always contingent on local authorities' willingness to do so.[38]

Yet, as part of tsarist power, the OMSA's viability and legitimacy as an Islamic institution were matters of imperial concern. Despite the government's frequently ad hoc approach to its function, it sought to maintain the hierarchy's exclusive purview over the religious sphere and also its Islamic correctness: as Crews notes, the empire promulgated a certain state-centric understanding of Islam, using the OMSA to channel Islamic piety towards its own practical goals, which was possible only insofar as the religious hierarchy remained authoritative in Muslims' eyes. The government thus took pains to both guarantee the OMSA's religious standing and legitimise its link with the state, presenting itself as protector and patron of the *sharīᶜa* and quite explicitly promoting loyalty to the empire as a central part of Islamic morality, conflating the two.[39] Muslims, accordingly, addressed claims to the administration in Islamic terms, emphasising the need for the state to support their proper and correct adherence to the *sharīᶜa*.[40]

This put the administration in the position of supporting Islam and as a stakeholder in Islamic institutions and their moral authority. Such an approach was awkward, given the government's link with Russian Orthodoxy, and many tsarist administrators were ambivalent about the Islamic hierarchies and the government's sanction of Islamic institutions. As Islamophobia grew in the second half of the nineteenth century, so did the sense that the OMSA prevented Muslims' conversion to Orthodoxy and fostered disloyalty towards the empire. While calls to disband the OMSA went unheeded, moves were made to weaken it. Areas of the Kazakh Steppe were removed from its jurisdiction, and, with the selection of Salimgarei Tevkelev (r. 1865–85), a Muslim military officer and landowner, as *muftī*, the appointment of scholars to the position effectively ceased.[41] It was also at this time that the imperial government began relying on academic Orientalists to oversee the OMSA and verify its judgments, and it explicitly rejected the establishment of an official *ᶜulamāᵓ* hierarchy for the newly conquered territories of Central Asia.[42]

These measures reflect the contradictions present in tsarist imperial rule. The Russian state wanted both to weaken Muslims' adherence to Islam and to use Islam to promote their loyalty to the empire. For the latter, the government needed the OMSA to serve as the exclusive and binding source of religious authority for Muslims, but the former was hindered by vibrant Islamic institutions, leading the state to simultaneously support and undermine the OMSA. Similarly, the government utilised political messaging to Muslims in terms of '*sharīᶜa*', while at the same time it denounced Muslim exhortations to '*sharīᶜa*' that were not pro-state as examples of intractable fanaticism.[43]

It has been pointed out that state power is not uni-directional, but, rather, it can both exploit subject peoples and be manipulated on their behalf.[44] This is precisely the role played by the OMSA, which served as a vehicle both for the extension of tsarist rule to Muslim communities and Muslim representation with the imperial government. And Muslims used the state's presence within their communities to press their claims and interests to the administration as well as one another. As Crews writes, 'The regime did not have to resort to force to penetrate Muslim communities. In villages and towns throughout the territory under the jurisdiction of the Orenburg Assembly, lay people drew the state into the mosque.'[45] The link between the religious hierarchy and state power allowed Muslims access to the latter through the former.

As such, simple narratives of the decline of the *sharīᶜa* or of Muslims' Russification or reflexive resistance thereof under state control obscure a much more entangled relationship. Tsarist legal structures certainly fell into direct conflict with some Islamic legal structures, but not with other aspects of the *sharīᶜa*, and, moreover, the founding of the OMSA made space for Islamic law within the Russian bureaucracy.

The function of the *sharīᶜa* underwent tremendous change as a result of its interaction with state power. By assigning a particular jurisdiction to the OMSA, the government effectively defined what was, and more importantly what was not, part of the *sharīᶜa*, creating a bounded Islamic religious sphere coterminous with the OMSA's areas of competence. In strictly legal terms, the *ᶜulamāᵓ* retained authority over most matters of family and personal status law, while all other types of cases – thefts, debts, assaults, property disputes, sales, contracts – were made the exclusive purview of the tsarist administration; officially speaking, they were no longer subject to Islamic law, and all cases not clearly within the OMSA's competence were considered government matters.[46] The scope of the *sharīᶜa* was narrowed to the realm of the mosque – namely religious ritual and education – and the duties of the imam.

The impact on Islamic religious institutions was marked. Islamic law became the purview of the newly formed religious hierarchy, which was, in turn, subordinate to the imperial bureaucracy. The transfer of authority from legal experts, whose mastery of the texts and methodologies of *fiqh* was recognised as authoritative for the Muslim community, to imams, who generally lacked the same training and proficiency in jurisprudence, directly contributed to significant transformations in how the *sharīᶜa* was applied in the Russian Empire and how Muslims conceived of it. Far from a complex set of interactions that ordered society, the *sharīᶜa* was rendered an overwhelmingly legal ethic, inextricably linked with formal administrative structures. Its function was brought closer to the domain of European 'law' (something implied in its very name: the Spiritual Assembly of Mohammedan *Law*, with the Russian *zakon* equivalent to the English 'law'[47]) as *ᶜulamāᵓ* moved away from *fiqh* as interpretation to the implementation of legal norms carried out within an official, bureaucratic hierarchy with a defined jurisdiction validated and enforced by the state.[48] Iza Hussin insightfully describes this transformation as moving from Islamic *law*, comprising the socio-legal aspects of Islam, to *Islamic* law, necessarily implying the simultaneous coexistence of 'other kinds of law, authorised by another source of organisational power: commercial, criminal, administrative, and Islamic law is one department among them, applicable in certain cases to certain people'.[49]

It was thus not a matter of the decline of the *sharīᶜa*, which certainly persisted under the OMSA, but rather that its discourses and function in society were quite radically changed by tsarist control. The very fact of a bounded sphere allotted to the *sharīᶜa*, which was marked by its absence in other areas of society, altered its character. The establishment of a formalised hierarchy for *ᶜulamāᵓ* supported by the state further impacted the role and function of Islamic law. Indeed, as Talal Asad writes, speaking of the similar changes to the *ᶜulamāᵓ* in nineteenth to twentieth-century Egypt, 'what happens to the *sharia* is best described not as curtailment but as transmutation. It is rendered into a subdivision of legal norms (*fiqh*) that are authorised and maintained by the centralizing state.'[50] In this way, Islamic institutions became another arm of the imperial legal structure, utilised in support of the tsarist autocracy.

Such a transmutation was both a matter of the enforcement of particular directives (or the imposition of particular structures) and of negotiation, over the scope, function and meaning of the *sharīᶜa* shaped by state power, carried out among Muslims and between them and the various levels of the tsarist administration. Hussin refers to the 'politics' of Islamic law, the interactions, institutions, contestation and power relations involved in the manifestation of the law and its form and content.[51] In this regard, although Muslims' responses were not univocal or without contradiction, their agency in the continued articulation of the *sharīᶜa* cannot be overlooked. These negotiations, even within the Muslim community, operated neither in a vacuum nor in a neutral space. Imperial states represented both 'an institutional political order and a condition of being', with the effects of government power not limited to the specific instruments of that power and its attendant structures. Although not omnipotent, state power forms a background that colours the society under its control, even where it is not directly present or, indeed, actively opposed.[52]

State power, both directly and indirectly, shaped Muslims' conception of the *sharīᶜa* and its modus operandi, altering both the Islamic legal discourse in the empire as well as its politics (in Hussin's sense). Following the establishment of the OMSA, the latter were characterised by debates and contestation over the nature of interpretive authority – who could legitimately engage in religious and legal interpretation, and how.

The Politics of ᶜUlamāᵓ *Authority*

Outright resistance to the OMSA, although present, does not seem to have been overwhelming or even widespread among Muslims.[53] In fact, there were (ultimately unsuccessful) calls from Muslim subjects for the founding of new, additional assemblies on the local level as early as 1802.[54] But there does not seem to have been blanket acceptance of the religious hierarchy either. A not-insignificant proportion of *ᶜulamāᵓ*, particularly in the decades following the OMSA's founding, went unlicensed, whether wilfully, through indifference to tsarist regulations or administrative gaps.[55] Effective oversight of *ᶜulamāᵓ* was difficult, given the empire's vast size and the wide dispersal of Muslim communities, and the government seems to have addressed such issues only as problems arose. Nevertheless, scholars – licensed or not – who ran afoul of state directives were subject to imprisonment, corporal punishment and internal exile.[56] Resistance by *ᶜulamāᵓ* was largely focused on particular policies and measures towards Muslims, rather than Russian rule or the OMSA per se, and, indeed, defence of the latter's standing and jurisdiction was a major priority for the Muslim community.[57]

Changes to the makeup and function of the *ᶜulamāᵓ* brought by the religious hierarchy would have been apparent to Muslims (even with lax enforcement of its measures by tsarist officialdom), such as government and muftiate approval for scholars to take a position, or that Muslims were legally required to follow their imam once appointed. As an example of the latter, in 1815, the Kazan *ākhūnd* Ibrāhīm bin Khūjāsh (1750s–1826) sent an official letter to residents of a nearby village ordering them to pray only behind the licensed imam, citing decree no. 283 from the Ministry of Religious Affairs.[58] The power structures underlying the OMSA likewise became apparent, especially in the leadership of Muftī Khusainov. Dogged by charges of official corruption and personal scandals, he was widely resented by Muslims, a fact noted even by his Russian superiors.[59] He nevertheless was the highest Islamic authority in the region, a position he held for some thirty-five years.

These changes certainly had an impact among *ᶜulamāᵓ*. Notably, two scholars active at the turn of the nineteenth century, Abū n-Naṣr al-Qūrṣāwī (1776–1812) and ᶜAbdarraḥīm al-Ūtiz-Īmānī (1754–1834), were both deeply critical of contemporary scholars and concerned with what they saw as a widespread shortage of necessary religious knowledge. Al-Qūrṣāwī viewed the situation in terms of a lack of scholarly understanding among the *ᶜulamāᵓ*, necessitating scepticism towards received wisdom, while al-Ūtiz-Īmānī for his part focused on scholars' immorality and acquiescence to Russian rule, and he was one of the most vocal rejectors of the Spiritual Assembly.[60]

Although they shared this critical perspective, they put forward diametrically opposed ideas for reform. Al-Ūtiz-Īmānī insisted upon an extreme conception of *taqlīd*, holding that legal reasoning of any kind had ceased to be possible, with all Muslims obliged to follow the norms laid out in the main texts of Ḥanafī *furūᶜ*, avoiding any action not deemed explicitly permissible in them.[61] Al-Qūrṣāwī, by contrast, argued that legal interpretation was needed to maintain the link between *fiqh* and the texts of revelation in light of social reality, but also to exclude and emend erroneous positions that were widespread within existing scholarship. As such, *ijtihād*, which he defined as *fiqh* interpretation generally, but including absolute *ijtihād*, was an obligation upon each Muslim, who should learn Ḥanafī jurisprudence in order to determine proper action for themselves, without relying necessarily on scholars.[62]

To be sure, many, perhaps most, scholars did not share these reformists' belief in the need for drastic changes. Fatḥullāh al-Ūriwī (1767–1843), one of the most prominent *ᶜulamāᵓ* of the early nineteenth century, saw little issue with continuing established methods of *fiqh* reasoning within the OMSA.[63] His judgments as *ākhūnd* show him engaging in secondary reasoning, utilising *furūᶜ* in deciding family law cases – predominantly marriage disputes – referred to him.[64]

Al-Ūriwī's judgments in this regard show continuity with legal opinions from pre-OMSA *fuqahāᵓ*. Although sources from this period are few, writings like Yūnus bin Īwānāy's *fatwā* on the *ᶜushr* tax (cited above) evince a similar use of secondary reasoning, with scholars formulating opinions reliant on existing *furūᶜ*.[65] For example, Amīr bin Nūr Muḥammad (?–*c.*1779), *ākhūnd* in a village near Ufa, settled a case granting a divorce to a woman whose husband had been missing for four years by appealing to positions established in Ḥanafī *fiqh*.[66] Early *ᶜulamāᵓ* under the OMSA such as Ākhūnd Ibrāhīm b. Khūjāsh engaged in the same types of interpretation, as can be seen in his ruling on a marriage dispute from 1818.[67]

Indeed, it seems that the view that *fuqahāᵓ* at this time were obliged towards strict *taqlīd* of their school's doctrine, regardless of their expertise or mastery of the law, was widespread. An anonymous text from Kazan copied in the early nineteenth century describes the structure of the Ḥanafī school based on the progression of generations (*ṭabaqāt*). Beyond the first three generations after Abū Ḥanīfa (699–767), scholars are mere *muqallid*s, limited to reasoning between the various opinions of the *corpus juris*.[68] Indeed, al-Ūriwī, a well-regarded and learned *faqīh*, was considered barred from *ijtihād* by his place in history, regardless of his ability in law: a contemporary biographical notice states that 'if the gate of *ijtihād* had not been closed, of course he would have been a *mujtahid*' (*Agar bāb-i ijtihād masdūd dīmasik albatta mujtahidlardān ūlmaqı*).[69]

Al-Ūriwī himself supported the regime of *taqlīd* that underpinned Hanafism, writing that its limits helped to ensure correctness in legal interpretation.[70] And he seems to have seen little difficulty in maintaining this within the religious hierarchy, whose activities he describes in terms conventional for *ᶜulamāᵓ*. Labelling the referral of a case to him by tsarist officials as '*istiftāᵓ*' (a request for a *fatwā*), he writes that 'within our religious court (*maḥkama-i dīniyyamizda*) [that is, the OMSA] there are arbiters (*ḥukkām*) who protect the people of Islam and judges (*quḍāt*) who are worthy of respect, and they will receive a great reward and an abundant bounty from God'.'[71]

Al-Ūriwī was set against both al-Ūtiz-Īmānī and al-Qūrṣāwī, particularly rejecting the latter's embrace of *ijtihād*, which he saw as undermining known doctrine.[72] In 1810, he sent an official letter to Muftī Khusainov seeking al-Qūrṣāwī's removal from his post as imam for religious errors, first among them 'claiming to be a *mujtahid*' (*mujtahidlik da*ᶜ*wāsını qılūb*).[73] It seems to have been ignored by the *muftī*. Al-Ūtiz-Īmānī likewise attacked al-Qūrṣāwī,[74] who himself was harshly critical of ᶜ*ulamā*ᵓ who insisted upon *taqlīd*.[75] Michael Kemper notes that the disputes between these scholars and their followers coloured Volga-Ural religious discourse throughout much of the nineteenth century.[76]

Despite their significant differences, al-Ūtiz-Īmānī and al-Qūrṣāwī both put forward a rethinking of religious authority and its link with legal discourse in response to the establishment of the OMSA and its impact on Islamic institutions. In light of these structural changes, questions arose about authority: how it is – or should be – exercised or made manifest, where precisely it lay. For al-Ūriwī, these were non-issues; authority remained, as ever, with the ᶜ*ulamā*ᵓ, whose knowledge and standing allowed them to interpret and articulate the *sharī*ᶜ*a* on behalf of the community, which they must do bound by *taqlīd* of their school. But if the ᶜ*ulamā*ᵓ were incapable of fulfilling this duty, then Muslims would have to ensure their own religious adherence through other means, to maintain a link with the normative basis of the *sharī*ᶜ*a*. Al-Ūtiz-Īmānī believed they should rely on the pre-existing Ḥanafī *corpus juris*, the texts of which preserved known and accepted guidance. Al-Qūrṣāwī, however, saw the answer in the use of Ḥanafī legal theory, and his understanding of authority was grounded in knowledge of *uṣūl al-fiqh* (methods of jurisprudence) and its application, particularly in primary legal reasoning.[77]

Al-Qūrṣāwī accordingly downplays secondary reasoning, although it still has a role within his stance on *ijtihād*. Instead, he considers the Ḥanafī *fiqh* methodology, rather than the school's substantive positions, as its centre.[78] In turn, he viewed *furū*ᶜ with some scepticism, holding that judgments – including Abū Hanīfa's – should be investigated to determine their *fiqh* correctness, in order to exclude wrong positions that *taqlīd* had allowed to proliferate.[79] Although al-Qūrṣāwī's position that *ijtihād* is an obligation on all Muslims is radical, it nevertheless retains a major function for the *madhhab*, and does not render everyone an absolute *mujtahid*. Indeed, he affirms significant limits to *ijtihād*, placing points of consensus (*ijmāᶜ*) and foundational religious issues – namely in ritual and creed (*ᶜaqīda*) – beyond its scope.[80]

The conflict between these scholars over *taqlīd* found particular relevance in the question of the *ᶜishāᵓ* (night) prayer, which was perhaps the most important and far-reaching debate among Volga-Ural Muslims in this period. The controversy regarding the prayer revolved around the timing of its performance, understood as after the disappearance of dusk. But this point never occurs around the summer solstice at extreme latitudes, and the long-standing Ḥanafī position on the matter was that the prayer should therefore be omitted in those months, as the proper time never arrives.[81] In the late eighteenth century, however, some Volga-Ural *ᶜulamāᵓ* began arguing against its omission, including al-Qūrṣāwī, who held the view that the scriptural duty to carry out all the daily prayers superseded the *fiqh* reasoning that held the prayer to be contingent on the correct time. He writes that it is absolutely obligatory to perform the prayer, while its timing in summer is a question to be answered through *ijtihād*.[82] By contrast, al-Ūriwī and al-Ūtiz-Īmānī both stuck by the more established doctrine of the Ḥanafī school, against the prayer's performance.[83]

Behind this debate lies an issue of religious authority: who could determine how the prayer should be handled, and how such a determination could be made. For those who believed that the question of the prayer had already been settled within the broader Ḥanafī *corpus juris*, it was the earlier generations of Ḥanafīs collectively who possessed the authority to answer it. For those who held that the short summer nights invalidated the conventional position, a new position better suited to the setting was therefore necessary, and, by declaring it a matter for *ijtihād*, al-Qūrṣāwī implied that he, or any qualified scholar, had the authority to determine the prayer's timing.

ᶜIshāᵓ was certainly a thorny question without a clear answer. Critically, it was not settled by Muftī Khusainov's 1819 *fatwā* declaring that the prayer should be performed.[84] Although it was within the *muftī*'s power to regulate prayer (it was expressly listed as part of the Spiritual Assembly's original jurisdiction[85]), and his *fatwā*, in theory, constituted the final word on the matter, it seems that there was little interest in enforcing it, and any attempt to do so would necessarily have involved tsarist authorities, who were disinclined to interfere in Muslims' affairs when imperial order was not threatened.

With the stability and permanence for Islamic institutions brought by the establishment of the OMSA came a flourishing of religious scholarship, with more scholars contemplating and questioning – in increasingly diverse ways – religious matters like the performance of the *ᶜishāᵓ* prayer.[86] Somewhat paradoxically, the religious hierarchy seems to have made addressing complex issues more difficult. The vibrancy of discourse was spurred by often-fractious *ᶜulamāᵓ*, yet existed ostensibly under the supervision of the *muftī*, who was empowered by the state but lacking in religious legitimacy. Indeed, despite Muftī Khusainov's *fatwā*, Volga-Ural Muslims requested pronouncements on *ᶜishāᵓ* from the amir of Bukhara and *muftī*s in Damascus and Mecca (who all affirmed the prayer's performance),[87] and the debate, in fact, continued into the twentieth century.

Out of this debate comes a very interesting text, the *Nāẓūrat al-ḥaqq fī farḍiyyat al-ᶜishāᵓ wa-in lam yaghib al-shafaq* by Shihābaddīn al-Marjānī, imam of Kazan's First Mosque (now Marjānī Mosque) and perhaps the single most important figure of the nineteenth-century *ᶜulamāᵓ*. Although explicitly addressing the performance of *ᶜishāᵓ* (its title translates as 'The View of the Truth on the Absolute Obligation of *ᶜIshāᵓ*, Even if Dusk Does Not Disappear'), the work takes an expansive view of the topic, connecting it not only with a discussion of *taqlīd* and *ijtihād*, but also with a treatment of the relevant jurisprudence and the makeup of the Ḥanafī school. Al-Marjānī here includes a significant historical perspective, looking at how legal authority had been constructed among Ḥanafīs, as well as offering a detailed history of the debates specific to the issue of *ᶜishāᵓ*.[88]

Substantively, al-Marjānī adopts a position similar to al-Qūrṣāwī's, that the prayer must be performed daily, with the timing determined through *ijtihād*. Al-Qūrṣāwī in fact represents the major influence on al-Marjānī's thought in general, and the latter uses many of the same premises in his defence of *ijtihād* as a necessary part of scholarship, against the widespread insistence upon *taqlīd*. Al-Marjānī, however, does not take the radical stance that *ijtihād* was an individual obligation. Rather, he sees it only as the domain of *ᶜulamāᵓ* learned in *fiqh*, with a narrower understanding than al-Qūrṣāwī of what kinds of reasoning constitute *ijtihād*, and which are forms of *taqlīd*. This is particularly important. While al-Marjānī holds that laypeople are unquestionably *muqallid*s – although he allows for following obvious norms from scripture, without a scholar's judgment – a large proportion of *ᶜulamāᵓ* are for him likewise compelled towards *taqlīd*, in the sense that they are strictly limited to secondary reasoning.[89]

Fragmentation of Authority

Al-Marjānī was a much more central figure than al-Qūrṣāwī among *ᶜulamāᵓ*, and he was far less critical of his fellow scholars (although he was not without his controversies). But he also was writing in a different historical environment. By the time he was appointed imam in Kazan in 1849, the religious hierarchy had become an established part of Muslims' communal existence. Yet in the second half of the nineteenth century there is evidence of an altered relationship between the *ᶜulamāʾ* and the community, as scholars' authority and its basis were increasingly called into question.

This change represents the fragmentation of Islamic authority, which Dale Eickelman and James Piscatori have described as a historical phenomenon in which *ᶜulamāʾ*'s foremost ability and authority to determine and articulate Islamic norms is questioned and undermined by lay Muslims 'compet[ing] to speak for Islam' on a level playing field with scholars.[90]

The hierarchical structure of the OMSA encouraged lay involvement and contestation with *ᶜulamāʾ* over religious issues. Its appellate function, Crews argues, 'substantially broadened lay opportunities to engage in controversies about Islamic interpretations' by providing a venue in which virtually any decision by a scholar could be formally questioned by a member of the community.[91] Furthermore, it was common for lay Muslims to make claims to the government of religious impropriety and incorrectness on the *ᶜulamāʾ*'s part, on the grounds that a scholar's decision was unfounded under the *sharīᶜa*, which often stemmed from legitimate religious disputes. As much as the OMSA was ostensibly the exclusive forum for determining such issues, laypeople turned to Russian officials to press their claims over and against the *ᶜulamāʾ*, using explicitly religious terms.[92]

The tsarist state unwittingly promoted contestation over religious interpretation by creating a bounded sphere for the *sharīᶜa* while undermining the *ᶜulamāʾ*'s standing within that sphere. Muslims of all stripes were attached to, and felt ownership of, the space for Islam carved out by the government and institutionalised in the OMSA, and they vied for influence and authority in matters of religious and communal importance (which, given the confessional structure of Russian governance, were almost necessarily and officially linked). Moreover, the restrictions placed on the OMSA's jurisdiction left whole areas of social life beyond the scope of effective Islamic institutions, leaving Muslims' quotidian adherence to *sharīᶜa* to a large extent free of scholars' guidance.

Patronage represented a major avenue for lay Muslims to shape the religious sphere. Despite state sanction, the government generally did not provide financial support for Islamic institutions, which came from the Muslim community. The responsibility for funding mosques and madrasas often fell to wealthier Muslims, whose contributions, Allen Frank points out, were viewed as an almost expected beneficence, without which institutions struggled to even remain open. (The *waqf*, so prevalent elsewhere in the Muslim world, was virtually non-existent in the Volga-Ural region.)[93] It was thus common for the Muslim merchant elite to support institutions and *ᶜulamāʾ*, with whom merchants were closely connected through marriage and family ties.[94] Patronage allowed merchants to exert a degree of influence by promoting and rewarding certain scholars or institutions over others, and, without the *waqf*'s permanence, financial support could be removed or altered based on the patron's wishes.

Publishing was an important area for patronage. The development of Arabic-script printing in the region was in fact led by wealthy merchants. Two merchants opened and operated Kazan's first press in the first decade of the nineteenth century. A boom in the 1850s saw the opening of innumerable publishing ventures supported by patrons who promoted particular types of works, genres and subject matter.[95] Wealthy elites also played an enormous role in the spread of Arabic-script periodicals, which greatly expanded after the Russian Revolution of 1905, becoming a major venue for Muslims' religious, social and cultural discourse.[96]

Print is a main factor in the fragmentation of authority, as it brings with it greater diversity in available texts, and, by extension, ideas, viewpoints and forms of knowledge. It promotes widespread literacy and education as well, of course, but also independent reading practices outside of scholarly guidance, all of which contributes to a weakening of reliance upon the *ᶜulamāʾ*.[97]

There is a strong overlap between the growth of printing in the Volga-Ural region and contemporaneous shifts in Muslim education, and pedagogical reformers like ᶜAbdalqayyūm an-Nāṣirī (1825–1902) and the famed Ismāᶜīl Gasprinskii (1851–1914) used publishing to further their efforts, both in promoting their vision of reform and in providing texts for teaching purposes.[98]

The push for education reform grew across the nineteenth century, driven by changing ideas of how Muslim schools should operate, in terms of what Muslims should learn and how they should learn it. As early as 1818, Muftī Khusainov proposed to the government the creation of European-style secondary schools for Muslims, to prepare them for careers as civil servants, translators or schoolteachers, or for study in Russian universities. These schools were needed, the *muftī* argued, due to the general lack of education among Muslims and the impractical and inefficient character of Islamic education.[99]

Although Khusainov's proposal was ultimately unsuccessful, the sense that Islamic education did not suit contemporary needs was growing, spurred in part by the influence of Muslims within Russian academia.

A number of important educational reformers were connected with Orientalist institutions in Kazan and elsewhere, such as an-Nāṣirī and Ḥusayn Fayḍkhanov (1823–66), who sought to reshape the madrasa through formalised curricula with modern subjects and publishing textbooks.[100] Particularly towards the end of the nineteenth century, similar goals were put forward by Muslims educated largely in Russian institutions or reformed Ottoman schools, or even in Western Europe, as growing numbers of Volga-Ural Muslims were choosing European-style schools, foregoing the madrasa.[101]

For many, conventional Islamic education paled in comparison to modern, European schools, which accordingly served as the primary point of emulation. Reformers sought to turn madrasas into schoolhouses or gymnasiums, with classrooms and teaching equipment, utilising standardised curricula consisting of modern subjects and the latest pedagogical approaches. These changes were at the heart of the *uṣūl-i jadīd*, the 'new method' of Islamic education popularised by Gasprinskii, from which Jadidism, the famed early twentieth-century modernist reform movement, takes its name.

The major proponents of new-method education were the Muslim mercantile elite. More urban and connected with Russian society than most of their co-religionists, Muslim merchants and industrialists towards the end of the nineteenth century tended to view conventional Islamic education as impractical and ineffective, and Muslims' lack of contemporary education as a hindrance to the community.[102] Many in the mercantile elite openly supported new-method schools, joining with reformers, activists and intellectuals instead of conventional *ᶜulamāᵓ*, and they used their financial clout to further their spread. By promoting a distinct form of education, rather than merely particular scholars, they were able to shape the religious sphere to a greater extent than they had previously. Virtually all the major new-method madrasas, as well as the newspapers and publishing houses that supported reform, were connected with wealthy and influential patrons.

The communal impact of educational reform is difficult to overstate. Islamic learning had long been the main point of cohesion within the community, tying lay Muslims and scholars together through a shared frame of reference. As Frank notes, an imam and his *maḥalla* were linked by education, 'the imam simply ha[ving] a deeper knowledge of the same texts and ideas that the villagers had themselves studied in their *maktab*s and *madrasas*'.[103] To possess this education was to have entry into the discourses and debates that helped define the community.

New-method schooling, however, represented a break with the long-established tradition of Islamic learning. It instilled different knowledge through different methods, leading to graduates who were learned in different discourses and with a different frame of reference. The spread of educational practices adopted from the West, Danielle Ross rightly argues, 'resulted in the replacement of a single uniform body of knowledge with multiple, competing ones'.[104] Once a point of communal cohesion, schooling now served as a marker of divergence. The separation between the different types of education was reflected in the distinction that had developed, according to Stéphane Dudoignon, between the terms 'imam' and '*muᶜallim*' (teacher), with the latter signifying a teacher without religious qualifications or position. While schooling had long been the domain of the former, by 1900 the latter had emerged as a competing category with growing social prestige.[105]

The split between conventional and new-method schools also brought with it competition over the community's financial resources, which laid out the religious and ideological debate over education into stark, practical terms. New-method schools were expensive, and their founding, particularly in *maḥalla*s with a pre-existing madrasa, diverted funds that many thought were better used elsewhere. In addition, proponents of educational reform often sought their own sources of support, whether from wealthy patrons, charitable societies or even Russian municipal councils (*zemstvos*), while those opposed to it sought to pool and distribute charitable contributions (primarily from *zakāt*) through the Spiritual Assembly.[106]

Education thus represented a major flashpoint for Muslims, and at the heart of these disputes was a question of authority: whether the *ᶜulamāʾ* should be Muslims' primary leaders and representatives, with judgment over matters of communal importance accorded to them, or whether other segments of society should have a say on these issues equal or superior to that of scholars. This question, despite its obvious significance, was precipitated by the very fact that lay Muslims had begun to vie for authority in these areas alongside scholars, and, in this environment, there was little that could be done to prevent it. The OMSA lacked the power itself to enforce and maintain the *ᶜulamāʾ*'s authority. Individual scholars were, instead, left to denounce reformers in petitions to the government, which, for its part, supported the religious hierarchy only with half-measures.[107] At the same time, lay Muslims increasingly used every channel available to them to assert themselves alongside members of the *ᶜulamāʾ*, whether through the structure of the OMSA, the press, civic organisations, Muslim schools or Russian institutions, even regarding religious issues: for instance, a massive 1910 protest in Kazan against a tsarist policy on religious holidays was led not by *ᶜulamāʾ* but merchants and lay activists, who had been further empowered by the loosening of restrictions on political activity following the Russian Revolution of 1905.[108]

Ijtihād

The more-or-less equal participation by lay Muslims alongside scholars over religious matters was the essence of the fragmentation of Islamic authority as a historical phenomenon, but it also directly relates to the issue of the continued validity of the scholarly tradition and the degree to which it remained authoritative. On a basic level, fragmentation was an issue of knowledge. As *ᶜulamāʾ*'s (lit. 'those who know') ability to speak for Islam and their standing as interpreters and guides were based on their mastery of Islamic scholarship and religious sciences (*ᶜulūm*; forms of knowledge), non-scholars' claims to these roles carried the implication that religious authority could or should be based on something else, thus devaluing or disregarding scholarly knowledge and the intellectual and interpretive frameworks – the 'scaffolding' – thereof.

The bureaucratic structure of the OMSA, along with providing opportunities for lay contestation with *ᶜulamāʾ*, formally separated knowledge from authority, or at least from institutional power. But educational reform laid this issue of knowledge bare. New-method education was premised on the abandonment of the practices and methodologies that had underpinned Islamic scholarship, on the grounds that this tradition was no longer relevant or useful. As Mustafa Tuna notes, its spread led to more and more Muslims holding the tradition in low regard.[109] As the basis for the *ᶜulamāʾ*'s authority, the diminution of the tradition's importance and its normative force within the Muslim community led necessarily to the diminution of their authority. And, indeed, for many proponents of Jadidism, the rejection of the conventional madrasa went hand-in-hand with a rejection of the scholarly tradition and the *ᶜulamāʾ*, and supporters of educational reform put forward new-method schooling as religiously superior.[110]

The impact was felt in terms of religious interpretation, leading to further contestation over legal and theological matters. Muhammad Qasim Zaman, following Eickelman and Piscatori's analysis, has argued that the fragmentation of authority is accompanied by a weakening of scholarly consensus, marked by both the opening of established points of doctrine to reinterpretation and the end of the restriction of interpretation to the canonical *madhhab*s. In effect, not only were previously settled questions subjected to revision, but the scope of possible interpretations was also greatly expanded.[111]

This move towards interpretation outside of the scholarly tradition was presented under the heading of '*ijtihād*', which now signified scepticism towards, or abandonment of, the tradition, through the interpretation of scripture directly, outside the limits of the *madhhab* and without deference to any prior position, both of which were seen as hindrances to necessary religious reform. *Taqlīd* was accordingly recast as strict, obscurant adherence to the tradition, against reform. It became associated with following the *ᶜulamāᵓ*, and proponents of *ijtihād* criticised it as backwards and unthinking.[112]

The issue with *taqlīd* was not merely closed-mindedness or obsolescence, but that it tied Muslims to outmoded (or downright incorrect) beliefs determined by *ᶜulamāᵓ* centuries earlier. Proponents of reform considered the edifice of the tradition, its 'scaffolding', unnecessary for the articulation and fulfilment of Islamic morality, at best irrelevant and at worst obscuring true religious knowledge (in arcane commentaries, for instance). Reformers argued instead for a model of Islam stripped of these extraneous elements and focused on what they saw as both essential to it and of current relevance. Prominent figures such as Mūsā Jārullāh Bīgī (Bigiev) (1875–1949) and Riḍāᵓaddīn bin Fakhraddīn (1859–1936) embraced this conception of *ijtihād*, arguing that Muslims' communal decline and stagnation was caused by religious error propagated by *taqlīd*. *Ijtihād* was the solution, representing, as Bīgī writes, the sole 'path to salvation and the road to progress' in economics and culture.[113]

Bīgī argued for legal thinking responsive and flexible to different societies and contexts, which he saw as necessitating *fiqh* unbound by the strictures of the *madhhab* and above all based in the texts of scripture.[114] (He condemns the *madhhab* particularly, blaming its formation – the so-called 'closing of the gate of *ijtihād*' – for preventing the use of 'reason' in Islamic civilisation, destining Muslims to fall behind Europeans.[115]) While past models and positions should not be rejected out of hand, *fuqahāᵓ* should be allowed to utilise whichever views are relevant and useful to deal with social realities. For instance, he translated and published a Tatar version of the Andalusian Maliki Abū Isḥāq Ibrāhīm ash-Shāṭibī's (?–1388) *Muwāfaqāt*, a work that argues for grounding *fiqh* in a larger ethical framework, known as the *maqāṣid al-sharīᶜa* (the goals or objectives of the *sharīᶜa*), which is one of the most influential ideas in twentieth-century legal reform due to its perceived ability to adapt to social circumstances.[116]

A lesser-known figure associated with Bīgī, Dhākir Āyūkhānov (1889–1961), took a more extreme position on the role of the *madhhab* and the use of interpretive methodologies in *fiqh*, declaring them illegitimate and promoting engagement with scripture to determine legal and moral issues (*istikhrāj al-aḥkām*) anew, in light of modern forms of knowledge.[117]

This is the context for Manṣūrov's article cited at the beginning of this essay. For more conservative Muslims, the idea that religious or scriptural interpretation without *taqlīd* could be correct – much less superior – was absurd. Manṣūrov argues that following one of the four canonical *madhhab*s was an absolute necessity for '*mutāba*ᶜ*a*', continuity with the Prophet, his companions, the Rightly Guided Caliphs and the early masters of the *sharī*ᶜ*a*, which only *taqlīd* can ensure across the passage of time. Determining the norms (*aḥkām*) of the *sharī*ᶜ*a* without their guidance, Manṣūrov writes, leads to error and illegitimate religious dissension (*iftirāq*).[118]

*Dīn wa ma*ᶜ*īshat*, where this article was published, was the leading conservative journal in the region, and reformist figures, Bīgī in particular, were accused in its pages of religious deviation and likened to Salafis and Wahhabis.[119] These accusations were not entirely without merit; these movements were similarly premised on an embrace of scripturalism and rejection of the scholarly tradition under the guise of *ijtihād*, with selective use of major scholarly figures from the past. Bīgī also studied with pioneering Salafis in Cairo and the Hijaz (as did Āyūkhānov in the former).[120] And, in fact, the references to the early community in Manṣūrov's defence of *taqlīd* appear aimed at Salafi-like claims of Islamic correctness and authenticity.

Such positions are extremes, to be sure, but they are representative of the terms of the debate, which revolved around whether *taqlīd* had any legitimate role in religious interpretation. Yet this is precisely not the contention in earlier debates over *taqlīd* and *ijtihād*. Al-Qūrṣāwī and al-Marjānī explicitly understood the latter as part of the *madhhab*, and thus *ijtihād* and *taqlīd* were not mutually exclusive, as they were for the reformists cited above.[121] Even absolute *mujtahid*s, who follow their own legal methodology, must first attain total understanding of their school's doctrine, and their status as absolute *mujtahid*s depends on their mastery of Islamic legal theory.[122]

This final point illustrates well the disconnect between these earlier scholars and later proponents of *ijtihād*. Al-Qūrṣāwī and al-Marjānī, despite their reformist posture, continued to rely on the edifice of Islamic scholarship, with *ijtihād* – or legal reasoning generally – grounded within broader intellectual frameworks, operating within limits and in reference to other aspects of scholarship, for instance the epistemology of Islamic theology (*kalām*), upon which *uṣūl al-fiqh* is based, and the established consensus of the community. For many twentieth-century reformists, *taqlīd* encompassed the very acceptance of this extant framework. Al-Marjānī, in fact, emphasises the need for religious interpretation by *ᶜulamāʾ* because of their knowledge of scholarship, and he takes pains to stress that laypeople must follow a *madhhab* in order to avoid falling into confusion and religious error.[123] Such a view has much in common with Manṣūrov's, and we can see al-Marjānī's stance in part as responding to ongoing changes to Islamic authority in the second half of the nineteenth century, including burgeoning fragmentation (which Manṣūrov is likewise against, instead reaffirming *ᶜulamāʾ* authority).

Similarly, the disputes among al-Qūrṣāwī, al-Ūtiz-Īmānī and al-Ūriwī revolved around how to understand the basis of the *madhhab*'s authority, to what degree it was grounded in its positive doctrine or its methodology and what precisely was scholars' proper role within it. These concerns are quite distinct from those of the twentieth century, in which the sheer abandonment of the *madhhab* and legal interpretation divorced from the scaffolding of *fiqh* were at issue.[124]

A transitory point in this history comes with the debate between ᶜĀlimjān Bārūdī (1857–1921), a prominent reformist *ᶜalīm* and follower of al-Marjānī, and the staunch anti-Jadidist Īshmuḥammad bin Dīnmuḥammad (1842–1919), widely known as Ishmī Ishān, held at the end of the nineteenth century. Īshmuḥammad, whose account we unfortunately have only in a brief summary by Bārūdī, holds that the perfection or mastery (*kamālāt*) necessary for *ijtihād* renders it impossible, and abandoning *taqlīd* entails religious dissension (*iftirāq*).[125] Bārūdī's position in turn focuses on learned people's ability to engage in *ijtihād*. He points to al-Marjānī as an example of a contemporary capable of *ijtihād* and argues that madrasa education is sufficient for people to engage in legal interpretation.[126]

Initially, it seems that Bārūdī is merely making explicit what is present in the writings of al-Marjānī and, especially, al-Qūrṣāwī, namely that *ijtihād* does not require special status and that educated people have the potential to perform it. But his discussion here – although admittedly short – does not delve into the specifics of *fiqh*, upon which the earlier figures' positions rely, nor the methods of legal theory. In fact, he says that texts such as the *Mukhtaṣar al-wiqāya* convey the knowledge necessary for *ijtihād*.[127] This work, although important in classical Hanafism, is a text of *furūᶜ*, not *uṣūl*, and to say that this is sufficient for legal derivation (he uses the terms *taḥṣīl* and *istidlāl*) is to build an argument on substantively different premises, namely that knowledge of *uṣūl al-fiqh* is not necessarily required for legal interpretation.

Indeed, Bārūdī bases his position on the availability and quality of education in local madrasas, and he himself was a proponent of pedagogical reform, operating his own new-method school, Kazan's Muḥammadiyya. However, the Muḥammadiyya's curriculum not only lessened the importance of *fiqh* in favour of subjects such as geography, history and mathematics, but *fiqh* was predominantly studied through *furūᶜ*, with little role for *uṣūl*.[128]

Bārūdī's position thus falls largely outside the *fiqh* tradition and its scaffolding, specific knowledge of which holds seemingly less importance for him. As such, his view has more in common with later reformists like Bīgī than earlier *ᶜulamāᵓ* such as al-Marjānī. Similarly, Īshmuḥammad's criticism that *ijtihād* would lead to dissension – also found in Manṣūrov – makes sense as a defence of the coherence ensured by the *madhhab*, which *ijtihād* in Bārūdī's conception would undermine. Looking then at the progression of this issue from the beginning of the nineteenth century to the beginning of the twentieth, we can see how the discourse had changed, as debates *within* the legal tradition gradually gave way to debates *about* the tradition and its continued validity.

But education had transformed discussions of *taqlīd* and *ijtihād* by rendering them increasingly moot. Beyond the authors who took part in these debates and their dichotomous positions was an increasingly educated, literate populace of Muslims, who, as Ross shows in her contribution to the present volume, were engaged with religious discourses and sought relevant knowledge for themselves, particularly, it seems, on legal issues, with Muslims seeking to ensure their adherence to the *sharīᶜa* without necessarily relying upon the *ᶜulamāᵓ*. For instance, in 1910, *Dīn wa maᶜīshat* responded to questions from readers about *taqlīd*, whether they had to follow a *madhhab*, or if they could make their own judgments following scriptural proof (*dalīl*).[129] The journal supported *taqlīd* of *ᶜulamāᵓ*, but the questions themselves speak to how notions of authority were shifting in laypeople's eyes.

*Fatwā*s such as these represent an important element in the legal discourse of the period. They were a regular feature in *Dīn wa maᶜīshat*, with most issues beginning with questions on myriad legal and religious subjects, with answers from the journal's editorial board (*idāra*). But requests for *fatwā*s and accompanying responses appear in reformist journals such as *Tarjumān* (which were answered by Gasprinskii, the editor, who possessed virtually no training in *fiqh*[130]), and *Shūrā* regularly featured 'questions' (*masᵓalalar*) from readers on a range of religious, moral and social topics, similar to those in *Dīn wa maᶜīshat*.[131]

The *fatwā* has a long history as an avenue for the *ᶜulamāᵓ*'s exercise of authority, of course, but these *fatwā*s operate in a novel fashion, put forward as abstracted norms functioning as religious guidance for a broad audience. They lack the interaction between a particular *mustaftī* and *muftī* that was traditionally part of the process of *iftāʾ*, but impossible in a newspaper. Thus, the publication of *fatwā*s alters their character and function. They become radically decontextualised, almost literally disembodied: an answer to a generalised question given to a mass readership, ostensibly to follow in similar cases in their own lives.[132]

Therefore, even if abiding by a *fatwā* can be considered a form of *taqlīd*, publication alters its operation, as they are delivered to the entirety of the journal's audience, who then determine which (if any) are applicable to themselves. This dynamic is representative of the ongoing changes in authority, how it was exercised and constructed and – more importantly – how it was received. It was up to the public to determine which positions and approaches were persuasive or compelling, to whom to turn for guidance (if anyone) and which pieces of guidance to accept and follow, with diverse voices competing among them for influence. There was also an ever-growing body of sources of religious knowledge and perspectives available to them. In addition to published *fatwā*s and exhortations in the press, works on Islamic law were popular in the imperial period, including older texts of Ḥanafī *furūʿ*, many of which were published in multiple editions,[133] alongside writings on ethics and comportment (the genre of *ʿilm-i ḥāl*) and moralistic novels, which begin appearing in the vernacular in the 1880s. In sum, members of the public could freely engage in different kinds of self-authority that did not necessarily map onto understandings of *taqlīd* and *ijtihād*, but, nevertheless, show them exercising a large degree of agency in their own religious adherence.

This situation was largely unique to the early twentieth century. It resulted from the spread of reformed and European education and particularly the growth of the periodical press, both of which brought new styles of reading, interpretation and discourse. These phenomena in turn contributed to the ongoing fragmentation of authority, which itself had its origins in the structure of the OMSA as established in 1788, but had evolved over the course of the nineteenth century.

The discourse over *taqlīd* and *ijtihād* likewise changed over time. The debates in the early nineteenth century were distinct from those 100 years later, with different premises, terms, stakes and contexts. Most significantly, the participants' conception of *taqlīd* and *ijtihād* was different, shifting from discussions of the precise forms of *fiqh* reasoning and the construction of Hanafism, to whether the *madhhab* and knowledge of the legal tradition necessarily had any role in legal interpretation. These discussions were all part of the politics of Islamic law in the empire, which were by no means static across the imperial period. As discourse over the adaptation of *fiqh* and legal practice circulated and developed, questions about the legal tradition, its function and application, its continued relevance and its normative force became inevitable. Debates about the validity of particular elements of the tradition morphed into debates about the validity of the tradition itself. In the face of the growing numbers of Muslims who called for its wholesale reform or outright abandonment, its continuity could no longer be presupposed, thus eliciting a full-throated defence of the kind put forward by Manṣūrov. Although expressed in terms of *taqlīd* versus *ijtihād*, the contours of the debate in his article were unique to the twentieth century, and quite distinct from earlier discourses.

Notes

1. The article was published in three parts: Aḥmad Fāʾiz Manṣūrūf, 'Taqlīd wa mutābaᶜa', *Dīn wa maᶜīshat*, 28 May 1910, pp. 339–40; *Dīn wa maᶜīshat*, 4 June 1910, pp. 359–60; *Dīn wa maᶜīshat*, 11 June 1910, p. 370.
2. See M. Kemper, *Sufis und Gelehrte in Tatarien und Baschkirien, 1789–1889: Der islamische Diskurs unter russischer Herrschaft* (Berlin: Schwarz, 1998); M. Tuna, *Imperial Russia's Muslims: Islam, Empire and European Modernity, 1788–1914* (Cambridge: Cambridge University Press, 2015); J. H. Meyer, *Turks across Empires: Marketing Muslim Identity in the Russian-Ottoman Borderlands, 1856–1914* (Oxford: Oxford University Press, 2014); A. Khalid, *The Politics of Muslim Cultural Reform: Jadidism in Central Asia* (Berkeley, Los Angeles and Oxford: University of California Press, 1999).
3. Such anachronism is an important shortcoming of Ahmet Kanlidere's otherwise useful work on Volga-Ural Islamic modernism. See A. Kanlidere, *Reform within Islam: The Tajdid and Jadid Movement among the Kazan Tatars (1809–1917): Conciliation or Conflict?* (Istanbul: Eren, 1997).
4. R. D. Crews, *For Prophet and Tsar: Islam and Empire in Russia and Central Asia* (Cambridge, MA: Harvard University Press, 2006).
5. Here, I make use of relevant literature from post-colonial and Islamic legal studies in further addressing these issues. Generally speaking, these fields can offer valuable insights for the study of *sharīᶜa* in the Russian setting (and vice versa).
6. N. Calder, 'Al-Nawawī's Typology of *Muftī*s and Its Significance for a General Theory of Islamic Law', *Islamic Law and Society* 3:2 (1996), pp. 137–64.
7. W. B. Hallaq. *Authority, Continuity and Change in Islamic Law* (New York: Cambridge University Press, 2001), p. 140. As Hallaq has noted, this type of interpretation allowed later jurists to delve critically into the law as elaborated, thus creating new theoretical and hermeneutical conceptions

within *fiqh*, ibid., pp. 86–120. Calder, citing the prominent thirteenth-century Shafiᶜi Nawawī, also makes note of this. See N. Calder, 'Al-Nawawī's Typology of *Muftīs*', p. 156.

8. Sherman Jackson uses the analogy that scholars within this framework are freed from continuously having to reinvent the wheel and can 'devote themselves to the more practical enterprise of building a car'. See S. Jackson, '*Taqlīd*, Legal Scaffolding and the Scope of Legal Injunctions in Post-Formative Theory: *Muṭlaq* and *'Āmm* in the Jurisprudence of Shihāb al-Dīn al-Qarāfī', *Islamic Law and Society* 3:2 (1996), p. 172.
9. For example, B. Johansen, 'Legal Literature and the Problem of Change: The Case of the Land Rent', in C. Mallat (ed.), *Islam and Public Law: Classical and Contemporary Studies* (London: Graham & Trotman, 1993), pp. 29–47.
10. S. Jackson, '*Taqlīd*', pp. 167–72; B. Weiss, 'The Madhhab in Islamic Legal Theory', in P. Bearman et al. (eds), *The Islamic School of Law: Evolution, Devolution, and Progress* (Cambridge, MA: Harvard University Press, 2005), pp. 1–9.
11. On the importance of the *madhhab* in relation to political and military elites, see S. Jackson, *Islamic Law and the State: The Constitutional Jurisprudence of Shihāb al-Dīn al-Qarāfī* (Leiden: Brill, 1996); B. Tezcan, *The Second Ottoman Empire: Political and Social Transformation in the Early Modern World* (Cambridge: Cambridge University Press, 2010); G. Burak, *The Second Formation of Islamic Law: The Ḥanafī School in the Early Modern Ottoman Empire* (Cambridge: Cambridge University Press, 2015).
12. Cf. G. Makdisi, 'The Guilds of Law in Medieval Legal History: An Inquiry into the Origins of the Inns of Court', *Cleveland State Law Review* 34 (1985–6), pp. 3–16. Validation within the school came by way of the *ijāza* (lit. 'permission'), one of the very few formal credentials in pre-modern Islamic education, wherein a teacher acknowledges a student's knowledge as of an acceptably high level. In the case of the *ijāzat al-tadrīs al-iftā*ᵓ (permission for teaching and giving *fatwās*), a *fiqh* teacher would grant a student the ability to represent the *madhhab* – to become a member of the guild, as it were – as a legal authority.
13. M. Fadel, 'The Social Logic of *Taqlīd* and the Rise of the *Mukhtaṣar*', *Islamic Law and Society* 3:2 (1996), pp. 193–233.
14. W. B. Hallaq, *Shari'a*, p. 543; W. B. Hallaq, 'What Is Shari'a?' in *Yearbook of Islamic and Middle Eastern Law, 2005–2006* (Leiden: Brill, 2007), vol. XII, p. 155.
15. Cf. N. Spannaus, 'The Decline of the *Ākhūnd* and the Transformation of Islamic Law under the Russian Empire', *Islamic Law and Society* 20:3 (2013), pp. 202–41 and, more broadly, A. J. Frank, *Muslim Religious Institutions in Imperial Russia: The Islamic World of Novouzensk District and the Kazakh Inner Horde, 1780–1910* (Leiden: Brill, 2001).
16. M. Romaniello, *The Elusive Empire: Kazan and the Creation of Russia,*

1552–1671 (Madison, WI: University of Wisconsin Press, 2012); A. S. Donnelly, *The Russian Conquest of Bashkiria 1552–1740: A Case Study in Imperialism* (New Haven, CT: Yale University Press, 1968).

17. Shihābaddīn al-Marjānī, *Qism al-Awwal min Kitāb Mustafād al-Akhbār fī aḥwāl Qazān wa Bulghār* (Kazan: Tipografiia E.L. Dombrovskogo, 1897); Shihābaddīn al-Marjānī, *Qism al-Thānī min Kitāb Mustafād al-Akhbār fī aḥwāl Qazān wa Bulghār* (Kazan: Tipo-litografiia imperatorskogo universiteta, 1900), reprinted as Şehabeddin Mercani. *Müstefad'ül-ahbar fi ahval-i Kazan ve Bulgar*, 2 vols (Ankara: Ankara Üniversitesi basımevı, 1997), vol. ii, p. 188. Yūnus, whose father was also an *ākhūnd*, had a remarkable, but not anomalous, scholarly career. He studied for a time in Bukhara, penned a commentary on the major Ḥanafī *fiqh* work *Farāʾiḍ sirājiyya*, and twice went on pilgrimage to Mecca (ibid., pp. 187–9; Riḍāʾ al-Dīn Fakhr al-Dīn, *Āthār* (part 1) (Kazan: Tipo-litografiia imperatorskogo universiteta, 1900), p. 30; Riḍāʾ al-Dīn Fakhr al-Dīn, *Āthār* (part 2) (Orenburg: Tipografiia G.I. Karimova, 1901–8), pp. 38–9; Muḥammad Murād Ramzī, *Talfīq al-akhbār wa-talqīḥ al-āthār fī waqāʾiʿ Qazān wa-Bulghār wa-mulūk al-Tatār*, 2 vols (1908), ed. Ibrāhīm Shams al-Dīn (Beirut: Dār al-kutub al-ʿilmiyya, 2002), vol. 2, p. 338.
18. M. Kemper, *Sufis und Gelehrte*, pp. 217, 290–4; A. Bustanov, 'The Bulghar Region as a "Land of Ignorance": Anti-Colonial Discourse in *Khʷārazmian* Connectivity', *Journal of Persianate Studies* 9 (2016), pp. 184–5.
19. D. Azamatov, *Orenburgskoe magometanskoe dukhovnoe sobranie v kontse XVIII–XIX vv.* (Ufa: Gilem, 1999), p. 18; Spannaus, 'Decline', pp. 218–19.
20. The region under the *ākhūnd*s' oversight, it should be noted, was divided along Russian administrative divisions. On the state sanction for *ʿulamāʾ*, see D. Azamatov, *Orenburgskoe magometanskoe dukhovnoe sobranie*, pp. 14–19; D. Azamatov, 'Russian administration and Islam in Bashkiria (18th–19th centuries)', in M. Kemper, A. von Kügelgen, D. Yermakov (eds), *Muslim Culture in Russia and Central Asia from the 18th to the Early 20th Centuries* (4 vols) (Berlin: Klaus Schwarz Verlag, 1996), vol. 1, pp. 91–112; N. Spannaus, 'Decline', pp. 211–15.
21. This body is called the Orenburg Assembly due to its location within the Orenburg governorate, but since its founding it has only been headquartered in Ufa, never in the city of Orenburg as often reported; D. Azamatov, *Orenburgskoe magometanskoe dukhovnoe sobranie*, pp. 24–5. A second assembly was founded in Crimea in 1794 and granted jurisdiction over Muslims in the western provinces, such as Ukraine and Belarus. Two more were founded for the Caucasus in 1872. Only the Orenburg assembly will be addressed here.
22. See D. Azamatov, *Orenburgskoe magometanskoe dukhovnoe sobranie*; N. Spannaus, 'Decline'; R. D. Crews, *For Prophet and Tsar*; M. Tuna, *Imperial Russia's Muslims*, esp. pp. 37–56. On the Spiritual Assembly's founding, see *Polnoe sobranie zakonov Rossiiskoi Imperii*, Series 1, 40

vols (St Petersburg: Gosudarstvennaia tipografiia, 1830), xxii, nos 16710, 16711; xxiii, no. 16759; *Materialy po istorii Bashkirskoi ASSR* (7 vols) (Moscow and Leningrad: izd-vo Akademii Nauk SSSR, 1936–60), vol. 5, pp. 563–6.

23. R. D. Crews, *For Prophet and Tsar*, p. 50.
24. Ibid., p. 162.
25. P. Werth, 'In the State's Embrace?: Civil Acts in an Imperial Order', *Kritika* 7:3 (2006), pp. 433–58. Registers were introduced for Orthodox parishes in 1722.
26. M. Mamdani, *Citizen and Subject: Contemporary Africa and the Legacy of Late Colonialism* (Princeton: Princeton University Press, 1996); J. Comaroff and J. Comaroff, *Of Revelation and Revolution: Christianity, Colonialism, and Consciousness in South Africa* (Chicago: University of Chicago Press, 1991).
27. The undermining of the nobility in the seventeenth century had left scholars as the primary Muslim elites, and efforts at governing Muslims, both hostile and conciliatory, focused on *ᶜulamāᵓ* as important social authorities; cf. D.Azamatov, *Orenburgskoe magometanskoe dukhovnoe sobranie*, pp. 14–15; A. J. Frank. *Islamic Historiography and 'Bulghar' Identity among the Tatars and Bashkirs of Russia* (Leiden: Brill, 1998), p. 28.
28. A note on legal status in the Russian Empire: imperial society was divided between estates (*sosloviia*) that determined the status of all tsarist subjects, with attendant privileges and obligations, in five main groupings: the nobility (which included military officers), clergy, merchants, townspeople and peasants. Islamic scholars, unlike their Orthodox counterparts, were never included in the clerical estate. See P. Werth, '*Soslovie* and the "Foreign" Clergies of Imperial Russia: Estate Rights or Service Rights?', *Cahiers du monde russe* 51:2–3 (2010), pp. 419–40.
29. The Russified form of Muslims' names will be used for figures widely known by that form, or with both forms included, as here.
30. R. D. Crews, *For Prophet and Tsar*, pp. 59, 66, 158; D. Azamatov, *Orenburgskoe magometanskoe dukhovnoe sobranie*, pp. 40–8; also D. Azamatov, 'The Muftis of the Orenburg Spiritual Assembly in the 18th and 19th Centuries: The Struggle for Power in Russia's Muslim Institution', in A. von Kügelgen, M. Kemper and A. J. Frank (eds), *Muslim Culture in Russia and Central Asia from the 18th to the Early 20th Centuries*, Vol. 2: *Inter-Regional and Inter-Ethnic Relations* (Berlin: Klaus Schwarz Verlag, 1998), pp. 356–64.
31. Cf. N. Spannaus, 'Decline', p. 207.
32. Riḍāᵓaddīn bin Fakhraddīn, *Āthār*, part iv, pp. 191–2; Riḍāᵓaddīn bin Fakhraddīn, *Āthār*, part v, pp. 233–5; N. Spannaus, 'Decline', pp. 222–4.
33. R. D. Crews, 'Empire and the Confessional State: Islam and Religious Politics in Nineteenth-Century Russia', *American Historical Review* 108:1

(2003), pp. 50–83. Despite the differences between the various institutions, they all were functionally based on the Russian Orthodox Synod, a body created as part of the sweeping reforms of Peter the Great (r. 1689–1724) to place the Church under direct control by the imperial government; see J. Cracraft, *The Church Reform of Peter the Great* (Stanford: Stanford University Press, 1971).

34. A. J. Frank, *Muslim Religious Institutions*, p. 140.
35. Cf. N. Spannaus, 'Decline'. In *Āthār*, there are reports from a number of cases brought before members of the *ᶜulamāʾ* in which claimants had gone to various government departments in addition to the Spiritual Assembly, or the case was referred to the *ᶜulamāʾ* by a government official who was unwilling to hear it.
36. D. Azamatov, *Orenburgskoe magometanskoe dukhovnoe sobranie*, p. 22.
37. R. D. Crews, *For Prophet and Tsar*, pp. 154-8.
38. Ibid., p. 98.
39. Ibid., pp. 74–9.
40. Ibid., passim; J. H. Meyer, 'Speaking Sharia to the State: Muslim Protesters, Tsarist Officials, and the Islamic Discourses of Late Imperial Russia', *Kritika* 14:3 (2013), pp. 485–505.
41. Tevkelev had little religious or legal education and often sought answers on *sharīᶜa*-related questions from Russian Orientalists. His successor, Mukhamed''yar Sultanov (r. 1885–1915), also a former military officer, had even less knowledge, knowing neither Arabic nor even Tatar. See D. Azamatov, 'Muftis', pp. 375–7, 380–1; D. Azamatov, *Orenburgskoe magometanskoe dukhovnoe sobranie*, pp. 40–78.
42. R. D. Crews, *For Prophet and Tsar*, pp. 177–89, 224–36.
43. J. H. Meyer, 'Speaking Sharia', pp. 490–4, 498–502.
44. Cf. S. Hirsch and M. Lazarus-Black, 'Performance and Paradox: Exploring Law's Role in Hegemony and Resistance', in M. Lazarus-Black and S. Hirsch (eds), *Contested States: Law, Hegemony, and Resistance* (New York: Routledge, 1994), pp. 1–31.
45. R. D. Crews, *For Prophet and Tsar*, pp. 93–4.
46. Ibid., p. 164.
47. On the significance of the usage of 'law' in terms of the *sharīᶜa*, see W. B. Hallaq, *Sharīᶜa*, pp. 1–6.
48. The application of Ḥanafī *furūᶜ* by scholars was encouraged by tsarist oversight, which relied on canonical *fiqh* texts as the source of correct legal doctrine to which *ᶜulamāʾ*'s judgments should conform (cf. R. D. Crews, *For Prophet and Tsar*, pp. 25, 76–9, 163–6, 177–80). The usurpation of legal authority by the government is a central feature of the alteration of Islamic law in the modern period. See W. B. Hallaq, *Sharīᶜa*, pp. 355–543; N. Brown, 'Sharia and State in the Modern Muslim Middle East', *International Journal of Middle East Studies* 29:3 (1997), pp. 359–76; A.

Layish, 'The Transformation of the *Sharīʿa* from Jurists' Law to Statutory Law in the Contemporary Muslim World', *Die Welt des Islams* 44:1 (2004), pp. 85–113.

49. I. Hussin, *The Politics of Islamic Law: Local Elites, Colonial Authority, and the Making of the Muslim State* (Chicago: University of Chicago Press, 2016), pp. 7–8.
50. T. Asad, *Formations of the Secular: Christianity, Islam, Modernity* (Stanford: Stanford University Press, 2003), p. 227.
51. I. Hussin, *The Politics of Islamic Law*, pp. 9–10.
52. J. Comaroff and J. Comaroff, *Of Revelation and Revolution*, pp. 4–6; M. Foucault, 'Truth and Juridical Forms', in J. Faubion (ed.), *Power: Essential Works of Foucault 1954–1984, Vol. 3* (London: Penguin, 2001), pp. 1–89; M. Foucault, 'Two Lectures', in C. Gordon (ed.), *Power/Knowledge: Selected Interviews and Other Writings 1972–1977* (New York: Pantheon, 1980), pp. 78–108.
53. Cf. A. J. Frank, *Islamic Historiography*, pp. 37–8; A. Bustanov, 'Bulghar Region'.
54. D. Azamatov, *Orenburgskoe magometanskoe dukhovnoe sobranie,* pp. 33–4; D. Azamatov, 'Russian Administration', pp. 108–9. These calls elicited considerable support from provincial administrators, but it seems that the Spiritual Assembly in Ufa was ultimately able to retain its original and exclusive authority.
55. Kemper notes that in the Kazan district, a majority of religious personnel were unlicensed as late as 1829; M. Kemper, *Sufis und Gelehrte*, p. 43.
56. See the undated list of *ᶜulamāᵓ* appointed by Mufti ᶜAbdassalām b. ᶜAbdarraḥīm/Gabdessaliam Gabdrakhimov (r. 1825–40) as replacements for thirteen recently incarcerated scholars from Orenburg province; Riḍāᵓaddīn bin Fakhraddīn, *Āthār*, part vii, p. 375.
57. The government periodically infringed upon the Spiritual Assembly's ostensible control over Islamic religious matters – for instance, an 1827 law regarding human burials or an attempted takeover of Islamic education in the 1870s – which scholars felt pressure by lay Muslims to reverse. Cf. R. D. Crews, *For Prophet and Tsar*, pp. 67–71; M. Tuna, *Imperial Russia's Muslims*, pp. 63–96.
58. Riḍāᵓaddīn bin Fakhraddīn, *Āthār,* part v, pp. 231–2.
59. Riḍāᵓaddīn bin Fakhraddīn, *Āthār*, part iv, pp. 184–6; Azamatov, 'Muftis', pp. 357–60; D. Azamatov, *Orenburgskoe magometanskoe dukhovnoe sobranie*, pp. 42–5.
60. On these important figures, see M. Kemper, *Sufis und Gelehrte*, passim; N. Spannaus, 'Formalism, Puritanicalism, Traditionalism: Approaches to Islamic Legal Reasoning in the 19th-Century Russian Empire', *The Muslim World* 104:3 (2014), pp. 354–78; N. Spannaus, *Preserving Islamic Tradition: Abu Nasr Qursawi and the Beginnings of Modern Reformism* (New York: Oxford University Press, 2019).

61. See ᶜAbdarraḥīm bin ᶜUthmān al-Bulghārī [al-Ūtiz-Īmānī], *Risālah-i Dibāghāt*, MS Kazan, Institut iazyka literatury i istorii Respublika Tatarstan (IIaLI RT), fond 39, no. 46, 19 pag. Facsimile printed in G. Utyz-Imiani al-Bulgari, *Izbrannoe*, ed. R. Adygamov (Kazan: Tatarstan knizhnoe izd-vo, 2007), n.p.; ᶜAbd al-Raḥīm b. ᶜUthmān al-Bulghārī [Ūtiz-Īmānī], *Jawāhir al-bayān*, MS Kazan, IIaLI RT, fond 39, no. 2982, fols 23–87. Facsimile printed in G. Utyz-Imiani al-Bulgari, *Izbrannoe*, ed. R. Adygamov.
62. Abū Naṣr al-Qūrṣāwī. *al-Irshād li-l-ᶜibād* (Kazan: lito-tipografiia I. N. Kharitonova, 1903). Reprinted with introduction and Russian translation as Abu-n-Nasr 'Abd an-Nasir al-Kursavi, *Nastavlenie liudei na put' istiny*, intro. and trans. Gul'nara Idiiatullina (Kazan: Tatarskoe knizhnoe izd-vo, 2005).
63. N. Spannaus, 'Formalism', pp. 372–4.
64. See his decisions recorded in Riḍāʾaddīn bin Fakhraddīn, *Āthār*, part ix, pp. 12–72.
65. Cf. Sh. Marjānī, *Mustafād al-Akhār*, vol. 2, p. 188.
66. Riḍāʾaddīn bin Fakhraddīn, *Āthār*, part ii, pp. 53–4. Amīr's ruling also cites a position attributed to Mālik b. Anas (founder of the Maliki school of law), which is significant, as Ḥanafī doctrine on the divorce of a missing person (*mafqūd*) is relatively strict, an issue that also arose in the predominantly Ḥanafī environment of India. See M. Q. Zaman, *The Ulama in Contemporary Islam: Custodians of Change* (Princeton: Princeton University Press, 2002), pp. 27–30.
67. Riḍāʾaddīn bin Fakhraddīn, *Āthār*, part v, pp. 233–5.
68. *Ṭabaqāt al-ḥanafiyya*, MS Kazan, Kazanskii Federal'nyi Universitet (KFU), inv. no. A-1010, fols 21b–45a, fols 21b–22b. This fits with Aleksandr Kazem-Bek's (1802–70) description, where he considers the *taqlīd* practiced by these later generations an elevated form of the *taqlīd* of laypeople; see Mirza Kazem Beg, 'Notice sur la marche et les progrès de la jurisprudence parmi les sectes orthodoxes musulmanes', *Journal asiatique* 4:15 (January 1850), pp. 207–13. Kazem-Bek was a prominent Russian Orientalist who worked at Kazan and St Petersburg universities.
69. Ḥ. Amirkhan, *Tawārīkh-i Bulghāriyya* (Kazan: Maṭbaᶜat Wiyācheslāf, 1883). Reprinted with Russian translation as Kh. Amirkhanov, *Tavarikh-e Bulgariia (Bulgarskie khroniki)*, ed. A. M. Akhunov (Moscow: izd-vo Mardzhani, 2010), p. 42.
70. Fatḥullāh bin Mullā Ḥusayn [al-Ūriwī], [Untitled,] MS Kazan, KFU, inv. no. T-3571, fols 1a–3a, fol. 1a.
71. Riḍāʾaddīn bin Fakhraddīn, *Āthār*, part ix, p. 41.
72. al-Ūriwī, [Untitled,] MS Kazan, KFU, inv. no. T-3571, fol. 1a.
73. Riḍāʾaddīn bin Fakhraddīn, *Āthār*, part iii, pp. 108–9.
74. Riḍāʾaddīn bin Fakhraddīn, *Āthār*, part vi, pp. 308–9.
75. For example, al-Qūrsāwī, *al-Irshād*, pp. 3–5.
76. M. Kemper, *Sufis und Gelehrte*, p. 59.
77. In addition to his *Irshād*, which is largely devoted to explaining the methods

of Ḥanafī *uṣūl*, al-Qūrṣāwī also composed an extensive commentary on legal theory in the *Mukhtaṣar al-Manār* by Ṭāhir ibn Ḥabīb al-Ḥalabī (1340–1406). See Abū n-Naṣr ᶜAbdannaṣīr bin Ibrāhīm [al-Qūrṣāwī] al-Ghazānī [*sic*] al-Ḥanafī, *Sharḥ mukhtaṣar al-Manār*, MS Tiumen', Tiumenskii Gosudarstvennyi Muzei, VF 6765, no. 19064.

78. He writes that the *madhhab* is not located in any position or doctrine, but rather in its method of interpretation. Making a pun on the meaning of '*madhhab*', he writes, 'It is the way *to* something (*madhhab ilayhā*), not the way *in* something (*madhhab fīhā*) . . . [So] the way of the person headed to Kufa, for example, is the route to Kufa, not Kufa itself. And [correct] Ḥanafī *ᶜulamāᵓ* see the necessity of following the ways and methods of Abū Ḥanīfa in *ijtihād* and [legal] derivation (*istinbāṭ*)'; al-Qūrṣāwī, *al-Irshād*, p. 62; emphasis added.
79. Cf. ibid., pp. 29, 32.
80. Ibid., p. 27.
81. See M. Kemper, *Sufis und Gelehrte*, pp. 278–86; M. Kemper, 'Imperial Russia as Dar al-Islam? Nineteenth-Century Debates on *Ijtihad* and *Taqlid* among the Volga Tatars', *Encounters* 6 (2015), pp. 95–125.
82. al-Qūrṣāwī, *al-Irshād*, pp. 58–9.
83. Cf. M. Kemper, *Sufis und Gelehrte*, pp. 280–3.
84. Sh. Marjānī, *Mustafād al-Akhār*, vol. 2, p. 290.
85. *Materialy po istorii Bashkirskoi ASSR*, vol. 5, p. 564.
86. Theological issues were for many *ᶜulamāᵓ* (including al-Ūrıwī and al-Qūrṣāwī) of even greater importance than legal questions; see M. Kemper, *Sufis und Gelehrte*, passim; N. Spannaus, 'Šihāb al-Dīn al-Marǧānī on the Divine Attributes: A Study in *Kalām* in the 19th Century', *Arabica* 62:1 (2015), pp. 74–98; N. Spannaus, *Preserving Islamic Tradition*.
87. M. Kemper, *Sufis und Gelehrte*, pp. 282–3.
88. Shihābaddīn al-Marjānī, *Nāẓūrat al-ḥaqq fī farḍiyyat al-ᶜishāᵓ wa-in lam yaghib al-shafaq* (Kazan: n.p., 1870).
89. Cf. ibid., p. 27. Al-Marjānī also addresses the limits on scholars' interpretations in a major *kalām* work: Shihābaddīn al-Marjānī, *Kitāb al-Ḥikma al-bāligha al-jāniyya fī sharḥ al-ᶜaqāᵓid al-ḥanafiyya* (Kazan: Maṭbaᶜat Wiyāchesläf, 1888), pp. 145–6. This work has been reissued in facsimile with an introduction and Russian translation as Shigabutdin Mardzhani, *Zrelaia mudrost' v raz''iasnenii dogmatov an-Nasafi: Kitab al-Khikma al-baliga al-dzhaniiia fi sharkh al-'akaid al-khanafiiia* (Kazan: Tatarskoe knizhnoe izd-vo, 2008).
90. D. F. Eickelman and J. Piscatori, *Muslim Politics* (2nd edn) (Princeton: Princeton University Press, 2004), p. 131.
91. R. D. Crews, *For Prophet and Tsar*, p. 166; R. Garipova, 'Where Did the *Akhunds* Go? Islamic Legal Experts and the Transformation of the Socio-Legal Order in the Russian Empire', *Yearbook of Islamic and Middle Eastern Law, 2016–2017* (Leiden: Brill, 2018), vol. XIX, pp. 38–67.

92. R. D. Crews, *For Prophet and Tsar*, pp. 94–8, 128–9, 134–42 and passim. For a discussion of this issue in light of Crews' analysis, see P. Werth, *The Tsar's Foreign Faiths: Toleration and the Fate of Religious Freedom in Imperial Russia* (Oxford: Oxford University Press, 2014), pp. 98–100.
93. A. J. Frank, *Muslim Religious Institutions*, pp. 179–80, 195-203, 232–5; M. Tuna, *Imperial Russia's Muslims*, p. 22.
94. See Sh. Marjānī, *Mustafād al-Akhbār*, vol. 2, p. 333–48.
95. A. G. Karimullin, *U istokov tatarskoi knigi: ot nachala vozniknoveniia do 60-kh godov XIX veka* (Kazan: Tatarskoe knizhnoe izd-vo, 1992). I use the term 'Arabic-script' printing as presses published texts in different languages, including multiple regional Turkic varieties and vernaculars, but also Arabic, Persian, Ottoman and Chaghatay.
96. A. Bennigsen and Ch. Lemercier-Quelquejay, *La Presse et le mouvement national chez les musulmans de Russie avant 1920* (Paris: Mouton, 1964); D. Usmanova, 'Die tatarische Presse 1905–1918: Quellen, Entwicklungsetappen und quantitative Analyse', in *Muslim Culture in Russia and Central Asia*, vol. 1, pp. 239–78.
97. Cf. D. Eickelman and J. Piscatori, pp. 42–4, 58–9 and passim; R. Schulze, 'The Birth of Tradition and Modernity in 18th and 19th Century Islamic Culture – the Case of Printing', *Culture & History* 16 (1997), pp. 29–72; F. Robinson, 'Technology and Religious Change: Islam and the Impact of Print', *Modern Asian Studies* 27:1 (1993), pp. 229–51.
98. See Gasprinskii's list of publications from 1900 in E. Lazzerini, 'Ǧadidism at the Turn of the Twentieth Century: A View from Within', *Cahiers du monde russe et soviétique* 16:2 (1975), pp. 259–77.
99. Cf. M. Kemper, *Sufis und Gelehrte*, pp. 61–4.
100. C. Lemercier-Quelquejay, 'Un Réformateur tatar au XIXe siècle 'Abdul Qajjum al-Nasyri', *Cahiers du monde russe et soviétique* 4 (1963), pp. 117–42; Riḍāʾaddīn bin Fakhraddīn, *Āthār*, part xiv, p. 432–43; Kh. Faizkhanov, 'Reforma medrese (Islakh madaris)', trans. I. F. Gimadeev, *Khusain Faizkhanov: Zhizn' i nasledie*, ed. D. V. Mukhetdinov (Nizhnii Novgorod: Izd-vo Medina, 2008), pp. 12–28.
101. A.-A. Rorlich, *The Volga Tatars*, pp. 101–2.
102. C. Noack, 'State Policy and its Impact on the Formation of a Muslim Identity in the Volga-Urals', in S. A. Dudoignon and H. Komatsu (eds), *Islam in Politics in Russia and Central Asia (Early Eighteenth to Late Twentieth Centuries)* (London: Kegan Paul, 2001), pp. 3–26.
103. A. J. Frank, *Muslim Religious Institutions*, p. 227.
104. D. Ross, 'Caught in the Middle: Reform and Youth Rebellion in Russia's Madrasas, 1900–10', *Kritika* 16:1 (2015), p. 60.
105. S. A. Dudoignon, 'Status, Strategies and Discourses of a Muslim "Clergy" under a Christian Law: Polemics about the Collection of the *Zakat* in Late Imperial Russia', in *Islam in Politics in Russia and Central Asia*, pp. 43–73.
106. Ibid.

107. Claims to the tsarist administration by anti-reform activists were often couched in political terms, as the state was more inclined to intervene against 'revolutionary' activities; cf. J. H. Meyer, *Turks across Empires*, pp. 145–9; C. Noack, 'Retrospectively Revolting: Kazan Tatar "Conspiracies" During the 1905 Revolution', in J. Smele and A. Heywood (eds), *The Russian Revolution of 1905: Centenary Perspectives* (New York: Taylor & Francis, 2005), pp. 119–36.
108. Norihiro Naganawa notes that one of the major changes of the post-1905 environment was that now 'a wide range of local Tatar leaders were allowed to sit alongside religious scholars (*ᶜulamāᵓ*) and make their voices heard'; see his 'Holidays in Kazan: The Public Sphere and the Politics of Religious Authority among Tatars in 1914', *Slavic Review* 71:1 (2012), p. 26.
109. M. Tuna, 'Madrasa Reform as a Secularizing Process: A View from the Late Russian Empire', *Comparative Studies in Society and History* 53:3 (2011), pp. 540–70.
110. For example, R. Majerczak, 'Notes sur l'enseignement dans la Russie musulmane avant la révolution', *Revue du monde musulman* 34 (1917–1918), p. 193.
111. M. Q. Zaman, *Modern Islamic Thought in a Radical Age: Religious Authority and Internal Criticism* (Cambridge: Cambridge University Press, 2012).
112. Cf. A. Kanlidere, *Reform within Islam*, pp. 60–5; T. Zarcone, 'Philosophie et théologie chez les djadids: La question du raisonnement indépendant *(iğtihâd)*', *Cahiers du monde russe* 37:1–2 (1996), pp. 53–63.
113. Helpful translations of key writings on *ijtihād* have been published in a collection that demonstrates well the commonalities between Volga-Ural reformers and contemporary figures elsewhere in the Muslim world; see Musa Jarullah Bigi, 'Why Did the Muslim World Decline While the Civilized World Advanced?', in C. Kurzman (ed.), *Modernist Islam, 1840–1940: A Sourcebook* (Oxford: Oxford University Press, 2002), pp. 254–6; Rizaeddin bin Fakhreddin, 'Ibn Taymiyya', ibid., pp. 238–43; Abdullah Bubi, 'Is the Period of *Ijtihad* Over or Not?', ibid., pp. 232–7.
114. Mūsā Jārullāh Bīgīyif, *Qawāᶜid-i fiqhiyya* (Kazan: èlektro-tipografiia Urnek, 1328 [1910]).
115. Bigi, 'Why Did the Muslim World Decline', pp. 255–6.
116. A. G. Khairutdinov, 'M. Bigiev ob obnovlenii musul'manskoi pravovoi sistemy', in D. V. Mukhetdinov et al. (eds), *Bigievskie chteniia: bogoslovskaia mysl' rossiiskikh musul'man XIX–nachala XX vv* (Moscow: Dom Medina, 2015), pp. 73–84; A. Kanlidere, *Reform within Islam*, pp. 94-6. Cf. on Shāṭibī's contemporary influence E. Moosa and Sh. Tareen, 'Revival and Reform', in Gerhard Bowering (ed.), *Islamic Political Thought: An Introduction* (Princeton: Princeton University Press, 2015), pp. 202–18.
117. I. A. Zaripov, 'Z. Aiukhanov-tatarskii neozakhirit', in *Bigievskie chte-*

niia, pp. 66–72; cf. Dhākir Āyūkhānuf, 'Fiqh', *Shūrā* (1 December 1914), pp. 726–8; *Shūrā* (1 January 1915), pp. 17–20.

118. Manṣūrov, pp. 359–60.
119. For example, ^{c}. K., 'Firaq-i ḍālla jadīdalardan shikāyat', *Dīn wa ma^{c}īshat* (4 June 1910), pp. 360–2; ^{c}Abdalḥaqq b. al-^{c}Imād Sīmī-Pūlāṭī, 'Bīgīyif ^{c}aqīdasina', *Dīn wa ma^{c}īshat* (19 March 1910), pp. 180–3; *Dīn wa ma^{c}īshat* (26 March 1910), pp. 198–9; *Dīn wa ma^{c}īshat* (2 April 1910), pp. 216–17.
120. Cf. A. Kanlidere, *Reform within Islam*, pp. 53–4; E. Akhmetova, 'Musa Jarullah Bigiev (1875–1949): Political Thought of a Tatar Muslim Scholar', *Intellectual Discourse* 16:1 (2008), pp. 49–71; I. A. Zaripov, 'Z. Aiukhanov-tatarskii neozakhirit', p. 66. It is important to note that during this period 'Salafism' was a much more fluid and amorphous category than it is today and, also, more accepting of internal diversity. On the development of Salafism across the twentieth century, see H. Lauzière, *The Making of Salafism: Islamic Reform in the Twentieth Century* (New York: Columbia University Press, 2016).
121. Indeed, *taqlīd*, for al-Qūrṣāwī and al-Marjānī, was juxtaposed not with *ijtihād* but with *taḥqīq* ('verification'), a mode of reasoning common in pre-modern Islamic theology that involved analysing a position's logical and philosophical bases and implications; cf. Kh. El-Rouayheb, *Islamic Intellectual History in the Seventeenth Century: Scholarly Currents in the Ottoman Empire and the Maghreb* (Cambridge: Cambridge University Press, 2015).
122. Cf. Shihābaddīn al-Marjānī, *Nāẓūrat al-ḥaqq*, pp. 56–7.
123. Shihābaddīn al-Marjānī, *Kitāb al-Ḥikma al-bāligha al-jāniyya*, pp. 145–6.
124. This is to say nothing of more secularist Jadids, for whom *ijtihād* represented a rejection of Islamic religious authority per se. See, for instance, the influential Marxist author ^{c}Abdraḥmān [*sic*] Sa^{c}dī (1889–1956), who describes *ijtihād* dating back to al-Qūrṣāwī and al-Marjānī in explicit terms of Europeanisation; ^{c}Abdraḥmān Sa^{c}dī, *Tātār adabiyātı tārīkhı* (Kazan: Tātārstān dawlat nashriyātı bāsmāsı, 1926). On this work's considerable influence in the twentieth century, see N. Spannaus, 'The Ur-Text of Jadidism: Abū Naṣr Qūrṣāwī's *Irshād* and the Historiography of Muslim Modernism in Russia', *Journal of the Economic and Social History of the Orient* 59:1–2 (2016), pp. 93–125.
125. ^{c}Ālimjān Bārūdī, [Untitled,] MS Kazan, KFU, inv. no. 1614-T, fol. 1b.
126. [G. Bārūdīnıng Ishmī Ishāngā yazgān khātı], MS Kazan, KFU, inv. no. T-1615.
127. Ibid., fol. 3a; cf. [Ṣadr al-sharī^{c}a] ^{c}Ubaydallāh b. Mas^{c}ūd Maḥbūbī, *Mukhtaṣar al-wiqāya fī masā$^{\circ}$il al-hidāya*, ed. Mirza Kazem Beg (Kazan: n.p., 1844).
128. ^{c}Ālimjān Bārūdī, *Madrasa-i Muḥammadiyyaning niẓāmnāmase*, MS Kazan, KFU, inv. no. T-1535.
129. *Dīn wa ma^{c}īshat* (19 March 1910), pp. 178–80.

130. Cf. M. Tuna, *Imperial Russia's Muslims*, p. 141.
131. Of note is an explicit *istiftāʾ* in *Shūrā* where the question (about *ṣalāt*) had already been addressed to *muftīs* in Bukhara and Tashkent. See *Shūrā* (15 September 1908), pp. 573–6; cf. S. A. Dudoignon, 'Echoes to *al-Manār* among the Muslims of the Russian Empire: A Preliminary Research Note on Riza al-Din b. Fakhr al-Din and the *Šūrā*, (1908–1918)', in S. A. Dudoignon, H. Komatsu and Y. Kosugi (eds), *Intellectuals in the Modern Islamic World: Transmission, Transformation, Communication* (New York: Routledge, 2006), p. 113, n. 65.
132. As Brinkley Messick points out in his study of radio *fatwās* in Yemen, such use of the *fatwā* 'represent[s] both a significant continuity in the venerable Islamic institution of iftāʾ' and, through their mass-media dissemination, 'an equally significant discontinuity', in B. Messick, 'Media Muftis: Radio Fatwas in Yemen', in M. Kh. Masud et al. (eds), *Islamic Legal Interpretation: Muftis and Their Fatwas* (Cambridge, MA: Harvard University Press, 1996), p. 310.
133. The frequency with which such texts were published by presses owned by Russians speaks to their profitability.

3

Debunking the 'Unfortunate Girl' Paradigm: Volga-Ural Muslim Women's Knowledge Culture and its Transformation across the Long Nineteenth Century

Danielle Ross

Introduction

In ᶜAyaḍ al-Isḥāqī's novel, *The Hat-making Girl* (1902), fifteen-year-old Qamar is seduced by her employer's son. Distressed by her loss of honour, she seeks the advice of an older woman, who counsels her to take up a life of prostitution. Left poor, alone and without work, she eventually leaves the city and wanders the countryside in search of charity. By the end of the novel, she dies during childbirth, her body fatally weakened by starvation and illness.[1]

The journalistic and fictional writings of ᶜAyaḍ al-Isḥāqī and other early twentieth-century Tatar social activists have strongly shaped the way that historians think about Muslim women and Muslim cultural, educational and legal reform in late imperial Russia's Volga-Ural region. These writers' depictions of Tatar society have been used to support a heroic narrative whereby male reformers strove to improve the lives of Tatar women by promoting women's education, health and rights within the family that supposedly had not previously existed in their society.[2] However, as al-Isḥāqī and other reformist writers used the periodical press and literary realism to forge images of helpless women in a degenerate Muslim society, they passed sweeping, harsh, highly subjective judgements on nineteenth-century Muslim women's education and knowledge culture. They ridiculed patterns of knowledge transmission among women and claimed to possess a greater understanding of childrearing, cooking, housekeeping and home medicine than traditionally educated female authorities. Muslim cultural reform of the 1890s to 1910s did not liberate women from an oppressive 'traditional' order. Rather, it initiated a struggle for authority over the domestic sphere and a transformation of women's knowledge culture into something more closely resembling Muslim men's educational and intellectual life. Women who wished to take part in reformist circles and to have their views taken seriously by the members of those circles were forced to conform to this new set of cultural and professional practices.

The literature on women penned by reformist writers of the Volga-Ural region in the late 1800s and early 1900s stands at the intersection of discourses on nation and colonialism. In the context of nation-building, female literary characters served as abstract symbols for the emerging nation while new emphases on women's status, health, education and honour were bound up with visions of women as mothers and nurturers of future national citizens.[3] In the colonial context, reformist discourses on women's status reflected the efforts of colonised intellectuals to lay claim to and re-shape the 'inner domain' (family, household, social life) once they had been stripped of power in the 'outer domain' of politics.[4] They also represented a response to European narratives of native women as victimised by 'barbaric' non-European men, narratives that often served as a pretext for intervention by colonial officials, intellectuals and missionaries into colonised communities.[5] Colonial and post-colonial reformers obscured the separation between the improvement of women's condition and the state of the community as a whole. As a result, their programmes often carried within them the potential to transform women's bodies into ideological battlefields and to make them targets for physical violence.[6]

These new understandings of the complexities of the relationship between women and modernising projects are present in historical scholarship on Russian Central Asia. Adeeb Khalid and Marianne Kamp, in their examination of Central Asian reformers' writings on women's rights, point out the conservative views on familial relations expressed therein, and, in particular, reformers' promotion of the ideal of the educated, but submissive and homebound wife-mother.[7] They are also reflected in Agnès Kefeli's studies of Christian apostates to Islam in nineteenth-century Russia, in which she argues that reformers' rejection of popular poetic works as decadent and immoral resulted in the excision from the literary canon of stories with strong female protagonists that had previously provided Muslim women with models for expressing and reflecting on their faith.[8] Historians who focus on Volga-Ural Muslim society have made much less progress in distinguishing between reformers' use of women as literary symbols of the nation and the impact of reformers' projects on actual Muslim women. Tatar and Russian-language scholars continue to accept at face value reformers' assessments of women's lives.[9] Rozaliya Garipova, in her recent articles on female *qāḍī* Mukhliṣa Būbī, discusses the existence of pre-reform women's intellectual culture and the nationalist dimension of reformers' rhetoric on women's roles, but gives little attention to the differences between the views of male and female reformers and the contradictions inherent in male reformers' visions of the 'modern' woman.[10] Marianne Kamp's analysis of the 1917 Muslim Women's Congress offers an intriguing view into women's involvement in the Russian Revolution, but the subject and timeframe of the article limit the degree to which Kamp can contextualise this moment with regards to the longer history of women's roles and culture in the Volga-Ural region.[11]

This chapter challenges the assertion that the dawn of Muslim cultural reform in the Volga-Ural region brought about the liberation of Muslim women. Building upon previous work by Khalid, Kamp and Kefeli and turning to a range of untapped print and manuscript sources, it argues that the situation of Muslim women living in the mid nineteenth-century Volga-Ural region was not nearly as constrained as male reformers asserted. Before the arrival of Muslim cultural reform, women wielded significant agency and responsibility in religious life and household affairs. Although most women did not study in the madrasas, literate women studied and mastered the same bodies of folk medicine, Sufi literature and Islamic legal knowledge as educated men did and acted as transmitters of Islamic knowledge to non-madrasa-educated Muslim women.

When reformers introduced a 'new' body of knowledge on running the household and the family, they disseminated and debated it in spheres other than those in which women acted as bearers and transmitters of knowledge. To become bearers and transmitters of the new knowledge, women had to adapt themselves to the terms of male-dominated reformist society. In this way, the 'modernisation' and 'liberalisation' of Muslim society in Russia led not to the empowerment of women, but to their dis-empowerment and marginalisation. Transformed in reformers' narratives into victims or bearers of outmoded, useless types of knowledge, women's only path to the 'new' sanctioned knowledge was through entry into an intellectual world dominated by men.

The Structure of Women's Education before the 1880s

During most of the nineteenth century, women's education and the transmission of knowledge among Muslim women was often gender segregated and tended to take place in non-institutional settings. The central figure in this process of transmission was the *abıstay* or *ostazbika*, an older and/or authoritative educated woman who was usually a wife or other female relative of a local imam. She was responsible for the education of very young children of both genders and of pre-pubescent and pubescent girls until they left to marry or take up work to support their families. An *abıstay*'s teaching was carried out in her home, in the home of a merchant sponsor, or in a public space made available for the purpose. The education she imparted included the Arabic alphabet, reading and (sometimes) writing in vernacular Turki, basic knowledge of the principles and rituals of Islam, prayers and recognition of specific formulas in the Arabic language. To achieve this task, she turned first to children's primers such as *Iman Shartı* and, then, to the *Haft-i Yak* and a variety of literary texts including *Badavām*, *Qiṣṣa-i Yūsuf*, *Baqırghān kitābı*, *Tawarīkh-i Bulghāriyya*, *Risāla-i ᶜAzīza*, *Muḥammadiyya* and *Qiṣāṣ al-Anbiyāʾ*. These texts continued to play a role in women's devotional activities after their studies ended.[12]

Women's education differed in important ways from men's education. First, women's educational experiences and social relevance are not well-documented in Muslim sources. Madrasas provided fixed sites for educating and socialising future scholars. This allowed for the formation of stable networks not only within generations of scholars, but across generations, as the madrasa's directorship was passed from father to son, to other male relatives, or to authoritative figures within a scholarly lineage. For nineteenth-century Volga-Ural Muslim men, madrasa attendance, induction into Sufi networks, marriages and the training of students and disciples are painstakingly documented in biographical dictionaries, *shajara*s, *silsila*s, *marthiyya*s and local histories.[13] These acts of documentation highlight how central men's education was for the processes of social networking, establishing public reputations and gaining access to financial resources and political power. Women's education lacked both the institutional permanence of male education and the thorough documentation of education-related networks. Aside from mentions of marriages among *ᶜulamāʾ* families and the occasional quoted letter or poem, women are rendered largely invisible in Volga-Ural Muslim historical records.[14]

Second, women's education differed from men's education in terms of its end goal. For men, a madrasa education was meant to confer both social prestige and vocational training. Because, in theory, any Muslim man could attain the ranks of jurist, teacher or Sufi shaykh through education, Volga-Ural Muslims saw the madrasa as a site of social mobility. It was difficult for a peasant's son to ascend to the ranks of the licensed *ᶜulamāʾ*, but with native intelligence, hard work and careful networking it was possible. The rapid growth in the number of Volga-Ural licensed *ᶜulamāʾ* during the nineteenth century was due in large measure to such upstarts from non-*ᶜulamāʾ* families.[15] While, for men, education could determine social status, the case for women was different. Whether a girl belonged to an *ᶜulamāʾ* family determined if she would receive an education that went beyond basic Islamic literacy. At present, there is no evidence that promising girls from non-*ᶜulamāʾ* families were trained as future *abıstays* in the same way that peasant boys might work their way through the madrasa into the *ᶜulamāʾ*.

This difference had ramifications for women's network-building. Boys might travel tens or hundreds of miles to study at a specific madrasa and/or with a specific teacher.[16] Lodging at or near their madrasa and socialising with their teachers and fellow students, they became integrated into regional, empire-wide and transnational networks of Muslim scholars. They became part of a brotherhood whose members shared an intellectual culture and linked together the diverse and dispersed communities within which they worked. By contrast, women received their education within their own communities. This does not mean that they were unaware of regional or transnational trends, but it does mean that any ties they forged through education were likely to be with other women in their immediate community and kinship group rather than with women from more remote locations.

Muslim women did not usually travel long distances to study, but their education also did not begin and end in the *abıstay*'s house. Within the Muslim household, men were encouraged to educate their wives. A mid-nineteenth-century Naqshbandi Sufi text entitled 'On the Duties of Women' (*Khātınnarda būlghān ḥaqqlarnıng bayānı*) portrays women as subordinate to their husbands in matters of religion. It relates the story of a woman who approaches the Prophet to beg a piece of bread and to ask how much a husband can limit his wife's duties. The Prophet answers that a wife must obey her husband's commands. If she decides to undertake fasts above and beyond that required for Ramadan, she can do so only after gaining her husband's permission. If she fasts without her husband's permission, the merit she earns for fasting will go to him. If a wife leaves her house without her husband's permission, the angels will curse her on Judgement Day.[17] However, the same text notes that, in return for being obedient to her husband, refraining from becoming involved in matters outside the home and running a proper Islamic household, a wife has the right to be instructed by her husband on the fundamentals of the faith, the proper methods for ablutions and the five daily prayers. If a husband shirks this duty, he will face torment in the afterlife.[18]

Poet and jurist ᶜAbdarraḥīm al-Ūtiz-Īmānī al-Bulghārī (1754–1834) repeatedly advocated the education of women in his early nineteenth-century writings. He encouraged men to instruct their wives in Islamic law.[19] In *Jawāhir al-Bayān*, he argued:

> The Prophet, may God's blessing be upon him, said: 'Seeking knowledge is obligatory for every Muslim man and woman'. By knowledge, what is meant is knowledge of social relations, knowledge of the faith, and acting upon or rejecting information. It is not obligatory for all Muslims to seek out all knowledge, but it is obligatory for them to acquire knowledge of *ᶜilm al-ḥal*, *ᶜilm uṣūl al-dīn*, and *ᶜilm al-fiqh*.[20]

Women also received information on Islamic law, ritual and morality through communal gatherings and rituals. The early nineteenth-century *Risāla-i Ḥabībullāh Ishān al-Ūriwī*, a list of instructions and admonitions penned by Shaykh Ḥabībullāh of Ūri village, Kazan province for his disciples, offered guidance on proper behaviour and religious practice that was applicable for both men and women. In the section 'Obligations of the Faith' (*Imānnıng wajībları*), he also included a piece of advice specifically for women: Muslim wives were supposed to serve and obey their husbands.[21]

Volga-Ural Muslim women are documented as participants in Sufi gatherings and Muslim apocalyptic movements from at least the mid-1700s. In the 1760s, Mullā Murād, who predicted that the world would soon end and that the throne of Adam would descend upon the ruins of Bulghar, attracted hundreds of male and female followers. Women were a constant presence in the followings of Sufi shaykhs in the 1800s, although they are usually only referred to collectively. For example, in poet ᶜAbdalmajīd al-Ghafūrī's account of an evening at the home of Naqshbandi-Khalidi shaykh Zaynullāh Rasulev in Troitsk in 1894, women are described as coming to receive blessings and healings from Rasulev.[22] The women of ᶜAlī Ishān al-Tūntārī's household attained a high level of education and played an active role in his Sufi network.[23] Bahāᵓaddīn al-Bulghārī Vaisov, the leader of a Muslim revival movement in the Volga-Ural region that refused to recognise the authority of the OMSA or to pay most taxes to the Russian government, also attracted women as followers. When the Russian police moved to arrest Vaisov in 1885 for non-payment of his taxes, an armed standoff ensued between them and Vaisov's followers, in which a number of Muslim women came to Vaisov's defence.[24] Leadership of the movement fell into female hands, namely, those of one of Bahāᵓaddīn's wives, until his sons came of age.[25]

Mixed-gender and exclusively female community gatherings also became sites for transmitting and re-enforcing Islamic knowledge among women. Al-Ghafūrī, in his memoir, gives a vivid description of a communal reading of Qūl Sulaymān Baqırghanī's 'The Book of the End Times' (*Akhırzamān kitābı*) at which his mother, siblings and neighbours, women as well as men, listened and shared their views and interpretations of the text.[26] Kefeli, in her study of Christian Tatars' conversion to Islam in nineteenth-century Russia, emphasises the importance of women in spreading Islamic knowledge within apostate communities. They did this by teaching as *abıstay*s and through the recitation of Islamic texts in communal rituals and life events.[27]

For *ᶜulamāᵓ* daughters and the average Muslim woman, Islamic education was much more spatially diffuse than was the case for *ᶜulamāᵓ* sons and Muslim men. Whereas the madrasa served as a central site for the transmission of Islamic knowledge among men, there was no equivalent site for women. While women participated in the Sufi orders, most of their educational experiences were rooted in their homes and native village or urban quarter and, often, in rituals closely connected with the lives of their families and the households immediately surrounding them. They did not usually form the transnational networks that educated men did. However, their close integration into their immediate communities did grant them considerable ability to mobilise locally.

Men's Knowledge versus Women's Knowledge in the 1860s

In the 1860s, manuscript production in the Volga-Ural region reached its zenith. In addition to being recipients and beneficiaries of knowledge on Islamic law, Sufism and folk medicine, by the 1860s, Volga-Ural men and women recorded such knowledge for their own use. Madrasa students copied down textbooks. Sufi disciples copied down instructions and advice given by their shaykhs. The copying of poetry, dream-interpretation manuals, spell books, miracle stories, morality lessons, prayer books and folk ballads, underway since the late 1700s, exploded by the middle of the century, as literacy rose and paper prices fell.

With only a relatively small range of Tatar and Arabic titles available in print and, among those, only a handful of the textbooks and law digests popular in the Volga-Ural madrasas, students of Islamic law depended heavily upon hand-copied books and notes to preserve and retain information. In addition to copying major textbooks, they also transcribed poetry and songs, their teachers' writings, compositions of their own and pieces of information that they found useful.[28] Madrasa youth continued to produce these 'student notebooks' (*shakird daftarlare*) even after the expansion of the Muslim commercial presses in 1905–6. Similar notebooks were kept by literate women.[29]

The notebooks of brother and sister Shāh-i Aḥmad and Bībī ᶜĀᵓisha, the son and daughter of a village imam named Batırshāh, offer a window into the worlds of men's and women's education in the mid-1800s. Shāh-i

Aḥmad composed his notebook in 1866 while in residence at the madrasa of ᶜAlī Ishān (1772–1874) in Tūntār village, near the town of Malmyzh, about 140 kilometres northeast of Kazan.[30] Bībī ᶜĀᵓisha composed her notebook in 1869 while living in the town of Cheboksary, 123 kilometres northwest of Kazan. Neither of them was prominent enough to merit inclusion in the biographical dictionaries of the late nineteenth century and early twentieth. However, both represent a class or category of Muslims that was growing rapidly in the mid-1800s: people knowledgeable in Islamic law, doctrine and ritual who filled the roles of imam, muezzin and *abıstay* in small provincial towns and less wealthy villages. They were not of the 'great' *ᶜulamāᵓ*, the families who monopolised posts in the major urban centres and important rural madrasas, but, through education and Sufi relationships, they could join the networks of one or another prominent scholar and gain his patronage. Both Shāh-i Aḥmad and Bībī ᶜĀᵓisha appear to have been attached to the network of ᶜAlī Ishān at-Tūntārī.

Shāh-i Aḥmad's notebook consists of seventy-seven folios divided among seventeen texts composed in Tatar, Arabic and Persian as well as miscellaneous notations on the intervening blank pages. Fifteen of the texts were copied by Shāh-i Aḥmad himself, while two others were copied by another of ᶜAlī Ishān's students, Fatḥullāh bin Ḥabībullāh, in the late 1850s.[31]

The notebook begins with a lengthy poem in Persian. The second text is a brief text entitled 'Fārḍ ᶜAyn', which lists, in Persian-language verse, the basic obligations placed upon the individual Muslim believer.[32] This is followed by a longer text entitled 'ᶜAqīda-i Manẓūma', a poetic summary of the tenets of the Islamic faith according to the Hanafī *madhhab*.[33] After this text, Shāh-i Aḥmad transcribed two poems in the Turki vernacular of Kazan. The first is structured around the *shahāda* and exhorts Muslims to avoid worldly passions and immoral behaviour and, instead, follow the path laid out in the books of the faith and the *ṭarīqa*. If one does so, it promises that one will 'burn with passion' for God and righteousness.[34] The second poem invokes Uways al-Qaranī (594–657), a Yemeni mystic who was martyred while fighting for the caliph ᶜAlī against Muᶜāwiya in the First Fitna (656–61) and who was later associated with the belief that a righteous Muslim could gain knowledge from a spiritual leader he had never physically met by making telepathic contact with this leader on the spiritual plane.[35] Next, Shāh-i Aḥmad copied down three prayers in Arabic, including 'A Prayer Transmitted on the Night of Power'[36] and 'In Your Compassion, Oh, Merciful One'.[37] The latter prayer is accompanied by an explanation that ᶜAlī Ishān had commanded his followers to recite it on particular days of the year.[38]

Bībī ᶜĀᵓisha's notebook contains seventy-six folios divided among eight texts composed in Arabic and Turki. One of the Turki-language texts transcribed by Bībī ᶜĀᵓisha summarises the functions of the so-called 'seven sultans': Bāyazīd Bisṭāmī, Khwaja Aḥmad Yasawī, Ibrāhīm bin Adham, Ismāᶜīl, Maḥmūd Ghaznawī, Sanjar Mahdī and Mahmūd Khosrow. Each of these men was either a Sufi shaykh or figured prominently in Sufi literature.[39] By recalling or invoking the names of one or more of these figures, one could achieve various results. For example, recalling the name of one of the sultans while reciting the Ya Sin *sūra* from the Qurᵓān and devoting it to his soul, once every day for one year, would ensure that one's important affairs would turn out well.[40] Each day of the week is to be dedicated to one of the sultans: Saturday to Bāyazīd, Sunday to Yasawī, Monday to Ibrāhīm bin Adham, Tuesday to Ismaᶜīl, Wednesday to Maḥmūd Ghaznawī, Thursday to Mahmūd Khosrow, Friday to Sanjar Mahdī.[41] Different days of the week are also designated as auspicious for performing particular acts. Thursday is a good day to give birth and one should perform prayers twice on Friday.[42] Reciting the Ya Sin *sūra* is also prescribed as a cure for a variety of misfortunes, including hunger, thirst and fear.[43] Near the end of the text, Bībī ᶜĀᵓisha informs the reader that salvation was assured for all who followed this advice. The universality of that promise is emphasised through the use of both the masculine and feminine forms of the words 'Muslim', 'martyr' and 'believer'.[44]

Bībī ᶜĀᵓisha's collection includes a lengthy Arabic-language text that lists the sayings of the Prophet regarding various interpersonal relationships and religious obligations. The section entitled 'What Comes to Husbands and Wives', includes a saying that promises that the man who hits his wife more than three times will experience the worst possible debasement on Judgement Day.[45] Another saying from the same section claims that if a woman should leave home without her husband's permission, all things in the world will curse her, and only after the sun and the moon rise together will her husband be pleased with her again.[46] Yet another promises that if a wife curses her husband, God will curse her seven times.[47]

The journal also includes a *qaṣīda* dedicated to an unnamed Sufi shaykh. After relating the life of the shaykh, text promises that if the *qaṣīda* is read a prescribed number of times, the reader may achieve different results. The person who seeks wealth should read the *qaṣīda* 700 times. The 'door of wealth' will then be opened to him or her. Reading the same *qaṣīda* 110 times will enable a woman to bear a son. Reading the *qaṣīda* to one's infant son will guarantee that he will live a long life.[48]

Notations in the margins and on the blank pages between the main texts give further glimpses into the kinds of knowledge that Bībī ᶜĀᵓisha recorded and transmitted. On a blank page, she includes notes on how long a woman must wait to remarry if her husband dies or divorces her. A woman who was not pregnant when her husband died should wait four months and ten days before remarrying. A woman who had been divorced should wait three menstrual cycles.[49] On another page, Bībī ᶜĀᵓisha jotted down how to convert between various monetary units and how to convert units of length and distance.[50]

Shāh-i Aḥmad and Bībī ᶜĀᵓisha's notebooks both confirm and challenge existing views on Volga-Ural Muslim education in the 1860s. The contents of both notebooks show strong Sufi influences. Both include the recitation of designated prayers and formulas to bring blessing, protection and prosperity. Both notebooks show clear links between the copyists and the Sufi shaykh, ᶜAlī Ishān. Also, both authors were clearly familiar with a pantheon of Sufi saints and martyrs that reached well beyond Kazan and its environs. Links to the nineteenth-century Persianate world are clearest in Shāh-i Aḥmad 's notebook but are also present in Bībī ᶜĀᵓisha's.[51]

Studies of Muslim women's education in the Volga-Ural region have emphasised the importance of Sufi mystical literature as an avenue by which women learned about and engaged with Islam.[52] However, the notebooks of Shāh-i Aḥmad and Bībī ᶜĀᵓisha do not bear this pattern out. Tūntār Madrasa was one of the most highly regarded madrasas in the Volga-Ural region in the mid-1800s, and Riḍaᵓaddīn bin Fakhraddīn describes ᶜAlī Ishān as teaching *tafsīr*, hadith, *fiqh* and Arabic literature at Tūntār. Indeed, ᶜAlī Ishān's lessons in *tafsīr* and hadith were supposedly so well regarded that students from other madrasas travelled to Tūntār village to attend them.[53] However, there is nothing in Shāh-i Aḥmad's notebook to suggest that he was training intensively in these fields. Aside from a few prayers and *sūra*s (heavily marked with diacritics to show the reader the proper pronunciation of each word), there is little evidence that he could comprehend basic Arabic, much less tackle scripture or complicated law commentaries. The *tafsīr*, *ᶜaqīda* and *fārḍ ᶜayn* sections of his notebook take up less than two pages each and their content does not reach beyond the most basic level of Islamic knowledge.[54]

ᶜAlī Ishān travelled and studied in Bukhara and India and was especially renowned for his mastery of the Persian language and Persian poetry.[55] This Persianate influence is very clear in Shāh-i Aḥmad's notebooks, which abounds with Persian and Chagatai-language Sufi poetry. Given the strong focus on mysticism, poetry and elementary knowledge of Islamic doctrine in his notebook, it is possible that Shāh-i Aḥmad's goal in attending Tūntār Madrasa was to become a poet or mystic rather than a jurist or theologian. It is also possible that Sufism made up a much larger portion of the curriculum at ᶜAlī Ishān's madrasa than early twentieth-century accounts suggest. In any case, Shāh-i Aḥmād's notebook demonstrates that Sufi poetry, *munājāt*-singing and striving for individual salvation through moral behaviour and renunciation of the material world were as much a part of men's spiritual life as of women's in the mid-1800s.

Bībī ᶜĀᵓisha's notebook presents a markedly different set of knowledge. While Sufi prayers and rituals are described in her notebook, these take up only a small fraction of the manuscript. In contrast to Shāh-i Aḥmad's notebook, there are no Persian-language texts. Arabic-language texts predominate. Those texts include not only prayers, but also long lists of hadiths sorted by topic and maxims on how Muslims should behave in various situations. Notes taken on blank pages and in the margins of the notebook often relate to Islamic legal questions. With such a collection in hand, Bībī ᶜĀᵓisha would have been well equipped to answer basic questions her neighbours might pose to her about worship, morality, commerce and family life. The fact that Bībī ᶜĀᵓisha omits diacritic pronunciation aids from the lengthy Arabic-language texts she copied suggests that she in fact was more comfortable reading Arabic than Shāh-i Aḥmad was. Far from being limited to vernacular mystical and didactic texts, Bībī ᶜĀᵓisha had access to the same hadiths and Ḥanafī formulas that madrasa-educated men did.

The different kinds of knowledge found in Shāh-i Aḥmad and Bībī ᶜĀᵓisha's notebooks reflect the differing roles that the siblings were expected to play in mid-nineteenth-century society. For Shāh-i Aḥmad, mastery of Sufi knowledge was part of the process of socialisation into ᶜAlī Ishān's *khānaqāh*, and, by extension, into wider, transnational Naqshbandi networks. Being able to perform Naqshbandi Sufism properly was critical if he was to be recognised by other Naqshbandi shaykhs and disciples as one of their brotherhood. Such recognition would open the door to further educational opportunities, employment and, eventually, perhaps, ascent to the ranks of the region's great *ᶜulamāᵓ*. By contrast, Bībī ᶜĀᵓisha's future was based less on her personal educational accomplishments than on the reputations and connections of her male relatives. Once married and settled in her new husband's *maḥalla*, she would have been expected to provide basic Islamic education and Islamic legal guidance to the girls and women of the district and to take the lead in the female rituals surrounding childbirth, marriage and death. In this context, the ability to compose a moving religious poem in Persian or to perform in public as a Sufi shaykh was less valuable than a solid knowledge of Islamic law.

Masculine Modernity and Feminine Backwardness (1880s–1910s)

As reformist trends made their way across the Volga-Ural region in the 1880s, certain male scholars began to challenge Islamic education and the knowledge culture of their communities. They questioned the effectiveness of teaching from books written in Arabic and Persian rather than in the Turkic vernacular.[56] They decried the predominance of Aristotelian logic and medieval philosophy in the madrasa curriculum and called for greater focus on the primary sources of Islamic law and the basic processes of deriving the law.[57] They ridiculed the emphasis on mysticism that permeated madrasa education as well as Muslim cultural life.[58] They attacked the highly personalised system of madrasa education by which students formed strong ties with a single teacher and in which teachers often insisted on absolute exclusivity in shaping their students' education, arguing that such methods created unnecessary factional strife within the Muslim community.[59] Reformers sought educational methods and processes that would permit rapid, reliable, efficient learning comparable to what they believed to exist in Russia and Western Europe.

By the end of the nineteenth century, a new kind of madrasa sprang up in the Volga-Ural region. Tightly organised around grade-levels and subject classes, it resembled in structure a Russian gymnasium. In terms of curricular content, it placed greater emphasis on mathematics, natural sciences, geography and history than the mid nineteenth-century madrasas had, while, simultaneously, introducing Russian-language courses and promoting an Islamic legal and theological curriculum that emphasised Arabic language, Qurʾān, hadith and *fiqh* at the expense of Persian language, speculative theology and Sufi culture. The founders of these new madrasas justified these changes in curriculum by pointing to the threat posed by European colonial expansion. They voiced concerns over whether Islam could adapt itself to a modern world in which it was no longer the dominant culture or political power.[60]

Muslim women and women's education did not fare well within this new rhetorical framework of colonialism, modernity and backwardness. In a subplot of Musa Aqeget's 1886 novella, 'Mullā Ḥusāmaddīn' (1886), a young woman, Ḥanīfa, appeals to a local *abıstay* to help her evade the man her parents wish her to marry. The *abıstay* at first refuses to help her and laments how young people have been spoiled. When Ḥanīfa threatens to kill herself if she is forced to go through with the marriage, the *abıstay*, although still reluctant, relents and permits Ḥanīfa to hide at her house for a few days. This gives the reform-minded Ḥusāmaddīn time to come to her rescue.[61] In Muḥammad Zahīr Bīgī's 'Thousands, or the Beautiful Girl Khadīja' (*Ulūf, yākī guzal qız Khadīja*) (1887), the male characters use logic and forensic science to investigate the death of one woman and aid another.[62] These extremely passive, non-descript women contrasted starkly with the much more active female characters of *Qiṣṣa-i Yūsuf* or *Qiṣāṣ al-Anbiyāʾ*.

Bīgī's second novel, *Great Sins* (*Gunāh-i Kabāʾir*) (1890), forges an even stronger and more explicit link among femininity, passivity and cultural backwardness. 'Great Sins' contains only two significant female characters: a merchant's wife who becomes pregnant while cheating on her husband and an elderly woman who helps her deliver the child, promises to care for it and, ultimately, drowns it in the river.[63] The latter – the ignorant, superstitious woman who inadvertently or intentionally misleads impressionable young people – was to become a stock character in the new literature of the Volga-Ural region at the turn of the nineteenth–twentieth centuries. Reformist writers contrast the moral corruption, greed, lust and ignorance of male villains (often middle-aged or elderly merchants, imams and shaykhs) with the virtuous, selfless, socially useful actions of young male reformers. However, it is difficult to find a similar dichotomy among the female characters in reformist fiction. Male reformers in their writings usually allotted women two roles: helpless victims and perpetuators of false, anti-modern knowledge. Mystical and folk practices that had once constituted an acceptable body of knowledge for educated people of both genders were now depicted as the failings of women and uneducated men.

A scene from Fatīḥ Amirkhan's utopian novel, *Reverend Fatḥullāh* (*Fatḥullāh Khaḍrat*) (1908), neatly captures the process of gendering backwardness in the Volga-Ural Muslim community. At one point in the novel, Reverend Fatḥullāh, a 'backward' imam who dies at the beginning of the twentieth century and is brought back to life in 1958 by his son, a prominent scientist, prepares to attend mosque with his grandchildren. Unable to find a turban and robe (clothing that Muslims eschew in Amirkhan's imagined future), Fatḥullāh dons his granddaughter's robe and goose-down hat.[64] Fatḥullāh is not simply backwards and old-fashioned in his mode of thought. For Amirkhan, the fact that he thinks in these ways feminises him.

As reformers promoted strict regimentation and thorough institutionalisation of education and embraced a combination of empirical thinking, pragmatism and scripture-based legal interpretation, they characterised the prevailing education and knowledge cultures as backward, rural and feminine. Men could escape this backward sphere by applying to the new madrasas, subscribing to reformist publications and joining reformist scholarly networks. Such escape was not technically difficult because, despite their rejection of many aspects of mid-nineteenth-century intellectual life, reformers adopted much of its structure: madrasas as sites of male socialisation, the formation of transregional networks and patronage of fellow network-members. Despite the introduction of the newspaper, which provided an additional tool for attracting and connecting network members, Naqshbandi and reformist networks were structurally very similar.

*Abıstay*s, *ostazbika*s and other female transmitters of Islamic knowledge were less well equipped to adapt to the changes in men's education and knowledge culture. In the nineteenth-century madrasas, *ᶜulamāʾ* daughters had sometimes sat in on their male relatives' lessons.[65] The reformed madrasas, with their admission systems, grade cohorts, large populations of students in residence and impersonalised systems of instruction, left little space for such informal arrangements. Moreover, the reformed madrasas, like earlier madrasas, provided no formal means by which an intelligent girl from a non-*ᶜulamāʾ* family could attend. At the same time, as the madrasas became more institutionalised, their supporters loudly criticised all forms of informal education, including Sufi gatherings and women's circles. Any kind of education that was not carried out in a designated, hygienic space at a fixed time under the watchful eye of properly trained pedagogues was, at best, inferior, and, at worst, socially harmful. Women's education, carried out in homes or at social events, failed to meet reformers' standards for proper, 'modern' education.

The ability of late nineteenth-century educated women to respond to reformers' critiques was limited by the fact those critiques were carried out in spaces that were not usually opened to women. As reformist networks built on the pattern of earlier Sufi networks, late nineteenth-century Muslim print culture arose from earlier manuscript culture. Writing down one's opinion and circulating it in educated society in one's own district and beyond was largely a male activity. The initial change that the printing press brought to male intellectual culture was that scholars could produce more copies of their works more rapidly and circulate them to a larger audience. Meanwhile, women's contribution to legal culture was mostly oral, local and interpersonal. While this mode of engagement was effective for spreading knowledge within close-knit communities, it was not well-suited to taking part in empire-wide discourses. This structure of knowledge transmission made it relatively easy for male reformers to talk about women – and, ultimately, 'other' them – without directly engaging in debate with them.

As in the discourses of other colonial societies, in Volga-Ural Muslim reformist discourse, the plight of the abstract Muslim women was conflated, first, with the fate of Russia's Muslims and, then, with the fate of a nascent Tatar national community. Reformers used women to embody the 'backward' state of the Volga-Ural Muslim society and, simultaneously, made their reform vision concrete: if they could save women from ignorance and abusive men, they would take a significant step towards saving Volga-Ural Muslim society. The conflation of women and the nation occurs regularly in Tatar literature of the 1890s to 1910s, from the exploited girls of al-Isḥāqī's 'The Hat-making Girl' (*Kalapushche qız*), Zakir Hādī's 'The Unfortunate Girl' (*Bakhatsez qız*) and al-Ghafūrī's 'The Famine Year, or the Prostitute' (*Achlıq yıl, yākī sātlıq qız*) to the titular heroine of Amirkhan's *Ḥayāt*, who seeks a future husband who embodies the right balance of progressive thought and adherence to Tatar national culture.[66] Most of the young female characters in reformist novels are noticeably passive. While reform-minded heroes actively protest backwardness and embrace 'modern' formats (newspapers, textbooks, novels) to do so, their female counterparts are much more restricted in their actions: the most active female characters write letters protesting unwanted marriages or dare to venture into public to meet a young man; many more of them take no action at all.[67] Women seem to have contributed little of intellectual value to male reform authors' imagined world of cultural reform. Rather, the liberation of Muslim women by Muslim men was equated with the salvation of the Muslim world as a whole.[68]

Reclaiming Authority: The Creation of Public Writing, Transregional Networks and Institutional Education for Women

As women joined late nineteenth-century modernist movements, they introduced two major changes into the sphere of women's knowledge. First, they shifted from acting as guides and advisors to women in their immediate communities to joining the male-dominated empire-wide discourses. Educated women, including *ᶜulamāᵓ* wives and daughters, became public commentators on Islamic law and women's roles and began to publish and disseminate their work in formats previously exclusive to male scholars. They also began to place greater emphasis on producing original works of literature and Islamic law rather than copying, memorising and transmitting existing texts.

By the 1890s, female writers began to compose works intended for publication. ᶜAlīma al-Banāt Bīktīmeriyya (1876–1906), a daughter of an imam from Qıshlaush village in Kazan province's Arsk district, was one of the first rural female educators to publish her writings. Her pamphlets 'The Teaching of Girls' (*Targhīb al-Banāt*), 'Just Guardianship' (*Ḥusna aw-Wiṣāya*) and 'Rules of Social Relations' (*Muᶜāsharat adabı*) reproduced the kinds of information that would, in previous generations, have been transmitted locally from *abıstay*s to their female students and their neighbours.[69] All three pamphlets were primarily didactic in nature and focused on problems of education, child-rearing and maintenance of domestic harmony. In 'Rules of Social Relations', Bīktīmeriyya urges husbands to set a positive example for their families by being 'shepherds' of their households. She advises women to familiarise themselves with their husband's habits and tastes and to avoid behaviours that would annoy him.[70] The revolutionary aspect of 'Rules of Social Relations' was its published format, not its content.

By the early 1900s, more women entered the Muslim publishing industry. Khabira Naṣīriyya (1882–1912), niece of educator-ethnographer ᶜAbdalqayyūm an-Nāṣirī, published a Persian–Arabic–Turkish dictionary in 1901 and a collection of anecdotes in 1902.[71] Māhrui Muẓaffariyya (1873–1945), the wife of a Kazan imam, began publishing poetry in the Tatar newspapers in 1907.[72] Maḥbūbjamāl Akchurina (1869–1948), the daughter of an imam from Dimau village in Saratov province, began to publish prose fiction, advice columns and literary criticism in the Tatar newspapers in 1908, launching a writing career that continued until 1915.[73] Farkhana Alusheva (née Bakhatguzina) (1886–1958), a school teacher from Achinsk, Siberia, began to publish on the lives of Siberian women in 1906.[74] At least a small number of women also took part in the technical and managerial sides of publishing, most notably, Zuhra Akchurina (of no immediate relation to Maḥbūbjamāl), the daughter of Asfandiyār Akchurin, a wealthy industrialist of Simbirsk, and the wife of Crimean educator-publisher Ismāᶜīl Gasprinskii. Akchurina made significant financial contributions to her husband's newspaper *Tarjuman*, an important press organ for Volga-Ural reformers, especially before the relaxing of Russia's censorship laws and the expansion of Arabic-script printing that followed the 1905 Revolution. She also handled much of the paper's accounting and communications with contributors, subscribers and sponsors until her premature death in 1903.[75]

Women who took up careers in Muslim publishing in the late 1800s and early 1900s tended to come from two social groups. The first group consisted of *ᶜulamāʾ* wives and daughter. In earlier decades, these women would have taken on the roles of *abıstay*s and *ostazbika*s and ministered to the women in their male relatives' *maḥalla*s. Some of these women were drawn into publishing through their *ᶜulamāʾ* husbands, fathers or brothers, who joined the reform movements. The first generation of reformers valorised the husband–wife team who worked in unison to transform their *maḥalla*s and schools. Other *ᶜulamāᵓ* women appear to have entered the publishing world on their own or through the advice of female friends and relatives.

The second group of women writers hailed from the post-Great Reforms provincial towns. They came from middling or wealthy urban families engaged in trade, manufacture or civil service. They received their education from private tutors, girls' gymnasia and teachers' schools. As a result of this education, they were fluent in the Russian language and had been exposed to academic disciplines that *ᶜulamāᵓ* daughters had not: Russian and European literature, geography, history and the natural sciences. They were also more likely than *ᶜulamāᵓ* daughters to have Russian acquaintances and to be familiar with Russian discourses on the 'woman question'.

It was through mass printing and the male networks that formed around early newspapers and printing houses that Russian-education urban Muslim women and traditionally educated *ᶜulamāᵓ* daughters began to meet and exchange views and experiences. The new models of women's education and women's literary production emerged from a fusion of the knowledge commanded by these two kinds of women. These women now had to contend with an increasingly male-dominated discourse on family life, childrearing and proper female behaviour. Within reformist circles, male jurists devoted great attention to the nuclear family as the primary site for training healthy, responsible members of the religious community, and, increasingly, the nation. In 1899, Fatīḥ Karīmī translated Shamsaddīn Samībek's 'The Position of Women' (*Khātınnar waẓāᵓifi*) from Turkish to Tatar.[76] ᶜAbdullāh Būbī published 'Polygamy and the Preservation of Health' (*Taᶜaddud zawājati hifẓ ṣiḥḥatihi taṭbīq*) in 1901 and 'Happiness in Marriage' (*Tazawwujda saᶜādat*) in 1902.[77] In 1903, Riḍaᵓaddīn bin Fakhraddīn published 'Family', a guide to relationships within the nuclear family. 'Family' was re-published seven times from 1903 to 1917.[78] His 'People of the Family: An Essay on Necessary Lessons for Girls and Women' (*Ahl-ᶜāᵓil: Qız balalar wa khātınnar uchūn kira kulan adablarne bayān ilmesh bi-risāla*) appeared in print for the first time in 1908 and again in 1910.[79] Riḍaᵓaddīn bin Fakhraddīn also published guides focused on the role of specific members of the family: 'The Educated Father' (1898), 'The Educated Mother' (1898), 'The Educated Child' (1898), and 'The Educated Wife' (1899). Most of these appeared in multiple editions during the first decade and a half of the twentieth century.[80] By the early 1900s, male reformers also initiated discussions concerning appropriate clothing for Muslim women and veiling.[81]

While some women began to publish and disseminate their writings, others sought to re-shape female education practices. The girls' schools founded by many early women's education reformers arose together with or as offshoots of reformed madrasa and *maktab* projects initiated by their male relatives. In the 1890s, one of the first Muslim girls' schools in inner Russia was opened in the village of Zoyabashı, Sember province with the financial assistance of the Akchurin family.[82] In 1891, Māḥrui, wife of jurist and madrasa director ᶜĀlimjan Bārūdī, opened a girls' school in Kazan adjacent to her husband's reformed Muḥammadiyya Madrasa.[83] ᶜAlīma al-Banāt Bīktīmeriyya opened her girls' school in her husband's village of Yaubash in Riazan province in 1897. She modelled its curriculum on the education she and her sisters had received from their father.[84] The Izh-Būbī girls' school, founded by Mukhliṣa Būbī (1869–1937), was located on the same grounds as Būbī Madrasa and its affiliated *maktab*, which were operated by Mukhliṣa's brothers ᶜAbdullāh and ᶜUbaydullāh. Mukhliṣa began the school when she returned to Izh-Būbī village, having escaped an unhappy marriage.[85] In running the school, she was assisted by Nafīsa and Ḥusnī Faṭīma, her brothers' wives.[86] In 1908, a woman named Bāghubustān Khanım founded a girls' school in Orenburg with financial backing from the city's wealthiest Muslim merchant family, the Ḥusaynovs.[87] By 1909, the Muslim Women's Society of Ufa was financing three girls' madrasas, an orphanage and a home for young women. All these institutions were administered and staffed by women.[88]

Just as publication signalled a shift in the production and presentation of women's intellectual activity rather than the beginning of it, the appearance of girls' schools in the 1890s and early 1900s represented a change in educational practices rather than the beginnings of Muslim female education in the Volga-Ural region. In the new girls' schools, women's education gained the institutional structure already present in men's education. Classes met in buildings and rooms designed and reserved for educational purposes. As was the case in men's reformed madrasas, these rooms were equipped with desks, maps, blackboards and bookshelves. Lessons were held according to a fixed schedule and the day was neatly divided into instructional hours devoted to specific academic subjects.[89] Newly published textbooks replaced Sufi poetry and didactic stories. The teachers received salaries and, increasingly, they were expected to present documentation of their qualifications to teach. This institutionalisation was necessary to bring legitimacy to women's education, or, more precisely, to remove it from unregulated sites such as private homes and women's gatherings and from the influence of morally questionable figures (Sufi shaykhs, local wise women), sites and authority figures that had been stigmatised by the modernist movement.

In reformist writings of the 1890s, male reformers lamented the plight of Muslim women and equated the demeaned state of women with the state of Muslim society as a whole. Reformist discourses emphasised women's lack of agency in 'traditional' Muslim society and women's ignorance, a condition brought about by their lack of access to educational institutions. This rhetoric overlooked or denigrated existing methods of transmitting knowledge among women as well as specific kinds of knowledge (mysticism, witchcraft and folk medicine) that reformers associated with women.

Serpent Queens and Female Jurists (1905–17)

In the years after the 1905 Revolution, a network of girls' schools emerged across inner Russia. Like the all-male madrasas, the most prominent of these schools attracted girls and women from diverse regions and relied on complex regional and transregional networks for financial and professional support. For example, by 1907, the girls' school in Izh-Būbī village enrolled pupils from Ufa, Kazan, Moscow, Sember, Tashkent, Samarkand, Semipalatinsk, Tiumen, Astrakhan, Pishpek, Kasimov and Zaisan.[90] Bāghubustān Khanım's girls' school in Orenburg employed female teachers from Perm and Bukhara.[91] The latter school also hosted visiting lectures by male jurists, theologians and writers. Despite efforts by some male reformers to remove Sufism from education, Sufi shaykhs were also invited to speak at some of the new girls' schools.[92] In this way, these schools' pupils not only gained access to views of male religious-legal scholars and reformers but continued the longer tradition of women's engagement with Sufism, albeit within the setting of a formal classroom. The girls' madrasas of Ufa received their operational budgets and necessary resources (food for the students, cloth for uniforms) from a network of *ʿulamāʾ*, merchant and bureaucratic families, including the Tevkelevs, the Akchurins, the Yaushevs, the Yenikeevs, the Ramievs and the Janturins.[93] In a few cases, prominent men made donations to these schools, but most of the support came through an exclusively female charitable society that brought together women of various socio-economic levels from across Ufa province.[94]

In terms of their official programmes of study, the girls' schools echoed trends evident in the new or reformed madrasas. Būbī girls' school and Bāghubustān Khanım's school offered courses in Arabic language and literature, Russian language, ethics, arithmetic, native-language reading and writing, geography, physics and zoology.[95] Meanwhile, Persian language, Sufi literature and folk medicine disappeared, at least from the official curriculum. Like the madrasas, the girls' schools encouraged familiarisation with the Qurᵓān and the hadith in Arabic. They also emphasised the importance of the 'worldly' sciences – mathematics, geography and the natural sciences – for understanding one's faith as well as navigating daily life. Finally, these schools promoted both native-language literacy and functionality in the Russian language.

The girls' schools were not simply women's madrasas. The reformers' primary goal was not to create a female scholarly cadre that would fulfil the same functions as madrasa-trained men. Rather, for male reformers such as ᶜAbdullāh Būbī and Riḍaᵓaddīn bin Fakhraddīn, the primary purpose of women's education was to strengthen Muslim households by creating competent, 'modern' wives and mothers. The importance of the 'practical' side of girls' education was also emphasised in modernist fictional works such as Aḥmadgaray Ḥasanī's play 'ᶜAlī the Officer's Orderly' ('Denshchik ᶜAlī') (1907), in which a military officer's career is ruined when his superior is invited to dinner at his house and discovers that his highly educated young wife does not know how to cook.[96] Such works communicated that a woman's worth lay in her ability to run a household and not in her mastery of languages, mathematics or Islamic law.

While girls' schools offered courses in reading and writing, arithmetic, geography and basic Islamic ritual and doctrine, they often lacked the advanced courses in jurisprudence, logic and hadith studies offered at many madrasas. In place of those subjects, they offered courses in handicrafts, household management and childcare.[97] The drive to teach women 'scientific' means of housekeeping was in no way unique to the Volga-Ural region. It reflected broader interests across the nineteenth-century world in applying engineering and scientific models to all aspects of life.[98] In the case of the Volga-Ural modernist movements, this institutionalised training for wives granted reformers greater power to shape household practices and the views of the families who might one day send their children to the reformed madrasas. By focusing on this blend of basic religious knowledge, languages and household skills, the girls' schools also served as facilities for training a new cadre of reformist female teachers to replace the traditionally trained *abıstay*s in rural education.

However, the experience of the female teachers and students within the girls' schools reveal far more complexity than male reformers' writings on women's education suggest. For the young women studying at these schools, institutional education was much more than a path to enlightened motherhood. Poems written by girls studying at Bāghubustān Khanım's girls' school in Orenburg make no reference to marriage or childrearing. One untitled poem calls upon Tatar girls to educate themselves, unite, spread knowledge and fight for their place in society against those who would oppose them. The opening line reminds readers that 'we girls have no friends [but ourselves]'.[99] Another poem exhorts girls to study hard at school in to order to find happiness.[100] In addition to these gender-specific poems, the collection also includes works such as 'The Khan's Mosque' (*Khān masjide*), a poem from al-Ghafūrī's 1907 volume 'Love of the Nation' (*Millāt maḥabbate*), which circulated widely in oral and manuscript form among Volga-Ural madrasa students.[101] The presence of this poem demonstrates the porousness of the barrier between male and female education in reformist circles, in which male teachers were permitted to lecture to female students and in which female students socialised with their male counterparts from the reformed madrasas in theatrical performances, musical evenings and mutual aid societies.[102] Despite Riḍaʾaddīn bin Fakhraddīn and ʿAbdullāh Būbī's vision of women's education as a tool for promoting a form of domestic harmony rooted in science and Islamic law, girls' schools became sites for political radicalisation and youth networking in the same way the men's reformed madrasas did.[103] The first generation of reformers had attempted to 'fix' women's education by introducing models and methods from men's intellectual culture. The younger generation of educated women, who came of age within this new system, strained against its boundaries and pushed for further integration of women into male-dominated intellectual life.

Whereas male reformers often used the abused woman as a metaphor for the state of the Muslim community, female writers emphasised the ways in which men exploited the rules and conventions of Muslim society to mistreat or take advantage of women. Ashrāf al-Banāt at-Tājiyya, writing to the Crimean journal *Women's World* (*ʿĀlam-i niswān*), lamented that women were driven to commit adultery by negligent husbands who disappeared from the household months or years at a time, failed to provide for their families or carried on affairs with dancing boys.[104] Maḥbūbjamāl Akchurina, in her novel *The Merciless Father* (*Shafqatsız ata*) (1914), examines the double standard relating to men's and women's sexual transgressions. While a man faced few, if any, social consequences for carrying on an extra-marital affair, a woman's life could be turned upside down by a false accusation of sexual misconduct.[105] Female reformers, like their male counterparts, noted the importance of women's education for the health of the family, but they also stressed the need for women to gain intellectual and emotional independence. They decried the view that had arisen in upper- and middle-class Muslim households of the 1890s and the early 1900s that family honour was bound up with female virtue and that virtuous women should depend entirely upon their fathers and husbands for their economic and emotional well-being.

Girls' schoolteachers turned to the Turkic-language mystical literature of the nineteenth century to seek positive female role models. A collection of books and manuscripts from Bāghubustān khanım's girls' school in Orenburg contained two different versions (one in verse and one in prose) of the tale of the serpent queen Shāhmarān, a character originating in Turkic or Indo-Iranian folklore.[106] In the most basic version of the story, a young man named Jamsab accidently stumbles into the kingdom of the snake people. He is taken in by their beautiful queen, Shāhmarān, and chooses to remain with her for years, and she imparts to him all her knowledge. Eventually, Jamsab returns to his family and uses what he has learned to become a physician. When the sultan of Jamsab's land is struck ill, it is rumoured that the only cure is to eat Shāhmarān. The sultan and his wazir eventually convince Jamsab to take them to Shāhmarān. Knowing she has been betrayed, Shāhmarān instructs Jamsab to boil her and serve her to the sultan and his wazir. The sultan eats her boiled flesh and is saved while the wazir drinks the broth and is poisoned. The sultan appoints Jamsab as his new advisor.[107]

Kefeli has drawn attention to how Muslim women took inspiration or guidance from female characters in Muslim mystical literature.[108] However, Shāhmarān is a very different character from Zulaykhā, Khadīja or Maryam. First, Shāhmarān's status is not defined by her relationship as wife or mother of a male prophet. Second, the Turkic adaptations of the Shāhmarān story are free from the misogynistic passages found in certain popular works that feature female characters, such as Rabghūzī's *Qiṣaṣ al-Anbiyā'*.[109] Third, Shāhmarān is not a sinner in need of redemption (like Zulaykhā) or a virtuous supporter of a male prophet (like Khadīja). Shāhmarān is a bearer and transmitter of knowledge in her own right and a teacher of others, including men. She is defined through her personal knowledge and accomplishments rather than through her relationship to husband and household.

The tension in reform movements between training 'modern' mothers and preparing autonomous women capable of holding their own in male-dominated spheres such as publishing and public discourse also emerged in the field of Islamic legal interpretation. By the early 1900s, women armed with Islamic legal training gained at home or at their fathers' madrasas began to make their voices heard in published discourses on Islamic law. Of these women, Mukhliṣa Būbī, who, in 1917, was appointed as the first female *qāḍī* in the history of Russia, has received the most attention.[110] However, she was not the only woman to engage in debate with male scholars on matters of Islamic law.

Fakhr al-Banāt bint Ṣibghatullāh as-Sulaymāniyya (b. 1852 or 1857) was the daughter of an imam and madrasa director from Ūri village in Kazan province. She received her education at her father's madrasa. Her husband was appointed a *qāḍī* of the Orenburg Muslim Spiritual Assembly and he and as-Sulaymāniyya moved to Ufa, where she worked as a teacher.[111] In 1898, the couple moved to Saba village, where they founded a school for boys.[112] In the early 1900s, as-Sulaymāniyya began to publish translations and original legal treatises primarily through the Karimov–Husaynov Publishing House in Orenburg. As-Sulaymāniyya's writings on women's education very much resembled those of Riḍaʾaddīn bin Fakhraddīn and ᶜAbdullāh Būbī insofar as they focused on the training of efficient, scientific, modern housewives. In 'Family Lessons' (*ᶜĀʾila dareslare*), as-Sulaymāniyya explained how a wife should interact with her relatives and organise her household.[113] Her two-part 'Girls' Education' (*Qızlar tarbiyase*) included a small section on the importance of reading and writing, but offered numerous lessons on housekeeping, including how to select nutritious foods for her family, cook soup, prepare jams and preserves, do laundry, iron and sew.[114] 'A Girl's Teacher' (*Muᶜalīmat al-banāt*), a primer for children just beginning to read, contained paragraph-long stories presenting the fundamentals of Islam and the important relationships in a young girl's life (with her parents, her teachers and her age mates).[115]

In addition to writing these textbooks, as-Sulaymāniyya also took part in debates with male legal scholars through the Muslim press. In her 'Scissors of Fanaticism in Reply to the Mirror of Regret' (*Miqrāḍ al-taᶜaṣṣub fī radd mirʾāt al-taʾassuf*) (1907), she took on legal questions ranging from women's education to proper attire for Muslim men. When addressing issues of Islamic dress and ritual (especially prayers and fasting), she argues that outward trappings of piety are meaningless if they are not supported by sincere faith. She compares an impious Muslim who prays and wears a robe and turban to an empty nutshell, a thing that serves no purpose because it lacks the very object that it is meant to cover.[116] As-Sulaymāniyya does not discourage Muslims from praying and fasting but insists that such actions must be accompanied by moral behaviour, solid knowledge of Islam and genuine belief. She likewise rejects distinctions between Muslim and non-Muslim clothes by arguing that clothing is culturally and historically contingent and that much of the 'Muslim' clothing worn by men in the Volga-Ural region was not truly Muslim (not explicitly mentioned in the Qurʾān and hadiths) in any case.

In the same treatise, as-Sulaymāniyya challenged other jurists' assertion that it is unlawful for women to leave the household to seek education or to take work as teachers, doctors, telegraph operators or shop clerks because it is the first duty of a Muslim woman to live in accordance with the will of her husband.[117] She argued that nowhere in the Qur'ān, hadiths or the legal decisions of the great *mujtahids* were women characterised as being less than human beings. She claimed, moreover, that the age of ignorance had ended, and the age of science and knowledge had begun. In this new age, women were no longer slaves, but individuals with rights, including the right to education.[118]

In another treatise, 'Advice, or a Mirror' (*Irshād, yaki Kuzge*) (1909), as-Sulaymāniyya refutes the folk belief that mead-drinking is *ḥalāl* (permitted under Islamic law). She supports her argument for the forbidden nature of mead through analogy (*qiyās*) based upon injunctions in the Qur'ān and the hadiths against the consumption of wine.[119] She also argues against mead-drinking by noting its effects on family life, highlighting the connection between drunkenness and domestic abuse as well as the social and economic consequences of having a husband or a father who is chronically intoxicated.[120]

As-Sulaymāniyya's treatises on Islamic law differ little in style and approach from those of male reformers. Her calls to consider historical and cultural context when interpreting the Qur'ān and hadiths closely resemble the approach of reformist jurists such as ᶜAbdullāh Būbī and Mūsā Bīgī.[121] Her insistence on the need to return to and re-interpret the primary sources of revelation rather than adhere to the views expressed by later law digests, shaykhs and madrasa directors identifies her as a follower of late nineteenth- and early twentieth-century reformers such as Muḥammad ᶜAbduh. She also references Ottoman cultural reformers such as Ahmad Midḥat Pāshā, defending them against accusations of atheism and elevating them as models of how to serve one's faith and community.[122]

When Education Was Not Enough: The Tale of Two Girls

Reform of women's education transformed the goals and stakes involved in schooling Muslim daughters. The opening of the girls' schools, the growing networks of educated women structured around the Muslim press and local charitable societies, and the mass-printing of the works of female writers and legal experts gave young literate women and, especially, *ᶜulamā'* daughters aspirations to take up careers (journalists, novelists, legal commentators, school directors) that had formerly been open only to men. Also, merchant and *ᶜulamā'* families began to view education as a quality likely to improve their daughters' marriage prospects. These expectations were directly comparable with the beliefs of the sons of peasants, muezzins and poor village imams who entered the madrasa: time devoted to education and self-improvement would eventually be rewarded with economic gain and social prestige.[123] Men and women who became invested in reform imagined *ᶜulamāᵓ* society as a meritocracy. They often found reality to be somewhat different.

Fāṭima-i Farīda bint Murtaḍa Wahabov was born into a wealthy merchant family in Chistopol, Kazan province in 1889. As an only child, she received the full benefit of her parents' wealth and attention. At age four, her father enrolled her in a primary school in Istanbul while he was there on business. By the time she was six, the family had returned to Chistopol, where they hired a private *abıstay* to teach her. At age six, her parents noted that she read well, but wrote poorly, so they sent her to Kazan for three or four months to improve her writing.[124] Upon her return, her father tried to enrol her in Chistopol's girls' gymnasium, but she was denied admission because she could not speak Russian.[125] Undaunted, her father took her to Kamāliyya Madrasa for which he was a sponsor. The madrasa director's adult son agreed to tutor Fāṭima-i Farīda alongside his own daughters. This arrangement continued until Fāṭima-i Farīda was twelve, at which point the director's son left for Mecca to continue his studies. Fāṭima-i Farīda was now taken by her grandmother to Kazan, where she was enrolled in the girls' school organised by ᶜĀlimjān Bārūdī's wife, Māḥrui. Fāṭima-i Farīda studied there for a few years before returning to Chistopol, where she resumed taking lessons from her former teacher at Kamāliyya Madrasa. From ages three to sixteen, she had studied Arabic grammar, Persian language, logic, ethics, the Qurᵓān, history, literature and geography. She took lessons in Russian from a private tutor.[126] In 1906, at age seventeen, she began publishing articles in the Uralsk-based journal *al-ᶜAṣr al-Jadīd*, beside prominent reformist writers such as ᶜAyāḍ al-Isḥāqī and Riḍaᵓaddīn bin Fakhraddīn and emerging youth writers such as ᶜAbdullāh Tuqaev, Najīb Dūmāwī and Fatīḥ Amirkhan.[127]

Munīra bint Saᶜdaddīn, the scion of an *ᶜulamāᵓ* family, also received her education in the late 1800s. Like Fāṭima-i Farīda's father, Munīra's father, a village imam, placed great importance in educating his daughter. Munīra learned Arabic grammar at home under her father's tutelage. At age eighteen, Munīra was given in marriage to a rural imam who appeared to have good prospects.[128] However, after the wedding, relations between the newlyweds quickly deteriorated. The *mahr* promised by Munīra's new husband never materialised. Meanwhile, he enquired as to when his new father-in-law (Munīra's father) would send them money for a carriage and the construction of a new house. Munīra's husband, clearly from an impoverished family, had dedicated twenty-eight years of his life to studying in the madrasa in hopes of obtaining an imam's post and marrying into a wealthy *ʿulamāʾ* family. Munīra's father had invested years in her education to make her a suitable bride for a prosperous legal scholar. These two poor but ambitious young people had tried to barter education for social advancement and instead ended up married to each other.[129] When the couple was finally able to afford a home, it was barely the size of a bathhouse. Munīra claimed that she was perfectly willing to spend her life advising and teaching 'common' women and children, but not to do so in abject poverty.[130] Five years and three children later, the couple divorced, but not without a final dispute over the unpaid *mahr*, the division of their meagre property and the custody of their children.[131]

The stories of Fāṭima-i Farīda and Munīra highlight changing perspectives on Muslim women's education, the limits of education's transformative power and the disconnect between reformist rhetoric and cultural realities. Both young women (and their parents) subscribed to the belief that education could provide a path to socio-economic advancement. However, the wealth and connections possessed by Fāṭima-i Farīda's family gave her access to resources and people that poorer rural girls such as Munīra could only dream of. An Islamic legal education combined with the proper social contacts could launch a young woman into a marriage with a well-to-do husband, a writing career or the directorship of a girls' school. In the absence of such contacts, by contrast, an Islamic legal education offered learning without a clear path to advancement. Munīra's relationship with her husband became intolerable to her not only because of their poverty, but because that poverty gave the lie to an ideal that was embedded in nineteenth-century Volga-Ural Muslim society and particularly emphasised by reformers: namely, that education was valuable and benefited both the individual and the community. As Munīra saw the matter, she, her ex-husband and their children were condemned to live in penury because Russian Muslim society did not, in fact, value educated people.[132]

The contrast between the experiences of Fāṭima-i Farīda and Munīra complicates the heroic narrative of 'Jadid' promotion of women's education. Behind the stories of triumphant 'firsts' (first Volga Muslim woman to attend the Sorbonne, first Russian Muslim actress, first female *qāḍī*) lurk darker tales of social exclusivity, thwarted ambitions and broken relationships. Neither the opening of the girls' schools nor the entry of women into publishing and Islamic law necessarily improved the lives of Volga-Ural Muslim women, because the very structure of Volga-Ural Muslim society limited which women (and how many) could avail themselves of these new occupations. As was the case with imams, madrasa directors and male teachers and journalists, there were only so many *abıstay*s, *ostazbika*s, female writers, girls' schoolteachers and jurists that Volga-Ural merchants, *maḥalla*s, charitable societies and newspaper subscribers could support. Turkic-language guides to cooking, gardening and housekeeping were aimed overwhelmingly at urban women living on middle-class incomes.[133] Rural women equipped with a solid Islamic legal education still had to cope with poverty and limited access to the goods and services available in the provincial towns by the late nineteenth century. These problems posed much more immediate and pervasive obstacles to improving the lives of rural Muslim women (and men) than did the lustful shaykhs and devious old women who appeared as villains in modernist novels and propaganda.

Conclusion

Throughout the nineteenth century, both men and women in Volga-Ural Muslim society enjoyed the benefits of expanding mass-printing and growing merchant-industrial wealth. Educational opportunities expanded for both genders. However, educational culture and institutions developed in two different directions, with the madrasa becoming the heart of male education and intellectual culture while female knowledge transmission developed in a more diffuse manner, transpiring in the homes of imams' wives, communal gatherings and life-event rituals. Whereas educated men were socialised into far-flung Sufi networks, women's networks remained more closely confined to their immediate communities. While promising sons from non-*ᶜulamāᵓ* families could aspire to careers in the *ᶜulamāᵓ*, the education and future status of girls was usually contingent upon their father's status. Intelligent daughters of *ᶜulamāᵓ* families mastered the same foreign languages and religious-legal scholarship as their fathers and brothers. In some cases, girls may have excelled in relation to their brothers in these fields. However, women did not usually take part in the male-dominated occupations of leading prayer, composing legal decisions, teaching Islamic law and producing texts for mass consumption.

When Muslim cultural reform took root in the Volga-Ural region in the 1880s and 1890s, it initiated a re-organisation of women's knowledge transmission and education culture. Institutionalisation and systematisation of education had been underway in madrasa education since the late 1850s and became the new standard against which women's education was measured and found wanting. At the same time, reformers forged a multi-layered narrative of colonialism and backwardness in which Muslim women were cast as surrogates for the nation and/or the Islamic community and imbued with all its perceived flaws: ignorance, underdevelopment, helplessness. Reformist narratives at once denigrated the intellectual activities of nineteenth-century women, promoted a vision of female subordination and domesticity and insisted that women's educational and intellectual life be made to more closely resemble that of men.

Male reformers' views on women were riddled with tensions. These reformers imagined that Muslim girls' schools would train a new generation of 'modern' wives and mothers. However, permanent schools and mass printing enabled female teachers and their students to develop transnational networks in the same way that male scholars did and to pursue careers as legal specialists, school directors and authors – activities that were not necessarily compatible with the reformist vision of the submissive housewife. If male reformers imagined women's Islamic education as means of creating domestic bliss, female teachers and students saw it as a source of personal empowerment and means of curtailing the everyday misbehaviour of men. Also, in positing education as a cure-all for social ills and a path to a brighter future, male reformers overlooked the economic and social conditions that made their existence possible. Even with rapid growth in the fields of education and publishing, Volga-Ural Muslim society could only support so many *ᶜulamāʾ*, teachers and writers. As women's education was re-shaped to resemble men's education, educated Muslim girls fell victim to the same ambitions and economic pressures as their male counterparts. Reformist schools and publications promised Muslim girls that, through education, they would not only become better wives and Muslims, but would gain a foothold in the emerging middle class. In reality, reformers' commitment to women's improvement often faltered once girls ceased to be students. More than one woman discovered that it was possible to be well versed in Islamic law as well as economically marginalised and painfully aware of the 'modern' domestic life that lay beyond her reach.

Notes

1. Muḥammad ᶜAyaḍ al-Isḥāqī, *Kalapushche qız* (Kazan: Tipografiia B. L. Dombrovskago, 1902).
2. A.-A. Rorlich, *The Volga Tatars: A Profile in National Resilience* (Stanford: Hoover Institution Press, 1986); M. Tuna, *Imperial Russia's Muslims: Islam, Empire and European Modernity, 1788–1914* (Cambridge: Cambridge University Press, 2015); T. A. Biktimerova, *Stupeni obrazovaniia do Sorbonny* (Kazan: Tatarskoe knizhnoe izdatel'stvo, 2011); A. Makhmutova, *Pora i nam zazhech' zariu svobody!: Dzhadidizm i zhenskoe dvizhenie* (Kazan: Tatarskoe knizhnoe izdatel'stvo, 2006); A. Makhmutova,

Vaqıt inde: bez dä torīq (Jädidchelek häm khatın-qızlar khäräkäte formalashu) (Kazan: Tatarstan kitap näshriyatı, 2012).

3. M. Warner, *Monuments and Maidens: The Allegory of the Female Form* (Berkeley and Los Angeles: University of California Press, 1985); A. Parker, M. Russo, D. Sommer and P. Yaeger (eds), *Nationalisms and Sexualities* (New York and London: Routledge, 1992); S. Ranchod-Nilsson and M. A. Tétreault, 'Gender and Nationalism: Moving Beyond Fragmented Conversations', in S. Ranchod-Nilsson and M. A. Tétreault (eds), *Women, States, and Nationalism: At Home in the Nation?* (London and New York: Routledge, 2000), pp. 4–6; B. Baron, *Egypt as a Woman: Nationalism, Gender, and Politics* (Berkeley and Los Angeles: University of California Press, 2007); N. De Mel, *Women and the Nation's Narrative: Gender and Nationalism in Twentieth-Century Sri Lanka* (Lanham, Boulder and New York: Rowman and Littlefield, 2001).
4. P. Chatterjee, *The Nation and Its Fragments: Colonial and Precolonial Histories* (Princeton: Princeton: Princeton University Press, 1993).
5. G. Chakravorty Spivak, 'Can the Subaltern Speak?', in P. Williams and L. Chrisman (eds), *Colonial Discourses and Post-Colonial Theory: A Reader* (Hertfordshire: Harvester Wheatsheaf, 1994); L. Mani, *Contentious Traditions: The Debate on Sati in Colonial India* (London: University of California Press, 1998). Another response to these European interventions was the complete rejection of Western values and reform projects in favour of culturally 'authentic', native forms, values and customs, see D. Kandiyoti, 'Introduction', in D. Kandiyoti (ed.), *Women, the State, and Islam* (Philadelphia: Temple University Press, 1991), pp. 1–21.
6. H. Yilmaz, *Becoming Turkish: Nationalist Reforms and Cultural Negotiations in Early Republican Turkey, 1923–1945* (Syracuse: Syracuse University Press, 2013); D. Northrop, *Veiled Empire: Gender and Power in Stalinist Central Asia* (Ithaca: Cornell University Press, 2004); M. Kamp, *The New Woman in Uzbekistan: Islam, Modernity, and Unveiling under Communism* (Seattle: University of Washington Press, 2006).
7. A. Khalid, *Muslim Cultural Reform: Jadidism in Central Asia* (Berkeley and Los Angeles and London, 1998), p. 226; M. Kamp, *The New Woman in Uzbekistan*, p. 40. Two of the main authors they cite, Riḍāʾaddīn bin Fakhraddīn and Fakhr al-Banāt al-Sulaymāniyya, were, in fact, from the Volga-Ural region.
8. A. Kefeli, 'The Tale of Joseph and Zulaykha on the Volga Frontier: The Struggle for Gender, Religious, and National Identity in Imperial and Postrevolutionary Russia', *Slavic Review* 70:2 (2011), p. 381.
9. T. A. Biktimerova, *Stupeni obrazovaniia do Sorbonny*; A. Makhmutova, *Pora i nam zazhech' zariu svobody!*; A. Makhmutova, *Vakyt inde: bez da toryik.*
10. R. Garipova, 'Muslim Female Religious Authority in Russia: How Mukhlisa Bubi Became the First Female *Qāḍī* in the Modern Muslim World',

Die Welt des Islams 57 (2017), pp. 135–61; R. R. Garipova, 'Muslim Women's Religious Authority and their Role in the Transmission of Islamic Knowledge in Late Imperial Russia', *Tatarica* 5 (2015), pp. 152–63.

11. M. Kamp, 'Debating Sharia: The 1917 Muslim Women's Congress of Russia', *Journal of Women's History* 27:4 (2015), pp. 13–37.
12. A. Kefeli, 'The Role of Tatar and Kriashen Women in the Transmission of Islamic Knowledge', in R. P. Geraci and M. Khodarkovsky (eds), *Of Religion and Empire: Missions, Conversion, and Tolerance in Tsarist Russia* (Ithaca and London: Cornell University Press, 2001), pp. 250–73; T. A. Biktimerova, *Stupeni obrazovaniia do Sorbonny*, pp. 10–13; A. Makhmutova, *Vaqıt inde: bez dä tordiq*, pp. 19-22; R. R. Garipova, 'Muslim Women's Religious Authority', p. 156.
13. See, for example, Riḍāʾaddin bin Fakhreddin, *Āthār*, 2 vols (Orenburg: 'Karīmov, Ḥusaynov wa Sharkāsı" maṭbuᶜası, 1901–8); Muḥammad Murad Rāmzī, *Talfiq al-akhbār wa talqiḥ al-Athār fī waqāʾiᶜ Qazān wa Bulgār wa mulūk al-Tatār* (Orenburg: al-Maṭbuᶜa al-Karimiyya wa Ḥusayniyya, n.d.); Qurbānᶜali Khālidī, *An Islamic Biographical Dictionary of the Eastern Kazakh Steppe, 1770–1912*, trans. and ed. A. J. Frank and M. A. Usmanov (Leiden and Boston: Brill, 2005).
14. Women did occasionally receive mention and brief description in biographical treatments of their husbands or fathers. Riḍāʾaddīn bin Fakhraddīn's *Famous Women* (*Mäshhür khatınnar*), published in 1904 and augmented subsequently, but not republished, is currently the only known prosopography of Volga-Ural Muslim women. See R. R. Garipova, 'Muslim Women's Religious Authority', pp. 155, 157–9. Shihābaddīn al-Marjānī included biographies of some of his female relatives in his biographical dictionary, *Wafayāt al-Aslāf* (K(P)FU-ORRK No. 615 AR (6 vols), pp. 269ob, 271, 274, 282. These sources offer views of women's lives and intellectual culture filtered through male informants.
15. On the rapid growth in the number of mosques and licensed Muslim religious personnel during the nineteenth century and early twentieth, see I. Zagidullin, *Islamskie instituty v Rossiiskoi imperii: Mecheti v evropeiskoi chasti Rossii i Sibiri* (Kazan: Tatarskoe Knizhnoe Izdatel'stvo, 2007), p. 143.
16. S. Sharaf, *Marjānī* (Kazan: 'Maᶜārif' maṭbuᶜası 1915), pp. 28–86; Y. Akchūrā-ughlı, *Dāmellā ᶜĀlimjān al-Bārūdī: Tarjama-i ḥāle* (Kazan: Sharaf maṭbuᶜası, 1907), pp. 24–64.
17. [No author or title page], pp. 77–8. This manuscript is held at the Central Mosque in Semei, Kazakhstan.
18. Ibid., pp. 78–9.
19. Gabderäkhim Utız-Imänī al-Bolgarī, 'Näzmı Gabderäkhim Bolgarī fī ḥaqqı Qāḍīzadä', in Ä. Sharipov (ed.), *Gabderäkhim Utız-Imänī al-Bolgarī: Shigır'lär, poemalar* (Kazan: Tatarstan kitap näshriyatı, 1986), p. 37.
20. Gabdrakhim Utyz-Imani al-Bulgari, 'Jawāhir al-Bayān', in D. Shagaveev

(ed.), *Antologiia tatarskoi bogoslovskoi mysli: Gabdrakhim Utyz-Imani al-Bulgari* (Kazan: Tatarskoe knizhnoe izdatel'stvo, 2007), n.p.. English translation from the Arabic facsimile.

21. '*Risāla-i Ḥabībullāh Ishān al-Ūriwī*', Institut Iazyka, Literatury i Iskusstva im. G. Ibrahimova, AN RT, (hereafter IIaLI) fond 39, opis 1, delo 3442, p. 36.
22. M. Gafuri, 'Tärjemä-i ḥalem', in F. Ibrahimova (ed.), *Mäjit Gafuri: Äsärlär dürt tomda* (4 vols), (Kazan: Tatarstan kitap näshriyatı, 1981), vol. 4, p. 433.
23. Garipova, 'Muslim Women's Religious Authority', pp. 155–7.
24. I. Rämi and R. Dautov, 'Vaisilar khäräkäte', *Ädäbi Süzlek (Elekke tatar ädäbiyatı häm mädäniyatı buencha qısqa beleshmälek)* (Kazan: Tatarstan kitap näshriyatı, 2001), p. 66.
25. M. Kemper and D. Usmanova, 'Vaisovskoe Dvizhenie v zerkale sobstvennykh proshenii i poem', *Ekho vekhov* 3–4 (2001), pp. 93–4.
26. M. Gafuri, 'Tärjemäi ḥalem', *Mäjit Gafuri*, vol. 4, pp. 356–7.
27. A. Kefeli, *Becoming Muslim in Imperial Russia*, pp. 60–116.
28. 'Shäkert däftärläre', in R. Mähdiev (ed.), *Mädräsälärdä kitap kichtäse: Mäshhür mäg'rifät üzäkläre tarikhınnan* (Kazan: Tatarstan kitap näshriyatı, 1992), pp. 224–32.
29. A. Kefeli, 'The Role of Kriashen Women in the Transmission of Islamic Knowledge', p. 255.
30. ᶜAlī bin Sayfullāh at-Tūntārī was the most prominent Naqshbandi-Mujaddidi shaykh of the Volga-Ural region in the mid-1800s. His disciples numbered in the thousands. He appears as an influential figure in the council of *ᶜulamāᵓ* responsible for vetting Shihābaddīn al-Marjānī before nominating him to a post of imam-*mudarris* in Kazan. Kefeli identifies him and his disciples as partly responsible for circulating Islamic literature and ideas among baptised non-Russian populations. For the biography of ᶜAlī at-Tūntārī, see R. Fäkhreddin, 'Gali Ishan', in L. Göbäidullin and R. Mingnullin (eds), *Mäshhür adamnar: 'Shura" zhurnalı sähifälärennän* (Kazan: Rukhiyat, 2012), pp. 36–47; R. Fäkhreddin, *Asar: Öchenche häm dürtenche tom*, eds L. Baibulatova et. al (Kazan: Rukhiyat, 2010), pp. 16–42; R. Sh. Zaripov, *Gali Ishan häm Tüntär mädräsăse* (Kazan: 'Iman" näshriyatı, 2002).
31. 'Rukopisnyi sbornik, perepischik: Shahiäkhmät bine Batyrshah, 1866', IIaLI-RT, f. 39, del. 3772, p. 76ob.
32. Ibid., pp. 6ob–7ob.
33. Ibid., pp. 8ob–11ob.
34. Ibid., pp. 11ob–12ob.
35. Ibid., pp. 12ob; 'Uways al-Ḳaranī" and 'Uwaysiyya', *The Encyclopaedia of Islam: New Edition* (12 vols), eds P. J. Bearman et al. (Leiden: Brill, 2000), vol. 10, p. 958.
36. Laylat al-Qadr*:* the night on which the first verses of the Qurᵓān were revealed to Muhammad. It is supposed to be one of the last days of the month of Ramadan.

37. IIaLI-RT, f. 39, del. 3772, p. 13.
38. Ibid.
39. 'Bībī ᶜĀᵓisha bint Batırshāh, [No Title], 2ob. (Manuscript purchased at antique store 'Ligiia' in Kazan. It is currently in the possession of the author.)
40. Ibid., p. 2.
41. Ibid., p. 2ob.
42. Ibid., pp. 2ob–3.
43. Ibid., p. 3.
44. Ibid., p. 4ob.
45. Ibid., p. 28.
46. Ibid.
47. Ibid.
48. Ibid. pp. 45ob–46.
49. Ibid., p. 62.
50. Ibid. p. 61ob.
51. On the Persianate sphere in early modern Inner Asia, see J. R. Pickett, 'The Persianate Sphere during the Age of Empires: Islamic Scholars and Networks of Exchange in Central Asia, 1747–1917' (PhD dissertation, Princeton University, 2015).
52. A. Kefeli, *Becoming Muslim in Imperial Russia*; R. R. Garipova, 'Muslim Women's Religious Authority', p. 156.
53. R. Fäkhreddin, 'Gali Ishan', p. 42.
54. IIaLI-RT, f. 39, del. 3772, pp. 6ob–7ob, 8ob–11ob, 15–15ob.
55. R. Fäkhreddin, 'Gali Ishan', p. 44.
56. ᶜA. Bayazitov, *Islām Kitabı* (Kazan: n.p., 1880), p. 7.
57. R. Fäkhreddin, *Asar, Tom III–IV*, ed. M. Gosmanov (Kazan: Rukhiiat näshriyatı, 2010), p. 19; M. Bigiev, *Adabiyat ᶜarabiyya* (Kazan: Lito-Tipografiia I. N. Kharitonova, 1909), pp. 2–4.
58. G. Tukai, 'Murīdlar kaberstānında ber awaz', *al-ᶜAsr al-Jadīd* 4 (1906); A. Sh., *Murīd* (Kazan: Tipo-litografiia I. B Ermolaevoi, 1907); [no author], *Murīd Ḥāle* (Kazan: n.p., 1910).
59. Kh. Fäezkhanov, 'Risāla', *Shäkheslärebez: Khösäen Fäezkhanov*, p. 81; F. K. *Ber shakird ilä ber student* (Kazan: Tipografiia B. L. Dombrovskago, 1899), p. 36.
60. On the reform of men's education in the Volga-Ural region, see the previous chapter.
61. M. Aqeget, 'Khisamattin Menla', in A. G. Yakhin (ed.), *Qaraurmannı chıqqan chaqta . . .: XIX gasır ädäbiyatı* (Kazan: Mägarif, 2001), pp. 34–9.
62. Z. Bigiev, 'Ölüf, yaki Güzäl qız Khadicha', *Zahir Bigiev: Zur Gönahlar*, ed. R. Dautov (Kazan: Tatarstan kitap näshriyatı, 1991), pp. 221–53.
63. Z. Bigiev, 'Gönahe Kabair', ibid., pp. 254–88.
64. F. Amirkhan, 'Fätkhulla Khäzrät', in N. Sadikova (ed.), *Fatikh Amirkhan: Äsärlär* (4 vols) (Kazan: Tatarstan kitap näshriyatı, 1985), vol. 2, p. 30.

65. I. Rämi and R. Dautov, *Ädäbi süzlek*, p. 273.
66. Muḥammad ᶜAyaḍ al-Isḥāqī, *Kalapushche qız*; M. Gafuri, 'Achlıq yıl, yaki satlıq qız', *Mäjit Gafuri: Äsärlär*, vol. 3, pp. 18–35; Z. Hadi, 'Bäkhätsez qız', *Zakir Hadi: Saylanma Äsärlär*, ed. M. Kh. Gainullin (Kazan: Tatknigoizdat,1957), pp. 22–63; F. Amirkhan, *Ḥayāt: millī ḥikäyät* (Kazan: Lito-tipografiia I. N. Kharitonova, 1911).
67. F. Amirkhan, *Ḥayāt*; Z. Hadi, 'Jihanshah Khäzrät', *Zakir Hadi*: Sailanma äsärläre (Kazan: Tatknigoizdat, 1957)., pp. 140–86.
68. Qāṣimbek Amīn, *Taḥrīr al-Marᵓa*, trans. Zākir al-Qadīrī (Kazan: Elektro-tipografiia 'Urnek", 1909); *Khanımnara hidāya: Berenche kitap: Muslimalarneng Islamiyyattage ḥāllare* (Kazan: Tipo-litografiia Imeratorskago Universiteta, 1909).
69. 'Galimatelbanat Biktimeriia, 1876–1906', *Ömet yoldızları: XIX yöz akhırı häm XX yöz bashı tatar khatın-qız yazuchıları äsärläre*, ed. M. Gainullin (Kazan: Tatarstan kitap näshriyatı, 1988), pp. 40–2.
70. ᶜAlīma al-Banāt al-Biktimeriyya al-Yaubashiyya al-Khankirmaniyya bint al-Akhūnd Latifullāh al-Sulaymanī, *Muᶜāsharat adabı* (St Petersburg: Tipo-Lit. i Boraganskago i Ko., 1898), pp. 3, 9.
71. 'Khabira Nasiriya, 1882–1912', *Ömet yoldızları*, pp. 52–3.
72. 'Mahrui Mozaffariya, 1873–1945', *Ömet yoldızları*, pp. 65–6; A. Kh. Mäkhmütova, 'Mahrui Mozaffariya', *Vaqıt Inde: Bez dä torīq* . . ., pp. 343–61; A. Kh. Mäkhmütova, 'Mahrui Mozaffariya', *Millät Anaları*, pp. 163–93.
73. 'Mäkhbübjämäl Akchurina, 1869–1948', *Ömet yoldızları*, 70–1; A. Kh. Mäkhmütova, 'Mäkhbübjämäl Akchurina', *Millät Anaları*, pp. 97–101.
74. 'Farkhana Alusheva, 1886–1958', *Ömet yoldızları*, pp. 132–3.
75. R. Fäkhreddin, 'Zohra Khanım', in M. Usmanov (ed.), *Shäkheslärebez: Ismägyil' Gasprinskii: Tarikhī-dokumental' jıentıq* (Kazan: Jıen näshriyatı, 2006), pp. 222–4.
76. Shamsaddīn Samībek, *Khātınnar waẓāᵓifı*, trans. Muḥammadfatīḥ al-Karīmī (Orenburg: Tipo-litografiia B. Breslina, 1899).
77. ᶜAbdullāh al-Makhdūmī, *Taᶜaddud zawājati hifẓ ṣiḥḥatihi taṭbīq* (Orenburg: Tipografiia Gil'man Ibrahimovicha Karimova, 1901); ᶜAbdullāh al-Makhdūmī, *Tazawwujda saᶜādat* (Orenburg: Ghilmān Ibrāhīm-ughlı Karīmov maṭbuᶜası, 1902).
78. Rizaᵓaddīn bin Fakhraddīn, *ᶜĀᵓila* (Orenburg: Tipografiia Gaz. 'Vakt', 1902).
79. Rizaᵓaddīn bin Fakhraddīn, *Ahl-ᶜāᵓil: Qız balalar wa khātınnar uchūn kira kulan adablarne bayān ilmesh bi-risāla* (Orenburg: Tip. Gaz. 'Vakt", 1910).
80. Rizaᵓaddīn bin Fakhraddīn, *Tarbiyale ata* (Kazan: n.p., 1898); Rizaᵓaddīn bin Fakhraddīn, *Tarbiyale ana* (Kazan: n.p., 1898); Riḍaᵓaddīn bin Fakhraddīn, i*Tarbiyale bala* (Kazan: n.p., 1898); Rizaᵓaddīn bin Fakhraddīn, *Tarbiyale khatın* (Kazan: n.p., 1899).
81. Ḥasanjān bin Aḥmadjān al-Ḥusaynī, *Bayān al-ḥaqq fī ḥaqq al-ḥijāb*

(Kazan: Tipo-litografiia Togovago Doma 'Brat'ia Karimovy", 1906); G. D., *Adabsezlar arasında ḥijabsez qız* (Kazan: Tipo-litografiia 'Umid", 1915).

82. A. Kh. Mäkhmütova, *Vaqıt inde*, p. 22.
83. Ibid., p. 122.
84. Ibid., p. 24.
85. A. Makhmutova, 'Mukhlisa Bubi, (1869–1937)', *Tatarskie Intellektualy: Istoricheskie portrety* (Kazan: Izdatel'stov Magarif, 2005), p. 157.
86. Ibid., p. 158.
87. *Un yıllıq ᶜilmī khidma* (Orenburg: Tip. Gub. Kom. po Mus. Delam, 1918).
88. *Ufada Musulmān khanımnar jamᶜiyatınıng khisābnāmase – otchet 1909 nche yıl üchün* (Ufa: Tipografiia 'Vostochnaia Pechat', 1910).
89. On these and similar changes implemented in men's educational institutions in the Volga-Ural region, see chapter three of this volume.
90. Gabdulla Bubi, 'Bubi mädräsäseneng qısqa tarikhı', p. 42.
91. *Un yıllıq ᶜilmī khidma,* p. 10.
92. Ibid.
93. *Ufada Musulmān khanımnar jamᶜiyatınıng khisābnāmase,* pp. 36, 38.
94. Ibid., pp. 36–7.
95. Gabdulla Bubi, 'Bubi mädräsäseneng qısqa tarikhı', 41.
96. Ä. Khäsäni, 'Denshchik Gali', in D. F. Zahidullina, A. D. Battalova and L. N. Iozmokhammatova (eds), *Shäkheslärebez: Äkhmätgäräi Khäsäni: Fänni-biografik jıentıq* (Kazan: 'Jıen" năshriyatı, 2011), pp. 33–49.
97. Ibid., p. 41; *Un yıllıq ᶜilmī khidma,* p. 10.
98. B. M. Pietsch, *Dispensational Modernism* (Oxford: Oxford University Press, 2015), pp. 26–9; R. Horowitz, *Putting Meat on the American Table: Taste, Technology, Transformation* (Baltimore: The Johns Hopkins University Press, 2005), p. 10.
99. ['Bez bārābız da tātār qızı . . .'], [untitled girls' school notebook, Orenburg, 1912–13], p. 1. The original manuscript is held at Sulaymaniyya Mosque in Arenda District, Orenburg, Russia.
100. ['Ilahi imtiḥān kutarne shādlıq berlān utkar . . .'], [untitled girls' school notebook, Orenburg, 1912–13], p. 3ob.
101. 'Khān masjidneng shighre', [untitled girls' school notebook, Orenburg, 1912–13], pp. 4–4ob.
102. ᶜAbd al-Majīd al-Ghafūrī, 'Ber Tātār shakirdınıng Qazānda mashhūr khān masjideneng manarasını kurganda inshād itedege shigridir', *Millāt maḥabbate nām ashᶜarı*, pp. 34–5.
103. D. Ross, 'Caught in the Middle: Reform and Youth Rebellion in Russia's Madrasas, 1900–1910', *Kritika: Exploration in Russian and Eurasian History* 16:1 (Winter 2015), pp. 75–7.
104. Khoqandlı Ashrāf al-Banāt at-Tājiyya, 'Idāraya maktūblar', *ᶜĀlam-i Niswān* 36 (1906), p. 574.
105. Makhbūbjamāl Āqchūrīnā, *Shafqatsez ātā, yākī mīshārlār tūrmıshı*

(Orenburg: Tipo-litografiia tovarishchestva 'Karimov, Khusainov i Ko.', 1914).

106. [No author], *Qiṣṣa-i Shāhmarān* (n.p.: n.d.), pp. 35–40; [No author], *Shāhmarān* (n.p.: n.d.), p. 21.
107. A version of this story can be found in 'The Queen of the Serpents', in *The Book of the Thousand Nights and One,* trans. John Payne (London: Herat, 1901), pp. 49–148. In the Arabic version, the youth is named Hasib rather than Jamsab. Beyond this, it is not possible to assess whether the Turkic versions are simply a translation of the Arabic original or a significant digression from it because the Turkic texts currently in the author's possession contain only Shahmaran's narration of the adventures of Balokiya and fragments of the story of Jānshāh.
108. A. N. Kefeli, *Becoming Muslim in Imperial Russia*, pp. 88–97.
109. A. Kefeli, 'The Tale of Joseph and Zulaykha on the Volga Frontier', pp. 384–5.
110. A. Makhmutova, 'Mukhlisa Bubi', *Tatarskie Intellektualy,* pp. 156–71; A. Makhmutova, *Vaqıt Inde: bez de torīq . . .*, pp. 122–45, 322–41; *Millät Analarɪ*, pp. 208–94; R. Garipova, 'Muslim Female Religious Authority in Russia', pp. 135–61.
111. I. Rämi and R. Dautov, 'Fäkhrelbänat Khanım Söläymaniya', *Ädäbi Süzlek,* p. 272.
112. Ibid., p. 273.
113. Fakhr al-Banāt Sulaymāniyya, *ᶜĀᵓila dareslare: Qızlar maktabe uchūn* (Kazan: Lito-tipografiia T. D. 'Br. Karimovy', 1913).
114. Fakhr al-Banāt Sulaymāniyya, *Qızlar tarbiyase: Berenche juzᵓ* (Orenburg-Ufa, 'Karīmov, Ḥusaynov wa sharkāsı" nıng paravoi maṭbuᶜası, n.d.); Fakhr al-Banāt Sulaymāniyya, *Qızlar tarbiyase: Ikenche juzᵓ* (Orenburg-Ufa: 'Karīmov, Ḥusaynov wa sharkāsı" nıng paravoi maṭbuᶜası, n.d.).
115. Fakhr al-Banāt Sulaymāniyya, *Muᶜalīmat al-banāt: Berenche juzᵓ* (Ufa: Elektro-pechatnaia 'Vostochnaia pechat'", n.d.).
116. Fakhr al-Banāt bint Ṣibghatullāh as-Sulaymāniyya, *Miqrāḍ al-taᶜaṣṣub fī radd mirᵓāt al-taᵓassuf* (Orenburg: Kärimov wa Sharkāsı maṭbuᶜası, 1907), p. 6.
117. [Anonymous], *Mirᵓāt al-taᵓassuf* (Kazan: Kharitonov maṭbuᶜası, n.d., p. 9.
118. Fakhr al-Banāt bint Ṣibghatullāh as-Sulaymāniyya, *Miqrāḍ al- taᶜaṣṣub fī radd mirᵓāt al-taᵓassuf*, pp. 8–9.
119. Fakhr al-Banāt bint Ṣibghatullāh as-Sulaymāniyya, *Irshād, yaki Közge* (Orenburg: Parovaia tipo-litografiia tovarishchestva 'Karimov, Khusainov i Ko.', 1909), pp. 3–6.
120. Ibid., pp. 8–9.
121. ᶜAbdullāh Būbī, *Ḥaqīqat, yaḥūd tūgriliq: berenche juzı* (Kazan: Lito-Tipgrafiia I. N. Kharitonova, 1904), p. 12.
122. Fakhr al-Banāt bint *Ṣibghatullāh* as-Sulaymāniyya, *Miqrāḍ al-taᶜaṣṣub fī radd mirᵓāt al-taᵓassuf*, p. 5.

123. D. Ross, 'Caught in the Middle', pp. 77–9.
124. 'Fatimai-Färidä khanımnıng üz kulı belän yazılghan köndälek däftäre', *Millät Analarι*, pp. 486–8.
125. A. Kh. Mäkhmütova, 'Fatimai-Färidä', *Millät Analarι*, pp. 441–2.
126. 'Fatimai-Färidä khanımnıng üz kulı belän yazılghan köndälek däftäre', *Millät Analarι*, pp. 488–92.
127. Fāṭima-i Farīda, 'Bezeng khatın wa qızlar', *al-ᶜAṣr al-Jadīd* 1 (1906), pp. 11–12.
128. Mönirä bint Sägdeddin, 'Tatarlarnıng khatın aerui', *Ömet yoldızları*, p. 198.
129. Ibid., p. 198.
130. Ibid., pp. 198–9.
131. Ibid., p. 200.
132. Ibid.
133. The authors of one early twentieth-century cookbook admitted in their introduction that their book, *Master of Food and Drink: A Guide to Preparing the Various Foods and Drinks That Should Be in Every Household*, was targeted to the middle-class (*ūrtā ḥālda tūruchι*) housewife. The book's recipes, which included eight different kinds of ice cream, four kinds of wafer and twenty pages of meat dishes, demanded specialised culinary equipment and a budget beyond the means of most rural housewives. See *Ash-sū ustādhι: har ᶜāʾilada bulunduruwι tiyesh būlub turle ash sūlar khazerlar uchūn yūlbāshchι* (Kazan: n.p., n.d.), p. i.

4

Between Imperial Law and Islamic Law: Muslim Subjects and the Legality of Remarriage in Nineteenth-century Russia*

Rozaliya Garipova

Introduction

Although the Russian state left the arbitration of family matters, such as marriage and divorce, to the jurisdiction of the religious law of every community in the empire, the nineteenth-century laws and regulations aimed at better integration and control of the population turned the previously intra-communal issues of marriage and divorce into imperial issues. These legal changes created new challenges for the Muslim women and the Muslim community of the Volga-Ural region. The issue of divorce and remarriage in the case of a husband's exile proved to be especially problematic. The prevalent school of Islamic law in the region – the Ḥanafī school of law – did not grant divorce to women whose husbands went missing or absent (*mafqūd*), but legal experts in the Volga-Ural region had found interpretations to circumvent this legal obstacle before marriage and divorce became imperial issues. I argue that the new laws on exiles and their wives were a part of state policy to further integrate Muslim subjects into the empire, but they created social problems that had larger socio-religious and ethical implications for the Muslim community. Looking at petitions of Muslim women to the Orenburg Muslim Spiritual Assembly (hereafter, the OMSA)[1] I explain the consequences of these legal changes and explore how Muslim religious scholars and the OMSA tried to cope with them.

On 5 December 1852, a resident of the village of Novoe Arslanovo of Troitskii uezd, Khalilzada Kalkamanova,[2] wrote to the Tsar asking to dissolve her marriage and to allow her to marry a person of her choice. She wrote that the Military Court Commission of the Orenburg Military Battalion (Komissiia voennogo suda pri orenburgskom voennom batal'one) tried her husband, Muhamedsharif Bazekeev, for several crimes and sentenced him to exile in Siberia for settlement (*na poselenie*). Since she did not have any material support from her husband she was staying with a relative and intended to marry another man. However, the *maḥalla* imam of Novoe Arslanovo, Gatikam Araslanov, had to get permission from the OMSA to perform the second marriage and therefore 'did not dare' to do it. The OMSA contacted the Military Court Commission and received a letter of confirmation that Muhamedsharif Bazekeev was sued for robbery and other crimes, and that on 19 August 1850 he was sentenced to 300 lashes and was exiled to Siberia for settlement. Therefore, on 20 December 1852, the OMSA allowed Kalkamanova 'to enter a second marriage with a person of her choice' on the basis of art. 36 of vol. 10 of Digest of Laws (svodzakanov Rossiiskoi imperii), published in 1842. The OMSA also instructed imam Araslanov 'to perform Kalkamanova's marriage and register it in the parish register (*metricheskaia kniga*) on a legal basis (*na zakonnom osnovanii*)'.[3]

In another case that the OMSA received and resolved in the 1850s, a former convict who had his sentence altered to military service, asked for the return of his wife Ḥusnijamāl, who married another person. The plaintiff, Raḥmatullāh Muḥammad Sharīf-ūghlī, married his wife in 1833 but was convicted for stealing a horse exiled to Siberia in 1835. In the meantime, Ḥusnijamāl gave birth to a daughter and, lacking any material support (*nafaqa*), she was forced to return to her paternal home. Later, Ḥusnijamāl's father asked a prominent *ākhūnd* of the region Fatḥullāh Ḥusayn-ūghlī bin ᶜAbdelkarīm al-Ūriwī[4] to authorise a divorce for Ḥusnijamāl. On 18 May 1840, the *ākhūnd* gave a *fatwā* to Ḥusnijamāl granting her divorce on the basis of her husband's inability to provide financial maintenance and her extreme hardship. On 7 August 1840 Ḥusnijamāl married for the second time, on this occasion to a Tatar peasant Ḥabībullāh Ḥamīd-ūghlī. Imam Najmaddīn Muḥammad Sharīf-ūghlī officiated their marriage and recorded it in a parish register. In the meanwhile, in 1838, Raḥmatullāh, the first husband of Ḥusnijamāl, had his sentence changed from exile to military service.[5] In 1849 he came back to his village on leave from the army (*v otpusk*). Learning that his wife had married another man, he sought the help of the commander of his unit to take his wife back. On behalf of his soldier Raḥmatullāh, the commander sent a request to the land court (*zemskii*) of Tsarevokokshaisk to resolve this issue. On 13 February 1850, the court decided to send the case to the OMSA for resolution because it did not fall under the jurisdiction of the secular authorities (*ne podlezhaschee resheniiu svetskogo pravitel'stva*). After investigating the case, the OMSA ruled on 28 June 1850 that Ḥusnijamāl's divorce from her first husband was not valid and, therefore, her marriage with Ḥabībullāh was illegal. The OMSA ordered the annulment of the marriage, the registration of this decision in the parish register and the separation of the couple. Imam Muḥammad Sharīf-ūghlī was sentenced to short-term imprisonment for performing an illegal marriage. A little later, the Kazan land court informed the OMSA that Ḥusnijamāl's separation from her second husband had been enforced and she went to her relatives' house in the village of Urazlino.[6]

These are two examples of numerous petitions by women or their guardians to the OMSA from the early 1850s. As these cases reveal, in certain situations, the involvement of imperial authorities including the OMSA became a necessity to resolve the problem of divorce and remarriage of Muslim women. In the first case, *mullās* needed permission from the OMSA to perform divorce and remarriage. The woman had to obtain a document from the court confirming her husband's sentence to exile in order to ask permission for remarriage. Divorce could be performed only on the basis of this document. In the second case, although a local *ākhūnd* performed divorce and officiated the second marriage, the OMSA ruled out that the *ākhūnd* was not supposed to perform these rites without its permission and annulled them. Why did women have to ask the permission of the OMSA to divorce and remarry when performance of marriage and divorce was under the jurisdiction of *maḥalla* imams and *ākhūnd*s? Why were some women able to remarry while others were not? Answers to these questions lie in the changing nature of the relations between Russian imperial and Islamic law in the nineteenth century.

The legality of Muslim marriage and divorce was a complex issue in nineteenth-century Russia. Starting from the 1830s, Muslim understanding about what constitutes legal marriage and divorce began to change. According to Russian imperial law, Muslim marriage was considered legal only if it was performed by a licensed (*ukaznyi*) imam of the congregation (*maḥalla*) to which the bride belonged. Only the marriage of a couple who reached the legal age of marriage as defined by imperial law – sixteen for women and eighteen for men – was recognised as valid.[7] In addition, for marriage and divorce to be considered valid and legal, they had to be registered in parish registers by a parish imam. These rules were institutionalised through Russian imperial law as an attempt to better regulate social life of Muslims in the empire.[8]

The Russian state began to institutionalise religion and construct a multi-confessional establishment in 1721 with the creation of the Holy Synod for Orthodoxy, a process that culminated in a series of laws for Russia's different religious communities in the Digest of Laws in 1857. Paul Werth defines this process as 'domestication'. Through this process, the Russian state apparatus would communicate, intervene and regulate its population of diverse religious backgrounds until the end of the empire.[9] For the Muslims of the Volga-Urals and Western Siberia, such institutionalisation started with the establishment of the OMSA in 1788 and continued throughout the nineteenth century. Werth describes how this order was constructed, paying attention especially to the legislative dimension. Non-Orthodox religious communities gained recognition and a certain level of religious liberty through this process of institutionalisation. This institutionalisation, however, created a 'tension' between the traditions of these non-Orthodox communities and the political and social aims of the modernising Russian state. He also suggests that the tension between the state and religious laws led to the questioning of the religious authority in different religious communities, including the Muslim community.[10] However, he does not delve into the social impacts of this tension on the lives of the imperial subjects.

Robert Crews demonstrated another side of this institutionalisation of religion in the Volga-Ural Muslim community. He has looked at how the tsarist regime tried to solidify closer relations with *ᶜulamāᵓ* and engage them and laypeople in empire building. Muslim laity resorted to the help of Russian institutions and officials. By bringing their family issues, they dragged imperial authorities into the Muslim family.[11] While there were indeed occasional cases of cooperation between the *ᶜulamāᵓ* and Russian officials in which they worked together to solve *sharīᶜa* disputes according to orthodox Islamic precepts, I suggest that most often the *ᶜulamāᵓ* experienced difficulties when trying to balance the requests of their parishioners and the requirements of imperial law. Russian officials usually returned petitions of Muslims to the OMSA claiming them to be 'under the jurisdiction of Muslim authorities' and stating that they did not know what to do with them, as in the second case introduced at the beginning of this chapter. Therefore, this institutionalisation did not always result in cooperation between Russian state officials and the clergy of non-Orthodox confessions, but, as Werth argues, created uncertainty in many cases as the new imperial regulations made it unclear which institution was responsible to resolve certain legal issues.[12]

Jane Burbank interpreted the existence of multiple legal systems as a feature of imperial subjecthood, which was based on the idea of the 'imperial rights regime'. In this regime, all peoples inhabiting the empire had their own laws and customs. Burbank suggests that '[i]ncorporating these distinctive customs and laws into official governance was a means to enhance order and productivity in each region of the empire'.[13] Catherine's edict on 'the Toleration of All Faiths', announced in 1773,[14] marked the beginning of recognition of this diversity. In 1775, it was followed by another decree that stated that 'every people is allowed to perform marriages according to rules of one's own faith or custom'.[15] Burbank's concept of an 'imperial rights regime' helps us understand the legal basis for the functioning of a variety of legal systems – be it Jewish, Muslim or other – within the Russian imperial legal system. This system of 'imperial rights' granted legal protection for the social functioning of each religious community and also set the legal framework for interaction between religious communities and the state. But what happened in those cases that fell under the jurisdiction of both imperial law and Islamic legal practice of *sharīᶜa* as understood in this locality? This chapter aims to look at such cases of double jurisdiction and at the problems that arose from them.

Such reconfiguration of Islamic family cases within the imperial system not only impacted Muslim subjecthood and made Muslims even more integrated into the empire, but also affected the legality of the institution of marriage. Paolo Sartori suggests that imperial incursions into legal institutions affected the legal consciousness of Muslims. Through a study of legal cases of Central Asian Muslims living under Russian imperial rule, Sartori argues that Muslims 'learned to avail themselves of the new institutional arrangements offered by the colony' and 'accustomed themselves to a legal culture in which new institutions and new notions of justice mattered greatly in the pursuit of their own interests'.[16] Analysing the impact of laws and regulations that the imperial state introduced to the Muslim community of the Volga-Ural region in the nineteenth century, we can see a similar change in the understanding of what constituted legal marriage and divorce among the Volga-Ural Muslims.

While Werth, Burbank and Crews commonly focus on the interaction of non-Orthodox religious communities with the Russian state through institutionalised religious structures and laws, Allen Frank directs our attention to the fact that much of the legal debates in the Muslim community of northern and eastern Kazakh Steppe, which became a part of the empire in the nineteenth century, took place outside the Russian legal system, beyond the reach of the Russian state and outside of customary law courts established by the Russian authorities. At the same time, however, he points out that these legal debates show how Muslims adapted Islamic law to Russian rule.[17] When we look at a legal debate on divorce of wives of exiles that took place among the Volga-Ural *ᶜulamāʾ* in the 1890s we see that it developed beyond the purview of the state and Russian officials and there was no reference to Russian laws or institutions. However, the debate was triggered by a problem that developed as a result of the incorporation of Muslim family sphere into imperial law; it was triggered by a request in 1892 from imperial authorities in St Petersburg for the opinion of the OMSA on the permissibility of divorce; and the legal debate took place within the framework of a Russian imperial institution, the OMSA.

I suggest in this chapter that while the new laws on the exiles and their wives facilitated integration of Muslims into the empire, they also created social problems that had larger socio-religious and ethical implications for the community. Obtaining divorce from local religious authorities (imams and *ākhūnds*) became almost impossible as imperial law made it compulsory for women to seek divorce only from 'spiritual authorities' (*dukhovnoe nachal'stvo*), that is, the OMSA. As different imperial laws specifying who could ask for divorce were extended from the 1830s onwards to cover the Muslim population, the decisions of the OMSA depended on imperial laws, rather than Islamic legal regulations and practices. The 'substantial tension' between the state and the established Islamic legal tradition that Paul Werth writes about was a major reason for the increase in the number of women who could not officially obtain divorce and remarry and had to live with men outside of matrimony, which the tsarist officials labelled as 'illegal cohabitation (*nezakonnoe sozhitel'stvo*)'. Unresolved issues of marriage and divorce in the cases of exiled and disappeared husbands created serious problems for the wives of these men, for couples living together without an official marriage, for Muslim clerics who tried to help these people and, sometimes, for the whole Muslim congregation (*maḥalla*). The lack of a solution to the tensions between Islamic and imperial laws regarding the divorce and remarriage prompted *ʿulamāʾ* to collectively decide on a resolution to alleviate the tribulations of Muslim women that would be in congruence with Islamic legal traditions without circumventing or violating the imperial laws. This was an attempt to preserve the Islamic integrity of the community and to provide internal solutions to external challenges. In the following pages, I will describe how the problems relating to the wives of exiled and disappeared husbands created tensions between the state and the Muslim institutions and within the Muslim community, and how the *ʿulamāʾ* and the Muslim community of the Volga-Ural region dealt with these tensions.

Exile and Abandoned Wives

After the Russian conquest of Kazan, Muslims of the Volga-Ural region did not only lose the last political institutions of the Kazan Khanate; they also lost administrative, legal and other institutions, including their prerogative over punishing criminals. Muslims became subject to Russian law except in family and inheritance matters. Through the adjudication of criminal law, Volga-Ural Muslims were further integrated into the growing Russian Empire. With the development of exile as a means of punishment and imprisonment, the Russian state moved convicted Muslim men eastwards to Siberia, giving their wives an option to follow them.

Since the sixteenth century, exile was an integral component of empire building in Russia. Failing to find voluntary migrants to newly conquered territories, the state decided instead to populate Siberia with exiled criminals and mutineers. Daniel Beer states that '[t]he Petrine use of prisoners to harvest raw materials at labor sites across Siberia expanded as the state sought not simply to tap Siberia's natural resources but also to settle and colonize the land'.[18] In a century, these efforts were institutionalised and turned into 'a full-blown state-led project to colonize Siberian landmass'.[19] Culprits of serious crimes, participants in revolts and even people convicted of minor crimes such as theft of small property were chained up and sent over to Siberia. As Beer explains, the system was not only beneficial to the state, which could banish political or religious dissidents along with serious and petty criminals to Siberia. All levels of society, including peasant communes, land and factory owners and guilds, utilised exile to get rid of the 'troublemakers and the unproductive'.[20]

Since imperial criminal law was applied to Muslims like all other subjects of the Russian Empire, we see that many Muslim men were punished with exile for different crimes. Exile usually meant that a man would not come back to his home village or town. Convicts from different parts of Russia walked over to Siberia for months or even years under terrible conditions. If they could survive the journey, they would arrive at their destinations, where more hardship awaited them.[21] Even after the completion of their sentences the exiles continued to serve the state's goal of populating Siberia as they were allowed to stay anywhere in Siberia but could not easily return to their villages or towns. An exile had to obtain an official permission to return to his hometown or village in European Russia; he also had to secure the consent of his own peasant or merchant community, which was very often impossible. He furthermore had to pay for his return journey. As Beer suggests, the Russian state devised these legal and procedural obstacles intentionally in order to ensure that most of the exiles had to stay in Siberia.[22] Thus, convicts became participants of another – exile – society, which had its own rules and traditions.

The situation of the spouses of the exiled men was also regulated by law. If a person was sentenced to exile with the loss of all status rights, it meant that they also lost family rights. According to Article 31 of the Legal Code of Criminal and Corrective Penalties (*Ulozhenie o nakazaniiakh ugolovnykh i ispravitel'nykh*), dated 1845,

> The loss of family rights consists of the termination of marital rights, except for the cases when the wife of the convict or the husband of the convict voluntarily followed their spouses to their place of exile. Spouses who did not follow convicts to the place of their exile can request the absolute dissolution of their marriage, from their spiritual authorities (*dukhovnoe nachal'stvo*) which are guided by the rules of their confession in resolving this request. . . . If, however, according to the monarch's mercy or a new sentence of the court, the convicts are forgiven or recognized as innocent afterwards, and returned to their former place of residence, and their spouses have not asked for the dissolution of their marriage, then these marriages are recognized as remaining in force.[23]

What were the options for a Muslim woman after the exile of her husband? As the law stated, one option was to follow her husband to Siberia. Russian and Muslim women from European Russia often preferred not to accompany their husbands because of the difficulties of travel to Siberia on foot and harsh conditions at destinations for settlement. In our introductory case, Ḥusnijamāl refused to follow her husband to Siberia. As numerous petitions of Muslim women reveal, many other Muslim women also refused to do so. According to Beer, 'at the beginning of 1835, there were just under 3,000 women and male children who had followed their husbands and fathers to Siberia out of a total exile population of nearly 100,000.' The state tried to persuade the spouses of convicts to follow them across the Urals, with the aim to meet gender imbalance and disorder related to it, but it was difficult to do so. According to the 1822 Statutes on Exiles, 'wives of peasants and tradesmen who had been administratively exiled by their communities to Siberia were obliged to follow their husbands, whether they wished to do so or not. In 1828, the government extended this ruling to include the wives of all state peasants exiled by the courts to Siberia.' Still, at the end of the nineteenth century, only 5 per cent of exiles were women.[24]

Those women whose parents were alive could return to their parents' homes, like Ḥusnijamāl, but generally this was a temporary and an imperfect solution to their difficulty. The parents might not have the means or the will to support their daughters. Ḥusnijamāl was left with a young daughter and she returned to her father's house. During the interrogation Ḥusnijamāl's sixty-year-old father Fayḍullāh-ūghlī complained that his son-in-law failed to financially support his daughter during their marriage.[25] Indeed, from the very start of the marriage, she had depended on her father's financial help. Two years later their daughter was born but Raḥmatullāh failed to provide for the baby and so Ḥusnijamāl's father had to support his grandchild. He was resentful about his son-in-law:

'[Raḥmatullāh] had disappeared without notice several times, and squandered money. Finally, he was found guilty of robbery and was exiled to Siberia. He did not leave his wife and daughter a house or means to sustain themselves.' As a poor man, he told his daughter that he could not provide for her and her daughter anymore and requested that she find alternative means of sustenance.[26]

Women tried to find menial jobs like being in-home servants. In a petition from 1888, a woman complained to the Tsar that her husband, who was sentenced to imprisonment for six months, 'totally disappeared and has been absent for five years now', and that she earned her money on her own.[27] In another case, a woman, who was left with two children after her husband's exile to Siberia, started working as a hired servant (*rabotnik po naimu*). Later, she and the man for whom she worked started living together. During the interrogation, they claimed that the *maḥalla* imam had performed their marriage and they paid him twenty rubles for the marriage ceremony.[28] The questioning of another couple accused of illegal cohabitation reveals that another wife of an exile, Hazar Bulatova, went to the house of a certain Bashkir, Pitchin, and declared that she did not have anything to eat and asked him to take her into his house. Pitchin accepted her plea because he 'did not have a wife and expressed his intention to marry her'.[29]

Some women had relatives, but often the latter were reluctant to provide for them. If they were not able to find any other means to support themselves, they could not remarry and, in the absence of alternative options, found themselves having to beg or become prostitutes.[30] Imams were observing the tribulations of women in their communities. For example, the imam and mudarris Mūsā bin Fatḥullāh (Verkhneural'sk province) noted that in his twenty-three years as imam he had seen many women whose husbands went away and did not return for various reasons, and who did not receive the *nafaqa*, or financial support, that their husbands were supposed to pay them. Some of them started living with other men and others resorted to prostitution. *Ākhūnd* Muḥammad Shāfiᶜ Muḥammad Sharīf-ūghlī from the village of Urkī Irmat in Istarlītāmāq (Sterlitamak) province also underlined that

> young women, whose husbands disappeared without leaving provisions, are forced to roam in the streets and bazaars and even in places of crime and suspicion (*mawāḍᶜ tuhmat*). And this, in its turn, leads to disaster and chaos (*fitna*). Since they are not able to obtain divorce from their husbands, they fall into despair and start living with somebody in an adulterous life. I have sent several such cases to the consideration of the Orenburg Assembly.[31]

Remarriage: Ākhūnd *Fatḥullāh al-Ūriwī*

The most desirable course of action for such women was to find a man who would agree to marry and sustain her and her children, but obtaining divorce and remarrying was complicated. Sometimes, these issues were settled within the extended families. For example, in a case that was resolved in 1835 the in-laws of a woman whose husband was exiled to Siberia helped her to get a divorce. Her father-in-law told his son to grant divorce to his young wife before leaving for Siberia. The man therefore delegated divorce to his wife stipulating that she would be divorced after approximately one year of his absence: 'Let this Ramadan pass and after the next Ramadan she can marry whoever she wants.' There were several witnesses to this conversation. Even though the issue was settled within the larger family and the imam was informed about it, the woman wrote a petition to the Tsar to ask permission for remarriage.The issue was then sent to the OMSA for resolution. The OMSA ordered the local imam to investigate and confirm that the husband was exiled and had granted divorce to his wife. After the imam provided due confirmation, the OMSA granted the woman permission for remarriage.[32] The imam's report included the testimonies of the woman, her father-in-law, witnesses and the *maḥalla* imam. Such a case might have been resolved before the institutionalisation of religious institutions and legal norms within the *maḥalla* without resorting to the OMSA or to the Tsar. However, the legal changes that happened in the 1830s made this impossible.

In *Āthār*, Riḍāʾaddīn bin Fakhraddīn[33] recorded how a prominent *ākhūnd*, Fatḥullāh al-Ūriwī, handled cases of women whose husbands were exiled or disappeared for a long period of time in the 1830s. Fatḥullāh al-Ūriwī (d. May 10, 1843) was a prominent imam-*mudarris* and legal scholar. Some of his students became *qāḍī*s at the OMSA. He held high authority at the time of the *muftī* of the OMSA, Gabdessalam Gabdrakhimov (1825–40). According to Riḍāʾaddīn bin Fakhraddīn, members of the OMSA privately asked al-Ūriwī's opinion on many legal issues and used them in official decisions.[34] In this regard, one would expect that the OMSA would respect his decisions based on Islamic law, however, it was not always the case.

One of the cases was about a certain woman, Mahbūbjamāl, whose husband was conscripted into the army in 1829. Since military service was for twenty-five years[35] and many women refused to follow their husbands in this endeavour, the wives of soldiers shared the troubles of women whose husbands were exiled or got lost. Upon Mahbūbjamāl's request, her husband agreed to divorce her in front of witnesses before leaving the village with the other conscripts. Two years later, in December 1831, Mahbūbjamāl asked al-Ūriwī for a *fatwā* that would grant her divorce based on the exchange with her husband in front of witnesses. Al-Ūriwī agreed to grant her divorce in 1833 referring to the concept of *'adam īfā-i nafaqa* – the husband's failure to provide a place for living, money for food and clothing for his wife and his progeny. Al-Ūriwī also based his reasoning on the testimonies of the witnesses of the verbal exchange between Mahbūbjamāl and her husband, as well as on the permission of the OMSA to divorce women who could not secure material support from their husbands from 4 September 1831.[36]

Al-Ūriwī granted divorce to another woman in 1834, with the same legal reasoning – *'adam īfā-i nafaqa* – and based on the same permission from the OMSA to grant divorce to women who did not receive support from their husbands. In his reasoning, al-Ūriwī also cited the response of the Crimean *muftī* to the Head of the Department of Religious Affairs of Foreign Confessions (Departament dukhovnykh del inostrannykh ispovedanii) concerning permission of divorce and remarriage to women whose husbands were exiled to Siberia. In that case, the woman submitted the proof that her husband was found guilty of theft and was exiled to Siberia in 1833. The elders of her village and the imam confirmed her testimony. However, the husband of the petitioning woman, Ṣubḥiūghlī, demanded the annulment of al-Ūriwī's decision to dissolve his marriage and permission for his wife to marry another person. Ṣubḥiūghlī stated that he was in military service and his wife could not get a divorce as an imperial decree prohibited that. The decree was from 1835 and it was recorded in Article 94 of the Digest of Laws. According to said article, only the wives of conscripts who had a letter of divorce from their husbands that has been recorded in the parish register could request divorce.[37] In 1839 the OMSA questioned al-Ūriwī about his decision. In his response to the OMSA al-Ūriwī claimed that he was not aware that Ṣubḥiūghlī was in military service. He also noted that Ṣubḥiūghlī had been a convict and had his sentence of exile altered to military service, in accordance with Article 146 of the Penal Code. Moreover, he stated that he did not know about the imperial decree that Ṣubḥiūghlī mentioned in his petition until 1836 and he had written the *fatwā* in 1834 before said decree was promulgated. After he heard about the decree banning divorce to the spouses of soldiers, he stopped granting divorce to them.[38]

These three cases provide important insight into the ways that the resolution of marital issues of Muslims were changing in the first half of the nineteenth century. In the first case, a woman was trying to get legal affirmation of divorce she had already obtained from her husband.

Although the woman's claim was supported by witnesses including the parents of her husband, the local imam still sought the approval of the OMSA. The decision of the OMSA depended on the oral testimonies of the witnesses about the existence of the husband's declaration of divorce. Such evidence would not be enough when in 1835 the imperial law would require a divorce letter that was recorded in parish registers.

In the following two cases that al-Ūriwī handled the women were seeking *tafrīq,* which is to say the annulment of a marriage by a judge at the wife's request. Since Islamic law gives the right of divorce only to the husband, women were able to secure divorce only with a *qāḍī*'s permission. However, the problem on which al-Ūriwī based his decision – lack of financial support for women – is not recognised as a reason for *tafrīq* according to the Hanafī school of law that was followed in the Volga-Ural region. Al-Ūriwī was deriving his reasoning from other Sunni schools of Islamic law, as Hanbalī, Mālikī and Shāfiᶜī legal scholars consider that providing maintenance is an obligation of the husband and therefore lack of maintenance was a valid reason to ask for divorce.[39] Using the legal methods of other Sunni schools of law was not an unusual practice. However, al-Ūriwī apparently did not consider the flexible usage of *fiqh* regulations to be a sufficient foundation for a legal decision. He found and recited precedents in the OMSA's previous decisions and referred to the legal responses of the Crimean Muftī to Russian authorities on the status of wives of exiles.[40]

In the third case, the preeminence of imperial laws over Islamic law became apparent. After the promulgation of an imperial decree establishing the right of divorce for the wives of soldiers only in cases where there was a recorded divorce letter, the OMSA revoked the decision of al-Ūriwī, which had hitherto been deemed acceptable. For a woman to secure a divorce, it was no longer enough to present the testimony of witnesses confirming the husband's consent. Moreover, in all the cases we also see that the OMSA, as a higher religious and legal institution, limited the authority of *ākhūnd*s and imams by requesting reports from them or limiting their independent legal authority altogether.

These problems are most fully reflected in the case of Ḥusnijamāl that I outlined at the start of this chapter. From this case, we learn that Ḥusnijamāl was lucky to find another man with whom she could establish a stable married life. However, before she could marry him, she had to obtain a divorce letter from her husband, which was not possible as he was in exile. She needed a divorce decision from a religious authority, and, as the documents in her case attest, she knew whom she had to approach. After Ḥusnijamāl's father advised his daughter to find ways to maintain herself, she instructed him to explain her situation to the senior (*starshii*) *ākhūnd* of the village of Ūri (Sluzhilaia Ura) Fatḥullāh Ḥusayn-ūghlī (Fatḥullāh al-Ūriwī) and to request a statement of divorce (*razvodnoe pis'mo*) from Raḥmatullāh so that she could marry again. It was not a coincidence that Ḥusnijamāl instructed her father to seek the opinion and help of *ākhūnd* al-Ūriwī. The village of Ūri was located some 250 kilometres away from the village of Urazlino, on the other bank of the Volga river. There must have been other *ākhūnd*s closer to Ūri, however, Husnijamal specifically directed her father to al-Ūriwī. In *Āthār*, Riḍāʾaddīn bin Fakhraddīn emphasised that al-Ūriwī was famous for solving complicated *sharīʿa* disputes in his time. Muslims from faraway regions such as Simbirsk, Viatka and other provinces sought his legal opinion. It is highly probable that Ḥusnijamāl heard that Fatḥullāh al-Ūriwī could provide a legal solution to women in her situation.

As Ḥusnijamāl hoped, *ākhūnd* al-Ūriwī issued a *fatwā* on 18 May 1840 approving her request for divorce on the grounds that her husband had been convicted and exiled to Siberia, and allowed her to marry again. He based his *fatwā* on the principle of *'adam īfā-i nafaqa*.[41] As supporting proof, he cited the decree of the OMSA from 4 September 1831, no. 1256 on the dissolution of marriages when husbands left their wives without financial means and provision;[42] the *fatwā* of the Crimean Muftī dated 25 April 1832, no. 938; and the decree of the Holy Synod about the dissolution of marriages of exiles with their wives. Mullā Muḥammad Sharīf-ūghlī and a licensed imam of the village of Urazlino, Muḥammad Shah Sabit-ūghlī, were listed as witnesses for the issuance of this *fatwā*.[43]

Later, after the completion of the *'idda* period – the waiting period within which a divorced or a widowed woman cannot remarry – imam Muḥammad Sharīf-ūghlī performed Ḥusnijamāl's marriage to Ḥabībullāh on 8 August 1840. According to the testimony of imam Muḥammad Sharīf ūghlī, he performed and recorded the marriage on the basis of a divorce decision (*razvodnoi akt*) of the former ā*khūnd* of the village of Ūri, Fatḥullāh al-Ūriwī, on 18 May of the same year.[44] Thus, the Muslim community found a solution to the problem of an abandoned woman. However, Ḥusnijamāl found herself still facing a number of difficulties resulting from the transformation of the traditional socio-legal order in the Muslim community since the 1830s.

Imperial Law: Administrative and Procedural Problems

The transformation of the traditional socio-legal order of the Muslim community had a huge impact on the outcome of family problems. Some aspects of this transformation became points of contention in the case of Ḥusnijamāl. This relates to several rules and laws that the Russian state introduced into the Muslim community in the late eighteenth and early nineteenth century. These laws had a crucial effect on the outcome of the case of Ḥusnijamāl and those of many other women. The OMSA gave three reasons for not accepting the validity of *ākhūnd* Fatḥullāh al-Ūriwī's decision to grant a divorce to Ḥusnijamāl: first, *ākhūnd* al-Ūriwī did not record the decision in the civil register; second, *ākhūnd* al-Ūriwī granted a divorce to a woman who did not belong to his parish (*maḥalla*); and, third, the OMSA had not assigned the resolution of this case to al-Ūriwī, and the latter had issued the *fatwā* on his own volition.[45] None of the reasons pertained to the compatibility of *ākhūnd* al-Ūriwī's decision with Islamic law. Although the OMSA was considered to be the highest Islamic authority and the Islamic court of appeal, the reasoning for the annulment of Ḥusnijamāl's divorce and second marriage was based not on Islamic law but on imperial regulations.

The first imperial regulation concerned the introduction of obligatory registration. The Russian state introduced obligatory registration for its Muslim population in 1828. According to this requirement, *maḥalla* imams and *ākhūnd*s were obliged to register the births, deaths, marriages and divorces of the residents of their *maḥalla* in special parish registers. The form of the registers changed during the nineteenth century and the number of required categories of information increased. By the 1890s when recording a marriage, imams had to write down the names of bride and groom as well as their age, the date of the marriage, the name of fathers and grandfathers of the marrying couple and to which tribe (*tāʾifa*) they belonged. Imams also had to record whether the bride and groom had been previously married. There had to be witnesses and representatives (*wakīl*) from both sides and their names and signatures needed also to be recorded. The marrying couple could set conditions for marriage (*taʿliq*) and if they did so these conditions were also entered into the register. Another important category was about the dower (*mahr*). The imam had to record the amount of the dower, noting how much was paid up front (*muʿajjal*) and how much was deferred (*muʾajjal*). Since usually the dower was not paid in full, a person was named as the guarantor of the deferred amount, and the imam recorded that person's name in the entry for the marriage.[46] Finally, the imam who performed the marriage had to fill in his own name and signature as well as the names and signatures of other licensed imams who were present at the marriage ceremony (*majlis*).

The entry on divorce had to include the first and last names of a divorcing couple as well as the names of their fathers, grandfathers, their tribe and the witnesses. The imam had to record the type of divorce – *ṭalāq* or *khul*ᶜ.[47] If the divorce was of a *khul*ᶜ type, the amount of compensation (*badal khul*ᶜ) that a husband would receive as well as the reasons for divorce had to be recorded. The imam who performed the divorce had to sign the entry and indicate the date of divorce. The registration ascribed a new form of legality to Muslim marriages and divorces.[48] Only those marriages and divorces that were recorded in parish registers were considered legal. The OMSA ruled that since Ḥusnijamāl's divorce decision had not been registered, it was illegal.

The second imperial regulation was about the delineation of *maḥalla* boundaries, which led to a change from communal to individual adjudication of disputes. According to imperial law, an imam could only hear disputes of people who were registered as belonging (according to the list) to his *maḥalla* alone, and could not interfere in the affairs of other *maḥalla*s. Prior to this change, imams and *ākhūnd*s from different villages or *maḥalla*s had gathered for the resolution of complicated legal disputes. After the creation of the OMSA, *ākhūnd*s were limited in their independent legal authority. They were assigned to a *maḥalla* or several *maḥalla*s and had functions similar to those of imams.[49] Fatḥullāh Safargaliev was approved as *ākhūnd* in the place of Ākhūnd al-Ūriwī. Safargaliev reported that the village of Urazlino was under his jurisdiction but Ḥusnijamāl never asked him for a divorce from her first husband. Safargaliev was clearly not happy that a woman requested help from Ākhūnd al-Ūriwī instead of himself, as she was a resident of his *maḥalla*. He claimed that Ākhūnd al-Ūriwī did not have the right, without a special order from the OMSA, to divorce people who were not under his authority (*drugogo vedomstva*). Besides, we do not know the nature of the relationship between the former and the current *ākhūnd*s. There might be a certain degree of animosity between them. During the interrogation, Ākhūnd Safargaliev stated that he 'doubted the impartiality of the divorce letter' compiled by al-Ūriwī because Imam Muḥammad Sharīf-ūghlī was al-Ūriwī's son-in-law. Also, as al-Ūriwī's biography in *Āthār* reveals, while he held high authority at the OMSA under Muftī Gabdessalam Gabdrakhimov, his authority declined when Gabdulvakhid Suleimanov became the next *muftī* in 1840.[50]

The third imperial regulation concerned the limitation of the independent legal authority of *ākhūnd*s and imams. As I have explained elsewhere,[51] before the creation of the OMSA imams and *ākhūnd*s independently solved family and inheritance problems in the region. *Ākhūnd*s were considered to be specialists in Islamic law and for difficult cases people resorted to their arbitration. When Count Osip Igel'strom (1737–1823), the governor of Simbirsk and Ufa, was outlining his ideas about the creation of the OMSA, he suggested that Muslims should bring their disputes to the OMSA clerics if a case could not be solved by a *maḥalla* imam or a local *ākhūnd*. This appellate function of the OMSA was discussed for a while until it was confirmed in the 1820s. Thereafter, *maḥalla* imams and *ākhūnd*s were required to report to the OMSA on all the cases that were assigned to them by the *muftī* and *qādī*s. In 1836, a new regulation obliged the OMSA officials to keep journals (*zhurnaly zasedanii*) including summaries of all the petitions received from the Muslim population, along with the reports and investigation results of *ākhūnd*s and imam-*khatīb*s to whom the cases were assigned. Most importantly, in some specific cases Muslim laypeople could apply with their petitions only to the OMSA and the previously independent legal authority of *ākhūnd*s and imams turned to a simple investigatory role. One of these laws precisely concerned the right of women of exiled husbands to petition for remarriage.

The Issue of Imperial Law and Wives of Exiles for Settlement

We have seen how imperial law prevailed over a decision based on Islamic legal reasoning and how the OMSA restricted the judicial power of an *ākhūnd* in the case where al-Ūriwī granted divorce to the wife of an exile who then demanded his wife back claiming that he was a soldier.[52] During the nineteenth century laws to this effect continued to further restrict the Islamic law and the authority of Muslim legal experts.

Article 97 of the Penal Code (issued on 8 January 1836) extended the law about the wives of exiles to the Muslim population. This law allowed the wives of husbands who were exiled to Siberia with the loss of all status rights to request permission for remarriage from the OMSA (*dukhovnoe nachal'stvo*). The OMSA could grant divorce and permission to remarry after the criminal court (*palata ugolovnogo suda*) proved that a certain person was indeed exiled with the loss of all status rights.[53] Therefore, this law gave exclusive authority to the OMSA to deal with these issues, and the OMSA refused to recognise the independent legal authority of *maḥalla* imams and *ākhūnd*s with respect to these cases. Later, Article 98, issued on 3 November 1837, extended the law concerning the wives of disappeared (*bez vesti propavshikh*) husbands to the Muslim population and allowed Muslim wives whose husbands were missing to claim their right for divorce after five years of their husband's absence.[54]

Petitions of wives of exiled Muslim men from the 1860s onwards preserved in the archive of the Orenburg Assembly reveal that the OMSA easily granted divorce and the right to remarry to Muslim women whose husbands were exiled 'with the loss of all rights'. For this decision the OMSA demanded the fact and type of exile to be confirmed by local court or police. The OMSA requested an investigation about a man and, after receiving a written proof, it approved the wife's request for divorce and granted her the right to marry again. However, the law concerned only those wives whose husbands were exiled 'with the loss of all status rights' (*s lisheniem vsekh prav i sostoianii*), but not those who were exiled just 'for settlement' (*na poselenie*). Based on this law, the OMSA officials granted divorce to Muslim women whose husbands were exiled with the loss of all rights and privileges, and refused to grant divorce to the wives of exiles who were exiled for settlement. In all these responses (*postanovleniia*), the OMSA never mentioned Islamic family law. The OMSA *qādīs* and *mufti* did not discuss how these issues would and should be settled according to Islamic law. Decisions were only based on Russian imperial law.

As we saw in earlier examples, previously, a woman could obtain divorce from a local imam/*ākhūnd* on the basis of extreme hardship and non-provision. However, with the implementation of Russian laws limiting the right to get divorce only to the wives of exiles who lost all status rights, many women whose husbands were sent to exile without the loss of all status rights, or conscripted to the army, were adversely affected. Sometimes, imams tried to help women out and performed second marriages without registration and without informing the OMSA. For example, in one case a state peasant wrote to the Tsar a complaint that his son-in-law married a woman whose husband was exiled to Siberia. During interrogations, witnesses confirmed that the imam of their *maḥalla* had indeed performed their marriage illegally, because the first marriage of the woman had not been dissolved. The imam was indicted, and the second marriage was found illegal.[55] Imams often refused the requests of wives of exiled husbands for divorce, fearing the consequences that such an action might entail a punishment, ranging from a formal disciplinary warning to dismissal from office.

At other times, imams tried to help women out by petitioning on their behalf. In 1864, the imam of the village of Kayuki, in Riazan province, wrote to the OMSA asking permission to perform remarriage for a wife of an exile. The imam gave a highly emotive account of the position in which the woman found herself. He wrote that the woman was 'in a very difficult situation as she could not even find food'. However, the OMSA refused to grant the imam's request, stating that according to the imperial law only the wives of those exiles who had lost all status rights were eligible for divorce.[56] In 1869, Ākhūnd Munasipov from Perm wrote that a woman of his parish whose husband was exiled to Siberia had a baby and asked him to record the baby's birth in parish register. In his report, the *ākhūnd* asked the OMSA whether he should record the baby as legitimate or illegitimate (*zakonnorozhdennyi ili net*). The *akhūnd* also asked if he could perform her second marriage. The OMSA replied that he could perform her marriage only if her husband was exiled with the loss of all status rights.[57]

As the new understanding of legality of marriage and divorce settled in, we witness a change in the reaction of the imams and the Muslim community regarding the situation of wives of exiles. Thus, for example, in 1877, imams from Kurmasheva village in Ufa province denounced a couple to the OMSA, accusing them of illegal cohabitation. In their report the imams stated that one of their parishioners was exiled to Amur and his wife was living illegally with another man. The OMSA ordered Ākhūnd ᶜAbdulsattārov from the same village to investigate the case. The accused woman, Bībīṣafā, told that her husband divorced her (*ṭalaq*) before his exile to Siberia and that imam Nigmatullin performed her marriage with Muḥammad Salīm in presence of two female witnesses (imam Nigmatullin's wife and mother). Muḥammad Salīm, Bībīṣafā's new husband, explained their situation differently. He said that they informed the imam about their will to live together and the latter advised them to apply to the OMSA and request permission for marriage. None of the people whom Bībīṣafā and Muḥammad Salīm gave as witnesses corroborated their testimony of their marriage or inquiry with the OMSA. Even in Bībīṣafā's testimony about their marriage it was apparent that it was an unusual marriage ceremony in which the witnesses were only two women, namely the wife and the mother of the imam who allegedly performed the marriage. On the basis of the information that Ākhūnd ᶜAbdulsattārov gathered, the OMSA ordered the separation of Bībīṣafā and Muḥammad Salīm and ordered the village imams to make the couple repent and fast for their 'sinful act'.[58]

When we look at other cases of illegal cohabitation, the trials and tribulations of exiles' wives become clearer. In 1882 the OMSA received another complaint about illegal cohabitation and assigned Ākhūnd Baishev to investigate the marital situation of a woman whose husband was exiled. Ākhūnd Baishev questioned the woman, Dūshanbika ᶜAbdulkhāliq qizī, from the village of Yunusovo in the province of Ufa. Like Husnijamāl, Dūshanbika was left alone with two children after her husband's exile and she needed to find ways to feed herself and her children. She stated that she 'agreed, without the permission of the *maḥalla* imam, to cohabitate with a Bashkir man Ziainbaev in his house'.[59] She gave birth to a son in November 1882. Her partner also declared that he 'agreed and accepted Dūshanbika as his wife without marriage'.[69] When twelve people from their *maḥalla* were interrogated, they all acknowledged the illegal cohabitation of this couple and the birth of their son.[61]

It was apparent that Bashkir Zianbaev and Dūshanbika had to live together without *nikāḥ*, although they wanted to marry legally. The imam of their *maḥalla* could not marry them and the *maḥalla* community knew about their cohabitation. It was the *maḥalla* imam who complained to the OMSA about their illegal cohabitation in 1882, right after the birth of their son. The OMSA ordered to force the couple to repent and to separate them. Because the imperial law regulating the family rights of exiles did not grant divorce to the wives of exiles who had not lost all status rights, the imam could not marry the couple. Like the rest of the community, he might simply have ignored their cohabitation, but was unable to remain silent when a child was born because he had to give a name to the child and record the child in the parish register. This, however, was complicated because the infant's parents were not married legally and their marriage was not registered in the civil records.

Many other illegal cohabitations are recorded in the archive of the OMSA. Sometimes imams performed unofficial marriages without recording them in parish registers, thus waiving their responsibility for illegal marriage.[62] Sometimes marriages were performed by unofficial *ᶜulamāʾ*. At other times a couple might agree in front of several witnesses to live together, trying to find a communal legitimisation for their marital life. Children were born in these marriages. The *maḥalla* communities knew about such cohabitations but kept silent.

Attempts to Find a Solution and Religious Authority

As stipulated in the Digest of Laws, the spouses of exiles whose sentence did not entail 'the loss of all status rights' did not have the right to request divorce. Moreover, exiles did not have the right to request divorce themselves. This created practical problems for the settlement authorities in Siberia and elsewhere. Even those convicts who lost all status rights could not ask for divorce and marry in their destination of exile. In 1892, the State Council and the United Department of Civil and Religious Laws decided to remedy this situation. The attending parties to the meeting, prosecutor-general of the Holy Synod, ministers of Justice and Internal

Affairs, senator Vyacheslav Konstantinovich Plehve (later the Minister of Internal Affairs) and the representatives of the United Department of Religious and Civil Laws, stated that

> the existence of these limitations leads in practice to very adverse consequences. Siberian spiritual and secular authorities complain about the impossibility of dissolving the marriages of the majority of exiles and their spouses which condemns these people to eternal celibacy, extremely burdens their fate, promotes the development of extramarital affairs and largely prevents the correct arrangement of the family and household life of exiles.[63]

While the committee was ready to grant the right of divorce to the Orthodox exiles who 'lost major rights and property' and to their spouses, they were hesitant to extend this right to the exiles of other religious groups (*inovertsev*). Upon the suggestion of the Holy Synod, the members of the meeting decided that dissolution of the marriages of non-Russian Orthodox exiles had to be discussed with the religious courts (*dukhovnye sudy*) of respective religious communities.[64] The Minister of Internal Affairs was to ascertain the rules of dissolution of marriage for the people of other faiths who were exiled to Siberia with the loss of major rights and property, and for the people who were deported to Siberia for settlement.

When the issue was soon after discussed at the State Council, one of the members suggested that the state should not consult the non-Russian Orthodox religious authorities about the issue of the dissolution of marriage in the case of exile, since the reason for divorce – exile – was a matter governed by state laws, not religious ones. Despite this suggestion, however, the State Council decided to consult the religious courts of non-Russians, considering that 'the purpose of [the proposed amendment] was to establish the conditions under which the exiled and their spouses are allowed to apply for divorce, and not in determining the rules themselves, which should be accepted by spiritual courts when resolving such requests'.[65]

Subsequently, the Ministry of Internal Affairs asked the opinion of the Orenburg Assembly. The OMSA responded on 5 April 1893. The *qādīs* of the OMSA informed the Ministry that for exiled Muslims, the proposed amendments would affect only women, for Muslim men had the right of divorce in any case, and Muslim women did not have the right to divorce. The OMSA members clarified that Islamic law allowed women to request divorce from religious courts only under some exceptional situations. A woman could ask for divorce in the following cases: if her husband could not consummate the marriage; if the mental instability of the husband threatens his wife's life; if the husband could not provide daily food (*ezhednevnoe propitanie*). In these cases, Islamic law allowed courts to annul a marriage upon unilateral petition of a woman if the reasons for divorce would undoubtedly be proved. Referring to the above-mentioned special situations that allowed women to ask for divorce, the OMSA came up with a general rule: if the situation of a woman is extremely desperate, Islamic law gives her the right for divorce by the decision of religious court. Therefore, the OMSA responded to the Ministry of Internal Affairs that the marriages of the wives of exiles to Siberia who were deprived of major rights and property, and those who were deported to Siberia for settlement, could be annulled upon petition, if it could be established that the petitioning party was in a desperate position. Likewise, the marriages of men who did not want to accompany their exiled wives could also be annulled.[66]

The amendment of the law regarding the dissolution of marriages of exiles and the inquiry of the Ministry of Internal Affairs about the opinion of the OMSA on that amendment gave the OMSA an opportunity to solve the problem at the imperial level. With their response, the OMSA clerics issued an opinion that would affect all Muslim women in similar situations. However, the decision for divorce would still depend on the assessment of the situation of each petitioning woman, because the Hanafī legal school that was prevalent in the Volga-Ural region did not grant divorce to wives whose husbands had disappeared until such had time had passed that the husband's natural lifespan could be presumed to have come to an end.[67]

In 1896, Riḍāʾaddīn bin Fakhraddīn, one of the *qādī*s of the OMSA who compiled the response to the Minister of Internal Affairs, sent out an imperial-wide inquiry to the *ʿulamāʾ* under the jurisdiction of the Orenburg Assembly.[68] In the inquiry, he stated that in recent years the Orenburg Assembly had been inundated with petitions from women requesting that the OMSA annul/dissolve (*faskh*) their marriages because their husbands were missing. These women were 'legally bound to marriages that no longer had any emotional (*ḥissī*) or spiritual (*ma'nawī*) benefit for them'. These marriages, he wrote, caused a variety of problems both for the women in question and for Muslim society more generally.[69]

> As the Russian empire expanded and as traveling became easier, many Muslim men left their homes for distant cities and provinces in pursuit of better jobs (*kasb wa ish*), while others were exiled to Siberia for the crimes they had committed. Those men who left or were forced to leave their native homes failed to provide maintenance for their wives. Some men did not even inform their wives about their whereabouts. If a man died, information about his death might not reach his wife. These women, some of whom were still young and

had young children, were forced to roam from village to village and from house to house to find food.

Faced with a considerable increase in the number of petitions from exiles' wives requesting divorce, the Assembly decided 'to urgently take this into consideration and address this issue'.[70] Riḍāʾaddīn bin Fakhraddīn and the OMSA wanted to get the opinions of *ākhūnd*s and imams on the question of granting these women divorce and performing marriage with conditional stipulations to avoid future problems. Later, Riḍāʾaddīn bin Fakhraddīn compiled the opinions of sixty-three *ākhūnd*s and imams from different towns and villages of the Volga-Urals and Western Siberia into a volume titled *Muṭālaʿa*. In the inquiry Riḍāʾaddīn bin Fakhraddīn recommended the following stipulations to be added to marriage contracts of Volga-Ural Muslims:

1. A husband must not be absent for more than a year without ensuring the financial maintenance of his wife;
2. If a husband is sentenced to exile, he must divorce his wife before leaving for exile;
3. A husband must not beat his wife, consume alcohol or leave her without financial support;
4. A husband may not take a second wife if he is unable to ensure the financial support of the first wife.

The first question in the inquiry asked the Volga-Ural *ʿulamāʾ* whether it was appropriate to marry couples with a contract that would give a woman the right to announce herself divorced in the presence of a local parish imam, if one of the above-mentioned conditions is broken. The second question was about the legal (*shar'ī*) appropriateness of obliging all imams to compile marriage contracts with these stipulations. The third question asked the *ʿulamāʾ* if they could suggest other methods to facilitate the divorce of wives of absentee husbands.

In their responses several *ʿulamāʾ* explicitly and implicitly mentioned the importance of parish imams having independent legal authority. Ḥāfiẓaddīn Naṣraddīn-ūghlī claimed that 'in our country, each imam is a *qāḍī* (judge) over the question of marriage, divorce, funeral and other questions in his own *maḥalla*, and every imam is aware of what is going on in his *maḥalla*'. He proceeded to note that *maḥalla* imams were in fact best suited to solving this problem, as they directly knew their parish fellows and their families. Therefore, imams, in their capacity as judges, could independently perform the dissolution of marriage. Naṣraddīn-ūghlī thus maintained that every imam could take an independent legal decision based on his immediate knowledge of people, families and problems/

conflicts that were going on in his *maḥalla*, and he could propose his own *ijtihād* (legal interpretation) based on concrete factors within a given situation.

Other respondents also highlighted the importance of the independent authority of *maḥalla ākhūnd*s and imams. Jamāladdīn Sayfaddīn-ūghlī clearly emphasised that *Maḥkama-i Islāmiya* (the OMSA) must leave 'full autonomy (*kāmil mukhtariyya*) to *maḥalla* imams in divorcing such men'. In his opinion, *maḥalla* imams would be able to annul marriages upon the request of those women who had been left without maintenance (*nafaqa*) and whose men consumed alcohol and/or beat them without reason.

> The accuracy of legal decisions of *maḥalla* imams to divorce women whose husbands do not provide should not be subject to a second opinion, because these decisions are proven by the verse stating that in times of necessity everything is correct. And we do not know of any proof that the *umma* of our Prophet should follow a particular *mujtahid*. It is well-known that in times of necessity it is possible to borrow from another *madhab*. Therefore, there is no need to appoint a Shafi'ī or Mālikī or Ḥanbalī *nā^cib* ('representative') or a *qādī*.[71]

In this way, this imam called on the Orenburg Assembly to recognise the legal authority of *maḥalla* imams – an authority that was presumed in theory, according to Russian imperial law, but often overridden in practice by the authority of the Orenburg Assembly and by ordinary Muslims who increasingly opted to appeal to this latter institution during the second half of the nineteenth century.

Conclusion

Rather than dwelling on the integration or insulation paradigms to understand the place of Volga-Ural Muslim communities in nineteenth century Russia, in this chapter I have considered the legal and social transformations that occurred as a result of state policies regarding the empire's Muslim subjects. The ambiguities that the imperial penal system created in the marital status of women presented an important challenge for the individual and communal lives of Muslims, as well as for other subjects of the empire. Legality of marriage and divorce had to be defined according to the regulations of imperial laws rather than according to Islamic laws and tradition. Resolutions by Islamic scholars aimed at saving women from a legal quandary could be overturned by the spiritual authority (*dukhovnoe nachal'stvo*) of Muslims, the OMSA, since imperial laws concerning the wives of exiles recognised this latter as the sole authority empowered to grant divorce. Instead of applying to a local legal authority and acquiring the right to divorce through the implementation of an exceptional legal solution, that is, granting divorce because of lack of maintenance, Muslim women had to go through an arduous and time-consuming legal process through the OMSA. As a result, socially and religiously unacceptable situations such as illegal cohabitation became a common occurrence. Although the communities sometimes ignored such illegal cohabitations, the latter created further legal problems, such as illegality of children, and certainly bothered religious authorities who were the guardians of religious and moral order in the Muslim society. The problem regarding the wives of exiles was a problem created by the empire. The solution and the platform for the solution was also provided by the empire. The inquiry of state authorities about the Islamic approach to the annulment of marriages of spouses of exiles gave a legal ground for the OMSA and, later, with the initiative of the OMSA, for a group of religious scholars to discuss and offer solutions to this problem within the Islamic legal framework.

Notes

* I am thankful to the anonymous reviewers, Paul Werth, Paolo Sartori and colleagues at History Reading Circle at Nazarbayev University, for valuable comments and suggestions.

1. The Orenburg Muslim Spiritual Assembly was an institution established during the reign of Catherine II to better govern Russia's Muslim population. It was a collegiate institution formed by a *mufti* and three *qāḍī*s who collectively took decisions on different cases. It also functioned as a court of appeal for Muslims who were not satisfied with the decisions of parish Muslim clergy.
2. I use Cyrillic transliteration of names taken from documents written in the Russian language. For the transliteration of names and terms written in Arabic script I follow the *IJMES* Arabic transliteration guide.
3. Tsentral'nyi gosudarstvennyi istoricheskii arkhiv Respubliki Bashkortostan/ Central State Historical Archive of the Republic of Bashkortostan (henceforth, TsGIA RB), f. 295, op. 4, d. 2445 (1852).
4. Fatḥullāh Ḥusayn ūghlī al-Ūriwī (d. 10 May 1843) was born in 1767. He studied in Bukhara and, after returning therefrom, received licence and became imam in the village of Ūri in 1799. In 1814, he was appointed as *ākhūnd*, and in 1819 as senior *ākhūnd* (*starshii akhun*). Rizaeddin Fakhreddin (Riḍā al-Dīn bin Fakhr al-Dīn), *Āthār* (2 vols) (Orenburg: Karimof Matbaasi, 1905), vol. 2, part 9, pp. 7–13.
5. Exile sentences for light crimes could be changed to military service according to Article 146 of Russian penal code. See: *Ulozhenie o nakazaniiakh* (St

Petersburg: Tipografiia vtorogo otdeleniia sobstvennoi ego Imperatorskogo Velichestva kantseliarii, 1845), pp. 47–8.

6. TsGIA RB, f. 295, op. 3, d. 2809.
7. *Svod Zakonov*, vol. 10, part 1, Article 91 (St Petersburg, Tipografiia vtorogo otdeleniia sobstvennogo ego imperatorskogo velichestva kantseliarii, 1857), p. 18; R. Garipova, 'Married or Not Married? On the Obligatory Registration of Muslim Marriages in Nineteenth-Century Russia', *Islamic Law and Society* 24:1–2 (2017), pp. 112–41.
8. *Sbornik tsirkuliarov i inykh rukovodiashchikh rasporiazhenii po okrugu Orenburgskogo Magometanskogo Dukhovnogo Sobraniia 1836–1903* (Ufa: Gubernskaia tipografiia, 1905) (Reprinted: Kazan: Iman, 2004), pp. 15–18.
9. P. Werth, *The Tsar's Foreign Faiths: Toleration and the Fate of Religious Freedom in Imperial Russia* (Oxford: Oxford University Press, 2016), p. 47.
10. Ibid., pp. 47–8.
11. R. Crews, *For Prophet and Tsar: Islam and Empire in Russia and Central Asia* (Cambridge, MA: Harvard University Press, 2006), pp. 144–91.
12. P. Werth, *The Tsar's Foreign Faiths*, p. 67.
13. J. Burbank, 'An Imperial Rights Regime: Law and Citizenship in the Russian Empire', *Kritika: Explorations in Russian and Eurasian History* 7:3 (2006), p. 401.
14. A. Fisher, 'Enlightened Despotism and Islam under Catherine II', *Slavic Review* 27:4 (1968), p. 543.
15. *Svod Zakonov*, vol. 10, part 1, Article 90 (St Petersburg, Tipografiia vtorogo otdeleniia sobstvennogo ego imperatorskogo velichestva kantseliarii, 1857).
16. P. Sartori, *Visions of Justice:* Sharīᶜa *and Cultural Change in Russian Central Asia* (Leiden and Boston: Brill, 2016), p. 309.
17. A. J. Frank, 'Sharīᶜa Debates and Fatwas among Nomads in Northern Kazakhstan, 1850–1931', *Islamic Law and Society* 24 (2017), pp. 61–76.
18. D. Beer, *The House of the Dead: Siberian Exile under the Tsars* (London: Allen Lane, 2016), p. 18.
19. Ibid., p. 25.
20. Ibid.
21. Ibid., pp. 31–5.
22. Ibid., pp. 18, 27.
23. Ibid., pp. 26–7.
24. Ibid., pp. 27, 243–5.
25. According to Islamic law and local legal tradition a husband has to provide maintenance (*nafaqa*) for his family. See J. Tucker, *Women, Family, and Gender in Islamic Law* (New York: Cambridge University Press, 2008), p. 50.
26. TsGIA RB, f. 295, op. 3, d. 2809, l. 27.
27. TsGIA RB, f. 295, op. 4, d. 15505 (1888).
28. TsGIA RB, f. 295, op. 3, d. 1824 (1843–9).
29. TsGIA RB, f. 295, op. 3, d. 1845 (1843–6).

30. Riḍāʾaddīn bin Fakhraddīn, *Muṭālaʿa: Idāra-i Islāmiya-i Īrīnbūrgiya ūzārīna ʿālimlarimiz ṭarafīndan nikāḥ khuṣusunda yāzilmish afkārlarinin khulāsasī jamʿ īdilmish risāladir* (Kazan: Dumbrawski, 1897), p. 32.
31. Ibid., pp. 55–7.
32. TsGIA RB, f. 295, op. 4, d. 665 (1831).
33. Riḍāʾaddīn bin Fakhraddīn was a prominent Muslim scholar of the Volga-Ural region. He served as *qādī* of the Muslim Spiritual Administration from 1891(?) to 1906, and again from 1917 to 1920, and as *muftī* from 1920 until his death in 1936. He is well-known for his role in the development of Tatar Jadidism. He was the chief editor of the popular Jadid journal, *Shūrā*, and published numerous works on the social and religious problems of Russia's Muslim community. He also published several fiction and non-fiction works on Muslim women and their place in family and society.
34. Riḍāʾaddīn bin Fakhraddīn, *Āthār* (2 vols) (Orenburg: Karimof Matbaasi, 1905), vol. 2, part 9, pp. 7–13.
35. Until 1834 military service was for twenty-five years in the Russian Empire. It was decreased to twenty years in 1834. Allan K. Wildman, *The End of the Russian Imperial Army* (Princeton: Princeton University Press, 1980), p. 25.
36. Riḍāʾaddīn bin Fakhraddīn, *Āthār*, vol. 2, part 9, pp. 17–19.
37. Article 94, *Svod Zakonov*, vol. 10, part 1 (St Petersburg, Tipografiia vtorogo otdeleniia sobstvennogo ego imperatorskogo velichestva kantseliarii, 1857), p. 19.
38. Riḍāʾaddīn bin Fakhraddīn, *Āthār*, vol. 2, part 9, pp. 26–7.
39. J. Tucker, *Women, Family, and Gender in Islamic Law*, p. 52.
40. Riḍāʾaddīn bin Fakhraddīn, *Āthār*, vol. 2, part 9, pp. 26–7.
41. TsGIA RB, f. 295, op. 3, d. 2809, ll. 25–6.
42. Ukaz OMDS ot 4 sentiabria 1831 goda za no. 1256 o rastorzhenii brakov za ostavleniem muzh'iami zhen svoikh bez sredstv k propitaniiu. Ibid., l. 26.
43. TsGIA RB, f. 295, op. 3, d. 2809, ll. 27–8, 34–6.
44. TsGIA RB, f. 295, op. 3, d. 2809, l. 33.
45. For the analysis on the transformation of Islamic legal order, see R. Garipova, 'Did the Ākhūnds Disappear? Islamic Legal Experts and the Breakdown of the Traditional Islamic Legal Order in the Russian Empire', *The Yearbook of Islamic and Middle Eastern Law* 19 (2018), pp. 38–67.
46. J. Tucker, *Women, Family, and Gender in Islamic Law*, p. 47.
47. All schools of Islamic law recognise three types of divorce: The first type is *ṭalāq*, when a husband unilaterally repudiates his marriage. The second type of divorce is *khulʾ, which is to say* a negotiated divorce, and *is* usually initiated by a wife. The last type of divorce is *tafrīq*, requiring judicial intervention to end a marriage because of certain conditions. See, J. Carlisle, *Muslim Divorce in the Middle East: Contesting Gender in the Contemporary Courts* (Birmingham: Palgrave Macmillan, 2019), pp. 9–13.
48. See R. Garipova, 'Married or not Married? On the Obligatory Registration of Muslim Marriages in Nineteenth-Century Russia'.

49. Rossiiskii Gosudarstvennyi Istoricheskii Archiv/Russian State Historical Archive (henceforth, RGIA), f. 821, op. 150, d. 404, l. 71. The decree of the Governing Senate from 10 March 1893, n. 2384. Every imam and *ākhūnd* was assigned to a mosque *maḥalla* and was responsible to carry on his duties within his own *maḥalla*. Since the title was bound with certain duties, when an *ākhūnd* retired, he lost the title.
50. Riḍā'addīn bin Fakhraddīn, *Āthār* (Orenburg: Karimof Matbaasi, 1905), vol. 2, part 9, pp. 7–13.
51. R. Garipova, 'Did the Ākhūnds Disappear?', pp. 38–67.
52. *Svod Zakonov Rossiiskoi Imperii*, vol. X, Part 1, *zakony grazhdanskie* (Civil Laws) (St Petersburg: Tipografiia vtorogo otdeleniia sobstvennogo ego imperatorskogo velichestva kantseliarii, 1857), p. 19.
53. Ibid., p. 20.
54. Ibid.
55. TsGIA RB, f. 295, op. 4, d. 8342 (1871–8).
56. TsGIA RB, f. 295, op. 4, d. 4992 (1864).
57. TsGIA RB, f. 295, op. 3 d. 7120 (1869).
58. TsGIA RB, f. 295, op. 3 d. 9480 (1877).
59. TsGIA RB, f. 295, op. 3, d. 10653, l. 8.
60. TsGIA RB, f. 295, op. 3, d. 10653, l. 8 ob.
61. TsGIA RB, f. 295, op. 3, d. 10653, l. 9.
62. TsGIA RB, f. 295, op. 4, d. 8342.
63. RGIA, f. 821, op. 10, d. 655, delo ob izmenenii pravil rastorzheniia brakov, v sviazi ssylkoi odnogo iz suprugov v Sibir', 28 December 1892–7 July 1902, l. 20.
64. RGIA, f. 821, op. 10, d. 655, l. 22.
65. RGIA, f. 821, op. 10, d. 655, ll. 23–6.
66. RGIA, f. 821, op. 10, d. 655, ll. 39–41.
67. J. Tucker, *Women, Family, and Gender in Islamic Law*, p. 94.
68. Riḍā'addīn bin Fakhraddīn, *Muṭāla'a*, p. 22.
69. Ibid., p. 22.
70. Ibid., p. 25.
71. Ibid., pp. 50–1.

5

Islamic Scholars among the Kereys of Northern Kazakhstan, 1680–1850

Allen J. Frank

Introduction

A number of preconceptions regarding nomadic religiosity and Islam have strongly affected our understanding of the *ᶜulamāᵓ* among Qazaq nomads. These ideas are evident in much of the Russian writing on Qazaq history, and commonly maintain that Qazaqs, while nominally Muslims, did not constitute the same sort of Muslim society as their sedentary neighbours in the Volga-Ural region and Central Asia because they did not share the same sort of emotional or social attachment to Islam. Qazaqs were often described as 'shamanists' and their lack of immediately recognisable Islamic institutions, such as mosques and madrasas, was further evidence of their 'superficial' devotion to Islam. According to much of this Russian writing, 'pre-Islamic' customary law defined Qazaq legal culture, and *sharīᶜa* was an invasive species of law brought by outsiders, specifically Tatars and Central Asians. Qazaqs who administered customary law – *biys* – were understood to be secular tribal chieftains whose authority and homespun wisdom were similarly 'pre-Islamic', and, in any event, unpolluted by Islamic education. Furthermore, these scholars argue, Qazaq nomads, as 'shamanists', had no Islamic scholars of their own, and instead brought in (or were supplied with) Islamic scholars from their more recognisable Islamic neighbours in Russia and Central Asia to administer Islamic Law.[1]

Such a view reveals a substantial inability to assess Qazaq social history on its own terms. But it retains considerable currency in much of the scholarship on Qazaq history, particularly scholarship that is mainly derived from Russian sources, and not least in Kazakhstan itself.

At the same time, Qazaqs, including members of the *ᶜulamāᵓ* who examined the history of their own Islamic institutions, frequently assert the nearly total absence of Islamic scholars among Qazaq nomads up until about 1830. For example, writing in Russian periodicals in 1881, B. Daulbaev asserts that before 1830 there were virtually no 'mullahs' among the Qarabalïq Qïpshaqs in Torghay *oblast'*. Muhammad-Salih Babadzhanov, writing in 1861, made a similar observation regarding the Qazaqs of the Inner Horde.[2] The Bukhara-trained poet and scholar Mäshhür Zhüsïp Köpeyŭlï (1857–1931) and the theologian and historian Saduaqas Ghïlmani (1890–1972) wrote in manuscript works that the first Islamic scholars did not appear among the Arghïns of the Pavlodar and Aqmola (Akmolinsk) regions until the 1830s.[3] There is no reason to doubt these assertions, and in fact they illustrate one of the most significant challenges regarding Qazaq social history, namely the tendency of scholars to generalise about Qazaqs on the basis of information obtained from or relating to geographically restricted communities. This is particularly true for the travel literature on the Qazaqs produced over four centuries (admittedly, generalisation is the stock-in-trade of any travel writer). An emphasis on generalisation is perhaps more evident among Russian administrators, who, as bureaucrats, were tasked with applying centralised policies over Qazaq communities that diverged widely in terms of their own institutions and historical experience. Similarly, Soviet historiography focused especially on Qazaq national history and also favoured generalisation, while showing little, if any, interest in Qazaq Islamic institutions and networks. The pitfalls of over-generalisation are especially relevant when discussing such a geographically vast area as the Qazaq Steppe. To be fair to the Qazaq scholars mentioned above, they were explicit in restricting their observations to their geographic and chronological fields of vision. Nevertheless, the presence of Islamic scholars among steppe nomads before the nineteenth century was not unusual. As we shall see, Qazaq sources reveal that the presence of Islamic scholars in nomadic communities, at least by the eighteenth century, was by no means exceptional.[4] Beyond the Qazaqs, there is ample evidence for legal scholars among Noghay nomads of the Kuban and Black Sea steppe in the eighteenth century, a group sharing close historical and ethnic connections with the Qazaqs.[5]

The purpose of this paper is to broaden geographically and chronologically previous discussions of the Qazaq *ᶜulamāᵓ*: while not generalising about the situation on the Qazaq Steppe as a whole, the paper seeks to provide biographical information on Qazaq Islamic scholars in nomadic communities, demonstrating their presence well before the 1830s, and in fact as far back as the late seventeenth century. Another goal is to illustrate the shifting social and legal roles of nomadic Islamic scholars over the course of several centuries. The paper is based above all on a number of genealogical treatises and hagiographies produced among the Kereys, a major branch of the Middle Zhüz inhabiting modern-day Qostanay, North Kazakhstan and Qïzïlorda *oblast'*s in modern Kazakhstan. This historiography constitutes a remarkable collection of sources describing Islamic scholarly networks, educational institutions and Islamic religious and political authority. The works are based on a number of locally produced and preserved sources, including genealogies, memoirs, songs and poetry produced from the first quarter of the eighteenth century through the middle of the nineteenth, and published in independent Kazakhstan after 1991.[6] While the Kerey biographies offer a particularly detailed overview of the *ᶜulamāᵓ* within a particular community, we can also make use of biographical information on Islamic scholars in other nomadic communities in the eighteenth century and early nineteenth primarily – but not exclusively – from western Kazakhstan to fill out the picture as much as possible.[7]

The Kereys

The Kereys constitute one of the major tribal groupings making up the Middle Zhüz, and historically have been closely linked with the smaller, but genealogically distinct, Uaq tribe. Two major groupings constitute the Kereys. These are the Abaq Kereys, primarily located in eastern Kazakhstan, as well as in northern Xinjiang province in China, and in western Mongolia. The western division of the Kereys is the Ashamaylï Kereys, with whose historical traditions we are concerned here. They are located primarily in the North Kazakhstan *oblast'*, Kostanay *oblast'*, and in neighbouring areas of Kurgan and Tiumen' *oblast*s in Russia. The Ashamaylï Kereys are further divided into a number of branches, including the Köshebe, Siban and Tarïshï Kereys.[8] One genealogy compiled by the Köshebe branch of the Ashamaylï Kereys in western Siberia and northern Kazakhstan is said to have been first composed in the early seventeenth century, and was continually expanded into the nineteenth century. These Kereys trace their ancestry to an ancestor named Baghïlan-biy, whose genealogy is given as follows:

> Kerey-Oshïbay → Menglïqaghan → Arïstanbek → Naurïzkhan[9] → Ghali (Ashamaylï) → Baghdat-batïr → Töbey → Äzizbek → Tursïnkhan-sardar → Zharghaq → Qazhïkhan → Älmukhamed → Uïzbek → Zhanï-batïr → Baghïlan-biy.[10]

These Kereys established a particularly strong connection to Siberia in their genealogy. Ghaliy, the ancestor of all the Ashamaylï Kereys, is said to have been the first to come to that region. Baghïlan-biy is similarly a quasi-legendary figure, but he is considered the main ancestor (*tüp ata*) of many Kereys in northern Kazakhstan. His grave is today located in Russia, near the former Cossack settlement of Zverinogolovka, known to Qazaqs as Baghïlan, in Kurgan *oblast'*. Kerey tradition dates Baghïlan-biy to about the beginning of the fourteenth century CE, since his son Tanash-biy was said to have served Özbek Khan, ruler of the Golden Horde (r. 1313–41), who is also remembered as the Islamiser of the Qazaqs' ancestors. According to the Köshebe genealogy Tanash-biy was a 'just *qāḍī*' (*ädilqazï*). [11] In a poem specifically devoted to Tanash-biy Qozhabergen relates that he served not only Özbek Khan, but also Özbek's predecessor, Toqta Khan (r. 1291–1313 CE). Qozhabergen emphasises Tanash-biy's accomplishments in protecting the Muslim community, including 'shooting down the leader of the infidels' and bringing down their banner, and enjoying the approval of the Muslims.[12]

While the seventeenth- and eighteenth-century wars with the Zunghars figure prominently in the accounts of their heroes, the Ashamaylï Kerey accounts emphasise their conflicts with Russia, suggesting that these groups saw themselves as a sort of a frontier community, protecting their lands from Russia. In his poem *Elim-ay* Qozhabergen-zhïraw refers to the role of the Qazaq khan Shïghay in defending Siberia from Russian conquest in the 1580s, providing assistance to the Muslim khan of Siberia, Küchüm Khan and defending the 'Muslim lands' from 'the dog Yermak'.[13] The sources also make frequent mention of Muslim military and political solidarity between the Qazaqs, Siberian Tatars, Noghays and Bashkirs in opposing the Zunghars, as well as in maintaining autonomous religious institutions under Russian rule.[14] However, the Ashamaylï Kereys place particular emphasis on their opposition to the advancement of the Cossack fortified lines into their territory in the eighteenth and especially in the first decades of the nineteenth century. The fortified lines of the Siberian and Orenburg Cossacks largely conform to the modern boundary between Kazakhstan and Russia; the role of the Kereys in resisting its advancement, and defending what is seen as both Qazaq land and the realm of Islam, is clearly evident in these Kerey sources.[15]

The Kerey materials unequivocally depict their own nomadic community as a Muslim society possessing its own scholarly networks. They describe networks rooted in Central Asian cities, as well as scholarly institutions and networks in the Kerey encampments. Scholars who studied in Central Asian madrasas, specifically in Urgench, Bukhara and Samarqand, are frequently encountered in these accounts, and for the most part these figures form part of the political and military elite. While it could be countered that the frequent mention of scholars who studied in Central Asia may reveal a literary device typical of religious and genealogical hagiographies and oral sources, there is nothing particularly formulaic about the descriptions of these networks, and some of the accounts, such as the works of Qozhabergen-zhïrau, were passed down as manuscripts, indicating a textual tradition existing alongside an oral one. Furthermore, literary features typical of legendary sacred histories such as exist among the Siberian Tatars, and the Tatars and Bashkirs of the Volga-Ural region – including, for example the mention of famous Sufis and other major figures from the history of Islam, with distorted chronologies – are entirely lacking from the Kerey accounts. The contacts between historical figures in the Qazaq accounts are internally and chronologically consistent, and typically feature Sufi figures who are otherwise unknown. In other words, absent information to the contrary, there is no compelling reason to dismiss these accounts as ahistorical. Similarly, while it is not surprising that the published sources emphasise the connection of their ancestors with Qazaq statehood and place particular emphasis on the role of these ancestors in defending Qazaq sovereignty against Russian and Zunghar encroachments, there is no reason to doubt that the accounts of Maral Baba and Qozhabergen-zhïrau in particular contained these elements before Qazaq independence, that is,, before *c.*1470.

Qozhabergen-zhïrau

The central scholarly figure in the Kerey accounts is the *aqïn* (bard) and military commander Qozhabergen-zhïrau Tolïbayŭlï (1663–1762), a historical figure who served the Qazaq ruler Täuke Khan (r. *c.*1680–1718) as an advisor and military commander.[16] However, Kerey tradition – including Qozhabergen's own literary works – provides information on Qozhabergen's ancestors who had connections with Central Asian madrasas. Qozhabergen's father Tolïbay-sïnshï Däulenŭlï (1603–80) was a poet and military commander, as was Qozhabergen's grandfather Däulen Tauzarŭlï. Tolïbay, Däulen and Tauzar were all said to have been commanders 'in the three *zhüzes*', that is, in the unified Qazaq Khanate. Däulen is credited with being the first to compile the genealogy of the West Siberian Kereys. And Tolïbay-sïnshï is said to have commanded a joint military force of Qazaqs, Siberian Tatars, Bashkirs and Noghays against the Zunghars.[17]

While neither Däulen nor his son Tolïbay were scholars, the family had close connections with Islamic educational centres in Central Asia. Zhamal, the mother of Tolïbay-sïnshï, was the sister of the better-documented figure Zhalangtös-bahadur Seytqŭlŭlï (*c.*1580–1660), from the Törtqara people of the Älimŭlï division of the Junior Zhüz.[18] Zhalangtös (known in Persian and Turki sources as Yalangtush) ruled Samarqand and its surrounding towns during the late Shïbanid era, and is widely remembered for having built a number of structures in that city, including the well-known Shir-Dor and Tilla-Qari madrasas.[19]

This Kerey genealogy goes on to relate that because of his family's connections with these Central Asian cities Tolïbay-sïnshï sent eighteen of his twenty-four sons, including Qozhabergen, to study in madrasas in Urgench, Bukhara and Samarqand. According to the autobiographical sections of Qozhabergen's work *Elĭm-ay*, written in 1723, he studied in Samarqand for seven years, and then another two in Bukhara. He claimed to have completed his studies there, and to have become an imam by age seventeen, before taking up the *qobïz* (a type of Qazaq fiddle used in recitation of poetry and in healing rituals), and learning to be a poet and a singer.[20] Qozhabergen gained renown as a military commander, fighting the Zunghars from 1688 until 1710, and is closely associated with the Qazaq ruler Täuke Khan whom he served as an advisor. In particular, Qozhabergen is linked, at least in Kerey tradition, with the creation of Täuke Khan's law code, the *Zhetĭ Zharghï*, which only has come down to us in fragments but which formed the basis of the Qazaq customary law codes that Russian administrators compiled in the nineteenth century.[21] While Russian administrators typically sought to sequester Qazaq customary law from Islamic law, it should not be surprising that high-ranking Qazaqs such as Qozhabergen, who obtained educations in Central Asia, should have been influenced by Islamic legal thought in drafting the *Zhetĭ Zharghï*.[22]

There is also evidence that in the seventeenth century and early eighteenth there was a degree of Islamic education available in the Kerey encampments in Siberia. One of the commanders serving under Tolïbay-sïnshï, Zhänïbek-batïr Tölekŭlï, is said to have studied in a madrasa in Urgench. He was born near the modern-day village of Arkhangel'ka, in North Kazakhstan *oblast'* early in the seventeenth century and to have studied the Qur'ān and the hadiths. After serving in the wars against the Zunghars, he returned to his encampment and opened a school there. Similarly, Qara-biy Aldayŭlï, who was born in the second half of the seventeenth century, and is remembered as a student of Qozhanbergen-zhïrau's and as a warrior against the Zunghars, also studied in a madrasa in Urgench. He returned to the Ashamaylï Kereys after having fought the Zunghars and opened a school for children. He is remembered for having been an authoritative judge known for his sense of justice.[23] After the threat from the Zunghars had been parried Qozhabergen and his nephew Asqap Qarabasŭlï, who had also been educated in Central Asia, ordered the *biys*, commanders and warriors among the Kerey and Uaq tribes to build a school for every four encampments to train mullahs from among the young men in order to send them to madrasas in Central Asia.[24] It is unclear what the outcome of this initiative was, but a school in Qozhabergen's former encampment of Gültöbe bore the name Qozhabergen-Asqap madrasa, and was functioning in the first half of the nineteenth century.[25]

One of Qozhabergen's sons, Eset-batïr (1688–1772), is remembered as a military and political leader of the Siberian Tatars. He, too, according to Kerey tradition, studied in Samarqand, but like many of his kinsmen, his path to becoming a scholar was diverted by the need to fight the Zunghars. He is remembered in numerous poems for having commanded a combined force of Qazaqs, Bashkirs and Tatars against the Zunghars. According to these accounts, in 1746 Abïlay and Äbĭlmambet Khan, the ruler of the Middle Zhüz, responded to a request of the Siberian Tatars to send Eset-batïr to be their commander. The Tatar *biys* and *beks* bathed him in the milk of a white mare, dressed him in white clothing, raised him up on a piece of white felt and made him their military leader (*shora*), a position he held from 1746 until his death in 1772.[26]

The emphasis on Qozhabergen, and on his association with Täuke Khan, has parallels in the traditions of other Qazaq communities. Although there is some scant evidence in *khoja* genealogies on some figures active among the Qazaqs in the sixteenth century,[27] the first more-or-less detailed biographical information on Qazaq Islamic scholars dates precisely from Täuke Khan's reign, and associates these scholars with the *Zhetĭ Zharghï*. The figure most closely associated with the drafting of the law code was the Arghïn Änet Baba Kĭshĭkŭlï (1628–1723), who is remembered as 'the *biy's biy*' but also as an Islamic scholar educated in a madrasa in Bukhara.[28] The law code was announced soon after Täuke Khan's enthronement in 1680, at a gathering (*qŭrïltay*) at a place called Qŭltöbe near Türkistan. Another cycle of legends, from western Kazakhstan, tells about the election of a 'chief *pir* of the three *zhüzes*' at this gathering, and of a contest that took place between the three nominees from each of the *zhüzes*. Äyteke-biy, a leader of the Junior Zhüz, travelled to the madrasa of the chief *muftī* of Türkistan, Akhtan Sopï, to identify a candidate with sufficient holy qualities to become chief *pir*. There, with Akhtan Sopï's help, Äyteke identified a young man named Müsiräli (later known as Sopï Äziz) who went to the gathering with Äyteke, and prevailed in that contest.

Although Müsĭräli is remembered for the dramatic miracles he performed in the contest with his rivals, the accounts also emphasise Müsĭräli's status as an Islamic scholar. In addition to having been a student in a madrasa in Türkistan, he is remembered for administering a madrasa in the village of Shayan, along the lower Syr Darya, and his descendants constitute a long line of *ishans* active in Islamic education down through the Soviet period. He is the ancestor in a number of *khoja* lineages along the lower Syr Darya River and in Khorezm. In one account, the Zunghar ruler Galdan Tseren gave his daughter Maryam to Müsïräli, and from that union Qosïm-qozha, who succeeded Müsïräli as *pir* of the Junior Zhüz, was born in 1685.[29] His son Qosïm-qozha is remembered as a great scholar. He 'trained many students who spread religion in the central Qazaq steppe, along the Syr Darya, and in Qaraqalpaqstan'.[30]

These accounts reveal in explicit terms that the *bas pir* of the Qazaqs fulfilled a political role, or at least a politically symbolic role. The *bas pir* is remembered as both the chief religious figure of the united Qazaq Khanate, and the 'Chief Holy Figure to Täuke Khan' (*bas äzïret Täuke khangha*). The ceremony elevating Müsïräli to the rank of *bas pir*, in which Äyteke-biy raises him up on a piece of white felt, clearly mimics the accession ceremony of a khan to the throne, and perhaps suggests an equivalence between the legitimacy of the *khoja pir* and the Chingisid khan. The position of a chief *pir* as a political title is also attested for the late eighteenth century in Russian sources. In a document from 1785, in which Qazaqs from the Junior Zhüz petition Catherine II to keep the sons of the deposed khan Nūr-ᶜAlī away from the steppe, one of the signatories is ᶜAbd al-Jalīl-khwāja, who bears the title '*Qïrghïz yūrtīnïng pīrī*' in the Tatar document, which the Russian translator rendered as '*pir* of the entire Kirgiz-Kazakh people' (*pir vsego kirgiz-kazakhskago iurta*).[31]

Shaqshaq-biy Köshekŭlï

Shaqshaq-biy Köshekŭlï (1740–1832) was a prominent figure in narratives about Islamic education among the Ashaymalï Kereys, and more specifically in Qïzïlzhar (Petropavlovsk). He had studied in Samarqand, and he is remembered above all as a poet and a political leader in the first decades of the nineteenth century, when relations with the Russian state were particularly difficult. He is also remembered as local chieftain (*shora*) of the Kereys and Uaqs from about 1780 until 1819.[32] He opened a madrasa in Qïzïlzhar in 1767, which was attended by a number of Kerey scholars and poets who were to become prominent in the nineteenth century. These included the political leader Eseney Estemïsŭlï, the poet Segïz-Serï Bahramŭlï Shaqshaqov and the imam Tïlen-biy Montayŭlï.[33] Additionally, Shaqshaq is credited with founding a mosque in Qïzïlzhar, and these are the earliest references to such institutions in that city. It should not be surprising that these are not mentioned in Russian, or even Tatar sources, since at that period, before the establishment of the Orenburg Muslim Spiritual Assembly, such institutions, especially among the Qazaqs, fell outside of the scope of Russian legislation. How long the madrasa functioned is unclear, although in his description of the officially registered mosques and imams of Qïzïlzhar, compiled in 1919, the Muftī Galimjan Barudi does not mention any mosque existing in the city before the beginning of the nineteenth century.[34] The Kerey accounts recall Shaqshaq-biy as functioning essentially as a quasi-independent ruler, or at least a ruler who resisted Russian appropriation of Kerey lands in Siberia. The historical accuracy of such a depiction requires further investigation, although the biography of Shaqshaq-biy as it has come down to us suggests the continuity of political and religious authority among the Kereys in the period before the 1822 Speranskii reforms.

Eseney-biy Estemisŭlï

Typical of the association of political and religious authority is Eseney-biy Estemĭsŭlï (1798–1871), who was the subject of a biographical poem *Er Eseney* by Shaqshaq-biy's grandson, Segĭz-serĭ Bahramŭlï. He is remembered, like his ancestors, as a religious and political leader of the Ashaymalï Kereys, that is, as a *biy* and a *qāḍī*. He appears in Russian sources as Iseney Istimisov (or Istemesov). These Russian sources document his elevation to a number of positions within the administrative structure for the Siberian Qazaqs. He served as a *biy*, *starshina* and *zasedatel'* (Deputy Sultan) in the Kokchetav Outer District Office from 1834 to 1836 (where he served under the Senior Sultan Chingis Valikhanov), and a *volost' upravitel'* of the Siban-Kerey *volost'* (1842–53), as Senior Sultan of the Kushmurun Outer District Office (1853–9), and as councillor (*sovetnik*) to the Territorial Administration of the Siberian Qazaqs in Omsk (from May 1859), finally attaining the rank of major in 1860.[35] In specific versions of a Kerey tradition (published in independent Kazakhstan), however, he is remembered less for his service to the Russian Empire than for his resistance to it, at least before 1824.

Eseney was from a prominent lineage of the Siban Kereys. His great-grandfather was Aqpanbet and his grandfather was Seyĭt.[36] Seyĭt is said to have gone with his son Estemis on the hajj, and to have enjoyed friendly relations with Central Asian merchants in Qïzïlzhar and Omsk. His sons Estemĭs and Esĭrkep studied in Qïzïlzhar at Shaqshaq-biy's madrasa, and later in Urgench, evidently thanks to Seyĭt's Central Asian connections. Both sons studied well there, and, upon their return, Esĭrkep became an instructor in Shaqshaq-biy's madrasa, while Estemĭs gained renown as a wrestler and became *biy* of the Siban Kereys. Estemĭs's sons Eseney and Esenkeldĭ also studied in the Shaqshaq madrasa, and later went to Urgench, where they studied in the same madrasa as their father and uncle had before them. Eseney graduated from one of the Urgench madrasas in 1815, and upon returning home became a *murīd* of the Kerey Sufi leader Maral-ishan Qŭrmanŭlï (who will be discussed in more detail below). At some point before 1820 Eseney joined Maral-ishan's military resistance (*ghazauat*) to the Russians and soon became one of Maral-ishan's commanders. In 1819 Eseney succeeded Shaqshaq-biy as *shora.* He was proclaimed *shora* at a gathering at Qaq Kölĭ attended by prominent figures from the Kerey, Uaq, Atïghay and Qarauïl people, where Eseney was dressed in white and raised up on a piece of white felt, a clear reference to the Chingisid enthronement ceremony. The gathering was also attended by Tatar notables from Kurgan, Tiumen' and Qïzïlzhar. As *shora,* Eseney continued to support Maral-ishan by collecting horses for his troops.[37]

Kerey tradition also emphasises Eseney's substantial religious authority. The Kerey poet Zhanaq Qambarŭlï (1760–1857) praised him for his efforts as *shora* to spread to Islamic faith, including opening mosques and madrasas, and remarked that 'the Islamic faith was like a fortress to him'. He was also said to have had a hundred *murids.*[38] In 1823, evidently in connection with Qazaq resistance led by Eseney and Maral-ishan to the advancement of the Cossack *Gor'kaia Liniia* fortified line deeper into the Qazaq steppe, the chiefs of Qïzïlzhar province, Shaqshaq Köshekŭlï, Tĭlenshĭ Tangbayŭlï, Kiyĭkbay Aytughanŭlï, Toqsan Zhabayŭlï, Itĭke Zhandosŭlï, Mamanay Sardarbekŭlï and Qoldas Sandïqŭlï convened a meeting (*qŭrïltay*) where they decided to elect Eseney as chief of the Ashamaylï Kereys. Following his election, Eseney served as a *biy* and *qāḍī*, resolving disputes on the basis of the *sharīᶜa.* According to a poem by Shong Däuletŭlï, the Russian governors of West Siberia refused to recognise Eseney as the chief and *qāḍī* of the Sïban Kereys, and instead only were willing to grant him the title of imam. The Kereys replied:

> We are a Muslim people who submit to our *āqsāqāls*, muftis, *qāḍīs*, *shoras*, and khans, and who worship God. We don't pay any tax. We only agree to pay the smoke-hole tax in the amount that was paid during the time of Uali Khan.[39] We will unite and take up the former *ghazauat* of Maral-ishan.[40]

Maral-ishan Qŭrmanŭlï

Maral-ishan Qŭrmanŭlï (1780–1841) was a Kerey Islamic scholar, Sufi, and military leader who features in a number of traditions among Qazaqs in northern Kazakhstan, as well as in communities along the lower Syr Darya River, where he settled after fleeing Siberia, and where his descendants became prominent religious leaders in their own right.[41] He appears in Russian documentary sources, thanks to his armed resistance to Russian encroachment on Kerey lands in Siberia. The role of his religious authority in the Kerey's resistance to Russian authority appears to have completely excluded him from consideration in the politically convoluted Soviet studies of Qazaq resistance to Russia.[42] In Qazaq tradition, he is remembered as a *pir,* an Islamic scholar and a saint. As with Eseney-biy Estemïsŭlï, Qazaq traditions about Maral Ishan reveal in particular detail the social and political role of Islamic scholars in the Qazaq khanate.

Russian sources on Maral-ishan, while contemporary, are somewhat contradictory with respect to biographical information, and the Qazaq sources, while containing extensive hagiographical elements, appear generally consistent regarding the basic biographical facts, in particular with respect to the genealogies of his ancestors and descendants.[43] In general, furthermore, we find that the two bodies of sources agree on a number of details. In Qazaq tradition Maral Qŭrmanŭlï was born in 1780 into the Nŭrïmbet people in a place called Qayranköl, subsequently named Äuliyeköl (Saint's Lake) after him, located in modern-day Qostanay province. Like Qosïm-qozha, the son of the *pir* Müsïräli, Maral-ishan, was said to be the grandson of the Zunghar khan Galdan Tseren. His future religious authority was foretold in 1743 by Galdan Tseren's wife. Two years before, the Zunghar khan had captured Abïlay Khan, the future khan of the Middle Zhüz.[44] He then, however, decided to free Abïlay and return him to his people, together with thirty-five other Qazaq prisoners, including his own two daughters and his Qazaq wife. The girls' mother predicted to Abïlay that the first daughter would give birth to a hero, and the second one to a saint. When he returned to his people, Abïlay married the first daughter, and gave the second one to his healer, Qŭrman. Abïlay's wife gave birth to Qasïm-sultan, the father of Kenesarï (Kenesary Kasimov, in Russian sources), and Qŭrman's wife, named Fatima, gave birth to Maral.[45]

In 1793, Maral had a dream in which a Sufi named Zhalangayaq-ishan told him to come and find him. Maral and his mother set off there, and when they ran out of money, they took employment with a wealthy man named Qŭlanbay-ishan. Qŭlanbay, we read, soon recognises Maral's sacred powers, and offers his daughter Menglïbike to Maral. Maral insists on fulfilling his mission to find Zhalangayaq-ishan, and Qŭlanbay pledges his daughter to Maral upon his return. He finally finds Zhalangayaq-ishan, who maintains a mosque and a madrasa in a cave located between Bukhara and Kattaqurghan, and he becomes his student. Among the miracles attributed to Maral were those related to his military prowess, including leading his fellow *murids* in battle against enemies seeking to attack Zhalangayaq-ishan's madrasa.[46]

In 1810, Maral returned to his people near Qïzïlzhar, and began 'preaching Islam'. It is said he was elected chief *muftī* (*bas muftisï*) for the Muslims of western Siberia, and gained a following not only among Qazaqs, but among Tatars, Bashkirs and Central Asians as well.[47] Russian sources tell a slightly different story – that he was a healer among his people near Presnogorskaia Krepost', near Qïzïlzhar, and in 1803 or 1806 he and his family went to Shahrisabz, 'near Bukhara', where he studied with a Sufi named Kul'-Mukhammad (according to the Russian spelling). It appears that in the Emirate of Bukhara Maral-ishan used the name Isa, and wrote appeals using the name 'Isa-khazret'. Russian officials became alarmed when Maral began calling for the resurrection of the Qazaq Khanate and for the unification of Muslims in Siberia, Bashkiria and Khorezm against Russian encroachments. Maral and his followers were involved in raiding Russian settlements and other forms of armed resistance, activities that other scholars and political leaders, such as Eseney-biy Estemïsŭlï also supported, at least materially.[48]

Maral-ishan's activities alarmed Russian officials along the steppe, who tasked loyal Qazaqs with capturing him. Maral-ishan and his supporters were forced south, to the Torghay region. The Polish traveller Jan Witkiewicz related how he met an Orenburg Tatar in Bukhara who had deserted from the army in St Petersburg, fled to Troitsk and eventually stayed in Maral-ishan's encampment, along with several other Tatar deserters. Eventually, Maral-ishan was forced to flee to Qazaq communities along the Syr Darya River, who sought his protection against Khivan forces.[49] Later, after the Russian construction of fortresses in Turgai and Irgiz, Maral-ishan settled in the village of Qarmaqshï, where he became known as Maral Baba and where his descendants continued to function as *ishans* well into the Soviet era. Elders in Qarmaqshï related that in 1954 a Chechen scholar named Abdulkhamit came to Qarmaqshï to meet with Maral's great-grandson, Ämit-ishan, himself a scholar. Abdulkhamit claimed to have known of Maral-ishan when he was studying in Egypt, and recognised Maral-ishan as the founder of holy war (*ghazauat*) in Kazakhstan.[50]

Kerey Scholarly Networks and Institutions

The accounts are explicit about the connections between Qozhabergen's family and madrasas in a number of Central Asian cities. For example, his paternal grandmother Aqbïlek, the daughter of Aydabol-biy, a leader among the Süyïndïk Arghïns, was also the aunt of Zhalangtös-bahadur Seytqŭlŭlï, and in the Kerey traditions Aqbïlek is also remembered as a patron of madrasa construction in Samarqand.[51]

As we saw above, Tolïbay-sïnshï Däulenŭlï sent eighteen of his sons, including Qozhabergen, to study in Urgench, Bukhara and Samarqand, where they studied alongside the sons of Zhalangtös-batïr. Together with his nephew, Asqap-shora Qarabasŭlï, who succeeded Qozhabergen as military commander of the Kerey and Uaq peoples, Qozhabergen and Asqap decreed that every four encampments (*auïls*) should establish a mosque and a madrasa to train young men and send them to cities in the Khanate of Bukhara.[52] It is unclear how many mosques and madrasas were built, but it appears that the madrasa in Qozhabergen's encampment of Gültöbe, known as the Qozhabergen-Asqap madrasa, functioned at least into the 1820s. The poet Salghara Zhankïsïŭlï (1758–1859) studied there, and later went to Urgench to continue his studies, after which he became an imam and a madrasa instructor among the Kereys.[53] Qozhabergen's son Eset-batïr also studied in Samarqand, but had to cut his studies short to fight the Zunghars.[54] The grandson of Asqap-batïr, Shaqshaq-batïr Köshekŭlï, studied in Samarqand and became a talented poet. As noted above, he founded the Shaqshaq madrasa in Qïzïlzhar in 1767. He also went on the hajj. How long this madrasa functioned is not clear, since it is mentioned neither in Russian sources nor in Tatar sources on the history of Qïzïlzhar.

Other Kereys obtained learning in Central Asia. Zhänibek-batïr Tölekŭlï, who was born at the beginning of the seventeenth century near Qïzïlzhar, was one of Tolïbay-sïnshï's commanders. He studied in a madrasa in Urgench, and became an instructor to children after he returned. Another was Qara-biy, for whom we have no dates, but whose son Zhabay served as a warrior under Abïlay Khan. He is remembered as a famous *biy* who had studied in Urgench. A prominent poet named Tïlen-biy Montayŭlï (b. 1771) studied initially in the Shaqshaq madrasa, and later went to Samarqand. After graduating he returned to his *awïl* and opened a school there to teach children. He is remembered as a *qāḍī* who settled disputes on the basis of the *sharīᶜa*.[55]

Eseney Estemïsŭlï's family comprised a number of prominent religious and military leaders among the Kereys. Estemes and his father Seyït went on the hajj together, probably in the latter half of the eighteenth century.

Estemes and his brother Esïrkep first studied under a local mullah named Qazhïm, and then went to the Shaqshaq madrasa. Seyït travelled frequently to Omsk and Qïzïlzhar, and as a result made contacts with merchants from Bukhara, Khorezm and Khoqand. The brothers then went to Urgench to continue their studies. Esïrkep became a mullah and when he returned home, he became an instructor in the Shaqshaq madrasa, while Estemes gained renown as a wrestler and military commander.[56]

Estemes' sons Eseney and Esenkeldï followed the same path as their father. They studied with a local mullah, and then went to the Shaqshaq madrasa, and then to the same madrasa in Urgench that their father had attended. There they studied Arabic, Persian and Chaghatay, and in Qïzïlzhar they learned Tatar and Russian. Eseney graduated from the madrasa in Urgench in 1815 and became a *murid* to Maral-ishan, taking an active part in his *ghazauat* against the Russians in 1818 and 1819. Later he was elected Chief Muftī (*bas muftïsï*) of Western Siberia by Qazaqs, Tatars and Bashkirs.

Two figures who were prominent instructors in the Balatnay madrasa, founded in the present-day settlement of Novo-Rybinka evidently after 1822, were the imams Körpesh Bahramŭlï (1799–1851) and Imamghabit Ïrghïzbekŭlï (dates unknown), both of whom studied in Bukhara. They were said to have been keen legal scholars who have possessed the qualities of other khojas, mullahs, imams and Sufis. In addition, they excelled in skills particularly prized by Qazaqs, such as playing the dombra, wrestling and falconry.[57] Kerey scholarly networks were not restricted to Central Asia, but extended to the Volga-Ural region as well. A warrior named Iteke-batïr Zhandosŭlï (1759–1831) studied initially from a local mullah, and then went to Kazan to continue his studies.[58]

Islamic Law among the Kereys

In dividing *sharīᶜa* and *ᶜādat* into separate legal systems, Russian colonial officials, and many historians who rely on colonial sources, have divided *ᶜādat* judges (*biys*) and *sharīᶜa* judges (*qāḍīs*). The Kerey materials provide a corrective to such prescriptive accounts of Qazaq law, demonstrating that *biy* and *qāḍīs* before 1822 were often one and the same – and we know this was often the case after 1822 as well. Rather than emphasising titles, the Kerey sources focus instead on the function of individuals as judges. As further evidence of the flexibility of Qazaq nomenclature it is worth remembering that some groups of Qazaqs, for example, those on the Mangyshlak Peninsula under Khivan rule, lacked the title of *qāḍī* as such altogether, and Islamic law was administered by hereditary *ishans* who effectively filled the role that *qāḍīs* performed elsewhere on the steppe.[59]

The close relationship between *sharīᶜa* and *ᶜādat* would not come as a surprise to students of customary law in the Islamic tradition, and in fact the close relationship was even noted by some Russian officials, most notably d'Andre's report on Qazaq customary law from 1849 (a report that was only published almost exactly a century after it was compiled).[60] Historians of Muslim nomadic customary law, generally unfamiliar with Islamic history, do admit a degree of overlap between the two legal systems, but have generally flinched from engaging in a sustained comparison between the two, possibly intimidated by the prospect of engaging with the sources of Islamic law.[61] While steps have been made in this direction, at least among some Qazaq scholars, another approach would be to examine the biographies of *biys* and their relationship to Islamic legal studies.

The Kerey biographical materials, in fact, demonstrate that Qazaqs themselves obscured, or perhaps did not necessarily distinguish between customary law and Islamic law. It is typical in Russian accounts for *biys* to be identified as the representatives of indigenous 'shamanistic' Qazaq legal culture, with *qāḍīs* depicted by contrast as bearers of the supposedly 'foreign' *sharīᶜa*. The Kerey sources indicate quite clearly that in the Qazaq Khanate – and indeed after 1822 also – Qazaqs understood *qāḍīs* and *biys* to be one and the same. We have seen how an eighteenth-century poem by Qozhabergen-zhïrau identified his ancestor Tanash-biy as a 'just *qāḍī*' from the time of Özbek Khan. Even if we doubt the historicity of this claim, it demonstrates that such an association existed in the first half of the eighteenth century. We have the same epithet of 'just *qāḍī*' used for another prominent Kerey *biy* from the early nineteenth century, Qozhaghul-biy Bertĭsŭlï.[62] Similarly, prominent *biys* such as Shaqshaq-biy Kösheŭlï and Eseney Estemĭsŭlï were educated in Central Asian madrasas. We can also mention Qara-biy Aldayŭlï, born in the second half of the seventeenth century who was a student of Qozhabergen-zhïrau. He had studied in a madrasa in Urgench, and is remembered as a particularly famous *biy*.

The association of the positions of *biy* and *qāḍī* in Qazaq sources extended into the era of Russian administration. Eseney Estemĭsŭlï held a number of official positions as the Russian-appointed *biy* of various Kerey communities from 1824 to 1842.[63] Eseney is remembered for deciding cases on the basis of the *sharīᶜa*, as was the Samarqand-trained *biy* Tĭlen-biy Montayŭlï. The conflation of *biys* and *qāḍīs*, and their ability to rule on the basis of either *sharīᶜa* or *ᶜādat*, is even more widely documented for the period after 1822. This is perhaps most evident in d'Andre's report, for which his main sources on *ᶜādat* are *biys* who also bore the title of *qāḍī*.[64]

That *biys* could possess at times a high degree of Islamic education is also evident outside of the Kerey sources. Bayghara-biy Quttïbayŭlï (1699–1775), a leader among the Naymans in the Ayagöz region, in eastern Kazakhstan, was said to have studied under a prominent Sufi, Ghabdïlgani Äzizi, a Naqshbandi Sufi shaykh and imam in Türkistan. Bayghara's son, Aqtaylaq-biy (1720–1816), is remembered among the Qazaqs of the Middle Zhüz as a 'just *qāḍī*'.[65] Similarly, Qŭnanbay Öskenbayŭlï, the father of Abay Qŭnanbayŭlï (Abai Kunanbaev in Russian sources), who often appears in Russian sources as the quintessential powerful Qazaq *biy*, was evidently closely familiar with Islamic law, which he applied to resolving disputes. The Polish exile Adolph Januszkiewicz, who met Qŭnanbay and left us an important memoir of the Qazaq Steppe in the 1830s, remarked that people would constantly come to Qŭnanbay, and that every third phrase in the advice he gave was a Qurʾānic quotation.[66]

Islamic Scholars in Qazaq Society

The Kerey sources for the period before the 1830s demonstrate that Islamic scholars were engaged in wider aspects of social engagement beyond discussing and administering Islamic law. Tatar – and to a lesser extent Qazaq – biographical dictionaries from the late nineteenth century and twentieth generally present a somewhat intellectualised depiction of Islamic scholars, focusing above all on their Islamic scholarship and their scholarly credentials as jurists, theologians, grammarians and so forth. The Kerey traditions, however, to a large degree were not recorded by scholars, and if they provide little information on their scholarly networks and writings, which are the stock-in-trade of the later biographical dictionaries, they provide rich detail on their subjects' social roles, which appear to have changed over the course of the nineteenth century as Russia exercised increasing bureaucratic control over Qazaq law and political and religious life.

For the period before 1822 the Qazaq sources above all emphasise the role of the *ᶜulamāʾ* as political and military leaders of their communities. Like the khans, religious leaders, whether as 'chief *pirs*' or *muftī*s, were elevated on white felt during their appointment ceremonies. Many Kerey scholars were warriors and military commanders. These included most notably Qozhabergen-zhïrau, Eseney Estemïsŭlï and Maral-ishan, as well as a large number of less prominent figures. While the Kerey sources emphasise the origins of the scholars in the Kerey community as 'commoners' (*qara khalïq*), we also find genealogical connections to powerful political figures, most notably to the non-Muslim khan of the Zunghars Galdan Tseren, who, as we say above, is identified as Maral-ishan's grandfather. Such a linking of religious and political/military authority is evident among *khojas* as well, where, as we have seen, in the traditions of the Junior Zhüz, Müsïräli Sopï married his son Qosïm, the founder of a prominent *khoja* lineage along the lower Syr Darya River, to a daughter of Galdan-Tseren.

Similarly, Islamic education in the nomadic milieu appears to have involved more than studying religious texts of Islamic law. The accounts make frequent mention of madrasa instructors who excelled in other topics, such as falconry, music, wrestling and, above all, poetry. We have seen how Estemïs Eseneyŭlï is remembered as a famous wrestler, as were the madrasa instructors Körpesh Bahramŭlï and Imamghabit Ïrghïzbekŭlï. Qozhabergen-zhïrau himself as well as many of his nineteenth-century descendants were wrestlers as well. Biographical sources from the Qazaq Steppe are rich with instances of scholars famed as wrestlers. Along the lower Syr Darya this is true of many *ishans*. Äbdïsadïq-ishan (b. 1848) was a graduate of a Bukharan madrasa, and he is remembered for defeating the Emir's champion there. During the Soviet period Üseyïn-maghzŭm (1885–1964) was remembered as a great poet, hunter and wrestler, skills he reportedly obtained from his father Ayqozha, the founder of an important *ishan* dynasty in the Qïzïlorda region.[67] Äliyasqar Aytqozhaŭlï, an imam in Kökshetau (d., 1937) was a wrestler and came from a family of wrestlers. His father was remembered as a champion who once overcame a bear, and Äliyasqar used to wrestle with his students.[68] A nineteenth-century Tatar mullah in Semey (Semipalatinsk), Daulī Pahlawān, was remembered for having wrestled before the Tsar in St Petersburg, and for defeating the Russian champion. He also wrestled before the Emir in Bukhara and the Ottoman Sultan in Istanbul.[69]

The *mudarrises* Körpesh Bahramŭlï and Imamghabit Ïrghïzbekŭlï provide a good example of the range of topics Kerey scholars could teach their students. At the same time, it appears they attracted the ire of *khojas* and other Islamic scholars. In a Kerey genealogical treatise we read:

> Imamghabit and Körpesh had both studied in Bukhara, and they had many of the qualities of other *khojas*, mullahs, imams, and Sufis. Because they were also men with practical skills, they taught their students arithmetic, checkers, *qŭmalaq* [a type of divination], as well as the *dombra*, *sïbïzghï* [a type of flute], and the *qobïz*, in addition to writing songs, composing verse, and making riddles. Because of these activities some of the Tatar and Qazaq notables, mullahs, imams, and *khojas* did not like them.[70]

One of their students in the 1830s was the poet and singer Shärke-sal (Shärip) Qorabayŭlï (1824–1907), who studied Arabic Persian, and Turki, but also falconry (*qŭsbegilik*), archery and musical instruments. He travelled to Kazan where he made a name as a wrestler, performing feats of strength and defeating Russian opponents. He also obtained great honour by besting a Tatar mullah in an improvised poetry competition (*aytïs*).[71] Whether Shärke-sal (the epithet *sal* signifies his reputation as a poet and singer) can be considered a legal scholar is unclear, since the sources only indicate he had obtained a madrasa education, and emphasise a whole different body of skills. Nevertheless, the Kerey sources show the strong connection between Islamic education and the *ᶜulamāʾ* and Qazaq oral literature.

The connection between Qazaq oral literature and Islamic education has generally been obscured in studies of Qazaq literature. Like Qazaq 'customary law', outside observers have tended to depict Qazaq oral epics in strongly romantic terms, depicting it as an indigenous 'folk' art, fundamentally democratic in its origins and embodying the 'pure' culture of the nomads, and not that of the more-or-less foreign urban elites. This is evident among the pre-Revolutionary collectors and critics of Qazaq oral literature. Nikolai Katanov, for example, in his reviews of Arabic-script Qazaq poetry in mass-market Islamic book publishing at the turn of the nineteenth and twentieth centuries frequently commented on the linguistic 'pollution' of Tatar forms and Arabic spellings in these works, which he felt were inauthentic.[72] During the Soviet era, oral epics of Qazaq and other Turkic peoples were depicted as 'democratic' popular art. Soviet publications emphasised epics as historical literary works, and their performers and composers were separated from 'foreign' high culture. Both approaches reveal the view that Islamic education, and Islam itself, were foreign elements in Qazaq culture.

An examination of the Kerey materials, and of biographies of later Qazaq literary figures, demonstrates a close connection between madrasa education – especially Central Asian madrasa education – and Qazaq oral literature performers (*aqïns*). In one respect, it is natural that the Kerey materials would emphasise the literary legacy of their madrasa-trained ancestors, since much of what we know about them comes from their poetry. These figures were memorialised not by Islamic scholars, but by their descendants who were more likely to be exposed to literature than to Islamic scholarship. Nevertheless, despite the 'secularisation' of the transmitters of these traditions, the religious connections are remembered and are important elements of their ancestors' authority as leaders and artists.

The Kerey genealogical materials can be described as collections of literary biographies and biographies of the *ᶜulamāʾ*, particularly since all of the major scholarly figures are remembered above all as poets and performers. This is true for Qozhabergen-zhïrau and Shaqshaq-batïr Köshekŭlï, as well as for later figures, such as Niyaz-serĭ Bekdäuletŭlï (1818–93), who was trained in madrasas in the 'religious sciences' and was both a madrasa instructor in Western Siberia and a well-known poet, and Shaqshaq-batïr's grandson Segĭz-serĭ Bahramŭlï (1818–54) and his descendants.[73]

It is precisely the link between Islamic education and literary prominence that makes the Kerey genealogical and biographical materials such rich sources for the history of the Qazaq *ᶜulamāʾ*. The connection between literature and Islamic scholarship was not restricted to the Kereys, but is found throughout the Qazaq Steppe, particularly in the nineteenth and twentieth centuries. Among the most prominent poets/religious scholars we can point to the Arghïn poet, folklorist and religious scholar Mäshhür-Zhüsĭp Köpeyŭlï (1857–1931), who was trained in Bayanaul and Bukhara; Äbubäkĭr Shoqanŭlï Kerderĭ (1858–1912), who studied in Orenburg and Troitsk; the Chingisid poet Shädĭ Zhängĭrov (1855–1933), who studied in the Shayan madrasa, along the Syr Darya and then in Bukhara and Tashkent; and Oraz-molda Zhüsĭpŭlï (1814–68), who studied in Bukhara and Baghdad. In discussing the connections of these authors with their Islamic education, literary historians in Kazakhstan point out that 'oriental literature' was an academic focus for these madrasa students. Oraz-molda Zhüsĭpŭlï, for example, translated Ferdowsi's *Shahnama* into Qazaq. Shädĭ Zhängĭrov studied Persian classical literature extensively, which had a profound effect on his own works.The same can be said of Soviet-era figures, like Äbdĭrayïm Baytŭrsïnov (1897–1959) who studied in Bukhara. Similarly, Tŭrmaghanbet Ĭztĭleuov (1882–1939) began studying in Bukhara in 1899 and became strongly influenced by Persian literature, producing Qazaq versions of various classical Persian works. In 1934 he attended the first Congress of the Qazaq Union of Writers and subsequently joined the Communist Party.[74] Tatar and Bashkir scholars also contributed to Qazaq literature. Mullā Kashshāf ad-Dīn b. Shāh-i Mardān al-Manzalawī al-Qarqarālī was a student of Shihāb ad-Dīn Marjānī in Kazan, and he published a number of Qazaq verse works devoted, among other things, to a retelling of the battles of the Prophet Muhammad.[75]

Conclusion

The Kerey biographical and genealogical materials should encourage historians to re-evaluate much that has been previously written about

Islamic institutions and the *ᶜulamāʾ* among Muslim nomads, particularly for the period before 1822. Far from being passive recipients of Islamic learning coming from outside the community, Kereys participated directly in scholarly networks linking the West Siberian Steppe with the major centres of learning in Central Asia, especially with Khorezm, but with Mawarannahr as well. In addition, by the end of the eighteenth century they had established educational institutions in their encampments and in Qïzïlzhar where Kereys could obtain sufficient education to enable them to travel to Central Asia to engage in more advanced studies.

The Kerey narratives also offer us a much different picture of the Qazaq *ᶜulamāʾ* from what we have for the later, better documented, period starting in the second half of the nineteenth century. At that time the Qazaq *ᶜulamāʾ* on the northern steppe operated within the confines of Russian administrative policies, and Qazaq scholarly networks were linked above all with Tatar and Bashkir scholarly centres in the major Muslim cities of the steppe, such as Semey, Qïzïlzhar, Orenburg and, above all, Troitsk.[76] However, before 1822 – before the social, political and economic transformations brought about by direct Russian rule – we are able to see to what degree Russian rule restricted the social and political role that the nomadic Qazaq *ᶜulamāʾ* had played. We also are able to see how substantially these roles remained in place under Russian rule, and how the maintenance of these roles distinguished the social role of the Qazaq *ᶜulamāʾ* from that of its Tatar and Central Asian neighbours during the Imperial Russian and Soviet eras.

It is clear from the Kerey sources that their *ᶜulamāʾ* formed part of the nomadic elite. This is evident from their role as *qāḍīs* and *biys,* the association of early figures with the drafting of the *Zhetĭ Zharghï* law code of Täuke Khan and their role as military commanders.

The Kereys remember their greatest scholars also as their greatest warriors. While we have numerous accounts of Kerey warriors who perhaps happened to study in madrasas, but are remembered almost exclusively for their military careers, others are remembered no less for one role as for the other.[77] These include above all Qozhabergen-zhïrau, but also Maralishan, the founder of an important Ishan dynasty in southern Kazakhstan, and Eseney Estemĭsŭlï, and their role as military commanders – a role that we find attributed to members of the *ᶜulamāʾ* and prominent Sufis and *khojas* also in the other successor states of the Golden Horde, including among the nomadic Uzbeks, and in the Kazan Khanate, as well as in Siberian legends of Islamisation.[78]

Those with access to Islamic education earned prestige as legal scholars, but formal training in other arts, such as literature, music and even sports comprised forms of Islamic learning, to the degree they were taught by madrasa instructors, and are remembered as part of an individual's academic 'transcript'. This feature also characterises much of the Qazaq biographical material for the later era; however, in the case of the Kereys, there is a particularly full picture for the earlier period, particularly from the period spanning the eighteenth century through the early twentieth, when it is widely reported in both Russian and Qazaq historiography that Qazaqs were almost completely lacking Islamic scholars. These materials should encourage historians to look more closely at the range of Qazaq biographical and literary sources for the history of the Qazaq *ᶜulamāᵓ*. Above all they should encourage historians to look at Qazaq nomads on their own terms, as a clearly self-aware Muslim society.

Notes

1. See, for example, A. L. Saliev, 'O Vliianii musul'man-tatar na sudoproizvodstvo kochevykh narodov Turkestana (1865–1917) (po arkhivnym, pravovym i inym materialam)', *Vestnik Kyrgyzsko-Russkogo Slavianskogo Universiteta* 14:11 (2014), pp. 73–7. The writings of Chokan Valikhanov from the mid-nineteenth century have perhaps contributed most to the continued distortions in the historiography of Islam among the Qazaqs; see his 'Sledy shamanstva u kirgizov', 'O musul'manstve v stepi', and 'Zapiska o sudebnoi reforme', in Ch. Ch. Valikhanov, *Sobranie sochinenii v piati tomakh* (5 vols) (Alma-Ata: Glavnaia redaktsiia Kazakhskoi Sovetskoi Entsiklopedii, 1985), vol. IV, pp. 48–70, 71–5, 77–104.
2. B. Daulbaev, 'Razskaz o zhizni Kirgiz Nikolaevskago uezda Turgaiskoi oblasti s 1830 po 1880 god', *Zapiski Orenburgskago otdela imperatorskago russkago geograficheskago obshchestva* 4 (1881), pp. 102–3; Khadzhi Mukhamed-Salikh Babadzhanov, 'Zametka kirgiza o kirgizakh', *Severnaia Pchela* 4 (5 January 1861), p. 13.
3. A. J. Frank, 'Sufis, Scholars and *Divanas* of the Qazaq Middle Horde in the Works of Mäshhür Zhüsip Köpeyulï', in N. Pianciola and P. Sartori (eds). *Islam, Society and States across the Qazaq Steppe (18th–Early 20th Centuries)* (Vienna: Austrian Academy of Sciences, 2013), p. 219; S. Ghïlmani, *Biographies of the Islamic Scholars of Our Time* II, eds A. Muminov et al. (Istanbul: IRCICA, 2018), p. 189.
4. For example, in the western Qazaq Steppe the Sheктї scholar Qarazhïgït had emerged as an opponent of the Orenburg *muftī* and as an adviser to Arïnghāzī Khan in the late eighteenth century; see Z. Baydosŭlï, *Qarazhïgït* (Aqtöbe: A-Poligrafiia, 2008), pp. 23–6.
5. B. Keller-Heinkele, 'Crimean Tatar and Nogay Scholars in the 18th Century', in M. Kemper et al. (eds), *Muslim Culture in Russia and Central Asia from the 18th to the Early 20th Centuries* (Berlin: Klaus Schwarz Verlag, 1996),

vol. 1, pp. 279–96; Prince de Gouroff, *Des tatars-nogais dans le midi de la Russie européenne* (Khar'kov: n.p., 1816), pp. 72, 115.

6. These works include M. Mukanov, *Iz istoricheskogo proshlogo (rodoslovnaia plemen kerei i uak)* (Almaty: Qazaqstan, 1998); B. Tŭrgharayev (ed.), *Qozhabergen zhïrau (shïgharma zhinaghï)* (Petropavl: n.p., 2010); S. Zhŭmabayev and K. Zhalmaqanov, *Bĭrzhannïng belgĭsĭz ghŭmïrï – Nŭralï shezhĭresĭ* (Petropavl: n.p., 2009); S. Zhŭmabayev, *Ŭlïlar tughan ölke* (Petropavl: n.p., 2006); T. Sügĭrbayev, *Qïzïlzhar öngĭrĭnĭng ziyalï qauïmï,* (Petropavl: n.p., 2010); Qozhabergen-zhïrau, *Elĭm-ay*, ed. B. Tŭrgharayev (Petropavl: n.p., 2008); S. A. Kasimov (ed.), *Soltüstĭk Kazakhstan Qazaqstan öngĭrĭndegĭ täuelsĭzdĭk üshĭn küres tarikhï* (Almaty: Qazaq Entsiklopediyasï, 2010); B. Tŭrgharayev (ed.), *Eseney estelĭgĭ* (Petropavl: n.p., 2010).
7. The most extensive Qazaq biographical dictionaries of scholars date from the early and mid-twentieth century; see Qurban-'Ali Khalidi, *An Islamic Biographical Dictionary of the Eastern Kazakh Steppe, 1770–1912*, eds A. Frank and M. Usmanov (Leiden: Brill, 2005); S. Ghïlmani, *Biographies.*
8. For elaborations of Ashamaylï Kerey genealogies, see M. Mukanov, *Iz istoricheskogo proshlogo*; S. Zhŭmabayev and K. Zhalmaqanov, *Bĭrzhannïng belgĭsĭz ghŭmïrï*; G. Zhüsĭpŭlï, *Bäyimbet Batïr ĭzĭmen*, (Almaty, n.p., 2015), pp. 141–60.
9. Naurïzkhan appears as Naurïzbay in some genealogies, and he is also the father of Abaq, the ancestor of the Abaq Kereys. For Abaq Kerey genealogies see *Shezhĭrelĭk dastandar* (*Babalar sözĭ*, vol. 32) (Almaty: Foliant, 2006), pp. 359–72; H. Altay, *Eselĭkterĭm* (Istanbul: n.p., 1980), pp. 11–12.
10. S. Zhŭmabayev and K. Zhalmaqanov, *Bĭrzhannïng belgĭsĭz ghŭmïrï,* pp. 116–20.
11. S. Zhŭmabayev, *Ŭlïlar tughan ölke*, pp. 29–30; S. Zhŭmabayev and K. Zhalmaqanov, *Bĭrzhannïng belgĭsĭz ghŭmïrï,* pp. 116–17.
12. Beket Tŭrgharayev (ed.), *Qozhabergen zhïrau*, pp. 274–5.
13. Qozhabergen-zhïrau, *Elĭm-ay,* p. 7.
14. Beket Tŭrgharayev (ed.), *Qozhabergen zhïrau,* p. 5; S. Zhŭmabayev and K. Zhalmaqanov, *Bĭrzhannïng belgĭsĭz ghumïrï,* p. 154; S. Zhŭmabayev, *Ŭlïlar tughan ölke*, pp. 272, 277, 297, 370, 372; Sügĭrbayev, *Qïzïlzhar öngĭrĭnĭng ziyalï qauïmï,* pp. 107, 191.
15. This is particularly evident in recent scholarship; cf. the collection of articles in S. A. Kasimov (ed.), *Soltüstĭk Qazaqstan.*
16. On the appearance of Qozhabergen in documentary sources cf. G. K. Mukanova, 'Kitaiskie istochniki o Kozhabergen-batyre', *Soltüstik Qazaqstan*, pp. 444–7.
17. S. Zhŭmabayev, *Ŭlïlar tughan ölke*, p. 272.
18. In Russian sources he is known as Yalangtush-biy.
19. Zhalangtös ruled under the title of *atalïq,* nominally under the authority of the Khan of Bukhara, but in effect independently, cf. V. V. Bartol'd, *Sochineniia* II/1, ed. Iu. Bregel' (Moscow: Nauka, 1963), pp. 270–1; *Istoriia Uzbekskoi*

SSR (Tashkent: Fan, 1967), vol. I, pp. 574, 578. For Qazaq traditions on Zhalangtös see, *Qozhabergen Zhïrau*, p. 6; S. Aqatay et al. (eds), *Qazaqtïng fol'klor ŭlaghatï* (Almaty: Print Express, 2011), p. 159; K. Madanov, *Kĭshĭ zhüzdĭng shezhĭresĭ* (Almaty: Atamŭra, 1994), pp. 126–7; T. Üsenbayev, *Alshïn shezhĭresĭ* (Qïzïlorda: Tŭmar, 2003), pp. 377–8.

20. Q. Zhïrau, *Elĭm-ay*, pp. 6–8; one of Qozhabergen's students was the bard Buqar-zhïrau (*c.*1693–1787).
21. On the sources for the law code, see Zh. O. Artïqbayev, *Zhetĭ zharghï: oku qŭralï* (Almaty: Zang ädebiyetĭ, 2006); without elaborating Artïqbayev dismisses the reliability of descriptions of the *Zhetĭ zharghï* attributed to Qozhabergen-zhïrau; see also T. I. Sultanov, *Kochevye plemena Priaral'ia v XV–XVII vv* (Moscow: Glavnaia Redaktsiia Vostochnoi Literatury, 1982), pp. 64–77.
22. Fragments of the *Zhetĭ Zharghï* appear in some nineteenth-century sources; see T. I. Sultanov, *Kochevye plemena Priaral'ia*, pp. 64–7.
23. T. Sügĭrbayev, *Qïzïlzhar öngĭrĭnĭng ziyalï qauïmï*, pp. 24, 122–3.
24. S. Zhŭmabayev, *Ŭlïlar tughan ölke*, p. 285.
25. Ibid., p. 330.
26. T. Sügĭrbayev, *Qïzïlzhar öngĭrĭnĭng ziyalï qauïmï*, p. 107; S. Zhŭmabayev, *Ŭlïlar tughan ölke*, p. 297.
27. Some Qazaq *khoja* communities, for example, trace their ancestry to a scholar from Turkistan named Zhüsipqozha who came to the Qazaq Steppe during the reign of Qasïm Khan (ruled *c.* 1511–18), see S. Qŭrbanqozhaŭlï, A. Zholdasov and M. Omartayŭlï et al. (eds), *Ŭlï Payghambar zhäne ŭrpaqtarï* (Almaty: Foliant, 2014), p. 126.
28. S. Qaliyŭlï, 'Änet Baba – ŭlï bilerdĭng ŭstazï', *Qazaqtïng ata zangdarï* (Almaty: Zhetĭ zhargï, 2009), vol. 10, pp. 193–8.
29. Alpïsbay Mŭsayev, *Äyteke bi aymaghïnïng etnomädeni mŭrasï* (Aqtöbe: n.p., 2006), p. 67; Rïszhan Iliyasova, *Dalam tŭnghan shezhĭre* (Almaty: Zerde, 2007), p. 72; in another account, Maryam is identified as Galdan Tseren's sister-in-law; see S. Äshĭmŭlï, *Sïrgha tolï Sïr boyï: tarikhi-tanïmdïq zhazbalar* (Almaty: Foliant, 2009), p. 323.
30. Mŭsayev, *Äyteke bi*, p. 69; S. Äshimŭlï, *Sïrgha tolï Sïr boyï*, p. 323.
31. M. Viatkin (ed.), *Materialy po istorii Kazakhskoi SSR (1785–1828)* (Moscow-Leningrad: Akademiia Nauk SSSR, 1940), vol. IV, pp. 52, 54; ᶜAbd al-Jalīl was from the Khorasan-Ata lineage of *khojas*. According to a genealogy compiled by his grandson Turiadzhan Aryslanov in 1830, the family descended from the Caliph ᶜAlī. Turiadzhan's genealogy, however, makes no mention of his grandfather's position as a pir; see I. V. Erofeeva, *Rodoslovnye kazakhskikh khanov i kozha XVIII–XIX vv.* (Almaty: TOO Print-S, 2003), pp. 100, 117–18.
32. *Shora* was a title used for a local ruler used during the reign of Abïlay Khan (r. 1771–81). During the era of the Golden Horde it had the sense of 'vassal'.
33. S. Zhŭmabayev, *Ŭlïlar tughan ölke*, p. 377.

34. G. Barudi, *Qïzïlyar säfäre* (Kazan: Iman, 2004), p. 86.
35. G. S. Sultangalieva et al. (eds), *Kazakhskie chinovniki na sluzhbe Rossiiskoi Imperii: Sbornik dokumentov i materialov* (Almaty: Qazaq Universitetĭ, 2014), pp. 16, 43, 324.
36. Seyĭt's genealogy, according to Marat Mukanov, is as follows: Balgha → Siban → Qazhï → Zhänĭbek → Mayqï-batïr → Esĭl → Tau → Qortïq → Qoshqarbay → Aqpanbet; cf. M. Mukanov, *Iz istoricheskogo proshlogo*, pp. 125, 127.
37. Esneney's support for Maral-Ishan while *shora* is mentioned in the works of both Bahram Shaqshaqŭlï and Musayïn Segĭz-Serĭŭlï; S. Zhŭmabayev, *Ŭlïlar tughan ölke,* pp. 371–3.
38. Ibid., pp. 373, 377.
39. Uäli Khan (r. 1781–1819) succeeded his father Abïlay as khan of the Middle Zhüz. However, he ruled essentially as a Russian vassal.
40. Ibid., p. 375.
41. Qazaq traditions regarding Maral Ishan circulate among descendants in the village of Qaraqshï, near Qïzïlorda, and among his kinsman in northern Kazakhstan. For traditions among his descendants, see A. Zhontayeva and Sh. Sh. Äbdĭbayev, *Sïr elĭnĭng mädeni mŭralarï* (Qïzïlorda: n.p., 2005), pp. 69–70; Säden Nurtayŭlï, *Islam zhäne Maral Baba* (S.l.: n.p., s.d.); for traditions collected in northern Kazakhstan, see S. Zhŭmabayev and K. Zhalmaqanov, *Bĭrzhannïng belgĭsĭz ghŭmïrï*; S. Zhŭmabayev, *Ŭlïlar tughan ölke*, pp. 361–6, S. Bürkĭtbayŭlï, *Maral ishannïng nŭr shapaghatï* (Qostanay: n.p., 1998); for a partial overview of Maral in Qazaq epic tradition, see Z. Süleymenov, 'Maral Ishan – ŭlt-azattïq küresĭnĭng rukhani köshbasshïsï', in S. A. Kasimov (ed.), *Soltüstĭk Qazaqstan,* pp. 309–15. For Russian sources on Maral-ishan, see KRO I, 197-201; N. N. Kraft, 'Vdokhovennyi Kirgiz Maral Kurmanov', originally printed in 1899, see *Kirgizskaia Stepnaia gazeta: chelovek, obshchestvo, priroda, 1888–1902*, ed. U. Subkhanberdieva (Almaty: Ghïlïm, 1994), pp. 649–55; also reprinted in: *Iz kirgizskoi stariny* (Orenburg: Tipografiia F. B. Sachkova, 1900), pp. 83–90.
42. For a treatment of Qazaq revolts in Soviet historiography, see L. Tillett, *The Great Friendship: Soviet Historians and the Non-Russian Nationalities* (Chapel Hill: University of North Carolina Press, 1969), pp. 171–93.
43. One report, obtained from a Bukharan traveller in 1821, appears to confuse Maral with one of his sons; see KRO I, 197–8; for an overview and synthesis of the Russian sources, see E. Adil', 'Maral-Ishan: kharakter i ideinye osnovy national'no-osvoboditel'nogo dvizheniia', in *Soltüstĭk Qazaqstan,* pp. 215–21.
44. For a discussion of Ablay Khan's capture by Galdan-tseren based on documentary sources, see R. B. Suleimenov and V. A. Moiseev, *Iz istorii Kazakhstana XVIII veka* (Alma-Ata: Nauka, 1988), pp. 36–8.
45. S. Zhŭmabayev and K. Zhalmaqanov, *Bĭrzhannïng belgĭsĭz ghŭmïrï,* pp. 151–2.

46. Äbdibayev, *Sïr elining mädeni muralarï,* pp. 69–70.
47. S. Zhŭmabayev and K. Zhalmaqanov, *Bĭrzhannïng belgĭsĭz ghŭmïrï,* pp. 153–4.
48. *Kazakhsko-russkie otnosheniia v XVIII–XIX vekakh (1771–1867 gody)* (Alma-Ata: Nauka, 1964), pp. 197–9.
49. K. K. Kraft, *Iz kirgizskoi stariny* (Orenburg: Sachkov, 1900).
50. S. Nŭrtayŭlï, *Islam zhäne Maral Baba,* p. 41.
51. B. Tŭrgharayev (ed.), *Qozhabergen zhïrau (shïgharma zhinaghï)* (Petropavl: n.p., 2010), p. 5.
52. S. Zhŭmabayev, *Ŭlïlar tughan ölke,* p. 285.
53. Ibid., p. 339; T. Sügĭrbayev, *Qïzïlzhar öngĭrĭnĭng ziyalï qauïmï,* p. 285.
54. Ibid., p. 107.
55. Ibid., pp. 122, 326, 332.
56. S. Zhŭmabayev, *Ŭlïlar tughan ölke,* p. 370.
57. S. Zhŭmabayev and K. Zhalmaqanov, *Bĭrzhannïng belgĭsĭz ghŭmïrï,* pp. 25–6.
58. T. Sügĭrbayev, *Qïzïlzhar öngĭrĭnĭng ziyalï qauïmï,* pp. 152–3.
59. I. Bregel', *Khorezmskie turkmeny v XIX veke* (Moscow: Nauka, 1961), p. 173.
60. On the accounts of Russian officials who looked critically at the *sharī^{c}a/ ^{c}ādat* divide, see S. Fuks, 'Nekotorye momenty istorii kazakhskogo prava i 'Opisanie kirgizskikh obychaev' d'Andre', *Izvestiia Akademii Nauk Kazakhskoi SSR, seriia iuridicheskaia* 1 (1948), pp. 77 94; P. Sartori and P. Shablei, 'Sud'ba imperskikh kodifikatsionnykh proektov: adat i shariat v kazakhskoi stepi', *Ab Imperio* 2 (2015), pp. 63–105.
61. S. K. Kozhonaliev, *Sud i obychnoe pravo kirgizov do oktiabr'skoi revoliutsii* (Frunze: Izdatel'stvo Akademii Nauk Kirgizskoi SSR, 1963).
62. S. Zhŭmabayev and K. Zhalmaqanov, *Bĭrzhannïng belgĭsĭz ghŭmïrï,* p. 21.
63. T. Sügĭrbayev, *Qïzïlzhar öngĭrĭnĭng ziyalï qauïmï,* p. 106; *Istoriia Kazakhstana v russkikh istochnikakh* VIII/1, eds B. T. Zhanaev and I. V. Erofeeeva (Almaty: Daik Press, 2006), pp. 337–8, 565–6.
64. S. V. Iuskov (ed.), *Materialy po kazakhskomu obychnomy pravu* (Alma-Ata: Izdatel'stvo Akademii Nauk Kazakhskoi SSR), vol. I, pp. 117–58.
65. A. Mangabay (Wäli)ŭlï, *Äziz äulet: Shakhiakhmed Khazret pen onïng ĭnĭsĭ Fatikh imamnïng häm olardïng ŭrpaqtarïnïng shezhĭresĭ* (Almaty: Öner, 2001), pp. 144–5.
66. Z. Kasymbaev, *Starshii sultan Kunanbai Oskenbaev i ego okruzhenie* (Almaty: Kitap, 2004), pp. 23–6, 30.
67. Zh. Zhontayeva and Sh. Sh. Äbdĭbayev, *Sïr elĭnĭng mädeni mŭralarï* (Qïzïlorda: n.p., 2005), p. 86; Shaydarbek Äshĭmŭlï, *Sïr boyïndaghï äuliyeler* (Almaty: Atamŭra, 2000), p. 116.
68. S. Ghïlmani, *Biographies,* p. 277.
69. Qurban-'Ali Khalidi, *An Islamic Biographical Dictionary of the Eastern Kazakh Steppe,* ff. 44b–45b.

70. S. Zhŭmabayev and K. Zhalmaqanov, *Bĭrzhannïng belĭsĭz ghŭmïrï*, p. 26.
71. S. Zhŭmabayev, *Ŭlïlar tughan ölke*, pp. 395–6.
72. N. Katanov, *Vostochnaia bibliografiia* (Kazan: Iman, 2004), 30–1.
73. S. Zhŭmabayev, *Ŭlïlar tughan ölke*, pp. 329–34, 339–41.
74. Q. Makhanbet (ed.), *Sïr süleyler: XIX ghasïrda ömĭr sürgen sïrboylïq aqïn-zhïraulardïng ĭlgerĭde zhariyalanbaghan shïgharmalarï* (Qïzïlorda: n.p., 2003), p. 281; Q. Ergöbek (ed.), *XX ghasïr basïndaghï ädebiyet* (Almaty: Bĭlĭm, 1994), pp. 24, 30, 35; S. Aqatay et al. (eds), *Qazaqtïng fol'klor ŭlaghatï*, pp. 59–60, 64; 290, 369.
75. These works include *Qiṣṣa-yi Uḥud* (Kazan: Chirkova, 1897), and *Qiṣṣa-yi Badr* (Kazan: Chirkova, 1897).
76. This evaluation is based on Saduaqas Ghïlmani's biographical dictionary, which focuses on the Aqmola, Qïzïlzhar and Kökshetau regions.
77. Tŭrsïnbay-batïr Ertĭsbayŭlï (1701–1800), who studied at the Qarnaq madrasa near Türkistan and obtained a *khadïmsha khat* licence, see A. Tasbolatov, *Esĭmderĭ el esĭnde* (Almaty: Foliant: 2012), p. 92.
78. Zeki Velidi Togan, 'Kazan Hanlığında İslâm Türk Kültürü', *İslâm tetkikleri Enstitüsü Dergisi* 3:3–4 (1959–60), p. 196; N. F. Katanov, 'Predaniia Tobol'skikh tatar o pribytii v 1572 g, mukhammedanskikh propovednikov v g. Isker', *Ezhegodnik Tobol'skago Guvernskago Muzeia* VII (1897), pp. 51–61; B. Akhmedov, *Gosudarstvo kochevykh uzbekov* (Moscow: Nauka, 1965), pp. 99, 101.

6

Tinkering with Codification in the Kazakh Steppe: ^{c}*Ādat* and *Sharī^{c}a* in the Work of Efim Osmolovskii

Pavel Shabley and Paolo Sartori

Introduction

'I expected from you more mistakes than you actually made, something like your assuming that you can take on yourself the role of the *muftī* among Kazakhs and solve conflicts among them according to the Mohammedan law.' These sardonic words were committed to writing in 1856 by the then chairman of the Orenburg Border Commission (henceforth referred to as OBC) and the famous Orientalist Vasilii Grigor'ev (1816–81),[1] when writing to A. A. Bobrovnikov, a specialist of Mongolian studies who at that time acted as 'border administrator' (*popechitel'*) among Kazakhs in the Governorship of Orsk. This small fragment of an otherwise intense correspondence reflects two diametrically different ways in which Russian Orientalists and imperial officials alike came to view the law of the Kazakhs. Grigor'ev (and many others with him) cultivated the conviction that Kazakh customary law (Rus. *adat* < Arab. ^{c}*ādat*) was and had always been detached from *sharī^{c}a*. He thus emphasised differences between them because he believed that Islam would represent a menace to the Russification of the Kazakh Steppe. In his view, upholding ^{c}*ādat* would be an effective means of showing that Kazakhs were only superficially Islamised and therefore more amenable to assimilation than Muslim communities in Transoxiana. Bobrovnikov, by contrast, was guided by practical expediency and his judgment was informed by what one could term 'participant observation'. While serving in the capacity of *popechitel'*, he often had to visit Kazakh nomadic encampments (*aul*s) and thus took advantage of many opportunities to examine local legal practices. Enjoying privileged access to local knowledge, Bobrovnikov came to view *sharī^{c}a* as an integral component of Kazakh legal culture in the nineteenth century.[2] As we shall see, Bobrovnikov was not alone in nurturing this idea, an idea that encountered the forceful opposition of the echelons of Tsarist power in the Kazakh Steppe.

The purpose of this chapter is to show that the codification of Kazakh customary law (*ᶜādat*) was central to a policy pursued systematically by the Russian Empire from the 1820s to disentangle Kazakhs from their political and cultural ties with Central Asian Muslims. Such a policy was premised upon the assumption, widely shared within imperial bureaucratic circles, that Kazakhs were culturally different from the subjects of the Central Asian polities, being immune from that so-called Islamic fanaticism that, in Russian eyes, made Central Asians so potent a threat to the stability of the Tsarist Empire.

The disambiguation of customary from Islamic law was not specific to the Russian imperial project alone, to be sure. In fact, historians observed a similar movement in many a colonial setting: 'allocating different bodies of law to different segments of the indigenous population along pre-existing divides – for example, between ethnic groups or sedentary and nomadic population – could serve two complementary purposes: it could allow state authorities to employ a divide-and-rule policy, while camouflaging it as a modernizing project or as a "rhetorical continuity" with the tradition'.[3]

The codification of Kazakh customary laws was squarely centred on the notion of 'custom' (Rus. *obychai*), an imperial residual category that Russians deployed to address the broad domain of *oral* legal culture. Indeed, nineteenth-century Russian literature about Kazakhs differentiated between 'unwritten customs' and 'law', the latter identified with *sharīᶜa*, that is, a corpus of texts deemed normative, which ranged from the Qurʾān to *fatāwā* collections. This distinction between custom and law reflected a civilisational hierarchy according to which oral legal culture was a hallmark of less developed societies. Accordingly, Russians viewed Kazakhs performing judicial functions on the basis of customary law as culturally inferior to other Central Asian communities, which, instead, derived their legal culture from written texts. Key to such a distinction was the idea of what we may term 'judicial legibility', which endowed Islamic law with a certain degree of predictability by dint of its speaking on behalf of a written culture.[4]

That codification of Kazakh customary law was part and parcel of Russian imperial policies of Russian colonisation has been noted long ago. In her magisterial study of law among Kazakhs under Russian rule, Virginia Martin has argued that

> the study of Kazakh *ᶜādat* began in the nineteenth century both as an outgrowth of the study of folklore and everyday life of Russian and non-Russian subjects

> of the empire, as a result of the colonial encounter of Russian officials and scholars with the Kazakh nomadic community during the process of building the Russian Empire. As early as 1847, the Imperial Russian Geographic Society advocated the collection and study of 'popular judicial customs' of the Russian people (*narod*); with the emancipation of the serfs in 1861, the study of customs occupied a prominent place in the scholarly ethnographic and legal literature on Russian peasant life. The study of the laws and customs of the non-Russian people of the empire began during the reign of Tsar Nicholas I (1825–55), who undertook their codification as one aspect of the major project of codification of Russian imperial laws. By the 1870s, legal scholars were calling for the comparative study of laws of non-Russian people, which resulted in a large body of literature on the study of customary and Islamic laws among nomadic and settled people in Siberia, the Volga-region, Central Asia and the Caucasus, as well as among non-Russians in the western borderlands. The study of Kazakh customary law must be viewed within this larger scholarly and administrative project.[5]

Our study builds on the effort of Martin to read the scholarship produced in Russian by eminent representatives of the imperial administration against the background of Russian colonialism. At the same, it adds a further interpretive dimension. While Martin has put particular emphasis on how the study and codification of Kazakh *ᶜādat* was shaped by ethnographic sensibilities that manifested themselves at the all-imperial level, we equally want to pause to reflect on the specific transformative nature of the project underpinning such tasks. By codifying what they termed 'customary law', Russians sought in fact not only to record what they encountered as they penetrated the Kazakh Steppe, but also to achieve specific political purposes. We contend that the imperial agents' main aim was to distance the culture of Kazakhs *qua* subjects of the Russian Empire from the culture of other Central Asian Muslims who were subjects instead of the Uzbek khans. As we hope to be able to show, writing *sharīᶜa* out of the Kazakh juridical field was a forceful way to project into the past a separation between Kazakhs and other Muslim communities. Anatomising the compilation of digests of *ᶜādat* in the Kazakh Steppe allows us to expose the degree to which Russian Orientalists and government officials were implicated in the production of an episteme that obliterated *sharīᶜa* from the history of Kazakh legal culture.[6] Such an epistemic project was premised upon, among other things, the exclusion from the Russian academic canon of those dissenting studies that suggested that Kazakh legal practice had in fact long been informed by *sharīᶜa*. It is to one such study, an unpublished work crafted by one Efim Osmolovskii, that we shall turn our attention.

Before we proceed to examine Osmolovskii's digest of Kazakh customary laws and comment upon the concerted attempt of certain imperial agents to belittle the prominence of Islamic law in the Kazakh juridical field, a short historiographical excursus is here in order to clarify our approach and elucidate what this chapter is and what it not. Our aim here is not to argue that Kazakh *ᶜādat* should be regarded as a colonial discursive construct alone and that such a notion never existed among Kazakhs prior to Russian imperialism; nor is to claim to establish that *sharīᶜa* was more significant for Kazakhs than *ᶜādat* was. Rather, our major concern here is to highlight the *arbitrary* way in which *sharīᶜa* was decoupled from customary law.

In the recent past legal anthropologists have alerted historians of law in Muslim-majority regions that any attempt to distinguish between *ᶜādat* and *sharīᶜa* is an exercise doomed to failure. This is especially true when one superimposes a narrow juristic understanding of Islamic law (an understanding premised upon the assumption that *sharīᶜa* is first and foremost a legal doctrine while *ᶜādat* amounts instead to a *lex loci* of some sort unreflexively applied by laymen) without considering the cultural perceptions of the uninitiated. Judith Scheele has recently made an important intervention in the field by noting that a

> distinction [between Islamic and customary law] is often difficult to establish: not only does Islamic law frequently draw on custom as a material if not a formal source, but custom is often tributary to forms and concepts borrowed from Islamic law, while locally, people might fail to distinguish between the two. As a result, 'custom' can either be defined in local terms, as what people consciously describe as such – as is the case with Yemeni tribal agreements or Kabyle village *qawânîn*, for instance – or negatively, as practices that, whatever people think them to be, do not 'really' constitute Islamic law; two definitions that are likely to be at odds, while the latter puts the author in the untenable position of acting as an arbiter of Islamic orthodoxy.[7]

While the historiography of Kazakh customary law, especially in its Soviet incarnation, has followed a trajectory substantially distinct from the study of Islamic law in the West, we encounter therein many of the problematic assumptions about *sharīᶜa* and custom that are characteristic of Western Orientalism and that pose the same interpretive problems indicated by Scheele. We find, for example, the idea that Kazakh customary and Islamic law have always been two discrete legal systems and that such separation could be traced to epochs prior to Russian colonisation.[8] Thus, the historian Savelii Fuks posits that by the late eighteenth century Kazakh sultans began to view *ᶜādat* as an ineffective instrument of power, that they therefore turned to ostensibly 'stricter' legal norms (that is, to the *sharīᶜa*) and that, by ignoring traditional *biy* courts, they attempted to exercise judicial power primarily with the help of Muslim clerics.[9] As we shall see, the work of Fuks reifies in fact the standard, official views of Russian imperial scholarship on the distinction between customary and Islamic law, which regarded the former as 'flexible' and the latter as 'stricter'. While Soviet legal historians capitalised on Tsarist historiography to claim that Kazakhs were only superficially Islamised, their decoupling *ᶜādat* from *sharīᶜa* acquired a different meaning. Indeed, Soviet historiography made *ᶜādat* a marker of national culture among other things, an attribute that could distinguish Kazakhs from other Central Asian (Soviet) nationalities.

Moving from the Soviet to the post-Soviet period, we see that in Kazakhstan today the study of customary law is still substantially informed by notions developed in the Tsarist and Soviet period, with a continued emphasis on the separation of *ᶜādat* from *sharīᶜa*. In Western historiography, by contrast, the study of customary law has undergone a substantial interpretive turn. Virginia Martin's work, for instance, offers a considerably more nuanced approach to the study of the historical relationship between *ᶜādat* and *sharīᶜa*, suggesting that 'in the Kazakh steppe, as in other islamicized regions of the world, this *syncretism* formed the foundation of a complex web of judicial practices, many of which were simply called *adat* among nomads . . . it is important to recognize that *Shariat* and *adat* coexisted; in the minds of nomadic litigants, the distinctions between them could be blurred significantly.'[10]

Martin's recognition that Islamic law played some kind of role among Kazakhs is no doubt most welcome, although efforts to quantify and appreciate said role remain inadequate. But her recourse to the notion of syncretism is problematic. It is problematic for the term 'syncretism' is derived from the vocabulary of religious studies and conjures up the image of blending and reconciling of religions supposedly at odds. Historians of South Asia have convincingly demonstrated that emphasis on blending is in fact predicated upon an essentialised and thus ahistorical understanding of said religions and their attending systems of signification, which does not take into account the various processes of change they underwent. In addition, syncretism does more to obfuscate than to clarify the meaning that a practitioner of a given religion conferred upon a specific course of action. In sum, to call a religious practice 'syncretic' amounts in fact to measuring it against a preconceived and immutable system of signification, and to signal that said practice is 'heterodox' by dint of deviating from a canonical habitus of sorts.[11] Coming back to our case, if one speaks of syncretism between *ᶜādat* and *sharīᶜa* in the

Kazakh Steppe to emphasise the process whereby the two legal systems become mixed to the point in which people are unable to distinguish them, one is presented with at least two options. First, one should be able to define what *ᶜādat* and *sharīᶜa* were prior to their mixing and morphing into one syncretic legal system and, further, define the moment or the period in history in which the process of syncretism began. Needless to say, such an exercise would be entirely unconvincing for, as we noted, *ᶜādat* and *sharīᶜa* (like any other legal system) have always been subject to profound changes. Second, if in speaking of syncretism one's main concern is Kazakhs' legal consciousness and their inability to disambiguate *ᶜādat* from *sharīᶜa*, then one should contemplate the possibility to do away with such reified notions of Islamic and customary law and attempt to unpack the system of signification in which Kazakhs operated. While one could, in principle, pursue this task, Martin has taken a different tack: she chooses instead to focus in on *ᶜādat* and purposefully recuses herself from addressing *sharīᶜa*,[12] thereby implicitly suggesting that one could disentangle *ᶜādat* from *sharīᶜa*. If so, we wonder, does it still make sense to speak of 'syncretism'?

With this essay we seek to outline a different approach to the study of law among Kazakhs under Russian rule. It is plain that Russian imperial agents took measures to distinguish between customary and Islamic law and diminish the importance of *sharīᶜa* among Kazakhs, as much as it is apparent that Kazakhs of various walks of life internalised said distinction and endorsed the view that Islamic law did not belong to their culture. Equally, it is when one dissects Russians' attempts to pursue such courses of action that one can appreciate that Kazakhs navigated a system of legal signification that was based on inherent contradictions. Such contradictions manifest themselves in a number of ways. The semantic ambiguity with which Kazakhs variously referred to the law is one example. Another example (and our chief concern) is the process of codification from which it emerges that, while instructed to codify 'customary rules', Russian officials like Osmolovskii were unable to weed out references to what Kazakhs termed 'Islamic law'.

Codification in the Kazakh Steppe

The imperial push towards codification first manifested itself in 1822 with the statute on non-Russian subjects (*inorodtsy*), developed by G. S. Baten'kov under the leadership of the Siberian governor Mikhail M. Speranskii,[13] which instructed Russian officials 'to collect from respected people these laws in detail, . . . to soften all that is wild and cruel, to nullify whatever is incongruous with other statutes, and, having put everything in order, to report to the local administration for confirmation'.[14]

As we can see, the task consisted of singling out customary laws (whatever Russians understood them to be in a given context) and adapting them to the imperial legislative discourse. To reconstruct the genealogy of the application of the term *obychai* to the Kazakhs is beyond the scope of this chapter. However, we should at first consider that between the end of the eighteenth and the first quarter of the nineteenth century Russian officials, including the famous Speranskii, usually deployed the concept of 'Kyrgyz laws' by which they meant in fact *sharīᶜa*. It was only in the 1840s when Russians began to use the expression 'Kyrgyz customs' (*kyrgyzskie obychai*) to refer to legal practices in the context of the Kazakh Steppe. The military governor of the Syr Darya region Nikolai Grodekov was one of those who first took such a course of action by employing frequently the concept of *ᶜādat* (and, as an alternative, *zang*) for such purposes.[15]

The next step was to collect cases exemplifying the practice of customary law and order them into digests of laws, which were made available to educated Kazakhs, as well as to the Russian administration in Central Asia. Officials were expected to use these digests of laws to review legal cases, especially in contentious instances, thereby augmenting confidence in Russian state institutions among the indigenous inhabitants of the Kazakh Steppe. This process of collecting and systematising Kazakh customary laws was both partial and inconsistent, with the legal practices of some regions being privileged over those of others. While much attention was given to the study of *ᶜādat* among Kazakhs of the Middle and Junior Hordes (*zhüz*), it appears that Russians did little to study indigenous legal practice in the Senior Horde. This is due mainly to the fact that the three *zhüz*es were integrated into the empire in different periods and under changing circumstances, which in turn influenced the nature of the imperial policies with regard to codification and legislation. Jin Noda has recently argued that geopolitics played an important role in this respect. The Tsarist empire pursued, for example, a more moderate policy towards the Kazakhs of the Middle Horde than those of the Minor Horde because the former considered themselves subjects of Russia and China and their positions vis-à-vis St Petersburg was thus regarded as somewhat politically unstable. If, broadly speaking, we do not encounter major legislative acts to codify local laws from 1820 to the mid-1860s, then the situation looks remarkably different in the Minor Horde where in the years 1840 to 1850 several initiatives were undertaken to codify *ᶜādat*. We encounter yet another situation in the territories of the Kazakh Senior Horde, conquered by the empire in the years 1850 to 1860. Considering these latter territories' close proximity to major nodes within a dense network of Islamic educational infrastructure, the heterogeneity of local societies and lack of administrative, economic and other resources that would facilitate the integration of local societies into the empire, Russia tried to maintain legal diversity on the territory of the Syr Darya Valley. In accordance with this, imperial officials stationed to the forts along the Syr Darya line had to solve conflicts among Kazakhs, guided by *ᶜādat*, *sharīᶜa* and imperial laws,[16] an administrative arrangement that was typical of frontier societies in colonial situations such as the first phase of British colonisation in South Asia.[17]

The reform of the legal sphere was tantamount to a soft transformation of Kazakh society, as reflected in the principles for the administration of *inorodtsy* formulated by M. M. Speranskii. The latter believed that education was a means of advancing any 'backward' people along the 'ladder of civilization', acknowledging the possibility of moving from one status (*sostoianie*) to another (for example, from nomadic to settled), with the prospect of further progress to come.[18] According to this logic, it was necessary to adapt imperial legislation to the 'developmental stage' of *inorodtsy*, many of whom were nomads. The process of imposing imperial legal norms on them was to be implemented gradually, in accordance with the use of local (read 'customary') law as collected and edited by Russian officials.[19]

In practice, the implementation of this plan – producing a compendium of customary laws in accordance with the requirements of imperial institutions – proved impracticable for various reasons. The legal material assembled in such digests was, to a significant degree, collected and classified *arbitrarily* by officials operating on the spot. Thus, certain legal practices were classified as criminal acts, while others were declared 'savage' in accordance with imperial legal taxonomies. In this vein Russian authorities designated the widespread practice of stealing cattle as a compensation for damage (*barymta*) as a crime, mainly to remove such cases from the jurisdiction of courts presided over by individuals versed in the practice of Kazakh customary law (*biy*s).[20] According to this discretionary, not to say vague, taxonomy, other practices such as marriage among kin (Kazakh *amangerliq*) was regarded as 'savage customs'.[21] This did not, incidentally, prevent the Russian authorities from nevertheless tolerating *amangerliq* and other such practices as means of reassuring people that the empire posed no threat to local tradition.

To distinguish Kazakh customary law from *sharīᶜa*, however, proved challenging in many respects. The push towards codification of Kazakh *ᶜādat* and its disambiguation from Islamic law coincided with a phase of profound cultural transformation within the Muslim communities inhabiting the Kazakh Steppe, a phase that is now commonly referred to with the term of art Islamic revival.[22] It was in the nineteenth century that Kazakhs took advantage of a boom in Islamic educational infrastructure, which favoured the production and circulation of Islamic legal knowledge. An immediately visible consequence of this 'Islamic revival' was that a significant portion of the Kazakh elite was schooled in the madrasas of southern Central Asia[23] and the border regions of the Russian and Chinese empires.[24] In addition, individuals presiding over Kazakh customary law courts (*biys*) performed in fact also the duties of mullahs and the judicial tasks of *qāḍī*s among Kazakhs' communities.[25] The resulting effect of the Islamic revival in the local juridical field was that the purported distinction between *ᶜādat* and *sharīᶜa* became in fact inconsistent with the practice of law among the Kazakhs. One is put in mind of the eloquent example of the Kazakh sultan Arïnghazï (1783–1833). 'Several tribes in the Kazakh tribal confederation known as the Junior Zhüz', writes Allen Frank, 'elevated Arïnghazï Khan to the status of khan in 1815 or 1816, and he maintained a firmly pro-Russian foreign policy directed primarily against the Khanate of Khiva'. However, Arïnghazï is also remembered for administering justice among the nomads under his control using *sharīᶜa* courts in which a Muslim scholar by the name of Qarazhigitmolda undoubtedly played a central role. Although the degree to which Islamic law was discussed in Arïnghāzī's *sharīᶜa* court is not known, there is no question that *sharīᶜa* norms were used to suppress raiding and feuding between Kazakh groups. There appears to have been a political advantage in this as well, as Arïnghāzī's strict punishments are said to have contributed to 'his popularity among the nomads'.[26] With regard to Arïnghāzī as a Kazakh ruler enforcing Islamic law, it is equally important to note that he encouraged his constituency to apply the *sharīᶜa* in order to prove themselves better imperial subjects than the affiliates of Shirghāzī Khan (r. 1812–24), whose reign was characterised instead by recourse to *barymta*, which was regarded by imperial officials and indigenous subjects alike as a hallmark of Kazakh customary law.[27] Other authoritative representatives of the Kazakh elite manifested their attachment to *sharīᶜa* even more forcefully. In response to the exclusion of Kazakhs from the jurisdiction of the Orenburg Muslim Spiritual Administration, a group of *aqsaqal*s from the Ural'sk *oblast'* demanded the appointment of a new *muftī* in 1888 who would dispense justice among Kazakhs.[28]

While Kazakhs' involvement in networks of trans-regional Islamic education deeply influenced their self-perception and complicated even further the process of cross-pollination between Islamic and customary law, Russian officials pursued a selective and, indeed, narrow understanding of both *ᶜādat* and *sharīᶜa,* which obliterated present and past mutual borrowings. It is to one such case of denial that we will turn our attention now. This case reveals the degree to which codification was pursued and, ultimately, endorsed by the highest echelons of Russian bureaucracy only when it reinforced a colonial legal episteme. By 'colonial legal episteme' we mean a fundamental body of ideas accepted as true knowledge, which conveyed an essentialist conception of *sharīᶜa* as jurists' law, that is, a law that was the preserve of legal scholars (*ᶜulamāᵓ*), most notably the *muftī*s. Such a narrow notion of *sharīᶜa* originated from an Orientalist, mostly philological approach to Islamic written culture, which was divorced from the study of the practice of Islamic law.[29] Seen from this point of view, the codification of Kazakh *ᶜādat* did not reflect any particular ethnographic sensibility cultivated by the Russians to appreciate vernacular understandings of law. In fact, it represented a typical colonial intervention to redefine customary law.

Osmolovskii and his Compendium of Kazakh Customs

Efim Iakovlevich (Iosif Ioakimovich) Osmolovskii was born on 9 September 1820 into a Catholic gentry family in Surazh district of Vitebsk province. In September 1840, he entered the Oriental Department at Kazan University, which at the time was dominated by Orientalists of German origin.[30] At that time an Orientalist education included not only the cultivation of specific linguistic skills, the study of religions and 'mores of Asian societies', but also the exploration of their 'regional peculiarities'. Students had to develop a professional strategy of 'approaching' local populations ('to conduct themselves as modestly, cautiously, and courteously as possible'), in addition to examining and acquainting themselves with literature.[31] From 1840, students were required to familiarise themselves with Oriental-language materials in both printed and manuscript form; hence their strong philological background.[32]

After graduating from the university in May 1844, Osmolovskii was invited to St Petersburg to serve as a translator at the Foreign Ministry's Asiatic Department.[33] The metropolitan libraries and archives provided excellent opportunities for research. In 1846, Osmolovskii published an article entitled 'Research on the location of Sarai, the capital of the Kipchak or Golden Horde' in the newspaper *Severnaia pchela*.[34] Attempting to determine the precise location of the city of Sarai, the author drew on sources in Arabic and Persian, and made extensive use also of scholarship in German and French.

In March 1848, Osmolovskii was sent by the Foreign Ministry to the OBC for a temporary assignment 'in the dragoman unit'.[35] While stationed in Orenburg, he not only had to craft translations of printed and manuscript documents, but was also entrusted with 'special assignments', which allowed him to make frequent trips to areas inhabited by Kazakhs.[36] During 1848 and 1849, Osmolovskii had further opportunities for scholarly pursuits in Orenburg[37] and he honed his skills in Kazakh and Chagatai in addition to Turkish, Arabic, Persian, Tatar and Chinese, which he had studied earlier.[38] Later, the head of the OBC, Grigor'ev, highly praised the abilities of his subordinate, especially when they were attending to various tasks in the Kazakh steppe, noting that Osmolovskii 'thoroughly [knew] the Kyrgyz [Kazakh] language'.[39] In this same period, Osmolovskii was tasked with assembling a compendium of government decrees and laws in the Trans-Ural Horde from the time of its incorporation into the Russian Empire.[40] In addition to his scholarly pursuits and bureaucratic occupations, Osmolovskii was also a man of action. Having completed his ethnographic forays into Kazakh *auls* near the Syr Darya line, he joined Lieutenant General I. F. Blaramberg for an ostensible reconnaissance expedition to the area, on 12 August 1852.[41] This was, in fact, a military-intelligence campaign, during which General Blaramberg attempted to conquer the fortress of Ak Mechet', a stronghold of the Khoqandi army. The assault failed, but Osmolovskii proved helpful for subsequent negotiations with Khoqandi forces.[42] Appreciating the outstanding quality of his service, the Governor-General of Orenburg and Samara, V. A. Perovskii, wrote in a report addressed to the Minister of War that without the help of 'this excellent officer', I. F. Blaramberg would have experienced great difficulties when it came to interacting with Khoqandis and the Kazakhs.[43]

In 1849, the OBC tasked Osmolovskii with the crafting of a digest of Kazakh customary laws. This work took him several years. In 1849–51, Osmolovskii made several trips to the Kazakh Steppe. He visited the eastern, central and western parts of the Trans-Ural Horde, as well as the Bukei Horde. The result of this work was his 'Collection of Kyrgyz Customs Having the Force of Law in the Horde'. While putting together this digest, Osmolovskii also completed a number of additional assignments for the Orenburg administration – he made lists of influential and distinguished Kazakhs from the eastern part of the Trans-Ural Horde and took part in court proceedings.[44] On the one hand, such diverse activities allowed him to deepen the study of Kazakh everyday life, and to appreciate the varied nature of local legal practices, probing ways to translate his findings about Kazakh legalism into Russian. On the other hand, Osmolovskii could not simply proceed as he saw fit. The instructions he received from the OBC ultimately informed his academic work. Thus, for example, Osmolovskii was instructed to examine the collection of Kazakh customary laws drawn up in 1848 by Sultan A. Dzhantiurin,[45] the ruler of the eastern part of the Trans-Ural Horde, compare it with the digest of customary laws assembled by his predecessor Lev d'Andre,[46] determine their similarities and shortcomings, and then supplement these materials by collecting new information, incorporating the latter and removing superfluous material. The expedition was also assigned the responsibility to determine '*adat*'s relationship to the Qurʾān and the Sunnah',[47] the latter expression bringing further testimony to the OBC's and specifically Grigor'ev's obsession with Islam.

Unlike d'Andre, who spent only two and a half months in the Kazakh Steppe (from 13 July to 21 September 1846),[48] Osmolovskii devoted several years to the fulfilment of his assignment. As we mentioned earlier, in 1849–50 he travelled to the Trans-Ural and Bukei Hordes, and then worked on collating and systematising his materials.[49] In 1852, Osmolovskii had the opportunity to move further south towards the borders of the Kazakh Steppe with the khanates. He continued to think about complementing the materials he had collected in 1849–50 with new data, but his participation in the campaign against Ak-Mechet' in 1853 and his subsequent appointment to service far beyond Orenburg prevented the implementation of these plans.[50]

Initially, the materials collected during Osmolovskii's first expedition to the eastern part of the Trans-Ural Horde (9 July to 22 December 1849) were meant to represent the main body of the digest. Osmolovskii abandoned this idea, however, and decided to compare the different regional variants of *ᶜādat*. Exactly one year later, in the period from July to November 1850, he completed his second trip, this time travelling to the central and western parts of the Trans-Ural Horde as well as the Bukei Horde.[51] Drawing attention to the regional peculiarities of Kazakh customary law, this orientalist official demonstrated the difficulty of making broad generalisations about Kazakh law and the highly contextualised nature of *ᶜādat*. He emphasised that Kazakh customary law had been subject to a complex process of transformation under the influence of internal and external factors that had changed conceptions of Kazakh identity, including certain ideas about the law.[52] Observation of the practice of conflict resolution in different regions of the Kazakh Steppe led Osmolovskii to distinguish aspects of *ᶜādat* as distinct from earlier legal traditions.[53] In addition, Osmolovskii emphasises that a substantial number of perceived innovations in the legal sphere of the Kazakh Steppe originated from the interactions between Kazakhs, Khivans and Bukharans (interactions, which, of course, had been intense and culturally meaningful also in earlier periods). Thus, for example, he recorded among Kazakhs the use of the vernacular term *zarkefil* (< Per. *zar-kafīl*) denoting the notion of guarantor,[54] namely someone who undertakes to keep in custody suspects and individuals under investigation, a concept that was widely used to craft records of conflict resolution in Khiva. It is unclear at this point whether in speaking of 'innovations' Osmolovskii was merely voicing the concern of his Kazakh interviewees who had witnessed how the integration into the empire had led to a transformation of what they termed *ᶜādat*, or if his main preoccupation was to manufacture an idealised version of customary law, untainted, so to speak, by spurious Islamic elements.

In organising his study, Osmolovskii attempted to avoid the errors of his predecessors, and he attributed the slow pace of his work to the need to attract new informants, so as 'not to be subjected to one-sided descriptions of customs'.[55] At the same time, he was concerned about possible distortions in the codification and systematisation of Kazakh legal norms by European-educated colonial officials, so he thought it necessary to test out the materials on their 'target audience'. Thus, having completed his research in the eastern part of the Trans-Ural Horde, Osmolovskii stopped on his way back to Orenburg. Learning about a meeting of *biy*s and Kazakh notables in the Mikhailovskii fortress, he felt compelled to read to them from his collection and ask 'whether they found it in any way lacking or contrary to the Kyrgyz way of life'.[56]

Returning to Orenburg in November 1850, Osmolovskii immediately set out to finalise the preparation of his digest into that version that has come down to us as 'Kyrgyz Customs Having the Force of Law in the Horde'.[57] This text was completed on 21 December 1851. Osmolovskii separated his text into two parts, one that illustrated the principles of Kazakh customary laws, the other their applications. The structure of the first section does not display significant originality and is similar to other digests of customary law.[58] The first chapter describes the social groups inhabiting the Kazakh Steppe, the type of information that opens many collections of customary law.[59] The second and third chapters present the norms of family and property law, delineating the differences between various parts of the Trans-Ural and Bukei Hordes. The commentary included in the collection reflects of Osmolovskii's attempt to avoid artificial uniformity in recording the rules of local law, showing divergent legal practices, including the application of both *ᶜādat* and *sharīᶜa*. The fifth, sixth and seventh chapters contain information on legal proceedings, crime and punishment among the Kazakhs.[60] In contrast to the earlier digests of customary laws, Osmolovskii's work was not designed as a legal code to be used by imperial officials. The considerable mixing of material, including references to punishments according to *sharīᶜa* and legal practices that, he noted, had already fallen out of use, means that Osmolovskii's work can be seen as an ethnographic text, aimed at filling in the gaps in terms of knowledge of local law.[61] It is true, of course, that those who compiled digests of customary laws in the Kazakh Steppe and elsewhere, could not avail themselves of any all-imperial unified programme to guide them through the systematisation and rendering of their ethnographic observations. People such as Osmolovskii had little to gain from the schematic instructions that they received from imperial authorities and, therefore, had to turn their attention to other ethnographic publications, which best exemplified how to make sense of their own observations. It is difficult to say whether in the middle of the nineteenth century Russian officials were following any particular trend of ethnographic writing. It is plain, however, that it is only in the late 1840s that we first encounter a structured set of instructions (*programma*) designed for ethnographers studying Slavic peoples.[62]

The second part of I. A. Osmolovskii's text is the more original. Entitled 'Special Notes on the Collection of Kyrgyz Customs', it sees the author's attempt to clarify the relationship between *ᶜādat* and *sharīᶜa*. By supplementing this section with various comments based on Islamic legal literature, Osmolovskii clearly tasked himself with representing Kazakh legal culture as a mix of the two.[63]

A Code that Ought Not to Be Published

What was the fate of Osmolovskii's work? His materials were first submitted to the OBC, which evaluated the digest as 'complete and satisfactory'.[64] At this time, the chairman of the OBC was M. V. Ladyzhenskii. An outstanding topographer, formerly a professor of military history and strategy at the military academy, Ladyzhenskii was known for valuing the assistance of men of letters, an attitude best exemplified by his collaboration with A. Vengrzhikovskii, a friend of Taras Shevchenko.[65] Ladyzhenskii's humanistic sensibilities notwithstanding, Osmolovskii's collection never saw the light of the day. In April 1853, V. A. Perovskii (who, as we shall see, played an active role in the fate of the digest), noted quite cynically that 'the case is still stuck in [the Orenburg Border] Commission',[66] an unfortunate situation resulting from multiple circumstances. First, in 1852 Osmolovskii set himself the goal of becoming acquainted with the legal practices of Kazakh nomads living on the border with the Central Asian khanates. He therefore decided in 1853 to collect additional materials to supplement his digest, a decision complicating further the completion of his task. Second, bureaucratic considerations also intervened. Ladyzhenskii fully supported the idea of codifying *ᶜādat* and even suggested a separate section of Russian imperial law for the Kazakhs based on Osmolovskii's collection. Ladyzhenskii's praise and endorsement worked against the publication of Osmolovskii's digest, because he was accused by Grigor'ev, who replaced him as chairman of the OBC, of corruption and malpractice.[67] In those years a new statute for the administration of the Orenburg Kazakhs was being drafted, which further complicated the status of Osmolovskii's work: should the digest of Kazakh customary laws be prepared for publication in accordance with the 1844 statute, or should publication wait until after the approval of the new statute? In 1851 the Ministry of Foreign Affairs, advised by the deputy director of the Asian Department N. I. Liubimov, recommended that the publication of the collection be expedited given that 'systematic arrangement' of the articles 'is not an important issue; the main thing is that there be no omissions and inaccuracies'.[68] Governor-General V. A. Perovskii partly shared this view and suggested that the collection be published without waiting for approval of the draft Regulation on the Administration of the Orenburg Kazakhs. In his opinion, 'combining this customary legal code with the Regulation itself would put off approval of the latter for an indefinite period'.[69]

In the autumn of 1853, the office of the Samara and Orenburg Governor-General sent the collection back to the OBC with a request that its review be accelerated. Almost immediately, on 13 September, the OBC decided to create a special commission consisting of two officials from Orenburg, three Kazakh representatives of the Trans-Ural Horde and one Cossack officer. The participation of Kazakhs themselves was considered necessary in order to resolve various 'misunderstandings and inaccuracies' in the preparation of the code, and to add items that had been overlooked.[70]

In the meantime, Osmolovskii was no longer working for the OBC. After the Ak-Mechet' expedition, he was transferred to the Syr Darya fortified line.[71] He was replaced by the famous orientalist V. V. Veliaminov-Zernov, who was sent to Orenburg in 1851. As a specialist in Oriental languages (especially Kazakh and Arabic), Veliaminov-Zernov had to evaluate the Russian translation of two texts on Islamic law housed at the OBC,[72] and, also, to examine the materials produced by Osmolovskii.[73] Our documentation does not assist us to shed light on the position taken by Veliaminov-Zernov with regard to the digest. In any case, the commission evaluating Osmolovskii's digest of Kazakh customary laws reached a dead end[74] most probably because Veliaminov-Zernov had been outspoken about his disapproval of Osmolovskii, as recorded in his correspondence to Grigor'ev.[75]

The fate of the collection was ultimately decided by the 1854 appointment of Grigor'ev as the new head of the OBC. Guided by a distinctive ideological doctrine close to Slavophilism, Grigor'ev did not oppose the codification of Kazakh customary law. Indeed, he considered it necessary for the Kazakhs to finally recover 'their own law' and thus be allowed to decide their legal affairs on the basis of *ᶜādat*. As chairman of the OBC, Grigor'ev determined that this institution could not cope with its current inflow of cases and lacked sufficient resources to conduct investigations in the Kazakh Steppe. He therefore supported the proposal of the new Orenburg and Samara Governor-General A. A. Katenin to delegate the investigation and review of all Kazakh cases, including criminal proceedings, to a separate judicial system for Kazakhs, which consisted of courts presided over by *biys*.[76] In advocating a strengthening of the role of *biys*, Grigor'ev contended that the imperial intervention into Kazakh customary law had failed.[77] In particular, he opposed the introduction of the institution of guardianship,[78] based on imperial law, into the steppe, considering it 'contrary to basic Kyrgyz conceptions of tribal property'. While fostering the gradual development of 'civic-mindedness' among the nomadic population, it was necessary to prepare the ground as to enable the Kazakhs' adoption of imperial legal culture:

> With the development of civic consciousness among the Kyrgyz under the guardianship of the Russian administration, we must gradually replace and supplement their rough customs with the norms of the Russian legislation.[79]

Combining the idea of the Russian Empire's civilising mission with a belief in the 'natural predisposition' of every nation to cultivate its own legal principles, Grigor'ev rejected the idea of Kazakh customary law embodying elements derived from Islamic law. Believing that imperial authorities would help the Kazakhs achieve a higher stage in the process of evolution by dint of their good example and their benevolent approach to the 'good savages', Grigor'ev in fact hoped that Kazakhs would naturally assimilate into Russian culture, thereby renouncing their very cultural identity.[80] From this perspective, Islam was perceived as the main obstacle impeding the Kazakhs' adherence of their 'authentic' customs and hindering the Russian civilising mission. Grigor'ev was therefore ready to protect the nomads from mullahs and 'all Central Asians', who, he said, 'spoil and confuse our Kyrgyz', who had only superficially adopted Islam.[81] These views predetermined the fate of Osmolovskii's digest, which promoted instead an understanding of the laws of Kazakhs, which was premised upon the cohabitation of *ᶜādat* with *sharīᶜa*.

In 1857, Grigor'ev was assigned the task of completing the work begun by the special commission, which had studied Osmolovskii's digest. Grigor'ev not only opposed its publication, but also criticised the work of his predecessors. By claiming that the digest contradicted governmental policies[82] and reflected not 'native Kyrgyz customs' but 'Mohammedan sharia',[83] Grigor'ev insisted on the fundamental distinction between *ᶜādat* with *sharīᶜa*.[84] He once again reminded the government that the publication of the digest could function as a step towards 'consolidating Mohammedanism in the steppe'[85] and prevent 'the improvement over time of the public and moral life of the Kyrgyz'.[86] Nevertheless, Grigor'ev did not abandon the idea of shaping Osmolovskii's materials into a conceptual framework that he deemed more appropriate, and notified the Orenburg and Samara Governor General, A. A. Katenin, of his desire to personally fulfil this task. He was not prepared to guarantee the success of this endeavour, however, noting that 'to purify the digest . . . of the Mohammedan element, with which it is imbued, requires both considerable time and several trips into the steppe'.[87] He himself did not find time for a new large-scale project of this nature. A letter written by the new Orenburg and Samara Governor General A. P. Bezak reveals that as of 1861, Grigor'ev had not yet started to work on the collection.[88] The following year he left Orenburg to pursue his academic career in St Petersburg.[89]

Unable to edit Osmolovskii's collection as he wished, Grigor'ev equally did not want to lose control over such a 'dangerous' manuscript. Probably fearing that, in his absence, the new administration in Orenburg would revive the idea of publishing the digest, Grigor'ev took it with him to St Petersburg, along with other papers, and kept it away from other eyes. This unprecedented initiative taken by a public servant – removal of an official document (a legal collection prepared at the behest of the OBC that had been discussed by various administrative authorities) and its concealment – can be explained by the value that Grigor'ev attached to this document, which he considered potentially harmful to Russia if it fell into 'unskilled hands'. The title page of the collection manuscript uncovered by us contains a revealing postscript:

> Vasilii Vasil'evich guarded the manuscript closely and considered it highly valuable, but at the same time, caring for the welfare of Russia, he kept it concealed in light of the fact that in various instances our officials and administrators have enacted anti-patriotic measures when they failed to properly understand a given situation.[90]

Grigor'ev's attitude towards Osmolovskii's collection of customary laws explains why no other copies of the text have been found in the archives of the Orenburg administration. They were most likely destroyed or taken away by Grigor'ev himself. Such initiatives meant that the rich heritage of Osmolovskii's work was made inaccessible not only to his contemporaries, but also to future generations of scholars. For example, at the end of the nineteenth century, A. I. Maksheev noted in his recollections of Osmolovskii that 'his remarkable work is still buried in the archives'.[91] N. I. Grodekov, yet another Russian official who cultivated a fascination for Kazakh customary law, lamented in the preface to his famous *Kirgizy i karakirgizy Syr-Dar'inskoi oblasti* that 'his work (Osmolovskii's – P. Sh., P. S.) was not published, and is thus useless to the [imperial codification] project '.[92]

In all fairness, it must be acknowledged that Grigor'ev's ideological considerations were not the only factor determining the fate of Osmolovskii's collection. By the 1840s, different groups within the imperial administration and in the steppe took advantage of the artificial separation between *ᶜādat* with *sharīᶜa* to pursue their own interests. In the 1840s and 1850s, we observe serious conflicts between the imperial administration in the metropole and in the colony. The Ministry of Foreign Affairs tried to accelerate the codification of Kazakh customary law as a basis for new projects aimed at reforming the administrative and judicial system (it was for this purpose that L. d'Andre and I. A. Osmolovskii were sent to Orenburg in 1846 and 1848 in their capacity as officials of the Ministry's Asian Division). Local officials, however, feared that the codification of Kazakh customary law would make them hostage to the 1844 *Statute on the Administration of Orenburg Kyrgyz*, paragraph 60 of which stated: 'The Kyrgyz, if they wish, can settle their affairs orally at a Border Commission court; otherwise the Commission will examine such cases, conforming to Kyrgyz customs and possibly simplifying legislation.'[93] In fact, the OBC had no control over *biy* courts and lacked the resources to carry out its judicial functions. Orenburg officials were extremely critical of the 1844 *Statute*. The only way to ignore the requirements of the paragraph cited above was to refer to the lack of a comprehensive code of Kazakh customs. When seen in the light of this article, the publication of Osmolovskii's digest would have complicated the task of OBC officials. This is most probably the reason why the manuscript was transferred from one commission to another, each of which did not dare to take responsibility for the final decision to publish it.

Representatives of the Kazakh elite, for their part, also used the artificial opposition between *ᶜādat* with *sharīᶜa* to lobby for their interests in a language that was comprehensible to the imperial administration. In the mid-1850s, the Chinggisid Chokan Valikhanov,[94] then serving as the adjutant to the West Siberian Governor-General G.Kh. Gasfort, advocated for the necessity of withdrawing the Kazakhs from the jurisdiction of the Orenburg Muslim Spiritual Assembly on the basis that 'Muslim laws were never accepted by the Kyrgyz and were introduced to the steppe at the government's initiative'.[95] This demand served to increase the authority of the representatives of the tribal nobility, which had been undermined after the incorporation of the Kazakhs into the Russian Empire, at least in part due to the consolidation of judicial functions. From the perspective of the imperial administration, Valikhanov's opinion represented the position of the 'Kazakh people'.

Finally, the mid-1850s saw systemic changes in imperial political calculations, leading to the rejection of plans for further codification and supplementation of legal statutes within the empire. This was to a large extent due to the government's response to resistance that had sprung up under the banner of Islam, led by Imam Shamil in the Caucasus, Kenesary Kasymov in the 1830s and in the 1840s and Eset Kotibarov and Zhankhozhi Nurmukhamedov in 1840s and 1850s.[96] The 1863 January uprising in Poland increased the government's fear of separatism, and with it the fear that granting local law official status would entail the dissolution of the empire.[97] It is instructive at this point to consider that in the 1860s Russian legislators produced a draft of the new statutory law (*polozhenie*) for the administration of the Kazakh Steppe. Therefore, a special commission was put together to study Kazakh customary laws. Proceeding from this, the Ministry of Internal Affairs requested the archives of the Regional Government of the Orenburg Kazakhs (OPOK) to supply the members of said commission with the digest crafted by Osmolovskii who, according to metropolitan officials, was to offer key guidance in the preparation of the new statutory laws. However, OPOK, not without surprise, replied that such digest was not among the records held in its archives.[98]

Thus, for all of its scholarly innovation, Osmolovskii's digest of Kazakh customary laws stood in contradiction to the main political tendencies of its time, as well as to the jurisprudential dogma of the separation of *ᶜādat* and *sharīᶜa*.

Conclusion

In which ways can Osmolovskii's digest be distinguished from other Russian codes of Kazakh customary laws? First, Osmolovskii drew attention to the fact that Kazakh customary law cannot be described in generalising terms as 'tradition', or as a set of legal practices 'common to all Kazakhs'. He did not extract from the material collected during his first trip to the eastern part of the Trans-Ural Horde information to project on the practice of Kazakh customary law, which could be observed in other parts of the steppe. In addition, he consciously 'refrained from putting forth a general view of Kyrgyz customs and from determining their relationship to the Koran or to sharia in general'.[99] This resulted in a complex and multi-faceted vision of the laws of the Kazakhs, which included materials from the Western and Central parts of the Trans-Ural Horde and the Inner Horde.

Second, seen from today's perspective Osmolovskii's approach to the study of law among the Kazakhs looks surprisingly independent from and critical towards imperial policies in Central Asia. Following d'Andre, he took stock of Kazakhs' hybrid legal culture and cultivated a holistic approach to the study of Kazakhs' juridical field by analysing disputes heard by *qāḍī*s, hearings of *biy* courts and appeals to Russian authorities. He therefore had an expanded understanding of the functions and legal sources of *biy*s. His observation that *biy*s were guided not only by 'folk customs' but also by *sharīᶜa* stood in stark contrast with the prevailing view of Kazakhs relying on an ostensibly traditional judicial system that ignored the principles of Islamic law. In this regard, personal acquaintance with influential *biy*s, some of whom were also mullahs, was key to his original approach. One among the most notable informants of Osmolovskii was Ileman Tiulegenev, who was known both as a *biy* of the Eastern Trans-Ural Horde and as a *qāra mullā* ('black mullah', a tribal subgroup of the Minor *zhüz*).[100]

Third, Osmolovskii did not limit himself to his observation of the hybrid nature of Kazakh customary law. He also examined *ᶜādat* from a historical point of view, which took into consideration contemporary cultural changes in the Kazakh Steppe, especially in conjunction with the circulation of texts of Islamic jurisprudence,[101] texts representative of the Ḥanafī school of law.[102] Osmolovskii was also sensitive to the transmission of madrasa education, and especially of Muslim literacy, in the eastern part of the Trans-Ural Hordes, which resulted from contacts between Kazakhs and Central Asian subjects.[103] Commenting on the materials gathered in the chapter titled 'On Custody', Osmolovskii noted, for example, that, while the Kazakhs lacked the concept of *walī* (Ar. 'guardian') and *nāẓir* (Ar. 'supervisor'), an analogous practice of guardianship did nevertheless exist, whereby supervision of a minor's property was entrusted to the eldest male kin and thus resembled the institution of *walī*. Osmolovskii further explained Kazakhs' unwillingness to follow the *sharīᶜa*-based rule that property of an underage child should be taken under supervision in the presence of witnesses, not as a lack of legal literacy but as reliance on a different, more important provision originating from Islamic law. Kazakhs could refuse witnesses, because 'the Koran says that God will never forgive someone who misuses even the most insignificant part of a minor's inheritance'.[104]

The historian concerned with the study of legal pluralism will inevitably note the apparent parallels between the North Caucasus and the Kazakh Steppe under Russian rule. Almost simultaneously, the colonial administration in both regions began to pursue a separation of *ᶜādat* from *sharīᶜa* in order to reduce the influence of certain Muslim communities and social groups. One remembers that the Russian decision to uphold customary law in the Caucasus reflected a desire to weaken the resistance of the local population, which had been mobilised by deploying an Islamic discourse governed by puritanical sensibilities, especially during the movement of Imam Shamil (1830–59).[105] Such apparent similarity is misleading, however, for the two cases in fact differed considerably. While in the North Caucasus the distinction between customary and Islamic law pre-dated the Russian military penetration into the region,[106] in the Kazakh Steppe the separation between *ᶜādat* and *sharīᶜa* was entirely artificial. The history of codification of *ᶜādat* and the attempted marginalisation of *sharīᶜa* once again demonstrates the illusory nature of the idea that the Russian Empire pursued a single religious policy vis-à-vis Islam.[107] As demonstrated by attempts to codify customary law in the Kazakh Steppe, we can posit instead that policies of colonisation designed in the metropole often conflicted with the day-to-day practice of colonial administration (Osmolovskii's unpublished digest being an eloquent statement to such conflicts) and thus precipitated a cascade of institutional adjustments and cultural realignments among the local population. Among such change one should count the Kazakh's either manipulating or internalising the artificial separation between Islamic and customary law.

Notes

1. N. Knight, 'Grigor'ev in Orenburg, 1851–1862: Russian Orientalism in the Service of Empire', *Slavic Review* 59:1 (2000), pp. 74–100; A. Etkind, *Internal Colonization: Russia's Imperial Experience* (Cambridge: Polity Press, 2011), pp. 164–8.
2. N. I. Veselovskii, *Vasilii Vasily'evich Grigor'ev po ego pis'mam i trudam* (St Petersburg: Imperatorskoe Russkoe Arkheologicheskoe Obshchestvo, 1887), pp. 218–19.

3. P. Sartori and I. Shahar, 'Legal Pluralism in Muslim-Majority Colonies: Mapping the Terrain', *Journal of the Economic and Social History of the Orient* 55:4–5 (2012), p. 650.
4. D. Kestl', *Dnevnik puteshchestviia v godu 1736-m iz Orenburga k Abulkhairu, khanu Kirgiz-Kaisatskoi Ordy. Per. s nem. V Shtarkenberga, V. Skorogo* (Almaty: Zhibek-Zholy, 1998), pp. 106–7; I. G. Georgi, *Opisanie vsekh v Rossiiskom gosudarstve obitaiushchikh narodov: v 4 ch* (St Petersburg: Imperatorskaia Akademiia nauk, 1887), vol. 2, p. 125; P. Rychkov, 'Nizhaishchee predstavlenie o sostoianii kirgiz-kaisatskikh ord i o sposobakh k privedeniiu ikh k spokoinomu prebyvaniiu i ko ispolneniiu poddannicheskikh dolzhnostei', in I. V. Erofeeva (ed.), *Istoriia Kazakhstana v russkikh istochnikakh XVI–XX vekov. IV tom: Pervye istoriko-ètnograficheskie opisaniia kazakhskikh zemel'. Pervaia polovina XIX veka* (Almaty: Daik Press, 2007), pp. 197, 201.
5. V. Martin, *Law and Custom in the Steppe: The Kazakhs of the Middle Horde and Russian Colonialism in the Nineteenth Century* (Richmond: Curzon, 2001), p. 3.
6. A. J. Frank, '*Sharīᶜa* Debates and Fatwas among Nomads in Northern Kazakhstan, 1850–1931', *Islamic Law and Society* 24:1–2 (2017), pp. 61–76.
7. J. Scheele, 'Councils without Customs, Qadis without States: Property and Community in the Algerian Touat', *Islamic Law and Society* 17:3 (2010), p. 351 fn. 3.
8. *Materialy po kazakhskomu obyhnomu pravu*, vol. I, ed. S. K. Iushkov (Alma-Ata: Izdatel'stvo Akademii Nauk Kazakhskoi SSR, 1948); T. M. Kul'teev, *Ugolovnoe obychnoe pravo kazakhov* (Alma-Ata: Izdatel'stvo Akademii Nauk Kazakhskoi SSR, 1955); S. L. Fuks, *Obychnoe pravo kazakhov v XVIII–pervoi polovine XIX veka* (Alma-Ata: Nauka, 1981).
9. See his *Ocherki istorii gosudarstva i prava kazakhov v XVIII i pervoi polovine XIX v* (Astana: Iuridicheskaia kniga, 2008), pp. 132–8.
10. V. Martin, *Law and Custom in the Steppe: The Kazakhs of the Middle Horde and Russian Colonialism*, p. 25; our emphasis.
11. Carl W. Ernst and Tony Stewart, 'Syncretism', in P. J. Claus, S. Diamond and M. A. Mills (eds), *South Asian Folklore: An Encyclopedia* (New York: Routledge, 2002), pp. 586–8; Carla Bellamy, *The Powerful Ephemeral: Everyday Healing in an Ambiguously Islamic Place* (Berkeley: University of California Press, 2011), p. 20.
12. This has been first noted by Allen Frank in his '*Sharīᶜa* Debates and Fatwas among Nomads in Northern Kazakhstan, 1850–1931', 62 fn.2.
13. See, for example, V. O. Bobrovnikov, 'Chto vyshlo iz proekta sozdaniia inorodtsev? (otvet Dzhonu Slokumu iz musul'manskikh okrain imperii)', in *Poniatiia o Rossii: K istoricheskoi semantike imperskogo perioda* (Moscow: Novoe Lilereturnoe Obozrenie, 2012), vol. 2, pp. 259–91.
14. Polnoe sobranie zakonov Rossiiskoi imperii (PSZ RI), Series 1, vol. 38,

no. 29126 (St Petersburg: Tipografiia II Otdeleniia Sobstvennoi Ego Imperatorskogo Velichestva Kanzheliarii, 1830), p. 398.

15. D.Ia. Samokvasov, *Sbornik prava sibirskikh inorodtsev* (Warsaw: Tipografiia Imeni N. Noskovskogo, 1876); *Materialy po kazakhskomu obychnomu pravu. Sbornik*, ed. S. V. Iushkov (Alma-Ata: Izdatel'stvo Akademii Nauk Kazakhskoi SSR, 1948); N. I. Grodekov, *Kirgizy i kara-kirgizy Syr-Dar'inskoi oblasti: iuridischeskii byt'* (Moscow: Vostochnaia Literatura, 2011), p. 34, first edn, tom 1, Tashkent: Tipolitografiia S. I. Lakhtina, 1889).
16. J. Noda, *The Kazakh Khanates between the Russia and Qing Empires: Central Eurasian International Relations during the Eighteenth and Nineteenth Centuries* (Leiden and Boston: Brill, 2016); TsGARK, f. 383, op. 1, d. 88, ll. 74–5. The situation changes once again in 1864, when the administration of the Sir Darya valley passes from the supervision of the Ministry of Foreign Affairs to the Ministry of War.
17. S. A. Kugle, 'Framed, Blamed and Renamed: The Recasting of Islamic Jurisprudence in Colonial South Asia, *Modern Asian Studies* 35:2 (2001), pp. 257–313.
18. According to Marc Raeff, Speranskii also saw progress as possible among the people who were labelled *inorodtsy* by means of assimilation. They could even move further down the road towards progress than representatives of societies that were formally more 'advanced'. In this regard, the Kazakh nomadic Chinggisids were more likely to develop within imperial structures than were their neighbours, the settled inhabitants of Central Asia. M. Raeff, *Michael Speransky: Statesman of Imperial Russia (1772–1839)* (The Hague: Martinus Nijhoff, 1957), p. 276.
19. See Zh. Kadio, *Laboratoriia imperii: Rossiia/SSSR, 1860–1940* (Moscow: Novoe Literaturnoe Obozrenie, 2010), pp. 90–1; A. D. Gradovskii, *Nachalo russkogo gosudarstvennogo prava* (Moscow: Zertsalo, 2006), vol. 1, p. 416; V. O. Bobrovnikov, 'Chto vyshlo iz proekta sozdaniia inorodtsev?', pp. 262, 265.
20. V. Martin, *Law and Custom in the Steppe: The Kazakhs of the Middle Horde and Russian Colonialism*, p. 92. On *biys* in nineteenth-century Khorezm, see P. Sartori, 'Murder in Manghishlaq: Notes on the Application of Qazaq Customary Law in Khiva (1895)', *Der Islam* 88 (2012), pp. 217–57.
21. V. Martin, 'Barymta: obychai v glazakh kochevnikov, prestuplenie v glazakh imperii', in *Rossiiskaia imperiia v zarubezhnoi istoriografii* (Moscow: Novoe Izdatel'stvo, 2005), p. 368; Tsentral'nyi gosudarstvennyi istoricheskii arkhiv Respubliki Bashkortostan (TsGIA RB) f. I295 op. 4 d. 2978, 'Po raportu imama M. Sadzhanova Kushmurunskogo uezda Tobol'skoi gubernii o protivozakonnykh postupkakh kirgiza Murzagalieva', 1855, l. 5.
22. A. J. Frank, 'Islamic Transformation on the Kazakh Steppe, 1742–1917: Toward an Islamic History of Kazakhstan under Russian Rule', in

T. Hayashi (ed.), *The Construction and Deconstruction of National Histories in Slavic Eurasia* (Sapporo: Slavic Research Center, 2003), pp. 262–3.
23. See especially Allen J. Frank's contribution to this volume. See also P. Sartori, 'Exploring the Islamic Juridical Field in the Russian Empire', *Islamic law and Society* 24:1–2 (2017), pp. 15–16 and P. Sartori, 'On Madrasas, Legitimation, and Islamic Revival in 19th-century Khorezm: Some Preliminary Observations', *Eurasian Studies* 14 (2016), pp. 98–134.
24. Qurbān ᶜAlī Khālidī, *An Islamic Bibliographical Dictionary of the Eastern Kazakh Steppe, 1770–1912*, eds A. J. Frank and M. A. Usmanov (Leiden and Boston: Brill, 2005).
25. Paolo Sartori, 'The Birth of a Custom: Nomads, *Sharīᶜa* Courts and Established Practices in the Tashkent Province, ca. 1868–1919', *Islamic Law and Society* 18:3–4 (2011), pp. 301–9.
26. Frank, '*Sharīᶜa* Debates and Fatwas among Nomads in Northern Kazakhstan, 1850–1931', p. 64.
27. *Materialy po istorii Kazakhskoi SSR (1785–1828 gg.)* (Moscow and Leningrad: Izdatel'stvo Akademii Nauk SSSR, 1940), vol. 4 , pp. 315–16.
28. RGIA f. 821 op. 8 d. 602 l. 172.
29. I. Agmon and I. Shahar, 'Theme Issue: Shifting Perspectives in the Study of Shariᶜa Courts: Methodologies and Paradigms', *Islamic Law and Society* 15:1 (2009), p. 4.
30. A.I. Mikhailovskii, *Prepodavateli, uchivshiesia i sluzhivshie v Imperatorskom Kazanskom universitete (1804–1904 gg.), Materialy dlia istorii universiteta, chast' 1* (Kazan: Tipolitografiia Imperatorskogo Kazanskogo Universiteta, 1901), p. 256.
31. E. A. Vishlenkova, R. Kh. Galiullina, K. A. Il'ina, *Russkie professora: universitetskaia korporativnost' ili professional'naia solidarnost'* (Moscow: Novoe Literaturnoe Obozrenie, 2012), p. 172. One such text was Abū l-Ghāzī's famous *Shajara-yi Turk*. See National Archive of the Republic of Tatarstan, f. 87, op. 1, d. 3308, l. 44ob.
32. K. F. Foigt, 'Obozrenie khoda i uspekhov prepodavaniia aziatskikh iazykov pri Kazanskom universitete', *Zhurnal Ministerstva narodnogo prosveshcheniia (ZhMNP)* 1843, no. 39: 69.
33. GAOO f. 6 op. 10 d. 7611, 'Formuliarnyi spisok o sluzhbe starshego chinovnika MID Osmolovskogo', 1860, l. 2.
34. I.Ia. Osmolovskii, 'Issledovanie o meste Saraia, stolitsy Kipchaka ili Zolotoi Ordy', *Severnaia Pchela* 1846, nos 80–1.
35. On the office of dragoman (usually held by Tatars) in the nineteenth-century Kazakh Steppe, see G. Sultangalieva, 'Tatary v obshchestvenno-politicheskikh sobytiiakh i voennykh kampaniiakh', in I. Zagidullin et al. (eds), *Istoriia Tatar s drevneishikh vremen. Tom VI: Formirovanie tatarskoi natsii XIX – nachalo XX v* (Istanbul: İmak Ofset, 2013), chap. 2, pp. 351–7.
36. GAOO f. 6 op. 10 d. 7611 l. 7 ob.
37. According to A. I. Maksheev, from 1848 to 1849 Osmolovskii was in

Orenburg without any strictly defined assignments and therefore devoted a significant amount of time to research; see his *Puteshevstviia po Kirgizskim stepiiam i Turkestanskomu kraiu* (St Petersburg: Voennaia Tipografiia (v Zdanii Glavnogo Shtaba), 1896), p. 246. This should not be taken to mean that Osmolovskii was not busy with his official duties; it is known that from 27 September 1848 to 9 January 1849 he was sent to the western part of the Trans-Ural Horde on official business. See GAOO f. 6 op. 10 d. 7611 l. 7 ob.

38. RGIA f. 853 op. 1 d. 66 l. 64 ob; O. M. Khlobustov, 'Gosbezopasnost' Rossii ot Aleksandra I do Putina', www.rummuseum.ru/portal/node/2537 (accessed 4 April 2019).
39. V. V. Grigor'ev's praise carries significant weight, as he was generally inclined to criticise the intellectual capabilities of OBC officials. After entering into state service, he said that among the regional administration only N. F. Kostromitinov and A. A. Bobrovnikov rose to the level of 'first-class Orientalists'. It is all the more remarkable that Grigor'ev could rely on Osmolovskii's opinion on important political issues. For example, in 1862, the OBC chairman supported Osmolovskii's doubts on the question of settling Russian farmers along the Sir Darya. On the basis of his subordinate's memorandum, Grigor'ev wrote a letter to the Orenburg and Samara Governor-General, A. P. Bezak, stating that this measure would not only fail to promote the development of 'arable farming' among settlers, it would also make cultivation more difficult for the Kazakhs. See N. I. Veselovskii, *Vasilii Vasil'evich Grigor'ev po ego pis'mam i trudam, 1816–1881* (St Petersburg: Imperatorskoe Russkoe Arkheologicheskoe Obshchestvo, 1887), pp. 18, 23, 33–4.
40. RGIA f. 853 op. 1 d. 66, 'Otchet general-ad"iutanta Perovskogo po upravleniiu Orenburgskim kraem za 1853–1854 gg', l. 65.
41. GAOO f. 6 op. 10 d. 7611 l. 6.
42. I. F. Blaramberg, *Vospominaniia* (Moscow: Nauka, 1978), pp. 245–6.
43. GAOO f. 6 op. 10 d. 7611 l. 9ob.
44. I. V. Erofeeva and B. T. Zhanaev (eds), *Istoriia Kazakhstana v russkikh istochnikakh XIX–nachala XX v* (Almaty: Daik-Press, 2006), vol. 6, book 2, pp. 144–5.
45. TsGA RK f. 4 op. 1 d. 2382 l. 79ob.
46. Lev d'Andre (? –1848) was an official serving the Asiatic Department of the Ministry of Foreign Affairs. In 1846, the DCC commissioned him to prepare a collection of materials on Kazakh customary law. D'Andre's digest was dismissed as insignificant because, like in the case of Osmolovskii's oeuvre, it reflected the extent to which *sharīʿa* informed Kazakh customary laws. See S. L. Fuks, 'Nekotorye momenty istorii kazakhskogo prava i "Opisanie kirgizskikh obychaev' d'Andre"', *Izvestii Akademii Nauk Kazakhskoi SSR, seriia iuridicheskaia* I (1948), pp. 77–94.
47. Ibid., l. 71, 78–79ob.
48. *Materialy po kazakhskomu obychnomu pravu*, p. 119.

49. Otdel rukopisei i redkikh knig Rossiiskoi natsional'noi biblioteki (OR RNB), f. 224 op. 1 d. 6 l. 188 ob.
50. Nevertheless, we were unable to locate the results of this work. This publication is based on materials from 1849 to 1850, which were collected by Osmolovskii in the territory of the Trans-Ural Horde and the Bukei Khanate. It is possible that there existed a separate draft of his observations on the customs of the Sir-Darya Kazakhs. If so, its fate is unknown to us.
51. Although the name of the text ('A Collection of Kyrgyz [Kazakh] Customs Having the Force of Law in the Horde') does not tell us anything in terms of so-called regional specificities, the notes compiled by Osmolovskii on the basis of interviews with Kazakh *biys* constantly make reference to various particular features of ᶜādat in different parts of the Kazakh Steppe.
52. TsGA RK f. 4 op. 1 d. 2382 l. 111 ob.
53. That Grodekov too paid attention to customary practices perceived as innovations (such as recourse to written deeds and judgments issued in absentia of *biys*) suggests that indeed Kazakhs must have been aware of the fact that certain forces of historical change such as the process of bureaucratisation ushered in by colonisation had engendered also new legal practices. N. I. Grodekov, *Kirgizy i karakirgizy Syr-Dar'inskoi oblasti: iuridischeskii byt'*, pp. 32–3.
54. RGIA, f. 853, op.2, d. 65, l. 79.
55. TsGA RK f. 4 op. 1 d. 2382 l. 104. Osmolovskii's sense of responsibility in approaching this task is attested to by his desire to achieve a greater degree of objectivity than his predecessors. Thus, in a report dated 12 October 1849, he noted that he needed more time for travel in the Kazakh Steppe, as he had discovered 'many subjects that are not mentioned in the collections' (those of L. d'Andre and A. Dzhantiurin–P.Sh., P.S.), and 'the subjects set forth in the collections require considerable supplementation, and in some parts also correction' (ibid. l. 103).
56. Ibid. l. 107.
57. RGIA, f. 853 op. 2 d. 65, 'Opis' bumag i bumagi, napravlennye turkestanskomu gubernatoru Cherniaevu', 1851–62.
58. The formulaic nature of many collections of customary law concerning various regions of the Russian Empire is clear. See, for example, on the North Caucasus, M. Kemper, 'Araboiazychnaia ètnografiia adata po russkomu zakazu?' in A. P. Shikhsaidov (ed.), *Dagestanskie sviatyni* (Makhachkala: Izdatel'skii Dom 'Epokha', 2013), vol. 3, pp. 176–7.
59. Ibid., p. 176.
60. RGIA f. 853 op. 2 d. 65.
61. For an explanation of how a collection of customary law becomes an ethnographic text, see M. Kemper, 'Araboiazychnaia ètnografiia adata', pp. 175–90.
62. A. I. Vaskul, 'Ètnograficheskaia programma Russkogo geograficheskogo

obshchestva', in M. V. Reili (ed.), *Russkii fol'klor: Materialy i issledovaniia* (St Petersburg: Nauka, 2012), pp. 460–71.
63. RGIA f. 853 op. 2 d. 65 l. 70–120.
64. TsGA RK f. 4 op. 1 d. 2382 l. 205 ob.
65. 'Istoriia Orenburzh'ia', http://kraeved.opck.org/biblioteka/index.php.
66. GAOO f. 6 op. 10 l. 48.
67. RFIA, f. 853, op. 2, d. 210, l. 1.
68. *Materialy po istorii politicheskogo stroia Kazakhstana*, pp. 252–3.
69. GAOO f. 6, op. 10, d. 5716, l. 48.
70. Ibid. l. 50 ob.
71. From 1853 to 1862, I.Ia. Osmolovskii was acting supervisor of the Syr Darya Kazakhs. In 1862, he died at Fort Karmakchi following a stroke, TsGA RK f. 383 op. 1 d. 88 l. 3; d. 106 l. 4, 32 ob.
72. We can only assume that these two books on *sharīᶜa* formed the basis for commentary on Kazakh customary law included in the compilation. It is probable that the Russian translation and selection of materials was carried out by Osmolovskii himself.
73. GAOO f. 6 op. 10 d. 5716 l. 50, 52.
74. GAOO f. 6 op. 10 d. 5716 l. 51.
75. RGIA, f. 583, op. 2, d. 183, l. 7ob.
76. N. I. Veselovskii, *Vasilii Vasil'evich Grigor'ev: Prilozhenie*, pp. 37, 40.
77. Ibid. p. 56.
78. On Russian imperial legislation intruding into the Islamic law of guardianship, see P. Sartori, 'Constructing Colonial Legality in Russian Central Asia: On Guardianship', *Comparative Studies in Society and History* 56:2 (2014), pp. 419–47.
79. GAOO f. 6, op. 10, d. 5716, l. 54.
80. Ibid. l. 55. In this respect, Nathaniel Knight's thesis – that Grigor'ev's academic scruples and sympathies for Kazakh society meant that his position lacked an explicitly Orientalist (in the Saidian sense) character, and made the Russian civilising mission less violent in nature – is unconvincing; see N. Knight, 'Grigor'ev in Orenburg, 1851–1862: Russian Orientalism in the Service of Empire', p. 81. We observe, in fact, that Grigor'ev not only sought to predetermine the Kazakhs' future, he also decided what was to be considered natural for them and what had been introduced from outside and was therefore hostile to their ostensibly true interests.
81. See M. A. Batunskii, *Rossiia i islam* (Moscow: Progress-Traditisiia, 2003), vol. 2, pp. 275–80.
82. In his opinion, the government's aim in introducing the 1844 Regulation on the Administration of the Orenburg Kazakhs was one distinct from the goals pursued by Orenburg officials. According to Grigor'ev, the primary task was information-gathering: 'to gain closer knowledge of the Kyrgyz nomadic way of life and the resultant civil relations'. The second goal was supervision: 'while allowing the Kyrgyz to retain their courts in accordance

with their customs, to be able to oversee the actions of Kyrgyz judges, to see whether judges decide specific cases in accordance with national customs or in accordance with their own arbitrary will'. Finally, the third aim was prescriptive: 'with the development of [the notion of] citizenship among the Kyrgyz, under the guardianship of the Russian government, they will gradually replace and supplement their crude customs with the provisions of Russian legislation', GAOO f. 6, op. 10, d. 5716, l. 54 ob.

83. It was specifically the second part of the collection ('Special Remarks on Kyrgyz Customs'), which aimed to determine the nature of *sharīᶜa*'s influence on Kazakh *ᶜādat* and contained seventy-nine commentaries on Islamic jurisprudence (*fiqh*), that drew the greatest ire from Grigor'ev.
84. For more on this, M. A. Batunskii, *Rossiia i islam*, p. 227.
85. This trope was widespread in the empire's political discourse in the second half of the nineteenth century, finding its way into numerous scholarly works and public rhetoric. For example, at the beginning of the twentieth century a scholar of the Orenburg diocese, N. M. Chernavskii, regarded the establishment of a muftiate with jurisdiction over the Kazakh Steppe as a measure that would unwillingly contribute to the strengthening of Islam among the Kazakhs. See N. M. Chernavskii, 'Orenburgskaia eparkhiia v proshlom i nastoiashchem', *Trudy Orenburgskoi uchenoi arkhivnoi komissii, vypusk 10* (Orenburg: Tipografiia Orenburgskoi Dukhovnoi Konsistorii, 1901–2), pp. 8–9. See also M. A. Miropiev, *O polozhenii russkikh inorodtsev* (St Petersburg: Sinodal'naia Tipografiia, 1901); E. N. Voronets, *Nuzhny li dlia Rossii mufti?* (Moscow: Tipografiia A.I. Snegirevoi, 1891); M. A. Mashanov, *Sovremennoe sostoianie tatar-mukhammedan i ikh otnoshenie k drugim inorodtsam. Doklad professora Kazanskoi Dukhovnoi Akademii M. Mashanova missionerskomu s"ezdu 1910* (Kazan: Tipolitografiia I.S., 1910).
86. GAOO f. 6, op. 10, d. 5716, l. 55.
87. Ibid. l. 55 ob.
88. Ibid. l. 56 ob.
89. N. I. Veselovskii, *Vasilii Vasil'evich Grigor'ev po ego pis'mam i trudam*, p. 225.
90. RGIA f. 853, op. 2, d. 65, l. 1.
91. A. I. Maksheev, *Puteshestviia po Kirgizskim stepiam i Turkestanskomu kraiu*, pp. 246–7. Being a close acquaintance of Osmolovskii, Maksheev most probably was shown the manuscript. Nikolai Grodekov, instead, must have heard about Osmolovskii's work either from Maksheev or from one of Osmolovskii's subordinates.
92. N. I. Grodekov, *Kirgizy i karakirgizy Syr-Dar'inskoi oblasti*, p. 7.
93. *Materialy po istorii politicheskogo stroia Kazakhstana*, p. 222; O. I. Brusina, 'Obychnoe pravo kochevogo naseleniia Turkestana v sisteme Rossiiskogo upravleniia', *Sredneaziatskii ètnograficheskii sbornik* 5 (2006), pp. 228–9. For a critical discussion of Brusina's article, see P. Sartori, 'Murder in

Manghishlaq: Notes on an Instance of Application of Qazaq Customary Law in Khiva (1895)'.

94. I. W. Campbell, *Knowledge and the Ends of Empire: Kazak Intermediaries and Russian Rule on the Steppe, 1731–1917* (Ithaca: Cornell University Press, 2017), passim.
95. Ch.Ch. Valikhanov, 'Zapiska o sudebnoi reforme', in Ch.Ch. Valikhanov, *Sobranie sochinenii v piati tomakh*, vol. 4 (Alma-Ata, 1985), p. 99; 'O musulmanstve v stepi', in Ch.Ch. Valikhanov, *Izbrannye proizvedeniia: Seriia: Biblioteka kazakhskoi ètnografii*, vol. 1 (Astana: Altyn Kitap, 2007), pp. 115–16.
96. V. Martin, *Law and Custom in the Steppe*, p. 46.
97. Ibid.
98. TsGARK, f. 4, op. 1, d. 2382, l. 213.
99. TsGARK f. 4 op. 1 d. 2382 l. 111 ob.
100. Osmolovskii noted that Tiulegenev was 'an intelligent man, educated, literate, and distinguished by his beautiful Tatar handwriting, . . . he is considered a scholarly person', I. Ia. Osmolovskii, *Vedomost' o vliiatel'neishikh i pochetneishikh ordyntsakh vostochnoi chasti ordy*, pp. 152–3.
101. There is no doubt that the individual texts used in the collection could have reached Osmolovskii via Muslim scholars or merchants living in the Kazakh Steppe. In 1845 the famous text of Islamic jurisprudence *Mukhtaṣar al-wiqāyat fī masāʾil al-Hidāya* (written by a Bukharan scholar named ᶜUbaydallāh b. Masᶜūd Ṣadr al-Sharīᶜa al-Thānī al-Maḥbūbī, d. 1346) was edited and published in Kazan' by the Orientalist Alexander Kasimovich Kazem-Bek at the request of Khan Jangir, the ruler of the Kazakh Inner Horde and a Muslim of Chinggisid descent. Two thousand copies were distributed among the members of the Bukei Horde, B. T. Zhanaev, V. A. Inochkin and S. Kh. Sagnaeva, *Istoriia Bukeevskogo khanstva, 1801–1852 gg.: Sbornik dokumentov i materialov* (Almaty: Daik-Press, 2002), pp. 432, 436; M. Iu. Iliushinna, 'Arabskie rukopisi iz kataloga A. K. Kazem-Beka 1852 g. v vostochnom otdele nauchnoi biblioteke SPbGU', *Vestnik SPbGU* 13:1 (2011), p. 70.
102. In particular, he used works such as the *Jāmiᶜ al-rumūz*, known in Central Asia also as *Sharḥ-i nuqāya*, a work by Shams al-Dīn Muḥammad b. Ḥusām al-Dīn al-Quhistānī (d. 1554), which is a commentary on the *al-Nuqāya* (or *Mukhtasar al-wiqāya fī masāʾil al-Hidāya)*, see A. Idrisov, A. Muminov and M. Szuppe, *Manuscrits en écriture arabe du Musée regional de Nukus (République autonome du Karakalpakstan, Ouzbékistan). Fonds arabe, persan, turkī et Karakalpak* (Rome: Istituto per l'Oriente C.A. Nallino, 2007), p. 95; and the *Durr al-mukhtār*, a work by ᶜAlāʾ al-Dīn al-Ḥaskafī (d. 1677).
103. TsGA RK f. 4, op. 1, d. 2382, l. 11lob.
104. RGIA f. 853, op. 2, d. 65, l. 74ob.
105. M. Kemper, '*'Adat* against *Shari'a*: Russian Approaches towards Daghestani

'Customary Law' in the 19th Century', *Ab Imperio* 3 (2005), pp. 147–74; V. O. Bobrovnikov, *Musul'mane Severnogo Kavkaza: obychai, pravo, nasilie* (Moscow: Bostochnaia Literatura, 2002), pp. 137–41. On colonial empires pitting customary and Islamic law in opposition to each other, see P. Sartori and I. Shahar, 'Legal Pluralism in Muslim-Majority Colonies: Mapping the Terrain'.

106. M. Kemper, 'Communal Agreements *(ittifāqāt)* and *ᶜādāt*-Books from Daghestani Villages and Confederacies (18th–19th Centuries)', *Der Islam* 81:1 (2004), pp. 115–51.
107. R. D. Crews, *For Prophet and Tsar: Islam and Empire in Russian Central Asia* (Cambridge, MA: Harvard University Press, 2006), pp. 10–24.

7

Taqlīd and *Ijtihād* over the Centuries: The Debates on Islamic Legal Theory in Daghestan, 1700s–1920s

Shamil Shikhaliev

Introduction

In scholarly literature, the history of the development in Daghestan of Islamic legal theory (*usūl al-fiqh*), in general, and the polemic on *taqlīd* and *ijtihād*, specifically, continue to receive little study. The few works that do address this topic do not fully reveal the depth of this polemic within the framework of Shāfiᶜī legal tradition, which spread in Daghestan from the beginning of the eleventh century, the reasons it emerged or how it functioned from a historical perspective.[1]

The main shortcoming of most existing works on Islamic law in Daghestan is that they do not consider the multi-layered character of *ijtihād* or the subtleties of discussions among the Daghestani Muslim elite concerning this topic. With rare exceptions, scholars study the problem of *ijtihād* without connecting it to the internal and external factors at play during the appearance and development of the *ijtihād* discourses. Also, there is still a tendency in Russian-language scholarship to present *ijtihād* as existing in opposition to *taqlīd*.[2] However, as can be seen in Arabic-language Daghestani sources, *ijtihād* and *taqlīd* cannot be viewed as opposing or exclusive processes. Elements of *ijtihād* were never fully purged from the Shāfiᶜī legal tradition. In fact, the boundary between *ijtihād* and *taqlīd* in the Daghestani written tradition is less than clear; those jurists who are described in the local tradition as supporters of *taqlīd*, in fact permitted the use of certain kinds of *ijtihād*. In other words, all the discussions of *taqlīd* and *ijtihād* in Daghestan were not based primarily upon the opposition of the two methods to each other, but, rather, focused on the permissibility of different levels of *ijtihād*.[3]

These debates continued with varying degrees of intensity for several centuries and they were carried on across several historical epochs: the pre-colonial period, the colonial period and the early Soviet period. The variations in intensity of the polemic can be explained by several factors, including the outside influence of the great Islamic legal authorities of the Middle East. However, the discourses were also influenced by the internal socio-economic and political transformations of Daghestani society: the struggle of Daghestani jurists against the ascendancy of customary law (*ᶜadāt*), the period of *jihād* against the Russian Empire and the Great Reforms of the second half of the nineteenth century, when Daghestan was integrated into the social and economic framework of the Russian Empire.

The end of the legal discourses among Daghestani Muslim elites can provisionally be set at the end of the 1920s, when Soviet rule in Daghestan had grown strong enough to pursue concentrated anti-religion campaigns. At that time, Islamic legal education was liquidated, *sharīᶜa* courts were closed, the *waqf* lands belonging to mosques and *madrasa*s were given to the peasants' committees and many representatives of the Muslim scholarly elite were repressed.[4]

Ijtihād *and* Taqlīd*: A Few Theoretical Questions*

Once the Islamic legal schools (*madhhab*) solidified in the tenth and eleventh centuries, the Sunnis ceased to make further use of absolute *ijtihād* (*al-ijtihād al-muṭlaq*) for general questions concerning Muslim religious observances (*ᶜibāda*); regarding these questions, they considered 'the doors of *ijtihād* closed'[5]. At the same time, the adherents of the legal schools maintained the possibility of performing *ijtihād* within the framework of a specific school (*al-ijtihād fīl-madhhab)* when considering individual questions relating to the spheres of interpersonal and societal relations (*muᶜāmala*). Parallel to this, another group of Daghestani jurists, while theoretically acknowledging the permissibility of *ijtihād* within the boundaries of a legal school, in practice rejected the possibility that a scholar of adequate authority to perform *ijtihād* existed in their era. This stance was a characteristic one for scholars of the Muslim regions of the Volga Basin, the Urals and the North Caucasus in the eighteenth and nineteenth centuries.

Over the centuries, there were scholars in the Muslim world who rejected the concept of the 'closing of the doors of *ijtihād*' and called for a return to the basic sources of Islam – the Qurʾān and the Sunna – while using their own methods of investigation as well as the basic methods of the legal schools.

Modern researchers have already recognised that Muslim scholars had divergent views on the degrees or levels of *ijtihād*. Rudolph Peters has called attention to the fact that if, in the early days of the Muslim tradition, the level of 'absolute *ijtihād*' was natural and inherent only to the founders of the legal schools, in later eras the views of Muslim scholars changed somewhat, so that '*ijtihād*' itself, as they perceived it, was divided into several categories.[6]

In the Daghestani legal tradition, where the works of authors belonging to the Shāfiᶜī legal school enjoyed wide popularity, there were detailed descriptions of the different levels of *ijtihād*. With some small variations, the following kinds of *ijtihād* were designated in the legal literature that circulated most widely in Daghestan:

1) The very first and 'highest' level of *ijtihād* was referred to as 'absolute, independent *ijtihād*' (*al-ijtihād al-muṭlaq al-mustaqill*). Inherent in this kind of *ijtihād* was its own specially designed system of studying the fundamental sources (the Qurʾān and Sunna) and the additional sources (*ijmāᶜ*, *qiyās*) of Islamic law on the basis of the derivation and analysis of evidence (*istinbāṭ min al-adilla*).[7] *Mujtahid*s of this level developed their own principles and methods for studying the sources and, preferring one or another principle, handed down a decision for a given question. [8] Insofar as one of the main conditions of this level of *ijtihād* was the development of personal methodologies and principles, the *mujtahid*s of this level were not supposed to follow (*qallada*) the opinion of another *mujtahid* on a question, but were supposed to independently examine that question by means of their own individual effort (*ijtihād*), using their own methodologies and principles. Muslim tradition counts the founders of the legal schools (Abū Ḥanīfa al-Nuᶜmān, Mālik b. Anas, Muḥammad b. Idrīs al-Shāfiᶜī and Aḥmad b. Ḥanbal) among the *mujtahid*s of this level. [9] Besides the founders of the legal schools, there were other *mujtahid*s of this level. However, their decisions were not compiled and classified and have not come down to us, with the exception of a few individual opinions.
2) The next level of *ijtihād* can be characterised as 'relatively independent *ijtihād*' (*al-ijtihād al-muṭlaq al-muntasib*).[10] This kind of *ijtihād* is tied (*intasaba*) to the well-known legal schools and, in the process of deriving laws from the sources, its practitioners used the methodology of the founder of a chosen school. However, this kind of *ijtihād* is still considered 'absolute *ijtihād*' insofar as the jurist demonstrates independent effort (*ijtihād*) in studying the question by extracting and analysing arguments and evidence from the fundamental sources of *fiqh*. At the same time, the scholar-*mujtahid* does not develop his own methodology, but, rather, uses the principles of analysis of a given legal school. In other words, a *mujtahid* of the second level is one who hands

down his personal judgment or decision using the methods of his imam (for example, the preference for '*raʾy*' or '*istiḥsān*' among the Ḥanafīs, '*istiṣlāḥ*' among the Mālikīs, '*istiṣḥāb*' among the Shāfiʿīs or the minimisation of '*qiyās*' and stricter adherence to the hadiths among the Hanbalīs). Using the juridical principles of a given *madhhab*, a *mujtahid* has the right to hand down his own legal decisions, which may diverge from the opinions of the founder of that legal school. Working within the boundaries of the methodologies of Shāfiʿī or Ḥanafī *fiqh,* he can put forward a different point of view concerning a concrete legal decision than the one given by al-Shāfiʿī or Abū Ḥanīfa. For example, one may look to the activities of one of Abū Ḥanīfa's own students, Abū Yūsuf, who, working within the bounds of Ḥanafī legal theory, put forward his own opinions, which differed from those of his teacher. In this way, the main condition of this kind of *ijtihād* can be said to be that the *mujtahid* should use the methodology of his legal school, even if his opinion on a question ends up differing from the opinion of his teacher.[11]

3) The next level of *ijtihād* is *ijtihād* within the bounds of a legal school (*al-ijtihād fī 'l-madhhab*), which refers to the handing down of new legal decisions on issues that were not resolved by the early scholars of a given school. The main condition for a *mujtahid* of this level is that he follow the principles and methods of his legal school by which the school's founder constructed his own position. However, in those places where the founder did not give an opinion, a *mujtahid* of this third level may give a *fatwā* based upon his personal study. In doing so, he may not, by means of his own principles of analysis, violate the rules and basic conditions laid down in the works of the imam of his legal school. An example of this kind of *ijtihād* is the investigation of the question of when to begin and end the fast (*ifṭār*) during the month of Ramadan or how to perform the night prayer (*ʿishāʾ*) in the summer months in the far north.[12] Scholars of this level, in making their decisions, consult not only the Qurʾān and the Sunna, but also the legal works of their predecessors, and hand down a decision using, predominantly, the methods of casuistry or analogy. In addition, those who lay claim to the status of *mujtahid* within a *madhhab* are required to know the principles of deriving various arguments from the main sources of Islamic law.[13]

4) The last level of *ijtihād* is *ijtihād* within the bounds of issuing *fatwās* (*al-ijtihād fīl-fatwā*). This is when there exist two contradictory opinions on a question within one of the legal schools and the scholar, having studied the question using the principles and methodology of his school, gives preference to one of the two opinions.[14] The main

> conditions that must be met by a *mujtahid* of this level are: (1) that he should follow the methodologies of the scholars of the *madhhab* within which he is working, (2) that he know the principles of how each argument is derived from the basic sources of Islamic law and (3) that he should be competent to choose the stronger argument over the weaker (*tarjīḥ*).[15] In addition, according to the theory of Shāfiᶜī law, hierarchies have been constructed in relation to the preference for the opinions of particular jurists. For example, if there is disagreement on a specific question within the Shāfiᶜī *madhhab*, then, in making the final decision, preference is given to the opinions of the scholar al-Nawawī over those of the scholar al-Rāfiᶜī, whose opinions are, likewise, given preference over those of other Shāfiᶜī jurists. The opinions of Ibn Hajar al-Haytamī and Muḥammad al-Ramlī come next in the Shāfiᶜī hierarchy. No new *fatwā* issued within the framework of the *madhhab* may contradict the opinions of these scholars.[16]

For *mujtahids* of the *madhhab* and of the *fatwā*, the requirements are less strict. The main conditions for *mujtahids* of the last two levels is that they must know in every detail the principles and methods of investigation of their legal school.[17]

Many Muslim jurists agree that a scholar who is competent to perform the two above-mentioned levels of *ijtihād* is forbidden from following (*qallada*) the opinion of another scholar.[18]

In Muslim legal literature, strict requirements are applied to those who would undertake *ijtihād*. A *mujtahid* should live a disciplined and pious life, have a fluent command of the Arabic language, know the Qurᵓān by heart[19] and be well-versed in its commentaries. He should know the hadiths by heart, including the legal traditions (*ḥadīth al-aḥkām*) and their complete commentaries as well as the chains (*isnād*) of transmitters and their biographies. He should know which *ayāt*s and *hadīth*s are the repealing (*nāsikh*) and which are repealed (*mansūkh*). He should know the absolute (*al-muṭlaq*) and limited (*al-muqayyid*) laws related to various conditions. He should know the laws that are agreed upon by all *mujtahids*, and he should not cite the opinion of another *mujtahid* (that is, he should be independent in his reasoning).[20]

Taqlīd is strict adherence to the decisions of a legal school on all issues. A precise definition of *taqlīd* is 'the acceptance of the words of a scholar without analysis of the arguments and proofs that he puts forward'.[21] Scholars of this level practically never refer to the basic sources of Islamic law – the Qurᵓān and the Sunna – but appeal to the opinions and decisions of the major jurists of their legal school.[22]

The main discussion among the Muslim religious-legal elite of Daghestan revolved around the limits of the use of different kinds of *ijtihād*. As such, most scholars who allowed for the possibility of applying one of the kinds of *ijtihād* considered it forbidden to perform *ijtihād* to resolve questions on which there was already an opinion supported unanimously by representatives of all four *madhhab*s. Besides that, the application of *ijtihād* was not supposed to encroach upon the spheres of worship (*ᶜibāda*) and dogma (*ᶜaqīda*), but was to be limited to the sphere of interpersonal relations (*muᶜāmala*).

The overwhelming majority of today's jurists do not, in principle, reject the possibility of different levels of *ijtihād*. They argue that 'he who succeeds in handing down a correct decision will receive two bounties from God, and he who, in performing *ijtihād*, errs, will receive only one'.[23] In this way, jurists emphasise that even if a *mujtahid* is mistaken in his conclusion, his effort will not go unrewarded. The only limitation is that *ijtihād* should not be performed in the spheres of worship and ritual, for which direct, unambiguous instructions are given in the Qurʾān and the Sunna.

The overwhelming majority of Daghestani theologians over the centuries remained practitioners of *taqlīd*, rejecting the potential existence in their ranks of a scholar-*mujtahid* of even the third level, much less of the first or second levels. However, opinions on the practice of *ijtihād* varied widely in Daghestan at different times. At the end of the seventeenth century and in the eighteenth, there were discussions concerning the permissibility of different levels of *ijtihād*, and, in the sources, there are several Daghestani scholars from this period who are referred to as *mujtahids*. In the nineteenth century, Daghestani theologians believed that there was no scholar in their own time who met the strict requirements of a scholar-*mujtahid* and they put forward the thesis of the 'closing of the gates of *ijtihād*'. At the end of the nineteenth century and the beginning of the twentieth, the discussions of *ijtihād* were renewed with new intensity. In fact, arguments broke out not only over the permissibility of *ijtihād* or the impossibility of a *mujtahid* existing among the Daghestani *ᶜulamāʾ*, but over the possibility of performing *ijtihād* of the lower three levels. Regarding the first and highest level of *ijtihād* (absolute, independent *ijtihād*), Daghestani theologians, with a few rare exceptions, did not permit it even in theory, arguing that the founders of all four legal schools had already conceptualised and investigated all of the fundamental questions (*uṣūl*) of Islamic worship and ritual to such a degree that, if any questions remained unexamined, they were of a specific character (*khaṣṣ*) and related to the branches (*furūᶜ*) of Islamic law. Theoretically, the latter was entirely resolvable within the bounds of the third or fourth levels of *ijtihād*, but some Daghestani scholars considered that, even in this field, no topic remained opened for activities of a *mujtahid*.

The Beginnings of the Discourse on Ijtihād *in Daghestan (1600s–1700s)*

Arabic-language Daghestani sources allow us to identify the beginning of a discussion of *ijtihād* at the very end of the seventeenth century. This period was characterised by the beginning of a broad development of the Islamic legal tradition and, at the same time, the formation of a far-flung network of Islamic scholarly institutions within Daghestan. The latter process was closely connected with the Daghestani scholar Muḥammad b. Musa al-Quduqī (1652–1717). In this period, a flurry of intellectual activity began in Daghestan. Scholars began to produce original works on logic, rhetoric, theology, Arabic grammar and *fiqh*. The beginning of the formation of the Daghestani madrasas can be traced, at least, to the tenth and eleventh centuries.[24] However, by the seventeenth century, the education system in Daghestan underwent several changes. Some of the disciplines that Daghestani scholars had given great attention to in the pre-Mongol period (that is, hadith studies, Sufi literature) were replaced by new ones (such as rhetoric and logic), which had not been particularly popular before the 1600s.

Several factors internal to Daghestani society influenced the formation of the legal discourse there. One of these was the development of the village councils, which acted as independent political formations during this period. The legal culture of these councils in Daghestan was characterised by the ascendancy of customary law (*ᶜadāt*) with certain minor inclusions from the Shāfiᶜī legal system. Beginning with Muḥammad al-Quduqī, several major theologians of the eighteenth century tried to counterbalance the *ᶜadāt* legal proceedings by replacing them with the norms of the Shāfiᶜī legal system. But because that legal system had still only just appeared in the region, these scholars, who criticised the norms of customary law, could not always answer all questions (on inheritance, last will and testament, land disputes, marriage and so forth) brought before them. In other words, the newly formed Muslim spiritual elite did not accept the conditions and norms relating to certain questions (under Islamic law) that already had answers under the norms of customary law. However, they did not always find ready answers to these questions in Shāfiᶜī law itself, and they found it necessary to consult legal authorities in the Middle East.[25] These requests from the Daghestanis and answers from Arab jurists on certain legal questions were characteristic of much of the eighteenth century. Through this process, besides gaining practice in resolving individual questions, Daghestani scholars received a more profound education in the major scholarly centres of the Middle East: Damascus, Cairo, Aleppo, Mecca and Medina.

As Daghestani legal scholars handed down decisions, they faced the problem of choosing among methodologies of investigation and resolution. The beginning of the Daghestani discussions of *ijtihād* as a method of formulating new solutions to new questions also arose in connection with these developments.The Daghestani legal tradition connects the discussion of *ijtihād* with the Yemeni scholar Ṣāliḥ bin Mahdī al-Maqbalī al-Yamanī (1637–97), of whom Daghestani scholar Muḥammad b. Musa al-Quduqī was a student.

Ṣāliḥ al-Yamanī's name is well-known not only in Daghestani Arabic-language literature, but also in the Middle East, where his views have been discussed by many Muslim scholars. In Russian scholarship, the Soviet orientalist I. Yu. Krachkovskii wrote about him in detail.[26] In Daghestani Arabic-language works, the biography of Ṣāliḥ al-Yamanī can be found in Ḥasan al-Alqadarī's work *Jirāb al-Mamnūn*.[27]

Ṣāliḥ al-Yamanī is of interest in that, according the Arabic-language sources, he claimed for himself the status of 'absolute *mujtahid*'.[28] His adherence to *ijtihād*, together with several of his juridical decisions, which stepped beyond the bounds of the Shāfiᶜī school, sparked discussions concerning the admissibility of his rulings. In connection with this, Ṣāliḥ al-Yamanī was accused of adherence to the ideas of the Muᶜtazilis in matters of dogma and the ideas of the Zaidis in matters of *fiqh*. It was written in the margins of an anonymous eighteenth-century Daghestani manuscript, *Al-Risāla fī intiqād Ṣāliḥ al-Yamanī* ('The Treatise in Reproof of Ṣāliḥ al-Yamanī'), dedicated to criticisms of al-Yamanī's legal rulings on the treble process for divorce, that:

> It is known that Ṣāliḥ al-Yamanī was a Muᶜtazili, which is borne witness to in his words in the foreword of his work *al-Manār Sharḥ al-Baḥr al-Zakhkhār*. He said, 'For me, *madhhab*s do not exist.' And the *fatwā*s that he handed down contradicted all the Sunni *madhhab*s. His opinions are not worth giving attention to and following, because they are heresy (*murūq*). Likewise, it is generally known that, regardless of his claims to [being capable of performing] *ijtihad*, regardless of what he himself said about there being for him no *madhhab* but only one unified Islam, he was not an absolute *mujtahid*. He was a Muᶜtazili, for had he not been one, he would have followed one of the four *madhhab*s . . . Ṣāliḥ al-Yamanī was one who introduced harmful innovations into Islam (*al-mubtadiᶜ*), insofar as the mark of harmful innovation (*al-bidᶜa*)

> is contradiction of the followers of the Sunna (*ahl al-sunna*). And harmful innovation is that which did not exist in the time of the prophet Muḥammad and his companions. And if we acknowledged that he was among the followers of the Sunna, then, in that event, he should have followed one of the *madhhab*s or been a *mujtahid* within the bounds of one of the *madhhab*s. But he considered himself to be beyond all the *madhhab*s, and that speaks to his error. And the fact that he handed down rulings that contradicted the opinions of the imams of all four *madhhab*s disproves his claim that these were revealed to him by God. And he who hands down rulings not based on God's revelation is a non-believer (*kāfir*).[29]

The anonymous author's claim here about Ṣaliḥ al-Yamani's adherence to Muᶜtazili ideas probably has some basis in fact. One of Ṣāliḥ al-Yamanī's main teachers was the Zaidi scholar Mahdi b. ᶜAbd al-Ḥādi, well-known as 'al-Maḥsūsa', who, when answering questions of dogma, adhered to the views of the Muᶜtazilis.[30] Besides that, Yaḥyā b. al-Ḥusayn b. Al-Qāsim, one of the students of Ṣāliḥ al-Yamanī, was a Zaidi. This indirectly speaks to the fact that al-Yamanī shared certain ideas of the Zaidis, who, in matters of dogma, adhered to the views of the Muᶜtazilis.[31]

Al-Yamani's interest in the ideas of the Muᶜtazilis is indirectly confirmed by the fact that he wrote the sub-commentary *al-Itḥāf li ṭalaba al-Kashshāf* on the well-known *tafsīr*, *al-Kashshāf*, by the Muᶜtazili scholar Maḥmūd b. ᶜUmar al-Zamakhsharī.[32] Despite the fact that Ṣāliḥ al-Yamanī himself criticised certain points of al-Zamakhsharī's commentary in this work, in all of the other commentaries on this *tafsīr*, he confirmed that 'which was preferred (*rajāḥa*)' in the views of the Muᶜtazilis.[33] It is also noteworthy that Ṣāliḥ al-Yamanī completed this work in 1102/1690–1, that is, six or seven years before his death on 18 November 1697.[34] This, likewise, indirectly speaks to his interest in Muᶜtazili dogma, to which he adhered until his death.

Although the ideas of the Shāfiᶜī and Zaidi schools often intersected in Yemen, in Daghestan, Ṣāliḥ al-Yamanī was most often viewed negatively.[35] In the Daghestani manuscripts, we have found only one positive portrayal of Ṣāliḥ al-Yamanī, and that one is in the above-mentioned work *al-Itḥāf,* where he is called a 'profound scholar, who knew the finer points of the sciences'.[36]

Another scholar, Ḥasan al-Alqadarī (1834–1910), gives a somewhat more neutral characterisation of Ṣāliḥ al-Yamanī. In answer to a question posed by one of his correspondents concerning Ṣāliḥ al-Yamanī and whether one could follow his legal decisions, Ḥasan al-Alqadarī confirmed that some of al-Yamanī's rulings contradicted the unanimous opinion of the scholars of all four *madhhab*s. In light of this, Ḥasan al-Alqadari stated that it was possible to follow al-Yamanī's ruling only for individual questions relating to oneself.[37] However, his rulings could not be used to support a *fatwā* or argument in the Daghestani *sharīᶜa* courts, as al-Yamanī's conclusions contradicted the Shāfiᶜī legal system.[38]

The vast majority of Daghestani scholars' assessments of Ṣāliḥ al-Yamanī were of an extremely negative character. For example, the jurist Muḥammad ᶜAlī al-Chukhī wrote in his legal work:

> Concerning Ṣāliḥ al-Yamanī, he is well-known among us in Daghestan as a person who brought harmful innovation (*al-mubtadiᶜ*), who was himself in error (*ḍāll*) and led others into error (*muḍill*). Certain unwary Daghestanis studied with Ṣāliḥ al-Yamanī, thinking that he was an adherent of the Shāfiᶜī school. However, his works bear witness to the fact that he not only did not adhere to the Shāfiᶜī school, but went against all four legal schools. My brothers, do not follow the opinions of Ṣāliḥ al-Yamanī or you, too, will become those who engage in harmful innovation. Abu Bakr al-ᶜAimakī wrote a tract concerning Ṣāliḥ al-Yamanī in which he explained the adherence of the latter to the ideas of the Muᶜtazilis, and he wrote that Ṣāliḥ al-Yamanī was in error.[39]

Later in the text, the author gives the opinions of other Daghestani scholars, among them, Ḥasan al-Qudalī, ᶜAbd al-Latīf al-Ḥutsī and Muḥammad al-ᶜUbudī, who likewise accused Ṣāliḥ al-Yamanī of adhering to the ideas of the Muᶜtazilis and contradicting the four *madhhab*s with his rulings.[40] Another Daghestani scholar, Jamāl al-Dīn al-Gharabudāghī (1858–1947), also wrote about Ṣāliḥ al-Yamanī in a strikingly negative light, noting that he 'engaged in harmful innovation, was in error, and led others into error'.[41]

Yet another scholar, Abu Bakr al-ᶜAimakī (d. 1791), in answer to a question from one of his students concerning Ṣāliḥ al-Yamanī, who 'recognized only the Qur'ān and the Sunna, rejected *ᶜijmā'*, *qiyās*, and the *madhhab*s, and mixed the views of the Sunnis, the Muᶜtazilis, the Rafidis, and the Zaidis', gave a very negative response, noting that 'he who refuses to follow the *madhhab*s (perform *taqlīd*) and pretends to the status of absolute *mujtahid*, as Ṣāliḥ al-Yamanī did, is in error and his opinions cannot be used as a guide in legal questions'.[42]

An equally negative opinion of Ṣāliḥ al-Yamanī was given by yet another scholar of the eighteenth century, ᶜUmar al-Khunzakhī, who lived for a long time in Medina. Examining the opinions of those Daghestani legal scholars who adhered to the legal decisions of Ṣāliḥ al-Yamanī, ᶜUmar al-Khunzakhī wrote:

> The decisions that certain scholars hand down, following the rulings of al-Yamanī, should be considered incorrect. Al-Yamanī himself is not a fol-

lower of any of the four *madhhab*s and he is not even a Sunni (*Ahl al-sunna wāl-jamāᶜa*). And those who follow him will be resurrected together with him.

For all argumentation of his opinions, ᶜUmar al-Khunzakhī cited Arab scholars, with whom he had conversed on this issue.[43]

Negative opinions of Ṣāliḥ al-Yamanī were held not only among Daghestani jurists, but also among Arab scholars. As such, on the issue of Ṣāliḥ al-Yamanī's decision concerning the treble procedure for divorce, addressed to the *muftī* of Mecca, Saᶜid al-Makkī, the latter wrote the following:

> Certain Daghestani scholars, owing to their ignorance and carelessness, consider Ṣāliḥ al-Yamanī to be a Shāfiᶜī jurist. In fact, not only was Ṣāliḥ al-Yamanī not a Shāfiᶜī, but he worked outside of the frameworks of all four legal schools. Ṣāliḥ al-Yamanī was well-known among us [the scholars of Mecca] as a person who introduced harmful innovations into Islam (*al-mubtadiᶜ*), was, himself, in error (*ḍāll*), and led others into error (*muḍill*). Daghestani brothers, do not adhere to the opinions of Ṣāliḥ al-Yamanī, or you, too, will fall into heresy (*murūq*) and error (*ḍalala*).[44]

Although the Daghestani scholar Muḥammad al-Quduqī was a student of Ṣāliḥ al-Yamanī and followed his teacher's opinions on a variety of questions, practically all the accounts of him are complimentary. Muḥammad al-Quduqī received his education in various villages in Daghestan. From there, he set out for Egypt and the Hijaz with the goal of perfecting his knowledge. In Mecca, he met Ṣāliḥ al-Yamanī, with whom he studied for a long time.[45] After returning to his homeland, Muḥammad al-Quduqī founded a network of Islamic educational institutions that became well-known far beyond the borders of Daghestan.[46] Not long before his death, he went on a pilgrimage to Mecca. He fell ill and died in Aleppo in 1717.

Muḥammad al-Quduqī was the author of a number of works on Arabic grammar, logic, rhetoric and practical astronomy (*ᶜilm al-mikat*). Al-Quduqī did not leave behind a single work relating to *fiqh*. However, there are many glosses in the margins of Daghestani manuscripts of *fiqh* that cite legal decisions made by al-Quduqī concerning various questions.

Muḥammad al-Quduqī is considered the first Daghestani to turn away from *taqlīd* and promote *ijtihād*. The Daghestani scholar ᶜAlī b. ᶜAbd al-Ḥamīd al-Ghumuqī (1878–1943) wrote in one of his biographical works:

> Al-Quduqī was the first among the scholars of Daghestan to awake from the slumber of *taqlīd* and he instructed other scholars to use reason and thinking, so that, through this, they might distinguish between truth and lies. Al-Quduqī was the first to call them to freedom of thought, to freedom from the yoke of *taqlīd*,

> and to study religion and science from the fundamental sources, the Qurʾān and the hadiths, and to carry out analysis and set it upon the scales of the bases of *sharīʿa,* choosing the appropriate norms. The outstanding scholar al-Quduqī, during his time in Mecca fulfilling one of the pillars of the Islamic faith, met the *shaykh* Ṣāliḥ b. Madhi al-Yamanī, who had settled in Mecca and who lifted from his shoulders the yoke of *taqlīd.* Ṣāliḥ al-Yamanī chose from the decisions of the imams those in agreement with the foundations of Islam and ventured into innovations. Al-Quduqī learned from him and received sufficient knowledge; he favorably accepted his methods and his way. Then, al-Quduqī returned to Daghestan, bringing with him several new books from his *shaykh,* and began to call scholars to throw off the yoke of *taqlīd* and study the Islamic sciences from the basic sources: the Qurʾān and the hadiths. Unfortunately, very few people accepted his call and the majority met it with denial and rejection because of their weak faith in their own reasoning and their excessive veneration of the imams they followed. However, he did not carry out this activity in vain. Al-Quduqī's call found a response during his own life and after his death. And in Daghestan, scholars were always found who accepted his call and adhered to independent, free judgment, preferring it to the blind adherence of *taqlīd.* Al-Quduqī traveled a true and clear path. The decisions and *fatwā*s handed down by others were guided by him.[47]

This fragment of text is curious for several reasons. On the one hand, in Russian historical scholarship, Muḥammad al-Quduqī is attributed the status of 'absolute *mujtahid*'.[48] Similarly, ʿAlī al-Ghumuqī clearly states that al-Quduqī cast off 'the yoke of *taqlīd*' and began to formulate decisions on the basis of the Qurʾān and the Sunna. However, in al-Ghumuqī's text, there is a contradiction concerning al-Quduqī's status as an 'absolute *mujtahid*'.

As discussed above, the conditions for being an absolute *mujtahid* include: (1) developing one's own methodology and (2) when investigating a question, never following the opinion of another scholar but instead considering the matter independently. However, ʿAlī al-Ghumuqī's text clearly states that al-Quduqī 'chose from the decisions of the imams that agreed with the foundations of Islam'. In other words, he did not develop his own principles and methodology of selection and analysis of evidence. Rather, he followed the opinions of other jurists. It follows from this that, in the text cited above, al-Quduqī adhered to decisions that had already been formulated by other scholars of the various *madhhab*s, a course of action that would have been unacceptable for an absolute *mujtahid.*

There is a specific question that was fiercely debated over the course of almost three hundred years and that shows that al-Quduqī, in that specific case, followed the previous opinions of Taqī al-Dīn ibn Taymiyya and Ṣāliḥ al-Yamanī. This question concerned the treble procedure for divorce. According to the opinions of all four Sunni legal schools, if a husband gave his wife a divorce by saying the *ṭalāq* formula three times on a single occasion, then the divorce was considered valid. The spouses could not remarry until the wife had been married to another man and then divorced from him. There is, however, another opinion, which contradicts this unanimous decision of the four Sunni schools. Ibn Taymiya and Ṣāliḥ al-Yamanī considered a divorce valid only when the three *ṭalāq*s had been pronounced on different occasions. If the entire *ṭalāq* formula was pronounced at once, three times or even ten times, they considered this to count as only one pronouncement and believed that the husband still had the possibility of returning to his wife.[49] On this question, al-Quduqī did not develop his own opinion, but simply followed the opinion of Ibn Taymiyya and Ṣāliḥ al-Yamanī.[50] Insofar as an 'absolute *mujtahid*' cannot follow another scholar's opinion, but is obligated to independently investigate a given issue, al-Quduqī's performance of 'absolute *ijtihād*' in the above case can be called into question.

This opinion is indirectly supported by the words of another Daghestani scholar, Ḥasan al-Alqadarī, who wrote regarding al-Quduqī:

> In questions of dogma (*ᶜaqīda*), despite the fact that he (al-Quduqī) followed the way of the *shaykh* Abū al-Ḥasan al-Ashᶜarī, all the same, in certain questions, he broke the bonds of agreement with him (*ribq-e muwāfaqatni qatᶜ edüb*). Likewise, in questions of *fiqh*, despite the fact that he considered it necessary to follow (*mulāzamat taqlīd inde edüb*) [the school] of Imam al-Shāfiᶜī, all the same, he cut the bonds of agreement with him as well.[51]

Such different opinions from two scholars – al-Ghumuqī and al-Alqadarī – can be explained by the fact that ᶜAlī al-Ghumuqī himself was one of the supporters of *ijtihād* in Daghestan, and, naturally, al-Quduqī's great authority among Daghestani jurists and his supposed preference for 'absolute *ijtihād*' were, for al-Ghumuqī, solid arguments for his own use of the practice. Ḥasan al-Alqadarī, on the other hand, preferred to adherence to *taqlīd*, if it were done with care, but he was absolutely opposed to *ijtihād*.[52]

The authority of al-Quduqī among Daghestani jurists was, indeed, great. And explanations can be found in the works of later Daghestani scholars even for those of his decisions that contradicted the opinions of the Shāfiᶜī and other legal schools.

For example, Jamāl al-Dīn al-Gharabudāghī, in his citation of the decision of another Daghestani scholar, Ibrāhim al-ᶜUradī (d. 1771), writes the following: 'The legal decisions of al-Quduqī and his disciples were given not with the goal of having those decisions applied in practice, but with the goal of assessing those decisions (*mushāwara*).'[53] That is to say that, in Ibrahim al-ᶜUradī's opinion, some of al-Quduqī's legal decisions, when they diverged from the framework of *taqlīd*, were not *fatwā*s that had to be accepted in Daghestani courts. Rather, they were the personal opinions of one scholar, expressed with the goal of assessing a given question among Daghestani jurists.

The same Ibrahim al-ᶜUradī wrote in one of his commentaries: 'It came to me that Muḥammad b. Musa al-Quduqī, in relation to that question [that is, the treble procedure for divorce], rejected his preference (*tarjīḥ*) [in favour of a different opinion], which had been given earlier, and he did penance.'[54]

In the above fragment, the discussion again revolves around the question of the treble procedure for divorce. In this case, al-Quduqī had adhered to the opinion of his teacher, Ṣāliḥ al-Yamanī, at the beginning. Later, according to al-ᶜUradī, he rejected that opinion, preferring, instead, the opinion of the Shāfiᶜī school.

As such, an analysis of the sources shows that, despite the fact that certain modern researchers describe al-Quduqī as an 'absolute *mujtahid*', he, in fact, with a few rare exceptions, worked within the boundaries of the Shāfiᶜī legal school. Based on indirect evidence, his *ijtihād* may be characterised as the last two levels of *ijtihād*: *ijtihād* within the bounds of a school and *ijtihād* at the level of the *fatwā*. According to the sources, regarding certain questions, he stepped beyond the bounds of the *madhhab*s and held a divergent opinion. However, in these cases, there was no contradiction between the principles of *taqlīd* and *ijtihād* because, within the framework of the Shāfiᶜī tradition, scholars had not rejected all levels of *ijtihād*. At the very least, Daghestani scholars, including those who considered themselves adherents of *taqlīd*, acknowledged all three of the lower levels of *ijtihād*. However, many Daghestani jurists viewed the practice of *ijtihād* with trepidation, preferring to follow the opinions of past scholars. Al-Quduqī's authority in Daghestan was so great that later jurists did not dismiss the possibility that he could have achieved the status of *mujtahid*. However, they would have seen him not as an 'absolute *mujtahid*', as modern researchers have presented him, but as a limited *mujtahid* – a *mujtahid* of the *madhhab* or of the *fatwā* --, a status that was permitted in the Shāfiᶜī tradition.

In Daghestani sources, it is clearly stated that al-Quduqī achieved the status to investigate and give preference to one jurist's opinion over that of another (*tarjīḥ fīl-madhhab*), which is one of the principles of *ijtihād* of the *fatwā*.[55] If one approaches this question from the point of view of the dubious juxtaposition of *taqlīd* to *ijtihād*, then al-Quduqī, who sometimes resorted to *ijtihād*, should not have been well-accepted among the Muslim jurists of Daghestan. In my view, many Daghestani scholars held negative views of Ṣāliḥ al-Yamanī precisely because of his adherence to absolute *ijtihād*, which was considered unacceptable in the Daghestani Shāfiᶜī tradition. By contrast, they held positive views of his student, al-Quduqī, because he limited himself to *ijtihād* within the bounds of the *madhhab*, which did not go against the Shāfiᶜī tradition. However, thanks to the great authority that al-Quduqī enjoyed among Daghestani jurists, the early opinions of his teacher, Ṣāliḥ al-Yamanī, on certain questions enjoyed a degree of circulation in Daghestan.

At present, reconstructing a detailed portrait of al-Quduqī's views is difficult. The problem is that, to date, not one work on Islamic law by al-Quduqī has been located. The present historical accounts of al-Quduqī have been written based on several fragments left by later Daghestani jurists that contain references to him. However, in Daghestan, there are numerous private collections containing tens or, in some cases, hundreds of manuscripts. At present, just under 400 such collections are known. It is possible that, in the future, newly discovered sources and further research into the legal rulings of al-Quduqī will augment historians' understanding of him.

Al-Quduqī's ideas about *ijtihād* continued through the rest of the eighteenth century. The Daghestani theologian ᶜAlī al-Ghumuqī recalls several eighteenth-century Daghestani jurists who also promoted ideas about *ijtihād*:

> Damadan al-Muḥuwī knew to perfection all of the roots and branches of *sharīᶜa* and he was among those who considered that they should work from the fundamental, trustworthy sources – the Qurᵓān and the hadiths – and reject the decisions of jurists who contradicted those sources. He did not agree with the idea that he should follow the opinions of another (*qallada*), regardless of the status that person had achieved . . . Muḥammad al-Ḍarir al-Ghumuqī was among those scholars who worked from the bases of the legal sciences, that is the Qurᵓān and the Sunna, and cast the yoke of *taqlīd* from their shoulders. He spoke of the Qurᵓān and the Sunna as the primary sources of evidence and did not pay attention to anything else. Likewise, they say that he followed the opinions of Ṣāliḥ al-Yamanī and often approved of what al-Yamanī adhered to. He often defended [the opinions of Ṣāliḥ al-Yamanī] and carried on disputes with those who were not in agreement with the latter. . . . Muḥammad b. Ibrahim al-Qarakhī al-Huchuwī was a major scholar. He tended toward independent, free judgment and put forward evidence (*dalīl*), but not the opinions of people (*rijāl*) who contradicted what was generally accepted. He did this in the debates which took place between him and the scholar-jurist Mahdi Muḥammad al-Qarakhī, concerning the questions of oaths (*nadhr*) and the willing of inheritance (*waṣīya*).[56]

Through the polemics concerning the questions of *taqlīd* and *ijtihād* and, also, the resolution of certain juridical questions, we can see that *ijtihād* was practiced throughout the eighteenth century.

As was already noted above, the end of the seventeenth century and the beginning of the eighteenth were characterised by the more general development of the Islamic legal system. In the struggle against the ascendancy of customary law, many Daghestani jurists tried to find answers to recurring questions by new means. Some of them looked to the Islamic authorities in the Middle East. Others, taking into consideration the social and economic conditions of Daghestan, experimented with or adjusted the norms of the legal rulings existing in Shāfiʿī law by turning to analogy *fatwā*s. A third group tried to resolve many questions without an intermediary by turning directly to the sources of the law, the Qurʾān and the Sunna. Likely, Muḥammad al-Quduqī, as noted in the sources, preferred the ready-made decisions of the Shāfiʿī system in a form analysed and adapted to the realities of Daghestan. However, al-Quduqī also often turned to the method of independent judgment through direct consultation of the Qurʾān and the Sunna, using elements of *ijtihād* of the *madhhab*.

The discourses on *taqlīd* and *ijtihād* and these attempts to use *ijtihād* to resolve questions arising in the sphere of daily life and interpersonal relations (*muʿāmala*), which had emerged in Daghestan in the seventeenth century, began to subside by the beginning of the nineteenth century. On the one hand, this may speak to the fact that the more topical questions characteristic of Daghestan in that period had already been resolved. On the other hand, the diminishing interest in *ijtihād* was connected with the strengthening of the Shāfiʿī legal tradition during the period of *jihād* under the leadership of the three imams: Ghāzī Muḥammad (1828–32), Gamzatbek (1832–4) and Shamil (1834–59). During Shamil's imamate, the *ʿadāt* courts were liquidated and a new court system was created, which operated solely according to the norms of the Shāfiʿī school.

The Legal System in the Caucasus Wars Period (1828–59)

The first action of the first imam of Daghestan, Ghāzī Muḥammad (1828–32), was to continue the critique of customary law begun by eighteenth-century scholars. In his work, *Bāhir al-burhān li-irtidād ʿurafāʾ al-Daghistān*, Ghāzī Muḥammad called for the replacement of customary law with the norms of *sharīʿa*, which, in his understanding, meant following the ritual practices and juridical norms of the Shāfiʿī legal school.[57] It is curious that, in his own work, Ghāzī Muḥammad cited the opinion of Muḥammad al-Quduqī forbidding the consumption of the flesh of animals killed by those who lived by *ᶜadāt*, and, likewise, forbidding marriage contracts to be drawn up with such people. When he cited Muḥammad al-Quduqī, Ghāzī Muḥammad wrote nothing about *ijtihād*.

Later, the debates between the supporters and opponents of the imamate entered a new phase. Discussions arose concerning the Islamic legal bases of the imamate and the necessity for Daghestanis to emigrate from their territory (*hijra*), now under the rule of the Russian Empire (*dār al-ḥarb*), to the territory of the imamate (*dār al-Islām*). Those Muslims who preferred to live under the rule of the 'infidels' (*kāfir*) were called apostates (*murtadd*), against whom violence was permitted under the norms of the Shāfiᶜī system.

It is curious that, in this fierce polemic, no one among the supporters or the opponents of the imamate turned to *ijtihād* to justify their opinion. The written polemic between them shows that, in order to support their arguments, both sides referenced the works of Shāfiᶜī jurists, citing them without making the least effort to turn to an analysis of the primary sources of the law, the Qurᵓān and the Sunna.[58]

In Shamil's imamate, the question of *ijtihād* and *taqlīd* was not raised for several reasons. First, in the course of the eighteenth century, a strengthening of the Shāfiᶜī legal tradition had taken place such that, by the first half of the nineteenth century, many questions that had been the object of debate in the eighteenth century had been resolved. It should be added that, by the beginning of the nineteenth century, it had been established that the practice of *ijtihād* was impermissible in Daghestan, based on the opinion that it was not necessary and that it was impossible that qualified *mujtahid*s existed among the jurists of Daghestan. Despite the fact that Imam Shafiᶜī himself, like the other jurists of that school, had not rejected the various forms of *ijtihād*, the Daghestani Shāfiᶜī tradition preferred the practice of *taqlīd*.[59] However, as was noted above, the development of the *ijtihād* discourses in the eighteenth century had already resulted in many legal decisions on a range of questions (such as *nadhr*, that is, will and testament) and these decisions were widely used in Daghestani court proceedings by the beginning of the nineteenth century. At the same time, however, the nineteenth century saw the emergence of new questions, such as the negotiation of marriage contracts (*nikāḥ*) in native languages, the legitimacy of the imamate, the question of migration (*hijra*) and *jihād*, all of which demanded answers. Regarding marriage contracts, *ijtihād* was not necessary, as such questions had already been answered in the eighteenth century. Daghestanis simply referred to past precedents and decisions made by eighteenth-century scholars and argued in support of their own opinions using citations from the classical Shāfiʿī jurists Ibn Hajar al-Haytamī, Jamāl al-Dīn al-Mahallī and others.

For questions of *jihād* and the legitimacy of the imamate, there was also no need to perform *ijtihād*. Scholars' views on these polemics did not need to be supported with *ijtihād*, which all the *ʿulamāʾ* of Daghestan viewed with scepticism, but, rather, with the strong proofs from recognised authorities from the 'holy places' (Mecca and Medina) and the other cities of the Arab world.

The difference between the appeals of the Daghestani jurists to Arab scholars in the eighteenth century and those of the imamate period was that the two groups pursued different goals. In the eighteenth century, Daghestani jurists appealed to their Arab colleague on the basis that specific questions had arisen for the first time and they asked for simply argued legal decisions from Arab jurists regarding these questions. Alternately, some Daghestani scholars resolved these questions through the application of limited *ijtihād*.

In the *jihād* period in the nineteenth century, the supporters and opponents of the imamate appealed to Arab jurists to legitimate their decisions concerning the imamate, *hijra* and *jihād*, strengthening them with arguments in the form of '*fatwā*s from the holy places'. In this last instance, *ijtihād* was not only unnecessary, but even, at some level, 'harmful', insofar as the legitimation of such important issues as *jihād*, the imamate and *hijra* by means of Daghestani jurists' *ijtihād* would have raised doubts about those legal decisions within Daghestan itself. For Daghestani jurists, an argument coming from outside Daghestan was seen not only as more authoritative than an opinion from within Daghestan, but also gave the supporters of the imamate added legitimacy in their own activities. *Ijtihād*, for both the supporters and the opponents of the imamate in Daghestan, simply was not worth scholars' attention; although Daghestani jurists formally acknowledged the permissibility of several levels of *ijtihād*, they still did not believe that any of their contemporaries met the qualifications to be considered a *mujtahid*. As such, *ijtihād* in the time of the Caucasus Wars was viewed as equally harmful to the position of both the supporters and the opponents of the imamate. This explains why, despite the many decisions handed down by Daghestani jurists in this period, there is not a single word in the sources on the problem of *ijtihād* and *taqlīd*. Under the conditions of the Caucasus Wars, no such discussion was needed by either party.

In 1859, the Caucasus Wars ended in the eastern Caucasus on the following terms:

> the voluntary submission of the population, the promise to live peacefully and to obey the laws of our government's rulers, and we [Russians], for our part, are obligated not to interfere in their religion, rights, customs . . . and their bearing of arms; we are obligated never to levy taxes or tribute payments against them . . . and never to force them into military service.[60]

The key to the supporters of *jihād* accepting that the Caucasus Wars were at an end lay precisely in the fact that they were not ended by capitulation to the infidels, but by the conclusion of a temporary peace agreement. The degree to which Daghestanis viewed the peace between themselves and the Russians as a contract can be seen in their reaction to changes in the Daghestani tax system in the 1860s. During this decade, the imperial government began to collect taxes from the local population of the eastern Caucasus. Daghestani scholars saw this as a violation of the aforementioned 1859 agreement between Shamil and the Russian and as an opportunity to begin a new *jihād*.[61] This explains why, from 1863 onward, uprisings broke out periodically across the eastern and western Caucasus.

This situation changed abruptly after the 1877 uprising in Daghestan and Chechnya. The uprising was so brutally suppressed that Daghestani scholars understood that further *jihād*s were futile. Many members of the Muslim elite in Daghestan came to believe that since their land had fallen under Russian rule, it had become the 'house of war' (*dār al-ḥarb*). They preferred to emigrate, that is, to perform *hijra* to the 'lands of Islam', the territory of the Ottoman Empire. Another part of the Muslim elite was exiled to the interior of the Russian Empire. In Russian exile, some Daghestanis followed the example of Volga-Ural Muslims and adapted to the realities of life in Russia, while others escaped from their places of exile and fled to the Ottoman Empire or Central Asia.[62] After the 1880s, a new stage began in the history of the development of Islamic law in Daghestan. This new stage was characterised by the broad integration of Daghestan into empire-wide social institutions.

The Renewal of the Discourse on Ijtihād *from the Late 1800s to the 1920s*

After the uprising of 1877, it became clear to the Daghestanis that armed resistance against the Russian Empire was pointless. However, the inclusion of Daghestan into the social and economic structures of the empire led the Daghestani *ʿulamāʾ* to consider a range of new questions that had not been previously examined. With the new developments brought by the Great Reforms era, Daghestani jurists tried to find new answers. This led to a renewal of the discourse on *taqlīd* and *ijtihād* in Daghestan.

There were several reasons for the renewal of this discourse. The first reason was the exile of many Daghestani *ᶜulamāᵓ* to the interior of the Russian Empire. In exile, Daghestani scholars came into close contact with the Muslim legal scholars of the Volga-Ural region and had the opportunity to become acquainted with the works of the Ḥanafī jurists, who were popular in the Volga-Ural region and Central Asia. Upon their return to their homeland, these Daghestani scholars had already examined certain legal questions not only from the perspective of the Shāfiᶜī legal school, but also through a comparative analysis between the Shāfiᶜī and Ḥanafī schools.

Another factor was economic change. Colonial administration in Daghestan and the integration of the region into the Russian economy led, in part, to certain villages losing their economic niche. With the broad development of trade with the interior provinces of Russia, primarily representatives of the imperial elite controlled commerce and the wares of local craftsmen were unable to compete with Russian goods (manufactured goods, agricultural products, weapons). This led to the impoverishment of the Daghestani population. The transfer of village lands into the category of 'state lands' also led to the financial ruin of the local population. Residents of these villages were forced to become seasonal workers, travelling to other regions of the empire to find employment (in the oil fields of Baku in the early 1900s and in the interior provinces of Russia, including Kazan and Astrakhan). This also brought the Daghestanis into close contact with the other Muslims of Russia (mostly Ḥanafīs) as well as with the non-Muslim population of Daghestan and its surrounding regions. Such interactions raised new questions: Was it permissible to marry a Russian woman? How should one carry out one's prayers in the Ḥanafī way? Was it permitted to use a gramophone to listen to the text of the Qurᵓān? Was it permitted to wear the clothing of the 'infidels'? Was it possible to work for the 'infidels' for acceptable wages? Was it permissible to eat meat slaughtered by 'people of the Book'? Was it permitted to live under Russian colonial rule, or should Muslims emigrate to the Ottoman Empire?

Many of these questions had not presented themselves in the precolonial period or in the period of *jihād* under the three imams. As such, Daghestani jurists of the late nineteenth century had to find answers to these new questions.

A third factor was the travel of Daghestanis to Muslim lands beyond Russia's borders (Egypt, Syria, Istanbul) to begin or continue their religious education. The development of modern transportation networks (railways, roads, steamships) made these journeys more feasible than they had been in the pre-colonial period or in the period of isolation from the rest of the Muslim world that the Caucasus experienced during the *jihād*.

In addition, the development of mass printing made Muslim literature more readily available. Daghestanis also gained access to the Muslim press of Egypt, Istanbul, Bakhchisaray, Kazan, Ufa and Orenburg. All this gave Daghestanis the opportunity to become acquainted with new developments in Islamic legal thought. The ideas of Egyptian reformers Jamāl al-Dīn al-Afghanī, Muḥammad ᶜAbduh and Rashīd Riḍa and the works of Tatar scholars ᶜAbd al-Nāsir al-Qūrsāwī and Shihāb al-Dīn al-Marjānī became accessible, well-known and popular in Daghestan. Through Middle Eastern and Tatar literature, citations of authors who had previously been unknown or nearly forgotten began to appear in Daghestani legal writings.

Daghestani jurists responded in a variety of ways to the new developments of this period. For example, the Daghestani scholar Ḥasan al-Alqadarī, exiled in the town of Spassk in Tambov province, had the opportunity to closely study Ḥanafī legal literature, and he tried to answer a number of questions by means of a comparative analysis of the Shāfiᶜī and Ḥanafī legal systems. He examined these questions from the perspective of his adherence to *taqlīd*. However, in accepting this comparative method, al-Alqadarī was forced to seek a compromise between *taqlīd* and *ijtihād*, and, in fact, he did not see any reason why *ijtihād* should be forbidden. He often appealed to Muslim authorities who challenged the 'closing of the gates of *ijtihād*'. However, he viewed the practice of absolute *ijtihād* with great caution.[63] Nevertheless, al-Alqadarī was the first late nineteenth-century Daghestani jurist to return to the discussion of the boundaries of *ijtihād*.

A particularly active phase of this polemic began in the first years of the twentieth century. This was borne witness to in tens of compositions and articles in the Muslim press relating to *taqlīd* and *ijtihād*. The debates over *taqlīd* and *ijtihād* on the whole, as well as the discussions of the nuances of different levels of *ijtihād*, are reflected in detail in the works of twentieth-century Daghestani jurists, some of whom advocated some form of *ijtihād*. Below, I will try to reconstruct the chronology of the discourses and views of several jurists based on their Arabic-language works.

The first group was composed of those reformers who spoke in favour of the idea of absolute *ijtihād*. Among these scholars was ᶜAlī al-Ghumuqī (1878–1943). ᶜAlī al- Ghumuqī received his education at Al-Azhar. While in Cairo, he adopted the ideas of the Egyptian reformer, Rashīd Riḍa, with whom he worked for several years in the publishing house al-Manār. After returning to Daghestan, ᶜAlī al-Ghumuqī became the editor of the first Arabic-language Daghestani newspaper, *Jarīdat Daghistān*, in which he set forth the ideas of the Muslim reformers and called for the use of absolute *ijtihād*.[64]

In one of his works dedicated to the critique of *taqlīd*, ᶜAlī al-Ghumuqī wrote:

> Many of our scholars believe that *sharīᶜa* is only that which is written in the numerous works on Muslim law and in their commentaries and sub-commentaries. They also think that, by following the guidance of those books, they are adhering to *sharīᶜa*. And, if someone opposes what is written in those books, that person, in their opinion, opposes *sharīᶜa*, has strayed from the path of Islam, and follows the path of harmful innovation (*bidᶜa*) and heresy (*murūq*). Because of that, they call upon Muslims to follow the numerous books of *fiqh* and if they find an answer, they follow it almost verbatim. If they do not find it, then, after studying similar questions and examples, they will hand down a ruling by analogy (*qiyās*). However, they do not recognize that formulating a conclusion by analogy is one of the methods of absolute *ijtihād*. They perform *ijtihād*, a process that they themselves reject. In other words, by speaking out against *ijtihād* on the whole and using conclusion by analogy, which is one of the methods of *ijtihād*, they perform *ijtihād*, but do not admit to themselves that they do it . . . They say that absolute *ijtihād* was performed in the time of Aḥmad ibn Ḥanbal and that no one after him had the right to hand down decisions based upon conclusion by analogy (*qiyās*), while they themselves use that method. At the same time, they do not seek supporting evidence for their decisions in the Qurʾān and the Sunna and are not guided by what is evident in those sources, being limited [in their views] by the narrow confines of *madhhab* and being guided by that which is written in the books of Islamic law. Even when they see that a scholar's opinion contradicts the Qurʾān or a reliable hadith, they do not accept that the opinion is wrong. Instead, they accuse those who are guided by the Qurʾān and the Sunna of innovation and error . . . He who claims that he is a Ḥanafī or Shāfiᶜī cannot be considered as such, save on the basis of his own oral claim. The very understanding of 'adhering to a *madhhab*' (*tamadhhaba*) is possible only for those who command all the arguments and evidence, who know the various categories of *fiqh* and the *fatwā*s of various scholars . . . Adhering to this or that *madhhab* without a thorough understanding of *fiqh* is a form of fanaticism. If someone says that he adheres to a *madhhab*, he has the right to say so only if he follows the ways of the *madhhab*'s imam in scholarship, knowledge, methods of reasoning, and proofs. If he is a long way from understanding the principles and methodologies of the imam of his legal school, then he cannot claim to belong to a *madhhab* based on his words alone. Therefore, if it is said of a man that he does not understand *fiqh*, then, for him, the understanding of 'adhering to a *madhhab*' is unacceptable and meaningless. . . . Neither Allah nor his prophets commanded anyone among the people to limit themselves to the books of later scholar and blindly

> follow whatever was written in them . . . And not one of the imams wrote that it was necessary to be guided by some else's opinion in the case of personal questions.[65]

ᶜAlī al-Ghumuqī also wrote another lengthy article in which he criticised Daghestanis' adherence to *taqlīd* and promoted ideas about absolute *ijtihād*.[66] Importantly, ᶜAlī al-Ghumuqī did not simply criticise *taqlīd*, but also called for scholars to rely solely on the Qurʾān and the Sunna, especially when the evidence in the Qurʾān or the Sunna directly contradicted what was written by later jurists. At the same time, ᶜAlī al-Ghumuqī demonstrated that the methods used by the adherents of *taqlīd* to formulate new decisions, and, especially, judgment by means of analogy, were nothing but elements of *ijtihād*, a process that those same scholars rejected. Without a doubt, al-Ghumuqī's ideas about absolute *ijtihād* were formed under the direct influence of his teacher, Rashīd Riḍa, and the works of the other Egyptian reformers, which ᶜAlī al-Ghumuqī often cited in his writings.

ᶜAlī al-Ghumuqī had many students who wholly shared his views. In the early 1920s, one of these students, Masᶜūd al-Muhukhī (1889–1941), wrote the *Kharq al-Asdād 'an Abwāb al-Ijtihād*, in which he explained his own criticism of adherence to the legal schools and called for the use of absolute *ijtihād*:

> Many scholars in our day depart from the Qurʾān and the Sunna when formulating legal decisions. When issuing *fatwā*s, they rely on and are guided by the opinions of the later scholars, those who wrote books, commentaries on those books, and sub-commentaries. . . . These modern scholars of ours, who rely not on either the Qurʾān or the Sunna, but on the opinions of other scholars, do not know how this or that decision was formulated or what evidence or arguments it is based upon. They refuse to hand down a new decision, even when they see obvious evidence in the Qurʾān or Sunna. They say that the epoch of *ijtihād* ended many centuries ago and that it is necessary to be guided by the later books and opinions of scholars who wrote commentaries and sub-commentaries . . . In our time, it is relatively easy to meet the requirements imposed upon a scholar-*mujtahid*. The book of Almighty God is before us and the hadiths have all been collected into books. The compilers and commentators of the hadiths long ago determined the reliability or unreliability of each hadith, whether it was abrogated (*mansūkh*) or abrogating (*nāsikh*), the direct or interpreted meaning of each word in the hadiths, and so forth. Likewise, scholars have already written all about the consensus among scholars (*ijmāᶜ*), so there remains nothing on that subject which is unclear. It is left to us only to hand down a decision, being guided by all these sources . . . And there is no reason to reject *ijtihād*, except in those cases when a person is not a scholar

> (*ᶜawāmm*). It is necessary that all scholars, when handing down a decision, let themselves be guided by the Qurʾān, the Sunna, the consensus of the scholars, and judgment by analogy (*qiyās*), within the limits of their abilities and zeal. Even those who have not reached the level of *mujtahid* should be guided by evidence (*dalīl*) at the level that their understanding allows. And they should not follow anyone else's opinion, save in those cases when their understanding of *fiqh* is extremely weak. Although Abu Ḥanīfa knew the hadiths better than others and was more god-fearing than others, his students – Abū Yūsuf, Muḥammad (al-Shaybanī), Zufar (b. Huzayl), Ibn al-Mubārak, Bāqī (b. Jarrāh) – rarely followed his opinion in cases where they found obvious evidence in the Qurʾān or the hadiths. In our day, the ideas of reforming education, scholarship, and religion have spread. Scholars have begun to call for guidance from only the Qurʾān and the Sunna. And when these ideas appeared in Egypt, and, likewise, spread in India and in Russia, they were also noted in Daghestan, where certain scholars took a stand against the obduracy of *taqlīd* (*tajammud al-taqlīd*) and called for a return to the faith which had existed in the first centuries of Islam . . . Many of our scholarly contemporaries are guided by *fatwā*s that were handed down by their predecessors. As they do this, they claim that they are following the Shāfiᶜī or Ḥanafī schools. In fact, they are not following these schools, as they do not use even those books that were written by al-Shāfiᶜī and Abū Hanīfa, but use the *fatwā*s or commentaries of scholars who wrote later. In this way, it turns out that they do not follow even their own imams, to say nothing of the Qurʾān and the Sunna. Rather, they are guided in their own actions and decisions by the books of later scholars. However, the imams of these schools themselves forbid others from following their opinions in those cases when a *fatwā* contradicts the hadiths. In answer to the claim of the supporters of *taqlīd* that they are Shāfiᶜīs, one might call them 'Nawawīs', 'Ibn Hajarīs', 'Mahallīs', or 'Ramalīs', as they do not follow the opinions of Imam Shāfiᶜī, but, instead, the decisions of these Shāfiᶜī scholars (Muḥyi al-Dīn al-Nawawī, Ibn Ḥajar al-Haytamī, Jalāl al-Dīn al-Maḥallī, Shams al-Dīn al-Ramlī). In fact, they do not limit themselves to the books of these scholars, so, likewise, they even might be called 'al-Uradīs' and 'al-Qarakhīs', as they also follow the decisions of the Daghestani scholars Murtaḍā ᶜAlī al-ᶜUradī and Muḥammad Ṭāhir al-Qarakhī. Fanatically adhering to the *madhhab*, these scholars prefer the words of scholars to the hadiths, even when said scholars are not Arabs. In fact, they prefer the words of those non-Arab scholars to even the words of the founder of the *madhhab* that they claim to follow.[67]

This opinion of the supporters of absolute *ijtihād* received harsh criticism from those Daghestani scholars who supported *taqlīd*. For example, Jamāl al-Dīn al-Gharabudaghī wrote a critique of the work of ᶜAlī al-Ghumuqī, in which he noted:

> There is no doubt that it is necessary to follow one of the four legal schools (*madhhab*s). It is forbidden to work outside the framework of a given *madhhab*,

> to seek a simplified way within it, or to combine the opinions of different schools (*talfīq*), choosing whatever one likes. And, as to what ᶜAlī al-Ghumuqī wrote in his own works, I say to him that the appearance of a new legal school is impossible. And those words which ᶜAlī al-Ghumuqī wrote in his text are only the words and opinions of one person. These words are not a rule of the *sharīᶜa* that we should follow and guard against that which contradicts it. And the opinion of al-Ghumuqī that God and his prophets banned adherence to the opinions of someone else and that it is necessary to be guided only by the Qurᵓān and the Sunna can be attributed to al-Ghumuqī himself as well as to those like al-Ghumuqī who try to carry out *ijtihād* without possessing adequate knowledge and fear of God. As to being guided by the books of later jurists (*fuqahāᵓ*), that *is* following the Qurᵓān and the Sunna, as these very scholars were guided by the Qurᵓān and the Sunna in formulating their decisions. We choose for ourselves an imam [and *madhhab*] and follow that which he drew from the Qurᵓān and the Sunna. Our faith is Islam, the purist and most correct faith. And it is impossible to change something in it by handing down a dishonest (*fāsiq*) *fatwā* or by following those who pretend to the status of absolute *mujtahid*. And there is no harm in the fact that we do not follow the example of such people. Liars will be pierced by arrows.[68]

A second group of reformers approached the question of *ijtihād* more carefully. Acknowledging the impossibility that an absolute *mujtahid* could exist in their era, they called for extending of the boundaries of *ijtihād*. They accepted the practices of *ijtihād* of the *fatwā* and the *madhhab*, while criticising 'fanatical' (*ta'aṣṣub*) adherence to a *madhhab*.

A characteristic example of this stance can be found in the polemic that unfolded between Daghestani scholars Nadhīr al-Durgilī and Yūsuf al-Jungutī. This conflict reflects the nuances of the discourse on the various levels of *ijtihād* and whether some of them were permitted.[69]

The polemic began with a text that Nadhīr al-Durgilī wrote to the *qāḍī* Muḥammad b. Zayn al-Dīn al-Targhulī, in which al-Durgilī cited the Arab scholar Ibn Taymiyya. In response, Muḥammad al-Targhulī agreed with Nadhīr al-Durgilī's opinion, but reproached him for citing Ibn Taymiyya, whom the *qāḍī* considered a 'wayward scholar'. In response, Nadhīr wrote a second letter, in which he noted the major contributions of Ibn Taymiyya to developing *fiqh*. In answer, Muḥammad al-Targhulī wrote that heretics (*māriq*) such as Ṣāliḥ al-Yamanī, the Wahhabis and the Egyptian reformers based their work on the scholarship of Ibn Taymiyya, and one of their 'errors' was to promote *ijtihād*.[70] This prompted Nadhīr al-Durgilī to write a separate work, *al-Ijtihād wa al-taqlīd*, in which he laid out the following discourse between himself and Yūsuf from the village of Jungutai, who came into possession of Nadhīr's tract.

In his own work, Nadhīr examines several questions connected with the contradictions within the various legal schools. He raises seven examples of Ḥanafī decisions that contradicted Shāfiʿī opinions. He writes that some of the later scholars of these schools handed down decisions that contradicted the Qurʾān and the Sunnah. In such cases, writes Nadhīr, it is necessary to throw out the decision of the jurist and follow the evidence in the Qurʾān and the Sunnah. In his work, Nadhīr writes that, in matters of *ijtihād*, it is forbidden to meddle with the foundations of Islam, but it is possible and even necessary to examine those questions in the sphere of *fiqh* (*furūʿ*),[71] for which there was contradiction among the *madhhabs*.[72] However, Nadhīr approaches the problem of *ijtihād* with caution, noting:

> Although I wrote in relation to the necessity of practicing *ijtihād* in individual cases, I still consider myself to be an adherent of *taqlīd*. I do not reject the books [of *fiqh*] or what is written in them about the norms of the faith. It is obligatory (*wājib*) upon true believers (*mutadayyin*) to read the books of *fiqh*, and they should not be upset to find different opinions there. And may God preserve us from such contradictions, as much as from the slandering people in those groups that have appeared in our day and speak nonsense. They reject the books of *fiqh*, creating and spreading the greatest corruption (*fasād*). They are that group of Jadids (*al-ṭaʾifa al-jadīda*), who pretend to the status of absolute *mujtahid*s (*al-mujtahid al-muṭlaq*) and claim that they follow the Qurʾān and the Sunnah. The fact that they call upon anyone, including uneducated students, to perform *ijtihād* is a source of great harm and evil. God save us from them! And what I wrote [in this book] does not support their ideas. What I wrote were several examples with varying opinions, which were stronger in their argumentation. And these are examples of *ijtihād* were applied to several individual questions.[73]

In response to Nadhīr's text, Yūsuf al-Jungutī wrote a critique, which he titled *Al-Qawl al-Sadīd fī Ḥasm Mādda al-Ijtihād wa-l-Wujūb al-Taqlīd*.[74] In his critique, Yūsuf writes about the need to adhere to one of the four legal schools and oppose absolute *ijtihād*. Not rejecting *ijtihād* in framework of *madhhab* or in *fatwā* in principle, he writes that, in his time, there was not one scholar worthy even of the status of *mujtahid* of the *madhhab*, to say nothing of absolute *mujtahid*. He comments on Nadhīr's opinions and examples concerning the disagreement between the Ḥanafī and Shāfiʿī *madhhab*s, writing that even if there were disagreements, that was a great blessing for Muslims, because these disagreements related not to the foundations of Islamic law (*uṣūl*), but only to individual cases and rulings (*furūʿ*).

In addition to denying the possibility of practicing *ijtihād*, Yūsuf al-Jungutī harshly criticised the Wahhabis, who, in his opinion, called for absolute *ijtihād*. In connection with this, Yūsuf posits a sequence of 'heretical' ideas, which spread through the Islamic world from Ibn

Taymiyya, Ṣāliḥ al-Yamanī, Muḥammad ibn ᶜAbd al-Wahhāb and the Egyptian reformers – Jamāl al-Dīn al-Afghānī, Muḥammad ᶜAbduh and Rashīd Riḍa. For example, Yūsuf al-Junguṭī writes the following:

> Ibn Taymiyya, may God have mercy on him! Although he was a great scholar, all his good works were mixed in with bad ones. And, at the very least, he was heretical concerning the foundations of the faith and was mistaken in some of the individual questions. He did not follow the opinions of the majority of scholars of his epoch . . . His students – Ibn al-Qayyim al-Jawzī, Ibn ᶜAbd al-Ḥādī – were the same and followed his path . . . As far as Muḥammad ibn ᶜAbd al-Wahhāb al-Najdī, the leader of the Wahhabis and founder of this new corruption (*fasād*), is concerned, he followed the teachings of Ibn Taymiyya in his heresies, such that great evil was spread by him. He went out from Najd in the direction of the Hijaz, together with his amirs, at the head of a great army. They killed many people, seized the holy cities, and committed other evils acts . . . As far as those corruptors (*mufsidūn*) Jamāl al-Dīn al-Afghānī, Muḥammad ᶜAbduh, and his student, Rashid Rīḍa, the editor of the journal *Al-Manār*, they are also Wahhabis and so are their followers. They are unholy idols (*aṣnām*); they do not follow the true path; they stand in opposition to the great scholars and the saints (*al-awliyā*ᵓ); they toy with the *ayāt*s of the Qurᵓān and the hadiths of the Prophet Muḥammad; they are imperfect (*nāqiṣ*) in their faith; they lie and their masters are the Masons (*al-masunīya*) . . . It is enough that the English appointed Muḥammad ᶜAbduh as mufti over the Muslims without their agreement. The views of these corruptors and heretics is in agreement with the views of the Protestants (*brutistant*) of Europe, who likewise reformed the Christian religion, considering that beneficial for the people. The Egyptian reformers tried to bring reform (*iṣlāḥ*) to Islam and called Muslims to their new (*jadīd*) faith, in the same way that the Protestants did. And there is obvious agreement between the Egyptian reformers and the Protestants. Both published and distributed books with the goal of bringing confusion to the hearts and minds of the people and to turn them away from the true path.[75]

Two facts about Yūsuf al-Junguṭī's tract are interesting. First, Yūsuf theoretically allows for the possibility of *ijtihād*, while, in practice, denying the possibility of the existence of a new *mujtahid* and considering that all questions that required answers had already been resolved long ago by the Muslim jurists. He suggests that the differences between the Shāfiᶜīs and the Ḥanafīs that, in Nadhīr's opinion, caused problems for Muslims, in fact were a blessing, insofar as they gave greater possibilities to Muslims to choose to be guided by this or that practice.

Second, it is striking that Yūsuf al-Junguṭī argues that the Wahhabis and the later reformers were united in purpose, insofar as both groups based their view on the works of the 'corrupt' scholar Ibn Taymiyya and promoted the idea of absolute *ijtihād*.

However, such identification of the Wahhabis with the reformers is not seen elsewhere in the Daghestani Arabic-language written tradition. Other scholars emphatically distinguished these two groups. For example, the Daghestani scholar ᶜAbd al-Ḥāfiẓ al-Uḥlī wrote a work in which he criticised two groups of Muslims who 'destroy the integrity of Islam', bringing troubles among the Muslims. The first group he referred to as 'Wahhabis', and the second, 'worse and more harmful' group, he called the 'Jadids' (*ḥizb al-jadīdiyya*). He included among the Jadids the Egyptian reformers (Jamāl al-Dīn al-Afghānī, Muḥammad ᶜAbduh and Rashīd Riḍa) as well as their Daghestani followers.[76] ᶜAbd al-Ḥāfiẓ drew a clear line between the Wahhabis and the Jadids. It is curious that, in his works, there is not a single word of criticism directed towards those scholars who promoted ideas of reforming the Muslim education system. As we have seen in the writings of Nadhīr and ᶜAbd al-Ḥāfiẓ, the 'Jadids' were identified as those who promoted ideas about absolute *ijtihād*.

This clear division between Jadids and Wahhabis is explained by the fact that certain Daghestani scholars saw a distinct boundary between the two groups. Despite certain similarities in the rhetoric of the Wahhabis and the Jadids (their criticism of Sufism and the legal schools, the call to absolute *ijtihād*, their stance on certain legal rulings relating to the treble process for divorce and their citing of the same sources, including Ibn Taymiyya and his students), their ultimate goals were different. The Wahhabis did not like the situation of Islam in their day and they tried to change it by returning to the past, rejecting later additions and holding suspect all things 'European'. The reformers also disliked the state of the Muslim *umma* in their day, but they looked not to the past, but to the future, believing that Muslim society could become not only better than it was in the present, but better even than it had been in the past.[77]

To that end, the reformers did not reject the possibility of borrowing from Europe the best achievements of science, which they considered to be not purely 'European', but their own 'lost heritage of Muslims'. Allusions to the 'great past of the Muslims' in the rhetoric of the Jadids played the role of additional argumentation in their criticisms of Sufism and *taqlīd,* for, in the early Islamic period, there had been no Sufism and no legal schools. In this way, the Muslim scholars of Daghestan envisioned the Jadids as those who argued in favour of absolute *ijtihād* and not as those who wished to reform Muslim education. Most Daghestanis were fully in favour of the latter.[78]

In answer to Yūsuf's criticism, Nadhīr wrote yet another tract, *Ta'līq al-Ḥamīd 'alā al-Qawl al-Sadīd.*[79] Nadhīr criticised Yūsuf for writing that the four legal schools were a blessing for Muslim society. He noted that such disagreement among the legal schools in certain historical periods moved from the theological plane into mutual hostility. For example, in the thirteenth century, when the Mongols laid siege to Merv, the Ḥanafīs and the Shāfiᶜīs of the city's Muslim community began to fight with each other. As a result, both groups were so weakened by their enmity that the Mongols easily captured Merv and destroyed them both. A similar situation unfolded in the city of Rayy, where three groups fought for control: the Ḥanafīs, the Shāfiᶜīs and the Shi'ites. As Nadhīr writes:

> Fanatical adherence to *madhhab*s became the reason that the French invaded the western lands of the Islamic world (that is, al-Andalus) and captured them . . . In our own day, also we see that the Ḥanafīs, in theological questions, sometimes do not consider it possible to follow the Shāfiᶜīs and vice versa. They write tracts criticizing one another . . . We see that the followers of all four *madhhab*s pray separately from one another in Mecca and Medina, and each of them performs his prayers strictly in the mode of own imam, as if the followers of each of the *madhhab*s belonged to a different faith . . . Moreover, Abū Hafs, one of the great Ḥanafī scholars, said that the Ḥanafīs should not give their daughters in marriage to Shāfiᶜīs.[80]

In Nadhīr's opinion, such disagreements only weakened the Muslim community. To heal those schisms and unite the Muslim *umma*, it was necessary to use the practice of *ijtihād* and a direct examination of the Qur᾿ān and the Sunnah to resolve those questions that were disputed among the four legal schools.

Nadhīr writes that the Wahhabis did not call for absolute *ijtihād* but followed the Ḥanafī *madhhab*. Nadhīr likewise considers Yūsuf's criticisms of Ibn Taymiyya and his students to be baseless. In conclusion, Nadhīr writes that Wahhabism was not a religious schism, but a political one between the Egyptians and the people of Najd, and he noted the baselessness of Meccan *muftī* Zain al-Dahlān's criticism of the Wahhabis, pointing out that the latter was not very knowledgeable about their history and gave a lopsided portrayal of the Wahhabi movement.[81] For a more solid argument that the Wahhabis did not make claims to absolute *ijtihād*,[82] Nadhīr cited the Tatar scholar Riḍa᾿ al-Dīn b. Fakhr al-Dīn.[83]

In this way, we see that Nadhīr defended the necessity of performing *ijtihād*. However, he also criticised those of his contemporaries who promoted absolute *ijtihād*. As we can see from his tract, Nadhīr limited the permissible applications of *ijtihād* to the last two levels (*ijtihād* of the *madhhab* and the *fatwā*), considering it obligatory to perform *ijtihād* within the framework of a legal school and only 'in relation to specific, limited questions'.

As such, the substance of this polemic was that Nadhīr, seeing differing opinions in the Shāfiʿī and Ḥanafī schools, believed that such disagreement threatened the well-being of the Muslim community. In such cases, he proposed a departure from adherence to *taqlīd* and, for certain disputed questions, a turn to the practice of limited *ijtihād* (*ijtihād* of the *madhhab* or the *fatwā*). At the same time, Nadhīr approached the actual practice of *ijtihād* with caution and did not consider himself qualified to carry it out. He harshly criticised those who called for independent, absolute *ijtihād* outside the framework of the school, such as the Egyptian reformers and their followers among the Daghestani scholars, such as ʿAlī al-Ghumuqī and Masʿūd al-Muhukhī.

Yūsuf al-Jungutī debated with him over the fact that while, theoretically, the third and fourth levels of *ijtihād* were permitted, in practice they were not feasible, because the scholars of his own day had not received adequate preparation. Nadhīr demonstrated with citations from other scholars that the fourth level of *ijtihād* was not only permissible, but even obligatory, and he spoke out against 'fanaticism' in adherence to the legal schools.

In formulating all these opinions, both Nadhīr and Yūsuf stayed within the framework of the Shāfiʿī school. In their polemics, we see not an opposition of *taqlīd* to *ijtihād*, but, rather, how two supporters of *ijtihād* argued over the limits of permissibility of the lowest levels of *ijtihād* (of the *madhhab* and of the *fatwā*), which were in complete harmony with the Shāfiʿī theory of *fiqh*. Both Nadhīr and Yūsuf cited the same authors, including those who were widely known in the Shāfiʿī legal tradition as well as those from other *madhhab*s (Ḥanafī, Hanbalī). Sometimes, both theologians gave their own interpretation of these scholars' opinions or augmented them with material from alternative sources.

Both Nadhīr and Yūsuf agreed that absolute, independent *ijtihād* beyond the framework of the legal schools was not permitted. Likewise, they both agreed that those scholars who did not meet the criteria to be *mujtahid*s should follow the opinions of one of the four legal schools. Nadhīr's reasoning was more theoretical and abstract in character, implying a fundamental review of the permissibility of certain controversial rulings through the practice of *ijtihād* within the legal schools. Nadhīr's view of *ijtihād* as permissible on a case-by-case basis and within the framework of the schools was supported by another Daghestani scholar, the editor-in-chief of the Muslim journal *Bayān al-Ḥaqāʾiq*, Abū Sufyān al-Ghazanishī (1872–1932).

A similar polemic also developed between the above-mentioned ʿAlī al-Ghumuqī, who supported the ideas of absolute *ijtihād*, and Nadhīr al-Durgilī's teacher, Ghazanuf al-Gubdanī (d. 1942), who harshly criticised both the Wahhabis and the reformers, put himself forward as a defender of *taqlīd* and rejected the possibility that any form of *ijtihād* was possible in his era.[84]

Similar tracts and articles addressing the Wahhabis, the reformers, *taqlīd* and the various levels of *ijtihād* were written relatively often by Daghestani scholars in the first third of the twentieth century. This discourse continued in the manuscript tradition and in the pages of the Muslim press of the early Soviet period until the end of the 1920s.[85]

In the 1930s, we do not find a single tract on the issue of *ijtihād*. In my view, this is a result of the Soviet government's increasingly strict policies against Islam. Nearly all the participants in the *ijtihād* debates were repressed by the Soviet state. In 1929, Abū Sufyān al-Ghazanishī was exiled to a gulag, where he died in 1932. ᶜAlī al-Ghumuqī was sent to a gulag in Kazakhstan in 1939, where he died in 1943. Masᶜūd al-Muhukhī was sent to a prison camp in Magadansk District, where he died in 1941. Muḥammad ᶜUmarī al-Uḥlī, one of the students of ᶜAlī al-Ghumuqī, who also took part in the criticism of *taqlīd* and Sufism, was sent to a camp, where he died in the 1940s. Yūsuf al-Junguṭī was shot by the OGPU in 1929, at the age of sixty-seven. His colleague and a member of the staff of the journal *Bayān al-Ḥaqāʾiq*, Badawi-qadi Adil'bekov, was beaten to death in an OGPU prison in 1929. Some of the Sufi shaykhs, who had opposed *ijtihād*, were also repressed. The Naqshbandi shaykh Ḥasan al-Qaḥi was shot in 1937, at the age of eighty-five, and his successor, Muḥammad al-ᶜAsalī, who wrote several works criticising the views of the reformers, died in a prison in Daghestan in 1942.

The discourse on *taqlīd* and *ijtihād* was renewed after Second World War and gathered new momentum after the fall of the USSR, when the Sufis and the Salafis stepped forward as actors in this debate.

Conclusion

In the intellectual history of Islam, the case of the debates on *taqlīd* and *ijtihād* demonstrates how an idea can persist over the span of several centuries. These debates, which began in Daghestan at the end of the seventeenth century, passed through different phases: they emerged in the pre-colonial period, subsided during the time of the *jihād* in the Caucasus in the first half of the nineteenth century and then emerged once again and reached their highest level of development at the very beginning of the Soviet period.

The discourses on *ijtihād* and *taqlīd* in Daghestan were not abstract in character. Questions of Islamic legal theory were closely connected with the practical application of the norms of Islamic law in Daghestan. Emerging challenges in the spheres of social and political relations demanded the resolution of new questions in Muslim normative practices.

In the pre-colonial period elements of the Islamic legal system were integrated individually by various villages councils, with different levels of intensity, into the system of local courts of customary law (*ᶜadāt*). The development of a system of Islamic law in Daghestan coincided and coexisted with customary law. Over the course of the eighteenth century, Daghestani jurists tried to change that situation, handing down sometimes very harsh decisions against the norms of customary law. However, in trying to replace those norms with *sharīᶜa*, Daghestani jurists did not always find the answers to specific questions (inheritance, family and land law) appropriate to eighteenth-century Daghestani reality. To resolve these questions, many Daghestani jurists came to different conclusions: some tried to answer these questions by analysing the primary sources of Islamic law (the Qurᵓān and the Sunnah) through the process of *ijtihād*; others turned to the Muslim authorities of the Middle East. The latter approach was more characteristic for most of the eighteenth century. This was due to the fact that many Daghestanis continued their education in the great Muslim centres of Syria, Egypt, Yemen and the Hijaz, where Islamic intellectual life developed along many lines: Islamic law, logic, dogma and so forth.

For the entire eighteenth century, the theory and practice of Islamic law developed rapidly and widely in Daghestan, so that by the beginning of the nineteenth century, many questions had already been answered using *ijtihād* of the *madhhab* or *ijtihād* of the *fatwā*, to which Muḥammad al-Quduqī turned, or within a framework corresponding to the legal decisions of the Arab scholars of the Middle East. The work of Saᶜid al-Makki was an example of this latter practice. In the eighteenth and nineteenth centuries, Islamic legal theory in Daghestan developed to such an extent that the great majority of Daghestani scholars preferred to practice *taqlīd* when responding to various questions. However, the boundary between *taqlīd* and the various levels of *ijtihād* remained uncertain. Some jurists considered themselves part of the Shāfiᶜī *madhhab*, but still practiced certain forms of *ijtihād* within the bounds of that school.

The nineteenth century, and, especially, the period of the Caucasus Wars, raised new questions connected with the *jihād*. However, Islamic law was already well-developed in Daghestan during the eighteenth century, with many individual legal decisions and tracts having been handed down by Daghestani jurists. These included commentaries on legal works. In these works, finding answers to the question of the imamate's legitimacy, *jihād* and *hijra* did not present the Daghestanis with especial difficulty. In polemic works on these issues, both supporters and opponents of the imamate cited the works of the same Shāfiʿī jurists that had been widely studied in the eighteenth century. Communications with the Muslim authorities of the Middle East with questions relating to the imamate and the *jihād* were of a different character from those of the eighteenth century. Daghestani jurists did not demand new answers to questions concerning the legitimacy or illegitimacy of the imamate and the *jihād*, which they had already resolved. Rather, they wished to receive additional arguments to use in debates with their opponents, in the form of weightier evidence from the 'holy places' (Mecca and Medina). The practical necessity for any form of *ijtihād* vanished. Moreover, under these conditions, *ijtihād* was not only unnecessary, but uniquely harmful for both sides, insofar as, by the beginning of the nineteenth century, the vast majority of Daghestani jurists identified themselves as adherents of *taqlīd* and rejected the possibility of any form of *ijtihād* by their contemporaries. In this way, the decisions of jurists regarding the imamate, *jihād* and *hijra* formulated with the help of *ijtihād* would have raised scepticism from their rivals, who believed that, unlike among Middle Eastern scholars, among Daghestani scholar there was no one worthy of the status of *mujtahid*. For Daghestani scholars, the scholars of the Middle East continued to command greater authority.

In the colonial period, the integration of Daghestan into Russia's imperial institutions and the resulting social and economic transformations, raised new questions that the Daghestanis were unprepared to answer. The rapid growth of the non-Muslim population in Daghestan and contacts with the internal Muslim regions of Russia raised new questions connected with interpersonal relations. A number of scholars tried to answer these new questions (listening to the Qurʾān on a gramophone, the paying of *zakāt* in Russian paper money, the Russian tax system, Shāfiʿīs living among Ḥanafīs) through the practice of *taqlīd*, but that did not always provide them with adequate answers. In this period, at the end of the nineteenth century, certain Daghestani jurists understood that without some of the elements of *ijtihād*, it would be difficult to pose answers to these questions. There were no ready answers in Middle Eastern legal literature to fit the specificities of life in Orthodox Christian Russia. It was possible to resolve these questions only by using elements of *ijtihād*: analysis of the opinions of various jurists on a given question, investigation through analogy (*qiyās*) or a choice of the opinion with the stronger argument (*tarjīḥ*).

These new questions led to the renewal of debates over *ijtihād* and *taqlīd*: could answers to these questions be found within the framework of *taqlīd* or could they be resolved only through the practice of *ijtihād*? Once again, the discourse on *ijtihād* and *taqlīd* ceased to be an abstract discussion within the sphere of *fiqh* theory and became something closely intertwined with practical questions.

As in the eighteenth century, so too in the twentieth century external factors drove this discourse. Ideas of Islamic reform in Egypt and the spread of those ideas through the periodical press, book publishing and the travels of Daghestani scholars all led to wider discussion of *ijtihād* as a method that could help resolve (and had already partially resolved) practical questions in Daghestan. However, various Daghestani jurists, while seeing the necessity for *ijtihād*, approached the question in different ways. Some believed that these new questions and, likewise, the contradictory decisions within the various *madhhab*s, could be resolved through the practice of *ijtihād* on a case-by-case basis. Others turned to the practice of absolute *ijtihād* and were criticised not only by the supporters of *taqlīd*, but by those who called for *ijtihād* within the *madhhab*, as can be seen in the writings of Nadhīr al-Durgilī.

It is curious that, in the practice of Islamic law in Daghestan, political questions rarely arose among the Muslim elite. Except during the Caucasus Wars, we do not see a single legal decision that directly addressed colonial or Soviet rule. In Daghestani legal tracts of the first third of the twentieth century there is an almost complete lack of questions connected with the contemporary political conditions in the Russian Empire and the Soviet Union.

The anti-religion campaigns of the Soviet era, which grew stronger in the late 1920s, led to the repression of those who had been most active in the debates over *ijtihād* and *taqlīd*. But repression did not cause the polemic to disappear from Daghestan. It continued in the post-Second World War period and grew in intensity in the post-Soviet period. And, as in the eighteenth century and at the beginning of the twentieth, the driving force behind that discourse in the 1990s was once again an external factor: the education of Daghestanis in the great Muslim intellectual centres of Egypt, Syria and Saudi Arabia.

Notes

1. A. R. Navruzov, 'Diskussii ob idzhtikhade i taklide sredi dagestanskikh ulemov pervoi chetverti XX veka', *Pax Islamica* 2:11 (2013), pp. 31–8; *Dzharidat Dagistan*: *Araboiazychnaia gazeta kavkazskikh dzhadidov*

(Moscow: Mardzhani, 2012), pp. 174–80; Z. M. Abdulagatov, 'Vakhkhabizm i dzhadidizm v dagestanskom islamskom soznanii: paralleli i protivorechiya', *Tsentral'naia Aziia i Kavkaz* 6–48 (2006), pp. 108–20; M. A. Abdullaev, *Mysliteli Dagestana* (Makhachkala: Epokha, 2007), pp. 111–20.

2. See, for example: M. Kemper, *Herrschaft, Recht und Islam in Daghestan: Von den Khanaten und Gemeindebünden zum ǧihād-Staat* (Wiesbaden: Reichert Verlag, 2005), pp. 353–60; M. Kemper, '*Ijtihād* into Philosophy: Islam as Cultural Heritage in Post-Stalinist Dagestan', *Central Asian Survey* 33:3 (2014), pp. 2–3; R. Gould, '*Ijtihād* against *Madhhab*: Legal Hybridity and the Meanings of Modernity in Early Modern Daghestan', *Comparative Studies in Society and History* 57 (2015), pp. 35–66.
3. Sh. Shikhaliev and R. Gould, 'Beyond the *Taqlīd/Ijtihād* Dichotomy: Daghestani Legal Thought under Russian Rule', *Islamic Law and Society* 24:1–2 (2017), pp. 142–69.
4. V. Bobrovnikov, A. Nauruzov and Sh. Shikhaliev, 'Islamic Education in Soviet and post-Soviet Daghestan', in M. Kemper, R. Motika and S. Reichmuth (eds), *Islamic Education in the Soviet Union and its Successor States* (London and New York: Routledge, 2010), pp. 107–67.
5. W. B. Hallaq, 'Was the Gate of Ijtihad Closed?', *International Journal of Middle East Studies* 16 (1984), pp. 3–41.
6. R. Peters, '*Ijtihād* and *Taqlīd* in 18th and 19th century Islam', *Die Welt des Islams* 20:3–4 (1980), pp. 136–7.
7. *Al-istinbāt* is the extraction of evidence (*al-adilla*) from the main sources of Islamic law – the Qurʾān and the Sunna – while following a series of conditions, such as the strict adherence to a specific framework of lexical or semantic knowledge, the word order in a sentence, the accounts of the commentaries and the opinions of authoritative Muslim scholars. In their own turn, the evidence or proofs, (plural: *al-adilla*, singular: *al-dalīl*) come from the text of the Qurʾān or the sayings of the prophet Muḥammad (*ḥadīth*), which are divided into: (1) 'clear' (*naṣṣ*), which possess a single meaning; (2) 'manifest' (*ẓāhir*), which have two meanings, one of which is clearer that the other; (3) 'ambivalent' (*mujmal*), which require exegesis; and (4) 'intricate' (*mutashābih*), which have an allegorical meaning or several possible explanations.
8. This discussion most likely concerns the formulation of decisions in cases in which the Qurʾān and Sunna do not provide a clear answer. With the development of the system of Islamic law, *qiyās* (judgment by analogy) and *ijmāʿ* (consensus of authoritative jurists) were also included among the fundamental sources of the law. In the further development of Islamic legal theory, jurists worked out their own principle and methods. For example, in Ḥanafī legal theory, the practice of *istiḥsān* (when a jurist, examines controversial questions, which do not have clear answers in the Qurʾān or the Sunna, and lets himself be guided by the criteria of utility to the Muslim community, using individual subjective opinion (*al-raʾy*)) came into wide usage. Unlike

the Ḥanafīs, the Shāfiᶜī school did not embrace the principle of *istiḥsān*, seeing in it the expansion of the role of the jurist's subjective opinion and the threat of going beyond the fundamental sources of the law to seek answers from other sources. Shāfiᶜī legal theory was built on the principle of *istiṣḥāb* (in which the explanation of a decision demanded more direct proof, which minimised the role of the subjective opinion of individual jurists). Of course, Shāfiᶜ-i jurists also used logical, reasoned judgement. However, they were more precise in determining the boundaries of its usage, limiting it to the method of *qiyās*, and, then, only with the consensus of authoritative jurists. In this, they were close to another group, the *aṣḥāb al-ḥadīth,* who preferred to be guided by the evidence in 'weak' (*ḍaᶜīf*) hadiths to making wide use of subjective opinions. On the principle of *istiḥsān*: see Muḥammad b. Aḥmad b. Juzayy al-Kalabī al-Gharnātī, *Taqrīb al-wuṣūl ilā ᶜilm al-uṣūl* (Medina: n.p., 2002), pp. 399–403. On the principle of *istiṣḥab*, see: Taj al-Dīn ᶜAbd al-Wahhāb b. ᶜAlī al-Subkī, *Jamᶜ al-jawāmiᶜ fī uṣūl al-fiqh* (Beirut: Dār al-kutub al-ᶜilmiyya, 2003), p. 108; ᶜAlī Jumᶜa Muḥammad, *Al-Madkhal ilā dirāsa al-madhhab al-fiqhiyya* (Cairo: Dār al-salām, 2012), pp. 33–4).

9. Walī al-Dīn Aḥmad b. ᶜAbd al-Raḥīm al-ᶜIrāqī, *Al-Ghayth al-hamiᶜ sharḥ Jamᶜ al-jawāmiᶜ* (Beirut: Dār al-kutub al-ᶜilmiyya, 2003), pp. 693–701; ᶜAbd al-Ḥayy al-Laknawī, *Al-Nāfiᶜ al-kabīr sharḥ Jamīᶜ al-ṣaghīr* (Karachi: Idāra al-Qurᵓān, 1999), p. 14; See also A. Poya, *Anerkennung des Iǧtihād: Legitimation der Toleranz. Möglichkeiten innerer und äußerer Toleranz im Islam am Beispiel der Iǧtihād-Diskussion* (Berlin: Klaus Schwarz Verlag, 2003), pp. 250–77.
10. Shah Walī Allāh Aḥmad b. ᶜAbd al-Raḥīm al-Dihlawī, *ᶜIqd al-jīd fī aḥkām al-ijtihād wāl-taqlīd* (n.p.: Dār al-fath, 1995), pp. 48–50.
11. J. Schacht and D. B. Macdonald, 'Idjtihād', *The Encyclopaedia of Islam. New Edition. Volume III* (Leiden: Brill, 1971), pp. 1,026–7; M. M. Mutahhari, 'The Role of Ijtihad in Legislation', *Al-Tawhid: A Quarterly Journal of Islamic Thought & Culture* 4: 2 (n.d.), pp. 242–3; Th. P. Hughes, *Dictionary of Islam* (London: Allan, 1885), p. 199; W. B. Hallaq, 'Was the Gate of Ijtihad Closed?'; Shah Walī Allāh Aḥmad b. ᶜAbd al-Raḥīm al-Dihlawī, *ᶜIqd al-jīd fī aḥkām al-ijtihād wāl-taqlīd*, pp. 48–54; Abū Isḥāq al-Shaṭibī, *Al-Muwafaqat fī uṣūl al-sharīᶜa* (Beirut: Dār al-kutub al-'ilmiyya, 2004), pp. 774–867.
12. M. Kemper, *Uchenyie i sufii v Tatarstane i Bashkortostane, 1789–1889. Islamskii diskurs pod russkim gospodstvom* (Kazan': Idel-Press, 2008), pp. 383–93.
13. Shah Walī Allāh Aḥmad b. ᶜAbd al-Raḥīm al-Dihlawī, *ᶜIqd al-jīd fī aḥkām al-ijtihād wāl-taqlīd*, pp. 50-4.
14. Walī al-Dīn Aḥmad b. ᶜAbd al-Raḥīm al-ᶜIrāqī, *Al-Ghayth al-hamiᶜ sharḥ Jamᶜ al-jawāmiᶜ*, p. 700; Muḥammad ᶜAbd al-Ḥayy al-Laknawī, 'Masᵓala al-ijtihād wa inqirāḍ', *Jarīdat Dāghistān*, 29 October 1915, p. 4.
15. *Tarjīḥ* is the process of choosing between two arguments that contradict each

other by means of referring to the sources to determine which argument is weaker and making the necessary decision based on that determination. See: Muḥammad ᶜAmīm al-Iḥsān al-Mujaddidī al-Barakatī, *Al-Ta'rīfat al-fiqhiyya* (Beirut: Dār al-kutub al-ᶜilmiyya, 2003), p. 55; Manṣūr b. Muḥammad al-Samᶜanī, *Qawāti' al-adilla fī al-Uṣūl* (Beirut: Dār al-kutub al-ᶜilmiyya, 1997), pp. 404–9.

16. Sayyid al-Bakrī b. al-Sayyid Muḥammad Shaṭa al-Dimyaṭī, *Iᶜāna al-ṭālibīn* (Beirut: Dar iḥyaʾ turath al-ᶜarabiyyi, 1997), pp. 18–19; ᶜAlī Jumᶜa Muḥammad, *Al-Madkhal ilā dirāsa al-madhhab al-fiqhiyya*, pp. 65–6.
17. Walī al-Dīn Aḥmad b. ᶜAbd al-Raḥīm al-ᶜIrāqī, *Al-Ghayth al-hamiᶜ sharḥ Jamᶜ al-jawāmiᶜ*, p. 700.
18. Muḥammad Saᶜid ᶜAbd al-Raḥmān al-Bani al-Ḥusaynī, *ᶜUmda al-taḥqīq fī taqlīd wa talfīq* (Damascus: Dir al-Qadiri, 1997), pp. 341–2; M. M. Mutahhari, 'The Role of Ijtihad in Legislation', *Al-Tawhid: A Quarterly Journal of Islamic Thought & Culture* 4:4 (n.d.), pp. 242–3. See also A. Poya, *Anerkennung des Iğtihād – Legitimation der Toleranz*, p. 70; ᶜAbd al-Ḥayy al-Laknawī, *Al-Nāfiᶜ al-kabīr sharḥ Jamīᶜ al-ṣaghīr*, p. 17.
19. This is a requirement in the Shāfiᶜī legal system. In the other legal schools, for example, the Ḥanafī school, knowing the Qurʾān by heart is not required of a *mujtahid*.
20. Walī al-Dīn Aḥmad b. ᶜAbd al-Raḥīm al-ᶜIrāqī, *Al-Ghayth al-hamiᶜ sharḥ Jamᶜ al-jawāmiᶜ*, pp. 693–7, 712–13; ᶜAlī b. Muḥammad al-Amadī, *Al-Aḥkām fī uṣūl al-aḥkām*, mujallad 2 (Beirut: Dār al-fikr, 1997), p. 336; See also W. B. Hallaq, *The History of Islamic Legal Theories: An Introduction to Sunni Usul al-fiqh* (Cambridge: Cambridge University Press, 1999), pp. 117–19.
21. Jalāl al-Dīn Abū ᶜAbd Allāh Muḥammad b. Aḥmad al-Maḥallī, *Sharḥ al-waraqat fī ᶜilm uṣūl al-fiqh* (Makhachkala: Dār al-risāla, 2009), p. 76.
22. J. Schacht, *An Introduction to Islamic Law* (Oxford: Oxford University Press, 1964).
23. Jalāl al-Dīn Abū ᶜAbd Allāh Muḥammad b. Aḥmad al-Maḥallī, *Sharḥ al-waraqat fī ᶜilm uṣūl al-fiqh*, pp. 77–8.
24. For more details on this, see A. K. Alikberov, *Epokha klassicheskogo islama v Dagestane: Abu Bakr ad-Darbandi i ego* sufiiskaia entsiklopediia *'Raihan al-haqaiq' (XI–XII vv.)* (Moscow: Vostochnaia literatura, 2003).
25. Such legal decisions by Arab scholars regarding questions posed by Daghestanis are commonly found in private collections in the margins of manuscript law books or in separate statements.
26. A large part of his article is based on the biography of Ṣāliḥ al-Yamanī, written by another Yemeni scholar, Muḥammad b. ᶜAlī Shawkāni. See: I. Iu. Krachkovskii, 'Dagestan i Yemen', *Izbrannyye sochineniia*, Tom 6 (Moscow-Leningrad: Izdatel'stvo Akademii Nauk SSSR, 1960), pp. 574–84.
27. Ḥasan Efendi al-Alqadarī, *Jirāb al-Mamnūn* (Temir-khan Shura: al-Maṭbaᶜa al-islamiyya li Muḥammad Mirza Mawrayuf, 1912).
28. Muḥammad b. ᶜAlī Shawkāni, *Al-Badr al-Ṭāliᶜ bi maḥāsin man ba'd al-qarn*

al-sabi^c^, al-juz^ɔ^ al-awwal (Cairo: Dār al-kitab al-Islamiyyi, 1929–30), pp. 288–92. For a more detailed analysis of the views of al-Shawkānī on Ṣāliḥ al-Yamanī, see R. Gould, '*Ijtihād* against *Madhab*: Legal Hybridity and the Meanings of Modernity in Early Modern Daghestan', pp. 51–7.

29. *Al-Risāla fīl-intiqād ^c^ala Ṣāliḥ al-Yamanī*, Manuscript Collection of the Institute of History, Archaeology and Ethnography, Makhachkala (henceforth, IHAE), f. 14, no. 785b, l. 6a.
30. Ṣāliḥ b. al-Mahdi b. ^c^Alī al-Maqbalī al-Yamanī, *Al-Abḥath al-musaddada fī funun al-muta^c^addida* (Sana'a: Dār al-jīl al-jadīd, 2007 [1428]), p. 11.
31. Ibid, p. 15.
32. One of the early manuscript copies of the work of Ṣāliḥ al-Yamanī, *Al-Itḥāf li ṭalaba al-Kashshāf*, is held at IHAE, f. 14, no 545. This manuscript, dating from the beginning of the eighteenth century, was copied down by the Daghestani scholar Murtaḍa ^c^Alī al-Jarī, who was a student of another Daghestani scholar, Muḥammad al-Quduqī, who, in turn, was a student of Ṣāliḥ al-Yamanī himself.
33. Muḥammad b. ^c^Alī Shawkāni, *Al-Badr al-Ṭāli^c^*, p. 289.
34. There is a note about the composition of this work in 1690–1 and the death of Ṣāliḥ al-Yamanī on 18 November 1697 on the second page of the above-mentioned manuscript copy of this work, IHAE, f. 14, no 545, l. 2a.
35. For more details on this, see B. Eisenbürger, 'Muḥammad b. 'Alī aš-Šawkānī (gest. 1250/1834) – der große jemenitische Reformer', in H. von Stephan Conermann (ed.), *Seine rechtlichen, ideologischen und pädagogischen Vorstellungen* (Berlin: 'EB-Verlag Dr. Brandt', 2011), pp. 12–24.
36. Ṣāliḥ b. al-Mahdi b. ^c^Alī al-Maqbalī al-Yamanī, *Al-Itḥāf li ṭalaba al-Kashshāf*, IHAE, f. 14, no 545, f. 2a.
37. In the Shāfi^c^ī legal system, there exists a practice called 'internal *ijtihād*'. This is when one or another Muslim in an unresolvable situation uses his own power of reason to come to a decision. In such cases, the given opinion does not have legal standing and should not be made public in the form of a *fatwā* or a juridical ruling. This is also what Ḥasan al-Alqadarī meant when he wrote about following his opinion on personal questions. An example of the practice is when a Muslim is on a journey and, because of external factors (for example, fog or darkness) cannot precisely determine the direction of the *qibla* (the direction in which he should face while praying). In this case, he should, in agreement with his internal convictions, pray in the direction that seems most correct to him. Such a prayer is considered valid. However, he must not claim to others that the *qibla* is precisely in the direction in which he prayed. That is to say that his '*ijtihād*' is directed inward and not outward. Also, in questions to which there is a clear answer, Muslims do not have the right to perform this kind of *ijtihād*.
38. Ḥasan Efendi al-Alqadarī, *Jirāb al-Mamnūn*, pp. 279–81.
39. Muḥammad ^c^Alī al-Chuḥī, *Fatāwa al-Chuḥī* (Temir-khan Shura: al-Maṭba^c^a al-islamiyya li Muḥammad Mirza Mawrayuf, 1908), p. 526.

40. Ibid.
41. *Al-Taqrīrāt al-fiqhiyya li Jamāl al-Dīn al-Gharabudaghī*. This manuscript is from a collection held at a mosque in the village of Karabudakhkent, no 34, f. 41b. The copy of this manuscript is in private possession of author.
42. Notes from a legal work. The manuscript is held in the private collection of A. I. Magomedov (b. 1965), a resident of Makhachkala, № 13, l. 56a.
43. R. S. Abdulmazhidov and M. G. Shekhmagomedov, 'Obrashchenie Umara al-Khinzakhi k zhyteliam Dagestana: obshchaia kharakteristika i kommentirovannyi perevod', *Islamovedenie* 1 (2013), pp. 134–5.
44. 'Ibrahīm al-ᶜUradī Questions and Saᶜid al-Makkī's Answers', Notes from a manuscript (№ 16, l. 42a). The manuscript is held in the private collection of M. G. Shekhmagomedov (born 1981), a resident of Makhachkala.
45. On al-Quduqī, see A. Shikhsaidov, 'Al-Kuduki', in S. M. Prozorova (ed.), *Islam na territorii byvshei Rossiiskoi imperii. Entsiklopedicheskii slovar': Vypusk 2* (Moscow: Vostochnaia Literatura, 1999), pp. 51–2; R. Gould, '*Ijtihād* Against *Madhhab*: Legal Hybridity and the Meanings of Modernity in Early Modern Daghestan'; M. Kemper, '*Ijtihad* into Philosophy: Islam as Cultural Heritage in post-Stalinist Dagestan'; M. A. Musaev, 'Materialy k biografii Mukhammada, syna Musy al-Quduqi', *Vestnik Instituta IAE* 3 (2013), pp. 61–70.
46. Shihāb al-Dīn al-Marjānī al-Qazānī, *Mustafād al-akhbār fī aḥwāl Qazān wa Bulghār, qism al-thānī* (Kazan, 1900), pp. 219–20; Muḥammad Murād al-Ramzī, *Talfīq al-akhbār wa talqīḥ al-athār fī waqāᶜi Qazān wa Bulghār, al-mujallad al-thānī* (Orenburg: al-Maṭbaᶜa al-Karimiyya wa-l-Ḥusainiyya, 1908), pp. 413–14.
47. ᶜAlī b. ᶜAbd al-Ḥamīd al-Ghumuqī, *Tarājim ᶜulamāᵓ Daghistān*. The manuscript is from the private collection of I. A. Kayaev (b. 1964), no. 9, ff. 17–18.
48. M. A. Abdullaev, *Mysliteli Dagestana*, pp. 118–20.
49. ᶜAlī b. ᶜAbd al-Ḥamīd al-Ghumuqī, *Ṭalāq*, MS Makhachkala, IHAE, f. M.S. Saidova, Op. 1, no 50, ff. 1a–7b; Yūsuf al-Jungūtī, 'Masᵓala al-Ṭalāq', *Bayān al-ḥaqāᵓiq* 5 (1926), pp. 13–14; Ḥasan Efendi al-Alqadarī, *Jirāb al-Mamnūn*, pp. 66, 153–4.
50. Notes from a manuscript on *fiqh*. Manuscript No. 74. Date: first half of the nineteenth century, pp. 151–65. This manuscript is held in the private collection of M. Murtazaliev (died 1994) in Machada Village, Republic of Daghestan.
51. Ḥasan al-Alqadarī, *Athar-i Daghistān* (St Petersburg: n.p., 1894), pp. 232–3.
52. On al-Alqadarī's opinion on *taqlīd* and *ijtihād*, see Gould and Shikhaliev, 'Beyond the *Taqlīd/Ijtihād* Dichotomy: Daghestani Legal Thought under Russian Rule'.
53. The legal opinions of Jamāl al-Dīn al-Gharabudaghī, no 34, f. 40b.
54. Ibrahīm al-ᶜUradī's notes on legal questions. This manuscript is held in the private collection of Makhachkala resident M. G. Shekhmagomedov (born

1981). The manuscript was copied by Ibrahīm al-ᶜUradī, № 43, l. 26a.
55. Ibid., f. 44b.
56. ᶜAlī b. ᶜAbd al-Ḥamīd al-Ghumuqī, *Tarājim ᶜulamāʾ Daghistān*, ff. 19a, 47a, 53b.
57. A. Zelkina, *In Quest of God and Freedom* (London: C. Hurst & Co., 2000), pp. 138–9; M. Kemper, *Herrschaft, Recht und Islam in Daghestan*, pp. 219–24.
58. M. Kemper, 'The Dagestani Legal Discourse on the Imamate', *Central Asian Survey* 21:3 (2002), pp. 265–78.
59. *Al-Risāla lil-Imam Muḥammad b. Idrīs al-Shāfiᶜī, bi taḥqīq wa sharḥ Abi al-Ashkāl Aḥmad Muḥammad Shākir* (Cairo: Maṭbaᶜa Muṣṭafā al-Bābī al-Ḥalabī wa awlāduh, 1938), pp. 494–6.
60. A. P. Svistunov, *Ocherk vosstaniia gortsev Terskoi oblasti v 1877 godu* (St. Petersburg: tip. Gl. Upr. Udelov, 1896), p. 23.
61. M. A. Musaev, *Musul'manskoe dukhovenstvo 60-70-kh godov XIX veka i vosstanie 1877 goda v Dagestane* (Makhachkala: PBOYL Zulumkhanova, 2005), pp. 108–10.
62. M. Kemper, 'Daghestani Shaykhs and Scholars in Russian Exile: Networks of Sufism, Fatwas and Poetry', in M. Gammer and David J. Wasserstein (eds), *Daghestan and the World of Islam* (Helsinki: Finnish Academy of Sciences and Letters, 2006), pp. 95–107.
63. R. Gould and Sh. Shikhaliev, 'Beyond the *Taqlīd/Ijtihād* Dichotomy: Daghestani Legal Thought under Russian Rule'.
64. A. R. Navruzov, *Dzharidat Dagistan: Araboiazychnaia gazeta kavkazskikh dzhadidov*, pp. 38–74, 157–61. It is curious that the cycle of questions and thematic articles discussed in the newspaper *Jarīdat Daghistān* show remarkable agreement with the journal *al-Manār*, which was published by Muḥammad Rashīd Riḍa.
65. ᶜAlī b. ᶜAbd al-Ḥamīd al-Ghumuqī, *Risāla fīl-taqlīd wa jawāz al-talfīq*, MS Makhachkala, IHAE, f. M.-S. Saidova, op. 1, no. 37, ff. 101b–105a.
66. ᶜAlī b. ᶜAbd al-Ḥamīd al-Ghumuqī, 'Fī ḥaqq al-ijtihād wal-taqlīd', *Jarīdat Daghistān* (3 August 1913), p. 4.
67. Masᶜūd al-Muhukhī, *Ḥarq al-asdād fī abwāb al-ijtihād*, pp. 3, 10, 28, 30–2. This work was written in 1921. The copy of this manuscript cited above is in the private possession of the author.
68. Jamāl al-Dīn al-Gharabudaghī, *Taqrīẓ ᶜala baḥth ᶜAlī al-Chumuqī wa Ghazanuf al-Ghubdanī*, MS Makhachkala, IHAE, f. M.-S. Saidov, op. 1, no 37, f. 113a.
69. This discourse is included in a compiled manuscript consisting of four works and letters relating to *taqlīd* and *ijtihād*, criticism of and apologies relating to Ibn Taymiyya, the Egyptian reformers al-Afghānī, ᶜAbduh, Riḍa and, also, the Wahhabis. The discussion continued from 1928 to 1929, see MS Makhachkala, IHAE, f. M.-S. Saidov, op. 1, nos 35–141 ff.
70. Muḥammad b. Zayn al-Dīn al-Targhuli, *Mukataba bayna Nadhīr al-Durgilī*

wa Muḥammad al-Targhulī, MS Makhachkala, f. M.-S. Saidov, op. 1, no. 35, ff. 116-41.

71. Questions of Islamic dogma (*ᶜaqīda*), among them, things prohibited by Islam, questions of worship (*ᶜibāda*) and the clear texts of the Qurᵓān and Sunna, that possess only one meaning, belong to the roots (*uṣūl*) of Islamic law. In the opinion of the jurists, all this should be constant and performing *ijtihād* in relation to these questions is not permitted. The 'branches' (*furūᶜ*) of Islamic law include the spheres of interpersonal and community relations (*muᶜāmala*), where, in the opinion of a number of scholars, *ijtihād* is not only permitted, but necessary.
72. Nadhīr al-Durgilī, *Al-Ijtihād wal-taqlīd*, MS Makhachkala, IHAE, f. F. M.-S. Saidov, op. 1, no. 35, ff. 1a–30b. This work was written in 1928. 34 pp.
73. Ibid., ff. 26a–26b.
74. Yūsuf al-Junguti, *Al-Qawl al-sadīd fī ḥasm al-mādda al-ijtihād wa wujūb al-taqlīd*, MS Makhachkala, IHAE, f. M.-S. Saidov, op. 1, no. 35, ff. 32a–66a.
75. Yūsuf al-Junguti, *Al-Qawl al-sadīd*, ff. 63b–64b.
76. ᶜAbd al-Ḥāfiẓ al-Uḥlī, *Al-Jawāb al-ṣaḥīḥ lil-akh al-muṣlīḥ*, p. 20. This manuscript is in the possession of the author. See also Sh. Shikhaliev, 'Al-Jawab al-Sahih li-l-akh al-muslih 'Abd al-Hafiza Okhlinskogo' in A. K. Alikberov and V. O. Bobrovnikov (eds), *Dagestan i Musul'manskii Vostok. Sbornik statei* (Moscow: Mardzhani, 2010), pp. 324–40.
77. See, for example, I. Baldauf, 'Jadidism in Central Asia within Reformism and Modernism in the Muslim World', *Die Welt des Islams* 41:1 (2001), pp. 72–88.
78. See M. Kemper and Sh. Shikhaliev, 'Qadimism and Jadidism in Twentieth-Century Daghestan', *Asiatische Studien-Études Asiatiques* 69:3 (2015): pp. 593–624.
79. Nāḏir al-Durgilī, *Taᶜlīq al-ḥamīd ᶜala al-qawl al-sadīd,* MS Makhachkala, IHAE, f. M.-S. Saidov, op. 1, no. 35, 68a–103b.
80. Ibid., ff. 70a–70b.
81. This discussion concerns Aḥmad b. Zayn al-Dahlan. *Durar al-sinniyya fīl-radd ᶜala al-wahhābiyya* (Cairo: al-Maṭbaᶜa al-maymaniyya, 1896).
82. The discussion of Muḥammad ibn ᶜAbd al-Wahhāb's claim to absolute *ijtihād* continues to this day in Arabic-language sources. Many Arab theologians consider him an adherent of the Hanbalī legal school and believe that his ideas did not stray from the sphere of *fiqh*, but were directed, more than anything else, to the 'purification' of Islam of its later layers in the field of dogma (*ᶜaqīda*). Others wrote that this scholar went outside of the framework of the legal schools with his legal rulings, 'turning to the practice of absolute *ijtihād*'. See two polemic works with apologies and criticisms of Wahhabism: Muḥammad al-Baha, *Al-fikr al-Islāmī fī taṭawwurī* (Cairo: Maktaba wahba, 1981), pp. 70–9. Muḥammad Khalīl Harash, *Al-Ḥaraka al-Wahhābiyya* (n.p.: Dār al-kātib al-ᶜarabi, n.d.), p. 75. In any case, certain legal decisions by the followers of Muḥammad ibn ᶜAbd al-Wahhāb relating

to the sphere of *fiqh* contradict the decisions of all the legal schools and are based on the works of Ibn Taymiyya and his scholars, who sought to reform not only dogma, but, also, the sphere of Islamic jurisprudence. This, for examples, relates to the question of the process for divorce, where the opinions of Ṣāliḥ al-Yamanī, Muḥammad ibn ᶜAbd al-Wahhāb, al-Afghānī, ᶜAbduh and Rashīd Riḍa almost completely agree with and are based upon the decisions of Ibn Taymiyya, which contradict the decisions of all four of the Sunni legal schools. In this way, the figure of Ibn Taymiyya is of especial interest. His ideas have remained popular among the Muslims of the Russian Empire for nearly three hundred years, down to the present day. Many adherents of his ideas, such as Muḥammad ibn ᶜAbd al-Wahhāb, and, likewise, later reformers (ᶜAbduh, Riḍa, al-Ghumuqī, Riḍaᵓ al-Dīn b. Fakhr al-Dīn and others) often cited Ibn Taymiyya's works. In Daghestan, interest in the ideas of Ibn Taymiyya first grew (in the late seventeenth century and eighteenth), and then waned (in the nineteenth century), and then again increased (in the early twentieth century), and then again decreased (in the post-First World War period), and then re-emerged in the post-Soviet period among the Salafis, who were already widespread in all the Muslim regions of Russia.

83. Nadhīr al-Durgilī, *Taᶜlīq al-ḥamīd ᶜala al-qawl al-sadīd,* ff. 102a–103b.
84. Ghazanuf al-Ghubdanī, *Risāla fīl-radd ᶜala ᶜAlī [al-Ghumuqī]*, 5 ff., MS Makhachkala, IHAE, f. M.-S. Saidov, op. 1, № 37, ff. 107–11.
85. Abū Sufyān al-Ghazanishī, 'Masᵓala al-Ijtihād', *Bayān al-ḥaqāᵓiq* 3 (1926), pp. 2–5; '*Aḥwāl al-Ḥijāz wal-Ghaᵓila al-wahhābiyya*', *Bayān al-ḥaqāᵓiq* 1 (1925), pp. 2–4; Masᶜūd al-Muhukhī, '*Khiṭāb ilā ᶜulamāᵓ*', *Bayān al-ḥaqāᵓiq* 4 (1926), pp. 7–11; Ibrahīm Ḥajiyaw al-Tamirī al-Riknī, '*Mukālama fī ḥaqq dhamm al-Taqlīd*', *Bayān al-ḥaqāᵓiq* 6 (1927), pp. 15–17; ᶜAbd Allāh b. Qurbān ᶜAlī al-Ashilṭī, 'Fī ḥaqq al-ijtihād wal-taṣawwūf', *Bayān al-ḥaqāᵓiq* 7 (1927), pp. 6–8.

8

Kunta Ḥājjī and the Stolen Horse

Michael Kemper and Shamil Shikhaliev

Introduction

This paper is a contribution to the study of Kunta Ḥājjī al-Iliskhānī (1830?–67), the famous Chechen Sufi who is still enormously popular in Chechnya. Reportedly a representative of the Qādiriyya brotherhood, Kunta Ḥājjī established a Sufi network in Chechnya, Ingushetia and parts of Daghestan, and came into conflict with a rival brotherhood, the expanding Naqshbandiyya khālidiyya that had its stronghold in central Daghestan. According to Russian reports he was rebuked by *jihād* leader Shāmil (Shamwīl, Imām in central Daghestan and parts of Chechnya from 1834 to 1859), apparently on the issue of the loud *dhikr* ceremonies that Kunta and his disciples practiced, with round dances, chanting and musical instruments. Kunta is said to have rejected Shāmil's *jihād*, and to have called for non-violent resistance against the Russians instead. Many historians see him as a strong proponent of customary law (*ᶜādāt*) against Islamic law. According to the many Chechen and Russian accounts, Kunta escaped conflict with Shāmil by making a second hajj pilgrimage, from which he returned in 1862. He then gained more adherents who were dissatisfied with the long and unsuccessful militant resistance to the Russians, and placed his representatives in various villages. The Russian authorities soon became suspicious of Kunta's network, which they apparently saw as a parallel administration.[1]

In the last days of 1863, Kunta and some of his *murīd*s were imprisoned, and exiled to the Vologda area of Russia's north. In 1864, a rebellion of his remaining *murīd*s in Chechnya – armed with nothing but daggers, and apparently motivated by the expectation of the End of Times – was bloodily suppressed by the Russian military. The movement disintegrated into several groups called *wird*s (from the Arabic word for 'Sufi litany'), which were led by his disciples of the first and second generations. Next to the

'Kunta Ḥājjī' *wird* proper, today there are still other groups that emerged by names such as 'Bammat-Gireis', 'Ali-Mitaevs' and 'Chim-Mirzas'. These Sufi groups still exist today. Often with hereditary leaderships, these branches of the Kunta Ḥājjī network differ in their male headdress and the musical instruments they use, and some groups allow women to participate in their round dances while others do not. These *wirds* survived Soviet repression in the 1930s as well as the violent deportation of the whole Chechen and Ingush nations to Kazakhstan, in 1944; one *wird*, the 'Vis-hajjis', even came into being in Kazakhstan, and entered Chechnya when the deportees returned to the North Caucasus starting in the second half of the 1950s.[2]

Today these Sufi groups are again a political factor. As Mairbek Vatchagaev observed in 2015:

> With the advent to power in Grozny of the pro-Russian protégé Ramzan Kadyrov, Moscow's policy dramatically changed; it stopped supporting the creation of [political] parties and took on the Sufi fraternities as allies, specifically the Kunta-hajji order. Today they are found in all positions of power: in the government, the *muftiat*, mosques, and the *medrese*. Someone visiting the republic, unaware of the situation, may get the impression Chechnya consists wholly of Kunta-hajji's followers. Undoubtedly, the [Kunta-hajji] order is the largest of all the fraternities. Nonetheless, the total number of Naqshbandis in the republic may be greater than the total number of Qadiris. Naqshbandis and those Qadiris that do not support Kadyrov and remain outside of politics can only resent Moscow's alliance with a single brotherhood out of the twenty-nine [Naqshbandī and Qādirī *wirds* in Chechnya].[3]

To have a critical look into Kunta's writings is therefore a political minefield.

In what follows we intend to open up a new view on Kunta Ḥājjī, not as a Sufi in opposition to Islamic law but as a person who was well-versed in Islamic law and also applied it. This we do in five steps. We start with the translation of a brief undated text (see Figure 8.1), a hitherto unpublished Arabic letter from the quill of Kunta Ḥājjī. The original is preserved in the Oriental section of the Institute of History, Archeology and Ethnography of the Daghestani Scientific Centre of the Russian Academy of Sciences, Makhachkala, Daghestan.[4] In step two we reconstruct what this letter is all about, namely a legal case about a horse. In step three we contextualise this letter by placing it into the framework of what we know about legal relations in the nineteenth-century North Caucasus; this allows us to develop additional hypotheses about the purposes of Kunta's letter. The fourth section briefly reviews the Sufi writings that are ascribed to Kunta, and asks what this letter adds to our knowledge of the shaykh. Then we return to contemporary politics in Chechnya, in the line of Vatchagaev's observation quoted above; here the question is how the ongoing Islamisation of Chechen society under President Ramzan Kadyrov relates to Kunta's image as a peaceful saint, and to the conclusions that we draw from the letter – namely that Kunta positioned himself not only as a Sufi or saint but also as a scholar of Islamic law.

Step One: Translation

From the servant of Allah the Exalted, from Ḥājj Kuntā, to his truthful close companion and his smart friend Ḥājj-Muḥammad. Peace be with you, and Allah's grace!

In the following:

The things that happened concerning the restitution (*ḥaqq*) of your lost horse are well-known, and observed from the meal on the table at your place (*maᶜhūda min al-ṭaᶜām fī al-māʾida ladayka*) and at the places of others.

If I had given a compensation (*ḍamān*) for Ḥājj Arqa or for Aygum, or if I had taken over the debt (*in kuntu muʾaddiyyan al-dayn*) that was proven to be Ḥājj Arqa's or Aygum's, then I would not turn against you [now]. In fact, I know this better.

But I am turning against you because what I gave to you was not a compensation payment (*ḍamān*), and not a payment (*adāʾ*) [in a legal procedure]; I therefore now demand back from you what I paid (*dafaᶜtu*) to you. I [simply] gave you the silver in order to stop the litigation (*li-tawaqquf al-daᶜwā*). For I did not know the truth of this issue concerning Aygum, so I feared Allah ٢ the Great and therefore refrained from making the judgment (*an aḥkuma*) that the fine (*ghurm*) of the horse would fully fall on Ḥājj Arqa. I also feared him ٢ [that is, Allah] in case I put part of the fine (*ghurm*) of the horse on Aygum, for I did not find the evident proof [for this case] (*ṣarīḥ*) in the books. So I asked the scholars in the plain (*al-ᶜulamāʾ fī l-sahl*) [to solve this issue], and each of them said that apparently, Aygum ٢ made mistakes [that is, was negligent or falling short of fulfilling his obligations, *muqaṣṣir*] in the issue of this lost horse.

But neither in my eyes nor in my heart do I see the evident proof (*ṣarīḥ*) that would be the necessary foundation for me to decide (*li-an naqṭaᶜa*) that he ٢ [= Aygum] made mistakes. And I have been hopeful that the eyes of a more intelligent scholar could find the evident [proof] and detect [the truth]; I would ask him about this issue, and then I would pass a judgment (*aḥkumu baᶜda dhālika*) and ask my money back. And I have hoped [that the scholar would] reject (*an aᶜzala*) the judgment of Tarki (*qaḍāʾ*

Targhū). Then this *qāḍī* and scholar would take my place (*maqāmī*) and sit in the council (*majlis*) in my place. He will judge according to his own will (*yaḥkumu bi-mā arāda*), and according to what he finds is the truth.

So if [this scholar] judges (*ḥakama*) that I should take my money back from Ḥājj Muḥammad according to his vision [*ruʾya*] of the person ٢ from whom ٢ the price (*ḥaqq*) of the horse must be taken, then God the Exalted gave me what I asked from Him. My thanks go to God for this.

And you should not doubt the safe procedure (*amn*), for each person who deserves restitution (*ḥaqq*) will attain restitution.

And you continue to say that the fine (*ghurm*) for the horse should come to me [that is, that I should pay it]. However, I do not want this to fall on me, no matter from which side. This [to ask that I pay the fine] is not appropriate for you; rather, you should claim your lost and stolen horse from the person who deserves this [that is, from the real thief]. As you know well, I am not obliged to pay the fine (*ghurm*) for your horse.

You must understand my words, and act according to what is the truth. And do not be surprised by what I wrote to you earlier; it is not surprising that a man demands money (*ḥaqq*) from the person who owes him money.

Rather, surprising is what you wrote to me. You must pay me my money (*ḥaqqī*) [back], if you do not [intend to] do me injustice (*in lam taẓlumū ʿalayya*). Greetings!

Step Two: Reconstruction

As Kunta emerges here as a person of means and power, there is reason to assume that the letter stems from his last years in Chechnya (before his imprisonment in December 1863), when he was at the peak of his influence. The issue at stake is who has to pay compensation (*ḍamān*) for the loss of a horse, and who has to pay the fine (*ghurm*) that accompanies the restitution payment. As we have no other information about this particular case, we will first try to make sense of the text simply by re-narrating its content.

The addressee, Ḥājj Muḥammad, claimed that his horse was lost, and there are two men who may have been responsible for the loss, Ḥājj Arqa and Aygum. There is no information on how the horse was lost; perhaps Arqa and/or Aygum had been in charge of guarding it, perhaps there were indications one of them stole it.

Then the writer of this letter, Ḥājj Kunta, intervened by making a payment (in silver) to the owner of the horse, Ḥājj Muḥammad. Kunta now employs a legal argumentation: he argues that his payment was not a compensation payment (*ḍamān*), which would have been equivalent to acknowledging that Ḥājj Arqa or Aygum (or both) had indeed been legally responsible for the loss of the animal. Instead, Kunta claims he just wanted to stop the process of litigation without making his own statement on who of the two was to blame for the loss of the horse, because he did not find a clear solution 'in the books' (*al-kutub*). It seems Kunta had intervened to protect Ḥājj Arqa and/or Aygum, and to please his friend Ḥājj Muḥammad. To obtain a judgment Kunta then asked Islamic specialists 'in the plains', most probably, the Kumyk lowlands of Daghestan; this seems to have been a court in Tarki (an old political centre close to present-day Makhachkala), the only place name that is mentioned in the text. The legal specialists there decided that the responsibility falls on Aygum.

This, however, does not satisfy Kunta; he has doubts about Aygum's responsibility, and hopes that another (unnamed) scholar can be found who comes to a better judgment, perhaps by establishing Arqa's guilt, in any case by clearing Aygum from guilt. If this *qāḍī* confirms Kunta's view of the matter then he will take Kunta's seat in the *majlis* ('council', here perhaps: the court meeting). Kunta thus encourages the horse owner Ḥājj Muḥammad to continue to search for another *qāḍī* who would pass the desired judgment. The identification of the legally responsible person would be the basis for Kunta to get his money back from Ḥājj Muḥammad.

But the last section of the letter indicates that after having obtained the value of the horse from Kunta, Ḥājj Muḥammad insisted that Kunta must also pay the accompanying fine (*ghurm*) for the theft or loss. This seems to be the point that made Kunta furious: Kunta had been ready to compensate Ḥājj Muḥammad for the loss, but he was not willing to also pay the penal fine (which, traditionally, would go into the treasure of the claimant's community, but perhaps also to the owner), for it was not Kunta who stole the horse. Hence Kunta decided to emphasise that his payment was not a legal compensation payment (*ḍamān*) that would have established his own guilt, or the guilt of Aygum. Ḥājj Muḥammad's insistence on also getting the fine from Kunta seems to have put their relationship under strain, and may have been the reason why Kunta now demanded his money back. The initial reference to a lavish meal at Ḥājj Muḥammad's place was Kunta's reminder that Ḥājj Muḥammad had previously treated him with much honour.

For Arabists, an interesting feature in this letter are the syntactical signs: in Daghestani Arabic writings, authors often used extra symbols to clarify syntactical relations. Kunta employed a sign similar to the Arabic number '2' (٢), which is placed underneath 'Allah' and under 'him' (in 'I feared Him'), making clear Kunta feared Allah. The same sign is later on employed in two more cases, namely to connect Aygum with the 'he' in 'he made mistakes', as well 'the person' with 'from whom the price is demanded' (*man yastaḥaqqu minhu al-ḥaqq*).

Step Three: Contextualisation

This letter is a typical specimen of the legal literature from the North Caucasus of the nineteenth century and early twentieth, which has, in the absence of central archives of Muslim ruling houses (as we know them from pre-colonial Central Asia), largely come down to us in fragments. Letters are often preserved as loose sheets in Daghestani manuscript volumes; mostly written in Arabic or in Kumyk (the second lingua franca of the region), they report on donations, divorce cases, *waqf*, theft and compensation issues, to name but a few reoccurring legal subjects. We also have compilations of customary law 'agreements' (sg. *ittifāq*), that is, conclusions of legal cases either between two litigating parties, or among all fellow villagers, or between two or more village communities. Some communities gathered lists of historical *ittifāqāt* that they used as legal precedents, and that were constantly enlarged by new judgments and agreements. Such community agreements cover not only how to compensate for manslaughter, theft, arson or the loss of a limb; they also lay down the use of water and community-owned meadows and the organisation of the village's defence.[5] These customary law documents employ a sophisticated legal terminology that is partly derived from Islamic law, and they are a gold mine for historical anthropology. But also individual letters combine terms from Islamic and customary law. Equally in circulation were classical texts of Shāfiᶜī law, including commentaries, glosses, treatises and *fatwā*s, which were used as textbooks at the many small madrasas in Daghestan's mountains. The *jihād* leaders (esp. Ghāzī Muḥammad, Imām 1828–32, and Shāmil, Imām 1834–59) were from among the madrasa students who saw that most of the Islamic law that they studied with their masters was not applied in practice – and their *jihād* began as a rebellion against customary law, and only developed into war against Russia once the empire supported the traditional legal and political authorities in Daghestan who upheld customary law.[6]

Kunta's letter belongs to the genre of legal correspondence, and has therefore to be understood in the field of tension between Islamic and customary law. The letter contains a number of professional legal terms, such as *adāʾ* (making a payment), *dayn* (debt), *ḍamān* (compensation for theft or destruction) and *ghurm* (fine). Often the term *ḥaqq* is used, with various meanings depending on the context. The whole procedure is called *daᶜwā*, a formal legal process. The text also mentions experts of Islamic law (as *ᶜulamāᵓ*, 'scholars'), and more specifically the unnamed *qāḍī*; his job is to give a legal ruling (*ḥukm*). Whether this *qāḍī* was attached to any court institution is not clear; he may have been a freelancer. Kunta's own attempt at identifying the culprit is referred to as *qaṭᶜ*, 'to determine', which would precede the *ḥukm*. The decisive proof (or argument) necessary for a judgment is referred to as *ṣarīḥ*.

There is also a reference to the 'judicial decision (*qaḍāᵓ*) of Targhū'. A mountain on the Caspian coast (today a part of Makhachkala, the capital of the Republic of Daghestan), Tarki was the seat of the Shamkhāl dynasty, one of several old ruling houses in central Daghestan. The Shamkhāls for a certain period also owned lands in northern Daghestan and in the Chechen lowlands; and many regarded the Shamkhāl as the *primus inter pares* among Daghestan's Muslim noble families. Russia used the Shamkhāl family as their ally against the *jihād* movement of the three Imāms (1828–59), but after Imām Shāmil's surrender in 1859, they deprived the Shamkhāls of their political authority and established direct colonial rule. In the empire, Daghestan Oblast' (region) obtained a new legal system in which petty legal cases among Daghestanis were settled at local village courts, with one higher court of appeal. Here customary law and Islamic law were administered, under colonial supervision.[7] Based on the assumption that the litigation about the horse took place in the time after Shamil's surrender in 1859 and before Kunta's exile to North Russia in 1863, we might assume that 'the judgment of Tarki' refers to a legal procedure held at the seat of the Shamkhāl, or conducted by Islamic judges residing in Tarki, perhaps operating under a Russian constable.

The fact that Kunta first tried to find a solution to this case in 'the books' (of Islamic law) indicates that he saw himself as a person capable of using legal literature (in Arabic), and of passing an appropriate judgment once he identified a similar case in the books. The letter indicates that he was expected to resolve this case. He first did so by turning to more learned scholars, in Tarki. However, these 'scholars in the plain' did not produce the desired outcome, since they also blamed Aygum. Kunta makes it clear this is unacceptable for him, and therefore demands that the search for an appropriate *qāḍī* must go on. So, while Kunta is not himself posing as a full-fledged Islamic *qāḍī* here, he clearly takes the liberty to pick and choose from various judgments offered by professionals, and to reject the judgments of *qāḍī*s if they do not confirm his view of the affair. Let us add here that at least in one more surviving letter, in a different legal context (how to sell a house), Kunta is explicitly addressed as 'Qāḍī Ḥājj Kunta', indicating that Muslims in the North Caucasus saw him not only as a Sufi master but also as a legal authority.[8]

It remains to be asked why Kunta intervened in the first place. Did he pay money to protect Aygum or Arqa from prosecution, or to extend a favour to 'his friend' Ḥājj Muḥammad? If it was not meant as a *ḍamān*, how then should we define Kunta's payment – as an extra-legal gift or bribe, with the tacit understanding that Aygum or Arqa were indeed responsible for the loss? Or was it a security he hoped to get back once the culprit was identified and forced to pay?

And were Aygum and Ḥājj Arqa, or only Aygum, from among Kunta's Sufi *murīd*s? If so, this would imply that the master also took care of his disciples' financial liabilities. Money is then Kunta's instrument to protect his Sufi circle. But the document does not indicate that Kunta was particularly close to either of the two suspects.[9]

More probable is that Kunta wanted to terminate the legal case by an extra-legal payment because he knew that Ḥājj Arqa or Aygum would not pay restitution. This could have unpleasant consequences, especially if they were not from Ḥājj Muḥammad's own community; in this case the community of Ḥājj Muḥammad would be entitled to conduct a raid on the community of the defendants, and take *ishkīl*, in the form of an item equal to the lost horse. This could lead to long-lasting feuds between families and communities.

Ishkīl was a respected instrument of customary law (*ᶜādāt*).[10] Daghestan's Islamic scholars saw customary law as a remnant of the pre-Islamic 'period of ignorance' (*jāhiliyya*), and as a highly defective system that allowed for the self-enrichment of those village elders and local aristocrats who administered customary law. As the regulations of customary law were man-made, they were unjust and illegitimate. In his letter, Kunta Ḥājjī argues from the position of Islamic law, and his legalistic reasoning is quite sophisticated (for instance, when he argues that his payment did not belong to the category of *ḍamān*). And, finally, if his intention was to prevent Ḥājj Muḥammad from taking recourse to self-help (*ishkīl*), then Kunta acted in the spirit of Islamic law, against a customary law practice that would escalate the conflict.

The alternative to *ishkīl* is of course mediation by a respected outsider. Kunta seems to have taken on this role, and decided to pay for the lost horse from his own pocket, in order to preserve peace. This investment would have obliged all parties – especially Ḥājj Muḥammad! – to honour and respect him. Kunta only changed his mind once Ḥājj Muḥammad was so bold as to also demand the accompanying fine from him, that is, the punishment for negligence or theft. As Kunta's investment would not bring the expected dividends in terms of respect and authority, he demanded his silver back – and did so by turning to professional judges in the hope that they would identify the person responsible for the loss of the horse. Kunta would get his money back, and Ḥājj Muḥammad would perhaps also receive the fine.

Step Four: What Does this Letter Tell Us about Kunta Ḥājjī?

This letter is one of the few testimonies that we have from Kunta himself. While Kunta has been a major anchor point in every historical survey of Islam among the Chechens, hardly anybody has ever looked at his (or his followers') Arabic, Kumyk or Chechen/Ingush writings from his era. All that has come down from him are editions of his sayings written down by his disciples, in 'editions' that Kunta may or may not have authorised. So far we have discovered three books that present Kunta's words in direct speech, and that seem to have been written during his lifetime or shortly after his death.[11]

The most well-known book ascribed to Kunta is the *Maqālāt*, a loose compilation of Kunta's purported sayings. It also contains statements that are introduced as having come not from Kunta but from a certain Ghāzī-Ḥājjī, supposedly Kunta's master. Clearly, the *Maqālāt* was produced by one of his disciples, perhaps even after his death in 1867. The text was printed in lithograph form in 1910, in the Mavraev publishing house in Temir-Khan Shura (today Buinaksk, Daghestan). According to the preface to this edition, the work was originally written in Arabic, and then translated into Kumyk by Shikhammat-qadi Biibulatov from the Daghestani village of Erpeli. Following the classical tradition of theological and legal commentaries, in this edition the Arabic original is still preserved in the form of fragments (in brackets) between the Kumyk translation parts (also in Arabic script). One year later, in 1911, Mavraev also published a Chechen translation of the Arabic–Kumyk text of the *Maqālāt*.[12] Contentwise, the *Maqālāt* is completely devoted to Sufism, dealing particularly with the relationship between the Sufi master and his disciples, in addition to sections on dream interpretation. Some of the individual statements are clearly directed against Islamic scholars (*ᶜulamāᵓ*) who claim that Islam is all about the legal schools, and about studying the disciplines of law. To such statements Kunta replies that 'our Prophet revealed the *sharīᶜa* and made clear the Sufi path (*ṭarīqa*), and the latter is the root (*aṣl*) of the four law schools. And [the Prophet] was illiterate (*ummī*), and therefore he did not make the understanding (*maᶜrifa*) of the judgments of the four law schools dependent on the understanding (*maᶜrifa*) and reading of the books (*al-kutub*) that had been laid down [by men], because they are [just] a wisdom (*ḥikma*); and Allah gives the wisdom to whom he wishes.'[13]

We understand from this text that Kunta was in a dispute with scholars of Islamic law who reproached him – presumably for his Sufi practices, but maybe also because he opposed Shāmil's claim to political authority as Imām and *jihād* leader. These statements imply that Kunta placed mystical insight higher than pure knowledge of the books, without, however, rejecting the bookish interpretations of Islamic law out of hand; still, the emphasis on the Prophet's illiteracy stands in full opposition to Kunta's skilfully composed letter on the horse.

A second Arabic work connected with Kunta Ḥājjī is a collection seemingly composed in 1281 (1864/5)[14] by a certain ᶜAbdassalām al-Chachānī, that is, a Chechen; the latter gave it the title *Ajwibat al-ustādh li-masāᵓil al-murīd* ('The Master's Answers to the Murid's Questions'). This text exists in several Daghestani manuscript copies and in an Arabic print edition from 1330 (1912).[15] As ᶜAbdassalām noted, he had accompanied the saint (*walī*) Kunta Ḥājjī for a couple of months during their exile in 'Siberia' (a term that in North Caucasus literatures refers also to central and north Russia as a place of exile), and became his disciple. The text is structured along fourteen questions that ᶜAbdassalām posed to Kunta, with the latter's replies again in direct speech. Here as well we find a negative view on scholars of law: in one place Kunta complains about the *ᶜulamāᵓ* who imposed their rule during the Imamate of Shāmil.[16]

A third Arabic text, finally, is structured as Kunta's responses to claims of 'the Islamic scholars', evidently reflecting a debate with Daghestani *ᶜulamāᵓ*. Again, this text is authored by the above-mentioned ᶜAbdassalām, and presented as Kunta's direct speech, which ᶜAbdassalām again translated from Chechen into Arabic. This text is known from Daghestani manuscript copies and was also included in the 1330/1912 Syrian edition of ᶜAbdassalām's *Ajwibat*.[17]

All three texts therefore clearly present Kunta Ḥājjī as a charismatic saint who opposes the Islamic legal scholars and their legalistic approaches. Daghestani private libraries contain more text fragments written by Kunta, or on him; they might give more clues about Kunta's relationship to Shāmil and in particular to the Russian authorities. Suffice it to mention here that *Ajwibat* contains a section in which Kunta is reported to give advice on how service to Islam (*ᶜibāda*) can be upheld by those 'who fell into the hands of the infidels', that is, in Russian prison or exile, far away from their communities. Kunta here argues that as long as a Muslim is able to praise God, he is still a Muslim. The third text contains a separate section in which Kunta argues that fasting and prayers can be performed at other than the prescribed times if the situation forces the Muslim to do so, for instance, while being imprisoned by infidels or in exile; in such situations Muslims may follow the same norms that are applied during travels. The third text is also the only one of the three that mentions the Qādiriyya: Kunta here defends the loud (*jahr*) *dhikr* of the Qādiriyya against the silent (*khafī*) *dhikr* of the Naqshbandiyya, however without denigrating the latter. Kunta clearly developed his more ecstatic Sufi path against the 'sober' Naqshbandiyya khālidiyya in Daghestan, and against the legalistic approach of Shāmil's *jihād* state.[18] This opposition to the Naqshbandiyya may have had ethnic overtones: most Naqshbandis came from Daghestan, and accompanied Shamil's taking control of significant parts of Chechnya in the 1830s.

Step Five: On the Political Usefulness of Kunta Ḥājjī in Contemporary Chechnya

In the 1990s the Kunta Ḥājjī ritual – especially the fierce-looking dance in which men move in circles, clapping and shouting – was revived as national folklore, and used by the leaders of the Chechen separatist movement. In the first war between Russia and Chechnya (1994–6, ending with Russia's withdrawal), Chechen military formations were partly organised around the various Kunta Ḥājjī *wird*s, and the *muftī* of independent Chechnya, Akhmed Kadyrov, regarded the Kunta Ḥājjī brotherhood as a bulwark against the rise of the foreign-funded *jihādī* ('Wahhabi') groups. When the militants' pressure on the secular interwar government of Chechnya/Ichkeriia became overwhelming, Akhmed Kadyrov defected to Moscow. After Russia's victory over Chechnya (Ichkeriia) in the second Chechen war (1999–2000, with operations continuing for several more years), President Putin made Akhmed Kadyrov 'head' of the republic that was now again integrated into the Russian Federation. With significant financial support from the Kremlin, Kadyrov had the tombs of Kunta's mother Hedi and of many of Kunta's followers renovated.[19] His son Ramzan Kadyrov, president of Chechnya since 2007, continues the Kunta cult, and portrays the saint as the archetype of Chechen Islam. Also in neighbouring Ingushetia, the local *wird* of the Kunta network is portrayed as a pillar of the state[20] (although Ingushetia's leadership seems to be less attached to it, and enrages Chechnya's Kadyrov by signalling readiness to establish a dialogue also with Salafis in Ingushetia). In the Republic of Adygea (in the north-west Caucasus), a 'Russian Islamic University' bears the name of Kunta Ḥājjī.

There are still many unanswered questions about the actual influence of 'Kunta-Hajjism', in the past as well as today. Many observers hold that Chechen Muslims are by and large Sufis, and closely connected to the

Kunta Ḥājjī *wirds*; but we already saw from Vatchagaev's observation at the start of this paper that the picture is more complex. All arguments about the persisting influence of the Sufi groups and families are connected to assumptions about the 'traditional clan structure' of the Chechens and Ingush: many argue that clan identities are directly replicated in affiliations to specific *wirds*, in a unique 'ethno-religious' social structure.[21] But both the *wirds* and the clan structure must have been transformed, if not destroyed, by Soviet modernisation, urbanisation, violent exile and resettlement at places other than their original homes. On top of that, the two wars of the 1990s turned huge parts of the population into internally displaced people, and made others go into exile; and since the mid-1990s many Chechen and Ingush men have lived and worked in central Russia, as 'internal labour migrants'. All of these factors have influenced the way in which traditional Chechen clan structures have given way to flexible political and religious alliances.[22]

In this light the role of Kunta Ḥājjī remains highly ambiguous. He has been celebrated as a pacifist, and even as a Chechen Mahatma Gandhi.[23] But the Russian Empire, as a rule, did not send pacifists into exile. As there is no critical research on the sources from his time, Kunta has become an easy model for whatever one wants to see in him. It almost seems as if his written heritage is purposefully exempted from critical examination, since any serious investigation of the past might lead to political tensions in the present, especially among the competing *wirds* that claim his heritage. The saint's image remains stereotyped, with popular legends in place of historiography.[24]

For the current Chechen leadership, Kunta is important because he was Chechen, because he stood for a 'Chechen way of Islam' (against the overwhelming Islamic influence that came from Daghestan, and against Russia's Tatar *muftīs*) and because he was foundational for major religious communities of our times. The *dhikr* ceremonies that he introduced have become part of the Chechen national cultural heritage, and the tombs of his disciples adorn a Vaynakh (Chechen and Ingush) Islamic topography, which makes Kunta closely linked to Vaynakh soil. And Kunta's reported rejection of violence seems to fall on fertile ground today, after two recent wars, just as it did in the 1860s, after the failure of Shāmil's *jihād*.

But other features of Kunta's career are more difficult to integrate into this conventionalised picture. In particular, his Sufi thinking seems to have been shaped by eschatological expectations, which did not make him a state-builder. But, above all, his understanding of Islam seems to have defied the mainstream Sunni scholars of the time. All this while today's Chechnya is striving hard to be as orthodox as possible. Ramzan

Kadyrov's government is well-known for its enforcement of Islamic customs and norms, with Kadyrov posing as a native fighter – fearing God, caring for his dependants, but ruthless to his enemies. This image is not exactly in line with Kunta's rejection of violence, and certainly not with Kunta's Sufi message.[25]

Kadyrov's legalistic approach to Islam can be demonstrated with the example of a highly controversial Islamic congress that took place in Grozny in August 2016. With welcome messages transmitted from Vladimir Putin and Ramzan Kadyrov, the Chechen Muftiate convened several hundred Islamic authorities from Russia and other countries (including Egypt and war-torn Syria) to discuss 'who falls under the category of Ahl al-Sunna'. The event was meant to exclude Islamic radicals from Sunni Islam. The delegates allegedly gave their consent to a *fatwā* that defined Sunni Islam as the religion of those (1) who follow one of the four accepted Sunni legal schools, (2) who subscribe to Māturīdī or Ashᶜarī speculative theology (*kalām*) and (3) who honour the Sufism of Junayd al-Baghdādī (d. 910), Bahāᵓaddīn Naqshband (d. 1389) (remembered as the founder of the Naqshbandiyya) and ᶜAbdalqādir al-Jilānī (d. 1166, founding father of the Qādiriyya). In other words, Sufism (here termed *iḥsān*) is defined as an intrinsic part of what it means to be Sunni; who does not subscribe to this definition is excluded from that community.

More explicitly, this *fatwā* banned from Sunni Islam not only 'sects' like Ḥizb al-Taḥrīr (under legal ban in Russia anyway) but also 'Wahhabism', which in Russia is the catch-all term not just for the Islam of the Saudi establishment but for all trends of Salafism or radicalism. The document called for the establishment of a council of Islamic experts to support the Russian legal authorities in the identification of dangerous trends that misuse Islam, clearly with the aim to impose more official bans.[26]

Days later Saudi authorities began to protest against this call for a legal ban on Wahhabism. Several of the high-profile international guests realised the explosive character of the document, and tried to defend themselves by arguing that the *fatwā* was not properly discussed at the congress, and that all communication was conducted only in Russian.[27] While several *muftīs* from Russia's regions continued to support the *fatwā* (which they understood as a Kremlin demand that one cannot ignore), a major Islamic umbrella organisation, the Council of Russia's *muftīs* headed by Ravil Gainutdin in Moscow, openly opposed the Grozny resolution, arguing that Russia's Muslim leaders should not copy the *takfīrī* strategies of their radical and terrorist opponents.[28]

To Kunta, the Chechen Muftiate's attempt at defining 'good Islam' with the help of the Russian authorities, and at defining it by dogmatic schools, would probably have sounded preposterous. The three texts that report his Sufi positions describe him as an opponent of the Islamic legal scholars who define Islamic life by adherence to 'the books'.

But the horse letter allows us to draw a more balanced image of the saint: evidently, he was not just an ecstatic mystic but also a reasonable player in the field of legal relations, a role that he seems to have exploited as a means of strengthening his authority. Above we quoted his observing that the 'basis' of Islamic law is gnostic perception: he did not pose as an opponent of Islamic law but rather emancipated Sufism from the legal schools, and thereby from the purview of the scholars who reject Sufism or demand more 'sober' forms of Sufism. In this sense we can also interpret the only mystical reference in the letter: at one point Kunta writes that he does not see a clear text 'in his heart', indicating he might have given an earlier judgment (*ḥukm*) if he had seen a corresponding vision of the Prophet. Sufism is not just something added to *sharī^{c}a*; for Kunta, Sufism is the core of Islam!

This is, we believe, the main contribution that this document makes to our understanding of Kunta Ḥājjī. More research into his Sufi writings, but especially into the various fragmentary sources that we have about this important Sufi master, must take into consideration not only Kunta's rejection of specific Islamic scholars but also his use of Islamic law. And letters like the one discussed in this chapter might in fact reflect what the Russian administration saw as Kunta's 'parallel administration' in Chechnya. Perhaps the Tsarist authorities sent him into exile not because of his wild Sufi practices but because of his growing legal authority. At any event, Ramzan Kadyrov might be delighted to hear that Kunta was also a scholar of Islamic law – even though Kunta's legal thinking clearly developed in a Daghestani context.

Notes

1. The best study on Kunta to date is still V. Akaev, *Sheikh Kunta-khadzhi. Zhizn' i uchenie* (Groznyi: Nauchno-issledovatel'skii institut gumanitarnykh nauk Chechenskoi respubliki, 1994). See also M. Vachagaev, *Chechnia v kavkazskoi voine XIX st.: sobytiia i sud'by* (Kiev/Paris: Fond 'Istoriko-kul'turnoe nasledie chechentsev', 2003). C. W. Dettmering, *Russlands Kampf gegen die Sufis: Die Integration der Tschetschenen und Inguschen in das Russische Reich 1810–1880* (Oldenburg: Dryas, 2011), is very brief on Kunta (pp. 290–6).
2. Z. Ermekbaev, *Chechentsy i Ingushy v Kazakhstane. Istoriia i sud'by* (Almaty: Daik-Press, 2009), esp. pp. 220ff.

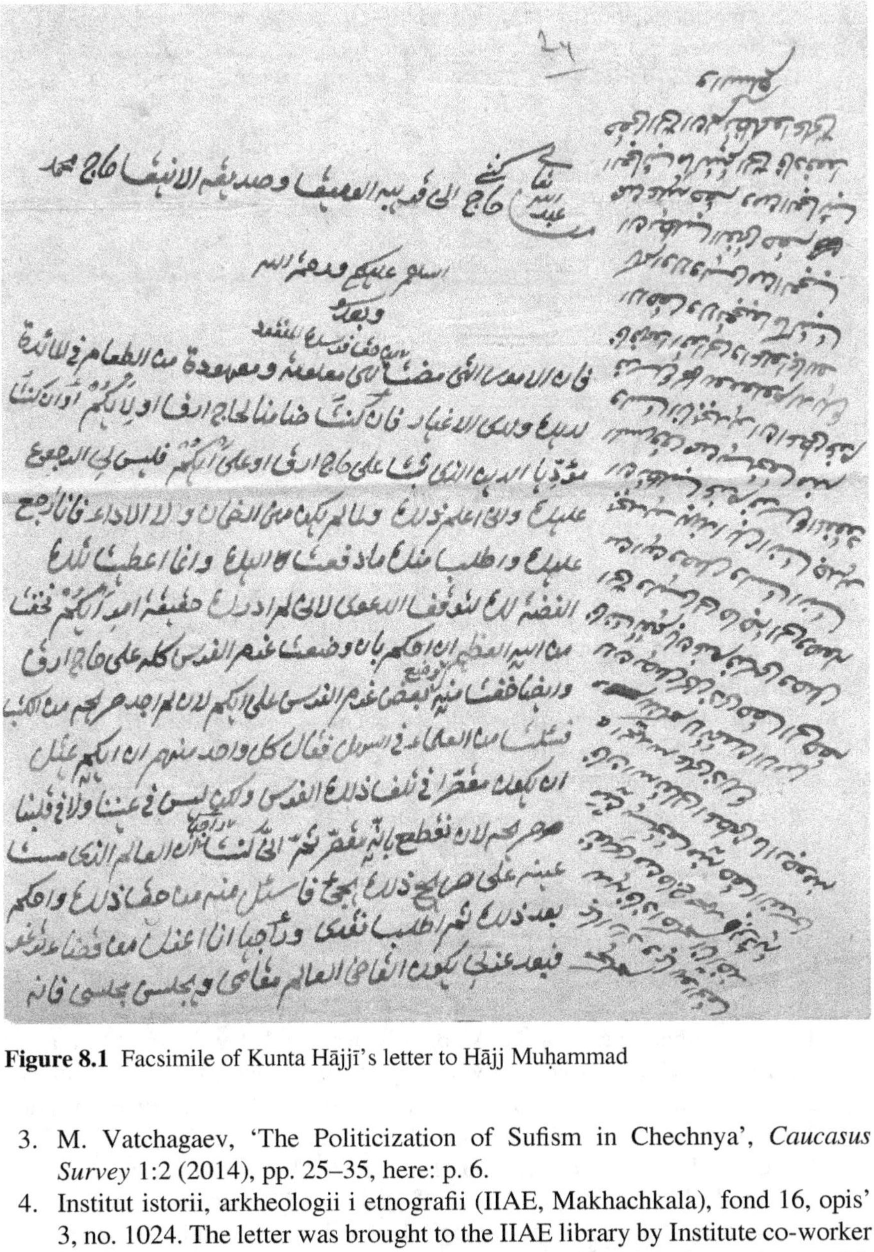

Figure 8.1 Facsimile of Kunta Ḥājjī's letter to Ḥājj Muḥammad

3. M. Vatchagaev, 'The Politicization of Sufism in Chechnya', *Caucasus Survey* 1:2 (2014), pp. 25–35, here: p. 6.
4. Institut istorii, arkheologii i etnografii (IIAE, Makhachkala), fond 16, opis' 3, no. 1024. The letter was brought to the IIAE library by Institute co-worker Magomed-Rasul Mugumaev, as part of texts collected during archeographical expeditions into the Kazbek and Gumbet raions of Daghestan in 1975–7. We extend our sincere gratitude to IIAE director Dr. Makhach Musaev for giving us permission to publish this letter in translation and facsimile.
5. V. O. Bobrovnikov, 'Ittifāq Agreements in Daghestan in the Eighteenth

– Nineteenth Centuries', *Manuscripta Orientalia* 8:4 (2002), pp. 21–7; M. Kemper, 'Communal Agreements *(ittifāqāt)* and *'ādāt*-Books from Daghestani Villages and Confederacies (18th–19th Centuries)', *Der Islam* 81 (2004), pp. 115–51.

6. M. Kemper, 'Ghazi Muhammad's Treatise against Daghestani Customary Law', in Moshe Gammer (ed.), *Islam and Sufism in Daghestan* (Helsinki: Finnish Academy of Sciences and Letters, 2009), pp. 85–100.
7. V. O. Bobrovnikov, *Musul'mane severnogo Kavkaza: Obychai, pravo, nasilie. Ocherki po istorii i etnografii prava Nagornogo Dagestana* (Moscow: Vostochnaia literatura, 2002).
8. IIAE, fond 16, op. 3, no. 1011 (a certain Aḥmad al-Ḥashīshī to Kunta, undated, on a question concerning the sale of a house: the author states that the transaction takes place when all items of the previous owner are removed).
9. At any event, their names do not appear in a surviving Russian list of Kunta's foremost disciples; cf. V. Akaev, *Sheikh Kunta-khadzhi*, pp. 39f.
10. V. Bobrovnikov, 'Verbrechen und Brauchtum zwischen islamischem und imperialem Recht: Zur Entzauberung des *iškīl* im Daghestan des 17. bis 19. Jahrhunderts', in M. Kemper and M. Reinkowski (eds), *Rechtspluralismus in der Islamischen Welt. Gewohnheitsrecht zwischen Staat und Gesellschaft* (Berlin: De Gruyter, 2005), pp. 297–315.
11. For a first overview of the manuscript material, see Sh. Sh. Shikhaliev, 'Kratkii obzor arabograficheskikh sochinenii Kunta-khadzhi Kishieva', in ed. M.S. Albogachieva (ed.), *Islam v Rossii i za ee predelami: istoriia, obshchestvo, kul'tura. Sbornik materialov mezhregional'noi konferentsii, posviashchennoi 100-letiiu so dnia konchiny vydaiushchegosia religioznogo deiatelia sheikh Batal-khadzhi Belkharoeva* (St Petersburg and Magas: Muzei antropologii i etnografii imeni Petra Velikogo RAN, 2011), pp. 71–5.
12. *Maqālāt al-Shaykh al-fāḍil wa l-ustādh al-kāmil al-Ḥājj Kunta al-Michighishī al-Iliskhānī*, Kumyk translation from the Arabic by Erfīlilī [from Erpeli, Daghestan] Shikhammat Qadi [*sic*] (Temir-Khan Shura: al-Maṭba^{c}a al-islāmiyya li-Muḥammad Mīrzā Māvrāyūf [Mavraev], January 1910). Another edition of the Arabic text was published by the Muftiate of Ingushetia, with an accompanying Ingush translation: *Maqālāt al-Shaykh al-fāḍil al-Ḥājjī Kunta al-Iliskhānī. Tarjamat bī l-lugha al-inghūshī* [sic]. Translator: Abū Bakr b. Aḥmad al-Sarkhūkhī [Ingush title: Galgai Respublika Muftiiato: *Vezacha Shaikha, Kamil Ustaza Ilaskha-iurtara Kunta-Kh'azhii 'K"ama'lash"* (Nazran: n.p., *c.* 2000)]. For a Russian translation of the *Maqālāt* see 'Poucheniia dostoinogo sheikha i sovershennogo ustaza Kunta-Khadzhi Chechenskogo . . .', introduction and translation from the Arabic and Chechen by A. M. Garasaev, in *Vestnik Moskovskogo universiteta*, seriia 13: Vostokovedenie, 2001, no. 4, pp. 99–112.
13. *Maqālāt al-Shaykh al-fāḍil al-Ḥājjī Kunta al-Iliskhānī* [Ingushetian edition, Arabic text], p. 21.

14. ᶜAbdassalām, *Ajwibat al-ustādh li-masāʾil al-murīd,* Arabic manuscript copy (of 1324/1906–7) from the private collection of Magomed Dalgatovich Dalgatov in the village of Somoda, Daghestan, 20 folios; here fol. 22a. The manuscript was detected (and registered under no. 146) by the archeographical expedition of the Institute of History, Archeology and Ethnography of the Daghestani Branch of the Russian Academy of Sciences.
15. *Kitāb Jawāb al-sāʾilīn fī ḥujjat al-murīd, wa-huwa al-kitāb al-mustaṭāb alladhī talqāhu al-fāḍil 'Abdassalām al-Chachānī 'an shaykhihi Quṭb al-wāṣilīn,* ed. Muḥammad b. al-Ḥājj Aḥmad al-Ghumūkhī (al-Qunayẓara/ al-Shām al-Sharīf: Maṭbaᶜat Jawlān, 1330). The text of *Ajwibat* – roughly equivalent to the manuscript version mentioned in the preceding footnote – goes from pages 18 to 39. In the print version the date of termination is given as 27 Ramadan 1288, which would imply that the manuscript version referred to above (which has 1281 as the date when the text or the copy were produced) is older, and not a copy from the print.
16. *Ajwibat al-ustādh li-masā'il al-murīd,* manuscript collection Dalgatov, fol. 15a.
17. *Kitāb Jawāb al-sā'ilīn fī ḥujjat al-murīd,* pp. 2–16.
18. On which see M. Kemper, 'The Daghestani Legal Discourse on the Imamate', *Central Asian Survey* 21:3 (2002), pp. 265–78.
19. For photographs and historical information on these tombs, see M. Vachagaev, *Sheikhi i ziiaraty Chechni* (Moscow: n.p., 2009).
20. J. Meskhidze, 'Shaykh Batal Hajji from Surkhokhi: Towards the History of Islam in Ingushetia', *Central Asian Survey* 25:1–2 (2006), pp. 179–91.
21. For a recent example of this mystifying obsession with clans and *wird*s in a political studies work see O. V. Vol'ter, 'Akhmat-khadzhi Kadyrov kak politicheskii lider v sovremennoi Rossii', *Vestnik Zabaikal'skogo gosudarstvennogo universiteta* 22:4 (2016), pp. 63–75, with many references to the traditionalist-esotericist Khodzh-Akhmed Nukhaev.
22. Cf. E. Sokirianskaia, 'Families and Clans in Ingushetia and Chechnya. A Fieldwork Report', *Central Asian Survey* 24:4 (2005), pp. 453–67; C. Dettmering, 'Reassessing Chechen and Ingush (Vainakh) Clan Structures in the 19th Century', *Central Asian Survey* 24:4 (2005), pp. 469–89.
23. V. Kh. Akaev, 'Sheikh Kunta-khadzhi Kishiev v dukhovnoi kul'ture chechentsev: osnovnye vekhi zhizni, sut' ucheniia i ego sovremennoe znachenie', *Islam v sovremennom mire* 12:1 (2016), pp. 95–108, here: p. 104.
24. For a similar post-Soviet context where historical studies are replaced by epics and hagiographies, see A. Bouma, 'Turkmenistan: Epics in Place of Historiography', *Jahrbücher für Geschichte Osteuropas* 59:4 (2011), pp. 559–85.
25. For a balanced analysis of Ramzan Kadyrov's policies see A. Malashenko, *Ramzan Kadyrov: rossiiskii politik kavkzskoi national'nosti* (Moscow: Rosspen/Carnegie Endowment, 2009).
26. T. Iusupov, 'Anti-salafitskaia Konferentsiia v Groznom prevrashchaet

Ramzana Kadyrova v pravitelia vsekh musul'man Rossii', *OnKavkaz*, 4 September 2016, http://onkavkaz.com/news/1223-anti-salafitskaja-konferencija-v-groznom-prevraschaet-ramzana-kadyrova-v-pravitelja-musulman-ro.html (accessed 30 December 2016).

27. A. Priimak, 'Saudity vozmushcheny otlucheniem ot Groznogo. Posle razgovora s Chechnei saudovskii bogoslov oproverg soobshcheniia o svoem prizyve k ubiistvu Ramzana Kadyrova', *Nezavisimaia gazeta*, 21 September 2016, http://www.ng.ru/facts/2016-09-21/6_saudi.html (accessed 30 December 2016).
28. D. Akhmetova, 'Smuta iz-za odnoi fetvy. Popytka perekroit' musul'manskoe pole Rossii obernulas' mezhdunarodnym skandalom', *Nezavisimaia gazeta*, 7 December 2016, http://www.ng.ru/facts/2016-12-07/7_411_fetva.html (accessed 30 December 2016).

9

What We Talk about When We Talk about *Taqlīd* in Russian Central Asia*

Paolo Sartori

Introduction

A half-century or more in which colonialism has been examined both in imperial history and Islamic studies has produced a colossal amount of scholarship. But it has also yielded a host of assumptions and narratives about colonial *sharīᶜa,* which are seriously in need of problematising and refining. One such narrative propounds that in the nineteenth century *sharīᶜa* underwent a process of transformation that ultimately led to what many observers have called a 'rupture'. Such a process is usually interpreted as the outcome of modernisation, that is, some kind of inevitable evolution in which the West imposed its legal episteme consisting of a new codification ethos, superimposed institutional rearrangements and imported secular normative sensibilities. In other words, we are dealing here with a narrative of irreversible decline according to which *sharīᶜa* fell apart and its broken pieces could not be glued back together.

Indeed, it does not take a great effort to very real changes in the Islamic juridical field under colonial rule. One notes, for instance, the following: (i) It is today common knowledge, for example, that Western empires that extended their power over Muslim-majority regions claimed an exclusive prerogative over punitive institutions and punishments, thereby truncating *qāḍīs*' jurisdiction and constraining this latter to the so-called personal status law, itself a colonial legal category.[1] ii) One notes the institutional arrangement common to many a colonial situation whereby Muslim legists were organised into a juridical hierarchy and made subject to judicial review, either by their Muslim peers or their colonial masters. Such arrangements affected the moral standing of *qāḍīs* and other members of the *ᶜulamāᵓ* whose rulings became easier to quash on grounds of judicial malpractice, either actual or purported.[2] (iii) Many have noted that the codification of *sharīᶜa* by means of translation and massive publication of a narrow selection of juristic sources had lasting effects that rigidified the very understanding of Islamic law and overhauled its basic governing principles.[3] (iv) One can detect changes at the semantic level: we are put in mind of the transformation of agrarian systems from a regime of usufruct to one of ownership, that is, from status to contract. Another major transformation in the field of Islamic law, which was ushered in by colonisation, is the possibility to free up property that once belonged to *waqf* assets.[4] Yet another change, which manifests itself in situations of colonialism, is the hybridisation of certain legal practices such as, for example, the Islamic procedure of oath-taking before the Russian justices of the peace.[5] (v) Also, notions of rupture and displacement are eloquently borne out by the testimony of Muslim intellectuals who lived through and reflected upon the effects of colonialism and the impact that the latter had on the domain of Islamic legal culture. The spread of scriptural Islam and the activation of puritanical sensibilities together with the rise of calls for independent legal reasoning (*ijtihād*) and hermeneutic eclecticism (*takhayyur*) are eloquent manifestations of the reaction of Muslim thinkers to colonialism.[6] (vi) Finally, the period of decolonisation, with its purported re-enactment of *sharīᶜa*, attests to the structural changes taking place in the colonial period, which had long-lasting effects in the way local jurists came to view *sharīᶜa*. Nigeria is a case in point. The reintroduction of Islamic law courts there and the ensuing debates on their jurisdictional boundaries reflect an understanding of the difference between criminal and civil law that was introduced under British rule.[7] But the same applies to the creation of discrete courts adjudicating according to customary law as well as the production of a discourse on the centrality of customary law within a specific community.[8] All this reflects the enduring legacy of colonial intervention, a legacy that is still significant today in Muslim-majority countries such as Indonesia,[9] Kyrgyzstan[10] and Morocco.[11]

While all these changes are self-evident, their reception among Muslims is in fact one of the most obscure issues in the history of colonial *sharīᶜa*, but also one of the most important. That is to say, it is unclear whether Muslims perceived the changes that I have outlined as integral to an experience of total change and one that ultimately transformed their behaviour and morality. It is unclear in part because of the impact of the Orientalist tendency to regard *sharīᶜa* as a jurist's law, which assumes that the evolution of *sharīᶜa* should be measured against the backdrop of a narrow selection of juristic models established either in the formative period of Islam[12] or in the Ottoman Empire, where the latter is usually taken as a metric to detect changes or aberrations from a putative 'canon' elsewhere in the Islamicate world.[13] It is also obscure because of the anti-

Orientalist and post-colonial Muslim critique that propounded a purist vision of the law, according to which everything colonial is contaminated because it reflects Western sensibilities – a vision that is integral to a post-colonial discourse about Islam and the centrality of *sharīᶜa* in the history of Islamic episteme.[14] The importance of the issue, likewise, rests not only on the need to understand colonialism that was so pervasive a phenomenon in many Muslim societies, but above all on the broader benefits that I believe will result from explaining why the colonial project of transforming *sharīᶜa* encountered only relative resistance along the way towards its realisation. Manifestations of resistance against non-Muslim forces, some of which included references to the urge of uphold *sharīᶜa*,[15] should be, of course, disambiguated from more articulate reactions by jurists against the imposition of other, non-indigenous systems of law.

There is one study, in particular, which attempts to explain this phenomenon, that is, what has been called 'muted opposition to codification'[16] in the Islamic juridical field in the modern period. In a remarkable *tour de force* on the history of Islamic jurisprudence over the late medieval and the early modern period in the Middle East, Ahmed Fekry Ibrahim argued that the superimposition of the Western legal episteme on *sharīᶜa* was favoured by a tectonic change within the tradition of Islamic law. Centuries prior to colonisation the office of the *muftī* underwent mutation as *sharīᶜa* shifted from a system based mainly on hermeneutical engagement to one in which jurists had to report only the accepted view within a given school of law. This entailed a shift from a situation of fluidity in which jurists could still contribute to the growing diversity of opinions to one of adherence to a school of law, that is, absolute *taqlīd*. One can trace such a shift to a change of meaning in the idea of preponderant view (*tarjīḥ*).[17] Until the thirteenth century, *tarjīḥ* signified the exercise of preponderance by evaluating and reporting the 'indicant' (*dalīl*) attached to an opinion.[18] Such an exercise amounted to examining the legal proof enabling the jurist to verify the degree of authority of a given legal opinion, that is, if the latter contradicted the Qur'an and the Prophetic traditions. Starting from the early modern period, we observe that the meaning of *tarjīḥ* is reduced to reporting the preponderant view; hence the rise of the genre of the juristic compendium (*mukhtaṣar*) and the *fatāwā* collection (*masāʾil*). What we ultimately learn from the works of Ibrahim is that the evolution of *taqlīd* in the early modern period pushed jurists to think of *sharīᶜa* in terms of content rather than in terms of process. Making sense of the history of Islamic law over the long term carries a broad implication for the study of *sharīᶜa* in the colonial period: the slow process of transformation taking place in the field of juristic hermeneutics in the early modern period as noted by Ibrahim prepared the ground for modern legal sensibilities, which further morphed into the ideology of codification.[19]

In general, this argument sounds remarkably persuasive as far as the history of Islamic law in post-Mongol Central Asia is concerned; and, as we shall see in this chapter, legal tracts originating from this region confirm the view propounded by Ibrahim as concerns the change in meaning of *taqlīd*. But this argument carries an attendant danger. There is a risk that, by looking for the local agency that 'anticipated' that major shift leading to legal codification, one actually ends up reinstating a remarkably tenacious idea that consists of imagining colonialism as an experience of total change. But knowing how colonialism changed Muslim legal culture, particularly how Western modes of thought became dominant, requires us also to know 'what was there to be changed', as Sheldon Pollock put it.[20] Unfortunately, this has not been done systematically with regard to the legal history of Islamic Central Asia prior to the Russian conquest, or India before British colonialism, for that matter. Also, it seems to me that this observation is particularly valid with regard to the role of the *muftī*, which has escaped so far the sustained attention of scholars. I'll come back to this topic in a bit.

In this chapter I intend to reflect upon the exercise of *taqlīd* or the recognition of and adherence to the most authoritative legal opinion within a certain school of law, in our case, the Ḥanafī *madhhab*. *Taqlīd*, historians of Islamic law explain to us, stands in diametrical opposition to the notion of 'independent legal reasoning' (*ijtihād*). The latter, in brief, denotes a method to engage the Islamic scriptures (the Qur'ān and the *ḥadīths*) hermeneutically and derive from them an opinion to answer a legal problem (*mas'ala*). Opposition between *taqlīd* and *ijtihād* does not mean mutual exclusion, however, and scholars of Islamic legal studies have repeatedly emphasised that the two juristic postures are mutually bound in a dialectical relationship, which has produced historically a continuum.[21]

The relationship between *taqlīd* and *ijtihād* has been the subject of ample academic commentary over the last two decades and it has been at the centre of many a study. However, for our purposes, it would be perhaps helpful to clarify that the historiography of Islamic Central Asia, in the West as well as in Russia and in Central Asia, is still marred by a somewhat imprecise understanding of these two terms. Indeed, at the turn of the twentieth century in Central Asia a self-contained group of Muslim intellectuals who condemned the perceived cultural backwardness of their communities became particularly vocal and thus acquired political prominence. Known in Western historiography today as 'the Jadids', such intellectuals were self-proclaimed 'modernists' for they pursued the progress of the Muslim nation and in this vein fashioned themselves as *taraqqī-parwar* (Pers. 'progressive'). Amid the various facets of their project of cultural change one finds that they regarded *taqlīd* as the worst of all sins for they saw in it the main cause for the stagnation of Islamic culture. The Jadids employed a derogatory understanding of *taqlīd* and one that was predicated upon the assumption that the scholars of Islam, in general, and the jurists, in particular, who rever the practice of *taqlīd* do little but uncritically follow their forefathers. The most eloquent advocate of this view was ᶜAbd al-Rauf Fiṭrat who in 1915 penned a theological tract entitled *Rahbar-i Najāt* ('A Guide to Salvation') in which he openly invited co-religionists to engage critically with the scriptures by means of *ijtihād* in order to avoid *taqlīd*, which he merely understood as a tool for imitation.[22] He further articulated such a view in the early Soviet period in a shorter work devoted to the seventeenth-century South Asian poet Mirzā ᶜAbd al-Qādir Bīdel and entitled *Bedil: Bir Majlisda* ('Bedil: In One Assembly') in which he wrote: 'One of the causes keeping the human unaware of his own power, [and one] that holds him back completely from normal, natural progress is "blind obedience" (*taqlid*).'[23]

Such a radical modernist rendering of the term *taqlīd* as we know it from the work of Fiṭrat obscures the fact that *taqlīd* reflected in fact a hermeneutic system designed for the low-rank *muftī*s to establish the preponderant opinion amid an assortment of sometimes contradictory juristic propositions and thus facilitated their task of issuing an opinion appropriate to the legal case at hand. We shall see this in more detail in the following section of this chapter. At the same time, ᶜAbd al-Rauf Fiṭrat and his modernist contemporaries also urged the need for the scholars of Islam (*ᶜulamāʾ*) to return to the scriptures and thus engage them directly by means of *ijtihād*. As noted elsewhere,[24] this view was based upon what we might call a 'rationalist' understanding of independent legal reasoning – an understanding, that is, which did not reflect the intellectual traditions as well as the writing practices that in Central Asia, as elsewhere in the Islamic world, had informed juristic discussion precisely on the topic of *taqlīd* and *ijtihād*. I call this a 'rationalist' understanding because modernists conceived of *ijtihād* not simply as a method of juristic analysis, but as a synonym for critical thinking, which in their view should have liberated local scholars and their Muslim communities from the shackles of backwardness.

Unconcerned as it was with the intellectual traditions and writing practices that characterised Muslim culture in Central Asia prior to colonisation, Cold War-era historiography conferred disproportionate significant upon the modernists. It presented them as the only intellectual force to react to Russian colonialism and regarded them as the only original voices among a community of passive observers. These perceived traits made them worthy of historical consideration.[25] Needless to say, in so doing, Cold War-era historians ended up reifying the language, the discourse and the cultural predicaments of Central Asia Muslim modernism, thereby not only distorting, but ultimately obliterating all the remaining cultural manifestations, including the pervasiveness of Islamic law in the society. This approach to the nineteenth- and the early twentieth-century history of Central Asia is now slowly changing, but the view of *taqlīd* as epitomising stagnation and *ijtihād* as representing the key that one day will open the door of progress is still dominant in Western scholarship.

What I want to do in this chapter is to argue something radically different from the dominant view on *taqlīd* in Central Asian modern history. I aim to show that it was precisely the profound level of formalism, stability and predictability achieved by *sharīʿa* in the age of *taqlīd* that allowed Muslim jurists to ignore colonial attempts to codify Islamic law.[26] I do not want to suggest that the nineteenth-century evolution of *taqlīd* in Central Asia anticipated the Western codification ethos. What I want to do, instead, is to draw a line between codification and canonisation and, therefore, to argue that the notion of *taqlīd* was endowed with a high degree of authority inside the Islamic juridical field of Central Asia. It was on account of such recognition of authority, I contend, that Muslims jurists preserved the integrity of the hermeneutical method of *taqlīd* according to which they used to issue their *fatwā*s prior to colonialism. In addition, I posit that manifestations of jurisprudential continuity in the Islamic juridical sphere can be observed in spite of the pressure exerted by colonial officials and the mounting critique of Orientalists and modernist Muslim thinkers against the intellectual practice of *taqlīd*. Such a manifestation of continuity in juristic thinking is indeed a remarkable feature of the colonial history of Central Asia for we observe this phenomenon in fact amid a good deal of substantive changes at the level of legal institutions and in the domain of popular legal consciousness.

This chapter will thus offer a discussion of the juristic thinking that informed the ways in which *muftī*s operated in Central Asia under Russian rule. To this end it will be important to remind ourselves at this point that the colonisers did not legislate on the position of *muftī* and one will search in vain in Russian statutory law for an entry regulating the duties of *muftī*s. This does not mean, however, that *muftī*s were left untouched and continued instead to operate within the same institutional system in which they had served their Muslim rulers prior to the Russian conquest. That system did not exist anymore, to start with.[27] Also, we should keep in mind that Russians' dismissive attitude towards the office of the *muftī* produced an institutional vacuum around this office. Let me explain what I mean by this. As they aimed to reform the Islamic juridical field, Russians preserved only the court of the *qāḍī*s, but they made it subject to an electoral system. By so doing they did away with a number of other important legal institutions, on the one hand; on the other, they retained de facto the *muftī*s who flanked *qāḍī*s in court. Given that *muftī*s and *qāḍī*s worked together but that only the latter were recognised *de jure*, appointment to the office of the *muftī* became often dependent on the will of *qāḍī*s. The resulting outcome was that, in term of power relations, *muftī*s were often subordinate to the *qāḍī*s with whom they worked. Indeed, we find that in the perception of both legal specialists and the laity, the role of the *muftī* too, in spite of having been left untouched by the legislative interventions of Russians, underwent substantial mutations.[28]

While as I said before changes are plain in the field of law under colonialism, I hope to be able to complicate the narrative according to which the history of *sharīᶜa* and colonialism is usually rendered and show that there are areas of the Islamic juridical field in which Muslims may well not have perceived colonialism as one experience of change alone. In this respect, I will try to show that Russians did attempt to push local jurists to issue legal opinions by doing away with the hermeneutic tradition of *taqlīd* and engaging directly the Qur'ān and the Sunna. As we shall see, the attitude of most *muftī*s to *taqlīd* did not strain under the pressure of the colonial episteme. Nor did their adherence to the established juristic practice of their *madhhab* push them to accept the codification of Islamic law.

'Muftī *Means* Muqallid'*: Juristic Ethics in Mid-nineteenth-century Bukhara*

What did it mean to be a *muftī* in pre-colonial Central Asia? A tentative answer to this question can be found by reading the *Risāla-yi Raḥmāniyya*, a legal tract penned in Bukhara in 1877 by one Mīr Rabīᶜ b. Mīr Niyāz Khwāja al-Ḥusaynī. It was compiled, its author claims, at the instigation of a scholar from Balkh who had turned to our Mīr Rabīᶜ and requested him to 'write down what I had listened about the rules and the precepts, either heard from or hidden in the reliable chains of narrators and the authoritative books [of law]'.[29] While the context of the *Risāla-yi Raḥmāniyya*'s composition remains obscure, we will see that the tract addresses mainly the duties of the *muftī* and as such belongs to the long-standing writing tradition of *adab al-muftī*, that is, a compositional genre defining the moral underpinnings as well as the hermeneutic ethics that were to guide him who issues *fatwās*. More specifically, the tract serves as a guide to making sense of the *masāʾil* literature, that is, legal treatises on novel cases and collections of *fatwās* compiled mostly in the late medieval and early modern period, upon which nineteenth-century jurists from Central Asia mostly relied when they were asked to deliver an opinion on a specific point of law. Indeed, the opening line of the introduction to the *Risāla-yi Raḥmāniyya* reads: 'Let it not be concealed that the objective of writing a collection of established opinions is to offer a clear reflection on a given legal problem, which the *muftī* can copy and upon which he can append his seal.'[30] Thus, the *Risāla-yi Raḥmāniyya* makes clear from the outset that it will address the relationship between *muftī*s and existing jurisprudence.

This text has come down to us in a single copy included into a *jung*, a term that Central Asian scholars deployed to refer to legal miscellanies that, along with *fatwās*, contain all sorts of juristic genres (mainly as copies), such as protocols of claims (*maḥḍar*s), legal issues (*masāʾil*), opinions (*riwāyāt*) and treatises (*rasāʾil*), as in this case. Such composite-type texts often resemble scrapbooks in their outlook, and it is unclear how they were used by jurists.[31]

The *Risāla-yi Raḥmāniyya* explains to us the virtues of the Islamic jurist by addressing first the meaning of the term *muftī*. It does so by disambiguating the latter from that of the earlier jurist (*mujtahid*; *faqīh*). With this move, the author of the *Risāla* accomplishes in fact two things. First, he creates a hierarchy of juristic authority whereby *mujtahid*s stand on a higher ground than *muftī*s. This is to say that he considers a nineteenth-century *muftī* as a low-rank jurist. Second, he premises such a juristic hierarchy on a periodisation, one in which *mujtahid*s represented the early jurists (like the founders of the four schools and the first generation of their disciples) and the *muftī*s are merely regarded as the contemporaries who have to take stock of the knowledge and the eloquence of preceding legal authorities.[32] Here is what Mīr Rabīᶜ says on this subject:

> It is mentioned in the *Quniya*[33] and also in the *Fatḥ al-qadīr*[34] that: 'By defining the conditions and [introducing the] virtues (*ādābhā*) which [are required to become a] *muftī*, current [jurisprudential] texts (*kutub-i mutadāwila*) refer to [the role of the] *mujtahid*; and they do so [by employing the term *muftī*] in its true meaning (*ba-irāday-i maᶜnī-yi ḥaqīqī*). However, the metaphorical (*majāzī*) meaning [of the term *muftī* is different and it] refers to a condition of perfection (*sharṭ-i kamāl*).' In these days [people usually deploy the term] *muftī* in its metaphorical meaning, i.e., he who adheres to a school of law (*muqallid*). While glossing the meaning of [the word] *muqallid*, the *Kifāya*[35] says: 'The scholar who knows all jurisprudential questions with its indicants (*dalāʾil*)

by way of direct inference (*instibāṭ al-ṣaḥīḥ*) is a *mujtahid*. Otherwise he is a *faqīh*. [Indeed], whoever learns [jurisprudential] questions from a teacher or the books, and he does so through the indicants, he is a *faqīh*; otherwise he is a *muqallid*.' The *Ghiyāth al-muftiyīn*[36] [in this respect] says that: 'But at the same time in order to follow [a school of law] (*taqlīd*) is enough to memorize the traditions [transmitted by] the great *imāms* and the authoritative books of *fiqh*.' When Imām Ẓahīr al-Dīn[37] was asked what was needed in our period to [become a *muqallid*], he said that it is enough to memorize the traditions of the authoritative books.

Let it be known to the *muqallid* that, [if he operates in this fashion], his *fatwā* will be deemed correct and he will be more eloquent (*afḍal*) than who disagrees [with his opinion] (*mukhālif*). It is not incumbent on a *muqallid* to know or report the indicant of the tradition [he refers to]. If he does, it is to pursue completeness.[38] It is obligatory for the uneducated who requests a fatwa to put in practice the opinion of the *muqallid*.[39] The *Majmū*ᶜ*a al-fatāwā*[40] says that: 'A quotation from [the great imams or the authoritative books means] for the *muqallid* what a Qur'anic verse or a Prophetic tradition (*naṣṣ*) means for the *mujtahid*. It is not incumbent on him [the *muqallid*] to provide legal reasoning (*ta*ᶜ*līl*)'. Likewise, in the *Fuṣūl* [*al-*ᶜ*Imādī*][41] [one finds] that: 'the word of a *mujtahid* is like a Qur'anic verse or a Prophetic tradition (*naṣṣ*); [to refer to it] is the right (*ḥaqq*) of a *muqallid*'. The commentary on the *Majma*ᶜ *al-Baḥrayn*[42] says that: 'It is harmful for a *muftī* who does not belong to the people of *ijtihād* to issue a fatwa even if he is knowledgeable in the sciences [of jurisprudence]; but he can transmit (*al-ḥikāya*) [the opinions] of the *mujtahid*s by memorizing their sayings.'[43]

We learn from this excerpt that the most important prerequisite for being a *muftī* in Bukhara in the second half of the nineteenth century was to follow the established juristic traditions.[44] This amounted to memorising the opinions of the first generation of jurists of Islam (*bi 'l-ḥifẓ min aqwāl al-mujtahidīn*) as well as the traditions (*bi 'l-ḥifẓ naqlan*) transmitted by legal texts of recognised authority (*al-kutub al-muṣaḥḥiḥa*). In other words, to issue a *fatwā* in pre-colonial Central Asia required that a *muftī* establish the most suitable opinion among those transmitted *within* the Ḥanafī school of law and repeat it in the form of a quotation (*riwāyat*). Such an exercise amounted to recognising the legal force of opinions conveyed by certain earlier authorities. He was not expected to seek an indicant (*dalīl*).[45]

It is important to pause to reflect on the equivalence between the term *muftī* and *muqallid*, for it signals to us that, to follow Ibrahim's distinction, the author of the *Risāla-yi Raḥmāniyya* regarded *sharī*ᶜ*a* more as a 'law-in-content' than as a 'law-in-process'. By excluding direct engagement with legal methodology and thus any form of independent juristic reasoning from the purview of the ideal nineteenth-century *muftī*, Mīr Rabī^c suggests that the *muftī* should consider the selective process of cumulating authoritative opinions as terminated. The resulting effect, as Ibrahim has noted, was that, faced with the task of issuing an opinion on a given point of law, the *muftī* was expected to deliberate by selecting from a self-contained pool of established opinions.

Indeed, the passage of the *Risāla-yi Raḥmāniyya* that I quoted above clarifies that the very understanding of *fatwā* in mid-nineteenth-century Bukhara was in fact restricted to the meaning of 'quotation' (*riwāyat*) from opinions endowed with recognised legal force, which had been issued earlier and therefore included in texts deemed authoritative. It is here that we begin to see why in nineteenth-century Central Asia the term *riwāyat* usually replaced that of *fatwā*.[46]

But to become a *muftī*, Mīr Rabī^c b. Mīr Niyāz Khwāja al-Ḥusaynī explains to us, required, in addition to performing this exercise, also mastery of several disciplines. Here again, however, it is important to emphasise that what amounted to specific knowledge allowed in fact the *muftī* to engage (and adjust to) a self-contained body of scholarship, itself the product of a cumulative as well as selective process that had begun after the establishment of the Ḥanafī school of law and that was regarded as independent from the engagement with legal methodology (*uṣūl al-fiqh*) and the exercise of juristic hermeneutics. He thus explains that to perform the tasks of a *muftī*, a scholar is expected to combine the mastery of different branches of Islamic knowledge, but it is sufficient to know only 'a definite quantity' (*miqdār*) of Arabic grammar, jurisprudence (*furū^c al-fiqh*) and theology as well as a certain amount of the law of inheritance and dogmatics (*^caqā^oid*):

> The substance of [my] proposition [can be derived from] what has been reported by current texts and other [books], what has been learnt from the words of the scholars, and what has been heard from reliable teachers. [For example] it is mentioned in the *Tarjima-yi Sharīfiyya* that: 'In these times to issue a fatwa is enough to have a person who is a facilitator for the believers (*taysīr al-mū^ominīn*), who is known for being a modest person (*mastūr al-ḥāl*), a person who has more rewards than sins, who knows a definite quantity (*miqdār*) of grammar and morphology of Arabic, *fiqh*, and theology (*kalām*); [he should know] a definite quantity of the law of inheritance (*farā^oiḍ*) and what are the requisites to read excerpts [from] fatwas; a definite quantity of what is required to pray and what concerns transactions [among individuals] (*mu^cāmala*); a definite quantity of what counts as sound in [the sphere of] doctrine (*^caqā^oid*); and he should be familiar with [customary legal] practice (*ta^cāmul*).' If he supplies a quotation [from jurisprudential authorities], the

> latter should be in conformity with the objective of the inquirer; this requires that he have the skills to articulate and explain in writing the purpose of the individual who poses the question.[47] [It is important] that no one should surpass him in knowledge in a given region, and that he should have studied with a reliable scholar, and become knowledgeable in the [jurisprudential] questions that he studied [with such a scholar]. In this case it is sound for such a person to write a *fatwā* and explain *fatwās* to the commoners. It is obligatory for the uneducated person to put into practice what such a person says.[48]

We can observe that our author puts great emphasis on the fact that for a *muftī* it was vital to know the customary practices that were current in a given locality, for such practices were endowed with more legal force than analogical reasoning (*qiyās*). Here again we are confronted with a vision of the *muftī qua* low-rank jurist who is completely disengaged from legal methodology (*uṣūl al-fiqh*). Such disengagement should not be regarded as a mark of decadence as modernist Muslim intellectuals would like us to think; instead, it reflects the outlook of Bukharan scholars who were aware of the progressive advancement of knowledge, one the one hand, and the growing importance accorded to social circumstances and extra-legal considerations by adjudicating authorities (governors and *qāḍīs* alike).

> A *muqallid* should be acquainted with the legal practice (*ta*ᶜ*āmul*) current in every city and village where he issues a fatwa so that he can supply a quotation (*riwāyat*) in agreement with that practice. It is so because the practice and the customs (ᶜ*urf wa* ᶜ*ādat*) of the people of Islam change over time. So it is said in the *Baḥr al-fatāwā*:[49] 'In every city or village commoners and aristocrats follow the practice because it has the same status of a Qurᵓanic verse or a Prophetic tradition (*naṣṣ*)'. In the *Dhakhīra*[50] [one finds] that: 'What is valid (*al-ṣaḥīḥ*) changes according to city, century, and epoch'. In the [*al-*] *Hidāya* [it is written] that: 'The use of analogy (*qiyās*) will be rejected in favor of [legal] practice.'[51]

Mīr Rabīᶜ b. Mīr Niyāz Khwāja al-Ḥusaynī draws once again our attention to the fact that the prominence of notions such as custom and established practice was premised upon an outright rejection of independent legal reasoning. A *muftī*, he claims, should accord pre-eminent importance to what has already become 'known' (*ma*ᶜ*lūm*) to him through the transmission of authoritative opinions. A *muftī*, that is, should not disagree (*mukhālif*) with the body of jurisprudential knowledge to which he has been exposed when studying in a madrasa:

> It is obligatory for the uneducated to put into practice what such a person says [that is, a *muftī* who fits all the requirements outlined above]. [Let it be known that this applies also to] a scholar without a following [because such a

> scholar] is like the uneducated. However, it is licit also for the scholar who has followers to put in practice [what such a *muftī* says]. He should not disagree with what is [already] known to him, especially [with what he learnt from] the [authoritative legal] texts, what he heard [from his teachers], and [what he learnt from] the scholars who had a following; otherwise, [such a disagreement] should be dismissed, as it is [written] in the *Jāmiᶜ al-rumūz*:[52] 'First and foremost it is sufficient [for a *muftī*] to adjust to the trustworthy *imāms* like al-Ṭaḥāwī and others. One should know the [mechanics of] analogic reasoning (*qiyās*), its principles, conditions, and judgments, and should be familiar with the consensus (*ijmāᶜ*) of the jurists and he should abstain from going against it. These are the requirements to perform independent legal reasoning (*ijtihād*) [when delivering] a judgment (*ḥukm*). But if [a *muftī*] proceeds independently to issue a decision [on a given legal problem regardless of the fact] that the *imāms* [that is, the *mujtahids*] have [already] accepted a decision, [he ignores the fact that] the requirement [to issue a judgment] is familiarity with the aspects of analogical reasoning (*qiyās*), and the latter's conditions, and what pertains to it. However, it is not necessary [for a *muftī*] to be knowledgeable in theology (*ᶜilm-i kalām*) and even less so in (*uṣul*) al-*fiqh*. Because in our period one can reach the position [in which one performs] *ijtihād* only with practice, as [stated] in the *al-Kashf* and other [texts] as well as in the *Sharḥ al-Birjandī*:[53] 'But the position of *ijtihād* in our period can be reached only by operating within the branches of jurisprudence (*furūᶜ al-fiqh*). This is the way to reach the *ijtihād* in this period'. And in *al-Hidāya* [it is stated] that: 'And some say that the requirement to master [the discipline of jurisprudence] is to know the customs' of people (*ᶜādāt al-nās*) for there are judgments which are based on such customs. And the remaining expressions [on this subject] can be found in the *Mukhtār al-ikhtiyār*.[54]

The *Mukhtār al-ikhtiyār* was a work with which local legists will have been familiar. Written in Herat during the reign of the late-Timurid rule Sulṭān Ḥusayn Bāyqarā (r. 1469–1506) by the famous jurist Ikhtiyār al-Dīn b. Ghiyāth al-Dīn al-Ḥusaynī, the work circulated widely in nineteenth-century Central Asia. And this text was adamant about the impossibility of performing independent legal reasoning:

> And if between them there is disagreement, then the preponderant view will be followed by exercising independent reasoning and discernment. But now the road to *ijtihād* is closed and the men of discernment have disappeared; and the way in which one should pose questions is evident and the quotations of the *muftī* are plain. It is incumbent upon the *qāḍī* to provide guidance by referring to the fatwas of the imams and issue judgments consistent with them.[55]

But if it is one thing to acknowledge that a *muftī* should attempt to follow the established opinion; it is an entirely different thing to establish what said opinion actually is. Indeed, *muftīs* were frequently confronted by cases in which jurists of earlier generations had expressed discordant, if not diametrically different views on the same question. Mīr Rabī^c^ thus tries to come to grips with this problem and outlines a method to disambiguate the most authoritative opinion from less sound alternatives. His method consists of first outlining a hierarchy of significance among the existing legal authorities that *muftī*s can and indeed should use to issue an opinion. In order to make sense of the following excerpt it is important to remind ourselves that for a nineteenth-century *muftī* to issue a legal opinion amounted to establishing the preponderant view, which he could quote. I employ here the term 'preponderance' for it is our author that accords particular importance to it as exemplified in the following quotation:

> [When answering to a question the *muftī*] should operate according to the opinion of that magnificent man the Imām A^c^ẓam [Abū Ḥanīfa], may God be pleased with him. [A *muftī* should proceed in this fashion] in each and every case when every other *imām* expressed a divergent opinion [on the same issue] and he [the *mufti*] did not hear that his teachers reported [such opinion] as established (*ma^c^mūliyyat*). [This rule also applies to the situation in which] a text [of an opinion] does not include the attribute (*ma^c^lama*) of *fatwā* referring to one of the sayings of the three [major] scholars [Abū Ḥanīfa and his two students, Abū Yūsuf and Muḥammad Shaybānī. In such a situation] the opinions of the three *imāms* are equal in the way they facilitate [the task of addressing a problem], otherwise he [the *muftī*] should put in practice the saying which is easiest [in its formulation]. As there is a rule in the *Mukhtār al-ikhtiyār*, which says that: 'When [a saying] of the Imām-i A^c^ẓam [which addresses the problem in question] has not been transmitted (*riwāyat na-shuda bāshad*), then he [the *muftī*] should put in practice the saying of Abū Yūsuf, may God be pleased with him, and, after him, the saying of Imām Muḥammad [Shaybānī], may God be pleased with him . . . As it is stated in the *Ḥayrat al-fatāwā*,[56] if the three *imāms* agreed on one pronouncement, in that case it is called *sawād-i a^c^ẓam* [that is, the agreement of the majority of the scholars], and it is obligatory to put into practice (*wājib al-^c^amal ast*). If [one deals with a question and finds that the pronouncement of] Imām Muḥammad [al-Shaybānī] is in accordance [with what was transmitted from Abū Ḥanīfa], [this situation] is called *ṭarafayn* [that is, an opinion held on two sides] and this [opinion] too should be put into practice. If a legal attribute is [to be found] in the pronouncement of Imām Muḥammad [al-Shaybānī], but it is absent in those of the *shaykhīn* [Imām Abū Yūsuf and Imām A^c^ẓam], one should put into practice the pronouncement of Imām Muḥammad [al-Shaybānī]. [So it is] because an attribute is a sign of preponderance (*zīrā-ki ma^c^lama ^c^alāmat-i tarjīḥ ast*). It is obligatory to follow the *mujtahids* and the later scholars.[57]

When facing different opinions on the same point of law, Mīr Rabī^c^ says, a *muftī* had to search for the preponderant view. He would do so by examining the attribute (*ma^clama*) that earlier jurists conferred upon opinions within an established chain of authority. But in evaluating the attributes of legal opinions other, more complex, challenges can present themselves. In the following passage, the *Risāla-yi Raḥmāniyya* breaks down for us several such cases and provides further guidance:

> If both sides [that is, the pronouncements of Imām Abū Yūsuf and Imām Aᶜẓam] show the attribute [of a *fatwā*], one should consider the force of such attribute [and opt for the stronger case] in order to avoid that a *qāḍī*'s judgment be based on a weak attribute; otherwise, one should put it in practice. This is the rule [to evaluate] the [legal] attribute [conferred upon] the pronouncements of the three *imams*; it also applies [to reviewing] two fatwas which have been already sealed. As this subject has been addressed in detail in the *Irshād al-muftiyīn*,[58] [we know that], if two [opinions] contradict each other, one should put in practice what has been stamped and what is closer to one's epoch and dismiss earlier *fatwās*. If the pronouncements of Imām Abū Yūsuf and Imām Aᶜẓam show the attribute [of a *fatwā*] and are equal in strength and weakness, for instance if they should be both regarded as the most valid (*al-aṣaḥḥ*) or sound (*al-ṣaḥīḥ*), one should pay attention to which of the two *muftīs* has a higher position and put in practice his *fatwā*. If both of them are of equal standing with regard to times, position, and experience, then one should consider their teachers. One should put in practice the *fatwā* of the *muftī* whose teacher was the most expert (*afqah*), the most learned (*aᶜlam*), and the most God-fearing (*awraᶜ*). If the two *muftīs* [studied] with the same teacher, then one should consider whether their opinion reflects the view of the majority of *imāms* [of the *madhhab*] or it is the pronouncement [of one *imām* alone]. If one [reflects the view of] the *madhhab* and one is a pronouncement or a quotation, then one should put in practice the opinion that is preponderant in the *madhhab*. If the two *fatwās* reflect either the *madhhab* [in that they come] from the *imāms* of the religion or the pronouncements [of individual jurists] or quotations, one should first consider the vehicle for their transmission (*rāwī*) and assess which one is trustworthy (*muᶜtamadiyya*) and then one should turn to the text reporting such views and put in practice the *fatwā* taken from the text [written by] modern scholars (*mutaᶜakhkhirīn*) such as the commentaries of the *Mukhtaṣar*[59] and in particular that of Mullā Shams al-Dīn Muḥammad Quhistānī.[60]
>
> If both opinions derive from one book, one should consider the *qāḍī* [or] the ruler (*ḥākim*) [who relied on such opinions], which one was knowledgeable of jurisprudential questions, who was a religious man, and who was closer to one's epoch and followed him. And if both of them are on an equal standing, one should consider which practice among them is most intelligible and most feasible. The one which is in accordance with the custom, practice, and habit (*ᶜādat*) should be put into practice. This explanation is taken from the *Ādāb al-muftiyīn*[61] and partly from the *Ādāb*[62] of Mīrzā Sharīf Aᶜlam. But

> sometimes among the cases and the matters mentioned above there will not be equivalence: if two *muftīs* report two quotations (*dū riwāyat*) from one teacher, which contradict each other and which both are considered established opinions (*ma*ᶜ*mūla*), it will not be suitable. In this case they can reject [such opinions] in order to expand the pool [of sources to issue a *fatwā*]. If there is disagreement between Qur'anic verses and Prophetic traditions, the latter should be put into practice because the Prophet, may God bless and cherish him, was well-conversant with the true meaning of the Qur'anic verses. If disagreement is between the Prophetic traditions and the juristic treatises (*masā*ʾ*il*), the latter should be put into practice because the *mujtahid*s, may God be pleased with them all, were well-conversant with the true meaning of the Prophetic traditions. If disagreement is between early and modern scholars, then one should follow the pronouncement of the modern scholars because the latter well understood the pronouncement of the early scholars.[63]

We now, finally, come to the section in which our author outlines his method to establish the most fitting among the established opinions available to him in order to issue a *fatwā*. As is evident in the passage below, his method follows certain rules of Arabic grammar to define the legal force of a given opinion as it was expressed by its accompanying attribute (*ma*ᶜ*lama*):

> With diligent research teachers found that the attributes of a *fatwā* are limited in number and that some should be preferred to others. In its opening [section] the *Muḍmarāt* [enumerates the following attributes]: ᶜ*alayhi fatwā* ('it should be ruled according to this opinion') and *wa bihi na*ᶜ*khudh* ('This is the opinion we follow'), *wa bihi yu*ᶜ*tamad* ('and [the opinion] depends on this'), *wa* ᶜ*alayhi al-i*ᶜ*timād* ('and [the opinion] depends on this'), *wa* ᶜ*alayhi* ᶜ*amal al-nās al-yawm* ('and upon this opinion the people act nowadays'), *wa* ᶜ*alayhi* ᶜ*amal al-a*ʾ*imma* ('upon this opinion the *imāms* act'), *wa huwa al-ṣaḥīḥ* ('and this [opinion] is sound'), *wa huwa al-aṣaḥḥ* ('and this [opinion] is sounder'), *wa huwa al-aẓhār* ('and this [opinion] is more evident'), *wa huwa al-ẓāhir* ('and this [opinion] is evident'), *wa huwa al-mukhtār* ('and this is the preferred [opinion]'), *wa* ᶜ*alayhi al-fatwā mashāyikhunā* ('This is the opinion upon which our masters [of the school/region] ruled'), *wa huwa al-ashbah* ('and this [opinion] is most resembling [the principles of the law]'), *wa huwa al-awjah* ('and this [opinion] is more relevant'). It should be known that the attribute *huwa al-ṣaḥīḥ* ('and this is sound') is stronger than *huwa al-aṣaḥḥ* ('this is most sound'). [And this is] in spite of the fact that *al-aṣaḥḥ* is [an adjective of] comparative degree and therefore above *al-ṣaḥīḥ*, which is a verbal noun. So it is because in order to put in practice [an opinion one should consider] the opposite meaning [of attributes] to what is transmitted in the *Mukhtār al-ikhtiyār* from the *Ḥāshiyah al-Pazdawī*: 'The term *aṣaḥḥ* presupposes that there can be [an opinion] more valid than it [that is, the opinion for which it serves as attribute], while the term *ṣaḥīḥ* denotes that there is nothing more

> valid than it'. Also it is mentioned in the *Mukhtār al-ikhtiyār* that: 'If [opinions] are accompanied by the expression *huwa al-aṣaḥḥ* ('and this [opinion] is more valid'), or *huwa al-awlā* ['and this [opinion] is more important'], or *huwa al-aysar* ('and this [opinion] is straightforward'), or *aftā bihi falānun* ('a certain individual issues a *fatwā* based upon this opinion'), or *akhadha bihi falānun* ('a certain individual accepted this [opinion]'), *ᶜalayhi fatwā fulān* ('there is an opinion on this of a certain individual') or similar such expressions, it means that a *muftī* can make a *fatwā* which is in disagreement with such opinions. But if [the opinion] is reported with expressions such as *huwa al-ṣaḥīḥ* ('and this is valid'), *wa ᶜalayhi fatwā* ('and [this is] the opinion on this'), or *huwa al-awjah li-al-fatwā* ('that suits for the *fatwā*'), or *bihi uftiya* ('the *fatwā* made upon this opinion'), and similar such expressions, this means that a *muftī* cannot issue an opinion which disagrees with them'. But this statement applies to a situation in which no one either heard about established opinions (*maᶜmūliyat hīch jānib masmūᶜ nashuda ast*) or could refer to a *qāḍī*'s decision, as it was mentioned. And this is what is reported about a certain Mīrzā Sharīf, may God be pleased with him, having ruled on this case (*dar īn bāb ᶜināyat farmūda*), which the scholars of Bukhara the Holy regard as worth of respect; also this is what is heard from teachers and known from authoritative books after rigorous investigation and diligent search.[64]

To sum up, to establish the preponderant view one has to compare the attributes given to legal treatises dealing with novel cases and in compendia of *fatāwā* collections.[65] We know that Bukharan jurists followed this method from at least the second half of the eighteenth century,[66] but the range of references found in the above-quoted passage suggests that the method may well have been in use in earlier periods also. However, it is worth reminding ourselves that, in fact, Mīr Rabīᶜ b. Mīr Niyāz Khwāja al-Ḥusaynī's understanding of the term *tarjīḥ* reflects a shift in the meaning of the term that must have occurred in the early modern period as the work of Ibrahim suggested on the basis of material coming mostly from the Ottoman Empire. This semantic shift reflects how jurists began to view *tarjīḥ* as an instrument to exercise preponderance among a self-contained number of possible interpretations of the law and thus opt for the strongest and most fitting opinion. This interpretation of the term was in fact far-removed from its intended original meaning of a tool to engage hermeneutically with the scriptures. While this may well sound like a somewhat dry philological exercise in reconstructing the history of an intellectual practice, it equally shows that, as noted, again, by Ibrahim in the Middle East, in Central Asian early modern history one can observe a tendency among jurists, which we find attested as early as the late Timurid period in the *Mukhtār al-Ikhtiyār*, to think of *sharīᶜa* in terms of its content, rather than of process. This is important to note for it may open new vistas on emic understandings of Islamic law, which may in fact suggest, as Muhammed Fadel has done in a ground-breaking work, that systematisations of Islamic legal knowledge led to a process of constraining the body of jurisprudential material available to *muftī*s in ways that are reminiscent of Western-type codes.[67]

The Challenges of a Muqallid *under Russian Rule*

From the outset of Russian rule, *muftī*s found themselves under the inquisitive pressure of the colonisers. In spite of their somewhat limited understanding of Islamic legal practice, Russian military officials who were administering the colonial bureaucratic apparatus did not shy away from tackling the mechanics of Islamic jurisprudence. Indeed, they often solicited from local jurists opinions on specific points of law by asking them either merely to supply 'quotations from the books of *sharīʿa*'[68] or to go back to the scriptures, thus by-passing the local jurisprudential tradition. In this latter respect, they clearly embodied the posture of the pretentious Orientalist who assumed that the true meaning of Islamic law was to be inferred from the Qurʾān and the Prophetic Sunna.

How did local jurists cope with such a pressure exerted by the colonial masters? In the remaining sections of this chapter I would like to show how Central Asian *muftī*s' established way of thinking did not capitulate before the prescriptive (and rather narrow) understanding of Russian bureaucrats. Indeed, we shall see how Muslim jurists frequently preserved the integrity of those juristic notions that we saw fully articulated by Mīr Rabīʿ b. Mīr Niyāz Khwāja al-Ḥusaynī. In putting emphasis on the *muftī*s' deliberate attempt to preserve such notions, I do not want to argue for yet another case of subaltern resistance to colonial rule. I want to draw the attention of the reader, instead, to the fact that juristic intellectual traditions proved to be just stronger than the epistemic forces deployed by Russians to enter the Islamic juridical field, intervene in decision-making processes at the *muftī*s' level and weed out the multiple layers of juristic authority, which they most probably deemed as unnecessarily complicated and unhelpful to achieve a clear and comprehensive understanding of Islamic law.

The following excerpt is taken from a rather long and complex missive that a *qāḍī* in Russian-ruled Tashkent, a certain Muḥyī al-Dīn Khwāja, wrote in February 1891 to the City Commandant. Muḥyī al-Dīn Khwāja had become by that time a close acquaintance of the colonial authorities. Born into a family of jurists who had served the Kokand Khanate, endowed with moral authority within the Tashkent city district of Sibzar and gifted with exceptional political acumen, Muḥyī al-Dīn Khwāja had elbowed his way through the civil-military administration of the Russian Governorship-General of Turkestan. As a result, he was able to be elected to the triennial post of *qāḍī* several times.[69] His standing both before the Muslim community, in which he operated, and before the Russian officers, however, did not prove particularly helpful when it came to dodging accusations of judicial malpractice and corruption. Indeed, Muḥyī al-Dīn Khwāja was made subject of multiple official inquiries, in which he was held repeatedly accountable for his ways of applying the law and thus obliged to fully disclose his juristic modus operandi. This situation led him to interact closely with the Russian authorities: and the following quotation beautifully exemplifies the kind of interaction he entertained with the colonial masters:

> The most excellent among the jurists (*mujtahids*) – Imām-i Aᶜẓam [Abū Ḥanīfa] and the most imitated among the jurists, Yūsuf, may God have mercy upon him and upon all the jurists who hold his words above anyone else's word, such as Abū Naṣr; Abū Laylā; Abū Jaᶜfar; ᶜUmar; Abū Jaᶜfar Kabīr; Abū al-Ḥasan Karḍī; Sarakhsī; Abū Layth Samarqandī; Imām Khwāhar-zāda; Abū Ḥafḍ-i Kabīr Bukhārī, may God have mercy upon them (they are the leaders of our religion) – have explained the rules of *sharīᶜa* in such a way that, with regard to the issue of division, there are [three rates:] one-twentieth, one-fortieth, one-half of one percent. However, they prescribed that, for the benefit of the people who have to pay, the one-twentieth rate should be excluded. They also ruled that, for the benefit of the person who is to receive the fee (*taqsīm ḥaqqī*), the rate of one-half of one percent should be excluded. The aforementioned [jurists] considered the one-fortieth rate, which is equal to the *zakāt*, and ruled that [such a fee] is to the benefit of both parties.

To prove himself innocent, and more specifically, to explain that he had asked for a commensurate and indeed fair fee when acting in the capacity of a notary during the division of inheritance, he attempted to clarify to the Tashkent City Commandant that the fee he levied was in accordance with *sharīᶜa*. To do so, he explained that prior to him a chain of recognised juristic authorities had opined on the issue of jurists levying a notary fee while dividing an estate and that their opinions corroborated the soundness of his actions. Anticipating the colonial obsession with independent reasoning (*ijtihād*), Muḥyī al-Dīn Khwāja first made sure that his Russian interlocutor could understand that the major *mujtahids* of the Ḥanafī school of law delivered opinions that were in accordance with the proceedings of the division of inheritance, which he had carried out.

Having thus established the authority of the *mujtahid*s, he could dwell a bit on the actual mechanics of *fatwā*-giving in nineteenth-century Central Asia and show that later juristic traditions (as exemplified by the genre of *masāʾil*) offered incontrovertible opinions on the specific point of law under consideration. To review the following quotation from his missive to the City Commandant is crucial to understand the degree to which *taqlīd*, that is, a method to determine the most fitting among the established opinions available to a *muftī* as we learnt from Mīr Rabīᶜ b. Mīr Niyāz Khwāja al-Ḥusaynī's work, impregnated the minds of local jurists. With regard to the following quotation one should appreciate the fact that here again Muḥyī al-Dīn Khwāja is conferring particular importance on the notion of 'attribute' (*maᶜlama*), which should be regarded, according to his reasoning, as conclusive evidence of the strength of a certain legal opinion, strength that should not be overlooked or disavowed by other jurists:

> Also, in the *masāʾil* [that address such problems] one finds these strong attributes (*katta ᶜalāmat*): 'and [this is] the opinion being advocated on it' (*wa bihi yuftā*), 'and [this is] the adopted opinion' (*wa ᶜalayhi al-fatwā*) and 'this is the selected [opinion]' (*wa huwa al-mukhtār*): one cannot apply a different opinion when [there is already a *fatwā*] labeled with such attributes.[70] Not a single *qāḍī*, *aᶜlam* or *muftī* can claim to have the right to do that.

A second eloquent example of the strength of *taqlīd* as an established practice as well as refined methodology of juristic reasoning can be found in a file cobbled together by the Russian colonial administration dealing with underage children, their ownership rights and the issue of guardianship.[71] The story begins in 1882 when a certain ᶜAẓīmbāy Rakhimbaev petitioned Russian agencies in Khojand on behalf of his wife Bībī Zībī Mirzabaeva. He explained that his father-in-law Mirzabai had made a will according to which the latter's wife ᶜAshūr Bībī would receive one-quarter of his estate and his daughter Bībī Zībī three-quarters. At the time the will was drawn up Bībī Zībī was six/seven years old. Prompted clearly by her husband, Bībī Zībī claimed at some point her share of her father's estate. However, she encountered an impediment. Four months after Mirzabai's death, ᶜAshūr Bībī had borne a son: and ᶜAshūr Bībī now produced a document notarised by a *qāḍī* of Khojand, according to which Bībī Zībī had willingly agreed to transfer to her underage brother three-quarters of what her father had left to her. Pursuing his own interests, ᶜAẓīmbāy did not recognise the validity of such a transfer of inheritance rights. He claimed that when that document was notarised his wife was underage and therefore unable to perform such a transfer. In addition, he asked for Mirzabai's will to be put into practice so that his wife Bībī Zībī could finally take possession of the share of her father's estate, which she was entitled to receive. He thus went to the *qāḍī* overseeing transactions among Muslims living in the district of Razzāq of Khojand, who made the document 'void' (*bīkār*). Unhappy with this decision, ᶜAshūr Bībī petitioned the City Commandant who transferred the case to an appellate court presided over by an assembly of *qāḍī*s. The latter decided, as often happened, in favour of ᶜAshūr Bībī, thereby reversing the previous judgment. ᶜAẓīmbāy did not give up, and he again petitioned the Commandant. This time he claimed that when the deed of transferral of ownership rights was notarised in favour of ᶜAshūr Bībī's son, Bībī Zībī 'was fourteen years old and could not dispose of immovable properties and, more specifically, she could not donate them on account of her minor age'. Also, ᶜAẓīmbāy claimed that 'had such a donation really occurred, then it should have been subject to the authority of a guardian or someone acting on behalf of the latter, against whom Bībī Zībī should now file a claim for the value of said properties donated to the underage child'.[72] At this point the Commandant of the Khojand District made a somewhat unusual move: he asked the *qāḍī*s who had decided against ᶜAẓīmbāy to explain *how* they reached such decision, i.e., by showing the authoritative texts upon which they relied to establish that the age of fourteen constitutes a threshold of maturity', which would have allowed Bībī Zībī to deal with her possessions as she saw fit.[73]

The file that has come down to us from what was once the archive of the chancellery of the Commandant of the Khojand district does not include the instructions that the colonial agency sent out to *qāḍī*s, which requested that they reveal what kind of sources they had used to issue their collegial judgment in favour of ᶜAshūr Bībī. However, from the replies that the *qāḍī*s sent to the Russian administration of Khojand we can infer that the Commandant had specifically asked them to include references to the Qur'ān, the Prophetic Sunna and the authoritative books of jurisprudence.[74] Indeed, we find that *qāḍī*s glossed the issue of puberty and maturity of girls by first referring to a verse of the Qur'ān, a saying attributed to the Prophet, and by reviewing the *masāʾil* literature. While commenting on the scriptures amounted to rely on an established exegetic text (*tafsīr*), selecting the most fitting opinion among those transmitted by the *masāʾil* books required the application of *taqlīd*. In this regard they unfailingly applied the method of *tarjīḥ*, which consisted, as we have seen, of selecting an opinion of authoritative attribution (*maᶜlama*). One of the *qāḍī*s wrote:

> Let us explain that with regard to the issue of establishing the age of maturity for a girl according to *sharīᶜa*, and accepting her acknowledgement concerning her disposing of her property as a mature individual according to the prescriptions of the law, the books say that it is required that she acknowledge having dreamt of sexual intercourse (*iqrār ba-iḥtilām*); and if this occurs to a nine-year old girl or a twelve year-old boy, this is right. If the acknowledgment of such a

> dream does not happen, then the age of puberty is set at fifteen years. And [this is] the adopted opinion (*ᶜalayhi al-fatwā*).[75]

Another one opined:

> [In replying] to the instructions [of the Commandant] issued on the 21st of Ramadan 1882, I explain by referring to the Qurᵓān, the Prophetic Sunna and the collections of *fatwā*s that, if the sign of puberty is not manifest, a minor needs a guardian in order to dispose of his possessions until the fifteenth year of age; and in our school of law it is said 'according to this opinion it should be ruled' (*ᶜalayhi al-fatwā*). However, if the sign of puberty appears, or if a girl up to the age of nine or a boy up to the age of twelve acknowledges having reached puberty, one can remove the guardian and said children can dispose freely of their possessions according to the law.[76]

These two quotations offer a snapshot of the Muslim legists explaining to the Russian agencies in Khojand how they had ruled on the case of Bībī Zībī from a jurisprudential point of view. They proceeded, like Muḥyī al-Dīn Khwāja did while writing to the colonial authorities in Tashkent, in a rather simplistic way. And they must have pursued simplicity in order to make their juristic thinking intelligible to the Russian officials. In the margins of such correspondence, however, one finds a great number of quotations from the *masāᵓil* literature (*Jāmiᶜ al-Rumūz*, *Mukhtaṣar-i Wiqāya*, *Sharḥ-i Wiqāya*, *al-Hidāya*), which showed the established opinions upon which those *qāḍi*s had relied to deliver their judgment. Here again one observes that such opinions are accompanied by all the required attributes of authority such as *huwa al-mukhtār* ('this is the chosen opinion'), *bihi yuftā* ('[this is] the opinion being advocated on it').[77]

Conclusion

To show that, amid times of change, the hermeneutic activity of *muftī*s in Russian Central Asia reveals a certain degree of continuity with precolonial practices period is important for several reasons that actually contradict most of the assumptions held about colonialism as a total experience of change and rupture with past practices. I shall name three here, but I am sure one can find more.

First, most of the students of colonial and imperial history are quick to assume that to translate, publish and spread certain Islamic juristic literature was an effective tool in the hands of the colonisers to dominate the juristic field. One may well concede to those scholars who are sympathetic to this views that such courses of action were replicated across various empires and different Muslim regions throughout the nineteenth century. However, it need not be that, by promoting this or that Islamic legal source, Western empires succeeded in canonising certain interpretations of *sharīᶜa*, which were specific to the colonisers' mindset; and we should not rule out the possibility that the selection and the promotion of a self-contained number of texts itself reflected *local* sensibilities. While historians all too often have turned to the example of the translation of *al-Hidāya* to signal the foundation of the Anglo-Muhammadan law, few have paused to reflect on the extent to which legists made recourse to *al-Hidāya* in British colonial courts, not to mention the fact that numerous other Ḥanafī texts were also translated and published, especially during the earlier phases of colonisation. The same applies to codes. We simply do not know whether *sharīᶜa* codes crafted by colonial lawmakers were actually employed by Muslim legists. As we sift through the details of court cases and dissect the procedures that Muslim legists followed in colonial courts, we often find that emphasis on single juristic texts reflected more a demand originating from Orientalists and colonial officials than a practice reflecting the conduct of Muslim jurists at court. In fact, we do not find among colonial administrations operating at different latitudes the same degree of confidence in such a tool of governance. One case in point was Sudan where British administrators purposefully avoided codifying customary law, for example.[78]

Second, periodisation in the history of Islamic law in the region is still an open issue. To think of ruptures as a pervasive feature of the Islamic juridical field of Russian Central Asia leads us to misunderstand, misinterpret or simply miss altogether the fact that Sovietisation had a substantially greater impact on the transformation of Islamic institutions, especially in the imaginary of Central Asian Muslims and what they have learnt to think of 'traditional' in Islamic law. I still recall the embarrassment I felt when in the wake of a paper that I gave in Tashkent in 2013, an Uzbek anthropologist lamented that my interpreting the *muftī* as 'jurist' was grossly inappropriate, since in Uzbekistan such a term is traditionally deployed to denote a counsellor or a sage of sorts, who advises the community on what is licit and what is not. Equally, the meaning of *fatwā* has undergone a dramatic change. Central Asian *muftī*s today purport to have revitalised the tradition of *fatwā*-giving that predates the Soviet experience. This is of course grossly improper. It seems to me that such a notion of traditionalism is itself a historical product of Sovietisation.

Third, in Central Asia Muslim modernising trends did not affect the sphere of legal hermeneutics directly, nor do we observe significant lateral transmissions. Starting from the 1880s we do encounter in Bukhara debates that reflect a rethinking of the relationship between the adherence to the *madhhab* (*taqlīd*) and independent reasoning (*ijtihād*). However, such debates originated in fact from the subordinate position of the *ᶜulamāʾ* vis-à-vis the local Uzbek dynasty in power (Manghits) and they do not seem to depend on the circulation of reformist literature. Debates on whether the application of independent reasoning was admissible in Bukhara speak more of a self-reflective approach to the juristic profession than of a reaction to Russian colonialism.[79]

Notes

* I would like to thank Guy Burak, Tom Welsford and two anonymous reviewers for their comments on earlier drafts.

1. L. Buskens, 'Sharia and the Colonial State', in R. Peters and P. Bearman (eds), *The Ashgate Research Companion to Islamic Law* (Farnham: Ashgate, 2014), pp. 209–21; A. Layish, 'The Transformation of the *Sharīᶜa* from Jurists' Law to Statutory Law in the Contemporary Muslim World', *Die Welt des Islams* 44:1 (2004), pp. 85–113.
2. P. Sartori, *Visions of Justice:* Sharīᶜa *and Cultural Change in Russian Central Asia* (Boston and Leiden: Brill, 2016), chap. 2.
3. Wael Hallaq has termed this process 'entexting'. See his *Sharīᶜa: Theory, Practice, Transformations* (Cambridge: Cambridge University Press, 2009), pp. 547–8; J. Strawson, 'Revisiting Islamic Law: Marginal Notes from Colonial History', *Griffith Law Review* 12:3 (2003), pp. 362–83; E. Giunchi, 'The Reinvention of *Sharīᶜa* under the British Raj: In Search of Authenticity and Certainty', *Journal of Asian Studies* 69:4 (2010), pp. 1,119–42; and Scott A. Kugle, 'Framed, Blamed and Renamed: The Recasting of Islamic Jurisprudence in Colonial South Asia', *Modern Asian Studies* 35:2 (2001), pp. 257–313.
4. C. Gazzini, 'When Jurisprudence Becomes Law: How Italian Colonial Judges in Libya Turned Islamic Law and Customary Practice into Binding Legal Precedent', *Journal of the Economic and Social History of the Orient* 55:4–5 (2012), pp. 746–70; P. Sartori, *Visions of Justice:* Sharīᶜa *and Cultural Change in Russian Central Asia*, chap. 4.
5. V. Martin, 'Kazakh Oath-Taking in Colonial Courtrooms: Legal Culture and Russian Empire-Building', *Kritika* 5:3 (2004), pp. 483–514. For cases of application of such a probative procedure in Kyrgyz-majority Tien-Shan, see P. Sartori, 'Exploring the Islamic Juridical Field of the Russian Empire: An Introduction', *Islamic Law and Society* 24:1–2 (2017), p. 7.
6. A. Layish, 'The Transformation of the *Sharīᶜa* from Jurists' Law to Statutory Law in the Contemporary Muslim World'; N. J. Brown, '*Shariᶜa* and State in the Modern Muslim Middle East', *International Journal of Middle East Studies* 29:3 (1997), pp. 359–76.

7. A. Christelow, 'Islamic Law and Judicial Practice in Nigeria: An Historical Perspective', *Journal of Muslim Minority Affairs* 22:1 (2010), pp. 185–204; S. Eltantawi, *Shari'ah on Trial: Northern Nigeria's Islamic Revolution* (Oakland: California University Press, 2017).
8. P. Sartori and I. Shahar, 'Legal Pluralism in Muslim-Majority Colonies: Mapping the Terrain', *Journal of the Economic and Social History of the Orient* 55:4–5 (2012), pp. 637–63.
9. F. and K. von Benda-Beckmann, *Political and Legal Transformations of an Indonesian Polity: The Nagari from Colonisation to Decentralisation* (Cambridge: Cambridge University Press, 2013).
10. J. Beyer, *The Force of Custom: Law and the Ordering of Everyday Life in Kyrgyzstan* (Pittsburgh: Pittsburgh University Press, 2016).
11. B. Turner, 'Translating Evidentiary Practices and Technologies of Truth Finding: Oath Taking as Witness Testimony in Plural Legal Configurations in Rural Morocco', in Y. Ben Hounet and D. Puccio-Den (eds), *Truth, Intentionality and Evidence: Anthropological Approaches to Crime* (London: Routledge, 2017), pp. 112–29.
12. I. Agmon and I. Shahar, 'Shifting Perspectives in the Study of *Shari*ᶜ*a* Courts: Methodologies and Paradigms', *Islamic Law and Society* 15:1 (2009), pp. 4–5.
13. On the pitfalls of using Ottoman history as a yardstick to measure changes and continuities in the history of Islamic law, see P. Sartori, *Visions of Justice:* Sharīᶜa *and Cultural Change in Russian Central Asia*, pp. 41–2.
14. A Salvatore, *Islam and the Political Discourse of Modernity* (Reading: Ithaca Press, 1997), pp. xiii, xv, xvii.
15. B. Babadzhanov, *Kokandskoe khanstvo: Vlast', politika, religiia* (Tokyo and Tashkent: NIHU Program TIAS, 2010), pp. 531–67.
16. A. F. Ibrahim, 'The Codification Episteme in Islamic Juristic Discourse between Inertia and Change', *Islamic Law and Society* 22:3 (2015), p. 220. Whether indeed the reception of codes and statutory laws amounted to 'muted opposition' alone, it is at present difficult to say given the state of the art of studies on Islamic law in colonial situations.
17. The most important work devoted to the idea of the preponderant view (*tarjīḥ*) is T. Al-Azem, *Rule-Formulation and Binding Precedent in the Madhhab-law Tradition: Ibn Quṭlūbughā's Commentary on* The Compendium *of Qudūrī* (Boston and Leiden: Brill, 2016).
18. 'For God did not reveal a law but only texts containing what the jurists characterize as indications (or indicants: *dalīl*s). These indicants guide the jurist and allow him to infer what he thinks to be a particular rule for a particular case at hand', W. B. Hallaq, *Sharīᶜa: Theory, Practice, Transformations*, p. 82.
19. For a different view on the transition to modernity in the field of Islamic law, see the later work of Avi Rubin on the Ottoman *mecelle*, 'Modernity

as a Code: The Ottoman Empire and the Global Movement of Codification', *Journal of the Economic and Social History of the Orient* 59:5 (2016), pp. 828–56.

20. Sh. Pollock, 'Introduction', in Sh. Pollock (ed.), *Forms of Knowledge in Early Modern Asia: Explorations in the Intellectual History of India and Tibet, 1500–1800* (Durham, NC and London: Duke University Press, 2011), p. 1.
21. See A. F. Ibrahim, 'Rethinking the *Taqlīd–Ijtihād* Dichotomy: A Conceptual-Historical Approach', *Journal of the American Oriental Society* 136:2 (2016), pp. 285–305.
22. S. Khan, *Muslim Reformist Political Thought: Revivalists, Modernists and Free Will* (Abingdon: Routledge, 2003), p. 96.
23. E. Allworth, *Evading Reality: The Devices of 'Abdalrauf Fitrat, Modern Central Asian Reformist: Poetry and Prose of ᶜAbdul Qadir Bedil* (Leiden and Boston and Köln: Brill, 2002), p. 138. See also A. Khalid, *Making Uzbekistan: Nation, Empire, and Revolution in the Early USSR* (Ithaca and London: Cornell University Press, 2015), pp. 248-9.
24. D. DeWeese, J. Eden, P. Sartori, 'Moving beyond Modernism: Rethinking Cultural Change in Muslim Eurasia (nineteenth–twentieth Centuries)', *Journal of the Economic and Social History of the Orient* 59:1–2 (2016), pp. 1–36; see also N. Spannaus, 'The Ur-Text of Jadidism: Abū Naṣr Qūrṣāwī's *Irshād* and the Historiography of Muslim Modernism in Russia', ibid., pp. 93–125.
25. D. DeWeese, 'It was a Dark and Stagnant Night ('til the Jadids Brought the Light): Clichés, Biases, and False Dichotomies in the Intellectual History of Central Asia', *Journal of the Economic and Social History of the Orient* 59:1–2 (2016), pp. 37–92.
26. In this respect, the work of Alexander Morrison has shown that the Russians attempt to involve local jurists in a project of codification of *sharīᶜa* ended in a remarkable fiasco; see his 'Creating a Colonial Shariᶜa for Russian Turkestan: Count Pahlen, the Hidaya and the Anglo-Muhammadan Law', in V. Barth and R. Cvetkovski (eds), *Imperial Cooperation and Transfer, 1870–1930: Empires and Encounters* (London: Bloomsbury, 2015), pp. 127–49.
27. For an overview on the Islamic juridical field in pre-Russian Central Asia, see P. Sartori, *Visions of Justice:* Sharīᶜa *and Cultural Change in Russian Central Asia*, chap. 1.
28. P. Sartori, 'An Overview of Tsarist Policy on Islamic Courts in Turkestan: Its Genealogy and its Effects', *Cahiers d'Asie centrale* 17:18 (2009), pp. 477–507.
29. Mīr Rabīᶜ b. Mīr Niyāz Khwāja al-Ḥusaynī, *Risāla-yi Raḥmānīya*, MS Tashkent, IVAN RUz, no. 9060/XII, fol. 403b.
30. *makhfī namānad ki murād az masāʾil-i maᶜmūla ān-ast ki muftī taṣwīr-i masʾala rā taḥrīr wa muhr karda bāshad*, ibid.

31. Further ruminations on the topic of *jung* can be found in the recent work of James Pickett, *The Persianate Sphere during the Age of Empires: Islamic Scholars and Networks of Exchange in Central Asia, 1747–1917* (unpublished PhD Dissertation, Princeton University, 2015), chap. 3.
32. It should be clarified here that the vision of the role of the *muftī*, as propounded by the author of the *Risāla-yi Raḥmāniyya*, represents in fact a common Ḥanafī perception of the juristic authorities within the *madhhab*; see G. Burak, *The Second Formation of Islamic Law: The Hanafi School in the Early Modern Ottoman Empire* (Cambridge: Cambridge University Press, 2015), chap. 3.
33. *Qunyat al-fatāwā* by Najm al-Dīn Mukhtār b. Maḥmūd b. Muḥammad al-Zāhidī al-Ghazmīnī (d. 1260), C. Brockelmann, *Geschichte der arabischen Literatur* (Leiden: Brill, 1996 [1st edn, 1943]), SI, p. 382 (656).
34. Most probably this title refers to Muḥammad al-Shawkānī's famous Koranic exegesis (*tafsīr*). See B. Haykel, 'Al-Shawkānī and the Jurisprudential Unity of Yemen', *Revue des mondes musulmans et de la Méditerranée* 67 (1993), pp. 53–65.
35. A work by Sayyid Jalāl al-Dīn b. Shams al-Dīn al-Gurlānī al-Khwārazmī (d. 768/1367), *GAL* I.376–8, pp. 466–70.
36. I have been unable to identify this reference.
37. Here the text most probably refers to the *Fatāwā al-Ẓahīriyya*, an unpublished Ḥanafī work composed by Ẓahīr al-Dīn Muḥammad b. Aḥmad b. 'Umar al-Bukhārī (d. 619/1222), otherwise known as Ẓahīr al-Dīn al-Kabīr (d. 506/1112). See Brockelmann, *GAL SI*: 379 (471).
38. *wa ḥājjat nīst ki muqallid dalīl-i riwāyat-i khwud rā dānad wa yā gūyad wa agar gūyad az kamāl ast.*
39. *wa wājib ast bar mustaftī-yi jāhil ki ᶜamal be-fatwā-yi ū kunad.*
40. I have been unable to identify this reference.
41. This is a work also known as *Fuṣūl al-iḥkām fī uṣūl al-aḥkām*, compiled in Samarqand by ᶜImād al-Dīn Abu al-Fatḥ ᶜAbd al-Raḥīm Zayn al-Dīn b. Abū Bakr al-Samarqandī (d. *c.* 1271). See *GAL* SI: 382 (656).
42. *Majma' al-baḥrayn wa multaqā al-nayyirayn* by Muẓaffar al-Dīn Aḥmad b. 'Alī b. Ṭa'lab b. al- Shā'ātī al-Baghdādī (d. 696/1296); see Brockelmann *GAL* II:383 (477).
43. Mīr Rabīᶜ b. Mīr Niyāz Khwāja al-Ḥusaynī, *Risāla-yi Raḥmānīya*, MS Tashkent, IVAN RUz, no. 9060/XII, fols 403b–404b.
44. As was the case in the Ottoman learned hierarchy as well, see U. Heyd, 'Some Aspects of the Ottoman Fetvā', *Bulletin of the School of Oriental and African Studies* 32.1 (1969), pp. 35–46.
45. And our author reinforced such argumentation by adding that the very meaning of *ijtihād* underwent a change: 'In the *Sharḥ al-Birjandī* [one finds] that: But in our period the duty of *ijtihād* can be performed only by operating within the branches of jurisprudence (*furūᶜ al-fiqh*). This is the way to reach the *ijtihād* in this period', Mīr Rabīᶜ b. Mīr Niyāz Khwāja

al-Ḥusaynī, *Risāla-yi Raḥmānīya*, MS Tashkent, IVAN RUz, no. 9060/XII, fols 404b–405a.

46. On nineteenth-century Central Asian jurists using the term *riwāyat* as a synonym for *fatwā*, see P. Sartori, *Visions of Justice:* Sharīᶜa *and Cultural Change in Russian Central Asia*, chap. 5. The use of the term *riwāyat* opens up an interesting parallel with *naql* (pl. *nuqūl*) as the latter was used in the Ottoman juristic field; see U. Heyd, 'Some Aspects of the Ottoman Fetvā', p. 45.
47. *wa riwāyatī ki mīnawīsad muwāfiq-i muddaᶜāy-i mustaftī bāshad yaᶜnī malika dāshta bāshad ki maqṣūd-i sāyil rā az nafs-i taḥrīr iẓhār wa mubayyin mīkarda bāshad.*
48. *dar īn ṣūrat ṣaḥīḥ ast bar īn shakhṣ taḥrīr-i fatwā wa taqrīr bar ᶜāmma khalq kardan wa wājib ast ba qawl-i way ᶜamal namūdan*, Mīr Rabīᶜ b. Mīr Niyāz Khwāja al-Ḥusaynī, *Risāla-yi Raḥmānīya*, MS Tashkent, IVAN RUz, no. 9060/XII, fols 404b–405a.
49. *Baḥr al-Fatāwā* is a jurisprudential work attributed to Kadizade Mehmet Erzani crafted in 1748. https://catalog.hathitrust.org/Record/006080023 (accessed 4 April 2019).
50. This work is an abridgment of the *Muḥīṭ al-Burḥānī* by Burḥān al-Dīn Maḥmūd b. Aḥmad b. al-Ṣadr al-Shahīd al-Bukhārī b. al-Māzah (d. ca. 1174), see *GAL* SI: 375 (642).
51. Mīr Rabīᶜ b. Mīr Niyāz Khwāja al-Ḥusaynī. *Risāla-yi Raḥmāniyya*. MS Tashkent, IVAN RUz, no. 9060/XII, fol. 405a.
52. Otherwise known in Central Asia as *Sharḥ-i nuqāya*, a work by Shams al-Dīn Muḥammad b. Ḥusām al-Dīn al-Quhistānī (d. 1554), which is a commentary on the *al-Nuqāya* (or *Mukhtasar al-wiqāya fī masāʾil al-Hidāya)* of ᶜUbaydallāh b. Masᶜūd Ṣadr al-Maḥbūbī al-Sharīᶜa al-Thānī (d. 1346), see A. Idrisov, A. Muminov and M. Szuppe, *Manuscrits en écriture arabe du Musée regional de Nukus (République autonome du Karakalpakstan, Ouzbékistan). Fonds arabe, persan, turkī et karakalpak* (Rome: Istituto per l'Oriente C.A. Nallino, 2007), p. 95.
53. Unidentified work, most probably a commentary (*sharḥ*) on the *Mukhtaṣar al-wiqāya fī masāʾil al-Hidāya (al-Nuqāya*, see fn. 15) a work by the Ottoman polymath ᶜAbd al-ᶜAlī b. Muḥammad al-Ḥusayn al-Birjandī (d. 1525), see A. Ėrkinov, N. Polvonov and H. Aminov, *Muhammad Rahimkhon II Feruz Kutubkhonasi Fehristi (Khorazmda kitobat va kutubkhonachilik tarikhidan)* (Tashkent: Yangi Asr Avlodi, 2008), pp. 22, 208. Excerpts of a legal work by Birjandī are also mentioned by A. Idrisov, A. Muminov and M. Szuppe, *Manuscrits en écriture arabe du Musée regional de Nukus (République autonome du Karakalpakstan, Ouzbékistan). Fonds arabe, persan, turkī et karakalpak*, p. 82.
54. Mīr Rabīᶜ b. Mīr Niyāz Khwāja al-Ḥusaynī, *Risāla-yi Raḥmāniyya*, MS Tashkent, IVAN RUz, no. 9060/XII, fol. 405a. See also P. Sartori, *Visions of Justice:* Sharīᶜa *and Cultural Change in Russian Central Asia*, p. 90.

55. *wa agar dar miyān-i īshān ikhtilāfī bāshad tarjīḥ-i qawl-i ba^cḍī ba-ṭarīq-i ijtihād va tamyīz khwāhad būd wa ḥālā rāh-i ijtihād masdūd ast wa ahl-i naẓar va tamyīz mafqūd wa ṭarīq-i istiftā^ʾ muta^cyyan wa riwāyāt-i muftīhā bayyin bas lāzim bāshad bar qāḍī rujū^c ba fatwāy-i ā^ʾyma hadī namūdan wa bar muqtaḍā fatwāy-i īshān ḥukm farmūdan*, Ikhtiyār al-Dīn b. Ghiyāth al-Dīn al-Ḥusaynī, *Mukhtār al-Ikhtiyār,* MS Tashkent, IVAN RUz inv. no. 2064, fol. 65a.
56. I have been unable to identify this reference.
57. Mīr Rabī^c b. Mīr Niyāz Khwāja al-Ḥusaynī, *Risāla-yi Raḥmāniyya*, MS Tashkent, IVAN RUz, no. 9060/XII, fol. 405a.
58. I have been unable to identify this reference.
59. The *Mukhtaṣar al-wiqāya fī masā^ʾil al-Hidāya* (otherwise known as *al-Nuqāya*) by ^cUbaydallāh b. Mas^cūd b. Tāj al-Sharī^ca al-Maḥbūbī al-Bukhārī was taught in madrasas and thus circulated widely in Transoxiana. It became so popular that Khorezmian rulers requested that its commentary (*sharḥ*) be translated into the vernacular. Under the rule of Abū al-Ghāzī Bahādurkhān (r. 1644–63) the commentary of a certain Dāmullā Muḥammad Ṣalāḥ (fl. sixteenth century) was rendered into Persian. Muḥammad Raḥīm Khān Firūz (r. 1864–1910) ordered the translation into Chaghatay of the commentary of ^cAbd al-^cAlī b. Muḥammad al-Ḥusayn al-Birjandī (d. 1525). See A. Erkinov, N. Polvonov and H. Aminov, *Muhammad Rahimkhon II Feruz Kutubkhonasi Fehristi (Khorazmda kitobat va kutubkhonachilik tarikhidan),* p. 208; and A. Idrisov, A. Muminov and M. Szuppe, *Manuscrits en écriture arabe du Musée regional de Nukus* (*République autonome du Karakalpakstan, Ouzbékistan*). *Fonds arabe, persan, turkī et karakalpak*, pp. 108–9.
60. The text here refers to the author of *Sharḥ-i nuqāya*; see footnote 52.
61. A work with this name is noted in A. Idrisov, A. Muminov and M. Szuppe, *Manuscrits en écriture arabe du Musée régional de Nukus (République autonome du Karakalpakstan, Ouzbékistan). Fonds arabe, persan, turkī et karakalpak*, p. 82, in the context of entry no. 19.
62. I have been unable to identify this work.
63. Mīr Rabī^c b. Mīr Niyāz Khwāja al-Ḥusaynī, *Risāla-yi Raḥmāniyya*, MS Tashkent, IVAN RUz, no. 9060/XII, fol. 405b.
64. Ibid., fols 405b-406a.
65. This practice has a long and established tradition in the Ḥanafī *madhhab*; see al-Azem, *Rule-Formulation and Binding Precedent in the Madhhab-law Tradition: Ibn Quṭlūbughā's Commentary on* The Compendium *of Qudūrī.*
66. P. Sartori, *Visions of Justice:* Sharī^ca *and Cultural Change in Russian Central Asia*, pp. 261–2.
67. M. Fadel, 'The Social Logic of *Taqlīd* and the Rise of the *Mukhtaṣar*', *Islamic Law and Society* 3:2 (1996), pp. 193–233.
68. P. Sartori, *Visions of Justice:* Sharī^ca *and Cultural Change in Russian Central Asia*, pp. 291, 293.

69. For more on this individual, see ibid., pp. 111–13.
70. *Ūl ᶜalāmat būlgānda anī khilāfīdagī masʾalagā ᶜamal qīlīb būlmāydūr*, TsGARUz, f. I–17, op. 1, d. 4785, l. 40. For more on this case, see P. Sartori, *Visions of Justice:* Sharīᶜa *and Cultural Change in Russian Central Asia*, chap. 5.
71. *O razreshenii voprosa o sovershennoletii i prava vladeniia imushchestvom po musul'manskomu zakonodatel'stvu*, TsGARUz, f. I–17, op. 1, d. 673.
72. Ibid., ll. 47ob–48*: usmotrev iz postanovlennogo po étomu delu resheniia s'ezda kaziev, sostavlennogo v pol'zu otvetchitsy i podannoi mne na oznachennoe reshenie prositelem zhaloba, chto doveritel'nitsa Bibi-Zibi, bivshaia 14 let, ne mogla raspologat' nedvizhemost'iu i osobenno darit', kak ne dostigshaia sovershennoletnogo vozrasta i ezheli podarok v deistvitel'nosti sostoial'sia to to delo dolzhen podlezhat' otvetstvennosti opekun ili zanimaiushee ego litso, k kotoromu i dolzhen byt' predliavlen isk Bibi-Zibi na summu po stoimosti nedvizhimosti, peredannoi maloletnomu.*
73. Ibid., l. 48.
74. Consider, for example, the following expression opening a *qāḍī*'s reply to the Russian official: *ṣaghīr kabīr nicha yāshda būlūb ūz mālīgha mutaṣarrif būlmāghīgha wa ham iqrār sharīᶜat būyūncha durustlīghīgha sharīᶜat ḥaddīcha riwāyat mushtamal bar āyat wa ḥadīth wa kutub-i fiqh īlān mangā maᶜlūm-nāma yāzīb birāsīz dīb farmāyish qīlghānlār*, TsGARUz, f. I–17, op. 1, d. 673, l. 9ob.
75. *Andāq maᶜlūm wa manẓūr qīlāmiz kim idnāy-i muddat-i bulūgh yaᶜnī kim muddat qīz-bala balāghīgha yitīb sharīᶜat būyūncha bālīgha būlūb ūz mulkīgha mutaṣarrif būlūb iqrārīnī sharīᶜat ḥaddīcha qabūl qīlmāghī . . . madhkūra bala iqrār ba-iḥtilām qīlsa agar chandī tūqqūz yāshda būlsa ham wa ūghūl-bala ūn īkkī yāshda būlsa durust dīb kitāblārda madhkūr dūr dīb wa agar iqrār ba-iḥtilām qīlmāsa muddat-i balāghatgā yitmāghī ūn bīsh yāshda ᶜalayh al-fatwā dūr*, ibid.
76. *1882-nchī yilinda Ramaḍān āynī 21-nchī kūnīda būyrūqlārīgha muwāfiq āyat ḥadīth wa masʾala-nī ḥāshīgha yāzīb maᶜlūm qīlāman kim ṣaghīr mulkīgha waṣī taṣarruf qīlmāghī agar ᶜalāmat-i bulūgh ṣaghīrgha ẓāhir būlmasa biznī madhhabīgha ᶜalayh al-fatwā qawlīda ṣaghīr 15 yāshgha kīrghūncha ᶜalāmat-i bulūgh ẓāhir būlsa qīz-bala 9 yāshgha ūghūl-bala 12 yāshgha kīrīb iqrār-i būlūgh qīlsa taṣdīq qīlīb sharīᶜat būyūncha waṣī bar-ṭaraf būlūb madhkūr balalār ūzlārī mutaṣarrif būlādūr*, ibid., l. 22.
77. Ibid., ll. 22, 25ob.
78. J. A. Sachs, 'Native Courts and the Limits of the Law in Colonial Sudan: Ambiguity as Strategy', *Law and Social Inquiry* 38:4 (2013), pp. 973–92.
79. P. Sartori, '*Ijtihād* in Bukhara: Central Asian Jadidism and Local Genealogies of Cultural Change', *Journal of the Economic and Social History of the Orient* 59:1–2 (2016), pp. 193–236.

10

Take Me to Khiva: *Sharīʿa* as Governance in the Oasis of Khorezm (Nineteenth Century–Early Twentieth)

Ulfat Abdurasulov and Paolo Sartori

Introduction

In the autumn of 2010 we toured Khorezm, a region nestled between modern Uzbekistan, Turkmenistan and Kazakhstan, to inspect private manuscript collections.[1] It was the end of September and, on account of the balmy weather favourable to our travelling, we thought it would be the most propitious moment to head to Nukus, the capital city of what is today Karakalpakstan. Our informants had told us about a manuscript library belonging to a local savant, himself scion of a family of scholars of Islamic sciences, called Sotiboldi Umarov. In fact, the library did not have many surprises for we had encountered similar collections along our way. As we leafed through the various items, however, we came across a rescript addressed to the chancellery of the Qonghrat Khans of Khiva, the last Muslim dynasty to rule over Khorezm prior to Sovietisation. The record offered a concise account of a dispute solved by representatives of the Qonghrats, a legal practice that we shall discuss further in this chapter. As we paused to read this record, the owner of the manuscript told us a story from his childhood memories. The story took place in the second half of the 1980s in Janbulak, a small village in Karakalpakstan located in a desert area to the east of To'rtko'l. His maternal grandmother, Umarov told us, an elderly and infirm woman, was staying in his uncle's house and he visited her quite often. During these visits his grandmother repeatedly complained about her eldest son who pressured her to bequeath her property, a house and a large garden, solely to him. Whatever the facts of the matter, the stubborn behaviour of his uncle forced his mother and aunt to act very cautiously in deference to their brother. It was decided therefore to resolve the situation by involving a former fellow village man and a distant relative, who at that time lived in Nukus and held a high position at the provincial *Ispolkom* (Rus. 'Executive Committee').

One Sunday morning, as had been agreed beforehand, Umarov's relatives travelled to Janbulak and waited for the man from the *Ispolkom* to arrive from Nukus. At some point someone cried *geldi, geldi!* thereby announcing that a white Volga had just arrived. The man from the *Ispolkom* got out of the car and, followed by a group of men and the 'village elder' (Uzb. *oqsoqol*), went to the house of Umarov's uncle. A ritual banquet was served for the men in the courtyard. But the mood soon soured, as greetings gave way to increasingly bitter accusations and recriminations between family members. As the *oqsoqol* realised that his exhortations for the parties to calm down were falling on deaf ears, he exclaimed with a voice full of reproach: 'Now listen! Stop it! Don't you have any sense of shame?! Let's solve the dispute! Have we bothered such a respectable person for nothing?' As he told us this story Umarov did not recall all the details of the discussion. However, he made clear that the *oqsoqol*'s exhortation had had its intended effect: a settlement was reached.

As we tried to make sense of this story, we wondered what could oblige the parties to find a suitable compromise in spite of their heated disagreement. Umarov told us that, ironically, the man from the *Ispolkom* neither entered his uncle's house that day, nor expressed any opinion on this issue. Nor did he take any measures to bring his obstinate uncle back to reason. Umarov said it was his mere presence that was key to the resolution of the conflict. That man from the *Ispolkom*, of course, enjoyed a certain authority among the community of Janbulak; he was a *katta*, a 'grandee', as Umarov put it. So, anyone who would not follow his call to solve the conflict would lose his benevolence in the future. But was this the sole factor that led the parties to reach a compromise? It appears in fact that the mere presence of the man from the *Ispolkom* gave a new dynamic to the discussion, which was now exposed to outside scrutiny: the party refusing the proposed settlement would not only have disappointed the expectations of the 'grandee' himself, but also would have let the whole community down, whatever the stipulations of the settlement.

For Umarov it was evidently natural to connect this story about the informal settlement of a dispute, which occurred in the 1980s, to the late nineteenth-century manuscript record we were holding in our hands. As we shall see, Umarov's story and the compositional genre embedded in that record have something in common: they show that the resolution of conflicts in Central Asia often involved not a *qāḍī* or some other judicial authority with which historians of Islamic law are all too familiar but rather just 'a man in power'. Umarov's story attests to the resilience and indeed the continued development of practices of non-judicial conflict resolution in the Soviet period, the roots of which may well be found at least in the second half of the nineteenth century.

This essay is about the pre-eminent role played by the Qonghrat khans and their officials in the resolution of conflicts in the oasis of Khorezm and the neighbouring regions. It argues that said khans and officials were in fact the primary judicial authorities to whom most petitioners addressed their claims. This chapter thus sets out to explore an Islamic juridical field (in the Bourdieusian sense) in which Muslims brought their affairs to state officials because they had the power to coerce parties to achieve a settlement and enforce a decision either formal or informal. Significantly, a clear sense of hierarchy rather than a notion of jurisdiction provoked decisions to take legal action in the first place. In nineteenth-century Khorezm responsibility for the resolution of conflicts fell on the royal court and the governors, while *qāḍī*s did not adjudicate of their own volition. The earliest attestation to this peculiar state of affairs comes from the Russian envoy to Khiva Nikolai Murav'ev who, in 1821, noted that *qāḍī*s 'do not have any right to hear cases . . . [except] only conflicts of little significance' and when they do so 'they have to report to the Khan about whatever wrongdoing and crime'.[2] In fact, judges usually heard cases only when the royal court or the governors instructed them to do so, mostly in cases in which respondents denied the claim (*inkār*) against them. As we shall see, a denial activated the transferral of a case to a *qāḍī*. We shall return to this topic and discuss the subordination of *qāḍī*s to Qonghrat court officials and their procedural limitations later.

The Qonghrats' pattern of governance calls into question the conventional understanding of the relationship between *sharīʿa* and the state. Indeed, studies on dispute resolution in the Islamic world, especially in Central Asia, tend to give greater importance to legists than to the state, that is, the Muslim ruler and his representatives in court. Indeed, it is usually held that the settlement of disputes in Muslim-majority areas depended on 'judges' (*qāḍī*s)[3] and 'arbitrators' (*ḥakīm*s)[4] who settled disputes independently or facilitated reconciliation by means of mediation, either judicial or extra-judicial.[5] In the resulting narrative, the state occupies only a marginal place in the judicial field.[6] As a consequence, a number of important studies on the subject of Islamic law suggest that the state provided either a court of second instance, by offering what is usually termed a *maẓālim* appellate system,[7] or a mechanism of governance that affected legal hermeneutics, by which it ultimately constrained juristic independence. The following quotation from the magisterial work of Wael Hallaq[8] may help the reader to appreciate what we mean:

> Aside from judicial appointments which were nominally, if not symbolically, hierarchical, the administration of justice was largely limited to the self-structured legal profession. If there was a hierarchy it was within the profession itself, and as in nature epistemic rather than political or social. Yet, the hierarchy within Islamic law was largely universal and self-sufficient, unlike the hierarchy existing in the judicial system of the nation-state, a hierarchy that ultimately reports to the higher political orders. The referential authorities of the *qāḍī* are other *qāḍī*s and *muftī*s. Hard cases were decided with the juristic assistance of the *muftī*, and appeals did not usually travel upward in a hierarchy, but were heard by the succeeding judge. And even when some complaints were made to the highest offices of the 'state' (as happened in the Ottoman Empire), they were made directly and given – with explicit intention – the personal attention of the ruler. This was a personal form of justice, not corporate.

In a recent article devoted to the *maẓālim* tribunals in the Mamluk period, Yossef Rapoport calls the view that 'the ideal form of Islamic law is independent of the state' the 'dominant paradigm'.[9] Over the last years, however, several scholars have shown that this view is untenable for the post-Mongol history of the Muslim world. Indeed Guy Burak[10] and Sami Ayoub[11] have clearly illustrated the degree to which in the Ottoman period jurists conferred legal authority upon sultanic orders and thus how Islamic jurisprudence depended on the intervention of the sovereign and his court.

By building on this recent literature, we contend in this essay that the dominant narrative in the field of Islamic legal studies creates an artificial opposition between the state and *sharīᶜa*, an opposition predicated on the reified notion of Islamic law as the exclusive preserve of Muslim legists (*ᶜulamāᵓ*), that is, as a self-contained juristic domain inaccessible to the uninitiated, and specifically, to state officials. While previous studies calling into question this binary interpretive model have focused exclusively on the Mamluks and the Ottomans, this chapter questions the supposed separation of *sharīᶜa* from political power on the basis of material from Central Asia.

Sultanic jutice entails people's travel to the centre. It might be argued, of course, that such travel might seem much easier in Khorezm than in the Ottoman Empire, given the two polities' relative size. However, distance was not the one and only factor that mattered for appellants when deciding whether or not to petition the royal court, as suggested by evidence from the Ottoman Empire. 'Despite the expense and danger of travel', James Baldwin reminds us, 'some provincial petitioners, including some from as far as Egypt, journeyed to Istanbul to present their petitions in person'.[12] Even if they opted not to make the journey themselves, the efficiency of postal communication in the Ottoman Empire allowed them to use courier networks to transport their petitions to the palace.[13] We here begin to see that categories such as 'small' and 'big' or 'far' and 'near' are insufficient to make sense of a culture of legality. True, Khorezm looks like a small region on a map. However, in the nineteenth century, travel presented more challenges to the inhabitants of the Khorezmian oasis and its surrounding regions than it did to Ottoman citizens who could avail themselves of infrastructures lacking in the Khanate of Khiva. Also, we know little about travellers' perceptions and even less about the subjectivities of petitioning to, and appealing to, a Muslim ruler. Why should one assume that Qaraqalpaqs living in nomadic encampments in the district of Chimbay imagined the Khivan royal court as 'closer' than, say, Levantines in Egypt thought of the *dīwān* in Istanbul? Consider the case of one Sayyid Aḥmad Khwāja, a nephew of the Bukharan ruler Amīr Ḥaydar. Sayyid Aḥmad Khwāja, who was the governor of Nurata, set out for hajj in 1851. Despite his royal pedigree, Sayyid Aḥmad Khwāja was unable to exit the emirate and join the globalised routes of Muslim pilgrimage. His travelogue opens with a shamefaced story about venturing into the domains of the Khans of Khiva as a result of hiring a local Turkmen scout who turned out to know as little about the surrounding region as he himself did. Thus, the introduction to Sayyid Aḥmad Khwāja's travelogue is in fact a series of anecdotes illustrating how easy it was to get lost when travelling into Khorezm through the Kyzylkum desert without any reliable form of 'local knowledge'. By peppering his *sayyāḥat-nāma* with contempt towards the inefficient Turkmen guide and detailing the route from one well to another, Sayyid Aḥmad Khwāja teaches us an important lesson not only about diversification in the business of hajj in the age of the steam engine, but also about our, often misguided, assumptions about what the process of travel might have entailed in the past.[14]

This chapter about law in nineteenth-century Khorezm has four parts. The first offers a brief historical background on the Khivan Khanate and the establishment of the Russian protectorate. The second explains the governmentality that shaped the system of conflict resolution known in Khivan sources as *ᶜarḍ-dād*. The third discusses some aspects of the court protocol during audiences at the Qonghrat royal court. The fourth addresses the mechanics of the system of conflict resolution as it is reflected in the available sources.

Background

In the early twentieth century, the chancellery of the Khanate of Khiva began systematically to preserve reports on matters pertaining to conflict resolution. Under Qonghrat rule, court attendants, governors and legists operating in the major urban centres in the oasis of Khorezm addressed such reports to the royal court in Khiva and, specifically, to the office of the *yasāwulbāshī*.

This chancery output reflected a bureaucratic disposition that manifested itself following the Russian subjugation of the Khivan Khanate in the nineteenth century. In accordance with the Gandumiam Peace Treaty signed in August 1873, the Qonghrat dynast Muḥammad Raḥīm Khān II relinquished to the tsar the lands east of the Amu Darya, while retaining limited sovereignty over the territories west of the river. Russia's subjugation of Khiva was similar, in certain respects, to France's 'protectorates' in North Africa. In 1881 the French intervened militarily and defeated the army of the Bey of Tunis in response to raids by the Khmir tribe into Algerian territory, which was part of the French Empire and its overseas territories (Outre-Mer).[15] Similarly, in Khorezm in 1873, the Russians decided to confront the army of the Khan of Khiva after the latter had sent his raiders into the Russian-ruled Kazakh Steppe to pillage.[16] Both France and Russia apparently were responding to a threat to the integrity of their dominion and sovereignty. In addition, the military operations that paved the way for France and Russia to expand their rule over Tunis and Khiva, respectively, were followed by peace treaties. In both cases, the treaty served to define legislatively the relationship between colonial masters and their subjects. The Gandumian Treaty (from Chaghatay, Gandūmqān), however, was a self-contained and vague set of regulations that did more to complicate than clarify the status of the Khanate of Khiva and its subjects vis-à-vis the Russian Empire.[17] The indeterminacy of the Gandumian Treaty may have reflected a purposeful political choice. Indeed, its vagueness endowed Russians with room to manoeuvre against the interests of the Khivans on subjects as complex as water rights.[18] But this form of governance was far from unique in the age of European colonialism. As Kristin Mann and Richard Roberts note about the history of African protectorates, 'significant ambiguities existed surrounding the legal authority that parties possessed to conclude these protection agreements and impose the new systems of colonial rule that developed'.[19]

There were also substantial differences between the Russian and French protectorates. Tunisia was home to several European communities, especially merchants: Italian and Maltese British subjects were living in Tunis when the Bey surrendered to the French army, the Italians outnumbering the French.[20] By contrast, before 1873 the European presence in Khiva was conspicuous by its absence, despite the presence of mostly British and Iranian agents who spied for the British and Qajar empires. The oasis of Khorezm, and Khiva in particular, was also known to various European merchants, Orientalists and adventurers. These figures did not, however, reside in the country. In sum, the largest non-native community in Khiva and its environs at the time of the Russian invasion consisted of Iranians and Russians, mostly slaves of the Qonghrat dynasty. In Tunisia prior to the French–Tunisian treaty (called the Bardo Treaty), European subjects could count on the notion of extraterritoriality. In the capitulation treaties that he signed with most of the European powers in the Mediterranean, the Bey of Tunis relinquished his jurisdiction over European foreigners. Thus, subjects of Austro-Hungary, Italy and Britain enjoyed legal immunity and could bring their affairs to their consular courts in Tunis. In this respect, too, Khiva was different. Russians were reluctant to install a resident with consular powers in Khiva, as they had done in Bukhara. Nor could they reach a decision on the issue of establishing justices of the peace in the territory of the protectorate, even though, during the first decade of the twentieth century, the community of Russian merchants had grown.[21]

The Russians did little to change the existing legal system in the protectorate. They did, however, hold the Khivans accountable when the latter heard complaints from or against Russian subjects. For example, if a Qazaq Muslim subject committed an offence in the territory of the Khivan protectorate, the aggrieved party would usually file a claim with the royal court in Khiva. Article 15 of the Gandumian Treaty required the royal court to report to the commandant in Petroaleksandrovsk (present-day To'rtko'l). The Russian official would write back to Khiva and instruct the royal court to hear the case. The case would then be transferred to a governor and, if the defendant denied the claim, to a judge or arbitrator. Every officeholder reported back to his superior: the judge to the governor, the governor to the Khivan royal court, the court to the commandant in Petroaleksandrovsk. The trial was the last link in a long chain of justice. We can trace this chain by following the surviving paper trail, which clearly reflects a process of bureaucratisation that affected recordkeeping in the Khivan chancery.

One unintended consequence of bureaucratisation was the increased visibility of dispute settlement in the documentary record. Indeed, the Russian takeover in Khorezm brought about a *formalisation* of certain chancery practices, which otherwise would not have come down to us.[22] One such practice consists of writing reports sent to the office of the *yasāwulbāshī* about the resolution of conflicts. These reports shed light on a legal system that operated in the region at least from the beginning of the nineteenth century. Since similar practices existed in the Emirate of Bukhara and the Khanate of Khoqand, this system may be regarded as representative of post-Chinggisid Central Asia.[23] Such a system reflects a shift from earlier political configurations that centred on notions of shared sovereignty,[24] to a highly centralised and bureaucratised state formation (whatever we may imagine this to be), which came into being in the wake of the ᶜArabshahid collapse of 1740.

It would be misleading, in our view, to explain the prominence of Qonghrat officials simply as a reflection of the so-called 'nomadic political tradition',[25] often said to have informed patterns of governance in the khanates of Central Asia and beyond.[26]. Indeed, there is little of Chinggisid pedigree in the ways in which Qonghrat officials articulated their legal authority over the resolution of conflicts in Khorezm. We learn from a Russian observer that prior to the rise to power of the Qonghrats 'adjudication belonged exclusively to the clergy, but with the establishment of dynastic rule in the khanate, the clergy lost almost all its judicial power'.[27] This statement suggests that the 'system' that we see reflected in the available evidence in which the Khans of Khiva and their officials enjoyed more legal authority than the *qāḍī*s, was certainly an innovation of the Qonghrats, at least in the oasis of Khorezm. To be sure, the Qonghrats were a dynasty of Uzbek tribal origin. However, nothing in our sources suggests that their Turko-Mongol ethnicity mattered more than *sharīᶜa* in the dispensation of justice.

Before we turn to a detailed discussion of the legal procedure in Khorezm known as *ᶜarḍ-dād* (or simply *ᶜarḍ*), a term that denotes a formal ceremony in which a subject submits a grievance to the ruler and files a claim with the royal court, two notes of caution are in order.[28] First, as elsewhere in the Islamic world, a petition (*ᶜarḍ*) represents a default mode of communication between the chancery and a subject, whether an officeholder or a member of the general populace. Indeed, any form of communication with the royal court, whether a plea of allegiance or a news report (*wāqiᶜa*),[29] was formulated as a petition and crafted in compliance with the requirements of this genre. However, under the Qonghrats, the terms *ᶜarḍ-dād* and *ᶜarḍ* were used specifically to denote a system of justice at the centre of which were the khan and his court. It would be misleading to characterise this system as a 'petitioning system', a term that connotes a larger body of textual practices that includes, but does not coincide with, the legal institutions under consideration. Historians of Islam usually regard petitions as part of the *maẓālim* system, which made it possible for Muslims to seek redress when confronting official malfeasance. The term *maẓālim* is conspicuous by its absence in Khivan bureaucratese. In addition, whereas under the Mamluks the royal court operated as a court of second instance,[30] this was not the case in Khorezm, where Qonghrat subjects brought their claims directly to the court of the khan, without first filing their lawsuits with judges. In this context, the Khivan royal court seldom served as a higher court with powers of judicial review.

Second, and more important, Khivan subjects presented their complaints to the khan orally, not in writing.[31] This marks a substantive and decisive difference from legal practices in other Muslim societies, which required that Muslims present their complaints to the ruler in form of a written petition.[32] Of course, it is possible that the Qonghrat polity also welcomed written petitions and that Qonghrat chancellery practices may have been as elaborate as elsewhere in the region. The Qonghrats promoted a culture of documentation that has left us the richest repository of Arabic-script texts from Central Asia covering the period from the late eighteenth century to the establishment of Russian rule (1873), the so-called Archive of the Khans of Khiva. This archive contains numerous documents that can be called petitions.[33]

Governance (1800–60)

Little is known about courtly life in Khiva and even less about justice in the oasis of Khorezm. There is no doubt, however, that the Qonghrats regarded *ᶜarḍ-dād* as an efficient instrument in upholding and dispensing justice. That hearing the affairs of their subjects was an important part of Qonghrat governance is attested both by court chroniclers and occasional observers, notably Russian military officials and European travellers. Readers conversant with treatises on the Islamic theory of government (*dawlat*) and the genre of mirrors for princes may note that the ability to dispense justice (*ᶜadālat*) has been regarded as one of the necessary attributes of the ruler since the beginnings of Islamic rule.[34] Significantly, Khivan court chronicles from the early nineteenth century draw attention to the fact that listening to the claims of his subjects and settling their disputes is a central activity of the sovereign himself (the khan). These chronicles offer vivid accounts of such activities.

One of the first Qonghrat rulers, Muḥammad Raḥīm Khān I (r. 1806–25), who undertook several military campaigns to restore the territorial unity of Khorezm, paid frequent visits to different parts of the khanate, where he heard petitions and complaints from the public.[35] By all accounts, this procedure was perceived by Khivan authorities as an important tool – together with military campaigns, resettlement policies and maintenance of the irrigation system – to ensure that the new dynasty could retain power over the new territories that had been brought under control. Khivan chronicles provide many accounts of how the royal court operated as an itinerant system of conflict resolution that followed the process of consolidation of Qonghrat power in the region. In these circumstances, Muḥammad Raḥīm Khān I acted in the capacity of peripatetic judge.

With the stabilisation of political life in Khorezm, this legal practice became more institutionalised and thus more visible. The seeds of such institutionalisation were planted under Allāh Qulī Khān (r. 1826–42), most notably with the construction of a new royal palace in Khiva called Tāsh Hawlī ('Stone Courtyard'). On the occasion of this monumental project, the ruler commissioned the construction of a 'chamber of petitions' (*ᶜarḍ-khāna*) that was designed to allow the khan to receive the claimants and hear their grievances directly. The chamber was built so that the hearing would be 'suitable to the royal status' of the rulers (*pādshālīqgha lāyiq*),[36] whereas, previously, hearings took place at the royal court (*kuhna arīkda* [*sic*]), that is, in the apartments of the khan, without any special procedure.[37] It is here that we can appreciate the importance of hearing the grievances of the populace for the Qonghrats: the dispensation of justice was not only a form of governance deployed to bring the ruler closer to the many concerns of the subjects, but also a physical and permanent attribute of sovereignty that was embodied in the architecture of the royal court.

A few mid-nineteenth-century texts recount how the royal court reacted to claims brought to the attention of the khan by the general public. The first such text is dated to 1858 and illuminates a case in which a tribal headman was accused of the unlawful detention of a woman:

> This is the royal order to Bīk-Fūlād Bī [endowed with] the vestiges of loyalty [to us]. A certain Yūsuf has now come here and claimed that you are keeping his wife at your home under duress (*zūrlīq qilīb*) and are not letting her go free. Now, if what Yūsuf says is true, you should return his wife to him. If you deny his claim (*ūzgā sūzīng būlsa*), you should both come to the royal court for a hearing (*qamtū dargāh-i ᶜālīgha kilīb*) and solve [the conflict]. So orders this royal instruction (*ᶜināyat-nāma*) that we wrote.[38]

The claimant, Yūsuf, was a layman who regarded access to the legal services of the royal court as a lever against the tribal headman (*bī*). Yūsuf probably understood that, had he filed a claim with a judge, the outcome would not have been favourable. A *qāḍī* might not have been in the position to summon a local notable such as Bīk-Fūlād Bī and hold a trial. Power relations mattered.

The second text elucidates the handling of homicide cases filed with the court of the khan:

> This is the royal order to ᶜAbdī. A certain ᶜAvaḍ-Murād has now come to the royal court and appealed (*ᶜarḍ*) to us, saying that he has a claim for blood-money

against you (*sanda khūn daᶜwām bār dīb*). Now, if what he says is true, they should both come to the royal court for a hearing (*qamtū dargāh-i ᶜālīgha kilīb*) and solve [the conflict]. This royal order was written on 28 Jumādī al-Thānī 1277 [11 January 1861].[39]

Several observations of the ruler performing the *ᶜarḍ-dād* at the royal court were recorded by Europeans who visited Khiva under various circumstances. One of the richest accounts comes from the pen of the Hungarian Orientalist Arminius (Ármin) Vámbéry, who happened to witness the hearings while staying at the residence of the ruler during his visit to Khiva in 1863:[40]

> Because at this hour *arz* [< *ᶜarḍ*], that is, an open audience, is held almost every day, in the khan's residence, by the main entrance and everywhere we went, there gathered a crowd of visitors of all ranks, genders, and ages. They were all dressed casually; many women even came with babes in arms. Nobody's presence was recorded, and those who gained admittance were therefore those who were best able to jostle . . . [After a short wait in the waiting room], two *yasaul*s respectfully took me by the hand, the curtain was raised, and I saw the khan of Khiva . . . He was seated on the dais, which had a view of the terrace, leaning with his left hand on a velvet pillow and holding a small golden scepter in his right.[41]

This practice is also attested in Russian sources from the period preceding the conquest of the khanate in 1873. The account of one eyewitness who found himself in Khiva in the 1860s invites us to consider whether or not the *ᶜarḍ-dād* was perceived as a 'court hearing' (*pravosudie*):

> Every day, around two o'clock, [the khan] goes to court to hear cases and complaints. In the summer quarters, court is held right in the courtyard, in which are arranged earthen couches; the khan sits on one of these, on a velvet pillow, leaning on his hand for greater comfort, and hears complaints.[42]

These accounts mention *ᶜarḍ-dād* as an established legal practice in Khiva and as a distinctive feature of the khanate's legal culture. These observations are strikingly similar to those found in local material, which emphasise that *ᶜarḍ-dād* was regularly conducted with the participation of the khan and the khanate's senior officials, in the 1860s and in the period following the Russian conquest of 1873. For example, the court historian Bayānī notes that Muḥammad Raḥīm Khān II (r. 1865–1910) spent an hour every day in his reception room, before sunset, dispensing justice (*ᶜadl-u dād mashghūl idīlār*) by hearing petitions from the public.[43] Further eloquent attestation of the importance of the ruler's participation in the regular hearing of lawsuits is found in a description left by Tarrāh Bābājān (1878–1971), who served Muḥammad Raḥīm Khān II as court poet and scribe (*mirzā*).[44] Describing the last years of the life and reign of the khan, the author reports that the deterioration of the ruler's health, especially his partial paralysis, made the regular holding of the *ᶜarḍ-dād* procedure very difficult.[45] The khan himself, according to Tarrāh, proposed that the hearing of complaints from the public be delegated to the hereditary prince, Isfandiyār Tūra. Clearly fearing rumours among the population and possible disturbances caused by the absence of the ruler, the khan's retinue was able to ensure his continual personal involvement in the procedure.[46] As Tarrāh relates, a special carriage was constructed to bring the khan to the 'chamber of petitions' immediately before the ceremony. During the reception of complainants, one of the court attendants, a certain Dawlat Murād, would prop up the khan's back as he sat on his throne. 'Thus', concludes Bābājān Tarrāh, 'Muḥammad Raḥīm Khān II heard the complaints of his subjects even within one year [of his death].'[47]

Khivan authors who report on long-term absences and illnesses of the ruler considered the complications that such situations caused for the hearing of complaints. In recounting Isfandiyār Khān's frequent absences from the country, one Laffasī informs us of the individuals who would replace the ruler and act as judges. Similarly, Tarrāh refers to physical difficulties that jeopardised the performance of the *ᶜarḍ-dād* as one of the complications in governance faced by the court elite because of the aged Muḥammad Raḥīm Khān's illness. The emphasis placed by local authors on the challenges posed to hearing the complaints is further evidence of the fact that the *ᶜarḍ-dād* was a prominent function of the ruler.

Protocol

Settling disputes at the royal court required compliance with official protocol. The khan and other court officials who participated in the *ᶜarḍ-dād* received complaints from the public and heard cases almost every day. The procedure, however, had a ceremonial aspect as well. There are two sources that may help us to recover some of the fundamental details of this ceremony as it was practiced at the court of the Khivan rulers at the beginning of the twentieth century. The first comes from Nil Lykoshin (1860–1922)[48] and comprises part of the official report to the chancellery of the governorship-general in Tashkent, which he wrote after his first visit to the court of Isfandiyār Khān in his capacity of commandant (*nachal'nik*) of the Amu Darya Department in late May 1912.[49] The second source was written in Uzbek by a local scholar,[50] Bābājān Safar ūghlī (Rus., Safarov). His description of the *ᶜarḍ-dād* is found in his *History of Khorezm* (*Khwārazm taᵓrīkhī*), a work written in 1957. This treatise elucidates the history of the region from the end of the nineteenth century to the beginning of the twentieth.[51]

Both narratives contain detailed descriptions of the protocol followed in the *ʿarḍ-dād* ceremony at court. Lykoshin's account, from the perspective of a bystander witnessing the ceremony by force of circumstance, focuses primarily on its formal aspects.[52] As a one-time observer of this procedure, Lykoshin offers only a snapshot of the event. His account obscures the ceremonial dimension of the performance and detaches it from its wider context, that is, the events preceding and following the ceremony. The author is inclined to see the ceremony as a primitive formalistic procedure that 'reeks of the past':

> About six o'clock in the evening, the usually deserted courtyard, decorated with tall columns in the Moorish style, suddenly perked up . . . Sometime later, the harem door opened, whence Isfandiyār Khān Bahādur proceeded to the place where he sits to mete out judgment and punishment. Not far from the only entrance into the courtyard there is a small stone platform, covered with a large felt mat. The khan sits on the dais in Asian style, and before him they lay out an ancient gun in its case and a small hatchet, also old – these are the insignia of power. The khan wears an expensive gold-trimmed saber of the Asian type, and on his head, in place of the usual fur hat, he has an equally large hat of lamb fur, but with a red top; this hat is the equivalent of a crown. By the khan's hand they place a kettle of green tea and a cup. Even before the khan's entrance, a *maḥram*[53] takes up a position not far from the khan's dais and stands perfectly still, with his head bare. From time to time, these *maḥram*s are silently replaced by others newly entered into the courtyard. The old man Yūsuf Yasāwulbāshī begins the ceremony . . . The time for parsing the people's complaints has come . . . The khan's subjects complain to him about each other and ask for the restoration of rights violated by others of his subjects. The petitioner, having entered through the door, stops at the entrance, quite far from the khan, so his complaint is pronounced in a very loud patter, the supplicant almost yelling, as if he hopes to prove the severity of his grievances and to penetrate the soul of the khan with his cries. The khan, having allowed the supplicant to finish his brief complaint, says only one word, turning to the Yasāwulbāshī. This is probably an order to sort out the case. The petitioner exits, another enters.[54]

Safarov's description differs considerably from Lykoshin's. It was not based on personal experience. Rather, the author probably conveyed common knowledge about the ceremony that was circulating among the inhabitants of Khiva. In fact, *Khwārazm taʾrīkhī* was composed four decades after the fall of Qonghrat rule in Khorezm, long after the events described. Together with other historical works written in Khiva at this time, Safarov's work may be categorised as a late development of what we may call vernacular historiography. A characteristic feature of his works is the attempt to continue the so-called Khivan historiographical tradition by maintaining the same structural elements and relying on both written texts and oral material.

At the same time, Safarov's writings lack the flowery phrases characteristic of pre-Soviet Khivan historiography. He also avoids laudatory assessments of the actions and intentions of Khiva's ruling circles. The greatest difference, however, concerns the exposition and layout of the material. Whereas traditional Khivan chronicles offer a sequential narrative of events in dynastic history organised around the rule of an individual sovereign, Safarov's works offer aggregated material gleaned from a variety of sources (often with bibliographic information), but they do not always have a single, logically connected and cohesive narrative outline. In addition, his account of the *ᶜarḍ-dād* brings to mind the epistemological paradigms that are typical of Soviet-period Uzbek historiography. This is apparent in the author's tendency to characterise certain administrative practices of the khanate as archaic and by his couching them in a discourse of corruption:[55]

> To receive petitions from the public (*fuqarālārnīng ᶜarḍdārlārī*), the khan dispenses justice (*ᶜarḍ-dād qīlādī*) on a daily basis, sitting on his throne for one hour. Beside him sit the *qushbigī*, the *mihtar*, the *naqib*, the *ātālik*, and the *shaykh al-Islām*. The *mīrshab*, together with ten other people – the *yuzbāshi* and the *jallād*s – stand beside the khan with sabers bared. Two *īshīk-āghā*s, armed with axes and knives, stand on either side of the gate, guarding the entrance to the reception room (*ᶜarḍ-khāna*). Summoning the [next] petitioner (*ᶜarḍchī*), the foremen (*dahabāshī*) with unsheathed sabers, lead him into the reception room, where the *yasāwulbāshī* stands between the khan and the petitioner, who stops thirty meters from the khan's throne. [The *yasāwulbāshī*] conveys the petitioner's greeting and his petition to the khan and transmits the khan's questions and decision to the petitioner. So it occurs and has become the custom (*ᶜurf-ᶜādat*), that the khan should not communicate directly (*ūz tūghrisīdān*) with his subjects (*fuqarālār*).[56]

These passages from Lykoshin and Safarov offer a glimpse of early twentieth-century practices and, specifically, recount an event that occurred during the reign of Isfandiyār Khān (r. 1910–18). Emphasising the ancient origin of the ceremony that, in his words, 'reeks of the past',[57] Lykoshin evidently assumed that what he saw reflected a long-standing legal practice taking place at the royal court. Similarly, Safarov's characterisation of the ceremony as 'custom' (*ᶜurf-ᶜādat*) attests indirectly to the perceived antiquity of this practice.

Lykoshin and Safarov illuminate two key elements of the *ᶜarḍ-dād* that point to the peculiarity of the institution. The first element, which is procedural, concerns the manner in which petitioners appealed to the ruler. Claimants always petitioned the khan orally and directly. Similarly, the ruler's response to a particular petition was delivered orally, through the medium of the *yasāwulbāshī*. It is tempting to see in the oral dimension of such petitions a manifestation of earlier juridical practices, when the khan heard public grievances. Such practices are attested during the rule of Muḥammad Raḥīm Khān I. But there is another aspect to orality. Addressing the khan orally was consistent with the peculiar etiquette of communication between sovereign and subject. This etiquette implies a direct personal communication, thus symbolising the expression of personal homage to the ruler and a humble willingness to put the decision on his question (as well as his fate) in the hands of the ruler.

The second key element of the *ᶜarḍ-dād* mentioned is the centrality of the *yasāwulbāshī*. This element is clearly institutional, for his function was not limited to attending the ceremony or to serving as an intermediary between the khan and the petitioner. The *yasāwulbāshī* and the special office under him (*yasāwulbāshī khidhmatī*) would be responsible for initiating and overseeing all subsequent investigations into petitions and their resolution, as well as for handling and archiving the documentation.

The regular hearing of public claims had to be ensured, even during periods when the supreme ruler found himself outside of the khanate. The Khivan historian Ḥasan-Murād Laffasī informs us, for example, that, during his periodic visits to St Petersburg for an audience with the Russian emperor, Isfandiyār Khān appointed proxies for receiving public complaints (*fuqarānīng ᶜarḍ-dādī ūchūn*).[58] This same practice was also used by the khan when he found himself outside of the capital in extraordinary circumstances.[59]

The Yasāwulbāshī *Office*

As we have seen from the accounts of Lykoshin[60] and Safarov,[61] the *yasāwulbāshī* took part in the *ᶜarḍ-dād* ceremonial at court and conferred on this institution a symbolic status. He acted as an intermediary by transmitting the content of the petition to the khan and by conveying to the subject the decision of the ruler.[62] In addition, the *yasāwulbāshī* played an important role in the resolution of disputes. Narrative sources and chancellery documentation are both clear that the *yasāwulbāshī* not only asked the supplicants about the content of their petitions but also referred the supplicants to other Qonghrat officials who would investigate the case and oversee the settlement of the dispute.[63]

Instructions

After a plaintiff had filed a claim with the royal court, the *yasāwulbāshī* would write an instruction, or *fatak*.[64] Conventionally addressed to the disputing parties, the instruction stipulated the appointment of a special attendant (*yasāwul*) who, acting as a plenipotentiary court representative, escorted the plaintiff back to the *locus rei*, initiated the investigation with the help of local Qonghrat officials (governors, legists and notables), and facilitated the resolution of the conflict. The results of the investigation, together with the stipulations of the settlement, were then brought to the *yasāwulbāshī* office and recorded, in brief, on the reverse of the *fatak*. These written reports were deposited at the office of the *yasāwulbāshī* as evidence, in the event of a future reopening of the case. The outcome of dispute settlements was duly recorded also in special registries (*daftar*s), containing the names of claimants (*dādkhwāhchīlār*) and stewards, and some basic information about the claim, as well as a summary of the resolution of the conflict.[65] Thus, *pace* Lykoshin, there is ample evidence that there were chancellery and archive practices associated with this system of conflict resolution. The *fatak* paper trail and the ensuing bookkeeping, of course, could not be produced without the clerks known as *dīwānī*s. The *yasāwulbāshī* also had at his disposal a handful of guards (*nawkar*) appointed to escort the plaintiffs who filed their claims with the royal court. In 1873 Alexander Kuhn, a Russian Orientalist of German origin, produced a survey of the political and administrative organisation of the khanate in which he noted:

> the *yasāwulbāshī* has at his disposal a few assistants, the so-called *yasāwul*s. As soon as he receives an order from the khan to investigate a case, he [the *yasāwulbāshī*] dispatches one of his assistants together with the claimant to the place in which the wrong occurred. At the end of the inquest the *yasāwulbāshī* collects from the claimant 3 ½ tenga, i.e. 70 kopecks for every 19 kilometers covered while on duty.[66]

In sum, the *yasāwulbāshī* presided over an 'office' called, in Khivan bureaucratese, *khidhmat*. This office occupied a separate room in the khan's residence.[67]

The following example illustrates how the *yasāwulbāshī* appointed a guard as attendant (*yasāwul*) and instructed him to settle the case by means of a *fatak*. The *fatak* sheds light on a conflict that arose in the wake of an engagement. A groom's father failed to deliver the deferred dower to the bride's family. Subsequently, the latter filed a claim with the royal court in Khiva. There the *yasāwulbāshī* issued the *fatak* and entrusted it to the guard. In the terse report written on the reverse of the document, the guard indicates that he assembled the parties and persuaded the groom's father to pay the deferred dower and commit to the defrayal of other wedding gifts. The guard's note also suggests that the agreement was solemnised before a *qāḍī* in the form of an acknowledgement (*iqrār*) made in the presence of two witnesses. The certificate in question was, no doubt, a marriage contract.[68]

> [*Recto*]
> Saᶜādat Bīka, daughter of Muḥammad Ṣafā, and Khāl Murād, son of Khudāy Bīrgān, are engaged (*fātiḥa-khānd ītib*). Although the [bride's parents] received thirty *ṭillā* as [part of] the customary dower (*qalīng pūlī*), the [groom] failed to pay the remaining sum and other liabilities relating to the wedding (*qālgan tūyāna lawāzim*). He avoided providing explanations, and four years have passed without his saying anything. For this reason, [Muḥammad Ṣafā] filed a claim against the [groom's side]. On this basis, let the parties come to the royal court of our lord, may his rule last forever, together with Sulṭān Yūzbāshī *yasāwul*, and settle the case. The attendant's fee should not exceed two *tanga* for each *farsakh*. This instruction was drawn up on Tuesday, 9 Shawwāl 1328 [14 October 1913].
>
> [*Verso*]
> Saᶜādat Bīka, the daughter of Muḥammad Ṣafā b. Yaᶜqub Bāy, who is a member of the Īsh Niyāz Bājbān community, returned to Khāl Murād, the son of Khudāy Bīrkān b. ᶜAwaz Muḥammad, who is a member of the same community. [This happened] in Manāq.[69] [The parties] then agreed on the wedding ceremony (*tūy ītib birmāk*) and [the bride's party] received [the deferred] customary dower (*qālīng mālī*). Khudāy Bīrkān said that he will deliver to Muḥammad Ṣafā new clothes together with other wedding gifts (*ṭūyānalār*). This [promissory note] was notarized (*iqrār yāzīldī*) in the presence (*shāhidlarī*) of the *yasāwul* and Gadāy Niyāz Bābā b. Ḥamīt Niyāz.[70]

Generally speaking, in nineteenth-century Central Asia a wedding consisted of three rituals. One was the betrothal. By reciting the opening sura of the Qurᵓān (*fātiḥa*), the bride and the groom commit to the wedding. The second was the solemnisation of the marriage (*nikāḥ*) in the form of a contract, usually before a mullah.[71] The third was the celebration (*tūy*).[72] The three rituals took place at the home of the bride, but the expenses of organising the celebration fell exclusively on the groom's family.[73] Such expenses, called *tūyāna*, consisted mainly of gifts to the bride's family. The groom's family also paid a dower (*qālīng*), which included a sum of money as well as clothes, and jewellery.[74] One would expect the dower to be paid directly to the bride and thus become her property.[75] However, our sources show that *qālīng* was usually paid to her parents.[76]

Khorezmian jurists opined that such payment should be regarded as temporary. That is to say, the dower was given in trust (*amānat*) to the parents, but the bride would recover her property after the solemnisation of the marriage.[77]

Rescripts

Writing practices connected to the *ᶜarḍ-dād* went beyond the *fatak* genre. Quite a few rescripts were addressed to the *yasāwulbāshī* office and stored there. They show that a provincial governor (*ḥākim*) might inform the *yasāwulbāshī* office in detail of the progress of an investigation into a claim filed with the royal court by reporting whether the parties to a dispute had resolved the conflict, or, less frequently, if one party intended, out of dissatisfaction with the course of the proceedings, to return the case to Khiva (*Khīwaga bārurman dīb*; *dargāh-i ᶜālīlarga bārurman*).

In July 1912, for example, the governor of Urgench reported to the *yasāwulbāshī* the settlement of a dispute concerning the disposal of water shares. The text demonstrates how the resolution of a conflict often required the participation of several actors representing different social forces. After a claimant had submitted a petition to the royal court in Khiva, the *yasāwulbāshī* appointed a guard to act as attendant. The latter did not act alone. He convened a hearing, probably in Urgench, in the presence of both the governor and the representatives of the community to which the parties belonged. The local notables who represented the locale no doubt had access to some kind of privileged knowledge – they must have known the details of the dispute, hence their attendance. The following text shows how the attendant and the governor pushed the parties to a settlement and sanctioned it:

> Let it be known to the office of Muḥammad Maḥram Yasāwulbāshī, refuge of the vizierate (*wizārat-panāh*) and repository of nobility (*najābat-dastgāh*), our lord (*āqā*), that a certain Muḥammad Yaᶜqūb from Chātkūfrūk went to the royal court (*dargāh-i ᶜālī*) and submitted a petition (*ᶜarīḍa*) [claiming] that Bābājān, Ṣābir, Dūndī Bīka, Karīm Birgān, Qālandār, and Saᶜādat Bīka do not let water flow into his water canal (*suv yūlī*). He also mentioned that these individuals had assaulted him and his brother. [The royal court thus] appointed Muḥammad Sharīf, the guard (*nawkar*) of ᶜAbd al-Sattār Says[78] [to the office of] attendant (*yasāwul*). [Muḥammad Yaᶜqūb] drove [the attendant to the locale]. The latter let the above-mentioned [individuals] reach a settlement (*madhkūrlārnī yarāshdīlār*) before us, together with the representatives of the local community (*ahl-i īlāt būlūb*). I wrote this notification (*khaṭṭ*) to inform your office on 27 Rajab [1330] [12 July 1912].[79]

Governors wrote such rescripts for various reasons. A deep sense of accountability no doubt shaped such practices, but the crafting of rescripts also acquired importance when a conflict affected the public. In the following case, a Turkmen appealed to the royal court in Khiva about a robbery. The royal court appointed a guard who proceeded to mediate the case. In the presence of the governor, the guard organised a public hearing with the headmen representing the communities of the two parties. A settlement was reached, but it seemed insufficient to prevent further escalation of the conflict. The notification of the settlement addressed to the office of the *yasāwulbāshī* thus acquires the status of a pledge indicating that the parties undertook to avoid new conflicts. From this we may infer that the actors in this dispute must have regarded the involvement of a *sharīᶜa* court as less effective than the royal court in achieving the purpose of avoiding further conflict.

> Let it be known to the *yasāwulbāshī*, the pivot of glory and happiness, our lord, that a certain Kildī Muḥammad, a Choudur,[80] claimed (*dīb*) that, in his absence, during the night, a certain Qūshān and ᶜAna Muḥammad broke into his house and robbed him of three hundred *manāt*. Accordingly, ᶜAyd Bāy, the guard of Ghāyib Yūzbāshi, was appointed [by the royal court] as attendant. [The latter, together with] the *kadkhudā*s of Kildī Muḥammad and his opponents (*sūzīnīng daᶜwāgarlārī*) – Qūshān and ᶜAna Muḥammad – came [before me] and reconciled the two parties (*īkkī ṭarafnī riḍālīqgha yitkūrdīlār*). And now, in order to avoid further disturbances among the people (*fuqarālārnī halāk būlmāslīqī wajhīdīn*), this notification was entrusted to the guard. We inform your office about this event. This report (*khaṭṭ*) was written in the year 1335 [1916–17].[81]

The Governors and the Qāḍīs

The *yasāwulbāshī* office produced reams of paper attesting to the participation of *qāḍī*s in the system of conflict resolution in Khorezm under Qonghrat rule. Rescripts to the *yasāwulbāshī* indicate that, after the issuance of a *fatak* precipitating the procedure we have illustrated in the preceding sections, the defendant's denial of the claim would lead the governor to activate the judges and thus transfer the case to them. In addition, while governors often transferred cases to the judges, it was usually the former alone who were held accountable for the resolution of the conflict and thus reported back to the royal court in Khiva. This suggests that *qāḍī*s generally held a position in the hierarchy lower than that of the provincial governors. Let us test this proposition.

A certain Ūrāḍ Bāy from the city of Gurlen owed 200 *ṭillā* to one Īsh Murād. According to a preliminary agreement, Ūrāḍ Bāy was required to pay Īsh Murād thirty *ṭillā* and entrust to another man, Muḥammad Yūsuf, a horse valued at forty *ṭillā*. The creditor, however, did not treat this payment as part of the debt. Consequently, Ūrāḍ Bāy decided to take legal action against both Īsh Murād and Muḥammad Yūsuf and travelled to Khiva to file his claim. An attendant escorted the claimant to meet the respondents. Muḥammad Yūsuf probably denied that the payment of the horse was connected to Ūrāḍ Bāy's debt to Īsh Murād. The lawsuit was then transferred to a *qāḍī*, before whom, after Ūrāḍ Bāy was unable to produce evidence, Muḥammad Yūsuf swore an oath and won the case. By contrast, the claim concerning the thirty *ṭillā* was heard on the spot. It is unclear who solved the dispute, but the attendant reported to the royal court that the claim was relinquished.

> [*Recto*]
> Ūrāḍ Bāy from Māylī Changul owes two hundred *ṭillā* [to a certain] Īsh Murād from the citadel of Khiva. [The debt has been] recorded (*khaṭṭlī*). [Ūrāḍ Bāy] entrusted to [a certain] Muḥammad Yūsuf from Māylī Changul a horse that was valued at fifty *ṭillā*, as part of his debt (*qarḍgha birmākchī būlūb*). He also paid thirty *ṭillā* [in cash] to the aforementioned Īsh Murād. [Nevertheless], the payments were not treated [as covering the debt], and, as a result, [Ūrāḍ Bāy] is still held liable to pay two hundred *ṭillā*. For this reason, [Ūrāḍ Bāy] has filed a claim (*daᶜwā*) against these individuals. Let them come to the royal court together with Jumᶜa Qulī Yasāvul, the guard (*nawkar*) of Bahādur Bāy Īshīk Āqāsī, and resolve [the dispute]. The attendant's fee is four *tanga* per parasang. This instruction was written on 17 Dhū l-Ḥijja 1328 [20 December 1910] to convey the royal order (*amr-i ᶜālī*) of our lord, may his rule last forever.

> [*Verso*]
> This claim was transferred to a *sharīᶜa* [court]. With respect to the horse valued at fifty *ṭillā*, Muḥammad Yūsuf took an oath. The claim against the aforementioned Īsh Murād concerning thirty *ṭillā* was not heard in a *sharīᶜa* [court]. [The dispute] was resolved and [the resolution] was notarized (*ṣaf būlūb wa khaṭṭlāshūb*). [The royal court] was informed on 22 Dhū l-Ḥijja 1328 [25 December 1910].[82]

The purpose of this section is to test the suggestion that *qāḍī*s were 'junior' to local administrators. The following example reflects a conflict between two communities (*dawr*) of water-users living along the banks of the lower reaches of the Qūshbigī Yāf canal,[83] a stream that flows northwest from Lavzan, the latter an important tributary of the Amu Darya.[84] On behalf of one community, two individuals filed a lawsuit with the royal court, claiming that the other water users had not fulfilled their duties of maintenance for the last two years. In Khorezm, maintenance of the irrigation system consisted of two main activities, *saqa qāzū* and *ābkhurī* *qāzū*. The first activity, which involved cleaning the upper channels (*saqa*) of a canal, was under the direct supervision of the central administration; the second activity, which involved cleaning the tributaries (*ābkhurī*), was carried out by the local communities.[85]

The communities of water users were required to organise this maintenance in accordance with established practices (*taᶜāmul*). In this case, the claimants lamented that, by neglecting its duties, the neighbouring community impeded the flow of water to the lower reaches of the canal, thereby complicating the irrigation process. In an attempt to resolve the conflict, the *yasāwulbāshī* ordered a governor to make further inquiries into the case. The governor was clearly endowed with powers to assess the veracity of the claim. If the claim was valid, he was expected to enforce maintenance obligations. If the respondents entered a counter-claim, the governor would transfer the case to the *qāḍī*s. Note that the formula used to describe this last procedure – 'we entrusted it to the *sharīᶜa*' (*sharīᶜatgha qūshdūk*/*sharīᶜatgha tāpshūrdūk*) – means that the case was transferred to local judges who would treat the dispute according to the probative procedures of Islamic adjudication. This does not mean, however, that, the governor (or the attendant) did not hear cases according to *sharīᶜa*. It means, rather, that the *counter-claim* triggered the *qāḍī*s' implementation of probative procedures, that is, (1) to request that the plaintiffs produce testimony, (2) to invite the respondents to swear an oath or (3) to ask the parties to bring legal opinions in support of their position. The implementation of such procedures was clearly the prerogative of *qāḍī*s. However, it should be mentioned that nothing in our sources suggests that governors (or attendants) implemented either customary laws or a body of laws that was regarded as non-*sharᶜī*.[86] They point, instead, to a procedural specialisation of *qāḍī*s within the Islamic juridical field whereby such specialisation was regarded (by jurists as well as by scribes in general) as a distinct activity, even if it was not discretely discontinuous from the *sharīᶜa* applied by representatives of the royal court.

Our source basis, and this document in particular, also shows that legal actors in Khorezm were aware of the legal instruments at their disposal. As soon as the respondents realised that the plaintiffs would produce testimony and win the case, the former informed the governor, Muḥammad Yaᶜqūb Bāy b. Jabbār Qulī Maḥram, that they would take the case to the royal court.

> Let it be known to the office of the *yasāwulbāshī*, the refuge of the vizierate, our lord, that Bābājān and ᶜAbdu Karīm from Manāq [claimed that] above their community (*dawr*), on the banks of the upper reaches of the Qūshbigī Yāf canal, [there is a group of people] that disposes of twenty water-shares (*sū*)[87]

under the supervision of Allāh Bīrkān Mīrshab and Nāvāḍā Mīrāb. During the last two years the latter group has not carried out the maintenance works (*qāzūshmāydūr*) in the lower reaches of the canal (*āyāq*). Since ancient times (*qadīmdīn*), it is established practice (*taᶜāmul*) that all water users should clean the local ditches proceeding from the lower reaches toward the main stream (*sāqā*). [As a result,] you ordered (*būyrūq*) that the aforementioned people be questioned and [if the claim is found to be sound], make them clean the canal according to the ancient practices. [You also established that,] if the [respondents] enter a counterclaim (*bāshqa daᶜwālār*), the dispute must be heard at a *sharīᶜa* [court]. We thus arranged for a hearing according to Islamic law. The *qāḍī-īshān*s from Manāq, who are skilled in *sharīᶜa,* ordered the appellants (*āriḍa-gūy*)[88] to produce their witness (*guwāh*). When the appellants were about to bring their witness, [the defendant] Allāh Bīrgān Mīrshab stated that he intended to go to Khiva (*Khīwāgha bārūrman dīb*) [and present the dispute to the royal court]. In wishing you well, we wrote this notification (*khaṭṭ*) to inform you about this [event] on 22 Jumādā al-Awwal 1335 [16 March 1917].[89]

Documentation originating in the office of the *yasāwulbāshī* indicates that there was a procedural distinction between the way in which conflicts were resolved by royal court attendants and governors, on the one hand, and by judges, on the other. One might say that the royal court attendants and the governors represented a tribunal of 'equity',[90] a quick way to dispense justice, while the *qāḍī*s followed the more elaborate rules of procedure and evidence typical of Islamic law.

In addition, one often observes that governors extorted a confession (*iqrār*) under duress (*siyāsat*), a procedure that the *qāḍī*s did not use. Several rescripts, however, complicate our effort to distinguish the practice followed by governors from that followed by *qāḍī*s. In some cases, royal court attendants and governors informed authorities in Khiva to apply the *sharīᶜa* – or this is at least what sources suggest. The next document deals with a dispute settled by a governor. A relative of a dead man filed a claim with the royal court and suggested that an assault might have caused the death. The court ordered the governor to make an inquest and settle the dispute. The governor summoned the relatives of the deceased, who stated that the man had been seriously ill before the fight; for this reason, they had no claim against the respondent. The claimant thus relinquished his claim, and the respondents received a release:

Let it be known to the office of the *yasāwulbāshī*, refuge of the vizierate and repository of power, our lord, that a certain Ḥaqq Muḥammad and a certain Sharīf from the community (*qavm*) [headed by] Mullā Yūsuf Āqsaqāl in Shāhābād[91] had a conflict. Because of the death of Sharīf, we [proceeded] in accordance with your instruction *(būyrūgh)* to investigate the claim [filed by his relatives] (*ālārnīng daᶜwālārīnī*), to resolve the conflict according to Islamic law on site (*shūl ṭarafda sharīᶜat farmāyishī bīla*) and report to [your office about the resolution]. We therefore summoned and questioned the heirs (*warathalārī*) of the deceased Sharīf, [namely] Jumᶜa Niyāz and Qurbān Bīka, [respectively] the son and the wife of Sharīf, together with his brothers, Rajab Bāy and Mullā Īsh Bāy. His heirs stated that Sharīf had quarelled violently [with Ḥaqq Muḥammad] three days before his death and that he was also sick (*kasal*). They thus acknowledged the relinquishment of the claim (*daᶜwāmīznī ūtdūk dīb iqrār qilīb*) against Ḥaqq Muḥammad. Subsequently, Jumᶜa Niyāz, son of Sharīf, acting on his own behalf (*ūz ṭarafīdīn*) and as proxy (*wakīl*) of his mother, Qurbān Bīka, with the testimony (*shahādat*) of his witnesses (*guwāhlār*), Yūsuf Āqsaqāl and Rajab Bāy, certified (*khaṭṭlāshtūrūb*) before the *qāḍī-īshān*s of Shāhābād the death (*mawt*) of his father and the relinquishment of his claim. This is the event (*ṣūrat-i wāqiᶜa*) that was recorded on 27 Shaᶜbān 1336 [7 June 1918] and was sent to your office.[92]

The following rescript exemplifies how difficult it is to disambiguate the law applied by the governor from the law followed by the *qāḍī*s, both referred to as *sharīᶜa*. When her husband was unable to consummate marriage due to sexual impotence, a woman declared her intent to divorce him, a decision that led to a violent altercation between the spouses' families. The bride's father submitted a petition to the royal court and filed a claim for battery and injury. The office of the *yasāwūlbāshī* instructed the governor (*ḥakīm*) to deal with the conflict. The latter did so, as the text emphasises, by hearing the case 'according to Islamic law'. In the absence of additional empirical information, it is unclear what the governor meant by this. He certainly urged the parties to reach a settlement, as we have seen governors do in other cases. During the hearing, however, the respondents must have manifested dissatisfaction with the stipulations proposed by the governor and denied the claim. The established procedure in such cases required that the governor transfer the case to the *qāḍī*s. Things seem, however, not to have changed substantially with the involvement of the judges. Unhappy with the outcome, the husband declared his intention to file a counter-claim with the royal court. This course of action left the governor no choice but to send the parties to Khiva.

Let it be known to the office of the *yasāwulbāshī*, refuge of the vizierate and repository of nobleness, our lord, that a certain Qurbān Dūrdī Qarādāshlī had appealed to the royal court (*darbār-i ᶜālīlārīgha ᶜarḍ ītib*) and was entrusted with an instruction (*nishāna*); his daughter Bāyrām Sulṭān decided to divorce (*āyirmāqchī*) her husband (*kuyuv*)[93] due to the latter's failure to consummate the marriage (*martnīng sharīᶜat īshīgā yārāmāghān sabablī*).[94] [As a result,] Ārtūq Nīyāz, Ūrāḍ Nīyāz, Mullā Jūmᶜa, ᶜĀshīr, and Khwājam Birdī

> beat (*ūrūb*) Qurbān Dūrdī's daughter, pulled her hair, and caused bodily harm (*jarāhatdār ītib*). On this account, the claim (*daᶜwā*) of the aforementioned individuals was heard according to *sharīᶜa*. Because [the parties] did not reach an agreement (*yutūshmagāndīn kiyīn*), I transferred [the case] to the judges (*sharīᶜatgha qūshūb*). However, when the groom appeared before them (*kuyuv ṭarafī sharīᶜatgha bārgānda*), they announced that they would go to the royal court (*dargah-i ᶜālīgha bārūrman*). For this reason, I have summoned the aforementioned [individuals] and dispatched them to your office. This petition (*ᶜariḍa*) was registered on 19 Dhū l-Ḥijja 1334 [17 October 1916].[95]

This text sheds light on the culture of accountability that informed the production of such rescripts. The governor's main concern was to inform the royal court that he and his subordinates, that is, the *qāḍī*s, had done everything in their power to settle the dispute. Indeed, the fact that the parties would turn once again to the royal court meant that the governor had failed to comply with the instructions that he had received from the office of the *yasāwulbāshī*. His mentioning that he had heard the case according to *sharīᶜa* may well have been a rhetorical move to claim that he had acted lawfully, that is, without making use of discretionary powers.

Conclusion

The *ᶜarḍ-dād* system had both practical and symbolic significance. The latter manifested itself in the ritualisation of the ceremony, which reflected the khan's willingness to delve into the concerns and needs of his subjects and to administer justice. For subjects throughout the khanate, this procedure was a unique opportunity to meet their ruler, convey their complaints to him personally and receive assistance in the resolution of their disputes. It is not by accident that Lykoshin characterises the procedure as 'a ceremony of singular service to the people, which gave the khan the reputation of being available to each of his subjects, personally listening to their complaints and restoring justice through his orders and decisions'.[96] The proximity of the Qonghrat subjects to the authorities in Khiva was not illusory but real. The Russian Turkologist Alexander Samoilovich, on a mission to Central Asia in 1906 and 1907, noted that 'the Khivan khan administers his people directly: every day he holds trials and dispenses justice, and every Khivan [subject] can attend his audience, unlike the Bukharan emir, who keeps himself far removed from his subjects behind a wall of officials and paperwork'.[97]

The motivations that prompted the populace to file their claims with the royal court varied considerably. They usually reflected the widely shared perception that agencies in Khiva were more powerful than provincial officeholders, such as *qāḍī*s, and that the royal court's sanctioning of a ruling would ensure its execution. This state of affairs manifested itself well beyond the borders of the Khanate. Qonghrat officials, for example, solved conflicts among the Qazaqs living in the Ust Yurt plateau and on the banks of the Uil river, who were formally Russian imperial subjects.[98]

To be sure, in Khorezm, as elsewhere in the Islamicate world, most claims were heard and resolved informally. The subject of this essay – the royal court's role in the resolution of conflicts – accounts for only a fraction of what occurred in villages and provinces, away from Khiva, where local notables and elders regularly settled disputes. Many such conflicts that never made it to Khiva were resolved, instead, by provincial governors who had the power 'to adjudicate small cases conclusively', but also 'to arrest criminals', 'deprive them of their freedom' and 'carry out physical punishments in cases involving ordinary people'.[99]

Deeds of acquittal (*ibrāʾ*) and amicable settlement (*ṣulḥ*) notarised by *qāḍī*s represent the lion's share of legal documents that surface today from private collections in Khorezm.[100] Such deeds of acquittal probably reflect the resolution of conflicts that first occurred informally, without the aid of a governor. Nor do we have evidence that *qāḍī*s participated in the achievement of such settlements. Indeed, it is likely that *qāḍī*s acted in these cases as mere notaries who certified settlements that had taken place prior to their crafting the deeds of acquittal. There is also, of course, the possibility that such amicable settlements were produced to secure the rights of a number of individuals who in fact never took legal action against one another. To say that informal settlements were integral to the local legal 'system' is to state the obvious. However, all these observations do not detract from the argument that power relations among state officials mattered. *Qāḍī*s were subordinate to representatives of the royal court, serving as deputies for Khivan officialdom. As noted above, parties would not bring their affairs to a judge unless they had agreed previously to have their dispute settled by a *qāḍī*, most probably in the hope of avoiding the expenses associated with an appeal to the royal court.[101] Equally, *qāḍī*s would more often than not hear cases only when ordered to do so by a representative of the royal court. Consider the following example. On 14 November 1916 Aman Kildī Dīwānbīgī, a prominent official in Khiva under the rule of Isfandiyār Khān, wrote to a *qāḍī* and instructed him to forgive the debts of a certain Bīrdī Shakūr, who had passed away. The *qāḍī* was ordered to send his own trustee (*amīn*), together with one Bābājān, the guard of Dawlat Bīk Īshīk Āqāsī, to a locality called Ālāchalī, to estimate the inheritance of the debtor and to sell his possessions in the presence of the creditors. Then, the trustee and the guard would divide the money among the creditors according to Islamic law (*sharīᶜat bīrlān*). Creditors who were also Russian subjects would be paid before Khivan subjects so that only the remaining sum would be divided among locals. Aman Kildī Dīwānbīgī concluded his order by requesting that the *qāḍī* report to him about the results of the division (*ākhīrīnī mūndā maᶜlūm ītmāklārī ūchūn*).[102] This and similar cases provide one possible clue to understanding how *qāḍī*s served in the Khivan judicial system and operated despite their structural lack of power.

In 1871 a Cossack serving the Russian imperial authorities in Orenburg, who was given the task of interrogating Khivan slaves released from captivity during 1869 and 1870, reported, 'Khivan subjects report to him [the khan] about everything happening during the day, [and bother him with] every trifle, every [insignificant] case.'[103] Qonghrat officials arguably devoted so much attention to the mundane affairs of their subjects because the *ᶜarḍ-dād* offered the central government the opportunity to monitor local affairs in a regular fashion and thus to make timely adjustments in response to changing social circumstances. Justice mattered to Qonghrat officials because it provided the state with knowledge about the society over which it ruled, while at the same time allowing the ruling dynasty to exploit fissures within local society and build trust. Equally, the Khivan legal system allowed subjects to speak and be heard. Justice was contingent on participation.

Notes

1. This is a revised and expanded version of an article published under the same tile in *Islamic Law and Society* 24:1–2 (2017), pp. 20–60. We are grateful to Brill for permission to reprint sections of it.
2. *Puteshestvie v Turkmeniiu i Khivu v 1819 I 1820 godakh gvardeiskogo general'nogo shtaba kapitana Nikolaia Murav'eva, poslannogo v sii strany dlia peregovorov* (Moscow: Tipografiia Avgusta Semena, 1822), part 2, p. 35.
3. J. Schacht, *Introduction to Islamic Law* (Oxford: Clarendon Press, 1965), pp. 188–98; W. B. Hallaq, *The Origins and the Evolution of Islamic Law* (Cambridge: Cambridge University Press, 2005), passim; M. Khalid Masud, R. Peters and D. Powers, 'Introduction', in M. Khalid Masud, R. Peters and D. Powers, (eds), *Dispensing Justice in Islam: Qadis and their Judgements* (Leiden: Brill, 2006), pp. 1-44. A notable exception to this trend is the work of M. Tillier. See, for example, his 'Judicial Authority and *Qāḍī*s' Autonomy under the Abbasids', *Al-Masaq: Journal of the Medieval Mediterranean* 26:2 (2014), pp. 119–31.
4. On arbitrators, see A. Othman, '"And Amicable Settlement Is Best": *Ṣulḥ*

and Dispute Resolution in Islamic Law', *Arab Law Quarterly* 21 (2007), pp. 64–90; W. B. Hallaq, *Sharīʿa: Theory, Practice, Transformations* (Cambridge: Cambridge University Press, 2009), pp. 159–64.

5. I. Tamdoğan, '*Ṣulḥ* and the 18th Century Ottoman Courts of Üsküdar and Adana', *Islamic Law and Society* 15:1 (2008), pp. 55–83.
6. On this view, see F. Pirie, *The Anthropology of Law* (Oxford: Oxford University Press, 2013), pp. 97–103.
7. On *maẓālim*, see J. S. Nielsen, *Secular Justice in an Islamic State: Maẓālim under the Baḥrī Mamlūks, 662/1264–789/1387* (Leiden: Brill, 1985), p. 9. On the role of the state in conflict resolution in the Ottoman period, see Y. Ben-Bassat, *Petitioning the Sultan: Protesters and Justice in Late Ottoman Palestine* (London: I. B. Tauris, 2013), pp. 24–8.
8. W. B. Hallaq, *Sharīʿa: Theory, Practice, Transformations*, pp. 362–3.
9. Y. Rapoport, 'Royal Justice and Religious Law: *Siyāsah* and *Sharīʿah* under the Mamluks', *Mamluk Studies Review* 16 (2012), p. 74.
10. G. Burak, 'The Second Formation of Islamic Law: The Post-Mongol Context of the Ottoman Adoption of a School of Law', *Comparative Studies in Society and History* 55:3 (2013), pp. 579–602.
11. S. Ayoub, '"The Sulṭān Says": State Authority in the Late Ḥanafī Tradition', *Islamic Law and Society* 23:4 (2016), pp. 239–78.
12. J. Baldwin, 'Petitioning the Sultan in Ottoman Egypt', *Bulletin of the School of Oriental and African Studies* 75 (2012), p. 507.
13. Ibid., p. 508.
14. *Sayyāhat-nāma-yi Sayyid Aḥmad Khwāja*, MS Tashkent, al-Beruni Institute of Oriental Studies of the Academy of Sciences of Uzbekistan, inv. no. 4292, fols 7b–12b.
15. M. Dewhurst Lewis, *Divided Rule: Sovereignty and Empire in French Tunisia, 1881–1938* (Berkeley: University of California Press, 2014), p. 1.
16. S. Becker, *Russia's Protectorates in Central Asia: Bukhara and Khiva, 1865–1924* (Cambridge, MA: Harvard University Press, 1968), pp. 13–20. Khivan raids into the Kazakh Steppe prompted a Russian military expedition against the Khivan Khanate in the winter of 1839, under the command of General Perovskii. The expedition failed miserably. A. Morrison, 'Twin Imperial Disasters. The Invasions of Khiva and Afghanistan in the Russian and British Official Mind', *Modern Asian Studies* 48:1 (2014), pp. 253–300. The formation of a discourse on the abolition of the Central Asian slave trade was instrumental in building a consensus in Russia against the Khanate of Khiva. See A. Matveev, 'Perceptions of Central Asia by Russian Society: The Conquest of Khiva as Represented by Russian Periodicals', in B. Eschment and H. Herder (eds), *Looking at the Coloniser: Cross-Cultural Perceptions in Central Asia and the Caucasus, Bengal, and Related Areas* (Würzburg: Ergon, 2004), p. 290.
17. For an English translation of the Gandumian Peace Treaty, see S. Becker, *Russia's Protectorates*, pp. 316–18.

18. A. Shioya, 'Who Should Manage the Water of the Amu-Darya? Controversy over Irrigation Concessions between Russia and Khiva, 1913–1914', in P. Sartori (ed.), in *Explorations in the Social History of Modern Central Asia (19th–20th Centuries)* (Leiden: Brill, 2013), pp. 111–36.
19. K. Mann and R. Roberts, 'Slave Voices in African Colonial Courts: Sources and Methods', in A. Bellagamba, S. E. Green and M. A. Klein (eds), *African Voices of Slavery and the Slave Trade, vol. 2: Essays on Sources and Methods* (Cambridge: Cambridge University Press, 2016), p. 134.
20. M. Dewhurst Lewis, *Divided Rule*, p. 8.
21. *O sudebnoi iurisdiktsii v Khivinskom khanstve*, 1906, TsGARuz, f. I–2, op. 1, d. 205, ll. 3–82 ob. (TsGARUz = Tsentral'nyi Gosudarstvennyi Arkhiv Respubliki Uzbekistan), Central State Archive of the Republic of Uzbekistan. Abbreviations used in references to Russian archives: f. (fond), holding; op. (opis'), inventory; d. (delo), file; l. (list), sheet; ob. (oborot), verso.
22. For other examples of the formalisation of chancery practices, see P. Sartori, 'Murder in Manghishlaq: Notes on an Instance of Application of Qazaq Customary Law in Khiva (1895)', *Der Islam* 88:2 (2012), pp. 217–57.
23. P. Sartori, *Visions of Justice:* Sharīᶜa *and Cultural Change in Russian Central Asia*, passim.
24. M. Dickson, 'Uzbek Dynastic Theory in the Sixteenth Century', in *Trudy XXV Mezhdunarodnogo Kongressa Vostokovedov* (Moscow: Izdatel'stvo Vostochnoi Literatury, 1960), pp. 208–16.
25. Y. Bregel, 'Tribal Tradition and Dynastic History: The Early Rulers of the Qongrats According to Munis', *Asian and African Studies* 16:3 (1982), p. 396.
26. A forceful critique against the ostensible Turko-Mongol traditions that supposedly shaped notions of sovereignty in early modern South Asia has been articulated by A. Anooshahr, 'On the Imperial Discourse of the Delhi Sultanate and Early Mughal India', *Journal of Persianate Studies* 7:2 (2014), pp. 157–76.
27. Anonymous, 'Turkmeniia i Khiva', *Vsemirnyi puteshestvennik* 8 (1870), p. 120.
28. The claimant is called *ᶜarḍ-dār* in Persian and *ᶜarḍchī* in Chaghatay.
29. On news reports (*wāqiᶜa-nawīsī*) and the ensuing compositional genre, see P. Sartori, 'Seeing Like a Khanate: On Archives, Cultures of Documentation, and Nineteenth-Century Khvārazm', *Journal of Persianate Studies* 9:2 (2016), pp. 228–57.
30. J. S. Nielsen, *Secular Justice in an Islamic State*, p. 9. The *maẓālim* courts did not only operate as a court of second instance for cases of judicial misconduct. See C. Müller, '*Maẓālim* Jurisdictions at the Umayyad Court of Córdoba (Eighth-Eleventh Centuries CE)', in A. Fuess and J.-P. Hartung (eds), *Court Cultures in the Muslim World: Seventh to Nineteenth Centuries* (London and New York: Routledge, 2011), pp. 93–104.

31. 'The subjects came and submitted their grievances to the khan orally' (*khalqlār kīlīb khāngha ᶜarḍīnī āghzākī sūzlāb*), ᶜAbdullah Bāltayif, *Khīwa-da Tāsh ḥawlī binā-sīning tāpāgrafiyasī*, Khiva 1950, MS Tashkent, al-Beruni Institute of Oriental Manuscripts, inv. no. 9321, fol. 24a; 'all the civil and criminal cases are referred to him directly . . . and are heard always orally' (*vse dela tiazhbennye i ugolovnye postupaiut priamo k nemu [khanu], . . . i proizvodiatsia vsegda slovesno*), G. I. Danilevskii, 'Opisanie Khivinskogo khanstva', *Zapiski Russkogo Geograficheskogo Obshchestva* V (1851), p. 134. Danilevskii was a Russian envoy to Khiva in 1842.
32. Y. Ben-Bassat, *Petitioning the Sultan*, pp. 24–8; M. Alam and S. Subrahmanyam (eds), *Writing the Mughal World: Studies on Culture and Politics* (New York: Columbia University Press, 2012), p. 160.
33. For a preliminary attempt to assess the scope of the Archive of Khiva compared to the archives of other Central Asian polities, see P. Sartori, 'On Khorezmian Connectivity: Two or Three Things I Know about It', *Journal of Persianate Studies* 9:2 (2016), pp. 133–57.
34. A. K. S. Lambton, 'Justice in the Medieval Persian Theory of Government', *Studia Islamica* 5 (1956), pp. 91–119; A. K. S. Lambton, 'Islamic Mirror for Princes', in *Atti del covegno internazionale sul tema, La Persia nel Medioevo (Roma, 31 marzo–5 aprile 1970)* (Rome: Accademia Nazionale dei Lincei, 1971), pp. 419–42; M. E. Subtelny, 'A Late Medieval Persian Summa on Ethics: Kashifi's *Akhlāq-i Muḥsinī*', *Iranian Studies* 36:4 (2003), pp. 601–14.
35. Shir Muhammad Mirab Munis and Muhammad Riza Mirab Agahi, *Firdaws al-iqbal: History of Khorezm*, trans. Y. Bregel (Leiden and Boston: Brill, 1999), pp. 423, 457.
36. ᶜAbdullah Bāltayif, *Khīwa-da Tāsh ḥawlī binā-sīning tāpāgrafiyasī*, Khiva 1950, BCOM, inv. no. 9321, fol. 3b, 5b.
37. *Awwal waqtdā ᶜarḍ sūrāsh ūchūn qīlinādūrghān ᶜimāratnī bāshlādī. Khīwanī pāytakhtī būlghān kuhna arīk awwalghī khānlārdīn qālghān īdāra būlghānī ūchūn būl jāy bitgāncha shūl kuhna arīkda ᶜarḍ-dād sūrāb ūltūrdī 1839-nchī mīlādīdīn kiyin shūl bināgha qūshūb ᶜarḍ-khāna binālārnī ham bāshlāb āltī yil īchindā ānī ham bitkāzdī 1254nchī hijrī yilindā khān ūyindā ūltūrghān waqtdā khalqnīng ᶜarḍlārīnī shūl banā qīlghān ᶜarḍ-khānadā sūrāshnī dawām qīldīrdī*; ibid., fol. 10a.
38. *Khukm-nama khivinskogo khana Said Mukhamada Bakhadurkhana prikazyvaiushchii beku Gulam Bi vernut' postradavshemu Iusupu ego zhenu, v sluchae nesoglasiia oboim iavit'sia v khanskii dvor dlia razbora étogo dela (1275/1858)*, TsGARUz, f. I–125, op. 2, d. 23, l. 1.
39. *Khukm-nama khivinskogo khana Said Mukhamada Bakhadurkhana povelevaiushchi poddannomu khana Abdi iavit'sia v khanskii dvorets vmeste s postradavshchim Avad Muradom, pretenduiushchim na krovnuiu mest' (1275/1858)*, TsGARUz, f. I–125, op. 1, d. 24, l. 1.

40. Vámbéry was in Khiva under the rule of Sayyid Muhammad Khan (r. 1856–64).
41. A. Vambery, *Puteshestvie po Srednei Azii*, 2nd edn (Moscow: Izdanie A. I. Mamontova 1874), pp. 112–13. The English version of his travelogue differs substantially from the Russian. See A. Vámbéry, *Arminius Vámbéry: His Life and Adventures*, 3rd edn (London: T. Fisher Unwin, 1884), pp. 200–1.
42. Seid-Mukhamed-Rakhim, 'Khivinskii khan, i ego priblizhennye', *Turkestanskii Sbornik* 42 (St Petersburg: Tipografiia Ministerstva Putei Soobshcheniia, 1872), p. 120.
43. Muḥammad Yūsuf Bayānī, *Shajara-yi Turk-i Khwārazmī*, MS Tashkent, al-Beruni Institute of Oriental Manuscripts, inv. no. 9596, fol. 298a.
44. Bobojon Tarroh Khodim, *Khorazm shoira va navozandalari*, eds A. Otamurodova and O. Abdurahimov (Tashkent: Tafakkur Qanoti, 2011), p. 30. Tarrāh was a court poet in the service of Muḥammad Raḥīm Khān II. According to the author, he was tasked by the sovereign with keeping a record of, among other things, the khanate's poets and writers (*shoir*) and their creative works. As a result, he was in close contact not only with court literary circles but also with many prominent officials who regarded the composition of poetry as an effective way to make a successful career at court. From 1965 to 1967, Tarrāh compiled an anthology of thirty-one court poets, along with his personal recollections. The first abridged edition of the text was published in 1994 as *Khorazm navozandalari. XIX asr okhiri-XX boshlarida Sayid Muhammad Rahimkhoni soniy davrida yashagan shoirlar haqida esdaliklar* (Tashkent: Ghafur Ghulom Nomindagi Adabiyot va San'at Nashriyoti, 1994).
45. *xalqni arz-dodiga chiqishga yaramas bo'ldi*, ibid., 30.
46. According to Tarrāh, one of the khan's closest and highest dignitaries, a certain Khudāyār Qūshbigī, justified his refusal to take over judicial powers in this manner: 'You have read history; it is not proper [for the ruler] during his lifetime to devolve his authority (*ikhtiyār*) to his heir.' Ibid.
47. *Khorazm shoira va navozandalari*, p. 30.
48. Nil Sergeevich Lykoshin (1860–1922) was an official of the Russian colonial administration in Turkestan as well as an Orientalist. He began his career in Turkestan in 1889 as a non-commissioned officer, advanced through the hierarchy, and, from 1914 to 1917, served as military governor of Samarkand District (*oblast'*) with the rank of major general. From 1912 to 1914 he served as head of the Amu Darya Department and was closely involved in relations with the Khivan administration on a wide range of issues. He was famous for his research on the history, culture and customs of Central Asia. On Lykoshin, see A. Morrison, 'Sufism, Pan-Islamism and Information Panic: Nil Sergeevich Lykoshin and the Aftermath of the Andijan Uprising', *Past and Present* 214:1 (2012), pp. 255–314.
49. N. Lykoshin, *Zapiska Nachal'nika Amu-Dar'inskogo otdela Polkovnika*

Lykoshina o sovremennom sostoianii Khivinskogo khanstva, 1912 god. TsGA RUz f. I-2, op. 1, d. 314, ll. 12–58.

50. B. Kazakov, *Bukharan Documents: The Collection in the District Library, Bukhara*, trans. J. Paul (Berlin: Klaus Schwarz, 2001), p. 44. See also D. Iu Iusupova and R. P. Dzhalilova (eds), *Sobranie vostochnykh rukopisei AN RUz. Istoriia* (Tashkent: Fan, 1998), pp. 236–7.
51. Babadzhan Safarov, *Khwārazm ta°rīkhī (1864–1934)*, MS Tashkent, al-Beruni Institute of Oriental Manuscripts, inv. no. 10231.
52. As Lykoshin acknowledges, he was an unintentional witness to this ceremony because the windows of the embassy premises at the Khivan khan's residence, where the Russian official was posted, looked out directly onto the outer courtyard of the palace, where the *ᶜarḍ-dād* took place. N. Lykoshin, *Zapiska*, ll. 15–16.
53. A *maḥram* was a proxy for the khan who carried out his personal instructions. According to Tarrāh, among the numerous *maḥrams* who served at court, a special position was occupied by the so-called *ᶜarḍ-khāna maḥramlarī*, who were responsible for preparing the reception room for the daily ceremony and were at the khan's disposal for its duration. See *Xorazm shoir va navozandalari*, p. 30.
54. N. Lykoshin, *Zapiska*, ll. 15–16 ob.
55. For example, Safarov notes that the administrative apparatus of the khanate consisted largely of illiterate persons appointed to their positions through patronage or bribes. See Babadzhan Safarov, *Khwārazm ta°rīkhī (1864–1934)*, MS Tashkent, al-Beruni Institute of Oriental Manuscripts, inv. no. 10231, fols 12–13.
56. N. Lykoshin, *Zapiska*, l. 18.
57. Ibid.
58. Ḥasan-Murād Laffasī, *Gulshan-i saᶜādat*, MS Tashkent, al-Beruni Institute of Oriental Manuscripts, inv. no. 7797, fols 8a–8b, 17b, 80b, 83b.
59. One such circumstance, for example, occurred in 1916, when Isfandiyār Khān travelled, with all of his officials, to Tash-Ḥawuz for a meeting with Lieutenant General A. Galkin, governor general of Sir Darya Oblast, after the latter had suppressed a large Turkmen uprising. At that time, the Khivan *qāḍī* Dāmullā Khudāybirgān Ākhund remained in Khiva in order to hear the claims of the public; ibid., fol. 64a.
60. N. Lykoshin, *Zapiska*, ll. 15–16 ob.
61. Babadzhan Safarov, *Khwārazm ta°rīkhī (1864–1934)*, fol. 18.
62. 'To everyone who entered with a petition, the *yasaulbashi* loudly posed the question, 'what is your petition (*arzing nimadur*)?'' M. Y. Yuldoshev, *Khiva khonligida feudal yer egaligi va davlat tuzilishi* (Tashkent: O'zbekiston SSR Davlat Nashriyoti, 1959), p. 283 n. 6.
63. A. L. Kun, *Ocherk istorii zaselenia Khivinskogo khanstva s drevnikh vremen, sostav ego sovremennogo naseleniia, administratsiia i goroda*

khanstva, 1873, Institute of Oriental Manuscripts, St Petersburg, Arkhiv Vostokovedov, f. 33, d. 8, l. 41 ob.

64. *Khorazm shoir va navozandalari*, p. 30; Babadzhan Safarov, *Khwārazm taʾrīkhī (1864–1934)*, fol. 21.
65. See, for example, TsGARUz, f. I–125, op.2, d.100. The register's header reads, 'Register of *yasauls* assigned to petitioners' complaints in the month of Muharram 1333 AH [November 1914]'.
66. A. L. Kun, *Ocherk istorii zaselenia Khivinskogo khanstva s drevnikh vremen, sostav ego sovremennogo naseleniia, administratsiia i goroda khanstva*, 1873, Institute of Oriental Manuscripts, St Petersburg, Arkhiv vostokovedov, f. 33, d. 13, l. 41ob. According to Gregor von Helmersen, the office of the *yasāwul* generated a substantial amount of money and therefore many attempted to be appointed to such a position. See his 'Izvestiia o Khive, Bukhare, Kokande i severo-zapadnoi chasti Kitaiskogo gosudarstva', *Istoriia Kazakhstana v zapadnykh istochnikakh XII–XX vv*, 10 vols (Almaty: Dayk Press, 2006), vol. 5, p. 36.
67. The existence of offices with separate premises at the disposal of the khanate's highest officials is mentioned in Vámbéry's account. During his stay in Khiva, he repeatedly had contact with the *mihtar*, who, in his words, 'together with his chancellery occupied one of the interior houses, just outside the entrance to the khan's palace'; see *Puteshchestvie po Srednei Azii*, p. 107. It follows that a dedicated space in the palace was probably assigned to the *yasāwulbāshī*.
68. See, for instance, A. Urunbaev et al. (eds), *Katalog khivinskikh kaziiskikh dokumentov XIX–nachala XX vv* (Tashkent and Kyoto: Izdatel'stvo Mezhdunarodnogo Institut po Izucheniiu Iazykov i Mira Kiotskogo Universiteta po Izucheniiu Zarubezhnykh Stran, 2001), doc. no. 205. There are several misinterpretations in the description of the document in question: for example, the term *ṣaghīr* is rendered as 'orphan' rather than 'minor'; cf. MS Tashkent, al-Beruni Institute of Oriental Manuscripts, Ashapberova Akliia, papka (folder) 3, unnumbered folio [5].
69. On the location of Manāq, see Shir Muhammad Mirab Munis and Muhammad Riza Mirab Agahi, *Firdaws al-iqbal: History of Khorezm*, p. 564, n. 277.
70. TsGARUz, I–125, op. 2, d. 633, l. 1–1 ob. The document is stamped with the seal of Shaykh Naẓar Yasāwulbāshī b. Muḥammad Murād Dīwānbīgī.
71. Apparently, the mullah needed the permission of an official (usually a *qāḍī*) to perform the marriage. *Katalog khivinskikh kaziiskikh dokumentov XIX–nachala XX vv*, doc. no. 842.
72. N. P. Lobacheva, 'K istorii slozheniia instituta svadebnoi obriadnosti (na primere kompleksov svadebnykh obychaev i obriadov narodov Srednei Azii i Kazakhstana)', in G. P. Snesarev (ed.), *Sem'ia i semeinye obriady u narodov Srednei Azii i Kazakhstana* (Moscow: Nauka, 1978), pp. 144–75, at p. 144. Lobacheva also suggests that settled Uzbeks (among whom we

count the population of Khorezm) usually agreed on the stipulations of the customary dowry before the engagement; ibid., p. 173.

73. S. N. Abašin, 'Qalïm und mahr in Mittelasien: Die moderne Praxis und die Debatten über Scharia und Adat', in M. Kemper and M. Reinkowski (eds), *Rechtspluralismus in der Islamischen Welt: Gewohnheitsrecht zwischen Staat und Gesellschaft* (Berlin and New York: de Gruyter, 2005), pp. 195–207.
74. Apparently, our sources do not distinguish between Islamic and customary dower, and we are led to infer that, in Khivan bureaucratese, *qālīng* was understood as, and used as a synonym of, *mahr*. This evidence supports the view expressed in Abashin. *Sharīʿa* court documents from Khorezm used, instead, only the term *mahr* in referring to dower: *Katalog khivinskikh kaziiskikh dokumentov XIX–nachala XX vv*, passim.
75. *EI*[2], s.v. 'Mahr' (O. Spies).
76. A. Layish, Sharīʿa *and Custom in Libyan Tribal Society. An Annotated Translation of Decisions from the* Sharīʿa *Courts of Adjābiya and Kufra* (Leiden: Brill, 2005), doc. 1; *Katalog khivinskikh kaziiskikh dokumentov XIX–nachala XX vv*, doc. no. 1076. In the description of the legal opinion, the dower is referred to as *kalym* (Russ. for *qālīng*); the term does not occur in the original text. See also TsGARUz, f. I–125, op. 1, d. 495, l. 9.
77. *Katalog khvinskikh kaziiskikh dokumentov XIX-nachala XX vv*, doc no. 1076.
78. Mukhamedjan Yo'ldoshev writes that, in the Khanate of Khiva, the term *says* means 'stable boy'; see M. Y. Yo'ldoshev, *Khiva khonligida*, p. 234. Babajan Safarov claims that, in Khiva, it denoted instead an office at the royal court. He notes that there were two *says* who commanded forty-five subordinates who were charged with the care of the Khan's stables; see Babadzhan Safarov, *Khwārazm taʾrīkhī*, fol. 15.
79. TsGARUz, f. I–125, op. 1, d. 498, l. 42.
80. The Choudurs were a group of Turkmens who lived in the Khorezmian oasis, most of them in the Pārsū district (N. Lykoshin, *Zapiska*: l. 24 ob.); smaller groups lived in the districts of Tahsauz, Shahabad and Ambar-Kala, see Y. Bregel', *Khorezmskie turkmeny v XIX veke* (Moscow: Nauka, 1961), p. 30.
81. TsGARUz, f. I–125, op. 1, d. 498, l. 94.
82. TsGARUz, I–125, op. 2, d. 633, l. 53–53 ob.
83. The Qūshbigī Yāf canal was built in 1857 by Ḥasan Murād Qūshbigī; see Ia. Guliamov, *Istoriia orosheniia Khorezma s drevneishikh vremen do nashikh dnei* (Tashkent: Izdatel'stvo akademii Nauk Uzbekskoi SSR, 1957), p. 231. Mirzā ʿAbd al-Raḥmān, a local scribe who assisted the Orientalist Alexander Kuhn in Khorezm at the time of the Russian conquest (1873), lists the Qūshbigī Yāf as one of the canals dug during the reign of Muḥammad Amīn Khān (1845–55), noting that it flows south of Urgench, *Dnevnik Mirzy Abdurakhmana, vedennyi vo vremia Khivinskogo pokhoda*,

Institute of Oriental Manuscripts, St Petersburg, Arkhiv Vostokovedov, f. 33 op. 1, d. 221, ll. 24–9. On Alexander Kun and Mirzā ᶜAbd al-Raḥmām, see O. Yastrebova and A. Azad, 'Reflections on an Orientalist: Alexander Kuhn (1840–88), the Man and His Legacy', *Iranian Studies* 48:5 (2015), pp. 675–94.

84. Y. Bregel, *An Historical Atlas of Central Asia* (Leiden and Boston: Brill, 2003), p. 67, map 33. On the Amu Darya and its waters breaching into the Lavzan in the nineteenth century, see Ia. Guliamov, *Istoriia orosheniia*, pp. 218, 292; A. Shioya, 'Irrigation Policy of the Khanate of Khiva regarding the Lawzan Canal. 1. 1830–1873', *Area Studies Tsukuba* 32 (2011), p. 116.
85. See Ia. Guliamov, *Istoriia orosheniia*, p. 261; Shir Muhammad Mirab Munis and Muhammad Riza Mirab Agahi, *Firdaws al-iqbāl*, p. 609, n. 607.
86. The involvement of *qāḍī*s usually led to a settlement (*ṣulḥ*), the stipulations of which were determined by local notables (*āqsāqāls*/*kadkhudā*s), giving ample room for the specifics of local circumstances, established practices and customary notions of justice.
87. In Khorezm, *sū* (lit. 'water') signifies a measure used to quantify a water-share. According to Iakh'ia Guliamov, the Qonghrats introduced standard irrigation units. They established that one *sū* was the quantity of water necessary to irrigate ten *ṭanāb* of land, and they allocated ten *sū* (called *jabdī*) to a community of landholders. Ia. Guliamov, *Istoriia orosheniia*, p. 295. The Qonghrat bureaucracy recorded (and updated) the allocation of water shares to communities. See TsGARUz, f. I–125, op. 2, d. 508 and d. 510, l. 4 (*ābkhūr yāflār*).
88. In the text, *āriḍa,* instead of *ᶜarīḍa,* for 'appeal'.
89. TsGARUz, f. I–125, op. 1, d. 498, l. 44.
90. We here draw on Y. Rapoport, 'Royal Justice and Religious Law: *Siyāsah* and *Sharīᶜah* under the Mamluks', p. 75.
91. The town of Shāhābād (Shavat) is located on the left bank of the middle section of the canal bearing the same name: A. L. Kun, *Ocherk istorii*, fol. 53; M. I. Ivanin, *Khiva i reka Amu-Daria* (St Petersburg: Tipografiia Tovarishchestva 'Obshchestvennaia Pol'za', 1873), p. 9; Shir Muhammad Mirab Munis and Muhammad Riza Mirab Agahi, *Firdaws al-iqbāl*, p. 564, n. 278. In the eighteenth century, Shāhābād was one of the Besh Qal'a ('Five Cities'), together with Khazarasp, Khanqa, Urgench and Kyat. The name Besh Qal'a is used in non-contemporary sources to refer to southern Khorezm. Ia. Guliamov, *Istoriia oroshcheniia*, p. 199; Shir Muhammad Mirab Munis and Muhammad Riza Mirab Agahi, *Firdaws al-iqbāl*, p. 573, n. 318.
92. TsGARUz, f. I–125, op. 1, d. 498, l. 86.
93. Uzbek *kuyov* means both 'groom' and 'son-in-law'. This word choice makes perfect sense here as it is the bride's father who recounts the events in this part of the narrative.

94. This phrase is clearly a circumlocution referring to sexual impotence. The term *mart* may well be a phonetic rendering of the word *mard* (male, masculine). The text reads literally, 'due to the latter's failure to do the legal thing that a man does'; cf. A. Layish, *Sharīʿa and Custom*, p. 37.
95. TsGARUz, f. I–125, op. 1, d. 498, l. 56–56 ob. The document is stamped with the seal of Muḥammad Karīm Yūzbāshī b. Ismāʿil.
96. N. Lykoshin, *Zapiska*, ll. 15–15 ob.
97. A. Samoilovich, *Opisanie rukopisei knig, khraniashchikhsia v Khivinskikh pridvornykh knigokhranilishchakh i knigopechatniakh*, MS St Petersburg, Russian National Library, fol. 671, d. 145, l. 1.
98. M. A. Terent'ev, *Istoriia zavoevaniia Srednei Azii s kartami i planami*, 4 vols (St Petersburg, 1906), vol. I, p. 179.
99. V. A. Girshfel'd and A. S. Galkin, *Voenno-statisticheskoe opisanie Khivinskogo khanstva* (Tashkent: Tipografia Shtaba Turkestanskogo Voennogo Okruga, 1903), part 2, p. 23.
100. *Katalog Khivinskikh kaziiskikh dokumentov XIX–nachala XX vv.*; E. Karimov, *Regesty kaziiskikh dokumentov i khanskikh iarlikov Khivinskogo khanstva XVII–nachala XX v* (Tashkent: Fan, 2007).
101. TsGARUz, f. I–125, op. 2, d. 606, l. 8.
102. TsGARUz, f. I–125, op. 1, d. 509, l. 145.
103. Esaul Lobasevych, 'Pokazaniia russkikh plennykh, byvshikh v Khive, dannoe 16 iunia Orenburgskomu general-gubernatoru (v 1869–1870)', in *Turkestanskii Sbornik* (St Petersburg: Tipografiia Ministerstva Putei Soobsheniia (A. Benke), 1871), vol. 42, p. 88.

Index

Abaq Kereys, 185, 204n9
Abay Qŭnanbayŭlï, 198
ᶜAbd al-Jalīl-khwāja, 190
ᶜAbdassalām bin Ḥasan, 42
Äbdïsadïq-ishan, 199
ᶜAbduh, Muḥammad, 143, 259, 265–6
ᶜAbdulkhāliq qizī, Dūshanbika, 173–4
ᶜAbdulsattārov (ākhūnd), 173
Abïlay, 189, 193, 195
abıstay, 122–4, 126–7, 131, 133, 135, 139, 144, 146
Abu Bakr al-ᶜAimakī, 248
Abū Ḥanīfa (Imām-i Aᶜẓam), 3, 52, 94–5, 115, 241–2, 262, 311–12, 316
Abū Yūsuf, 242, 262, 311–12
Achinsk, 135
adāʾ, 283, 286–7
adabiyyāt, 2
Adil'bekov, Badawi-qadi, 269
Adygea, Republic of, 291
Africa, 87
Aḥmad b. Ḥanbal, 241
Aḥmād Qāḍīzāda, 46
Akchurin, Asfandiyār, 135
Akchurina, Maḥbūbjamāl, 135
Akchurina, Zuhra, 135
Akchurins, 138
akhlāq (ethics), 2, 43–7, 52–5, 63–9, 73n23, 74n30, 78n102, 107, 138, 144
Akhtan, Sopï, 189
ākhūnd, 52, 84–6, 88–9, 93–4, 110n17, 157–8, 165, 168–73, 179n4, 182n49
Ak-Mechet', 219, 220, 223
Akmolinsk *see* Aqmola
Ālāchalī, 352
al-Afghanī, Jamāl al-Dīn, 259, 265–6, 278n69, 280n82
al-Alqadarī, Ḥasan, 246–7, 251, 259, 276n37, 277n52
Aᶜlam, Mīrzā Sharīf, 312–13
ᶜĀlam-i niswān, 140
al-ᶜAsalī, Muḥammad, 269
Al-ᶜAwāmil al-Miᶜa, 42, 72n14
al-Bukhārī, Muhammad, 2
al-Bulghārī, Muḥammad Karīm, 46
al-Būrindiqī, Manṣūr bin ᶜAbdarraḥman, 42
al-Chachānī, ᶜAbdassalām, 290
al-Chukhī, Muḥammad ᶜAlī, 248
Aldayŭlï, Qara-biy, 195, 188, 197
al-Durgilī, Nadhīr, 262–4, 268–9, 272,
Aleppo, 73n21, 246, 249
al-Farāʾiḍ as-Sirājiyya/as-Sirāj fīl-Mīrāth, 42
al-Gharabudāghī, Jamāl al-Dīn, 248, 251
al-Ghazanishī, Abū Sufyān, 268–9
al-Ghumuqī, ᶜAlī b. ᶜAbd al-Ḥamīd, 249–51, 253, 259–63, 268–9, 280n82
al-Gubdanī, Ghazanuf, 269
al-Hāmidī, Shākirjān, 67
al-Hidāya, 2–3, 26n7, 42, 53, 66, 73n25, 237n101, 237n102, 310, 319–20, 325n52, 325n53, 326n59
al-Ḥusaynī, Ikhtiyār al-Dīn b. Ghiyāth al-Dīn, 310
al-Ḥusaynī, Mīr Rabīᶜ b. Mīr Niyāz Khwāja, 305–6, 308–11, 314–16
al-Ḥutsī, ᶜAbd al-Latīf, 248
Al-i Burhān, 3
al-Iftitāḥ fī Sharḥ al-Miṣbāḥ, 42
Älimŭlï, 188
al-Jilānī, ᶜAbdalqādir, 293
al-Junguti, Yūsuf, 263–6, 268
al-Jurjānī, ᶜAbdalqāhir, 42, 72n14

al-Khunzakhī, ᶜUmar, 248–9
al-Kultasī, Shamsaddīn, 56
Allāh Qulī Khān, 337
al-Mahallī, Jamāl al-Dīn, 256, 262
al-Maḥsūsa *see* Mahdi b. ᶜAbd al-Ḥādi
al-Makkī, Saᶜid, 249, 270
al-Marghīnānī, Burḥān al-Dīn, 2, 28n15
al-Marjānī, Shihābaddīn, 11, 49, 53–4, 97, 104–6, 115n89, 118n121, 124, 149n14, 150n30, 201, 259
al-Muhukhī, Masᶜūd, 261, 268–9
al-Muḥuwī, Damadan, 253
al-Nawawī, Muḥyi al-Dīn, 262
al-Qaḥi, Ḥasan, 269
al-Qarakhī al-Huchuwī, Muḥammad b. Ibrahim, 253
al-Qarakhī, Muḥammad Ṭāhir, 262
al-Qaranī, Uways, 127
al-Qargalī, ᶜAbdalmanīḥ, 45
al-Qudalī, Ḥasan, 248
al-Quduqī, Muḥammad b. Musa, 245–6, 249–55, 270n32, 277n45
al-Qūrṣāwī, Abū n-Nāṣr, 11, 93, 95–7, 104–5, 114n77, 115n86, 118n121, 118n124, 259
al-Rāfiᶜī, 243
al-Ramlī, Muḥammad, 243, 262
al-Shāfiᶜī, Muḥammad b. Idrīs, 241–2, 251, 262
al-Shaybanī, Muḥammad, 73n25, 262
al-Ṭaḥāwī, 310
al-Targhulī, Muḥammad b. Zayn al-Dīn, 263
al-Tūntārī, ᶜAlī Ishān, 47, 125, 127, 129, 130, 150n30
al-ᶜUbudī Muḥammad, 248
al-Uḥlī, ᶜAbd al-Ḥāfiẓ, 266
al-Uḥlī, Muḥammad ᶜUmarī, 269
al-ᶜUradī, Ibrahim, 251–2, 262
al-Ūriwī, Fatḥullāh, 94, 105, 157, 165–70
al-Ūriwī, Ḥabībullāh, 125
Alusheva, Farkhana, 135
al-Ūtiz-Īmānī, ᶜAbdarraḥīm, 45–6, 75n40, 93, 95–6, 105, 124
al-Yamanī, Ṣāliḥ bin Mahdī al-Maqbalī, 246–51, 253, 263, 265, 275n26, 280n82
al-Zamakhsharī, Maḥmūd b. ᶜUmar, 247
amangerliq, 216
Amīr bin Nūr Muḥammad, 94
Amīr Ḥaydar, 332
Amirkhan, Fatīḥ, 132
Ämit-ishan, 194
Amu Darya, 333, 339, 347, 357n48
Amu Darya Department, 339
an-Nāṣirī, ᶜAbdalqayyūm, 52–3, 55–6, 65, 99, 100, 135
Āqāsī, Dawlat Bīk Īshīk, 352
Aqeget, Musa, 131
ᶜaqīda (doctrine, dogma), 38, 43–4, 46–7, 51–2, 55, 63, 65–7, 69, 70, 74n33, 83, 94–6, 102, 104–5, 127, 129, 139, 192, 244, 246–7, 251, 270, 279n71, 279n82, 308
aqïn, 187, 200
Aqmola, 184
Aqpanbet, 191
Arabic, 2, 4, 21, 25, 38–9, 41–6, 51–5, 59–60, 63–70, 123, 127–31, 135, 138–9, 144, 196, 200, 218–19, 223, 239, 243, 245–6, 249, 259–60, 266, 281–2, 285–7, 289–90, 308, 313
Arabic script, 25, 44, 47, 64, 99, 116n95, 135, 200, 336
ᶜArabshahid dynasty, 335
Araslanov, Gatikam, 157
ᶜarḍ-dād, 332, 335–6, 338–42, 345, 351, 353
Arghïn, 201
Arghïns, 184, 189, 195, 201
Arïnghazï (Sultan), 203n4, 217
Arkhangel'ka village, 188
Asad, Talal, 92
Ashamaylï Kereys, 185–6, 188, 192, 204n8
ash-Shāṭibī, Maliki Abū Isḥāq Ibrāhīm, 103
ᶜAshūr Bībī, 317–18
Asiatic Department, 218, 223, 233n46
as-Sulaymāniyya, Fakhr al-Banāt bint Ṣibghatullāh, 141–3
Astrakhan, 2, 9, 138, 258
Atïghay, 192
at-Ṭahṭāwī, Rifāᶜa, 56
at-Tājiyya, Ashrāf al-Banāt, 140
Äuliyeköl, 193
Austro-Hungary, 334
Ayagöz region, 198
Aydabol-biy, 195
Aygum, 283–5, 287–8
ᶜAyn al-ᶜIlm, 54, 66–7
Ayoub, Sami, 331
Ayqozha, 199
Äyteke-biy, 189
Aytqozhaŭlï, Äliyasqar, 199

Aytughanŭlï, Kiyïkbay, 192
Āyūkhānov, Dhākir, 103–4
Äziz, Sopï, 189
Äzizi, Ghabdīlgani, 198
az-Zanjānī, ᶜIzzaddīn, 42, 72n13

Babadzhanov, Muhammad-Salih, 184
Bābājān, Tarrāh, 338–9
Badavām, 123
Baghdad, 201
Baghïlan-biy, 185–6
Bāghubustān Khanım, 137–9
Bahramŭlï, Körpesh, 196, 199
Baishev (ākhūnd), 173
Balatnay Madrasa, 196
Baldwin, James, 331
Bammat-Gireis, 282
Bāqī b. Jarrāh, 262
Baqırghān kitābı, 123
Baqırghanī, Qūl Sulaymān, 125
Bardo Treaty, 334
Bārūdī, ᶜĀlimjān, 11, 67, 105–6, 137, 144, 191–2
barymta, 216–17
Bashkir uprisings, 16
Bashkirs, 9, 156, 164, 174, 186–9, 194, 196, 201–2, 320
Baten'kov, G. S., 214
Bayanaul, 201
Bāyazīd, 128
Bayazitov, ᶜAtāʾullāh, 52–3, 56
Baytŭrsïnov, Äbdïrayïm, 201
Bazekeev, Muhamedsharif, 156–7
Beer, Daniel, 162
Bekdäuletŭlï, Niyaz-serī, 201
Bertīsŭlï, Qozhaghul-biy, 197
Bezak, A. P., 225, 233n39
Bībī ᶜĀʾisha bint Batırshāh, 126–30
Bībīṣafā, 173
Bidān, 42
Bīdel, Mirzā ᶜAbd al-Qādir, 303
Bīgī, Muḥammad Zahīr, 132
Bīgī, Mūsā, 11, 103–4, 106, 117n113, 143
Biibulatov, Shikhammat-qadi, 289
Bīkbulātov, Sunᶜatullāh, 68
Bīk-Fūlād Bī, 337
Bīktīmeriyya, ᶜAlīma al-Banāt, 134–5, 137
Bīrdī Shakūr, 352
biy courts, 213, 226, 228
biys, 13, 183, 189–98, 202, 216–17, 221, 224, 228, 231n20, 234n51, 234n53
Black Death, 21
Black Sea, 184
Blaramberg, I. F., 219
Bobrovnikov, A. A., 209, 233n39
British Empire, 1, 3–5, 13, 22, 25, 216, 300, 302, 320, 333
Brower, Daniel, 10
Būbī Madrasa, 57–9, 63, 67, 137
Būbī, ᶜAbdullāh, 11, 60, 67, 136, 137, 139–40, 142–3
Būbī, Mukhliṣa, 121, 137, 141
Būbī, ᶜUbaydullāh, 137
Buinaksk, 289
Bukey (Bukei) Horde (Inner Horde), 12, 48, 184, 219–21, 234n50, 237n101
Bukhara, 2–3, 14, 16, 26n7, 42, 46, 51, 54, 72n10, 74n29, 74n31, 97, 110n17, 118n131, 129, 138, 179n4, 184, 186, 188–9, 194–6, 199, 201, 204n19, 305, 307–8, 314, 320–1, 334
Bukharan, 2–3, 27n9, 32n40, 54, 73n22, 199, 206n43, 220, 237n101, 309, 314, 332, 351
Bulatova, Hazar, 164
Burak, Guy, 331
Burbank, Jane, 159–60
Būstān Faqīh, 42

Catherine the Great (Catherine II), 9–12, 15, 32n40, 44, 86, 159, 179n1, 190
Caucasus, 1–2, 11, 20, 110n21, 211, 227
Caucasus Wars, 11, 254, 256–7, 270, 272
Central Asia, 1–3, 13–18, 20, 23, 25, 27n7, 32n40, 33n48, 41, 43–4, 70, 73n25, 74n29, 90, 121, 160, 183, 186–9, 191, 194–7, 200, 202, 210–11, 213, 215, 217, 222, 224, 228, 231n18, 237n102, 257–8, 286, 299, 302–8, 310, 314, 315, 316, 319–20, 325n46, 329–31, 335–6, 344, 351, 354n16, 356n33, 357n48
Cheboksary, 127
Chechen, 194, 281–3, 287–93
Chechnya, 24, 257, 281–4, 291, 293–5
Chimbay District, 332
Chim-Mirzas, 282
China, 1, 185, 215
Chistopol, 144
codification, 4, 7, 12–13, 19, 209–11, 214–16, 218, 221, 224, 226–7, 229, 299, 301–2, 304–5, 323n26
Crews, Robert D., 9–10, 82, 86, 88–90, 98, 115n92, 159–60

Crimea, 1, 20, 32n37, 110n21
customary law, 8, 22, 25, 300, 320, 348
Kazakh, 13, 15, 17, 24, 36n75, 160, 183, 188, 197, 200, 209–29, 233n46, 234n58, 234n61, 235n72
North Caucasian, 12, 229, 240, 245, 254, 270, 281, 286–8

d'Andre, Lev, 197–8, 220, 226, 228, 233n46
Daghestan, 12, 16, 239–41, 244–5, 247–59, 262, 266, 269–72, 281–2, 285–7, 289, 291–2, 295n4
dār al-Islām, 85, 255
Daulbaev, B., 184
Däulenŭlï, Tolïbay-sïnshï, 187–8, 195
Däuletŭlï, Shong, 192
*da*ᶜ*wā*, 286, 347, 351
dayn, 283, 286
dhikr, 281, 291–2
Dimau village, 135
*Dīn wa ma*ᶜ*īshat*, 81, 104, 106
divorce, 17, 94, 114n6, 156–8, 160–1, 164–79, 181n47, 246, 249, 251–2, 266, 280n82, 286, 350
Dīwānbīgī, Aman Kildī, 352–3
Dūmāwī, Najīb, 144
Dutch empire, 1, 4, 25
Dzhanturin, A., 220

Edict on the Toleration of Faiths, 10, 159
Eickelman, Dale, 98, 102
Enlightenment, 10
Erpeli village, 289
Eset-batïr, 189, 195
Esïrkep, 196
Estemes, 196
Estemïsŭlï, Eseney-biy, 190–8, 201
ethnographers, 12, 52, 135, 222

Fadel, Mohammed, 83, 315
faqīh, 73n22, 83, 88, 94, 306–7
Farīdaddīn ᶜAṭṭār, 45
Fatāwa Qāḍīkhan, 42
Fatāwa-i Hindiyya/Fatāwaī ᶜ*Ālamgīrī*, 42
Fawz an-Najāt, 45
Fayḍkhanov, Ḥusayn, 49–56, 100
Fayḍullāh-ūghlī, 163
First World War, 21, 280n82
Fiṭrat, ᶜAbd al-Rauf, 303
For Prophet and Tsar, 9
Foreign Ministry, 218–19
Frank, Allen J., 98–100, 160, 217
French empire, 3–5, 22, 25, 267, 333
French language, 51, 60, 63, 218
Fuks, Savelii, 212
*fuqahā*ʾ, 83, 94, 103, 263
*furū*ᶜ *al-fiqh*, 2, 24, 42–3, 73n20, 73n21, 73n22, 73n25, 308, 310, 324n45

Gabdrakhimov, Gabdessalam, 48, 113n56, 165, 170
Galdan Tseren, 190, 193
Gamzatbek (Imam), 254
Gandumiam Peace Treaty, 333–4
Garipova, Rozaliya, 121
Gasfort, G. Kh., 227
Gasprinskii, Ismāᶜīl, 57, 99–100, 106, 135
Gender, 5, 122, 125, 132, 140, 146, 163, 338
Ghafūrī, ᶜAbdalmajīd, 125, 134, 140
Ghaliy, 185
Ghāzī Muḥammad (Imam), 254–5, 286
Ghïlmani, Saduaqas, 184
ghurm, 283–6
Golden Horde, 2, 85, 186, 202, 205n32, 218
Grigor'ev, Vasilii, 209, 220, 224–6, 233n39, 235n80
Grodekov, N. I., 215, 226, 234n53, 236n91, 236n92
Grozny, 293
Gulistān, 45
Gültöbe, 189, 195
Gurlen, 346

Hādī, Zakir, 134
hadith, 2, 41, 43, 51, 54, 56, 63, 65, 67–69, 78, 129–31, 139, 142–3, 188, 242–3, 245, 250, 253, 260–2, 265, 273n7, 247, 302, 327n74
Haft-i yak, 44, 75n38, 123
Hajj Arqa, 283–5, 288
Ḥājj Muḥammad, 283–5, 288
Hallaq, Wael B., 19, 83–4, 108n7, 321n3
Ḥamīd-ūghlī, Ḥabībullāh, 157, 168
Ḥanafī, 2–3, 10, 17, 41–3, 66–7, 72n14, 73n21, 73n22, 72n23, 73n24, 73n25, 74n29, 81, 93–7, 107, 110n17, 112n48, 114n66, 114n77, 115n78, 127, 130, 156, 167, 176, 228, 242, 258–62, 264, 265, 267–8, 271, 273–4, 275n19, 302, 307, 308, 316, 320, 324n32, 324n37, 326n65
Ḥasanī, Aḥmadgaray, 139

Head of the Department of Religious Affairs of Foreign Confessions, 166
Hijaz, 51, 104, 249, 265
Ḥizb al-Taḥrīr, 293
Holy Synod, 158, 168, 175
Ḥusayn Bāyqarā (Sultan), 310
Ḥusayniyya Madrasa, 57, 60–2
Husaynovs, 137
Ḥusnijamāl, 157–8, 163–4, 167–9, 173
Hussin, Iza R., 91–2

Ibn ᶜAbd al-Ḥādī, 265
Ibn al-Mubārak, 262
Ibn al-Qayyim al-Jawzī, 265
Ibn Hajar al-Haytamī, 243, 256, 262
Ibn Taymiyya, Taqī al-Dīn, 250–1, 263, 265–7, 278n69, 280n82
Ibrāhīm bin Adham, 128
Ibrāhīm bin Khūjāsh, 93
Ibrahim, Ahmed Fekry, 301–2
Ibrahimov, ᶜAbdarrashīd, 67
ignorirovanie (benevolent neglect), 14–15
ijmāᶜ, 69, 96, 241, 261, 273n8, 310
ijtihad, 22–3, 81–3, 94–7, 102–8, 115n78, 117n113, 118n121, 118n124, 178, 239–46, 249, 251–3, 255–7, 259, 260–72, 276n37, 277n52, 278n69, 279n71, 279n82, 300, 302–4, 307, 310, 316, 321, 324n45
imam
  North Caucasus, 254, 258, 281, 286–7, 290
  of the *madhhab*s, 247, 250, 261–2, 307, 310–13
  prayer leader, 7, 14, 17, 23, 27n7, 38, 41, 46–8, 50, 63, 68–69, 81, 85–91, 93, 95, 97–8, 100–1, 122, 126–7, 132, 134–5, 142, 144–6, 150n30, 157–85, 161, 164–67, 169, 170–4, 177–8, 179n4, 182n49, 188, 190–2, 195–6, 198–9
Imperial Russian Geographic Society, 211
India, 16, 26, 48, 57–8, 73n25, 114n66, 129, 262, 302
Indonesia, 300
Ingush, 282, 289, 292
Ingushetia, 281, 291
Inner Asia, 3
Inner Horde *see* Bukey Horde
Inner Russia, 9, 48, 137–8
Iran, 1, 48, 74n33, 333–4
Ïrghïzbekŭlï, Imamghabit, 196, 199
Irgiz, 194
Isāghūjī, 38, 43, 66, 67
Isa-khazret *see* Maral-ishan Qŭrmanŭlï
Isfandiyār Khān, 339–42, 352
Isfandiyār Tūra, 339
Īsh Murād, 347
ᶜishāᵓ, 96–7, 242
Isḥāqī, ᶜAyaḍ, 120, 134
ishkīl, 288
Īshmuḥammad bin Dīnmuḥammad, 105
Islamic orthodoxy, 10, 82, 212
Islamic revival, 10, 14, 32n40, 217
Islamisation, 2, 202, 283
Ispolkom, 328–9
istiḥsān, 242, 273n8
Istimisov, Iseney, 191; *see also* Estemīsŭlï, Eseney-biy
Italy, 333–4
Itīke Zhandosŭlï, 192
ittifāq, 286
Izh-Būbī village, 57, 59, 137–8
Īztīleuov, Tŭrmaghanbet, 201

Jackson, Sherman, 83, 109n8
Jadids, 3, 11, 39, 57–8, 100, 102, 105, 118n124, 145, 181n33, 264, 266, 302–3
Jahāngīr Khan, 48
Jāmiᶜ ar-Rumūz, 42–3
Janbulak village, 328–9
Janturins, 138
Januszkiewicz, Adolph, 198
Jarīdat Daghistān, 260
Jawāhir al-Bayān, 46
jihad, 240, 254–9, 269–71, 281, 286–7, 290–2
Junior Horde (Junior *zhüz*), 12, 188–90, 199, 215, 217

Kadyrov, Akhmed, 291
Kadyrov, Ramzan, 282–3, 291, 293–4
Kalkamanova, Khalilzada, 156
Kamāliyya Madrasa, 144
Kamp, Marianne, 121–2
Karakalpakistan, 328
Karakalpaks, 332
Karīmī, Fatīḥ, 136
Kasimov (city), 138
Kasimov, Kenesary, 193, 227
Katanov, Nikolai, 200
Katenin, A. A., 224–5
Kattaqurghan, 194
Kayuki village, 172

Kazakh khanate (Qazaq khanate), 2, 187, 190, 193–4, 197
Kazakh Senior Horde (Senior zhüz), 215
Kazakh Steppe, 1, 12–18, 20, 24, 35n72, 36n75, 86, 90, 160, 209–29, 232n35, 234n51, 234n55, 236n85, 237n101, 333, 354n16
Kazakhs (Qazaqs), 12–13, 17, 23, 183–98, 203, 203n1, 209–29, 233n39, 234n50, 234n53, 235n71, 234n80, 234n82, 236n85, 352
Kazakhstan, 183, 185–91, 193–4, 198, 201–2, 206n41, 213, 269, 282, 328
Kazan, 2, 5, 9, 38, 42–6, 48–9, 51–3, 57, 62, 65, 68, 75n38, 77n64, 93–4, 97–101, 106, 113n55, 114n68, 125, 127, 129, 134–5, 137–8, 142, 144, 150n30, 158, 161, 196, 200–2, 218, 237n101, 258–9
Kazan University, 49, 52, 218
Keche Mui village, 38
Kefeli, Agnès, 121–2, 126, 141
Kemper, Michael, 95
Kenesarï *see* Kasimov, Kenesary
Kerderī, Äbubäkīr Shoqanŭlï, 201
Kerey (*ru'*), 22, 185–93, 195–202, 204n8, 204n9
Khalid, Adeeb, 121–2
Khiva, 2, 14, 16, 20–1, 24, 27n9, 28n15, 194, 196, 217, 220–1, 328–43, 345–7, 349–52, 354n16, 356n31, 356n33, 357n40, 357n48, 358n52, 358n59, 359n67, 360no74, 360n78, 361n84
Khojand, 317–18
Khoqand, 16, 196, 219, 334
Khorezm, 190, 194, 196, 202, 328, 330–7, 339–40, 346–8, 352, 360n72, 360n83, 361n87, 361n91
khulᶜ, 170
Khusainov, Mukhammedzhan, 87, 89, 93, 95–7, 99
Kirilov, Ivan, 16
Kīshīkŭlï, Arghïn Änet Baba, 189
Kitāb al-Miṣbāḥ fīl-Naḥw, 42
Kokchetau, 191, 199
Köpeyŭlï, Mäshhür Zhüsīp, 184, 201
Köshebe Kereys, 185–6
Köshekŭlï, Shaqshaq-biy, 190–2, 195, 197, 201
Kostanay, 185, 193
Kotibarov, Eset, 227
Kuban, 184
Kubrā, Najm al-Dīn, 2
Küchüm Khan, 186
Kuhn, Alexander, 343
Kumyk, 285–6, 289
Kunanbaev, Abai *see* Abay Qŭnanbayŭlï
Kunta Ḥājjī, 281–94, 296n8
Kurgan, 185–6, 192
Kurmasheva village, 173
Kyrgyzstan, 300
Kyzylkum Desert, 332

Ladyzhenskii, M. V., 222–3
Laffasī, Ḥasan-Murād, 339, 342
legal consciousness, 4, 9–10, 15, 20, 160, 214, 304
legal institutions, 4–5, 14–17, 19–20, 22, 160, 304–5, 335
legal reform, 11, 54, 103, 120
legal theory, 4, 9, 21–3, 25, 42, 63, 65–6, 95, 104–5, 114n77, 239, 242, 270, 273n8, 274
Liubimov, N. I., 223
Lykoshin, Nil, 339–43, 351

madhhab, 81–3, 95, 102–6, 109n11, 109n12, 115n78, 240, 242–4, 246–50, 252, 260, 262–4, 267–8, 270, 272
  Hanafi, 43, 107, 127, 267–8, 302, 305, 312, 321, 324n32, 326n65
  Shafi'ī, 243, 253–4, 264, 268, 270
madrasa, 22, 25, 38–60, 63, 66–7, 69, 70, 100–2, 105, 122–31, 137, 139–46, 188–91, 194–7, 199–201, 203, 228, 286, 309
Magadansk, 269
maḥalla, 86, 88, 100, 130, 157–8, 161, 164–5, 169–72, 174, 177–8, 182n49
Mahbūbjamāl, 165–66
Mahdi b. ᶜAbd al-Ḥādi, 247
Mahdi Muḥammad al-Qarakhī, 253
Maḥmūd Ghaznawī, 128
Mahmūd Khosrow, 128
Maḥmūd ᶜUbayd Allāh al-Maḥbūbī (Ṣadr al-Sharīᶜa), 3, 237n101, 325n52, 326n59
mahr, 169
Majmūᶜ al-Akhbār, 52
Makhachkala, 282, 285, 287
Maksheev, A. I., 226, 232n37, 236n91
maktab, 44, 46, 58, 62, 65, 69, 100, 137
Mālik b. Anas, 241
Malmyzh, 127
Maltese, 333
Mamdani, Mahmood, 87

Mamluks, 335
Manghits, 321
Mangyshlak peninsula, 197
Mann, Kristin, 333
Manṣūrov, Aḥmad Fāʾiz, 81–2, 104–6, 108
manṭiq (logic), 38–9, 42–3, 47, 51, 53–4, 63–7, 131–2, 139, 144, 245, 249, 270
Maral Baba *see* Qŭrmanŭlï, Maral-ishan
Martin, Virginia, 31n30, 210–11, 213–14
Marxist-Leninist, 5, 118n124
Mavraev publishing house, 289
Middle East, 12, 25, 29n19, 240, 245–6, 254, 259, 270–1, 301, 314
Middle Horde (Middle zhüz), 12–13, 185, 189, 193, 198, 206n39, 215
Middle Volga, 2, 9, 10, 18, 27n7
Mikhailovskii fortress, 221
Military Court Commission of the Orenburg Military Battalion, 156–7
Ministry of Education, 33n41, 49
Mirʾāt al-akhlāq, 43
Mirzabaeva, Bībī Zībī, 317–19
Mirzabai, 317
Mongolia, 185
Mongols, 2, 245, 267, 302, 331, 335, 355n26
Montayŭlï, Tīlen-biy, 190, 195, 197
Morocco, 300
muʾadhdhin, 86
mudarris, 41, 86, 164–5
Mufaṣṣal Anmūdhaj, 42, 67
mufti, 83–4, 107, 192, 218, 301–2, 315, 331
  Central Asia, 31n30, 118n131, 189, 303–15, 317, 319, 324n32
  Chechnya, 291, 293
  Crimea, 166–8
  Egypt 265
  Kazakh 194, 196, 198, 209, 217, 236n85
  Mecca, 249, 267
  Volga-Ural region, 10, 23, 31n30, 48, 86–90, 95–7, 99, 165, 170–2, 179n1, 181n33, 191, 203n4, 292
muftiate, 93, 282
Muhammad ᶜArif Bek, 67
Muḥammad Raḥīm Khān I, 336–7, 342
Muḥammad Raḥīm Khān II, 333, 338–9
Muḥammad Salīm, 173
Muḥammad Shāfiᶜ Muḥammad Sharīf-ūghlī, 164, 168
Muḥammad Yaᶜqūb Bāy b. Jabbār Qulī Maḥram, 348
Muḥammad Yūsuf, 347
Muḥammad Ṣābirjān bin ʿAbdalbadīᶜ, 68
Muḥammadiyya 52, 123
Muḥammadiyya Madrasa, 57, 60, 62, 106, 137
Muḥyī al-Dīn Khwāja, 315–16, 319
Mujtahid, 83, 94–5, 104, 143, 178, 241–8, 250–2, 255–6, 261–5, 268, 271, 271n19, 306–7, 310–11, 313, 316
mujtahid fī 'l-madhhab, 83
mujtahid muṭlaq, 83
Mukhtaṣar al-Qudūrī, 42, 43, 66–7
Mukhtasar al-wiqāya fī masāʾil al-hidāya, 3, 26n7, 43, 53, 66, 73n22, 79n116, 79n117, 105, 237n101, 237n102, 325n52, 325n53, 326n59
Mullā Kashshāf ad-Dīn b. Shāh-i Mardān al-Manzalawī al-Qarqarālī, 201
Multaqa al-Abḥur, 42
Munasipov (ākhūnd), 173
Munīra bint Saᶜdaddīn, 144–5
Murav'ev, Nikolai, 330
Mūsā bin Fatḥullāh, 164
Muscovy, 9
Müsiräli, 189–90, 193, 199; *see also* Äziz, Sopï
Muslim Question, 17
Muslim Women's Congress (1917), 122
Muslim Women's Society of Ufa, 137
Muṭarrizī, Abūʾl Fatḥ Nāṣir bin ᶜAbdassayyid, 42
Muᶜtazili, 72n14, 246–8
Muẓaffariyya, Māhrui, 135
Mysticism, 5, 8, 44, 71n1, 127, 129–32, 138, 141, 290, 294

Naqshbandiyya khālidiyya, 291
Naṣīb al-Akhbār, 43
Naṣīriyya, Khabira, 135
Naṣraddīn-ūghlī, Ḥāfiẓaddīn, 177
Native courts (*narodnye sudy*), 7, 14–15, 17, 25
Naymans, 198
Nicholas I, 211
Nigeria, 300
Noghay, 184, 186–7
North Africa, 16, 333
North Caucasus, 11–12, 14, 16–17, 24, 229, 240, 282, 286–7, 290
Novoe Arslanovo, 156–7
Novo-Rybinka, 196
Nukus, 328–9
Nūr-ᶜAlī Khan, 190
Nurata, 332

Nŭrïmbet people, 193
Nurmukhamedov, Zhankhozhi, 227

official Islam, 8
Omsk, 13, 191, 196
Orenburg, 5, 13, 48, 57, 61, 79, 113n56, 137–9, 141–2, 156, 186, 194, 201–2, 203n4, 209, 219–27, 233n37, 233n39, 235n82, 235n85, 259, 353
Orenburg Border Commission, 209, 219–20, 222–6, 233n39
Orenburg Muslim Spiritual Assembly (OMSA), 10–12, 14–15, 17, 31n30, 33n41, 36n75, 36n76, 47, 86–96, 98, 101–2, 107, 110n21, 125, 142, 156–61, 165–78, 179n1, 191, 217, 227
Orientalism, 100, 114n68, 209, 212, 218, 220, 223, 235n80, 237n101, 246, 300–1, 315, 338, 343, 357n48, 360n83
Orsk, 209
Orthodox Christianity, 14–15, 85–6, 111n25, 111n28, 111n33, 271, 175
Öskenbayŭlï, Qŭnanbay, 198
Osmolovskii, Efim, 24, 211–12, 214, 218–28, 232n37, 233n39, 233n46, 234n50, 234n51, 234n55, 235n71, 235n72, 236n91, 237n100, 237n101
ostazbika, 122, 133, 135
Ottoman, 52, 116n95
Ottoman empire, 1, 4, 21, 46, 48, 54, 56–8, 70, 73n20, 73n25, 74n30, 100, 116n95, 143, 199, 257–8, 300, 314, 322n13, 322n19, 324n44, 325n46, 325n53, 331–2
Özbek Khan, 186

Pahlawān, Daulī, 199
Pavlodar, 184
Perm, 173
Perovskii, V. A., 219, 222–3, 354n16
Persian
  language, 2, 4, 21, 25n7, 38, 41–2, 45, 51–3, 55, 63, 65–7, 70, 74n31, 116n95, 127, 129–31, 135, 138, 144, 188, 196, 200, 218–19, 326n59, 355n28
  literature, 46, 129, 201
Persianate, 2, 63, 129, 151n51
Peters, Rudolph, 240
Petroaleksandrovsk, 334
Petropavlosk *see* Qïzïlzhar
Piscatori, James, 98
Pishpek, 138
Plehve, Vyacheslav Konstantinovich, 175
Pollock, Sheldon, 302
post-Soviet, 3–5, 213, 272, 280n82, 297n24
Presnogorskaia Krepost', 194
Protestants, 265
Putin, Vladimir, 291, 293

qāḍī, 15, 23, 53, 121, 141–2, 145, 177–8, 181n33, 186, 191–2, 195–8, 263, 284–5, 287, 310, 312, 315–17, 329–31, 337, 344, 347, 349, 350, 352–3, 359n71
Qādiriyya, 281–2, 291, 293
Qajar Empire, 333
Qambarŭlï, Zhanaq, 192
Qaq Kölī, 192
Qarabasŭlï, Asqap-shora, 189, 195
Qarauïl, 192
Qarile village, 42
Qarmaqshï, 194
Qasïm Khan, 205n27
Qasim khanate, 2, 9
Qasïm-sultan, 193
Qayranköl, 193
Qazhïm, 196
Qazile village, 68
Qïpshaqs, Qarabalïq, 184
Qiṣāṣ al-Anbiyāʾ, 123, 132, 141
Qıshlaush village, 134
Qiṣṣa-i Sayfalmulūk, 45
Qiṣṣa-i Yūsuf, 123
qiyās, 69, 143, 241–2, 248, 260, 262, 271, 273–4, 309–10
Qïzïlorda, 185, 199, 206n41
Qïzïlzhar, 190–1, 194–6, 202
Qonghrats, 328, 330, 332–7, 340, 342–3, 346, 351–3
Qorabayŭlï, Shärke-sal (Shärip), 200
Qosïm-qozha, 190, 193
Qozhabergen-Asqap Madrasa, 189, 195
Quhistānī, Shams al-Dīn Muḥammad, 312
Qūl ᶜAlī, 45
Qŭlanbay-ishan, 193
Qŭltöbe, 189
Qŭrmanŭlï, Maral-ishan, 187, 192–4, 196, 198–9
Qūshbigī Yāf canal, 347
Quttïbayŭlï, Bayghara-biy, 197

Rafidis, 248
Rakhimbaev, ᶜAẓīmbāy, 317–18
Ramadan, 124, 150n36, 165, 242
Ramievs, 138
Rapoport, Yossef, 331
Rasulev, Zaynullāh, 125
raʾy, 242, 273n8
Razzāq, 317
Renan, Ernest, 56
Revolution of 1905, 99, 102, 135
Riazan, 172
Riḍāʾ addīn bin Fakhraddīn, 11, 42, 47–8, 68–9, 103, 129, 136, 139–40, 142, 144, 148n7, 149n14, 165, 168, 176–7, 181n33
Riḍa, Rashīd, 259, 261, 265–6, 278n64, 278n69, 280n82
Risāla-i ᶜAzīza, 45, 123
Roberts, Richard, 33
Romaniello, Matthew, 85
Ross, Danielle, 101, 106
Rūmī, Jalāladdīn, 45–6
Russian Islamic University, 291
Russo-Japanese War, 17

Sabit-ūghlī, Muḥammad Shah, 168
Saᶜdī, 45
Safargaliev, Fatḥullāh, 170
Safarov, Bābājān (Safar ūghlī), 339–42
Saḥīḥ al-Bukharī, 54
St Petersburg University, 49
Salafism, 29n19, 104, 118n120, 269, 280n82, 291–3
Samara, 219, 223–5, 233n39
Samarkand, 5, 138, 186–90, 195, 197, 357n48
Samībek, Shamsaddīn, 136
Samoilovich, Alexander, 351
Sandïqŭlï, Qoldas, 192
Sanjar Mahdī, 128
Sardarbekŭlï, Mamanay, 192
ṣarīḥ, 283, 287
Sartori, Paolo, 160
Sayfaddīn-ūghlī, Jamāladdīn, 178
Sayyid Aḥmad Khwāja, 332
sblizhenie (rapprochement), 16
Scheele, Judith, 212
secular (authorities), 157, 175, 183, 291
secularism, 3, 11, 59, 70, 299
Sember, 138
Severnaia pchela, 218
Seyït, 195–6
Seytqŭlŭlï, Zhalangtös-bahadur, 188, 195
Shafi'ī *see madhhab*
Shāh-i Aḥmad bin Batırshāh, 126–7, 129–30
Shāhmarān, 141
Shahrisabz, 194
Shamīl (Imam), 227, 229, 254–5, 257, 281–2, 284, 286–7, 290–2
Shamkhāls, 287
Shamsiyya Madrasa, 57, 60–1
Shaqshaq Madrasa, 195
Shaqshaqov, Segīz-Serī Bahramŭlï, 190–1, 201
Sharaf, Shahr, 54
Sharḥ ᶜAbdallāh, 42, 66
Sharḥ al-ᶜAqāʾid an-Nasafiyya, 43
Sharḥ-i Mullā Jamiᶜ, 38, 42, 67
sharīᶜa, 3, 7, 8, 11–14, 18–22, 24, 51, 82, 84–5, 87, 89–92, 95, 98, 103–4, 106, 108n5, 112n41, 159–60, 168, 183, 192, 195–7, 207n60, 209–18, 221–9, 233n46, 235n72, 236n83, 240, 248, 250, 253–4, 260, 263, 270, 289, 294, 299, 300–1, 304–5, 307, 314–16, 318, 320, 323n26, 328, 330–1, 335, 346–51, 353, 360n74
Sharīfūghlī, Najmaddīn Muḥammad, 157
Sharīf-ūghlī, Raḥmatullāh Muḥammad, 157–8, 164, 168
Shïghay Khan, 186
Shir-Dor Madrasa, 188
Siban Kereys, 185, 191–2
Siberia, 1–2, 9, 18, 28n13, 36n76, 46–7, 86, 135, 156–7, 159, 162–6, 168, 171–7, 185–6, 188, 191–4, 196, 201, 211, 290
Siberian Tatars, 186–7, 189
Sibzar, 315
sosloviia, 9, 16, 11n28
Southeast Asia, 1, 16, 29n19
Soviet, 2–5, 8, 19, 29n19, 29n21, 32n32, 81, 184, 190, 193–4, 199–200, 202, 206n42, 212–13, 239–40, 246, 269, 272, 282, 292, 303, 320, 330, 341
Speranskii, Mikhail, 12, 191, 214–16, 231n18
Statute on the Siberian Kirgizes (Ustav o Sibirskikh Kirgizakh), 12
Stepnoi Krai, 16
Sterlitamak, 164
Ṣubḥiūghlī, 166

Sufi, 2, 8, 11, 14, 17, 21, 23–4, 28n13, 39, 41, 45, 47, 52, 74n30, 84, 88, 122–31, 133, 137–8, 146, 187, 192–4, 196, 198–9, 202, 245, 269, 281–3, 287, 288–94
Ṣūfī Allāhyār, 44, 46, 52
Sufism, 2, 27, 45, 65, 70, 126, 129–30, 138, 266, 269, 289, 293–4
Sulaymānī, Muḥammad Shākir bin Muḥammad Dhākir, 68
Ṣunᶜatullāh bin Mullā Badraddīn, 38, 68, 70
Süyīndīk Arghïns, 195
syncretism, 213–14
Syr Darya, 190, 193–4, 199, 201, 215–16, 219, 223, 235n71

Tafsīr al-Jalālayn, 43
Tafsīr Yaᶜqūb Charkhī, 43
Tājaddīn bin Yālchīghul, 45
Taᶜlīm al-Mutaᶜallim Ṭarīq at-Taᶜallum, 42
Tanash-biy, 186, 197
Tanāyiḥ al-Afkār fī Kashf ar-Rumūz wa Asrār, 46
Tangbayŭlï, Tīlenshī, 192
Tanzimat, 56
taqlīd, 23–4, 81–3, 93–7, 103–8, 114n68, 118n121, 239–40, 243–4, 248–64, 266, 268–72, 277n52, 278n69, 299, 301, 302–5, 307, 317–18, 321
taraqqī-parwar, 303
Tarïshï Kereys, 185
tarjīḥ, 243, 252, 271, 274n15, 301, 311, 314, 318, 322n17
Tarjuman, 57, 106, 135
Tarki, 283, 285, 287
Tāsh Hawlī, 337
Tashkent, 5, 138, 201, 315–16, 319–20, 339
Taṣrīf al-ᶜIzzī, 42
Tatarification, 14
Tatars, 13–14, 17, 126, 183, 186–7, 189, 194, 196, 232n35
Täuke Khan, 187–90
Tauzar, 187
Tauzarŭlï, Däulen, 187
Tawarīkh-i Bulghāriyya, 123
Temir-Khan Shura, 289
Tevkelev, Alexei, 16
Tevkelev, Salimgarei, 90, 107n41
Tevkelevs, 138
Thabāt al-ᶜĀjizīn, 44–5
Tilla-Qari Madrasa, 188
Tiumen', 138, 185, 192
To'rtkul, 328, 334
Tölekŭlï, Zhänībek-batïr, 188, 195
toleration/tolerance, 9, 15, 32n40
Tolïbayŭlï, Qozhabergen-zhïrau, 186–9, 195, 197–9, 201–2
Toqta Khan, 186
Torghay oblast', 184, 194
Transcaucasia, 2
Transoxiana, 2, 209, 326n59
Trans-Ural Horde, 219–21, 223, 228, 233n37, 234n50
Troitsk, 65, 125, 156, 194, 201–2
Tuḥfat al-Mulūk, 42
Tuna, Mustafa, 58, 102, 33n41
Tunisia, 333–4
Tūntār Madrasa, 127, 129
Tūntār village, 57, 61, 127, 129
Tuqaev, ᶜAbdullāh, 144
Turkestan (governor-generalship), 14, 16, 18, 316, 357n48
Turkic, 2–4, 21, 25, 41, 45–6, 53–4, 65–6, 116n95, 131, 141, 146, 154n107, 200
Turkish, 37n85, 51, 54, 65, 67, 135–6, 219
Türkistan, 189
Turkmen, 332, 346, 358n59, 360n80
Turkmenistan, 328

Uaq, 185, 189–90, 192, 195
Ufa, 62, 81, 86, 94, 110n21, 113n54, 137–8, 142, 171, 173, 259
Uil river, 352
ᶜulamāʾ, 3, 10, 12, 14, 31n29, 39–41, 44–5, 47–56, 58, 63, 68, 70–1, 72n10, 81–106, 110n20, 111n27, 112n35, 112n48, 113n56, 115n78, 115n86, 117n108, 123–4, 126–7, 130, 133–6, 138, 143–7, 150n30, 159–61, 174, 176–7, 183–5, 198, 200–3, 218, 244, 256–8, 287, 289, 290, 299, 303, 321, 331
Umarov, Sotiboldi, 328–9
Ūrāḍ Bāy, 346–7
Ural Mountains, 1, 9, 46, 85, 163, 240
Ural'sk, 217
Urazlino village, 158, 168
Urgench, 186, 188, 191, 192, 195–7, 345, 361n91
Urkī Irmat village, 164
Üseyīn-maghzŭm, 199
Ust Yurt plateau, 352

uṣūl al-fiqh, 42, 95, 104–5, 239, 308–10
uṣūl-i jadīd (New Method), 100–2
ᶜUthmāniyya Madrasa, 57, 60, 62, 67
Uzbek, 3, 13, 15, 202, 211, 320–1, 335, 339, 341, 359n72, 361n93
Uzbekistan, 328

Vaisov, Bahāʾaddīn al-Bulghārī, 125
Valikhanov, Chingis, 191
Valikhanov, Chokan, 227
Vámbéry, Arminius (Ármin), 338
Vatchagaev, Mairbek, 282
Veliaminov-Zernov, V. V., 223
Verkhneural'sk, 164
Vis-hajjis 282
Volga basin, 47, 240
Volga River, 1, 168
Volga-Ural Muslims, 10–11, 15, 17, 23–4, 31, 33n41, 36n81, 39, 40, 44–5, 48, 50, 52, 55–6, 67, 72n9, 81, 96–7, 100, 120–1, 123, 125, 129, 132–4, 145–7, 149n14, 159–60, 162, 177–8, 275
Volga-Ural region, 2, 9, 11–17, 20, 22–3, 36n74, 36n76, 39–47, 55, 56, 63, 70, 72n10, 73n19, 73n20, 81, 84–7, 99, 120–2, 125–6, 129, 131–2, 137, 139, 142, 146, 148n7, 150n30, 151n60, 153n89, 156, 160–1, 167, 176, 181n33, 183, 187, 196, 258
Vologda, 281

Wahabova, Fāṭima-i Farīda bint Murtaḍa, 144–5
Wahhabis, 104, 263, 267, 291, 293
Wali Khan, 192
waqf, 18, 36n76, 99, 240, 286, 300
Werth, Paul, 86, 158–61
West Siberian Kereys, 187
Wiqāya al-riwāya fī masāʾil al-hidāya, 3
wird, 281–2, 291–2, 297n21
Witkiewicz, Jan, 194

Xinjiang, 185

Ya Sin *sūra*, 128
Yaḥyā b. al-Ḥusayn b. Al-Qāsim, 247
Yalangtush *see* Seytqŭlŭlï, Zhalangtös-bahadur
Yaᶜqūb village, 81
Yasawī, 128
yasāwulbāshī, 334, 340–9
Yaushevs, 138
Yenikeevs, 138
Yūnus bin Īwānāy, 72n19, 85, 94, 110n17
Yunusova village, 173
Yusuf Kitabı/Qiṣṣa-i Yusuf, 45, 123, 132

Ẓahīr al-Dīn (Imām), 307
Zaidis, 246–8
Zain al-Dahlān (mufti of Mecca), 267
Zaisan, 138
zakāt, 55, 101, 271, 316
Zaman, Muhammad Qasim, 102
zemstvo, 48, 101
Zhabay, 195
Zhabayŭlï, Toqsan, 192
Zhalangayaq-ishan, 193–4
Zhandosŭlï, Iteke-batïr, 196
Zhängïrov, Shädï, 201
Zhankĭsĭŭlï, Salghara, 195
Zhetï Zharghï, 188–9
Zhüsĭpŭlï, Oraz-molda, 201
Zoyabashı, 137
Zufar b. Huzayl, 262
Zunghars, 186–90, 193, 195, 199
Zverinogolovka, 186

EU representative:
Easy Access System Europe
Mustamäe tee 50, 10621 Tallinn, Estonia
Gpsr.requests@easproject.com

www.ingramcontent.com/pod-product-compliance
Lightning Source LLC
Chambersburg PA
CBHW071826230426
43672CB00013B/2768
9781474444309